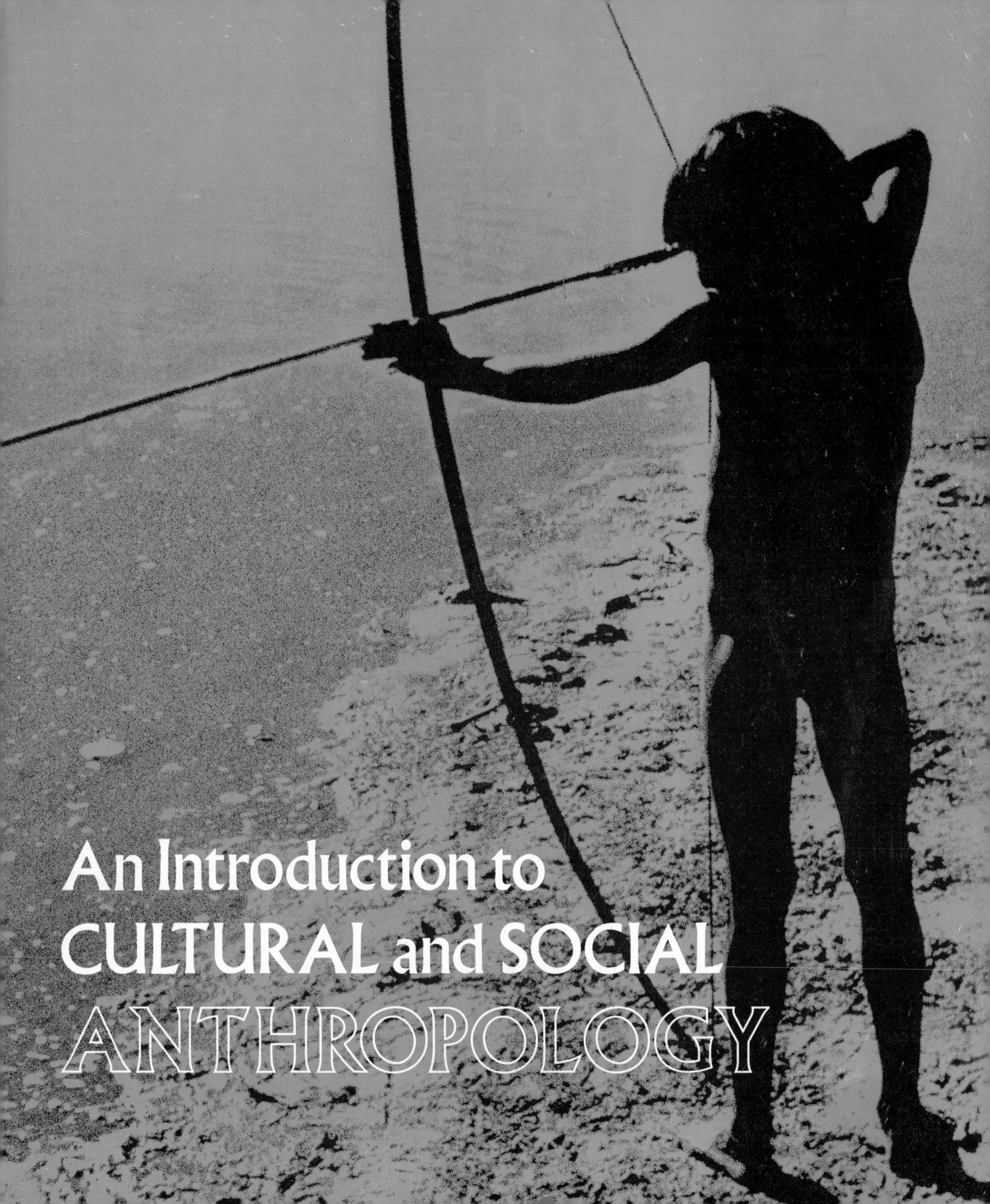
An Introduction to
CULTURAL and SOCIAL
ANTHROPOLOGY

An Introduction
to CULTURAL
and SOCIAL ANT

Peter B. Hammond

SECOND EDITION

HROPOLOGY

Macmillan Publishing Co. Inc.
NEW YORK
Collier Macmillan Publishers
LONDON

Printed in the United States of America

Macmillan Publishing Co., Inc.
866 Third Avenue, New York, New York 10022

Collier Macmillan Canada, Ltd.

Library of Congress Cataloging in Publication Data

Hammond, Peter B
An introduction to cultural and social anthropology.

Bibliography: p.
Includes index.
1. Ethnology. I. Title.
GN316.H35 1978 301.2 77-370
ISBN 0-02-349790-4

Printing: 1 2 3 4 5 6 7 8 Year: 8 9 0 1 2 3 4

Research on illustrations and photographic editing by the author.

To Azar F. Isfahani-Zadeh Hammond,
my wife and fellow worker

Preface

WHAT I have to say here about cultural and social anthropology follows from an effort to combine descriptive coverage of the basic aspects of society and the major categories of culture with a theory that suggests the causal interrelationships that unite them. I refer pointedly to the significance of these interrelationships not only for comprehending people, society, and culture in general, but for understanding ourselves and our own society and culture in particular.

Emphasis on both cultural evolutionary and cultural ecological interpretations follows from my judgment that these two related theoretical perspectives can be most effectively combined to develop a sound basic explanation of how cultures develop, societies "act," and peoples behave. This approach is complemented by frequent reliance on alternative theoretical orientations that, I hope, demonstrate the utility of synthesizing methods and theories that are sometimes too readily perceived as opposed.

In an introductory textbook it is often necessary to generalize in ways that make difficult the detailed analysis required for fully adequate coverage of certain highly specialized subfields. Some adherents of componential analysis, certain facets of structuralism, and ethnosemantics might feel their subjects have been dealt with too summarily. To counter this, at the end of each chapter, readings are suggested that will guide those who want to explore these and other topics in greater depth than is possible here.

Obviously, I owe a great debt to the work of others. The materials on technology and my emphasis throughout on the fundamental role of patterns of technoenvironmental adaptation in shaping the form and content of the other aspects of culture are the products of my response to the work of Robert McAdams, V. Gordon Childe, Henri Frankfort, Walter Goldschmidt, Marvin Harris, Darcy Ribeiro, Marshall D. Sahlins, Elman R. Service, Julian H. Steward, Andrew P. Vayda, and Leslie A. White. My treatment of economic organization has been strongly influenced by reading Paul Bohannan and George Dalton, A. Gunder Frank, Marion J. Levy, and Stanley Udy. The section on social organization owes much to what I know of the work of Gerald D. Berreman, Ronald Cohen, Elizabeth Colson, Robin Fox, Jack Goody, Kathleen Gough, Celia S. Heller, Joan Mencher, George Peter Murdock, A. R. Radcliffe-Brown, David M. Schneider, and Melvin M. Tumin.

The chapters on political organization reflect my reaction to the studies of Neville Dyson-Hudson, E. E. Evans-Pritchard, Morton H. Fried, Meyer Fortes, James L. Gibbs, Jr., E. Adamson Hoebel, Lucy Mair, John Middleton, Laura Nader, David Tate, and Eric R. Wolf. What I have written about ideology was stimulated by my reading of David Aberle, Clifford Geertz, Francis L. K. Hsu, Melford Spiro, Anthony F. C. Wallace, and J. Milton Yinger. My interpretation of "The Arts" was greatly influenced by past association with Warren L. d'Azevedo, William A. Bascom, James W. Fernandez, Richard M. Dorson, Alan P. Merriam, Jerome Mintz, and Roy Sieber. In the part of the book on anthropological linguistics my heavy reliance on the work of Joseph H. Greenberg and Dell H. Hymes is evident.

Gerald D. Berreman, Alan Fix, Lewis L. Langness, George E. Simpson, and Arthur Tuden have all suggested necessary revisions for this second edition. Working within uncomfortable constraints of time and space I have tried to make the most of their generously given good advice.

I am grateful to Kenneth J. Scott for his editorial cooperation, in preparing the second edition of this book, to Ronald C. Harris for his conscientious attention to its production, and to Andrew Zutis for his creative response to my gratuitous suggestions on its design.

The devoted assistance of Azar Hammond and the cheerfully irreverent support of our daughter, Alexa, have helped in more ways than either can know.

P. B. H.
N-Diol, Senegal, West Africa

Contents

Part One Introduction

Part Two Technology

Part Five Political Organization

Part Six Ideology

Part Seven The Arts

Part Eight Language

Part Nine Method and Theory

An Introduction to
CULTURAL and SOCIAL
ANTHROPOLOGY

Part One

Introduction

. . . culture is a biological adaptation, with nongenetic modes of transmission, which greatly supplements somatic evolution. . . .

SPUHLER (1965:1)

From the outset of the evolution of our species, our biologically based capacity to live in society and to learn to meet our needs by cultural means—our reliance on society and culture as a means of adaptation to relentlessly changing circumstances—has been the primal secret of human survival. Cultural and social anthropology is about the consequences of this human capacity, about the forms our societies take, about the ways our cultural behavior varies, about the causes of these variations, and about the processes by which they occur.

1

People, Society, and Culture

Anthropology Defined

Anthropology, the scientific study of humankind, is usually divided into three interrelated fields of specialization: physical anthropology, archeology, and (the subject of this book) cultural and social anthropology. Physical anthropologists are concerned principally with the study of human evolutionary origins, physical variation, and genetically determined human potential. Archeologists specialize in historical reconstruction based on the material evidence of cultural development through time. Many cultural and social anthropologists are interested in the historical development of culture also, but they focus more on the varying ways of life of contemporary peoples and the relatively recent aspects of their past.

This division of anthropology into three main branches is only an indication of differences in specific subject matter and methods of study, the inevitable consequence of necessary specialization. For achievement of a full understanding of people and their relation to society and culture the integration of knowledge from all three fields is required.

What the physical anthropologists have learned, for example, about human evolution and the gradual development of our biologically based capacity for culture is essential for an understanding of the way the development of culture has been affected, both facilitated and inhibited, by our

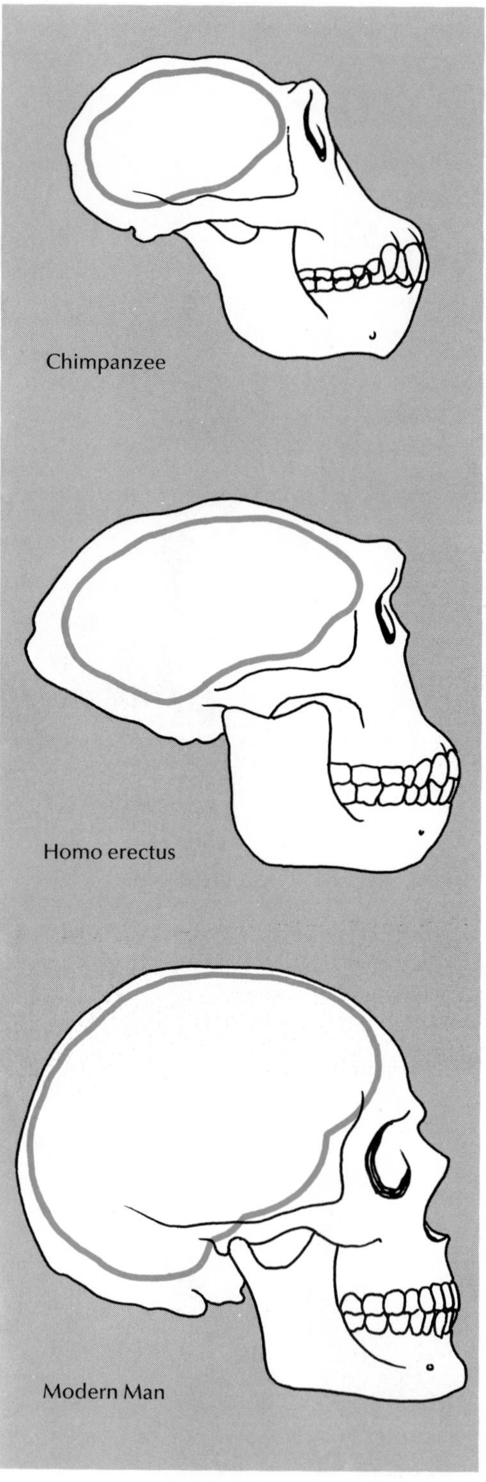

"What the physical anthropologists have learned . . . about human evolution and the general development of our biologically based capacity for culture. . . ."

Figure 1-1. As our brain grew larger, our face grew proportionately smaller. A comparison between the modern human *Homo erectus,* the first member of our own genus, and a chimpanzee. Red outline shows increasing brain size. (After Enid Kotsching.)

a

b

"What has been discovered of the essential biological sameness of all human beings as members of a single species supports a premise basic to the cultural and social anthropologists' approach. . . ."

Figure 1-2. *a.* Manipuri fishermen, India. (Courtesy of the Press Information Bureau, Government of India.) *b.* Town meeting, Woodstock, Vermont. (Courtesy of the Library of Congress.) *c.* Pottery seller at Segou, Mali. (United Nations.) *d.* Japanese boys. (Courtesy of the Embassy of Japan.)

c

d

"The basic question archeologists seek to answer—how cultures develop and change through time—is an equally fundamental question in cultural and social anthropology."

animal capacities and limitations. What has been discovered of the essential biological sameness of all human beings as members of a single species supports a premise basic to the cultural and social anthropologists' approach: that most differences in the patterned behavior of human groups cannot be explained by reference to inherited physical or "racial" differences but must be ascribed to differences in culture.

The work of the archeologist provides insights that are equally relevant to the interests of the cultural and social anthropologist. The basic question archeologists seek to answer—how cultures develop and change through time—is an equally fundamental question in cultural and social anthropology. Primarily it is the archeologists' methods of study that distinguish them; the concepts they deal with are the same.

In this book a composite term, *cultural and social anthropology,* is used for the third and largest basic field of specialization in anthropology. Most anthropologists in the United States prefer the shorter term *cultural anthropology.* By it they mean the branch of anthropology that is concerned with the scientific study of all aspects of the world's cultures—and of the factors that have affected their development—all dimensions of the differing ways of life of Africans, Middle Easterners, Asians, Aboriginal Australians, Pacific islanders, Europeans, and Americans, old and new. (The term *ethnology* is frequently used as a synonym for cultural and social anthropology.)

However, some anthropologists define the field of their interest more narrowly. Traditionally, they have regarded society, not the somewhat broader category of culture, as the appropriate subject of their inquiry. Like their British counterparts, they refer to themselves as social rather than cultural anthropologists and concentrate their attention on what they perceive as the more readily objectifiable, or concrete, aspects of people's ways of life—the organization of their social, economic, and political relations and the beliefs that accompany and support such organization. In contrast, most cultural

Figure 1-3. Temple of the Inscriptions, Chiapas, Mexico, an early center in the development of the complex culture of the Maya. (Courtesy of the Mexican Government Tourism Department.)

anthropologists take an approach that encompasses the study of all of culture, not just those aspects that constitute the structure of society. This means that in addition to their interest in social organization, economics, political systems, and religion, cultural anthropologists may be equally concerned with such cultural phenomena as technology, values, world view, the environmental conditioning of personality, art, and language.

But, as with differences between the other fields of anthropology, the differences that sometimes separate cultural and social anthropologists are principally ones of approach and emphasis. The compound term *cultural and social anthropology* is used herein because this book will deal both with those aspects of culture that social anthropologists have traditionally been most concerned about and with the broader aspects of people's ways of life as defined by cultural anthropologists. Wherever the term *culture* is used alone here, it is intended to encompass the somewhat more restricted concept of *society.*

Often linguistics is considered as still another separate field within anthropology. Because the capacity for language is both basic to the capacity for culture and one of its most important manifestations, the subject of language is included here as an integral part of cultural and social anthropology.

Our Evolutionary Origins

Anthropologists regard people, society, and culture as parts of nature. Human origins and the origins of society and culture are perceived as being closely linked, as having developed together from the outset. Humankind could not have evolved alone, without society and culture, and no one of them could continue to exist without the others.

First, our ancestors were animals. Gradually they acquired culture. Or more exactly, our animal attributes were largely established before we began to develop our capacity for living in society and using culture. This essential animality was and probably always will be a limiting factor in the development of culture. Conversely, once our early prehuman ancestors began to develop the ability to use culture, this new faculty had a similarly limiting effect on the physical aspects of their further evolution. Those who were best able physically and intellectually to utilize culture to live in society—to learn, store, speculate upon, and transmit their learning, to cooperate and communicate with others—had the best chances of surviving and passing on this valuable adaptive capacity. Those constitutionally less well equipped to use culture finally lost out and ultimately either were assimilated by their competitors or became extinct.

Like humankind itself, culture has also evolved. The several-million-years-long record of our evolutionary descent from ancient, not overly bright near human forebears is complemented by the material record of progressively more efficient adaptation that begins with evidence of the use of the simplest stone, bone, and wood tools and continues through the remains of early Middle Eastern and Asian farming communities, the complex societies of early America, and the Classic Period of the Mediterranean to the industrially based societies of the modern world. But the fascinating account of the interrelated origins and early evolutionary development of society, culture, and humankind is not our principal subject here. It is referred to only to support the premise that people, society, and culture, all having evolved together, are all the products of nature. If some sort of potentially discoverable order prevails generally in the relations between the other aspects of nature—between the elements, all other organisms, the earth, and the rest of the universe—then it follows logically that such order prevails also in the relations between people, society, and culture, and that the forces that govern this order can be known. This is the knowledge the anthropologist seeks.

"It is the biologically based need for nourishment that is demonstrably universal."
Figure 1-4. Waiting for lunch at a Philippine child care center. (Peace Corps.)

Animal Needs, Cultural Means, and Human Personality

As members of a single animal species, *Homo sapiens,* all people share a common set of fundamental needs derived from their common biologically determined requirements for survival. Among these are the need for nourishment and shelter, for the reduction of sexual tension, and for economic and social cooperation. This is a minimal list. Probably most anthropologists would want to alter or amplify it, each in his or her own way. At this point only the basic concept is critical: that all we humans share such needs and can meet them only by cultural means.

For example, people everywhere must eat, but the kinds of nutritive materials they consume and the ways they acquire and process their foods vary with their culture. It is the biologically based need for nourishment that is demonstrably universal. The specific means of meeting the need for food are cultural; all cultures, no matter how organized, must provide a system for getting food. Almost as essential is the human need for some kind of shelter from rain, snow, cold, wind, and sun and for protection from hostile fellow humans and predatory animals. The universality of people's need for the reduction of sexual tension again illustrates the distinction between the biologically determined sex drive common to all humans and the variety of patterned cultural means particular human groups have developed for channeling this basic impulse. The same can be said for the various ways people have worked out for coping with their need for some socially based system of cooperation: to make a living; to produce, protect, and provide for their families; and to get along with others.

Our status as the most adaptable of all the

". . . all cultures, no matter how organized, must provide a system for getting food."

Figure 1-5. Gathering coconuts in Kampong Riam, Sarawak, eastern Malaysia. (United Nations.)

animals derives from our reliance on culture to meet our needs rather than on genetically determined responses or structural changes. Our ancestors, often living under harshly uncomfortable natural conditions, in competition with each other and with other animals physically far stronger, survived and came ultimately to prevail as the dominant species through reliance on this capacity. Their adjustment to shifting environmental circumstances was dependent neither on discrete genetically determined changes in physique—the growth of a heavier shell, stronger teeth, or a keener sense of smell—nor on constitutionally dictated "instincts." Rather, it was dependent on their ability to

"Almost as essential is the human need for some kind of shelter. . . ."
Figure 1-6. Taos Pueblo, New Mexico. (Courtesy of the Library of Congress.)

think and to alter their behavior accordingly, to learn, unlearn, and relearn cultural behaviors necessary to their survival under changing conditions.

In the past many anthropologists regarded the human capacity for culture as unique, arguing that this ability distinguished us absolutely from all other animals. Now most would qualify any such assertion with reference to the growing evidence for impressive tool-making abilities and complex systems of communication and cooperation—all apparently learned—possessed by some of the great apes, our closest primate relatives (see Hewes 1973; Jay 1968; Jolly 1972; Premack 1971; Van Lawick-Goodall 1972; Washburn and Moore 1973).

Many anthropologists now assert that it is more accurate to think of this human capacity to use culture as a relative rather than an absolute distinction. But if the ability to use culture can no longer be regarded as wholly unique to our species (our closeness to the chimpanzees is becoming constantly more apparent, for example), the *extent* of people's reliance on society and culture as a principal means of adaptation still clearly sets us *Homo sapiens* apart.

Another anthropological premise so fundamental as to be almost a truism must also be stated: *Culture is learned,* in contrast, for example, to physical appearance and intellectual potential, which are primarily determined by heredity. A hypothetical Siberian

"Another anthropological premise so fundamental as to be almost a truism must also be stated: *culture is learned. . . .*"
Figure 1-7. An Indian family group from the Punjab. (United Nations.)

Eskimo infant taken from its family at birth and raised by Congolese Pygmies would grow up to look like its Eskimo parents. But the patterns of its cultural behavior and its specific personality would be similar to those of the Pygmies among whom it was brought up. A white Australian baby cared for from infancy to adulthood by Australian Aborigines would mature as white in appearance but Aboriginal in its cultural behavior. A newborn African black adopted by Native Americans would resemble its biological parents in appearance but would behave like the Indians in whose culture it was raised and whose personality type it had acquired.

This point is emphasized because much of cultural behavior, once learned, appears to be so "natural" that it can easily be perceived as instinctive, as biologically or

". . . so much of cultural behavior, once learned, appears to be so "natural" that it can easily be perceived as instinctive, as biologically or "racially" determined."
Figure 1-8. These young women from Senegal physically resemble many Americans. It is the culture they have learned that is different. (United Nations.)

"racially" determined. Take the culture of the United States, for instance, and the way American infants are gradually conditioned to meet their basic biological needs in the particular ways dictated by their culture. The formation of food habits illustrates this vividly. For all of the first and most formative years of their lives children in the United States are clearly trained in the culturally proper actions and attitudes related to eating: what they should eat and how, the appropriate combination of foods, the right way to serve them, the proper times to eat, the correct utensils to use, "good" table manners, and so on. Once the more intensive phases of this training period are past and the young are permitted, usually at adolescence, to begin to make their own decisions, they have already acquired strong feelings about food, definite likes and dislikes, sensations of pleasure and repugnance, often ideas of ritual purity and uncleanliness as well. From then on their food preferences may change over the years, but only within a quite narrow gamut of the total possible range. Present Americans with a toasted grasshopper, objectively nutritious and considered tasty by some Africans and most Japanese, and they would probably lose their appetites. A hungry but devout Moslem Middle Easterner would likely feel the same way about the offer of a ham-on-rye. High-caste Hindus in India and Pakistan are conditioned by their culture to abhor beef. Most thirsty Chinese would decline a proffered glass of cow's milk with a shudder of disgust. Further examples could be taken from the way North American children are trained to meet their other basic biologically determined needs: the carefully prescribed rituals of excretion and washing, for instance, or American ideas on the right and wrong forms of sexual behavior, appropriate dress, or any other type of conduct culturally defined as "correct."

Thus our basic human needs are perceived as universally similar, the consequence of our membership in a single animal species, but the particular means by which we meet these needs are determined by our culture, by where and specifically how we learn to cope with the needs we share with all other human beings. The fact that people meet their animal needs by cultural means creates for the anthropologist a paradox, for *Homo sapiens* is extraordinarily flexible, capable of more adaptive variability than any other animal. Yet once the human personality is developed and is conditioned by culture to meet individual needs in particular culturally approved ways, a person often becomes so set in these ways that he or she would rather perish than change. Perhaps this talent for maintaining a balance between the conservatism required for cultural stability and continuity and the flexibility essential for adaptation to continuously shifting circumstances has been the secret of our survival, at least so far.

Cultural Means and Anthropological Categories

Because people's fundamental biological needs can be met only by cultural means, it follows that all cultures, no matter how remarkably diverse they appear, must fulfill a number of common basic functions necessary to the support of human life. For this reason all cultures must resemble one another in their most essential attributes. These necessarily universal aspects of culture can be categorized as systems, as particularly organized ways of fulfilling requirements common to all people. At least seven of these systems or categories can be analytically separated. Each, no matter how varied in specifics of form, content, and function, is

"The term *technology* is used to refer to the system of tools, artifacts, and techniques used by particular people to modify conditions and resources in their environment to meet their basic material needs."

Figure 1-9. Georgian farmers at rest, U.S.S.R. (Courtesy of Novosti Press Agency, Moscow, U.S.S.R.)

discernible as an aspect of every people's way of life.

These categories will be referred to here as *technology, economic organization, social organization, political organization, ideology, the arts,* and *language.* Culture can be perceived as an integrated whole composed of these categorically separable systems, all meaningfully related and having as their principal reason for being the fulfillment of human needs. Perceived in this way, many of what otherwise seem to be striking and absolute differences between cultures are revealed as only variations of specific form and content on fundamental, universal themes.

Technology

The term technology is used to refer to the system of tools, artifacts, and techniques employed by a particular people to modify conditions and resources in their environment to meet their basic material needs.

"Among Japanese and Korean islanders in the Northwest Pacific, shellfish gathered from the ocean floor by women divers are an important part of the food supply."
Figure 1-10. Woman diver, Japan. (Courtesy of the Embassy of Japan.)

Again the need for food provides a basic illustration. Every people must have some system of techniques for getting food. It is the specifics of such systems that vary. Among Japanese and Korean islanders in the Northwest Pacific, shellfish gathered from the ocean floor by women divers are an important part of the food supply. In the Amazonian rainforest food is provided by hunters who bring down their game with blowguns and poison darts. In northern Norway, Sweden, and Finland nomadic Lapp herdsmen obtain most of their food from their reindeer. In Fiji and the Ivory Coast the inhabitants derive an important part of their food supply from cultivating tubers called taro. In the temperate regions of Southwest Asia, Europe, and North America farmers grow cereal grains as a major source of food. And now, in some places, nutritious foods are synthesized from chemicals. The human need for nourish-

"In the Amazonian rainforest food is provided by hunters who bring down their game with blowguns and poison darts."
Figure 1-11. Forest hunter, Brazil. (OAS Photo.)

"In the temperate regions of Southwest Asia, Europe, and North America farmers grow cereal grains as a major source of food."

Figure 1-12. Wheat farming in Canada. (The Photographic Survey Corp., Ltd.)

"The human need for nourishment is universal. What differ are the ways people meet it."

Figure 1-13. Indian rice farmers. (Courtesy of the Press Information Bureau, Government of India.)

"The need for shelter . . . is similarly universal."
Figure 1-14. Mbuti Pygmy camp in the Ituri forest, Zaire. (Courtesy of the American Museum of Natural History.)

". . . to the constructions of steel, preformed concrete, and polyurethane foam found in the urban centers of most industrialized parts of the world."
Figure 1-15. Nonoalco-Tlaltellolco, an urban settlement for seventy thousand in Mexico City. (Courtesy of the Mexican Government Tourism Department.)

ment is universal. What differ are the ways people meet it.

The need for shelter, for protection from weather and from predators, is similarly universal. The forms of shelter range from the simplest windbreaks of sticks, leaves, and dried skins still used by small groups of Aborigines in the Australian "outback" and the ice-built igloos of some Eskimo to the constructions of steel, preformed concrete, and polyurethane foam found in the urban centers of most industrialized parts of the world. The need for clothing and for a means of transport, and the variety of ways in which these requirements are met, further reinforces the point: Technology is a necessary system that is culturally universal. The forms technology takes are what differ.

Economic Organization

Economic organization, in the terms used here, encompasses the techniques utilized in organizing the production and allocation of

"They also require some system for organizing themselves for work. . . ."

Figure 1-16. Peruvian threshers. (OAS Photo.)

"They also must have a system for distributing the products of their work."

Figure 1-17. The market at El-Harrach, Algeria. (United Nations.)

"People can survive only within some framework of social relations that provides a basis for relating to and relying on other individuals and other groups for cooperation."
Figure 1-18. A Japanese nuclear family. (United Nations.)

the goods and services people require to meet their material needs. Every human group must have some system for allocating productive goods, the land and tools its members use to produce other goods. They also require some system for organizing themselves for work, whether they are shellfish divers, Amazonian hunters, Lapp pastoralists, or East German industrialists. They furthermore must have a system for distributing the products of their work. The need for some form of economic system is the universal. How the system is organized varies from culture to culture.

Social Organization

What is true of economic organization is also true of social organization. People can survive only within some framework of social relations that provides a basis for relating to and relying on other individuals and other groups for cooperation. The universality of this requirement is a consequence of our biological nature, particularly the long period of dependency in infancy and early childhood, when the young human is learning the behaviors necessary to survival. Because an individual must rely on learning rather than instinct as a means of staying alive, and because this learning should last at least up to early adolescence, the young must be protected and cared for until able to protect and care for themselves. For this and for other important reasons as well, some form of primary group, based initially on family ties, is a universal.

People everywhere also organize themselves into other kinds of social groupings

a

b

"... the young must be protected and cared for until able to protect and care for themselves."

Figure 1-19. *a.* A San Blas Indian mother and child. (OAS Photos.) *b.* A North Indian grandfather and his grandson. (Courtesy of the Information Office, Embassy of India.) *c.* Two Ladakhi matrons with a young kinswoman. (Press Information Bureau, Government of India.) *d.* A Tanzanian girl with an infant left in her care. (Courtesy of the American Museum of Natural History.)

c

d

"In every society some means must be provided for making decisions on matters that affect the group members' survival."

Figure 1-20. Election day in Kyoto. (Courtesy of the Embassy of Japan.)

that complement, extend, and occasionally replace the family: secret societies, clubs, castes, social classes, groups based on ethnic or sexual differences, and so on. The requirement for some system of social groupings is again the universal; the forms and processes of the system are the variables.

Political Organization

In every society some means must be provided for making decisions on matters that affect the group members' survival. There must be some way of controlling conflict within the society and some way of regulating relations with other societies. This need for the maintenance of internal order and for the governance of relations with other societies is the universal. The forms and processes by which the need is met range from small, autonomous family bands to populous, interdependent nation-states; from reliance on common custom to development of voluminous legal codes; from intrafamilial feuding to atomic war.

Ideology

Some guiding set of beliefs explaining the nature of the world and of people's relation to it and to the cosmos, always accompanied by some system of observances that symbolically reinforce these beliefs and sanction the actions they require, is still another universal aspect of culture. Among most of the world's peoples a major component of the ideological system is based on concepts of supernaturalism that usually entail belief in one or more beings endowed with miraculous powers: gods, spirits, angels, demons, prophets, and so on. Frequently these beliefs are described within the context of myths in which the origin of the world is recounted with apocryphal embellishments that serve both as a guide to good behavior and as a warning of the punishment in store for those who do "wrong."

An accompanying set of ritual actions, sacrifices, prayers, and other observances functions not only to reify and reinforce belief but also to provide people with a means for taking formal action to achieve or maintain a secure position for themselves in relation to the supernatural as they perceive it. Often these rituals are led by priests, religious specialists who act as intermediaries between human beings and the supernatural. Among a smaller but not insignificant number of the world's peoples, supernaturally based belief systems have been partially replaced by secular, nonreligious ideologies, frequently based on ethical

"... concepts of supernaturalism that usually entail belief in one or more beings endowed with miraculous powers: gods, spirits, angels, demons, prophets, and so on."

Figure 1-21. Ganesha, the elephant-headed god, Java. (Courtesy of the Library of Congress.)

"An accompanying set of ritual actions, sacrifices, prayers. . . ."
Figure 1-22. Canadian at prayer. (National Film Board of Canada.)

or political principles. Once more it is the presence of some system of beliefs that is the universal; the specifics of ideological form, content, and function are what differ.

The Arts

Some system of techniques for the exaltation of experience through manipulation of the senses is another universal aspect of cul-

a

b

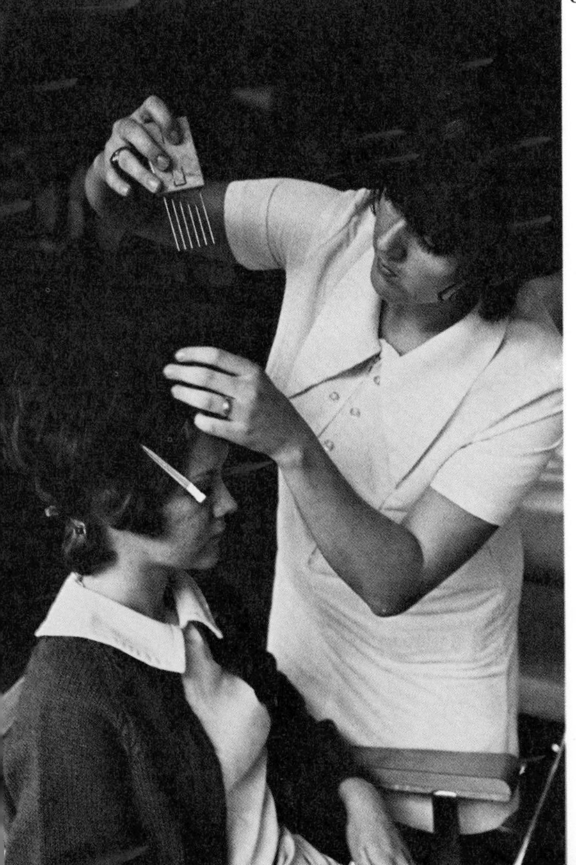

c

"The graphic and plastic arts, personal adornment, music, dance, drama, and oral literature are among the frequently combined forms through which this apparently universal need for aesthetic experience is expressed."

Figure 1-23. *a.* A Navaho sand painter. (Courtesy of the American Museum of Natural History.) *b.* Helmet mask, New Ireland, Melanesia. (Courtesy of the Museum of Primitive Art.) *c.* Cosmetology in Kentucky. (Jan W. Faul/Appalachian Regional Commission.) *d.* Balinese dancers. (Courtesy of the Cultural and Educational Division, Embassy of the Republic of Indonesia.)

d

ture. Among every human group there is to be found some such set of techniques, serving always to heighten and intensify feeling and thought. Often, but by no means invariably, this entails an effort to create in an object, in a movement, in a sound, or in a concept something beautiful. But it is the purposeful exaltation or intensification of experience, concern for the creation of a sensation that transcends mere "beauty," that appears to be the more fundamental attribute of such systems. The graphic and plastic arts, personal adornment, music, dance, drama, and oral literature are among the frequently combined forms through which this apparently universal need for esthetic experience is expressed.

"The universality of language and its integral relation to the processes by which culture is learned. . . ."

Figure 1-24. A language lesson in rural Afghanistan. (United Nations.)

Language

Language is the last of the major categories of culture to be considered here. The universality of language and its integral relation to the processes by which culture is learned, used, changed, and passed on are obvious. As with all other aspects of culture, it is the form, the particular content and certain specific functions of language, that differ from people to people.

How Culture Is Studied—And Why

Cultural and social anthropology as a discipline is based on the collection and theoretical analysis of information on nearly every aspect of the various ways of life of the world's peoples. Most of this information is collected by anthropologists working in the field. Anthropological, or ethnographic, fieldwork usually involves the careful study at first hand of the patterned behavior of a particular human group—a family band, a local community, one or more segments of some larger societal unit, a tribe, or a nation. The descriptive account written on the basis of such fieldwork is called an *ethnography.*

The methods used for collecting and analyzing ethnographic data depend on the anthropologist's subject and the specifics of his or her methodological and theoretical orientation. For example, an anthropologist may be intent on collecting all the information possible as fast as possible on an only recently "discovered" people whose traditional way of life is undergoing rapid change and may soon be irreversibly transformed as a result of contact with technologically more powerful outsiders. He or she may concentrate intensively on the testing of a few carefully selected hypotheses and consequently gathering data on only one or two aspects of a culture such as the subsistence technology, marriage system, political behavior, or music of a people whose basic way of life is already fairly well known.

In either instance the anthropologist's work is likely to entail two initial phases. First, he or she will become acquainted with the available literature on the people whose culture is to be studied. The anthropologist will try also to become acquainted with what is known of the ways of life of neighboring groups, on the often correct assumption that people who live in the same region and under similar circumstances are likely to have similar cultures. He or she will endeavor to learn as much as possible about their language.

Then the anthropologist usually goes to "the field" to live among the people being studied, for a period that may range from several months to several years. To increase the chances for observation, to shorten his or her cultural distance from the subjects, the anthropologist usually tries to participate in their culture to whatever extent possible, as much as they will allow. If the anthropologist finds the language especially difficult, or if time in the field is limited, an interpreter will probably be needed, at least at the outset. An interpreter who is a member of the culture may also serve as an important informant and as a helpful intermediary for the anthropologist in establishing the contacts and rapport essential to successful fieldwork.

At the same time that he or she will have an objective, scientifically derived system for approaching the study of the people's culture and for categorizing its aspects, the anthropologist will also be interested in learning how the people themselves perceive their way of life. Their image of themselves, their perception of their relation to their culture, and their ideas on how their society operates are also a part of the anthropologist's data.

Fieldwork is often difficult. The physical conditions under which the anthropologist must work are frequently much less comfortable than those to which he or she has been accustomed. Foods may taste strange; the water may cause sickness; unfamiliar insects and exotic bacteria are likely to attack. The fieldworker may miss accustomed surroundings and find it difficult to adjust to the very different life-style of the people he or she is living among and studying. Probably many of them will not like or trust the anthropologist. Undoubtedly the anthropologist will not like or trust all of them.

The need to learn everything about a people one has never seen before, who may find one's questions silly, impertinent, or threatening and who speak a language one can scarcely comprehend, may further complicate the task. To these difficulties will be added methodological and theoretical dilemmas related to the cross-cultural applicability of a variety of techniques of ethnographic data collection: testing, mapping, filming, recording, sampling, census taking, and so on. Because of other commitments the anthropologist may be able to stay in the field for only a few months during what turns out to be a wholly atypical time in his or her subjects' lives. The "group" to be studied may number several hundred thousand. The anthropologist may occasionally want to give up, but, happily, most persevere. For them the physical discomforts, psychological adjustments, and methodological difficulties of fieldwork are all potentially part of the data and are satisfactorily offset by the intellectual and emotional adventure of getting to know the "natives" of another culture, reaffirming some old truths about all people, perhaps learning a few that are new, and submitting what is learned to the critical scrutiny of colleagues with the hope that some part of the observations may be both of lasting scientific value and of benefit to the people who were studied.

Traditionally, anthropologists have tended to concentrate their attention on the study of "non-Western" or "non-European" peoples, those whose ways of life differ most markedly from the European and American middle-class cultural settings from which most anthropologists have so far come. As a result of the steady expansion of European colonial domination from the fifteenth through the nineteenth centuries, Europeans and non-Europeans found themselves in increasingly frequent and prolonged contact. Often, to justify colonial domination, missionaries were sent out to preach "the truth" and to guide native peoples in the abandonment of their "heathenish" ways. To maintain effective control over their colonial subjects the Europeans needed to understand them. Many of our earliest firsthand ethnographic accounts were provided by missionaries and colonial administrators. Frequently they were followed to "the field" by trained anthropologists employed by the colonial powers.

In accordance with an exploitative tradition that has proven discouragingly tenacious, the tribal and peasant peoples studied rarely had an opportunity either to assess the relevance to their needs of the anthropologists' research design or to react to their research conclusions. Usually these were published abroad and only in a European language. Recently a small number of "native" (or non-Euroamerican) anthropologists have begun to work among their own peoples, and in other cultures as well. This new and valuable research development should both enlarge the range of our knowledge of world cultures and deepen our awareness of the urgent problems of survival, emancipation, and self-determination that indigenous peoples face nearly everywhere.

So far most British anthropologists have worked primarily in Africa and Asia and in the British-controlled territories of the Pacific. French anthropologists have worked principally in the areas of Equatorial and West Africa under French colonial control and in French Oceania. Until the last decades the majority of North American anthropologists worked with American Indians. With the end of colonialism, some newly independent areas became accessible to anthropologists who were not citizens of the former colonial powers. Largely for these reasons the anthropological tradition of studying peoples variously, inaccurately, and objectionably termed "nonliterate," "primitive," "native," or "non-Western" first developed. And it persists. Because of this tradition the professional preparation of most anthropologists is still directed toward preparing them to work outside their own cultures, although answers to many of their scholarly queries might just as properly be sought through study of themselves and of their own ways of life. Tradition, habit, and lack of experience are the only significant obstacles. Ultimately they must be overcome, because "ultimately" (probably by the end of this century) the cultures that have been the principal object of the anthropologists' first-hand study—small, relatively isolated, exotic human groups—will almost all have come under cultural assault from technologically and politically more powerful peoples, and most will have disappeared. The chance to learn from them will then be lost forever. Considering this, perhaps the anthropologists' past propensity for the study of relatively small communities of technologically more primitive peoples has some justification. However, a shift in interest is already evident. Increasingly, young anthropologists are turning their attention to such equally compelling subjects as economic development, industrialization and its cultural prerequisites and consequences, race and ethnic conflict, mental health, overpopulation, the causes and characteristics of rural and urban poverty, sexism, economic imperialism, and modern warfare.

Obviously, the anthropologist working in the field reviews the data as they are being collected, checking discrepancies in information, shifting the direction of the investigation, the content of the sample, and the techniques of inquiry as circumstances change and his or her knowledge of the people's culture grows. However, it is often only when the anthropologist has returned from the field that there is time to analyze and organize the information in final form. Some of it may be written up and published in purely descriptive ethnographic reports. This kind of publication constitutes a basic contribution to the anthropological literature, a repository from which all other anthropologists can draw for teaching materials, in preparing their own research, in writing, and, increasingly, in working as partisans in the self-determination struggles of the still dominated peoples they have studied.

Or the returned fieldworker may attempt a theoretical analysis of the data gathered. The development of theory in cultural and social anthropology (or ethnology) proceeds from the collection of data in two phases. First the anthropologist works out a theoretical explanation of the information. He or she then tests the theory within the context of data on like phenomena collected by other anthropologists who have worked in other cultures. Increasingly anthropologists rely on statistical techniques to support their findings. Frequently the anthropologist returns to the field for more information, by this process working optimistically toward the confirmation of his or her conclusions, often discovering the need for further testing and the modification of the original explanation. Occasionally the anthropologist may decide to reject a first theory entirely and search for an alternative interpretation. Sometimes such testing is deferred; the explanation is left to stand as a hypothesis to be tested later by others.

In teaching, the anthropologist's first task is to introduce students to the wide variety of cultural ways in which people meet their common human needs. At the same time the anthropologist introduces them to those theoretical concepts that he or she believes serve best to make these cultural variations meaningful. Gradually this should lead the students toward a more objective appreciation of themselves and others, and of the combination of unique historical events, environmental circumstances, and universal processes that shape the lives of people and determine the forms of society and culture everywhere.

Beyond developing a greater tolerance for the differing ways of others and a greater objectivity about themselves, students of cultural and social anthropology may come to see familiar problems in new perspective. Poverty, family disorganization, racism and sexism, political exploitation, warfare, and ideological oppression can be perceived not as universal, irrevocable aspects of human fate but as products of particular sets of sociocultural circumstances, circumstances

"Poverty, family disorganization, racism and sexism, political exploitation, warfare, and ideological oppression can be perceived not as universal, irrevocable aspects of human fate, but as products of particular sets of sociocultural circumstances. . . ."
Figure 1-25. A West Virginia coal miner and his family. (Courtesy of the Library of Congress.)

that can in some instances be altered—if not to solve all human problems in any final sense, at least to reduce their severity and the suffering they cause.

From an anthropological perspective, whatever is learned about people anywhere is ultimately relevant to understanding people everywhere. The following chapters are organized to illustrate this premise, with ethnographic examples of the variety of cultural ways in which people provide for their common human needs, with some theoretical suggestions as to how such cultural variation can be explained, and finally with attention to the potential utility of anthropology in ameliorating some of humanity's most pressing current problems.

Summary

Anthropology, the scientific study of humankind, is usually divided into three related basic fields: (1) physical anthropology, the study of human evolution, variation, and growth; (2) archeology, the study of cultural development on the basis of the material remains of people's antecedent ways of life; and (3) cultural and social anthropology, the study of all aspects of the ways of life of contemporary or historically recent peoples.

We are cultured animals. During the several millions of years of our evolution those of our ancestors best able to use culture as a means of adaptation—to communicate and

". . . whatever is learned about people anywhere is ultimately relevant to understanding people everywhere."
Figure 1-26. A young Melanesian. (Courtesy of the American Museum of Natural History.)

cooperate with their fellows, to control their aggressive impulses for the sake of societal survival, to think out solutions to their problems, and to plan ahead—had the best chances of surviving long enough to pass on this valuable ability. By this process people, society, and culture evolved together.

Now, as members of a single species, all humans share a common set of fundamental needs: for food, for protection, for social cooperation, for belief, for esthetic experience, and for communication. These can be met only by cultural means. In order to survive, every culture must meet these needs for at least most of its members. Consequently, all cultures necessarily share certain fundamental attributes, the systems by which our universal human needs are met. These systems, or aspects of culture, are studied by anthropologists according to the following categories: technology, economic organization, social organization, political organization, art, and language.

The anthropologist studies culture, records variations in its component aspects, and develops and tests theories to explain them. The goal of such explanation is achievement of the objective understanding of people and their relationship to society and culture (and to the rest of the natural environment) that is essential for accurate prediction and effective human action.

Suggested Readings

In addition to other general introductory texts that deal with the subject of cultural and social anthropology there are several fairly recent, smaller books that take a sometimes different but essentially complementary approach to the one taken here. Among the best of these are Beals's *Culture in Process,* Peacock and Kirsch's *The Human Direction: An Evolutionary Approach to Social and Cultural Anthropology,* and Wolf's *Anthropology.* Hammond's *Cultural and Social Anthropology: Introductory Readings in Ethnology* is a collection especially designed to complement the text you are using.

For an idea of the essentially social anthropological approach try Bohannan's *Social Anthropology* or Mair's *An Introduction to Social Anthropology.*

On the relationships between the evolution of people and the evolution of society and culture see Spuhler's excellent collection *The Evolution of Man's Capacity for Culture.* Two other good general works dealing with aspects of the same subject are Birdsell's *Human Evolution: An Introduction to the New Physical Anthropology* and Campbell's *Human Evolution: An Introduction to Man's Adaptation.*

The interplay between people's biologically determined needs and their cultural means of coping with them is succinctly developed by Goldschmidt in the "Introduction" to his *Exploring the Ways of Mankind;* see also Alland's *Evolution and Human Behavior;* a collection edited by Montagu, *Culture: Man's Adaptive Dimension;* and Weiss and Mann's *Human Biology and Human Behavior: An Anthropological Perspective.*

For an excellent critical history of the development of cultural and social anthropology as a science see Harris's *The Rise of Anthropological Theory* and also Voget's *History of Ethnology.* Brew's *One Hundred Years of Anthropology* is an account that emphasizes the parallel development of physical anthropology and archeology.

Although there is no single general guide to anthropological fieldwork, a publication of the Royal Anthropological Institute, *Notes and Queries on Anthropology,* and Murdock's *Outline of World Cultures* illustrate the detailed variety of data anthropologists may collect in the field. See also the titles published in the Spindlers' series, "Studies in Anthropological Method," particularly Langness's *The Life History in Anthropological Science* and Williams's *Field Methods in the Study of Culture.* Naroll and Cohen's encyclopedic *A Handbook of Method in Cultural Anthropology* contains a long section on "The Field Work Process."

Many of the ethnographies listed in the references at the back of this book also contain descriptions of the problems of fieldwork in non-Western cultural settings. Among the best of the special works on ethnographic method are Golde's *Women in the Field,* Kimball and Watson's *Crossing Cultural Boundaries,* Spindler's *Being an Anthropologist: Field Work in Eleven Cultures,* and Wax's *Doing Fieldwork: Warnings and Advice.* Lewis's *A Study of Slum Culture* is a good example of the modification of traditional field techniques to meet the requirements of the growing number of anthropologists working in modern urban settings. On this same theme see "In the Field" in Hannerz's *Soulside: Essays in Ghetto Culture and Community.* For a now classic account of the ups and downs of life in the field see Bowen's *Return to Laughter,* Berreman's *Behind Many Masks: Ethnography and Impression Management in a Himalayan Village,* "The Politics of Field Work" in Diamond's *In Search of the Primitive,* and Read's *The High Valley.*

On the relevance of anthropology to the pressing problems of the contemporary world see Hymes's *Reinventing Anthropology* and Jorgensen and Truzzi's *Anthropology and American Life.*

Fried's *The Study of Anthropology* provides a lively introduction for anyone considering anthropology as a career.

Part Two

Technology

. . . culture is but a means of carrying on the life process of a particular species, Homo sapiens. *It is a mechanism for providing man with subsistence, protection, offense and defense, social regulation, cosmic adjustment, and recreation. But to serve these needs of man energy is required. It becomes the primary function of culture, therefore, to harness and control energy so that it may be put to work in man's service.*

WHITE (1949:367)

Technology is the aspect of culture that encompasses all the tools, artifacts, and techniques a people uses to meet its material needs. It can be usefully examined in terms of four basic categories: (1) food getting, (2) shelter, (3) manufacturing, and (4) transport.

In separating technology in order to look at its component aspects one at a time, it is important to keep in mind that such separation inevitably distorts cultural reality. The full workings and final significance of any aspect of any particular technology can be accurately comprehended only as it operates in interaction with the total system of technoenvironmental adaptation of which it is a part, and as that system itself has functioned through time in relation to the other aspects of culture.

2

The Quest for Food

OBVIOUSLY, all people must obtain food. What they get, how they get it, and how they process it for consumption vary in ways that are fundamental to an understanding of most other key aspects of their cultures.

Once people everywhere obtained their food by hunting, fishing, and gathering wild plants. In fact, for most of human history (that is, for 99 per cent of the last several million years) all people were hunter-gatherers. They first learned how to produce food relatively recently, no more than about ten thousand years ago. Thereafter this new and ultimately more efficient means of coping with the food quest gradually spread from people to people throughout most of the world, with revolutionary results.

Hunter-gatherers

However, there are still some culturally and/or geographically isolated people (about three million throughout the world) who have not yet discovered or borrowed food-producing techniques in even their simplest form, groups who still obtain their food by foraging (hunting wild animals and collecting wild plants) and for whom human muscle power is still the principal energy source. As their food-getting technologies are chronologically the oldest and comparatively the least productive, it is instructive to consider them first. Understanding how these still-existing primitive methods work is helpful both in understanding how more complex and more productive systems for obtaining food have developed and in assessing the social and cultural effects of this development. Also, the food-getting technologies of contemporary hunter-gatherers illustrate strikingly the fundamental, often causal relationship between technological adaptation to the environment and the form and content of other basic aspects of society and culture.

. . . "there are still some . . . people . . . who have not yet discovered or borrowed food-producing techniques in even their simplest form. . . ."

Figure 2-1. An Australian hunter trails a turtle, ready to spear it. (Courtesy of the American Museum of Natural History.)

Kalahari Hunter-Gatherers

The !Kung San hunter-gatherers of southern Africa are among the best studied of any present-day people living at this most primitive level of technological development (Bateman 1970; Jones and Doke 1937; Kolata 1974; Lee 1972a; Lee and DeVore 1976; Jordaan 1975; J. Marshall 1956, 1958; L. Marshall 1960, 1965; Schapera 1951; Story 1958; Thomas 1959; Tobias 1956). (The exclamation mark in *!Kung* represents an implosive click sound made with the tongue.) They are the descendants of an ancient people who once lived in more numerous groups scattered throughout most of the southern and eastern regions of the African continent. Centuries ago they began to be displaced by other Africans, people who had adopted—invented or borrowed—a more efficient means of making a living by growing food: farming and raising animals. Unable to compete for living space and natural resources with these technologically more efficient and consequently more numerous peoples, the !Kung were slaughtered, reduced to the status of serfs, absorbed, or driven out. The majority have survived only in the most inaccessible or undesirable parts of southern Africa, still autonomous only in areas others cannot reach or do not want. Today most of them live around the edges of the Kalahari Desert of Botswana and in the swamps nearby.

Because sources of wild food are sparse in the Kalahari region, and because the !Kung have few means of preserving and storing surpluses on those intermittent occasions when they are available, their life is necessarily organized around the continuous quest for fresh supplies of wild foods. They move, slowly but almost ceaselessly, over the hot sandy flats of the desert and its edges, searching always for newly grown wild plants, insects' nests, and the grazing grounds and watering holes of the wild animals that are their prey. Their meager surplus stores are rarely sufficient for more than a few days. When the available food in one area has been used up—when the game animals have grazed the grass down and moved on, when the usable plants have been gathered and eaten, when the water collected in surface ponds and the hollows of dead trees has been drunk—the Kalahari foragers must always move on.

Small bows and strongly poisoned arrows, spears, snares, throwing sticks, clubs, and digging sticks are the principal implements of the !Kung. These are complemented by a detailed and accurate knowledge of their prey's behavior and of the characteristics and growing conditions of wild food. The success of the !Kung as hunters is heavily dependent on their knowledge of the habits of their quarry: their ability to recognize a spoor and track it for miles and days over hard, rocky ground, their keen perception of the significance of any variations in the appearance of their habitat—a shriveled vine half hidden by rocks indicating the underground presence of an edible root; a tiny fissure in the surface of the sandy soil signifying that a tuber lies beneath; a parrot in a distant tree revealing that water must be nearby. All these aspects of !Kung technology are as important as the tools and weapons they use.

Almost any available form of animal or insect life is the !Kung hunters' prey: locusts, scorpions, ants, and bees; frogs, lizards, and snakes; guineafowl, bustards, and ostriches; aardvarks, elands, giraffes, and kudus. The !Kung hunt, kill, and eat them all.

Although game constitutes the smallest part of the !Kung's diet, its pursuit is always the subject of excited interest. Large animals such as giraffes are first sought out and then carefully stalked by hunters moving upwind of a herd that is grazing or gathered around a waterhole. An individual animal is selected, shot with a poisoned arrow, and then tracked until the poison has so weakened it that the hunters can move in safely to make the kill with a club or spear.

!Kung hunters also kill by poisoning the waterholes of their wild prey. Part of the water from a regular watering place, a pond or spring, is diverted into a shallow ditch and conducted off into a small pit a few yards away. There bunches of the poisonous euphorbia plant are thrown into the water, and stones are placed on top to hold them down. Gradually the juice exuded by the branches rises to the surface to form a lethal scum. The regular waterhole is then covered over with branches, forcing the animals to drink from the smaller poisoned pond. They drink, and die soon after, their meat apparently unaffected by the poison.

Ostriches are also killed with poison. A waiting hunter watches until a mother ostrich leaves her nest for a moment. Then, creeping stealthily up, he rams a poison-smeared stake into the earth, point up, among her eggs. When she returns to settle on the nest and cover the eggs, the sharp poisoned stake is driven into her rump and she dies in minutes. Smaller game is often caught with intricately engineered snares and traps.

The !Kung make use of all parts of the animals they kill. Sometimes pieces of flesh are cut off and eaten raw on the spot. If the hunters' camp is nearby, most of the meat of a large animal is cut up in chunks and carried home to be cooked by the women. Blood is collected and carried back in bags made from the stomach and intestines. Soft parts—the heart, lungs, and brain—are usually reserved for the old people whose teeth are poor. Like all !Kung fare, meat is cooked at an open fire, held over the flames at the end of a fire-hardened stick or placed in the hot ashes to bake. Tougher pieces of meat are sometimes softened by pounding with a stone. If the camp is located at so great a distance that there is danger of spoilage, all but the small portion of meat immediately consumed is cut into thin strips and dried before being carried home.

If leather is needed for cloaks or carrying bags, the hide is crudely tanned. Otherwise the skin is also eaten. The gristle of the ears and the mucuous membranes of the nose are consumed as well. Sinew is used to make bow strings, the cord for snares, and the wrappings for arrow points, cups, dippers, and spoons. The splinters of bones broken for their marrow are fashioned into projectile points to kill more animals. Nothing is left.

But !Kung hunters rarely bring down large game more than once or twice a month. As is true with most hunter-gatherers, the more certain and by far the larger part of the food supply (from 60 to 80 per cent) is collected by the women. Unless they are busy with other tasks, women and children go out foraging almost every day, ranging within a radius of several miles of the campsite and working preferably during the cooler hours of early morning and late afternoon. Using sticks from two to four feet long, sometimes tipped with a piece of bone, the women dig narrow holes into the earth where they think there may be an edible

"... they collect it in ostrich shells. ..."
Figure 2-2. Bushmen women collecting water in ostrich shell containers. (Courtesy of the American Museum of Natural History.)

root. When they find one, they tug it loose, pull it to the surface with their hands, and place it in a skin bag slung over their shoulders or across their backs. In addition to several varieties of roots and tubers, the women gather fruits, berries, nuts, melons (especially valued for the water stored in their pulpy flesh), mushrooms, truffles, and many kinds of insects.

Roots to be cooked are set directly in the ashes of the fire. Sometimes an empty but still-green melon rind or a piece of gourd is used as a pot for boiling some smaller vegetable. Foods that can be preserved by drying, such as nuts and melon seeds, are often collected in skin bags and buried or hidden in the crooks of trees to be used later. But the ability of the !Kung to acquire and preserve food surpluses is limited. Food must be consumed soon after it is found.

Insects usually are eaten raw. Occasionally they are held live over the fire, quickly toasted, and eaten hot.

Many surface sources of water—ponds, small streams, the water caught in the hollows of dead trees—disappear as the desert winter of hot, dry days and freezing nights progresses. As water becomes scarce, many wild plants die, grazing animals move off in search of new pasturage and other sources of water, and the !Kung follow, usually to the vicinity of a permanent spring. When water is more abundant, they collect it in ostrich shells fitted with stoppers made from wads of grass. These are buried or hidden in hollow trees and left to be returned to in times of drought.

Thirsty !Kung searching for water know that a patch of green vegetation in an otherwise arid region indicates the presence of water beneath the dry earth's surface. To reach it, a long reed tube tufted with a bunch of grass is pushed into the earth down to the water-bearing stratum. The liquid is painstakingly drawn to the surface by sucking and carefully transferred mouthful by mouthful to an ostrich eggshell container.

Despite (or perhaps because of) the productive limitations of their technology, the material needs of the !Kung are adequately met in all but the worst years. And they sustain a balanced, nondestructive relationship with the resources whose natural replenishment is essential to their survival.

Semang Hunters of Malaysia

Another group of people who still make their living in this most ancient way are the Semang of the Malaysian tropical forests (Evans 1927, 1937; Schebesta 1926a, 1926b; Skeat 1902; Skeat and Blagden 1906). They and others like them once lived throughout the greater part of Malaysia. Like the Bushmen, they have survived and maintained their traditional culture only where there has been no competition for territory from technologically more advanced intruders.

Despite its apparent lushness, the dense, humid rainforest habitat of the Semang is poor in available food resources. Yams, berries, nuts, roots, the tender young shoots of the wild plum, and the fruits of the durian tree provide the basis of a diet that is only rarely supplemented by such meager game as bamboo rats, squirrels, monkeys, lizards, birds, and an occasional wild pig.

The Semang have been described as living in the "Age of Bamboo." A treelike grass that grows in dense, sometimes almost impenetrable thickets throughout their forest, bamboo is one of the Semang's principal raw materials. Most of their tools are made from it. Short, sharpened sticks of bamboo are used as cutting instruments and for spears and arrows. Hollow bamboo tubes are used for carrying water and as vessels for cooking.

Among the Semang, also, women are the food gatherers. They collect snails and honey, a number of pulpy, tuberous plants, yams, nuts, and durian. Each family group has the right to collect fruit from particular durian trees. Often they camp nearby when the fruit is ripening, guarding it from wild bears and picking it as it matures.

Semang hunters use bamboo blowguns and strongly poisoned darts to bring down the rats and monkeys that are their principal prey. Their blowgun is made from a special variety of bamboo that has widely separated junctures. The tube of the gun, from six to eight feet long, is made from a single, smooth-barreled segment worked over the fire until it is absolutely straight. A second piece of bamboo, slightly larger in circumference, provides the casing. Seven-inch darts are made from the slender central spines of a palm. Just below their tip a slight nick is made in the shaft so that the poisoned point will break off in the flesh of the animal. Dart tips are dipped and turned until thickly coated in a paste made with the juice of several poisonous plants, among them a species of strychnos. Sometimes poison taken from scorpions, snakes, and centipedes is added. The dart is inserted at the end of the blowgun and fired by taking a portion of the lower part of the dart into the mouth, aiming, and expelling the air from the lungs so strongly that the dart is shot forward, striking the animal with such force that the poisoned tip is firmly embedded in its flesh. The fallen animal is finished off with the hunter's knife or a club.

Meat is skewered on a stick and cooked over the flames. The Semang eat most wild fruits raw. Tubers are set in the hot coals to bake. Leaves and the pulpy centers of edible plants are boiled in containers made from a single short length of green bamboo, closed at the bottom by the natural juncture of the stalk. Water is poured in at the top, and the bamboo vessel is stopped with a wadded leaf. Held over the flames at an angle, the container is turned constantly to prevent it from catching fire. When the food inside is cooked by the boiling water, the leaf stopper is removed and the contents are spilled out onto another leaf that serves as a plate.

Like nearly all foragers, the Semang are seminomadic. They adjust to changes in the distribution of wild foods by moving. When the supply of edible plants and game near their camp has been depleted, after a few days or a few weeks, they must gather their limited multipurpose possessions and move on—the women with babies and string collecting bags on their backs and digging sticks in their hands, the men with blowguns and quivers—for some fresh new camping place within their forest territory. There leaves are piled together to make beds, more leaves are tossed over a loose framework of sticks to construct a shelter, and the new settlement is established and ready to serve as another necessarily temporary base in the Semang's leisurely but continuous quest for food.

The Sociocultural Consequences of Foraging

The separate cultures of the !Kung and the Semang obviously developed independently. Yet in each instance similar causal factors were at work. Among each of these groups of hunter-gatherers, in fact among nearly all foragers, difficult environments and/or their invariably ingenious but always comparatively unproductive technologies are correlated with low population density and a relative lack of complexity or elaboration of the other aspects of society and culture.

For example, technological specialization is usually based on sex and age; nearly all foraging peoples are to some extent necessarily nomadic; beyond a few multifunctional tools and weapons, there is little possibility of property accumulation; most economic goods are allocated on a reciprocal basis; role differentiation is minimal; usually there are few important social groupings beyond the family; the community is small, flexibly organized, and unstratified; mobility serves as a major means of coping with conflict; political authority within the autonomous local band is usually exogamous (that is, its members must marry out into neighboring groups, thereby creating a useful basis for interterritorial cooperation); although often rich in abstract symbolism, ideology is parochial, ritual is confined to the life crises, and religious hierarchy is usually lacking; principal aesthetic forms are frequently non-material; and dialect differences are pronounced. Most exceptions to these generalizations (the Indian fishermen of the Northwest Pacific coast are a striking recent example) are found only among hunter-gatherers whose natural habitat is extraordinarily rich in wild food resources, making possible a greater degree of sedentarization, some increase in population size and density, and, often, the beginnings of internal differences in socioeconomic status.

Most of these causal propositions linking foragers' patterns of technoenvironmental adaptation and the other aspects of their culture still hold. But a few require reexamination in the light of new evidence. Perhaps partly because of earlier observers' biases, and also because few hunter-gatherers had been studied closely enough for sufficient time, certain features of their ways of life have been misinterpreted or exaggerated. The idea persists, for example, that the habitat of hunter-gatherers is invariably harsh and impoverished, making the food quest nearly ceaseless and often precarious, allowing little time for leisure or the elaboration of other aspects of culture, and making it difficult to support the sick and aged (the image endures of elderly Eskimo set adrift on the ice to die).

Generally it is true that foragers have managed to maintain their ancient ways of life only in areas too hot and arid or too bleak and cold to easily support an alternative technology. But this is not always so. In the forests of Zäire Pygmy hunters have lived for centuries in fairly stable symbiosis with Bantu farmers (Turnbull 1965, 1968). And recent reports by younger anthropologists who have shared the life of foragers in the Australian desert (Gould 1969), in the Dobe area in Botswana (Lee 1968, 1972a), and of the Hadza in northern Tanzania (Woodburn 1968, 1972) convincingly chronicle a life marked by moderate material comfort, considerable leisure, and few serious problems in caring for the infirm and aged. Where the natural habitat is less harsh, the foragers' persistent mobility is ascribed not alone to the pressures of the food quest but also to the pleasure of travel and the enjoyment of visiting kinsmen in neighboring territories.

Before the discovery of plant and animal domestication, when hunting and gathering were far more widespread, foragers frequently occupied much richer natural set-

". . . comparatively unproductive technologies are correlated with low population density and a relative lack of complexity or elaboration of the other basic aspects of society and culture."

Figure 2-3. An Eskimo seal hunter prepares to throw his harpoon. (National Film Board of Canada.)

tings than they do today. Their life then may have been even easier, especially where the weather was good. Even now latitude counts for a lot. The availability of vegetable foods is an especially significant variable. For example: because hunting is almost always harder than gathering, making a living among the east African Hadza is far less arduous and uncertain than among those northern Eskimo whose food supply still is almost solely dependent on hunting sea mammals on the arctic ice (Nelson 1973).

The Beginnings of Domestication

Similarly significant causal interrelationships of environment, technology, and the other basic aspects of society and culture are found among people who make their living at the chronologically and productively more advanced level of plant and animal domestication.

The discovery of food growing precipitated the first great sociocultural revolution in human history. This basic technological innovation made other sociocultural changes possible and in most instances necessary. For the first time ever people could settle down and stay in one place for longer periods of time, replenishing their stores of food by producing more where they were. As they learned to grow more food, they could feed more people. As human population grew and spread, knowledge of domestication spread also, and gradually was adapted to other environments, to different kinds of terrain and climate, and to other species of plants and animals. Where they could produce and preserve a surplus, some groups found it possible, rewarding, and occasionally necessary to take time out from farming to engage in other activities, to specialize in making tools and other artifacts or to provide their services as laborers and warriors or as religious and political leaders.

Probably the techniques of the earliest food producers were scarcely distinguishable from the food-getting activities of hunter-gatherers. By a gradual, initially perhaps almost imperceptible process, semisedentary

"The discovery of food growing precipitated the first great sociocultural revolution in human history."

Figure 2-4. A Javanese farmer sowing rice. (United Nations.)

collectors of wild grass seeds (probably mostly women) in the arid Middle East and in Middle America may have noticed that where dried seeds fell among the debris of their settlements or onto the rain-moistened earth new grasses sprouted and grew. In tropical Southeast Asia others may have observed casually that stalks of edible plants would often sprout when thrust back into the humid forest floor. Where, when, and most important *how* people first made this discovery, gradually realized its revolutionary potentialities, and slowly began to exploit it constitute the subject of compellingly important archaeological investigations (see Cambel and Braidwood 1970; Chang 1970; Harlan 1971; Harlan and de Wet 1973; Higgs 1972; Isaac 1970; Singh 1974; Solheim 1972; Streuver 1971; Tringham 1971; Waterbolk 1968; Wright 1971).

Horticulture, or Primitive Farming

A useful analytic distinction can be made between the primitive techniques of the earliest food growers and more recently developed and complex systems for growing food. In anthropology primitive farming is called horticulture. Use of this term usually means that farmers work their land with hand tools, use neither draft animals nor the plow, and make little or no use of irrigation, seed selection, or fertilizers. The ratio of laborers to acreage in cultivation is typically low. Gardens and small farm plots are commonly the units of land use. Where vegetation is heavy it is cleared by slashing and burning the trees and underbrush. Unless the soil is naturally very rich, the inability of horticulturalists to increase or replace its fertility usually means that after a few growing seasons they must abandon the land they have been working and allow it to regenerate naturally. Sometimes the whole community

"Use of this term usually means that farmers work their land with hand tools. . . ."

Figure 2-5. Two women cultivators at work with short-handled hoes, Upper Volta. (James Pickerell/International Development Association.)

then moves on to clear land in a new place, a technique called "shifting cultivation." Sometimes they can remain where they are for longer periods by rotating their crops and allowing a part of their land to lie fallow. Foraging usually continues as an important supplementary activity. Horticulture is the principal means of making a living in much of the Third World. Most of the farmers of sub-Saharan Africa are still horticulturalists. So are most of the peoples

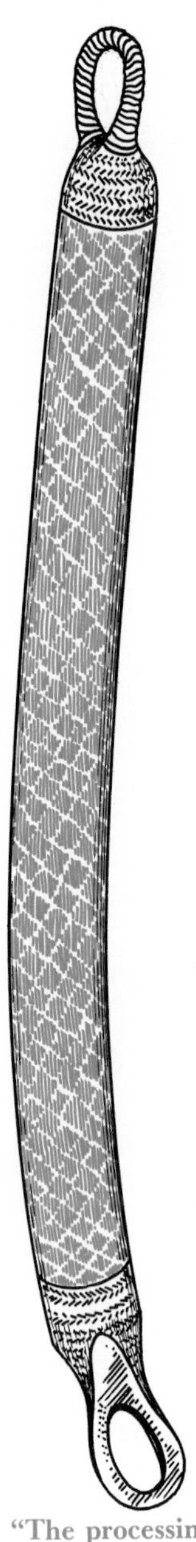

"The processing of the harvested plant is the most complex aspect of the Tupinambá food-producing technology.

Figure 2-6. Cassava squeezer, Guyana. (After I. M. Thurn.)

who live in the highlands of Southeast Asia, in Oceania, and in Latin America.

Although the food-producing technologies of primitive farmers vary in specifics of technique and in relative complexity and efficiency, they are generally more productive than the technologies of foragers and almost invariably less productive than those of the agriculturalists described later in this chapter. Most of the Indians of the tropical forests of South America are primitive farmers. Among the several root crops they cultivate, a tuber called manioc is especially important.

The Tupinambá of the Amazon

The Tupinambá (Métraux 1948), who live along the banks and out over the floodplains of the Amazon in northeastern Brazil, cultivate fine bitter manioc, which is poisonous, and nontoxic sweet manioc. Both types are processed to make a starchy sort of bread, which is the principal item in the Tupinambá diet.

Manioc cultivators clear their forest plots by cutting down the underbrush and felling the larger trees with axes (which used to be made of stone). After several months, when the dead trees have dried out, they are set afire; the potash enriches the soil. Near the end of the dry season cuttings are taken from the branches of mature plants and set out by the women, who thrust them into holes made in the soft earth of the garden with a sharp stick. The cuttings root quickly, and soon the surface plant reaches a height between five and six feet. The subterranean tubers develop in about four months, at which time they are pulled up.

The processing of the harvested plant is the most complex aspect of the Tupinambá food-producing technology. Preparation of the poisonous variety, bitter manioc, is particularly complicated. First the skin of the rough manioc tuber is peeled off with a piece of sharp shell and grated over a rough-surfaced stone or on a special grating board that is a wooden plank embedded with chips of stone or pieces of bone. The poisonous juice is then extracted by cramming the grated pulp into a narrow tubular basket about three feet long and ten inches in diameter with loops at each end. The top loop is fastened over one of the protruding ceiling beams of the Tupinambá house. A strong pole is passed through the loop at the lower end of the basket and set beneath a fulcrum created by attaching a stick at right angles to the house post. A woman then sits on the free end of the pole, stretching the tubular basket to diminish its diameter and squeezing the poisonous prussic acid out through the basket's interstices until only a pasty white mass remains inside. This is removed, pounded in a wooden mortar, passed through a basketry sifter, and emptied out as a starchy white powder onto a woven mat. Then it is baked on a clay grid into thin cakes or roasted on a large clay platter until it forms small, dry, pea-sized pellets, which, when baked and dried, can easily be stored until they are needed.

The Mossi of Yatenga

Like most peoples in Latin America, the Pacific, and much of Asia, the majority of the peoples of Africa still make their living by horticulture, or primitive farming. Only the Pygmies of the equatorial forests, the Bushmen, and a very few small East African groups have retained the older and less productive technology of hunting and gathering. Pastoral nomadic peoples are in the minority throughout the continent. In the forest regions African horticulturalists grow yams, taro, bananas, manioc, and other tropical food plants, using techniques essentially similar to or only slightly more complex than those of the South American Indians just described. In the more arid, less heavily forested regions of the continent (most of Africa is covered with rolling grassland, not jungle) in eastern and southern Africa and in the northwest just below the Sahara, most horticulturalists make their living by cultivating cereal crops: millet, sorghum, wheat, barley, and corn.

Millet and sorghum cultivation is the most widespread. They are the cereal grains whose cultivation might possibly have been discovered by the Africans themselves, perhaps somewhere in the warm, arid part of West Africa now occupied by people such as the Mossi, millet cultivators in the old kingdom of Yatenga, now part of Upper Volta (P. Hammond 1966).

Like all primitive farmers, the Mossi use only hand tools to work the land. Their principal implement is a short hoe, made from the forked branch of a tree, fitted transversely with a slightly curved iron blade. They use a mattock—part hoe, part hammer—to clear and clean the hard, dry earth of their fields for planting. This they do late in the spring, cutting down and setting fire to whatever underbrush remains after the long, dry winter. A field with especially poor soil is occasionally fertilized during the dry season by the herds of pastoral Fulani who graze their cattle on the unused land. To prevent erosion during the early rains, a network of branches is sometimes laid over a patch of especially thin soil. This is all the Mossi know of fertilizers and irrigation.

A month or so later, when rainfall has become more reliable, they return to their fields with dried millet seeds, which they sow by making a small depression in the earth with their hoes, dropping in a few seeds carried in a skin pouch or in a basket, tamping down the earth with the foot, and moving on. Later, beans, peanuts, and other crops are interplanted with the newly sprouted grain. Gradually, as the rains continue, the barren, dun-colored landscape is transformed. The millet springs up, and weeds and wild grasses are growing everywhere, turning the countryside into an endless thicket of deep green.

"In the more arid, less heavily forested regions of the continent . . . most horticulturalists make their living by cultivating cereal crops. . . ."

Figure 2-7. Mossi millet famers, Upper Volta. (Hammond 1966.)

Farmland must be cultivated between two and four times during the growing season to keep the maturing plants free of weeds, to turn the topsoil for ventilation, and to assure that precious rainwater is absorbed. The Mossi cultivate with the hoe and with their hands, moving slowly through their fields, often in groups, singing and working in unison to the accompaniment of a drum, pulling up or chopping out the weeds and leaving them to wither and die in the sun.

The harvest begins in late summer and continues through the fall, as different varieties of millet reach maturity at different times. The mature stalks are bent down by the harvester with one hand. He cuts loose the head of grain and with another slash lower down fells the entire plant. The heads of grain are stacked in the sun to dry and

". . . to be stored in mud brick granaries shaped like enormous earthen jars. . . ."
Figure 2-8. Three types of Mossi granaries; Yatenga, Upper Volta. (Hammond 1966.)

then carried back to the settlements to be stored in mud brick granaries shaped like enormous earthen jars, which are set up on foundations of sticks and stones to protect the harvested crop from moisture.

To prepare millet for consumption, the heads of grain are taken from the storehouses, laid out on a freshly swept spot of hardened earth, threshed with a stick or the branches of a tree, pounded in a wooden mortar and pestle, winnowed using a basket made from split millet stalks, and then ground on a flat stone set into the top edge of a circular mud brick platform. Millet flour is usually cooked in one of two principal ways: boiled to the consistency of a thick porridge in clay pots set over open fires or patted into small round cakes that are fried in oil squeezed from the fruit of the wild shea nut tree. Sometimes millet is mixed with water and drunk as a cold gruel. Some grain is used to make beer. With the cooked millet the Mossi serve sauces made from the leaves, flowers, and fruit of wild plants gathered by the women and children.

The few animals kept by the Mossi, mostly chickens and goats, are killed only on important occasions: as sacrifices in religious rituals or when there is an important guest to be entertained. Wild game is scarce in Yatenga. Of necessity the Mossi, like most other primitive farmers, are primarily vegetarian.

Horticulture and Its Sociocultural Correlates

So far it is most prudent to speak of the sociocultural consequences of horticulture, this more productive level of technological development, in terms of recurrent, possibly causal correlations. This is because the cultural adjustments of horticulturalists vary greatly as a function of differences in the relative richness of their environments and in the details of the history of particular peoples, especially as they affect the presence or absence of chances for cultural borrowing. However, some generalizations about causality can be confidently made.

In contrast to the majority of foragers, most horticulturalists have more secure and abundant food supplies that can support larger, more densely populated communities. However, reliance on hunting and gathering usually persists as an important supplementary food source. Nonetheless, greater sedentarization is possible, although the relative primitivism of farming techniques, especially the inability to get much beneath the topsoil to enrich the earth with fertilizers, usually means that farmers must rely on a system of shifting cultivation. Unless the environment is extraordinarily rich and population density is quite low, this in

". . . time and materials are usually available for an increase in part-time specialization in nonfarming activities."

Figure 2-9. A weaver at his loom, Benin. (United Nations.)

turn makes necessary the occasional movement of the farmers' households. Because of the relatively greater stability and abundance of the food supply and the possibility of longer permanent settlement, time and materials are usually available for an increase in part-time specialization in nonfarming activities.

Rights of land use tend to be codified. With a growing surplus and increasing economic specialization, intercommunity trade is likely to become more important. The transition from gathering and hunting to horticulture is also likely to result in a shift in social organization. Family systems that functioned to maximize female solidarity, more necessary where women gatherers are the more important suppliers of food, may shift to emphasize masculine cohesion.

With the possibility of property accumulation, in land, tools, and consumer goods, social status differences based on wealth may emerge. Systems for regulating descent and inheritance are more likely to develop. As the size of the community grows and economic relations with neighboring communities become more important, need develops for the regulation of economic and social relationships beyond the autonomous kinship-based group. Thus some measure of loose political centralization usually becomes necessary. Religious ideas and practices may be elaborated or changed to reflect the people's need for control over newly relevant aspects of their natural environment and as a means of sanctioning new economic, social, and political arrangements.

Pastoralism

"People probably learned how to domesticate animals at about the same time as or soon after they learned how to grow food."

People probably learned how to domesticate animals at about the same time as or soon after they learned how to grow food. The semiarid grassy plains suitable to the early domestication of cereal grains in the Middle East were also the natural habitat of a variety of herbivores. The first farmers in the Old World supplemented their vegetable diet with milk, the meat of the animals they captured, and probably eggs. Later other grass- and grain-eating animals—cattle, horses, donkeys, and camels, as well as sheep and goats, reindeer, and yak—were tamed and kept as sources of food. In time some human groups shifted from mixed reliance on farming and herding to become almost entirely specialized in animal raising. *Pastoralism* is the name for this form of subsistence technology, in which livelihood is based primarily on the nomadic or seminomadic herding of animals. Hardy livestock convert the rough herbage into human nourishment; they function as a means of storing live food, as a repository of wealth, as social security, as a medium of exchange, as a source of clothing and housing materials, and as a means of transport.

Figure 2-10. Mother elephant at work in a Burmese lumber camp. (United Nations.)

An extreme variant of animal domestication, subsistence herding probably developed most frequently because growing populations had spread to arid, too high, or too cold margins of farming regions, where food growing was arduous, horticulture impossible, and agriculture difficult without water for irrigation, or because isolated farming communities were too vulnerable to the attacks of nomadic desert raiders. Thus pastoralism became and continues to be a highly specialized sort of technological adaptation, one typically limited to desert fringes, open grasslands, mountain valleys, and steppes, where other means of making a living are even more difficult. Population density among pastoralists is typically low. Land area is vast, with only a fraction of the herdsmen's territory in use at any given time.

In a dry belt stretching from the Atlantic shores of North Africa across the Middle East to Central Asia, many peoples have made their living for centuries from their herds of sheep and goats, cattle, oxen, yaks, camels, and horses. The area in which herding is important extends southward as well, down through the grasslands of East Africa, from Somalia to Zambia, Zimbabwe and South Africa (Azania). The Lapps of northern Scandinavia make their living from herding reindeer. Recently the arid regions of the southwestern United States and the pampas of Argentina have been extensively utilized by herding peoples. However, in these last areas pastoralism takes the more modern form of ranching; livestock is raised primarily for market, not to meet the herdsmen's subsistence needs.

Many traditional herders are also farmers, living part of the time in rainy season settlements where they grow food for themselves and at least part of the forage for the animals they keep in pastures close by. Other pastoralists are more fully nomadic. They keep no permanent camps, rely on mobility as their principal means of environmental adaptation, and maintain symbiotic ties to neighboring cultivators, exchanging meat, dairy products, and hides for farm produce and trade goods. Often, particularly in the Middle East, several pastoral peoples may exploit a single flexibly bounded territory, but at different times or in different ways, some using it as the winter pasture for their sheep, others to herd camels, still others as a caravan route.

". . . to the arid . . . margins of farming regions."
Figure 2-11. Farming at the edge of the Libyan desert. (United Nations.)

Reliance on nomadism tends to increase in importance as a herding people's technological adjustment to the habitat becomes more fragile. The greater the aridity of the environment, the more sparsely scattered pasturage is likely to be, and the capacity for movement becomes proportionately more important to the efficiency of the pastoralists' adaptation. But such movement is never random. Although the equilibrium between herdsmen and their environment is always

". . . the capacity for movement becomes proportionately more important to the efficiency of the pastoralists' adaptation."
Figure 2-12. Sheep herders, northern Afghanistan. (United Nations.)

in flux, most pastoralists follow an orderly migratory regime, controlling the movement of their herds within fixed limits, constantly adjusting to environmental variation and seasonal shifts in the availability of water and pasturage. Many facets of the culture of most herdsmen, but particularly those that provide for societal flexibility and political cohesion, reflect the importance of this mobility to the maintenance of the pastoral nomads' way of life.

The Mongol Herdsmen of Central Asia

Since long before the time of Genghis Khan, the steppes of Central Asia have been the homeland of many pastoral peoples. Traditionally, most Mongols have made their living in this way (Krader 1955a, 1955b; Lattimore 1941; Wiens 1951). Their technology reflects the delicacy and fragility of the subsistence herders' adjustment to the unusually difficult environments in which they are typically found.

Central Asia is separated from the sea and from moisture-bearing sea air by distance, mountains, and prevailing winds. What rain there is falls in the summer. The winters are dry and cold. Farming is extremely difficult. Only one Mongolian acre in two hundred is under cultivation. The rest is used as pasture for cattle, for the long-haired oxen called yak, and for yak-cattle crosses, fat-tailed sheep, goats, small sturdy horses, and camels.

The Mongol herdsmen, whose survival depends on accurate perception of conditions on the land—the distribution of rainfall, water sources, and grass—see the apparently monotonous Central Asian steppe in terms of profoundly significant variations that must be accurately assessed if the poor environment is to be exploited with the efficiency necessary to keep themselves and their animals alive. Because evaluation of shifts in environmental conditions is critical, there must be maintained a constant, carefully thought out movement of people and animals from one source of pasturage and water to the next. Such movement is determined by the rate of depletion of grass and water in one area and an estimate of the probable rate of their replenishment. Thus the nomadism of the Mongols, like that of all pastoralists, is by no means haphazard. Rather, it must always be a precise accommodation to critical, ever-shifting environmental circumstances. The result for each Mongol herding group is a fixed round of migration from winter to summer grazing grounds, adjusted to yearly seasonal variations.

The relationship of the herdsmen to their animals is symbiotic. They protect their animals from wolves, thieves, and other predators. Sometimes they dig wells to get water for their herds. They build windbreaks to protect the animals against winter storms. They isolate sick animals to prevent the spread of disease. They assist them with difficult births and with the care of newborn young. Some Mongol pastoralists have techniques for improving their herds by selective breeding; some collect and store fodder to feed their animals in winter. In turn, the animals supply the Mongol herdsmen with food (milk and meat), fuel (dried dung), shelter and clothing (tents and most garments are made from animal hair and skins, wool, felt, and leather). The animals supply the herdsmen with transportation, with a means of storing food and wealth, and with their principal trade goods—the animals themselves and their by-products.

In modern times the relationship of Mongol herdsmen and their animals to the land has often ceased to be reciprocal and has become destructively parasitic, largely as the result of population growth and the reduction of range by the encroachment of settled farmers partially supported and protected by a new and more stable government. The herdsmen's wild resources are used to the point of near total depletion, and they have no means of restoring what they take. Grass is grazed to the bare ground, causing erosion. Manure that might serve as a fertilizer is collected for fuel. Waterholes are used until nothing remains but brackish, muddy dregs.

As a technological adaptation to the use of marginal resources, pastoral nomadic technologies can be regarded as efficient only where extremely harsh environmental circumstances and/or chaotic political conditions make sedentary farming impossible. In any environment where farming is equally feasible—now in parts of the Mongols' Soviet Central Asian habitat and in East Africa, for example—herding peoples tend to be driven out or pressured to settle down and take up farming, a way of life that centuries of sociocultural adaptation to pastoralism have conditioned them to abhor. As a result of the recent drought and growing evidence that the Sahara may be slowly spreading southward, the status of African pastoralists is now especially precarious.

The Borana Galla of East Africa

The Borana Galla of northeastern Africa keep zebu, humpbacked cattle with long horns (Huntingford 1955, Legesse 1973, Werner 1914). The relationship of people and animals is, again, symbiotic. The Galla protect their cattle from wild animals and from raiders, lead them to water and to fresh pasture, occasionally provide them with fodder, assist them in bearing and in caring for their young. At night animals are kept penned up in rough corrals made of thorny brush. Calves, and sometimes cows, are occasionally taken into their masters' own shelters. Cattle are watered twice daily at wells or nearby streams and supplied with salt licks.

Women milk the cows in the morning after they have been watered and allowed to graze for an hour or two, and again at night. Milk, caught and kept in woven fiber baskets sealed with cow dung (these are fumigated frequently and carefully cleaned with hot wood ash), is drunk fresh and sour. Curds are beaten up with a stick to form a thick paste. Butter is made by shaking milk in a gourd churn. Some is eaten fresh. To make semifluid ghee, butter is heated until it melts, then cooled, and the liquid is poured off. Butter is also used as a body unguent and as a dressing for the hair.

Animals, usually steers or barren cows, are

". . . the status of African pastoralists is now especially precarious."

Figure 2-13. A starving nomad child stands beside the tent of her dead parents, Mali. (United Nations.)

slaughtered for food only on important occasions. Then beef is eaten either raw or cooked, often served on a wood platter with salt and chili peppers. Meat not consumed at once is laid out on wooden platforms to dry in the sun. The skin of the slaughtered animals is used to make cloaks, pubic aprons, and sandals. Horn is made into spoons, mugs, and honeywine containers. Dung is used for sealing household containers, for fuel, for plastering walls and floors, and as a poultice for abdominal pain. No animal product of known value is wasted.

Nomadic Pastoralism As a Precarious Form of Adaptation

In East Africa, as elsewhere, groups entirely reliant on pastoralism have competed successfully for good land with farming peoples only where the herdsmen's greater facility for mobility and the greater cohesiveness of their social organization have made it possible for them to extend exploitative political domination over scattered, politically semiautonomous communities of sedentary farmers, exacting tribute from them in farm products and labor.

With the spread of farming fostered by stable central government and the implementation of new agricultural techniques, it is probable that, like the Borana Galla, the other peoples of East Africa who make their living primarily by subsistence herding will eventually be forced to abandon their traditional pastoral technology in all but the most marginal areas. And even there the stark facts of recurrent drought, growing herd size, and increasing overgrazing threaten their chances for cultural survival. So far most efforts at technological intervention proposed by outside "experts" have had limited and small-scale success. Starvation has been the more effective "remedy" for restoring balance in the pastoralists' relationship to their fragile habitat.

Agriculture

The Middle East was probably the first part of the world in which people discovered how to grow food. It was also one of the first regions in which primitive farming developed into agriculture. This term is used in anthropology to describe farming systems in which productivity is increased by the employment of more labor-intensive and efficient means of conserving and increasing soil fertility and plant growth, through selective breeding and the use of draft animals, the plow, irrigation, seed selection, and fertilizers—all techniques more complex than those used by horticulturalists and (in arid and temperate zones, at least) almost always more productive. From the archeological record it appears that the dryness of much of the Middle East and the early and widespread cultivation of cereal crops throughout the region were conditions conducive to the transition from primitive farming to agriculture. For in such areas where rainfall is sparse and uncertain, farmlands can be extended and cultivation carried on continuously—that is, during dry periods as well—only when some means is developed for collecting, storing, and redistributing water.

Irrigation Agriculture in Iran

In Iran, as elsewhere in the Middle East and in other parts of the world, the early development of irrigation-based agriculture was importantly related to the emergence of those other cultural institutions—technological and economic specialization, social stratification, political centralization and expansion, a growing religious hierarchy,

"In Iran . . . the early development of irrigation-based agriculture was importantly related to the emergence of . . . that more complex level of sociocultural evolution generally known by the term *civilization.*"

Figure 2-14. Frieze on the staircase of the Tachara Palace in Persepolis, capital of the ancient Persian Empire. (United Nations.)

the arts and sciences—that first marked the emergence of that more complex level of sociocultural evolution generally known by the term *civilization.*

Today, as they have been for at least the last five thousand years, most Iranians are still agriculturalists, farmers who know the use of fertilizers, the plow, draft animals, and irrigation.

Control of the water supply is probably the single most complicated and critical aspect of their farming system (Fisher 1928; Fitt 1953; Haas 1944; Hadary 1951; Noel 1944). Even in the extremely small portion of the total Iranian land area that is arable, rainfall alone is still inadequate. Water for farming can be secured at the necessary times and in the amounts required only

"... sloping gently upward to assure that water will be carried down by gravity." **Figure 2-15.** Mexican aqueducts work on the same principle. This one is in the arid state of Puebla. (Mexican Government Tourism Department.)

through the construction and maintenance of a system of water conduits called qanats, subterranean canals that lead from the plains up into the sides of often distant mountains, penetrating into deeply buried water-bearing strata. Construction of these canals begins in the arid lowlands and progresses back toward the mountains, sloping gently upward to assure that water will be carried down by gravity. As work proceeds, wells are sunk from the surface at twenty-yard intervals to mark the underground course of the canals; some reach down more than one hundred feet. Like manholes, these wells serve to remove soil during qanat construction and provide access for periodic cleaning and ventilation.

The canals themselves, about two feet wide and four feet high, are dug by men working crouched with a pick and spade, protected from cave-ins by luck and occasional supporting elliptical rings of burnt clay set in at intervals to strengthen the vaulted earthen ceiling. As one worker picks, another carries the mud back to the bottom of the nearest well, and a third draws it to the surface in a goatskin bucket. After the water-bearing strata are reached deep in the mountainside, other canals may be constructed, branching out laterally from the main tunnel to form a subterranean water supply system that can spread out for miles.

The water the qanats bring down from the mountains is carried underground across the lowlands and beneath the Iranian farmers' villages, where some of it is diverted to supply drinking water and to fill cool underground bathing pools. Then, still carried by gravity, it passes out on the other side and into the raised irrigation ditches of the farmlands lying below the level of the village site. From these ditches the water is directed into the farmers' fields, where it runs between plowed ridges that are opened and closed to the flowing stream with a spade.

The design, construction, and maintenance of the water system are complicated and costly. Qanat builders are full-time specialists. Regulation of the actions of all farmers who use the system is critical. A single individual who fails to keep his part of the canal open or whose carelessness causes a cave-in can threaten the welfare of an entire farming community. The problems—economic, social, political—related to the successful functioning of the qanat system illustrate both the interrelationships of technology and the other aspects of culture and, in microcosm, a centuries-old Middle Eastern dilemma: the interdependence of technological development, economic growth, and sociopolitical stability.

Iranian farmers work their land with a simple wooden plow equipped with an iron tongue and drawn by oxen, donkeys, or camels. If a farmer is too poor to own a plow, or if his field is small, his land may be worked almost entirely by hand, with the use of a spade. Some farmers till their fields by tying a rope around the spade just above the blade; one man then holds the spade handle at right angles to the earth while another uses the rope to pull it slowly forward through the soft earth.

"Iranian farmers work their land with a simple wooden plow. . . ."
Figure 2-16. Peasant cultivator in the Khuzestan region of southwestern Iran. (United Nations.)

A scythe or sickle is used for the harvest. Traditionally, grain to be threshed is trampled by animals attached to a revolving wooden wheel set up in the center of the threshing floor and is winnowed by being tossed into the air with a wooden pitchfork. The fallen heaps of grain are first passed through a coarse sieve and then ground to make a flour used to bake naan, a flat bread eaten by Iranians at nearly every meal.

". . . grain to be threshed is trampled by animals attached to a revolving wooden wheel. . . ."
Figure 2-17. Farmers in neighboring Afghanistan use the same techniques. (United Nations.)

"The fallen heaps of grain are first passed through a coarse sieve and then ground to make a flour used to bake naan. . . ."
Figure 2-18. Kurdish women grinding flour near Iran's western frontier. (United Nations.)

It should not be inferred that the greater productivity and increased sociocultural complexity resulting from the early transition to irrigation agriculture automatically resulted in a parallel improvement in the material well-being of the majority of Iranian farmers. In fact, increased productivity is never a guarantee of greater general prosperity. Most of the newly produced surplus goods were (and still are) drawn off to support growing urban centers whose inhabitants did little to better the peasants' lot. Even today taxes are high. Prices for agricultural products are chronically low and most good land is owned by a wealthy few. After thousands of years the majority of Iranian agricultural workers are still as poor as, or poorer than, many primitive farmers.

Agriculture in Japan

In the Far East, also, irrigation agriculture has repeatedly provided the material base for population increase, the development of urban centers, and a level of sociocultural complexity and economic prosperity from which the farmers themselves have been largely excluded. That was the case until quite recently in China; and in Japan.

Probably there is no place in the world where agriculture is practiced more intensively than in the Japanese Islands (Beardsley, Hall, and Ward 1959; Befu 1971; Cornell and Smith 1956; Hsu 1975; Ishida 1975; Embree 1939; Fukutake 1967; Ishino 1966; Smith 1970; Yamamoto and Ishida 1971). Population is large and still growing. Land is increasingly limited. Food production can be increased only by the technologically more efficient use of existing resources. Japan's average irrigated acre yields three tons of rice. All available land is used all the time. In the countryside the farmers' fields begin at the edge of one village and stretch on almost uninterrupted to the next. Terraced plots climb up the hillsides. As soon as one crop is harvested the land is quickly cleaned and prepared for replanting. The banks of irrigation canals are sown with vegetables. Mulberry, peach, plum, and chestnut trees line the field borders. Bamboo, tea bushes, and tobacco plants cluster at the edges of the farmers' vegetable gardens. Grass growing along roads and pathways is constantly cropped and collected for compost.

Intensity of human effort and the complexity of techniques of land use, rather than the complexity of tools, appear to be the critical factors in explaining the high productivity of Japanese farmers. Their implements are actually quite simple: a wooden plow, a hoe, a harrow for smoothing the soil, and a sickel used at harvest time. Now many farmers also use small machines, mechanical weeders, hand-operated seeders, spray equipment, and occasionally a power-driven threshing machine.

The fertility of the earth is replenished with night soil, dried fish, oil cakes, green

"In the Far East, also, irrigation agriculture has repeatedly provided the material base for population increase. . . ."
Figure 2-19. Japanese rice cultivators. (National Archives.)

"Terraced plots climb up the hillsides."
Figure 2-20. Japanese rice fields in winter. (Courtesy of the Embassy of Japan.)

"All the fields in a neighborhood are part of a larger, community-wide water system. . . ."
Figure 2-21. Part of the Aichi irrigation system, Japan. (United Nations.)

manure, and chemical fertilizers. Excrement is collected in tanks kept under the houses and emptied periodically into larger sunken receptacles near the edges of the fields. Near the towns extra human refuse is sometimes purchased from sewage carters. Usually night soil is left to stand for a day or so and then mixed with water and ladled out on the fields by hand from wooden buckets. Green manure is spread from baskets carried on shoulder poles. Chemical fertilizers are spread by hand from pails.

The cycle of rice cultivation begins in the spring with preparation of the seedbeds. First they are plowed and irrigated, then patiently and carefully worked over by hand until all the lumps and loose clods are broken up and the soil takes on a smooth, muddy consistency. Farmers experiment frequently with new seed varieties, always trying to find a type best suited to particular fields, to the chemistry and quality of their soil, and to the local climate. After careful selection, seed rice is soaked in a saltwater solution to cull out the infertile grains. The smooth, muddy seedbeds are painstakingly planted. Afterward they are often blanketed over with a thin layer of charred rice hulls as protection against birds, a technique that also serves to hasten germination by intensifying the heat. The seedlings begin to appear in about two weeks. Then they are thinned out by hand, and inferior plants are removed. The rest are ready to be set out in the paddy.

For maximum productivity the rice paddy must be so situated in relation to the irrigation canals that water levels can be maintained at precisely proper levels over the entire surface: raised and lowered as necessary for weeding and when the field is drained following the harvest. Each farmer's paddy is separated from his neighbors' by dikes. All the fields in a neighborhood are part of a larger, community-wide water system composed of gravity-flow ditches, irri-

". . . the complicated water system of each individual farmer is linked both to the community-wide system and to the still more extensive complex of embankment works, arterial ditches, and dams maintained by the central government."
Figure 2-22. Dam under construction, Japan. (Information Section, Embassy of Japan.)

gation pools for water storage, and wooden waterwheels. The system must be so maintained that each farmer's specific needs for water can be exactly met. A single water storage pond may contain as many as thirty outlets that pierce the pond's embankment at regular vertical intervals, each with a sluice leading water into the ditch below. Where the land is uneven or begins to rise toward the mountains, the paddy is terraced with connecting water channels designed to assure irrigation by streams and other water sources located at still higher altitudes. In this way the complicated water system of each individual farmer is linked both to the community-wide system and to the still more extensive complex of embankment works, arterial ditches, and dams maintained by the central government.

"It also feeds the growing number of workers who are leaving the farms for further education, for factory jobs. . . ."

Figure 2-23. Assembling a steam turbine in a Tokyo factory. (Information Section, Embassy of Japan.)

After planting in early summer the farmers work steadily in their fields until the harvest, fertilizing, weeding, hoeing, spraying for insects, and cleaning and repairing the irrigation and drainage canals. Rice is harvested with a sickle, hung to dry on bamboo racks in the fields, threshed by a hand-operated or power-driven threshing machine, further dried, and then stored in iron containers as protection against rats and mildew. Rice ready for consumption is usually boiled and steamed without seasoning and served with soup, pickles, green vegetables, soy sauce, and tea.

As soon as the rice is harvested the drained fields are cleared by chopping out the remaining rice stubble with a hoe. Then they are plowed, hoed again to break up the clods, and sowed with dry grain winter crops, usually barley and wheat.

The Japanese food-producing technology feeds the farmers and creates a surplus that provides capital both for continued agricultural innovation and improvement and for industrialization. It also feeds the growing number of workers who are leaving the farms for further education, for factory jobs, for business and professional offices, for laboratories, and for positions in the expanding governmental bureaucracy of what is now one of the world's most rapidly industrializing nations.

Agriculture and Its Sociocultural Effects

The sociocultural consequences of the development of agriculture have been paradoxically complex. The technological

a

b

c

"... development of the capacity to feed more people has accelerated population growth and intensified pressure on the earth's limited resources."

Figure 2-24. *a.* Women waiting at a birth control clinic in Tunisia. (United Nations.) *b.* At a Canadian filling station. (National Film Board of Canada.) *c.* A herdsman's wife gathers leaves to feed her starving children, Mali. (United Nations.)

progress, represented here by the development of advanced farming in Iran and Japan, defies easy assessment in terms of its worth in improving the lot of humankind. On the one hand it clearly represents a great improvement in people's capacity to adapt materials available in their environment to meet their subsistence needs. But, as we are increasingly aware, development of the capacity to feed more people has also accelerated population growth and intensified pressure on the earth's limited resources. Economic specialization and the development of trade have generally expanded the range of available goods and services, but they have also often facilitated economic and political exploitation.

The differential access to privilege and power that results from any system of social stratification arising out of increased material prosperity has frequently elevated the status of a few and debased that of the majority. The bureaucracies that first emerged to regulate the allocation of scarce resources (such as water for irrigation) and to regulate growing trade have often been discouragingly vulnerable to corruption. Newly codified laws have been as frequently enforced to protect the special advantages of the few as they have to assure justice for all. The material capacity to support a standing armed force has as often been used to uphold despotism and to support imperialist conquest as it has been employed for defense. The powerful position of religious hierarchies clearly has been a cause for persecution and suffering as well as a source of spiritual well-being. The benefits of the early development of science must be weighed against humankind's enhanced capacity to destroy itself.

In these days of mounting ecological imbalance we are all increasingly aware that technological progress can no longer be simplistically perceived as a self-evident "good." In brief, the sociocultural effects of the so far inexorable evolution of human technology represented by the development of advanced agriculture—and most recently of industrialization—can be more easily described than evaluated. More final judgment must at least be deferred until the relationship of technology to the other aspects of culture has been more thoroughly explored.

Summary

Obtaining food is necessarily the most fundamental aspect of any people's technology. The oldest and relatively least productive means of acquiring food, "per man-hour of energy expended," is by hunting and gathering. Once all humans made their living this way. Now, because of their inability to compete with technologically more advanced groups, most foragers survive only in marginal regions no one else wants.

Comparative study of this most primitive means of making a living serves as a simplified context for examining the ways in which a particular level of technological development may affect the form and content of the other basic aspects of culture. The Bushmen and the Semang are illustrative of these interrelationships. Compared to peoples whose cultures are based on a more advanced level of technological development, their ways of life, and those of foraging peoples everywhere, are usually marked by comparatively small population dispersed in scattered nomadic or seminomadic groups. Technological specialization is based only on age and sex. Economic relationships are essentially reciprocal. Each group is economically independent. Social organization is based primarily on the family band. Social stratification is absent. Authority is based on seniority within the largely autonomous kin group. Religious rituals relate

primarily to the life crises, and there is no hierarchy of religious specialists.

A similar parallelism between levels of technology and the form and content of other aspects of culture is observable among horticulturalists, peoples whose relatively primitive farming techniques provide a more abundant material base than that of hunter-gatherers, but one that is generally less secure and ample than provided by agriculture.

Typically, horticulturalists, represented here by the Tupinambá and the Mossi, are able to reside more permanently in settled villages whose larger populations usually include many nonkinsmen. There is greater possibility for the development of a degree of technological and economic specialization. This, combined with the production of surplus goods, generally results in increasing reliance on redistribution and on trade or market exchange as adjuncts to the still fundamental system of allocation based on reciprocity. Kinship systems are modified structurally to accommodate to changing needs resulting from the growing importance of farm labor and the need to regulate descent and the inheritance of property. Incipient social stratification is sometimes present. The locus of authority begins to

". . . technological progress can no longer be simplistically perceived as a self-evident 'good.'"

Figure 2-25. Burning discarded automobile batteries near Houston, Texas. (U.S. Environmental Protection Agency.)

shift from the family to the political system. Some degree of religious specialization occurs, and ritual life reflects the reliance of the population on control of those forces of nature most critical to their success as farmers.

Pastoralism represents a highly specialized technological adaptation to marginal environments in which farming is difficult or impossible. Pastoralists are likely to coexist with farmers only where the greater mobility and the greater cohesiveness often characteristic of the herdsmen's kinship-based sociopolitical systems make it possible for them either to dominate and exploit their sedentary neighbors or to live in a relationship of technoeconomic symbiosis with them.

Agriculture constitutes a further advance in the level of efficiency of human food-producing technologies. Its sociocultural consequences manifested by the early rise of complex cultures in the Middle East, Asia, West Africa, and the Americas are illustrated here with examples taken from Iran and Japan.

Although levels of technological development can never be regarded alone as *the* determinants of the form and content of a people's culture, they are always fundamental among those factors that must be taken into account if the history and present way of life of any particular society are to be properly understood, and if the processes of sociocultural change are to be accurately comprehended.

So far, for humankind as a whole, the evolution of technology from primitive to complex has been inexorable from the Stone Age to the present. Such advancement has been generally regarded as good. However, examined in the light of mounting evidence of the technological depredation of our planet's finite resources, this judgment must now be qualified.

Suggested Readings

For recent and comprehensive reviews of anthropologists' thinking about hunter-gatherers see Bicchieri's *Hunters and Gatherers Today,* Lee and DeVore's *Man the Hunter,* and Oswalt's *Habitat and Technology: The Evolution of Hunting.* Service's *The Hunters* develops in more detail many of the correlations between hunting and gathering technology and the other aspects of culture suggested in this chapter. Sahlins's "The Original Affluent Society" challenges conventional assertions about the supposedly hard life of foraging peoples. For several excellent ethnographic accounts of contemporary hunter-gatherers see Chance's *The Eskimo of North Alaska,* Nelson's *Hunters of the Northern Ice,* Gould's fascinating *Yiwara: Foragers of the Australian Desert,* Holmberg's *Nomads of the Long Bow: The Siriono of Eastern Bolivia,* and Turnbull's description of the Pygmy hunters of Zäire, *The Forest People.*

All standard works on the early phases of human history give lengthy attention to the discovery of plant and animal domestication and its cultural consequences. In addition to the sources already cited in the text see, for example G. Clark's *Aspects of Prehistory* and *World Prehistory* as well as G. Clark and Piggott's *Prehistoric Societies* and Hole and Heizer's *Introduction to Prehistoric Archaeology.*

For an excellent recent review see *The Domestication and Exploitation of Plants and Animals,* edited by Ucko and Dimbleby. On the specific regions in which domestication occurred at an early date see Anderson's *Children of the Yellow Earth: Studies in Prehistoric China,* J. D. Clark's *The Prehistory of Africa,* Flannery's "Origins and Ecological Effects of Early Domestication in Iran and the Middle East," and Patterson's *America's Past: A New World Archaeology.*

A good contemporary account of horticulturalists in Africa is provided by the Bohannans' *Tiv Economy.* For Asia there is Spencer's *Shifting Cultivation in South East Asia,* for the Pacific there are Barrau's *Subsistence Agriculture in Melanesia,* Heider's *The Dugum Dani: A Papuan Culture in the Highlands of West New Guinea,* and Waddell's *The Mound Builders.* For the Americas see Cancian's *Change and Uncertainty in a Peasant Economy: The Maya Corn Farmers of Zinacantan,* Harner's *The Jivaro: People of the Sacred Waterfalls,* and Meggers's *Amazonia: Man and Culture in a Counterfeit Paradise.* Sahlins's *Tribesmen* and *Stone Age Economics,* as well as Service's *Primitive Social Organization* explore the cultural consequences of this level of technological development in comparative terms. On the problems of increasing productivity among primitive farmers see Wharton's *Subsistence Agriculture and Economic Development.*

Zeuner's *A History of Domesticated Animals* and Leeds and Vayda's *Men, Culture, and Animals* offer a good introduction to the role of animal domestication in technological adaptation. On the general topic of pastoralism as a fragile mode of adaptation, see Dyson-Hudson and Irons' *Perspectives on Nomadism,* Johnson's *The Nature of Nomadism,* and Nelson's *The Desert and the Town: Nomads in the Great Society.* Middle Eastern pastoralism is analyzed in detail in Barth's *Nomads of South Persia,* in Salzman's "Movement and Resource Extraction Among Pastoral Nomads: The Case of the Shah Nawazi Baluch," and in Salzman and Spooner's *Nomads of the Iranian Plateau.*

The literature on agriculture, its development, and its cultural consequences is enormous. Among the most significant theoretical accounts are still Adams's *The Evolution of Urban Society: Early Mesopotamia to Prehispanic Mexico* and Braidwood and Willey's *Courses Toward Urban Life.* Three excellent collections are Sabloff and Lamberg-Karlovsky's *The Rise and Fall of Civilizations;* Spooner's *Population Growth: Anthropological Implications;* and Ucko, Trimingham, and Dimbleby's *Man, Settlement and Urbanism.* See also Ribeiro's "The Urban Revolution"; Flannery's "Archaeological Systems Theory and Early Mesoamerica"; Lee's *Sociopolitical Aspects of Canal Irrigation in the Valley of Oaxaca;* MacNeish and others' *The Dawn of Civilization* from the series "The Prehistory of Tehuacan"; and Weaver's *The Aztecs, Maya, and Their Predecessors: Archaeology and Mesoamerica.* For more detailed accounts of the consequences of the agricultural revolution in those areas in which it first occurred see Chang's *The Archaeology of Ancient China,* Treistman's *The Prehistory of Ancient China: An Archaeological Exploration,* G. Clark's "The Achievement of Civilization in South-West Asia," Starr's *Early Man: Prehistory and the Civilizations of the Ancient Near East,* Fairservis's *The Roots of Ancient India,* and Wheeler's *The Indus Civilization.*

Steward's *Irrigation Civilizations* is a classic that has had a profound theoretical impact on the work of all anthropologists interested in the role of technology in the development of culture. Among still more general theoretical works that emphasize the significant causal relationship between technological development and the other aspects of culture are Forbe's *The Conquest of Nature,* Spooner's *Population Growth: Anthropological Implications,* Steward's *Theory of Culture Change: The Methodology of Multilinear Evolution,* Sahlins and Service's *Evolution and Culture,* Service's *Cultural Evolutionism: Theory in Practice,* and Ribeiro's *The Civilizational Process.* The title of Carneiro's "A Reappraisal of the Roles of Technology and Organization in the Origin of Civilization," speaks for itself. See also Lustig-Areco's *Technology: Strategies for Survival.*

3

Meeting Our Other Material Needs

THE complexity of a people's food-getting technology, as already indicated, tends to be paralleled by the relative complexity of the other aspects of its system for making a living. The relationship is one of time, technical knowledge, available materials, and perceived necessity.

Where most of the energy of all able-bodied people is absorbed in the quest for food there is rarely the surplus of materials and time necessary for extensive specialization in other technological activities. Also, at least at the most primitive level of technological development—among contemporary foragers, for example—people must be on the move frequently in search of new sources of wild foods. Any accumulated goods other than food and the most necessary weapons would be an encumbrance. And, of course, the non-food-getting aspects of a people's technology are always affected by the environment—by climate and by the raw materials available—and by the opportunities for cultural borrowing from others. As for "perceived necessity": where a more abundant natural environment frees even hunter-gatherers from the constant food quest, they often elect to use this available time for other things they prefer over producing more goods, such as devoting more time to the maintenance of social relationships, to participating in religious activities, or simply to relaxing and enjoying themselves.

All of these limiting factors are reflected in the types of shelter people construct.

"The complexity of a people's food-getting technology . . . tends to be paralleled by the relative complexity of the other aspects of its system for making a living."

Figure 3-1. Multistoried revolving hen house, Japan. (Information Section, Embassy of Japan.)

Shelter

Hunter-gatherers must frequently move their encampments to adjust to the shifting availability of wild foods. Where the climate is relatively mild, they have no reason to build elaborate shelters only to abandon them when they must move on. Nor would it be convenient in most instances to dismantle them and carry them along, for usually they must transport their household goods on their heads and backs or in their arms. Temporary windbreaks of sticks and leaves or skins, rock shelters, and, occasionally, caves are usually the only shelter such peoples have. Where a somewhat more advanced food-getting technology makes it possible for people to remain for longer periods in a single place and to acquire more goods, more complex shelters made of mate-

"Where the climate is relatively mild, they have no reason to build elaborate shelters. . . ."
Figure 3-2. Bushmen huts of sticks and leaves, southern Africa. (Courtesy of the American Museum of Natural History.)

rials that require more processing are often found, such as the portable skin and bark tipis of American Indian hunters and the finely engineered winter houses constructed by the Eskimo.

Eskimo Snow Houses

At the start of the bitter cold winter on Hudson Bay, the Caribou Eskimo build themselves snug, dome-shaped houses of snow (Birket-Smith 1929). During the brief summer they live in skin tents. But in autumn, when the snowfall becomes regular, they begin to prepare their igloos. The snow must be just right: not too soft and loose, because it might powder and blow away in the high winds; not made of drift snow, because it forms in layers likely to crack. In

"... such as the portable skin and bark tipis of American Indian hunters. . . ."

Figure 3-3. An Arapaho camp. (Smithsonian Office of Anthropology, Bureau of American Ethnology Collection.)

order to be sure there is sufficient building material close at hand they use a probe made from reindeer horn, bone, or wood to test the consistency of the snow near the site selected.

The first snow block is the hardest to cut. Striking vertically into the snow with the long, narrow, slightly curved blade of his snow knife (now of steel but previously made of antler or bone fastened to a wooden handle), the Eskimo builder cuts all around the four sides of a block about three feet long, two feet wide, and a foot thick. Then he agitates it gently until it loosens at the base and can be lifted out. The next block is carved out beside it. One man cuts and removes the blocks to leave a circular depression in the snow; this will be the floor of the house. Another sets the blocks around the edges of the circle so that they lean almost imperceptibly inward. Then the next row of snow blocks is set on top of the first, and so on in a gradually mounting, continuous spiral that finally takes the shape of a dome as each higher, curving row of blocks inclines slightly more inward until only a small hole is left at the top.

The builder then cuts his way out through another hole that will become the door and places a last block of snow over the small aperture left in the roof, trimming it until the block falls down tightly into place. Ice forms on the interior walls to form a sealant. Any exterior chinks between the blocks are packed with loose snow, and more loose snow is thrown up all around the outside base of the house. Then, by use of the same technique, a sort of small tunnel is built out and down from the entrance at a level slightly lower than the floor of the inside room to prevent cold air from entering. Sometimes small storerooms are built leading off from the entrance tunnel at right angles. The outside opening of the tunnel is closed by a low door of boards. When the occupants of the house are away hunting or on a journey, a snow block is set in the entrance to seal it.

For light a window is cut into the wall of the snow house just above the entrance. A piece of clear, freshwater ice, cut earlier in the fall before the ice on the rivers and lakes has become too thick, is used as a pane. A

". . . the Eskimo builder cuts all around the four sides of a block about three feet long. . . ."

Figure 3-4. A Canadian Eskimo uses blocks of hard-packed snow to construct his igloo. (National Film Board of Canada.)

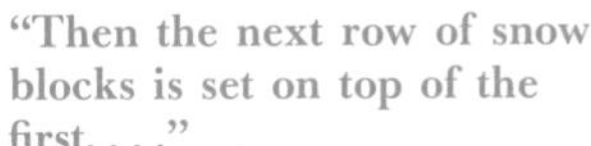

"Then the next row of snow blocks is set on top of the first. . . ."

Figure 3-5. Building an igloo for shelter on the trail. (National Film Board of Canada.)

"... when the food-getting technology allows people to stay longer in one place."
Figure 3-6. Indian house builders on the edge of the South American rainforest. (OAS Photo.)

small hole may also be cut in the roof for ventilation, especially if blubber lamps are burned in the house. Inside, a central raised platform, also made of snow, is spread with skins to provide a warm, dry place to sit, work, eat, and sleep during the short days and long nights of the Hudson Bay winter.

In warmer climates the construction of more permanent dwellings becomes more practicable when the food-getting technology allows people to stay longer in one place. Often the housing materials used by primitive farmers involve the same materials used by hunter-gatherers—sticks and branches, leaves, and mud—but worked with greater care to last a longer time. In a widespread technique of house building, mud or clay is added to a framework of sticks and branches. Slanting roofs are made of thatch, flat roofs by daubing mud in over the interstices of a tight network of branches. This technique, known as wattle and daub, is sometimes used to make the walls of the houses as well.

Bemba Huts in Zambia

The round mud and thatch huts of the Bemba of Zambia are made of wattle and daub (Richards 1950). A single dwelling takes about one hundred sturdy hardwood house posts from five to ten feet tall. Some are forked at the top for laying transverse beams that support the platform used in erecting the roof. Once cut and collected, trees are trimmed, smoothed, and sharpened at the end to be driven into the earth. Then, using a compass made from a peg and a length of bark rope, the Bemba builder traces a circle about twelve feet in diameter on the ground where his house is to be put up. Usually a high spot with good drainage is preferred.

A circular trench is then dug, the house posts are thrust into it, and the earth is packed solidly up around them. Onto these posts a wattle framework is built up of flexible branches tied securely to one another and to the house posts with strips of bark soaked in water to make them pliable enough to tie. Once the framework is completed, several large bands made from bark or branches are passed all around the house, over the frame near the base, half way up the wall, and at the top. Clay collected by the women is then mixed with water until malleable and sticky. Then it is thrown up against the sides of the house frame, where it adheres to the posts and the network of wattle. A thick, uneven coat of clay gradually covers the entire outside of the frame.

The inside walls are daubed in the same manner. Clay dries quickly in the sun, and by the time both sides of the framework have been thoroughly muddied and filled in, the mixture is firm enough to be smoothed with wooden scrapers. The result is a hard, solid wall from three to five inches thick.

The conical thatch roof of the Bemba hut is made from grass gathered at the time the builder is collecting logs, cut preferably during the rainy season when it grows longest, and tied together into bundles. At the center of the house an upright support for the roof is set up. A circular double band of bark is placed near the top of this supporting center pole. Into this band the ends of young saplings are set, firmly tied at the top, and allowed to fan out umbrellalike at the bottom to rest on top of the circular walls. Several bands of young saplings are bent and bound around this conical framework and securely fastened with wet strips of bark.

The thick bundles of long grass are then spread out over and around the lower edge of the roof frame and securely tied down. An overlapping layer of grass bundles is placed just above the first layer, and so on until the top of the frame is reached. A door of reeds or bamboo is placed between two sets of upright poles thrust into the ground at the entrance, and the house is complete and ready for use. With ten people working steadily the job can be completed in about five days.

Soon after, white ants begin to attack the walls, and the thatch dries and starts to blow loose in clumps. Within five years or so a new house is needed. As the Bemba are shifting cultivators, their land is usually exhausted in about that length of time, and they move on to clear new land for new gardens and to collect more logs, branches, and fresh grass for new houses to be built in another place.

Where a people's way of life is based on a more advanced farming technology that permits more permanent settlement, the need for sturdier, more durable construction

". . . the need for sturdier, more durable construction. . . ."
Figure 3-7. Pakistani bricklayers. (National Archives.)

". . . to the prefabricated, mass-produced multiple-unit buildings characteristic of industrial societies."

Figure 3-8. Contemporary apartment house, Montreal. (National Film Board of Canada.)

is reflected in the development of a still more elaborate shelter-building technology that may range from cottages of sod, logs, rough-hewn stone, or clay bricks to the prefabricated, mass-produced multiple-unit buildings characteristic of industrial societies.

Clothing

Peoples with the simplest subsistence technologies tend to have the simplest techniques of clothing manufacture; there is greater uniformity of style, and fashions change less rapidly. As technology becomes more complex and social stratification develops, clothing fashions reflect these status differences, and dress types become increasingly adapted to the performance of specific tasks. Hoopskirts are out for telephone linewomen and female astronauts. But the correlation between technological level and clothing style is by no means direct and unvarying. Humans dress to protect and adorn themselves and to signal their social position; some stylistic variation is almost always possible.

Nor can clothing ever be directly correlated with the kind of climate in which a people lives. Some Arabian desert dwellers—the Bedouin, for example—customarily protect themselves from solar radiation and blowing sand in several layers of loose, flowing garments that cover them from head to foot. Many of the indigenous inhabitants of the almost equally hot Australian desert wear nothing at all. Some Indians living in the colder parts of North America dressed themselves heavily in warm furs. Other Indians at the chilly tip of South America wore only a loose cloak of skins, and sometimes not even that—protecting their bodies only with a bit of animal grease mixed with clay.

Degrees of technological development (what people know how to make, whether they know how to weave or to tan and tailor hides, for example, or how to produce synthetic fibers); the specific activities entailed by particular subsistence technologies (polar bear hunting, deep-sea diving, or reindeer herding); the environment and the kinds of materials available (suitable plant and animal fibers or skins): all these variables affect every people's clothing technology. But the pattern of people's dress is affected by much more: by their social and political values—blue jeans all over campus and blue uniforms all over China—by their religious beliefs and practices, rank, sex and age, occupation, or the activity of the moment—getting married, playing a game, or sleeping—and, of course, by fashion. People's customs in dress are also affected by their cultural contacts with others, from whom they selectively borrow and adapt both new items of clothing and new ways of wearing them. In other words, a lot of factors, only

"Nor can clothing ever be directly correlated with the kind of climate in which a people lives."
Figure 3-9. Bedouin women at a loom, Egypt. (Library of Congress.)

"Many of the indigenous inhabitants of the almost equally hot Australian desert wear nothing at all."
Figure 3-10. An Australian preparing for the hunt. (Courtesy of the American Museum of Natural History.)

"It can then be decorated with designs made with strips of bamboo, leaves, and flowers dipped in dye."

Figure 3-11. Painted tapa cloth. (Courtesy of the Museum of Primitive Art.)

some of them strictly technological, influence what people wear, how they wear it, where, and when.

Most of the world's peoples are and always have been dressed in the skins and hair of animals—including, occasionally, the skin and hair of other humans—and in the leaves, bark, and fibers of plants.

The Polynesians (Brigham 1911; Ducret 1901; Koojiman 1972) make tapa cloth for kilts and cloaks from the soft inner bark of the mulberry tree. First the stiff outer bark is scraped away with a sharp shell. The inner fiber is then soaked in fresh water. When

". . . the fiber must first be spun out on a spindle."

Figure 3-12. A Laotian woman spinning cotton thread. (United Nations.)

thoroughly moist, it is spread out on a smooth log and beaten with a short square club with a grooved face until its fibers are well matted. As each strip is flattened, new ones are placed alongside with their edges overlapping and beaten until the fibers of the two intermeshed flaps adhere. By this process new strips can be added until the cloth is the size desired. After drying, the pure white material has the consistency of tough, soft paper. It can then be decorated with designs made with strips of bamboo, leaves, and flowers dipped in dye. Elsewhere bark fibers are twisted, twined, and braided to make garments.

The use of animal hair is strikingly varied. The Omaha Indians of the North American plains used the hair of the buffalo; the skin of the head, horns and all, was worn as a ceremonial headdress. Using a technique something like that of Polynesian tapa cloth makers, the Kazaks, Kirghiz, and other Central Asian herdsmen moisten, beat, and roll the matted hair of their sheep to make felt for their coats and hats.

More often plant fibers and animal hairs are woven to make cloth that ranges in quality from the coarsest cotton muslin made on the simplest Indian handloom to the finest, feather-light cashmere blends of modern textile mills. The manufacture of woven cloth is by far the most complex technique used in making fabric. Specifics vary, but always the fiber must first be spun out on a spindle. Looms vary also, but the principles of their operation, the basic relation of warp and weft, is universal. Parallel strands of thread, the warp, are stretched over a frame. The threads of the weft are then inserted at right angles between the strands of the warp, over and under.

Skin is the other material most widely used for making clothing. What varies is the way it is worked and how it is worn. The hunting shoe made by some Australian Aborigines is probably the simplest. The hide of a freshly killed rabbit is turned inside out and pulled over the foot just as it comes from the warm carcass. The skin of the neck is bunched up and bound over the toe; the hind legs are brought up around the ankle and tied in front above the instep.

"Looms vary also, but . . . the basic relation of warp and weft is universal."
Figure 3-13. Navaho weaver. (Bureau of Indian Affairs.)

People in many places use animal skins for foot coverings, belts, and carrying containers of various sorts. But it is the peoples of the northernmost regions of Europe, Asia, and America—the Scandinavian Lapplanders, the Reindeer Tungus of Siberia, and the Eskimo and Aleuts—who rely most extensively on animal skins and hair for clothing, because in the cold, barren places where most of them live the vegetation is always sparse, and sometimes almost entirely absent.

No trees grow on the islands inhabited by the Aleuts, and very few plants, none of them suitable sources of clothing materials. Traditionally, most Aleut garments (Collins and others 1945; Ivanov 1928) were made from walrus and sea lion hide. For hunting at sea men shielded themselves and retained body heat by wearing airtight parkas with drawstring hoods made from sea lion intestine split into long, thin strips and sewn together in lateral bands with needles made from the wing bones of seagulls and with thread of twisted gut. These parkas were worn with trousers made from the waterproof esophagus of the seadog sewn together with sinew that swelled when wet, making the seams impermeable. The sea hunters' boots were made from the gullets and the tough flipper palms of the sea lion. All garments were rubbed regularly with seal oil to keep them pliable.

"Skin is the other material most widely used for making clothing."

Figure 3-14. Drying hides, Brazil. (United Nations.)

The Aleuts made their underwear from the downy skin of the puffin; as many as forty tiny skins were sewn together for a single garment, which was worn feather side against the body. Children's clothing was usually made from the soft underskins of young eagles.

Hides were stripped from the carcasses of slain animals, scraped clean by the men, and given to the women, who stretched them out to dry over wooden frames. Intestines to be used for parkas were inflated and allowed to dry fully extended to the consistency of glistening parchment before being split with the fingernail into narrow bands. Some bird skins were soaked in stale urine to remove all the oil, washed and hung to dry, and then scraped and chewed until pliable.

Away from the sea the Aleuts usually went barefoot over the rocks and snow. (Cut feet were sewn up on the spot using a bone needle and sinew thread.) Their only dry-land garment was a loose skin cloak intricately embroidered with reindeer hair. Wearing nothing beneath this cloak, which reached to their bare knees, they warmed themselves periodically by squatting over a small lamp, allowing the heated air to rise around their bodies. Indoors they frequently went naked.

Manufacturing

Manufacturing, especially of productive goods, is obviously an integral aspect of many of the food-getting technologies already discussed. And the making of tools of stone, bone, wood, and metal and of containers for storage and for food preparation involves techniques that can be only partially separated analytically from those already examined in connection with getting food, constructing shelter, and making clothing.

Generally, foragers make the simplest tools, weapons, and containers, most often from materials that require minimal processing: shells, stones, pieces of bone and wood, leaves, and dried gourds, or simply worked animal skins and plant fibers. Many do not make woven baskets, most do not make pottery, and they usually know almost nothing of mining, smelting ore, or working metal.

Historically, the development of more complex manufacturing processes appears to have accompanied, or followed, the discovery of primitive farming, becoming progressively more intricate and refined with the transition to agriculture, and reaching its highest level of development with the advent of industrialization.

". . . the making of tools of stone, bone, wood, and metal. . . ."
Figure 3-15. An Australian hunter collects stone flakes to be used in making projectile points. (Courtesy of the American Museum of Natural History.)

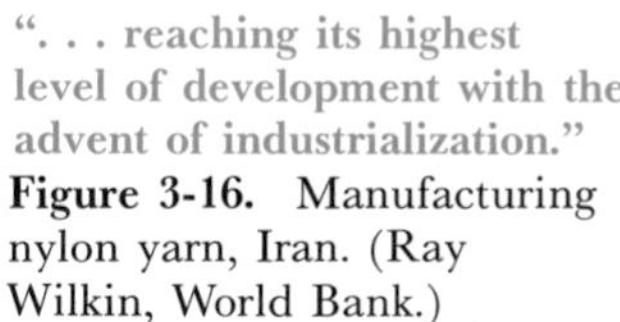

". . . reaching its highest level of development with the advent of industrialization."
Figure 3-16. Manufacturing nylon yarn, Iran. (Ray Wilkin, World Bank.)

"The strands of the weft, usually of equal thickness and pliability, are inserted at right angles and passed over and under those of the warp. . . ."
Figure 3-17. Weaving a palm leaf mat, India. (Press Information Bureau, Government of India, New Delhi.)

"In a third basic basketry technique, twining, the usually smaller and more pliable fibers of the weft are wrapped in, out, and around the parallel fibers of the warp. . . ."
Figure 3-18. An outrigger sail made by twining, New Guinea. (Courtesy of the Library of Congress.)

Basketry

The basic techniques of textile manufacture, involving the intermeshing by various means of plant and animal fibers, are quite like those used in making mats and containers, especially woven basketry (but, of course, no loom is used). In woven basketry the warp element consists of parallel pieces of fibers of such materials as grass, sea rushes, roots, rice straw, millet stalks, leaves, or split bamboo. Usually first soaked in water, these are then set out in rows. The strands of the weft, usually of equal thickness and pliability, are inserted at right angles and passed over and under those of the warp.

In a basketmaking technique called coiling, the baskets are built up from a single continuing strand or from a rod that is usually made of a cluster of strong but pliable fibers tied together to form a long, sturdy strand. As this is coiled flat, the bottom of the basket is formed. The sides take shape as the thick coil is gradually worked up from the edge of the base, each successive coil being fixed in place by the thinner strands of the weft worked in and out and up between the coils with an awl. In a third basic basketry technique, twining, the usually smaller and more pliable fibers of the weft are wrapped in, out, and around the parallel fibers of the warp, or the warp and weft are simply set on one another at right angles and intertwined with a third fiber, often of twine, creating an openwork design.

Pottery and Glassware

Because of the heavy kilns their manufacture requires and the fragility of the finished products, pottery and glassware are impractical for people frequently on the move. In Oceania ceramics were only minimally developed because of the lack of suitable clays and the wide availability of nut and shell containers. In both the Old World and the New World, ceramics are almost invariably associated with the development of a settled way of life based on farming.

As with many aspects of "primitive" technology, the manufacturing techniques for even the simplest ceramic or glassware require extensive understanding of basic chemistry and physics: the capacity for accurate recognition of a variety of raw materials, how they can and cannot be used, and the ways their physical conditions can be altered by heat, cold, dryness, and moisture or by the application of pressures by striking, pounding, kneading, stretching, and grinding.

The making of a pot, for example, requires accurate appreciation and precise use, properly combined and in correct sequence, of a number of raw materials with different properties and the application to them of carefully induced physical changes. Only certain types of earth, clays containing a high concentration of silica and aluminum oxide, are suitable for pottery making. These must be combined with tempers—mica, feldspar, pulverized potsherds, and sometimes blood, dung, and other materials—that serve to bring clay to the proper consistency: to make it malleable, to keep it from being sticky, and to prevent cracking. Then specific pressures must be applied: kneading, molding, and, finally, polishing. To dry the clay and fire it, just the right amounts of heat must be applied for just the right length of time.

A pot can be most simply formed by taking a single lump of clay and pressing it into or over a vessel of the shape desired (but reliance on this technique requires the ability to make the vessel that serves as the mold).

Coiling is also one of the most widespread and simplest ways to make pottery. From a

"Coiling is also one of the most widespread and simplest ways to make pottery."
Figure 3-19. Tewa women making coiled pottery, Arizona. (Smithsonian Office of Anthropology, Bureau of American Ethnology Collection.)

"... a potter's wheel, a turntable on which a lump of clay is worked as it is rotated...."

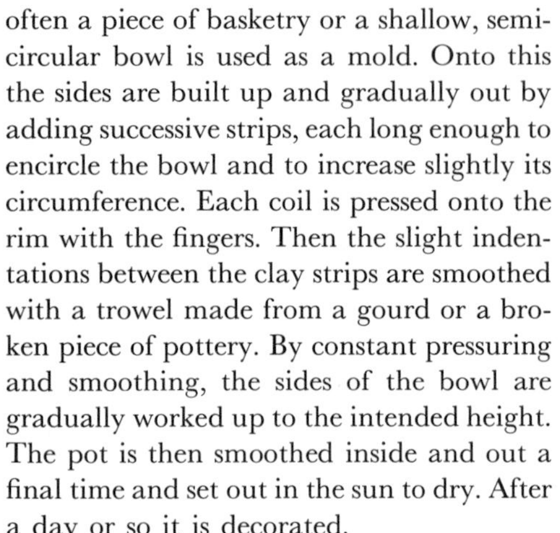

Figure 3-20. An Indian potter's wheel. (Information Office, Embassy of India.)

slightly concave, hand-molded base the sides of the vessel are built up by pressing successive coils of clay on top of one another and then rubbing or scraping the resulting surface until it is sufficiently smooth. Zuñi women make their pots by this method (Bunzel 1929). First they grind their clay to a powder and mix in a small amount of pulverized pottery as a temper. Water is added slowly until the clayey powder turns to a pasty mass. This is kneaded to remove all lumps and air bubbles. To begin construction of the clay vessel, a ball of clay is first molded to form what will be the base; often a piece of basketry or a shallow, semicircular bowl is used as a mold. Onto this the sides are built up and gradually out by adding successive strips, each long enough to encircle the bowl and to increase slightly its circumference. Each coil is pressed onto the rim with the fingers. Then the slight indentations between the clay strips are smoothed with a trowel made from a gourd or a broken piece of pottery. By constant pressuring and smoothing, the sides of the bowl are gradually worked up to the intended height. The pot is then smoothed inside and out a final time and set out in the sun to dry. After a day or so it is decorated.

First a white paint is applied. When this base dries, the pot is polished with a piece of sandstone. Then designs are painted on the surface using yucca needle brushes dipped in pigments made of water, yucca fruit syrup, and various clays that turn red, yellow, and brown when burned.

For firing, the pieces are placed on a few stones to raise them above the ground. An oven is then built over them, made by piling up dried manure collected from the sheep and goat corrals, turf, and greasewood. The temperature of the fire is carefully controlled, the heat gradually being increased to great intensity by adding fuel and then maintained by feeding the fire steadily for about two hours. Sometimes the pots are removed after the first firing and coated inside and out with the gummy juice of crushed cactus leaves and then fired again. This closes the pores in the clay surface and gives the interior a hard, shiny, dark glaze.

Pottery vessels can be more easily, quickly, and regularly shaped with a potter's wheel, a turntable on which a lump of clay is worked as it is rotated, turned by the hand or by a foot pedal. The potter's wheel first came into use in the Middle East or Asia. Archeologists associate its development with the transition from primitive farming to agriculture. It was apparently one of sev-

"Most hunter-gatherers who use metal obtain it in trade. . . ."

Figure 3-21. Australian kangaroo hunters with metal spears obtained in trade with white Australians. (Courtesy of the Library of Congress.)

eral more sophisticated manufacturing techniques like brickmaking and the fabrication of mosaic tiles, porcelain, and glass that paralleled the evolution of more complex subsistence technologies and ultimately became the full-time occupation of specialists.

Metalworking

Most hunter-gatherers who use metal obtain it in trade, and most often in the form in which they use it. If they shape it, they do so by crude cold hammering. A few, such as some Eskimo groups, find usable metal readily available in their environment. With rare exceptions none of them knows the complicated techniques involved in mining, smelting, and forging, processes usually necessary to transform metal-bearing ores into metal implements.

Metalworking also probably developed first among those peoples whose traditional way of life had already undergone the transition from horticulture to a technologically more advanced means of food production. Today the metalworking techniques of agriculturalists are almost everywhere more complex and efficient than those of primitive farmers.

Copper was one of the first metals to be freed by smelting from its base matrix of other ores and impurities. Then tin, then bronze (an alloy made from mixing molten copper and tin), and finally iron were discovered. Each new metal was superior to

". . . none of them knows the complicated techniques involved in mining. . . ."

Figure 3-22. Mine exit, Appalachia. (Appalachian Regional Commission.)

"Iron was best of all."
Figure 3-23. A blacksmith at his anvil as a young boy works the bellows, Yatenga, Upper Volta.

". . . ornaments, and other artifacts."
Figure 3-24. Two gold pendants from Colombia. (Courtesy of the Museum of Primitive Art.)

those already in use, harder and therefore more suitable to the manufacture of tools and weapons.

Iron was best of all. Once the special soils in which it was found were recognized, it was also far more widely available. Gradually the older tools of stone, bone, and wood were replaced by the sharper cutting edges of hand-forged metal knives, axes, adzes, scrapers, and drills, and by the more lethal projectile points of copper, bronze, and iron: all ancient forerunners of modern metal tools and weaponry. The new tools did the old jobs better. And, in another sense, they made new jobs possible and in some instances necessary. Specialists were needed in metalworking, in trading metal, especially metals like copper, tin, silver, and gold, which are not widely distributed in nature; and, with the new and improved means of killing, in making war. As with all more efficient technological innovations, metalworking gave those who adopted it a competitive advantage.

Like pottery manufacture and glassmaking, metalworking requires command of a complex body of knowledge concerning the properties and potentialities of a variety of raw materials and physical conditions. There are four phases to working metal: (1) mining, the extraction of ore-bearing materials from the earth; (2) smelting, the extraction of metal from ore or from sand by the application of intense heat; (3) alloying, the mixing of several metals to produce an amalgam harder, stronger, more malleable, or otherwise more useful; and (4) forging or casting, the methods by which metal is shaped into tools, weapons, containers, ornaments, and other artifacts.

Transport

As human technologies became more and more productive, surplus goods became available to trade or to sell to others also eager to acquire new and more varied goods. Specialists required raw materials they did not have at hand, and had to secure them from others. For these and other reasons it became advantageous and in some instances necessary to transport more people and more goods greater and greater distances. And so, gradually, techniques of transport have become more complicated and—usually—more efficient.

When people produce relatively few goods, consume most of what they produce, and move around in a comparatively small area, as is the case with most hunter-gatherers, they do not need much in the way of a transportation system. They can walk most places they need to go and can carry on their persons most of the goods they possess. These simplest systems of transport depend almost entirely on human energy. Only the dog is occasionally employed as a nonhuman burden-bearer or as a draft animal. Pathways, crude sandals, and hand-carried containers are the only "tools." With the exception of the Eskimo and some American Indians, such peoples use no vehicles. Watercraft are also rare among foragers. Objects that cannot be easily carried in the hand are balanced on the head, slung over the shoulder, or fastened onto the back. Numerous loose objects, such as roots and berries, birds' eggs, or shellfish, can be consolidated for carrying in crude sacks made by drawing together the edges of an animal skin or can be placed in a more carefully worked bag of leather or fiber netting or in a basket. Firewood, grass for thatch, and leaves to serve as mats can be bound together with twine for easy transport.

Despite the often impressive hardiness of many hunting and gathering peoples, the heavy burdens they can bear, and the long distances they can walk in the course of a hunt or in search of water or a new campsite, humans' carrying capacity and territo-

"... gradually, techniques of transport have become more complicated...."
Figure 3-25. Carrying stone and earth from the floor of a newly dug canal, Java. (United Nations.)

"They can walk most places they need to go...."
Figure 3-26. A traditional means of transport in West Africa, a mother and her child in Aguarra, Nigeria. (United Nations.)

"Only the dog is occasionally employed as a nonhuman burdenbearer or as a draft animal."
Figure 3-27. Dog sled team in the Canadian North. (National Film Board of Canada.)

rial range are limited; they can be significantly extended beyond relatively narrow limits only when people engage the auxiliary energy of animals and learn to make vehicles, boats, and flying machines.

The least efficient way of using most animals for transport is to have them carry things, people or goods, on their backs, for animals, like people, can pull more than they can carry. But there are exceptions: a

"But there are exceptions: a camel in the desert does better with its burden on its back."
Figure 3-28. A travel pause in the desert of Rajputana, India. (Government of India Information Service.)

"The American Indians developed what is probably the simplest animal-drawn vehicle. . . ."
Figure 3-29. A Cheyenne horse travois, Montana. (Smithsonian Office of Anthropology, Bureau of American Ethnology Collection.)

". . . wheeled vehicles are far more efficient."
Figure 3-30. Big wheels, British Columbia. (National Film Board of Canada.)

camel in the desert does better with its burden on its back. The dromedaries of the Bedouin herdsmen of Saudi Arabia, for example, are remarkably well adapted to the requirements of desert transport (Musil 1928). After the winter rains they can go for months without visiting a well, getting their water from shallow rain pools and from the heavy dew that lies on the sparse desert grass during the early morning. Camels bred as pack carriers can carry loads of more than four hundred pounds at a speed of about four miles an hour for a twenty-hour stretch. More lightly boned camels, bred for riding, can keep up a fourteen-mile-an-hour pace over the desert and are ideal for herding and raiding.

But it is only under rare circumstances, as in the particularly difficult desert terrain of the Bedouin, that it is more efficient for animals to carry loads rather than pull them.

The American Indians developed what is probably the simplest animal-drawn vehicle, the dog travois. This consists of two wooden shafts (often tipi poles) attached to the dog's shoulders in front and trailing on the ground at the back. Small burdens were lashed to a net or wood framework set between these shafts. The Eskimo dogsled represents a more efficient elaboration of the same principle. More animal power is harnessed, and the wooden runners move more smoothly and faster over snow.

On most land surfaces wheeled vehicles are far more efficient. The wheel's significance as an indicator of technological advancement is almost a cliché. But its development clearly did facilitate the transport of people and goods, especially during the last century or so, since rotary motion has been powered by steam, electricity, the combustion engine, and now by nuclear power.

Efficient means of water transport—floats, rafts, canoes, and plank boats—were developed somewhat earlier and faster than land vehicles. Perhaps this was because there were more opportunities for observing and copy-

". . . floats, rafts, canoes, and plank boats . . . were developed somewhat earlier and faster. . . ."

Figure 3-31. On the Nile near Alexandria. (National Archives.)

ing the means by which objects move on water. In Oceania, perhaps more than anywhere else in the world, water transport has for centuries been an essential aspect of traditional technology. Watercraft are used for fishing, for the interisland transport of trade goods, for warfare, and for migration. In fact, the ancestors of all Pacific islanders reached their present homes by travel over the sea, from other islands and originally from mainland Asia. Among these groups the Polynesians are relatively recent arrivals. Their canoes display in comparatively simple form the structural principles of the larger-scale vessels that elsewhere in the world, first in the Middle East and later in Europe, were an important part of the technological basis for the Age of Exploration, colonial expansion, and the development of the first systems of world-wide trade.

"In Oceania . . . water transport has for centuries been an essential aspect of traditional technology."

Figure 3-32. Navigational chart from the Marshall Islands, made of rattan. (Courtesy of the Museum of Primitive Art.)

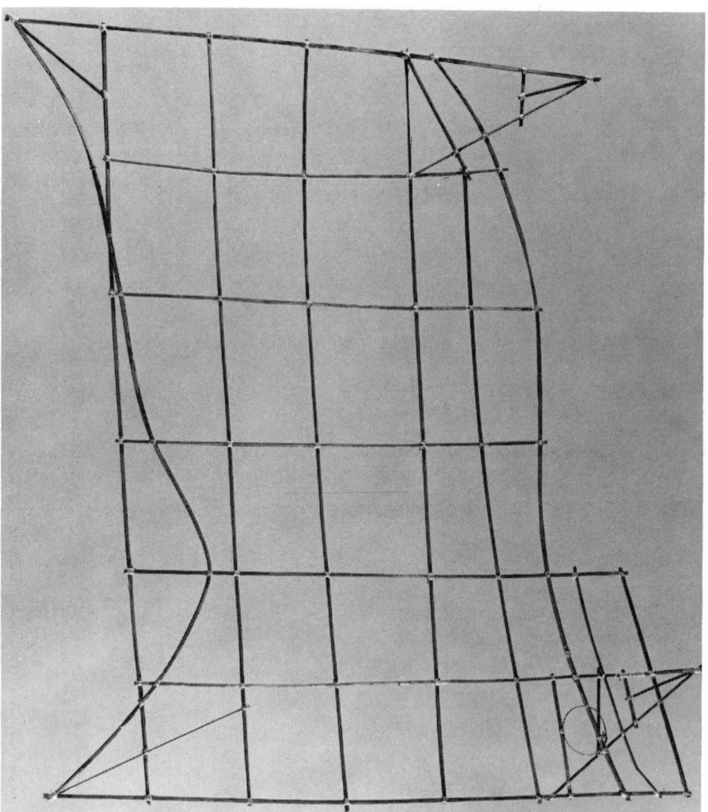

The hulls of Polynesian canoes are made from a single tree literally "dug out" with an iron adz (Sharp 1964; Suggs 1960). The sides are raised above sea level by the addition of washstrakes, planks attached to the hull along each side. The bow and stern are covered to further prevent the shipping of sea water. As a means of extending the surface base of support—to stabilize the canoe and keep it upright—one and sometimes two outriggers, lightweight wooden spans attached to log floats, project out from the sides.

Even such relatively uncomplicated aspects of a people's technology as these simple Polynesian craft can be fully understood and appreciated only by reference to the many other aspects of Polynesian technology and culture to which their construction, maintenance, and use are related: to Polynesian carpentry, as it involves the manufacture of the hull, the oars, the outrigger spans and floats; to Polynesian weaving and basketmaking techniques, as they are utilized in lashing together the component parts of the finished canoe and battening down its cargo; to Polynesian astronomy, the knowledge of the stars and of their movements as these affect the island navigator's effort to determine latitude; to Polynesian oceanography, as it provides familiarity with the currents and tides and the characteristics of the ocean floor; to island economic systems, as these structure the organization of the canoe builders' work and the composition of the crew; to the still larger social and political systems of which the work groups are a part; and, finally, to Polynesian religious beliefs and practices, ideas and observances concerning the supernatu-

". . . outriggers, lightweight wooden spans attached to log floats, project out from the sides."

Figure 3-33. Philippine outriggers off the coast of Zamboanga. (Philippine Tourist and Travel Association, Inc.)

ral qualities of the canoes themselves and of the ocean spirits believed to guard the sailors' welfare.

Technological Change

During our first several million years technological change and human evolution proceeded apace. Our capacity for culture was both cause and effect of the progressive development of our ability to make and use better tools. It is evident that every people's technology, particularly their subsistence technology, is linked causally with most of the other major aspects of their culture—their economic and social systems and their political organization and religion. This is apparent among Bushmen hunter-gatherers, where group composition and economic and political arrangements are largely determined by the foragers' patterns of technoenvironmental adaptation. The relationships between the development of advanced farming, population increase, and the emergence of socioeconomic stratification and centralized political authority is equally clear both from the record of the first rise of civilization and from the history of the agricultural point of takeoff for industrial modernization in Europe, America, and Japan.

". . . among Bushmen hunter-gatherers, where group composition and economic and political arrangements are largely determined by the foragers' patterns of technoenvironmental adaptation."

Figure 3-34. A Bushmen camp, southern Africa. (Courtesy of the American Museum of Natural History.)

As it is always a major causal factor in affecting the form and content of the other principal aspects of society and culture, when technology changes, other sociocultural changes must invariably follow. These days the question of technological innovation is most compelling as it is associated with changes meant to improve the productive capacity and the material conditions of life of the poor majority of the human population, most of whom live in the technologically less developed countries of the Third World.

As the industrialized sectors of the globe grow richer and politically more powerful and income distribution becomes steadily more lopsided, the rural peoples of Africa, Latin America, Asia, and the Pacific face increasingly straitened material circumstances. Their less productive technologies perpetuate an economic dependency that leaves them persistently vulnerable to foreign domination; this often takes the form of intervention that assures their continued

". . . when technology changes, other sociocultural changes must invariably follow."
Figure 3-35. A view of the Bhumiphol dam and hydroelectric power center, Thailand. (United Nations.)

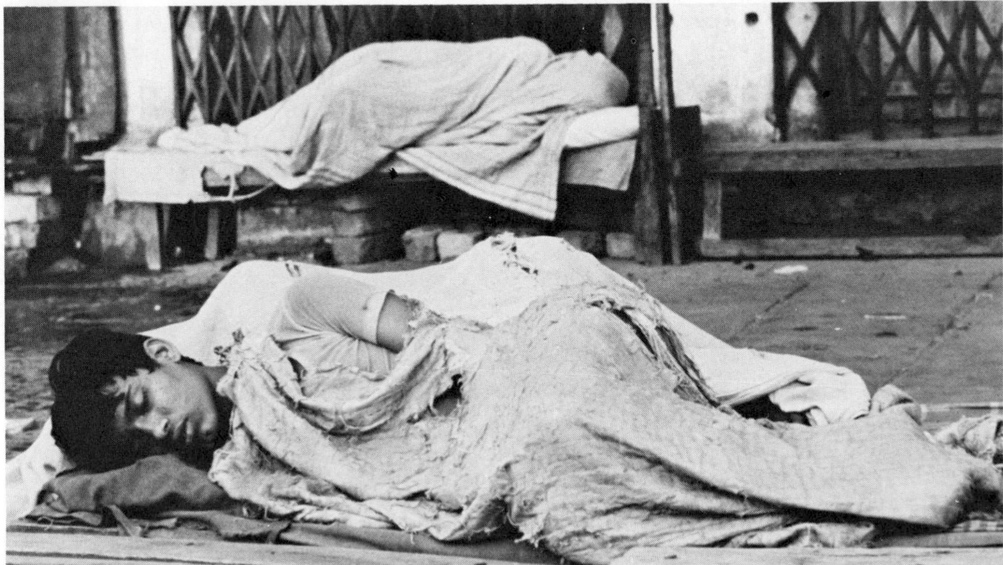

". . . the poor majority of the human population. . . ."
Figure 3-36. Sleeping in the streets, Calcutta. (United Nations.)

technological underdevelopment. Technical assistance, for example, is frequently offered in terms of loans or grants tied to the purchase of manufactured goods sold at high prices by the donor countries.

For the rural poor of Third World nations the basic problem of achieving effective technological change entails increasing the food supply through productive innovations in subsistence techniques at a rate fast enough to keep ahead of population growth. Today world climatic changes resulting in drought and the threat of recurrent famine critically undercut many poorer countries' already slim chances of winning this grim race.

"... at a rate fast enough to keep ahead of population growth."

Figure 3-37. Family Planning Pavillion at a Pakistani industrial exhibition in Karachi. (United Nations.)

Most Third World people live close to or below a subsistence level of technological development. This means that under the best of circumstances they can meet only their basic material needs for food, clothing, and shelter by applying their traditional skills to the processing of locally available raw materials. By custom the small surpluses they produce are generally redistributed among kinspeople or traded to other community members through the local market. Traditionally, such communities were technologically almost semiautonomous and politically self-sufficient. But in most places such "traditional" circumstances are now long past.

For most Africans, Asians, Pacific islanders, and Native Americans, technoeconomic self-sufficiency ended several hundred years ago when they were first conquered by European colonialists. Japan is an exception in that it avoided colonialization and thus was not artificially limited to the role of producer of raw materials for export. This, plus recent heavy support from the United States, may explain Japan's literally exceptional record of technological change, economic growth, and sociocultural transformation. For it was generally the colonizers' purpose to alter native people's traditional patterns of technoenvironmental adaptation to make colonial domination profitable. In

"... most of the cheaply exported goods were raw materials and agricultural products."
Figure 3-38. Lumber for export, Gabon, West Africa. (United Nations.)

some places this was accomplished by taking out minerals. In others, often the good land was taken over by European farmers. Especially in Africa and the Pacific, the people themselves were exported, as in the massive forced migration of millions of West Africans to the plantations of the Americas, of East Indians to the Caribbean and East Africa, and of Indochinese to the French-controlled islands of the Pacific. However, most of the cheaply exported goods were raw materials and agricultural products.

With independence from colonial control the problem persisted. Generally it has become worse. Ever since the Industrial Revolution the growth rate of the technologically more developed countries has expanded explosively. In the poorer nations the only explosion has been in rural population. Most new national governments are maintained only through foreign subsidies or by exorbitant levies on the surplus production of the already impoverished peasantry. For capital is needed both to support the growing governmental superstructure and to invest in new and varied forms of technology that may ultimately decrease the new nations' political dependency by expanding and diversifying their productive capacity.

So far, traditional technologies have become distorted in an effort to keep up. Land that should be left fallow to restore itself is put under continuous cultivation. Without the addition of costly fertilizers it is quickly exhausted. Pasturage is degraded to desert by overgrazing. Precious forest cover is cut away to create new farms for the expanding rural population. Millions must abandon the land entirely to become urban slum dwellers.

As cheap raw materials flow increasingly to the industrialized nations and high-priced finished goods are imported, the peoples of Third World nations grow progressively poorer. Most have lost the means of autonomous subsistence and are excluded from sharing in the profits of the exports they produce on land that is often no longer theirs. The comparatively lucky few who have so far succeeded in retaining their land make a marginal living almost totally outside the world economy. Ironically, it is often the aim of technical assistance missions to end even this tenuous technological self-sufficiency.

Against this background of exploitation by outsiders, traditional farmers have been understandably reluctant to abandon centuries-old survival strategies to follow the

"Pasturage is degraded to desert by overgrazing."

Figure 3-39. A hungry animal searches for forage in the West African Sahel. (United Nations.)

". . . traditional farmers have been understandably reluctant to abandon centuries-old survival strategies. . . ."
Figure 3-40. A Brazilian farmer observes the photographer with resigned dignity. (United Nations.)

directions of foreign experts keen on teaching them some new ways of using their limited resources to make a supposedly better living. Generally, the larger the scale of the attempted innovation—for example, installation of a dam and a new hydroelectric plant requiring massive population resettlement, or the conversion of large tracts of small landholdings to the mechanized cultivation of cash crops, or the forced sedentarization of pastoral nomads—the stronger has been the people's resistance and the higher the incidence of the experts' failure.

The reasons for such failure are usually abundant. But the most important single cause for present lack of success derives from the fact that large-scale, basic technological innovations can never be achieved in a sociocultural vacuum. This truism is emphasized simply because it is so persistently ignored, and at such a high human cost. The massive expertise directed to analysis of the suitability of Third World soils, seed types, climatic characteristics, and/or possible plant sites is almost invariably coupled with near total disregard for the sociocultural (that is, human) dimensions of the problems of introducing technological change. Too often it is simplistically assumed that the indigenous "target population" will somehow automatically perceive the obvious advantages of the outside experts' proposed innovations and quickly drop their previous technological bad habits. If they do not, this is used as evidence of their inability to recognize their own best interests and serves to justify continued foreign supervision. Rarely are those whom proposed technological innovations are allegedly intended to benefit effectively involved in planning. Only infrequently do they have an opportunity to evaluate the goals of the changes proposed or to suggest ways of increasing their effectiveness.

Considering this inattention to indigenous peoples' perspective on their problems, the notion of the innate conservatism of technologically primitive peoples has been asserted too simplistically. Their reservations are probably justified. Generally, those affected have no reason, aside from the verbal assurances of outside experts, to believe that they will truly benefit from the technological "improvements" proposed. If they recognize the risk of losing the security of their traditional subsistence technology in time to do something about it, they may successfully sabotage attempted innovations by strategies of indirect resistance. If they do not, they are liable to end up landless, underpaid, and powerless to reorganize against

"... they are liable to end up landless, underpaid, and powerless. ..."
Figure 3-41. Indian farm laborers, Bolivia. (United Nations.)

the results of a newly achieved higher level of productivity that mostly benefits foreigners and a small local elite.

Where large-scale efforts at technological modernization have succeeded in increasing gross national product, as in the Republic of South Africa, for example, the high human cost has been borne almost entirely by the nation's poorest: the black South African farmers deprived of land enough to be self-sufficient and forced thereby to seek work in white South African enterprises under exploitative conditions (Adam 1971). Another case is in Brazil (Gross and Harwood 1971), where farmers in the impoverished Northeast have been pressured to convert their small previously self-sufficient farms to the production of sisal, which they must sell at such a low price that all of their income is used up just to purchase enough food to give them the strength to cultivate more sisal.

No sort of technological change can ever be achieved without drastically affecting prevailing economic, social, and political institutions. Such changes may be good or bad, but they cannot be ignored. The problem of technological change always raises the issue of economics, the subject of this book's next part.

Summary

The relative complexity and efficiency of a society's food-getting technology are usually reflected in the degree of elaboration that marks the people's techniques for meeting their other material needs.

Among nomadic hunter-gatherers there is neither the time, the need, nor the opportunity to develop structurally complicated, permanent shelters that would only have to be abandoned when time came to move on. If they were dismantled they would have to be carried along on their owners' heads or backs, already overburdened with tools, weapons, food containers, and young children. Exceptions to this are the necessarily somewhat sturdier, structurally more complex snow houses of the Eskimo and others living in extraordinarily harsh climates or in natural settings rich enough to permit more permanent settlement.

The attainment of a more advanced level of food-producing technology, as it allows for greater sedentarization, is accompanied usually by the progressively greater elaboration of shelter construction. Initially, the sticks, branches, leaves, skins, mud, and stone requiring minimal processing that are typical of the most rudimentary house types are still the principal materials. But gradually, as it has become possible for larger populations to live sedentarily, this repertoire of ancient construction materials has been added to and finally replaced with concrete, structural metals, and prefabricated plastics.

Clothing is so closely related to considerations of social status and art styles, once manufacturing processes are beyond the most rudimentary level, that theoretically significant correlations between types of clothing and subsistence technology are difficult to establish.

As the general level of productivity of a people's subsistence technology increases, more time and materials are available to allow for the specialization necessary to the creation of a greater variety of other goods. Usually this begins with the part-time specialization of craft workers whose major occupation is still producing food. But with continuing increases in labor time made possible by increased productivity, and with the increased possibility of exchanging surplus goods for other commodities, basketry, ceramics, and metallurgy often become the specialized occupations of full-time workers whose techniques become progressively more sophisticated as their experience grows, as new materials become available, and as opportunities increase for borrowing and elaborating on the specialized skills of others.

It is within this context of a gradual increase in levels of technological development that systems of transport have also evolved: from hunter-gatherers compelled to carry all their goods on their persons through the greater increase in efficiency marked by the use of animal power, wheeled vehicles, and watercraft to the propulsive energy available in steam, coal, petroleum, electricity, jet fuels, and atomic power.

So far, for all humankind from the Paleolithic to the present, there has been a slow, inexorable increase in technological efficiency or productive capacity, from the first crude implements of stone, bone, and wood to atom smashers and the instrumental contemplation and calculation of potentially harnessable energy sources available in outer space. If this progressive evolution of technology continues, all the evidence from the past indicates that those cultures best organized to adjust to it—those with economic, social, political, and ideological systems so structured that they can adapt to continuing technological change—are most likely to compete successfully with others and thereby to prevail.

Today the achievement of technological change within a particular culture is dependent on the prevailing organization of economic, social, and political relationships, as is painfully illustrated by the dilemma of the nations of the Third World. As colonies they were prevented from developing and diversifying their technologies because of their value as producers of cheap raw materials. Now, as their rural populations grow increasingly more impoverished, newly independent governments are under heavy pressure to overcome this legacy of technological underdevelopment. Yet they must do so without relying so heavily on technical assistance from abroad that they remain vulnerable to political interference and continued foreign economic domination.

Suggested Readings

Much of the literature that deals specifically with material culture either is not available in English or can only be found in somewhat obscure publications: museum pamphlets, monograph series, or back issues of scholarly journals. The two-volume work edited by Singer and others, *A History of Technology,* is a good general source; so is Hodges's *Artifacts: An Introduction to Early Materials and Technology.* For a series of excellent summaries of what is known about the housing, clothing, and crafts of American Indians see Driver's *Indians of North America,* Kluckhohn and others' *Navaho Material Culture,* Osgood's *Ingalik Material Culture,* Tippett's *Fijian Material Culture: A Study of Cultural Context, Function, and Change,* and Spier's *Material Culture and Technology.*

For several sources that develop in detail the ways in which shelter construction reflects people's social organization and is affected by their religious ideas and practices see Beals and others' *Houses and House Use of the Sierra Tarascans,* Hart's *The Cebuan Filipino Dwelling in Caticugan: Its Construction and Cultural Aspects,* the Laubins' *The Indian Tipi,* LeBar's "Some Aspects of Canoe and House Construction on Truk," Morgan's classic *Houses and House Life of the American Aborigines,* Netting's "Kofyar Building in Mud and Stone," and Oliver's *Shelter in Africa.* See also Fitch and Branch's "Primitive Architecture and Climate."

Most of the anthropological literature on clothing deals primarily with its functions as an indication of status and as a means of aesthetic expression (see Chapter 14). See also Heider's "Attributes and Categories in the Study of Material Culture: New Guinea Dani Attire" and Ucko's "Penis Sheaths: A Comparative Study." A standard source on textile manufacture is Birrell's *The Textile Arts: A Handbook of Fabric Structure and Design Processes.* See also Amsden's *Navaho Weaving: Its Technique and History,* Koojiman's *Tapa in Polynesia,* Plumer's *African Textiles: An Outline of Subsaharan Fabrics,* Weir's *Spinning and Weaving in Palestine,* and Emery's *The Primary Structures of Fabrics: An Illustrative Classification.*

Mason's *Aboriginal American Basketry* is an important early work. O'Neale's "Basketry" provides a more recent review of basketmaking techniques among the Indians of South America, but most of the good descriptive accounts of basketmaking are embedded in larger, general ethnographies.

With the exception of the volume edited by Matson, *Ceramics and Man,* most material on pottery making is to be found in ethnographic sources that are either outdated or available only in a foreign language. Predictably, most of the literature in English is on pottery making among American Indians. In addition to checking with *The Handbook of South American Indians* series edited by Steward and the works of Hodges and of Singer and others already cited, see for a specialized study Fontana and others' *Papago Indian Pottery.* See also Fagg and Picton's *The Potter's Art in Africa* and Thompson's "Àbátàn: A Master Potter of the Egbádo Yorùbá."

On metalworking in the New World see Emmerich's *Sweat of the Sun and Tears of the Moon: Gold and Silver in Precolumbian Art,* and Root's "Metallurgy." For Africa see Evans-Pritchard's "Zande Iron-Working" and Cline's *Mining and Metallurgy in Negro Africa.*

Berg's *Sledges and Wheeled Vehicles* is a good example of the detailed studies of material culture typical of Scandinavian scholars. For a specific anthropological study linking transportation with the other aspects of culture see Ewers's *The Horse in Blackfoot Indian Culture.* The development of watercraft is the subject of Hornell's *Water Transport: Origins and Early Evolution.* Several interesting sources on water transport in Oceania are Gladwin's *East Is a Big Bird: Navigation and Logic on Puluwat Atoll,* Lewis's *We, the Navigators,* Reisenberg's "The Organization of Navigational Knowledge on Puluwat," and Sharp's *Ancient Voyagers in Polynesia.*

For references to technological change as it relates to economic development see the Suggested Readings for Chapter 5; also see Bernard and Pelto's *Technology and Social Change,* Bodley's *Victims of Progress,* and the new edition of Foster's *Traditional Societies and Technological Change.*

Part Three
Economic Organization

Anthropologists are concerned with structural connections between economic transactions and the rest of culture and social organization. In marketless communities and those with peripheral markets only. . . it is kinship or tribal affiliation—within constraints imposed by technology and physical environment—that dictates how land, labor, and products are produced and allocated.

BOHANNAN AND DALTON (1965:1)

People in every society need a system for organizing the productive goods—natural resources, tools, artifacts, techniques, and labor—involved in the operation of their technology. They must also have a system for organizing the distribution of the things their technology produces—more productive goods, consumption goods, and services.

So far economists in the United States have been most successful in explaining economic systems based on the market. But in much of the world the market, especially as it is known in North America, in Western Europe, and in parts of Asia, is not present at all. Or where it is, it is very differently organized and fulfills quite different functions, with considerably different cultural consequences.

In observing some of the various ways in which other peoples organize their economic systems, the effort should be made to understand the factors that cause or influence such variation. No economic system hangs suspended in a cultural vacuum. Its past development, its present form and function, and its future are directly related to other aspects of culture: to the people's culture history, to their technoenvironmental adaptation, to their social and political systems, and to their ideology, especially those beliefs that sanction the prevailing economic system and define economic "rights" and "wrongs."

Systems of Production

4

THE most fundamental function of any economic system is to organize the allocation of productive goods—natural resources, tools, artifacts, techniques, and labor—that are variously combined and used to produce the goods and services people require to meet their material needs.

The Allocation of Land and Other Natural Resources

"How is farmland acquired, held, and transmitted to others?"

Figure 4-1. Tea plantation, Ingirsky Collective Farm, Georgian S.S.R. (Novosti Press Agency, Moscow, U.S.S.R.)

First, some system of establishing and coordinating rights to use available natural resources is necessary. Every group of hunter-gatherers must have some principles that structure the allocation of rights of access to material goods: wild plants, animals, water, and other minerals needed to meet their basic subsistence needs. Who has the right to hunt and gather where? Who is denied such rights and how? Food growers face the same problem. How is farmland acquired, held, and transmitted to others? Pastoralists need a system for regulating rights to pasturage and watering places, and rights of access to the routes they use in moving their herds. Craft workers' rights of access to raw materials must be organized.

For foragers there is usually no reason for individuals to own land or to hold individual rights to the use of particular water resources. Rather, they require a system flexible enough to allow for the mobility to use land and wild food resources with maximum efficiency. This need increases in inverse relation to the stability and abundance of the resource supply. That is, where climatic and geographic variations are most critical in determining variations in the availability of wild foods, flexibility in the system of territoriality becomes most crucial

to the group's survival. Even if individually owned tracts were fairly large, sooner or later their proprietors would use up all the available resources, or a change in climate affecting the distribution of wild plants, the grazing habits of wild game, and the availability of water would make it necessary for them to move on in search of new herds, fresh stands of wild plants, and other water sources. If each family group had to stop when it reached the limits of its small territory, most members would probably starve.

Among the Shoshone Indians of the western United States (Steward 1955), who made their living principally by gathering pine nuts and other wild foods and occasional hunting, there were no such things as exclusive rights to land or to the plants, animals, and water found on it. The right of a family group to hunt and gather in a particular area was established by priority. Because food resources were scarce, sparsely distributed, and fluctuating in locale and abundance from season to season, and because population density was therefore low, it would have been useless for one group not to respect the prior rights of another. When pine nuts were available at all, they were available everywhere. There was no need for one family to enter an area where another was gathering. If it had, there probably would not have been enough pine nuts for either. Thus, temporarily exclusive rights were mutually recognized because they were adaptive. While gathering, each family stayed from several hundred yards to a mile or more apart. But the families did not own the land or the wild food on it. They owned as a group only what they had collected. Only after labor had been applied to natural resources—when nuts and other foods had been gathered and stored, for example—did they become "private property."

Significantly, in an especially rich part of the Shoshone territory, the Owens Valley of eastern California, the greater abundance of the natural water supply increased the availability of wild foods and made it possible for some Shoshone foragers to become sedentary. When this occurred they began to develop more fixed concepts concerning the territorial rights of particular groups. Thus, when a change in environment made nomadism unnecessary, this was reflected in changes in the rules of land use.

"For foragers there is usually no reason for individuals to own land or to hold individual rights to the use of particular water resources."

Figure 4-2. Karaja fisherman with his harpoon, Brazil. (Courtesy of the American Museum of Natural History.)

When the Semang gatherers of Malaysia (Skeat 1902) settle down around the durian trees to collect their ripening fruit, nomadism is also temporarily abandoned, and the Semang's usually loose sense of territoriality is slightly tightened up. Each family holds first right to collect the fruit of particular trees. Private proprietary rights emerge, but only temporarily.

Among most foragers the flexibility of territorial rights is extended to provide access, under certain circumstances, to the hunting and gathering grounds of neighboring peoples. Marriage serves most often as the basis of establishing the amicable relations with adjacent groups that assure at least some access to the resources available in contiguous areas. In-laws can usually move about freely in one another's territory, entering to pursue their game and, in time of drought, to search for water. But usually it is preferred that they first ask permission. Typically, the kinship-based right of access to adjacent territory is extended, figuratively, in a circle around each group, thus extending the provision for mobility essential to the forager's often nomadic life.

"... the flexibility of territorial rights is extended to provide access ... to the hunting and gathering grounds of neighboring peoples."

Figure 4-3. Pygmy net hunter with his spear, Zaire. (Courtesy of the American Museum of Natural History.)

Most primitive farmers also require a system for allocating rights to use land and water that is flexible enough to allow for changing environmental conditions, particularly changes resulting from the depletion of soil resources. Because they are technologically limited in their ability to restore what they take from the soil, to increase its fertility and productivity by the use of fertilizers, irrigation, or the plow, they must often rely on a system of shifting cultivation, leaving a part of their holdings to lie fallow after a few seasons so that it can regenerate naturally; or sometimes moving off entirely to a new area where new farms are started. For the system to work, the ratio of land area to farmers must remain low. As with hunter-gatherers, the importance of mobility as a land use technique is dependent on the relative natural richness of the horticulturalists' environment. In an alluvial valley, for example, where soil fertility is perpetuated by recurrent flooding, it may be possible for primitive farmers to work the land for many more years than would be possible where no such natural means of soil replenishment was available.

"Most primitive farmers also require a system for allocating rights to use land. . . ."

Figure 4-4. Mossi woman cultivating her millet field, Yatenga, Upper Volta. (Hammond.)

Typically, land rights among primitive farmers are established by tradition and maintained by use. As long as the members of a particular family group are using the land, either keeping it in cultivation or making known that they are leaving it to lie fallow, their rights are respected. But if their needs for land are reduced—because some members of the family work group move away or die, for example—others in need of land can usually secure permission to take possession from the head of the larger kin group of which the family is a part, or from the local political or religious authority. Within the family the rights of each individual to farm particular fields are adjusted in the same way, shifting frequently in response to changing needs.

Among Kpelle rice cultivators in Liberia (Gibbs 1965), for example, all farmland is theoretically owned by the paramount chief. Control over land is divided up by him among the village chiefs. At the village level the land control is further apportioned among the chief's immediate political subordinates, the village elders. They in turn control the allocation of rights to use land to particular family groups. All land is held by the family head and parceled out to family members for use on an individual basis. When an individual farmer no longer needs the land allocated to him, it reverts to the Kpelle family head to be reallocated within the kin group. When the overall land needs of the entire family group are reduced, the control over the fields they no longer require reverts to the village elders to be reallocated within the local community.

The important principle in such a system is the right of use for a limited period, not ownership. Because such land is not owned in any absolute or final sense by any individual or even by any group, it can be neither sold nor given away, nor by any other means permanently alienated from the community that has final residual rights to it. Many of the troubled relations between Europeans and "native" peoples throughout the world—between Dutch settlers and the Bantu in South Africa, between modern Australians and the Aborigines, between white colonists and American Indians—have resulted from failure to understand the fundamentally different principles that underlie European and non-European systems of landholding, especially the fact that foragers and primitive farmers must usually hold the right of access to more land than they appear to be actively "using" at any particular time.

"Typically, land rights among primitive farmers are established by tradition and maintained by use."

Figure 4-5. Indian farmer using a foot plow, Bolivia. (United Nations.)

The importance of mobility to pastoral peoples usually requires a similar provision for flexibility in the allocation of rights to land resources. Typically, each herding people has a territory within which it moves as a group. To survive, pastoralists must also have the right to more land than is actually used at any one time. When the available water has been used up, the salt licks have been depleted, and the grass has been grazed off, they must move on, frequently breaking up into smaller groups, to find new pastures and new watering places, to allow the land to regenerate naturally, or at least to await the seasonal changes that will replenish local water supplies and pasturage. Balance in relations among people, animals, and land is always delicate. Mobility—by transhumance, by migration, occasionally by usurpation of the grazing lands, animals, and other goods of peoples living at the fluctuating frontiers of their territory, or by expansion and contraction of group size—is the dominant mode of adaptation.

For example, the pastoral Fulani of West Africa (Stenning 1957) move with their ani-

"The importance of mobility to pastoral peoples usually requires a similar provision for flexibility in the allocation of rights to land resources."

Figure 4-6. Kashgai pastoralists on the way to their campsite, Iran. (Courtesy of the American Museum of Natural History.)

". . . the pastoral Fulani do not own land, nor do they need to."

Figure 4-7. Fulani women selling milk and butter in a market maintained by settled farmers, Yatenga, Upper Volta. (Hammond.)

mals almost constantly: north in response to the rains of late spring and early summer, which bring new stands of grass to the fringes of the Sahara; south when the winter dry season sets in and they must move off in search of new grazing lands. The pastoral Fulani do not own land, nor do they need to. Rather, through the mediation of the elders of their kin groups they maintain a flexible system of rights to access. These include permission to move their animals through particular farming communities, agreements to graze their herds on certain farmers' unused fields, authorization to use local wells or to allow their animals to drink from the farmers' ponds and from wet season streams.

Among agricultural peoples the concept of land ownership is more often found, in the sense that individuals or groups may have the right not only to use the land and its resources but also to reallocate it permanently, that is, to give the land away or to sell it. This is the prevalent system throughout most of the farming areas of mainland Asia and Japan, in Western Europe, and among most agricultural peoples in the Americas. A farmer (or a landlord) owns the land. He has acquired it by inheritance, expropriation, cash purchase, or gift. He can transmit it to others by the same means—by sale, by giving it away, or by disposing of it in his will—or it can be taken away from him, usually through government intervention, for failure to pay taxes, a fine, or a debt, or as part of a politically sponsored

"Among agricultural peoples the concept of land ownership is more often found. . . ."

Figure 4-8. Terraced rice fields, Indonesia. (Courtesy of the Cultural and Educational Division, Embassy of the Republic of Indonesia.)

program of land reallocation, redevelopment, or collectivization. Where land ownership is the prevailing system, an individual can apparently hold his land more absolutely or "privately" than is possible under any other system; but it is under such a system that his land can also be most irrevocably lost.

"Every people also requires a system for allocating the tools, artifacts, and techniques that are used in production."

Allocating Other Productive Goods

Every people also requires a system for allocating the tools, artifacts, and techniques that are used in production.

Hunter-gatherers usually make for themselves the tools and weapons they need, thus assuring first right to their use. Those who have assisted them in the task often share this right. A Bushman who gives an arrow he has made to another hunter then has a right to a share of the resultant kill. Sometimes a particular member of the group may have a special technical skill, or the right by virtue of his seniority or some other reason to exercise such a skill. He may make better traps or hunting charms than others. In his spare time he may specialize a little in such work, usually only as a favor in expectation that the person he assists will sooner or later reciprocate. Tools are privately owned in the sense that the person who produces them has the first right to their use and may dispose of them by giving them or lending them to others. But typically, all concepts of exclusiveness in the ownership of productive goods are tempered by awareness of the survival value of sharing. Among most foragers individuals own only those tools and weapons regarded as appropriate to their age or sex. Men possess weapons used in the hunt, women the tools they use for gathering wild foods. Young children often own crude toy replicas of the weapons and tools of their parents. By adolescence, if not before, they usually put aside their toy implements for the real things.

Sometimes certain important tools or weapons are held only by senior males. Possession of these valued implements both symbolizes their owners' superior status and serves as a means of reinforcing their authority. For example, among the Yir Yoront, Australian hunters (L. Sharp 1952), only older men could possess the polished stone axes hafted with bark to a wooden handle that were the principal tools used in almost all subsistence activities: in building shelters, in making other tools and weapons, in hunting and gathering, and, by the women especially, in cutting firewood. Every productive member of the group needed to use

Figure 4-9. Harvesting combines, Alberta. (National Film Board of Canada.)

"... control of productive goods is always a fundamental source of power."
Figure 4-10. Workers in a state-owned pipe factory, Morocco. (Bill and Christine Graham, World Bank.)

an axe from time to time, but only older men could own them. A woman or child who needed an axe always had to borrow one from a senior male relative, a necessity that reinforced the elder males' superior status and perpetuated the dependent and subordinate position of women and children—a vivid example of the widely operative principle that control of productive goods is always a fundamental source of power.

Among primitive farmers tools and weapons are produced either by the individuals who need them or by members of their kin groups. However, to the extent that there is technological specialization in making metal tools or in the manufacture of pottery such productive goods may be acquired either as gifts, through trade, or by means of money purchase. Small implements—hoes, knives, and spears, for example—are typically owned by the individual in the sense of having first right to use them and to transmit them permanently or temporarily to others. Usually the individual's reliance on relatives for assistance and support is such that any close relative will readily receive permission to use a particular tool or weapon. To refuse such a request for assistance would be to risk being refused oneself in future. As the family frequently works together as a single productive unit, it is in

"Small implements—hoes, knives, and spears, for example—are typically owned by the individual. . . ."
Figure 4-11. Clearing a field, Cameroun. (United Nations.)

the interest of each individual member to assist all others.

For example, among Mossi farmers (Hammond 1966) each man acquires his tools individually, as gifts from older kinsmen or from metalworkers with whom he is involved in a reciprocal exchange relation, or by commissioning their manufacture himself, paying for them in cash. Because he has acquired such implements through his own initiative he keeps them in his own house and has first right to their use. But if he is not using them any other close member of his family able to handle them properly may ask to borrow them. If a man were so unmindful of his own selfish interest in sharing as to refuse such permission, he would be punished with scorn. More importantly, he would jeopardize his right to seek similar loans himself. Although the right of ownership is, in this sense, less than exclusive, a man does have the right to give such a tool permanently to another, and, at least theoretically, he may sell it. However, if the goods he had sold in order to purchase it initially had been made with the aid of his kinsmen, this would limit his right to dispose of the tool in any such final way. Were he to do so, his kinsmen would have a strong right to share in the use of whatever he received in exchange. Thus, if he sold a knife purchased with a part of the money profits from the sale of a garden crop harvested with the aid of his younger brothers, all of them would have special rights to use whatever he purchased in its place.

As productive goods become more complex and more complicated or costly to make, and as they are thereby likely to be more critical to the success of the worker's endeavor and more difficult to replace, proprietary rights tend to become more absolute. The conditions under which others may use such equipment are likely to be

"As productive goods become more complex and more complicated or costly to make . . . proprietary rights tend to become more absolute."

Figure 4-12. Privately owned automobile factory, Japan. (Information Section, Embassy of Japan.)

more explicitly defined and carefully regulated. If a Tupinambá manioc cultivator lends his shell knife to a kinsman who breaks it or loses it during the course of the harvest, there may be some ill will or resentment until the implement is replaced. But no one's livelihood will be threatened by the loss, for the knife used in manioc cultivation is neither difficult to make nor costly to replace.

The iron plow of the Iranian and the power-driven threshing machine of the Japanese farmer, more complicated tools and part of a more complex technology, are much harder to make, more difficult to acquire, and more crucial to the functioning of the subsistence technology. Accordingly, rights to their ownership are more cautiously prescribed and rights to their use by

"... the larger productive goods—waterworks ... are almost always owned collectively, either by private groups or by the government."

Figure 4-13. Indus River dam, Pakistan. (Tomas Sennett for World Bank.)

others more tightly controlled. The Japanese farmer pays a set cash price for his farm equipment and receives a written receipt. Rights to use his equipment are strictly limited to those members of his family who farm with him, usually under his supervision, or to paid workers who use the equipment on his land only. Others have the right to use it only if they have participated in its purchase. In fact, larger pieces of farm equipment are often owned collectively in Japan, in the United States, in the U.S.S.R., and in many other modern agricultural nations. In each instance the contractual formality with which rights of access to such equipment are allocated is a reflection of its critical productive worth.

The Iranian qanat, a productive good crucial to the livelihood of the entire farming community, is usually owned by a single landlord, the only individual wealthy enough to afford the construction or maintenance of these subterranean canals. By means of a carefully calculated system of charges, peasants who use water from the qanat must pay for it with a portion of their crop. As the landlord has a monopoly, in the sense that farmers can neither move their farmland nor obtain their water from another source, he is usually paid the price he sets. Sharecroppers in the southern United States (Daniel 1972) must pay the owner whose fields and farm equipment they use, and often the charges have been just as rigidly and exploitatively set.

In most advanced agricultural societies and in those in which an important part of the subsistence base is derived from industry, the larger productive goods—waterworks, road systems, the capital equipment involved in the provision of public services (the mails, railways, ports, and airways), extractive industries, and factories—are almost always owned collectively, either by private groups or by the government. Allocation of the right to use them is a matter of rigidly codified contractual relations.

For nearly everyone in technologically primitive societies and for all but an elite minority in technologically advanced societies, the private ownership of productive goods is always sharply limited.

The Organization of Work

The organization of work, that is, the allocation of labor and the systematizing of the various phases of many productive ac-

"The organization of work . . ."
Figure 4-14. Laborers in a Nicaraguan ceramics factory. (International Bank for Reconstruction and Development.)

tivities—stalking, shooting, tracking, killing, cutting up, and preparing a game animal for consumption, for example, or the necessary steps to follow in making pots, building houses, cultivating crops, manufacturing computers, or providing social services—are importantly affected by the type and level of efficiency of the tools, techniques, and artifacts a people employs.

Work organization is also affected by environment, especially climate. How soon a hunter starts to stalk the game he has shot may be affected by the nature of the terrain the animal is moving over, what the weather is like, whether it is clear and looks as if it is going to stay that way, or whether it looks as if rainfall might soon cover the animal's tracks. Hunting animals that range widely in herds, such as buffalo, requires a different form of work organization than is necessary for hunting animals, such as bear, that often move alone and within a smaller territory.

The system of labor allocation is also often affected by the workers' sex and age,

"The system of labor allocation is also often affected by the worker's sex and age. . . ."
Figure 4-15. A Finnish street cleaner. (United Nations.)

their kinship affiliation, their social position, and, of course, the prevailing economic system and the political organization that sanction it. But the nature and requirements of a people's subsistence technology are always major formative factors.

Specificity and Diffuseness of Work Organization

There seems to be a relation between the overall simplicity or complexity of a people's technology and the *specificity* or *diffuseness* with which a worker's tasks are organized, that is, the extent to which he or she works continuously for a long time at a single task as opposed to working at a variety of quite different tasks within a comparatively short time span. The work organization of foragers is typically diffuse. An Andaman Island hunter, for example, might begin his work day by collecting a few shells to make into knives, scrapers, and arrow points (Radcliffe-Brown 1933). In doing so he might find a particularly well-shaped nautilus, which he would carry home to use as a drinking cup. There he might take a few minutes to repair a tear in one of his fishnets. Then a kinsman might ask for help in attaching a new outrigger float to his canoe. They might go out together by boat to hunt for sea turtles. Later in the day he might spend some time hunting for a wild pig he heard nearby or stand carefully quiet at the water's edge waiting to shoot a fish with his

"There seems to be a relation between the overall simplicity or complexity of a people's technology and the specificity or diffuseness with which a worker's tasks are organized. . . ."
Figure 4-16. A Peruvian spear fisherman at one of the many kinds of work he does in a single day. (OAS Photos.)

bow and arrow. On his way back to camp he might come across some wild fruit or some honey, which he would collect and carry home. Along the way he might stop to cut down a choice piece of bamboo, from which later that night he would begin to make a container for storing water.

During the course of this same day he might take a few minutes to help his wife build up the kitchen fire, to assist his young son in making his first arrow shaft, and to help a friend repair the roof of his hut. The following day he would probably work at some slightly different tasks, in different order. From week to week and season to season the pattern of his work would probably vary even more. Typically, he would engage in a constantly shifting variety of jobs, working sooner or later at almost all aspects of his society's technology. His organization of work would have been diffuse. In this same way the work of nearly all hunter-gatherers is diffuse.

In contrast, as subsistence technologies become more complex, as they involve more and different kinds of tasks, and as these tasks each require specialized skills, the work organization of individuals and of groups tends to become more specific; people specialize, many of them full time.

Although this tendency toward greater specificity is noticeable among horticulturalists, the work of most primitive farmers is still quite diffuse. Almost everyone can and does perform almost all the tasks regarded as appropriate to his or her age and sex. What specialization there is usually results from the proclivities of individuals, their personal preferences for or prowess at special tasks. As horticulture becomes more productive, some individuals can afford to take time off from producing food and from other basic tasks. They may choose to devote their spare time to perfecting particular skills, using them to produce special goods. In some instances whole groups in the local community may be associated with specialized work. In the West African Sahel certain kin groups specialize in metalworking, pottery making, and carpentry, but only in the dry season. During the rainy months of summer they work on their farms like everyone else. Only when the rains have ended and their harvests are in can they turn full time to their craft specialties.

Among pastoralists, specialized tasks are often assigned to subordinate or client

". . . certain kin groups specialize in metalworking, pottery making, and carpentry, but only in the dry season."

Figure 4-17. A Mossi blacksmith hammers a bracelet into place, Yatenga, Upper Volta. (Hammond 1966.)

groups, such as leatherworkers and metalworkers, who produce and maintain the pastoralists' saddlery and weapons in exchange for food and protection. But most specialized goods are acquired from nonpastoral peoples through trade or exacted tribute.

In contrast to the work of foragers and most primitive farmers, the work of people living in communities supported by agriculture tends to be more specific. Workers' tasks typically involve specialization in no more than a few of the diverse aspects of their technology. Rather than making for themselves most of the goods they consume, they concentrate on the production of a particular good or a special service, which is then exchanged for the goods and services produced by others.

Such specificity is greatest in those societies in which a major part of the technology is industrialized, where a worker's job may be confined to such highly specific tasks as polishing ball bearings of a particular caliber, stamping snaps on blue jeans, or monitoring a single set of dials on one of several hundred identical computer-operated machines.

As technology becomes more complex, especially in advanced agricultural and industrialized societies, the worker becomes progressively less autonomous. Because of the specificity of the task, the organization of his or her job and his or her performance become increasingly dependent on and critical to others' job performance and they are increasingly subject to external control from the boss, from the boss's boss, and from the sources of authority in the larger sociopolitical system that usually assumes increasing responsibility for the coordination of the ever more interindependent parts of an advanced agricultural or industrially based technology.

"Such specificity is greatest in those societies in which a major part of the technology is industrialized. . . ."
Figure 4-18. Television sets on the assembly line, Japan. (Information Section, Embassy of Japan.)

In the cultures of nearly all nonindustrialized peoples this is not yet the case. Most work is not organized on the basis of special skill or particular interest but rather is assigned on the basis of criteria that are essentially ascribed. In most cultures the most fundamental determinants of "who" a person is, and thus of what work he or she should perform, are sex and age.

Sex, Age, and the Organization of Work

In some very small-scale societies of hunter-gatherers, where everyone is likely to be related by kinship, sex and age are often the only important nontechnological determinants of work organization.

Among Bushmen hunters the tasks of very small children are usually undifferentiated by sex. Both small girls and small boys assist their mothers in collecting firewood, in gathering wild food, and in caring for still smaller infants in arms. But well before adolescence a division of labor based on sex begins to be established. Children begin to be encouraged to practice the skills categorized as appropriate to their gender. Little girls' responsibility for assisting their mothers in collecting food, cooking, and setting up their crude shelters is always more serious than that of their small brothers. Soon boys are drawn off to play at making the weapons and traps they use to hunt tiny game, insects, rats, lizards, and frogs, acquiring the skills they will be required to apply by late adolescence to support themselves and their young wives and children. All male Bushmen are primarily hunters; women are all

"Most work is not organized on the basis of special skill or particular interest, but rather is assigned on the basis of criteria that are essentially ascribed."

Figure 4-19. Dahomeyan fishermen. (Courtesy of the Library of Congress.)

ities ancillary to subsistence—in weapon and tool repair, food preparation, and the maintenance of household equipment—that gender is most important as a determinant of who does what work.

In most other societies, however, subsistence activities tend to be somewhat more rigidly separated on the basis of sex. Occasionally this sex-based division of labor appears to be related to sexually determined physiological differences; women who are very pregnant may be in poor shape to do most heavy construction work, for example. But the more important constraint on the organization of women's work appears to derive from their universal responsibility for child care. So far, no society has assigned this task principally to males. Brown (1970b) suggests that unless a culture provides an alternative means of caring for the very young, such as the use of older children as "nurses," reliance on cooperative co-wives, or still more formally structured child-care centers, most women tend to be assigned safe, repetitive work that can be easily interrupted and resumed and that permits them to stay close to home. Gathering allows for this. So do horticulture, participation in petty trade, and, of course, "housework." Thus, most factors limiting the tasks assigned to women appear to be neither physiological nor technological, but cultural. Once a way is worked out to take care of the kids (or to avoid having them—birth control devices may be the technological innovations most responsible for radically altering women's work) there are few jobs, especially in industrial societies, that can be logically assigned solely on the basis of sex.

Among most foragers the recognition of special skill is often combined with the criterion of seniority as the basis for organizing work. Although age is invariably important in the direction of critical activities that affect the livelihood of the entire group, it is usually weighed against considerations of

"In the fields members of both sexes work together, often side by side, doing the same things."

Figure 4-20. Threshing and winnowing barley in the Andean highlands, Peru. (United Nations.)

primarily food gatherers (and, as such, the chief suppliers of food).

For most primitive farmers and many agriculturalists gender is of greatest importance as a criterion for allocating household tasks and craft specialization. In the fields members of both sexes work together, often side by side, doing the same things. Sometimes a greater part of the responsibility for the more arduous work of cleaning and clearing the fields is taken by the men, especially if the female members of the work force are in the advanced stages of pregnancy, recuperating from childbirth, or burdened with the care of several small children. Otherwise, among primitive farmers and many agricultural peoples it is in activ-

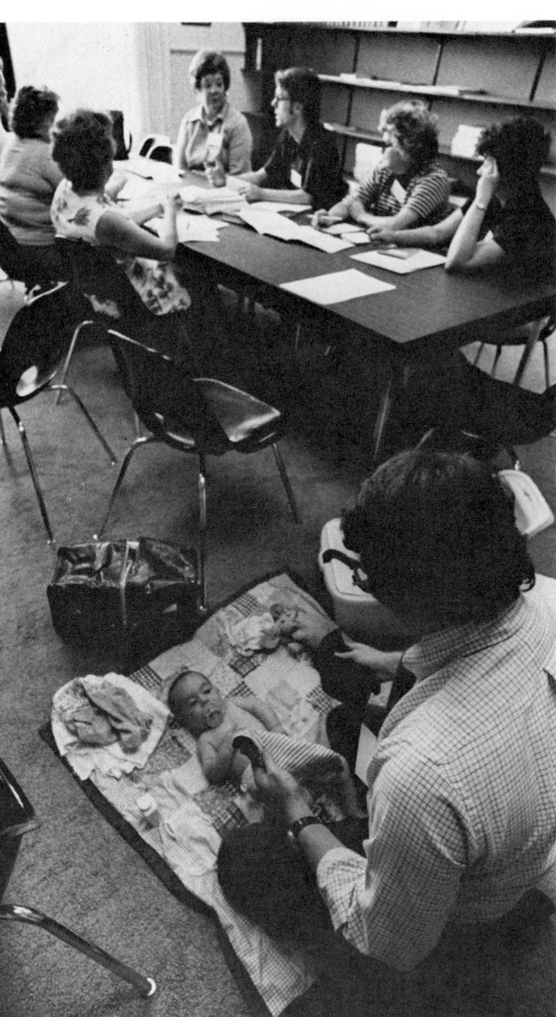

"So far, no society has assigned this task principally to males."
Figure 4-21. An exceptional man at work. (Appalachian Regional Commission.)

aptitude, inclination, and physical capacity. Material need is also an important variable. For example, Draper and Cashdan (1975) report that the rich food supply of !Kung foragers makes it unnecessary to bring children into the labor force. In contrast, among sedentary !Kung, who are making a difficult transition to farming, youngsters are put to work at an early age. For reasons that may be related as much to economics as to competence, age in industrial societies is often a major factor affecting work organization: determining entry into, advancement in, and retirement from the work force.

In many instances age as a basis for work organization is formalized by assignment of large segments of the population to age-based work groups. Most often they are assigned to military or agricultural tasks. Among the Zulu of South Africa, for example, all young men between certain ages were recruited into the king's army, where they served for a number of years as police, as collectors of the royal tribute, as warriors,

"... most factors limiting the tasks assigned to women appear to be neither physiological nor technological, but cultural."
Figure 4-22. Schoolteacher fulfilling a traditional female role. (Appalachian Regional Commission.)

and as laborers on the king's farmlands and keepers of his herds (Gluckman 1958). After about ten years they were retired as a group and could return to their villages, marry, and settle down to work their fields and tend herds of their own. Similarly organized age groups are currently deployed in Israel and China.

Kinship

In nonindustrialized societies family ties complement sex and age as the principal determinants of work organization. In societies with a very simple technology these three criteria provide almost the only basis for organizing work.

Among all foragers the nuclear family group, consisting of father, mother, and children, cooperates in accomplishing most of the activities basic to subsistence. A man and his sons hunt. His wife and daughters and his young children of both sexes gather wild foods. Membership in this most elementary of all work organizations is deter-

"In nonindustrialized societies family ties complement sex and age as the principal determinants of work organization."

Figure 4-23. Young Mossi herding their family's flock of goats, Yatenga, Upper Volta.

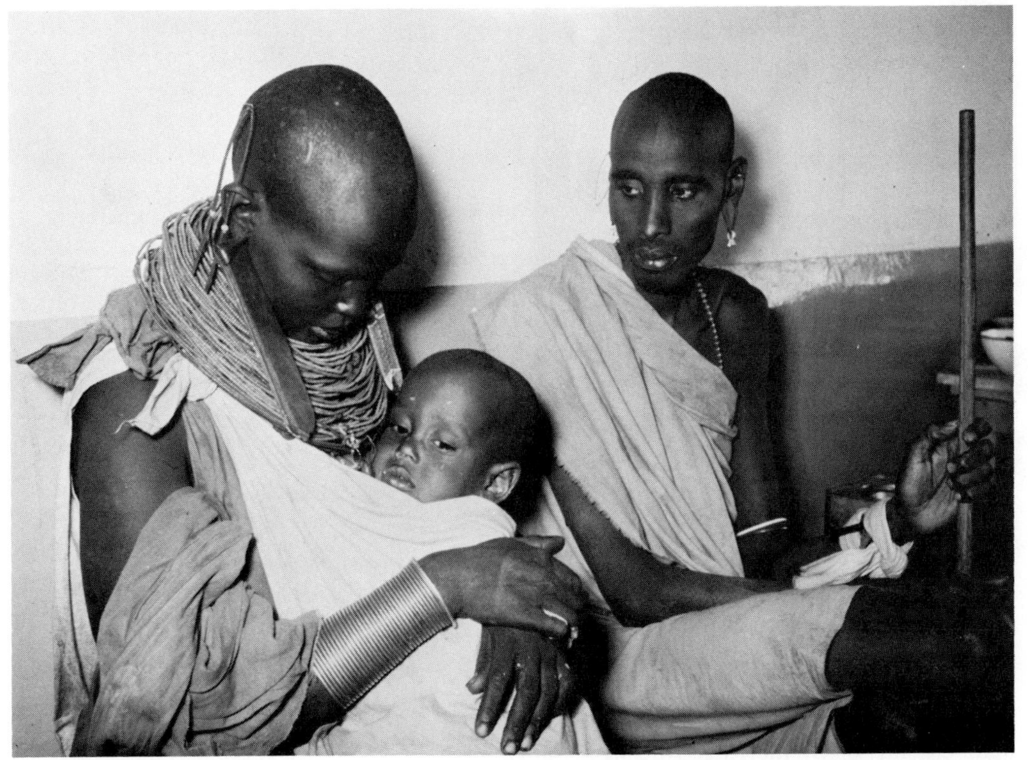

"Within the nuclear family the father is likely to be the final authority in the organization of tasks. . . ."
Figure 4-24. Young woman with her husband and child, Kenya. (United Nations.)

mined by kinship. Solidarity is reinforced by training and by a life experience that dramatizes for each individual his or her responsibilities to the other members of the domestic group, his or her dependence on them for material support and survival, and the benefits of subordinating private interests to concern with the well-being of the family.

Authority within the domestic work group typically rests with the elder or more experienced male members, as long as they remain vigorous. Within the nuclear family the father is likely to be the final authority in the organization of tasks and in the manipulation of the system of rewards and punishments that serve as work incentives. His wife acts as his immediate subordinate in organizing and directing the activities of female family members. Each child is usually assigned partial responsibility for directing the work of those younger than itself.

Among hunter-gatherers, work that includes nonmembers of the immediate family is still most often organized on the basis of kinship ties, being extended to include adult brothers and cousins, co-wives, in-laws, and others whose membership in a somewhat more extended domestic kin group serves as the basis for cooperation.

An Mbuti Pygmy, for example, hunts and shares his kill with his wife and children (Turnbull 1965). An Mbuti woman gathers wild food for herself, her husband, and her children and takes care of the campsite, cooks, and supervises the care of the very young. Children assist their parents. With rare exceptions every member of the local Pygmy band is related to every other by descent or marriage. A man hunts with his sons, his father, his brothers, and his father's brothers. Most other men in his hunting group are related by marriage, the husbands

"A man hunts with his sons, his father, his brothers, and his father's brothers."
Figure 4-25. And so it is among Nandi hunters as well, East Africa. (Courtesy of the American Museum of Natural History.)

"Family ties as the basis for work group solidarity are particularly valuable among pastoral nomadic peoples . . ."
Figure 4-26. Afghani shepherds guard their flock. (United Nations.)

of sisters, daughters, or other women in the family. A Pygmy woman works with other women who are related to her husband either by descent (his mother, sisters, and female cousins) or by marriage (the wives of his brothers or his father's brothers).

Frequently the organization of the domestic group is structured to foster solidarity among the female members of the work force. Among Indian horticulturalists in the tropical forests of the Guianas, for example, the organization of the domestic work group facilitates technoeconomic cooperation among women. For, aside from clearing the land, it is they who do most of the farm work. It is generally the rule among primitive farmers in this South American area that men live in their wives' villages after marriage (Steward and Faron 1959). Thus it is the female members of the local community who are related by common descent and who remain at home; their fathers come from other villages and so do their husbands. If women need help, they can call on their sisters or other female relatives who live close by. A significant correlation between technology, economic organization, and the kinship system seems apparent. The material survival of the group is primarily dependent on the cooperative work of the women, and this is clearly reflected in the society's rules of descent and residence.

An alternative arrangement illustrates the same point: among most farming peoples elsewhere in the South American tropical forests it is the males in the domestic work group who share common descent—especially where relations between neighboring groups are hostile. The resulting masculine solidarity serves as a useful basis for cooperation, loyalty, and acceptance of the authority of the elder males, all factors that strengthen the effectiveness of the men's work as warriors, in raiding other communities, and in protecting their own settlements from attack.

Family ties as the basis for work group solidarity are particularly valuable among pastoral nomadic peoples who must frequently defend their pastures and their herds from predators or organize themselves to expropriate the goods of others, invading their grazing areas, raiding for animals, exacting tribute from settled farming communities, attacking caravans, and engaging in other parasitic economic activities.

Among herdsmen in the Middle East and North Africa the males who live and work together are always closely related. Usually those who work closest with one another within some larger grouping of kinsmen are brothers, fathers, and sons, bound by blood ties that sanction cooperation, acceptance of the authority of senior males, and assurance of group loyalty in the face of external threat.

For example, the smallest domestic work group among Somali herdsmen, comprising a man, his wife or wives, and their children, would be insecure if it were to function independently, because of the harshness of the climate, the susceptibility of the animals to disease, and the constant danger of raids (I. Lewis, 1963). The nuclear family work group functions far more efficiently within the protective context of the strong relationship that prevails among a man and his brothers, their father, and their father's brothers, all of whom herd their flocks of sheep together, share the use of camels to

"Among herdsmen in the Middle East and North Africa the males who live and work together are always closely related."

Figure 4-27. Afghani herdsmen on the move. (United Nations.)

carry their household goods from one camp to another, and band together to fight in defense of the family and its herds.

From this relatively small family work group the principle of shared descent fans out over much of the territory in which Somali herdsmen circulate, providing the basis for the cooperation necessary for safe movement of animals and people in search of water, fresh pasturage, and new campsites and for protection from common enemies. The bonds of close kinship that structure the Somalis' organization of work are strengthened further by the form of marriage they prefer. Like young men among nearly all other pastoral peoples in the Middle East, a Somali youth is encouraged to marry his father's brother's daughter. A young girl's preferred mate is her father's brother's son. This correlation between technology and work organization is further substantiated by the diminished importance of kinship bonds among former pastoralists who have become sedentarized (see Barth 1953).

"... a large domestic work group is useful in order to best accomplish all the many tasks associated with food production."

Figure 4-28. But in India the relationship of family size to food resources is out of hand. Terai women preparing a meal while waiting for the rest of the family to return from the fields. (United Nations.)

Not only the composition but also the size of the kin group continuously working together is importantly affected by what is the most efficient size work group under a particular set of technoenvironmental circumstances. Among primitive farmers and many nonmechanized agricultural peoples a large domestic work group is useful in order to best accomplish all the many tasks associated with food production.

A Japanese farmer (see Beardsley, Hall, and Ward 1959; Fukutake 1967) can usually produce more food from his limited holding only by increasing the efficiency with which he works his land. Where farm mechanization is minimal or nonexistent, the many processes involved in the year-round task of intensive farming—field preparation and planting, irrigation, cultivation, and the harvest—depend on the patient and persistent work of many hands. A farmer with many children can be assured of the labor he needs. Peasants nearly everywhere regard a large family as desirable because it is the family that provides the farm work force. Seniority in the family sanctions authority in the organization of farm work, and dependence on the family—which is the primary unit of consumption—motivates individual farm workers.

The relationship of family work group size to technology is underscored further by

". . . because it is the family that provides the farm work force."
Figure 4-29. Preparing for the rice harvest, India. (Embassy of India Photo.)

what occurs whenever farming is abandoned for industry or commerce. The son of a Japanese farmer who becomes a bank clerk or a factory worker and moves to a small apartment in a suburban Osaka housing project, his Indian counterpart who leaves the countryside for a desk job in Calcutta, the Zambian farmer's son who migrates to the Copperbelt to work in the mines all are less likely than were their fathers to find maintenance of a large domestic group economically desirable.

Coercion

Where labor is allocated and organized by force, the avoidance of punishment or fear of an increase in punishment is the worker's principal "reward." Typically, such work systems are found in stratified societies dominated by a strong political organization. And, like work organizations everywhere, they are sanctioned, explained, and justified by the dominant ideology. Work organized on the basis of coercion can be structured in at least seven different ways.

1. Forced Labor. Under a forced labor system a previously free person is forced to work in a particular way at an assigned task for a set period of time—for a few hours, days, months, or years, or for life. The worker is principally motivated by a desire to escape further punishment: assignment to an even more arduous task; torture; denial of food, heat, adequate living space, recreation, or companionship; or the prolongation of sentence. Occasionally, positive rewards may also be offered that entail some amelioration of the worker's discomfort, such as a lighter task assignment, more comfortable quarters, or better food. In those instances in

"... a previously free person is forced to work in a particular way at an assigned task for a set period of time—for a few hours, days, months, or years, or for life."

Figure 4-30. Convict laborers, Georgia, U.S.A. (Courtesy of the Library of Congress.)

"The work organization of concentration camp inmates in Nazi Germany provides a particularly vivid example . . ."

Figure 4-31. Two Hungarians arrested for deportation to a Nazi concentration camp. (Courtesy of the Library of Congress.)

which workers are paid—as they sometimes are in prison, for example—one cannot assume that this constitutes just compensation for their efforts.

Often forced labor is assigned as a punishment for what those in political control define as criminality—for theft, murder, promoting prohibited political action, or belonging to an unpopular ethnic group. The work organization of concentration camp inmates in Nazi Germany provides a particularly vivid example of how such a system can work (see Kogon 1946; Lengyel 1947).

2. *The Corvée.* The Corvée is similar to certain kinds of forced labor. This French term was first used to refer to the system by which a feudal lord could compel his vassals to work for a specified number of days on his farmlands. Participation in the corvée is usually defined as a responsibility owed to the local political authority. Rendering the labor required is perceived as part of the worker's duty to compensate the political leader for his services in maintaining order in the local community or in leading his followers in battle against the enemy. Or it is justified as the means by which those politically in charge can assure that tasks necessary to the well-being of the community are accomplished. Where money is absent, the corvée may serve as an alternative means of taxation.

In accordance with a labor system called mita, commoners in the Inca Empire were required to contribute their labor to the construction and maintenance of all state-owned property: the mines, irrigation works, roads, and bridges that made up the impressive transportation system of the empire; the temples; the palaces of the nobles; and other public buildings (Rowe 1946; Steward and Faron 1959).

In preconquest Peru thirty thousand men at a time are said to have been employed in the construction of a single fortress above the Inca capital at Cuzco. Each local chief was assigned by the royal court a quota of laborers to be supplied by his district. He recruited them and supervised their work.

In the Americas, the Pacific, and Africa indigenous work organizations based on the corvée were frequently replaced by the European colonists with systems of labor recruitment intermediate in type between forced labor and the traditional corvée. Until the mid-1970s Africans in the Portuguese colonies of Angola and Mozambique were forcibly recruited by the police to labor both on public works projects and on the European-owned farms (see Harris 1959). That native workers benefited only minimally from the colonial systems they were required in this way to support may help explain the whites' frequent complaints about black workers' "laziness."

3. *Tenancy.* Tenancy involves an agreement between a landowner and those who work his land in which the workers' right to use a portion of the land for a given period of time is granted in return for their promise to compensate the owner by giving him a part of the harvest. Often the landowner provides the farmer-tenants with other goods as well, such as farm machinery and animals to use, fertilizer, seed, food, clothing, and money advanced to purchase other household items, to pay taxes, and to meet their other needs for cash.

Typically, at each harvest time accounts are settled between landlord and tenant. As the system actually operates, the tenant is often required to turn over so much of his harvest—from a third to more than half of his crop to cover the cost of advances already received—that the small portion he retains cannot be sold for enough to meet his cash needs for the coming year. Furthermore, as most of the small portion of land available to him has been used to produce a cash crop, he will have been unable to produce and keep enough food to feed himself and his family until the next harvest. So again he must ask the landlord for advances of goods he has not been able to produce, retain, or purchase. His indebtedness may be perpetuated from year to year. As the system operates in theory, the worker is free; as it usually operates in fact, exercise of his freedom is blocked by inescapable debt.

If the tenant leaves the landlord's farm without paying his debts, he is liable to court action, the imposition of a fine, or a prison sentence. In the plantation regions of the southern United States and northern Brazil (see Edwards 1969; Hutchinson 1957; Johnson 1971; Raper and Reid 1941; Wasserman 1967; Woofter and others 1936), where the system of tenancy has been operating for several centuries, farm laborers are frequently compelled to continue working the land by financial moves that keep the money value of cash advances so high and the price paid for the tenants' crops so low that workers are unable to leave the land, even when they might be able to find more rewarding work elsewhere. By manipulation of economic factors like loan rates and local market prices, and by political actions, especially the structuring of the contractual relationship between landlord and tenant as it relates to indebtedness, labor is allocated and work organized in accordance with a set of conditions that are imposed and enforced politically.

"... workers are unable to leave the land, even when they might be able to find more rewarding work elsewhere."

Figure 4-32. A Brazilian farm laborer and his family. Lack of alternative job opportunities compels many laborers in northeastern Brazil to accept the low wages paid on the coffee plantations of the area. (United Nations.)

4. Peonage. Analytically, tenancy becomes peonage at the point where the worker is almost totally immobilized by his debt. Under these conditions the political organization is typically more responsive to the interests of the debt holder and will lend its full strength to enforcement of the indebted peon's disadvantageous status and the protection of the debt holder's rights (see Daniel 1972; Good 1966). Interest is often applied at exorbitant rates to the amount of the original debt. If the wage paid the worker is kept sufficiently low, debt can be perpetuated indefinitely, even passed on at still-compounding interest to the worker's descendants.

The pearl divers in the Persian Gulf are organized on this basis (Bowen cited by Udy 1959:85–86). The captain (nakhoda) of a pearling ship takes on a crew of sailors and divers who are not paid a cash wage but receive advances in food, money, and other goods during the course of the voyage. When the ship returns to its home port after several months, a tallying of the captain's accounts usually reveals that the total cash value of the goods advanced to the seamen exceeds the amount of the wages they are owed. Not only do they receive no pay, they also are in arrears and forbidden by law to sign on any other ship until their debt is paid. So they must go to sea again with the same captain, drawing more advances. The interest on their original debt is regularly compounded, the total they owe increases steadily, and they are indefinitely bound to their work by debt.

5. Serfdom. Structurally, serfdom closely resembles peonage. Serfs are obligated to work by the fact of their residence on land controlled by a landlord. When rights to such land are transferred, rights to the labor of the serfs are transferred as well. Whereas land and serfs can be reallocated by those who control them, the serfs themselves cannot leave the land or refuse to work it according to the conditions imposed by the landlord. His coercive power is supported by the state.

In Tibet most farm laborers were until quite recently assigned in perpetuity to particular landholdings, which were granted by the Dalai Lama to the members of his court (Kawaguchi 1909; Goldstein 1971b; MacDonald 1929; Rockhill 1895; Shen and Liu cited by Udy 1959:83). They in turn reapportioned them to their agents, managers, and local headmen, who passed down directions concerning the use of the land and the employment of workers on it.

In parts of Iran (Lambton 1953) a similar

"Structurally, serfdom closely resembles peonage."

Figure 4-33. Russian villagers in the 1890s, twenty years after the abolition of serfdom. (Novosti Press Agency, Moscow, U.S.S.R.)

"It was only later . . . as plantation slavery expanded and became increasingly profitable . . . that slaves ceased almost entirely to be recognized as persons and became chattel."

Figure 4-34. People for sale. An eighteenth-century poster. (Courtesy of the Library of Congress.)

system prevails. The landlord owns a village, the surrounding farmland, and the right to organize the work of all local inhabitants.

6. Slavery. Slavery represents the potentially most extreme form of work organization based on coercion. As it was practiced in ancient Europe and in many parts of Asia and Africa, it was structurally somewhat similar to one or another of the coercive work organizations already described. People were enslaved if they were captured in war, fell into debt, or were the victims of some other unfortunate circumstance. In most instances it was possible for slaves to change their status by purchasing their freedom, by receiving it as a gift from their

Negroes for Sale.

A Cargo of very fine ſtout Men and Women, in good order and fit for immediate ſervice, juſt imported from the Windward Coaſt of Africa, in the Ship Two Brothers.—
Conditions are one half Caſh or Produce, the other half payable the firſt of January next, giving Bond and Security if required.
The Sale to be opened at 10 *o'Clock each Day, in* Mr. Bourdeaux's *Yard, at No,* 48, *on the Bay.*
May 19, 1784. JOHN MITCHELL.

Thirty Seaſoned Negroes
To be Sold for Credit, at Private Sale.

AMONGST which is a Carpenter, none of whom are known to be diſhoneſt.
Alſo, to be ſold for Caſh, a regular bred young Negroe Man-Cook, born in this Country, who ſerved ſeveral Years under an exceeding good French Cook abroad, and his Wife a middle aged Waſher-Woman, (both very honeſt) and their two Children. *Likewiſe.* a young Man a Carpenter.
For Terms apply to the Printer.

masters, by political proclamation, or by other legal means.

Under the Ottoman Turks slaves often attained high government office. Africans and most American Indians intermarried with their slaves or, in many instances, adopted them into their families, and the slaves' work was often no different from that of their masters. The slave was recognized as a person with limited but real social, economic, and religious rights. Even the first slaves brought to the Americas from Africa were regarded as bondsmen with a status and with rights analogous to those of the thousands of white indentured servants brought from Europe (see R. Morris 1946; A. Smith 1947).

It was only later, as the African slave trade was cut off and as plantation slavery expanded and became increasingly profitable, particularly in the southern regions of what became the United States, that slaves ceased almost entirely to be recognized as persons and became chattel. Not only their labor, and what they produced, but also the slaves themselves became property, productive goods like land and machines. The prevailing political system went to great lengths for a long time to maintain, protect, and assure the perpetuation of this most rigidly coercive system for organizing work (Blassingame 1972; Genovese 1965, 1972; Morgan 1975; Rawick 1972).

7. Total Mobilization. In total mobilization some aspects of the work of almost all members of the society are altered either by common agreement or by edict from those in permanent or temporary political control. What follows is not the total restructuring of existing work organization but the temporary imposition on it of controls that may affect both the rate of production and some modification of accustomed patterns of work performance.

Certain types of hunting organization exemplify the working of this system in its simplest form. At Shoshone communal antelope hunts (Steward 1955d), which were held at intervals of several years, all members of the nomadic family bands present within a particular region at a particular time (most but not all of them were related) were mobilized by the Antelope Shaman, a man believed to have the power to lure the antelope into a trap made by erecting a corral of brush with winglike extensions stretching out for several miles. For the duration of the hunt the otherwise autonomous Shoshone groups were mobilized under the Antelope Shaman's authority. Some were directed to build the corral, others to serve as drivers, first fanning out for several miles to form a line stretching across the entire valley, then slowly closing in. To escape from the advancing hunters, and drawn by curiosity toward the unusual figure of the shaman, the animals moved into the trap. During the hunt the Antelope Shaman had authority in the direction of all work. But once the hunt was over and the hunters were demobilized, his temporary authority came to an abrupt end. A similar work organization was activated by the Crow and other Plains Indian groups for hunting buffalo.

At levels of greater technological complexity, where authority is highly centralized on a long-term basis, modern nations are sometimes required to organize work the same way. During officially declared crises governments often impose extraordinary controls on all phases of work organization, directly allocating all vital labor for the duration of the critical period during a flood, earthquake, or other natural disaster; in wartime, when there is a threat of war; or during a period of "revolutionary reconstruction."

Voluntary Organizations

Beyond the kinship-based domestic work group, reliance on voluntary cooperation often provides a productive means of allocating labor and of organizing work. People everywhere work together with nonkinsmen at some tasks on a voluntary basis, grouping themselves to labor collectively without external coercion, usually motivated by recognition that assistance volun-

"People everywhere work together with nonkinsmen at some tasks on a voluntary basis. . . ."

Figure 4-35. Voluntary group at work in a millet field, Yatenga, Upper Volta.

"... they spread out in a line and set off through the field in unison, singing, stepping forward, and striking the earth to the time of the drummer's syncopated beat."
Figure 4-36. Haitian combite. (OAS Photos.)

tarily rendered to others will be reciprocated.

In most instances voluntary work organizations are permanently structured but activated only in response to specific needs. Typically, only a portion or segment of the total community is involved. When Aleut fishermen sight a whale, for example, all the sea hunters of the community set to work voluntarily, putting out to sea at once, some manning the oars, others standing ready to strike, still others preparing to bring the dead or wounded animal onto shore. Each man's specific responsibility is clearly understood by him and by all other participants. Work is organized without coercion. Participants are motivated by recognition of the benefits of cooperation (obviously, no Aleut could kill and bring in a whale alone), and so strong are the desire to be recognized as productive and the fear of being ridiculed as incompetent that the wholehearted participation of all workers is assured (Udy 1959).

Among many primitive farmers reliance on voluntary associations serves as a valuable complement to kinship-based work groups, especially when a particular task requires the concerted effort of a large number of workers for a relatively short time, in an activity such as house building, for example, or clearing a field for planting.

The peasants of Haiti (Herskovits 1964; Moral 1961) have retained from their West African cultural heritage a voluntary work organization called a combite, which is most often activated when a farmer needs assistance to prepare a field for planting and, as is usual with poor peasants in Haiti, is unable to hire the help he requires. The farmer notifies a neighbor of his need, usually a man who has organized voluntary work parties before. Often he gives a bottle of rum to seal the agreement and as a symbolic assurance that the workers will be rewarded. On the morning of the day agreed upon all those who want to participate gather in the farmer's field. One or more of them bring a drum. After receiving some general instructions on the work to be done, they spread out in a line and set off through the field in unison, singing, stepping forward, and striking the earth to the time of the drummer's syncopated beat. The sound of drumming and singing is a signal to the community that a combite is under way. Others come and join. As many as fifty or seventy-five people may accomplish in a day what it would take the individual farmer weeks to complete. When the work is finished, participants are rewarded by a feast prepared by the field's owner. Those who have worked best receive the most generous helpings, special thanks, and perhaps a coin or two placed on their plates beneath the food. Those who arrived late or worked listlessly are ridiculed, made the butt of jokes and sarcastic songs, and are given less to eat.

Haitian peasants participate voluntarily in the combite because they enjoy the company of their friends, the drumming and singing, the fine meal, and the free rum they are served by their host. But most importantly they cooperate because, lacking any other external source of economic support, they know that by responding to the request of a neighbor for aid they can be assured of assistance when they need it themselves.

Work Organization and Rank

Where a people's technology is complex and productivity relatively high, it is often possible for some individuals and groups to concentrate fully on particular productive activities that in time become their special prerogative. This often sets them apart socially, and, conversely, being set apart socially serves to reinforce their identification with particular kinds of work. Their social position comes to determine the work they do. In effect their labor is allocated by rank.

In those parts of the ancient world where the development of agriculture sometimes made it possible for groups to concentrate exclusively on the performance of tasks unrelated to food production—on metalworking, pottery manufacture, scholarship, government service, or the priesthood—the right or responsibility to perform such tasks often came to be confined to those whose ancestors had engaged in such work. Well-rewarded specialists frequently guarded jealously their monopoly on the performance of particular kinds of work.

The workers' guilds of medieval Europe represent one form that such specialization can take. An extreme case is represented by the community- and nationwide organization of work on the basis of caste affiliation characteristic of Hindu society, in which members of each caste inherit from their parents the right or requirement to engage in certain kinds of work: farm labor; the priesthood; cloth, pottery, or mat making; leatherworking; latrine cleaning; or story-

"Where a people's technology is complex and productivity relatively high, it is often possible for some individuals and groups to concentrate fully on particular productive activities that in time become their special prerogative."

Figure 4-37. An Indian potter at his caste-ascribed task. (Information Section, Government of India.)

". . . they are prohibited by threat of supernatural punishment . . . from performing tasks not regarded as befitting their caste status. . . ."

Figure 4-38. Indian women drawing water. If an outcaste person were to use this well it would be regarded as ritually polluted. (National Archives.)

telling. Traditionally they are prohibited by threat of supernatural punishment, and by force if necessary, from performing tasks not regarded as befitting their caste status (Freed and Freed 1972; Gough 1973; Khare 1970; Mahar 1972; Sinha 1967).

As a work organization the caste system is invariably reinforced by the ritual avoidance of close social contact with members of other castes: refusal to share food with, to intermarry with, or sometimes even to touch physically persons of a different caste, particularly if their rank is inferior. In India the caste system is further strengthened by the belief that Hindu society was originally divided into such groups by divine will (see Aggarwal 1971; Bouglé 1971; Weber 1958).

Within each caste, work is organized on the basis of sex, age, kinship, and subcaste status. The system encompasses the entire Hindu community, designating for each group the work appropriate to its caste, work that complements the assigned productive activities of the other castes to provide for the community-wide (but asymmetrical) organization of all work.

Class membership is also an important determinant in labor allocation (see Blau and Duncan 1967; Domhoff 1975; Kornblum 1975; Marx 1888; Mencher 1974a; Mhlongo 1975; Vogel 1971). In a class-structured society like that of the United States, certain socially useful jobs that entail cleaning and unskilled manual labor, such as garbage collection, street cleaning, and migratory farm work, are generally categorized as "low class." Usually they are held by people socially identified as low class. In effect, work is organized on the basis of class. At the top of the social class system success in the attainment of certain other positions, often ones of considerable power and prestige, in business, the professions, and government tends to be strongly affected by membership in the upper-middle or upper class; that exceptions are remarked upon proves the rule. At each end of the American social class continuum there are also people who do not work at all: certain members of the lower class whose poverty-related disabilities make them unemployable and some upper-class persons whose wealth, derived from the labor of others, makes work unnecessary (see Veblen 1953).

Where the social system is rigidly structured on the basis of either caste or class, compliance with the dictates of the rank-related work organization is usually assured by "tradition" backed up by the threat of force. Educated Hindu untouchables are frequently denied skilled jobs solely because of their caste position. The same thing happens to job applicants in Japan known to be Burakumin, members of an "outcaste" group that has for centuries been excluded from all but the most menial tasks (see DeVos and Wagatsuma 1967). In the United States, in Europe, and in the Republic of South Africa, qualified members of certain

". . . migratory farm work . . . generally categorized as 'low class.'"
Figure 4-39. Children and adults, all migrant laborers, U.S.A. (Steve Schapiro, Black Star.)

groups are frequently (sometimes invariably) refused access to particular types of work because of the social inferiority ascribed to all members of the ethnic group to which they belong.

Sometimes this forcible allocation of work is brutally explicit.

Contractual Work Organization

In many ways the several kinds of work organization so far discussed resemble contractual work organization. All are formally structured. There is usually comprehension if not acceptance of the conditions of work. Each worker understands his or her responsibility to members of the work group and what he or she can expect from them. Usually these circumstances are set by custom. Typically, a breach of the traditionally sanctioned pattern of work is quickly perceived and rectified, or punished. The recruitment of members, the sources of their motivation to participate, and the rewards they receive are all based on a series of particular external circumstances—the fact that they are all male kinspeople related in a particular way, residents of the same community with common interests, or members of a guild, caste, class, or ethnic group assigned by custom to the performance of particular tasks. Although all such workers are organized on the basis of agreement, that agreement is characteristically part of a larger framework of relations, and many aspects of work organization are affected by criteria not directly relevant to performance of the job—by considerations of sex, age, social status, ethnic identity, personal acquaintance, preference, or prejudice—all reflections of a somewhat extended, more complex, structurally more diffuse system of social groupings.

"... the expectations of laborers and employers are explicitly stated in terms of time, money, and other conditions of work. . . ."
Figure 4-40. Mine workers, U.S.A. (Appalachian Regional Commission.)

In contrast, in industrially based societies the relationship between workers and between workers and their employers generally tends to be more impersonal, limited to the requirements of the job and to the enforcement of compliance with a contractual agreement. In theory, these explicitly stated aspects of the work relationship replace consideration of factors that are irrelevant to job performance but that in nonindustrialized societies always play an important part in work organization. In industry and in jobs created by industry people tend to be recruited solely on the basis of their ability to do the job. Where recruitment is based on such nongermane criteria as class, race, sex, or kinship, labor is not allocated efficiently, and productivity suffers.

Where work is organized on the basis of contract the expectations of laborers and employers are explicitly stated in terms of time, money, and other conditions of work and are negotiated either in the "job market" or by the state.

Wage labor is the most common form of

contractually based work organization. It is universally absent among hunter-gatherers, nonexistent within the context of the traditional economic systems of most if not all primitive farmers, rare among pastoral peoples, and utilized only as a subsidiary basis for work organization among agriculturalists, usually as a supplement to the kinship-based work organization. It is only in industrializing societies, on mechanized farms, in factories, in service jobs, and in the bureaucracy necessitated by industrialization that formal contract and labor sold for money emerge as dominant bases for the organization of work.

Changes in the Organization of Production

By now it is apparent that the kind of technological change that is associated with economic growth and "development" inevitably precipitates changes in the traditional organization of production. Authority over the system for establishing and coordinating the right to use land and other natural resources tends to pass from the family and the local community to those at the center of the power structure, to private groups and/or government bodies. A parallel change occurs in the locus of authority for allocating other productive goods. Control over waterworks, power sources, tools, and factories is also increasingly centralized. Producers and owners tend to become opposed categories.

The traditional domestic mode of production associated with the family hunting territory, the family-owned farm, and pastoral nomadism is diminishing in significance and now persists only in the most ecologically marginal areas, in the very far north, in remote mountain valleys, and at the desert's edge. Everywhere else, the shift is well under way from domestic-oriented production to meet local workers' finite subsistence needs to production for the implicitly infinite goals of growth, development, and profit.

Given our planet's evidently limited resources, it is by no means certain that such objectives are either universally attainable or ecologically desirable. What is certain is that the quest to achieve them has already transformed the traditional production organization—the ways of work—of most of humankind.

Summary

The allocation of productive goods—natural resources, tools, artifacts, techniques, and labor—is a basic function of any economic system.

Among hunting and gathering peoples the requirements of technoenvironmental adaptation, especially the need to adjust to shifts in the availability of wild foods, make necessary a flexible system for allocating access to natural resources. Territorial rights are typically held communally.

Among primitive farmers systems of land tenure are also usually structured to assure rights of use based primarily on need within a system that provides for the reallocation of these rights as the needs of members of the community change and as shifting cultivation requires that certain lands be left fallow. Characteristically, the kinship system provides the organizing principles for the allocation of land among horticulturalists, with residual controls resting with local political or religious leaders.

An analogous sort of flexibility is built into the territorial systems of most pastoral peoples. Only among advanced farmers and in industrial societies does private land ownership become the dominant system. The resultant potential for the accumulation of wealth, social stratification, and centralization of political power makes possible the concentration of control of access to natural resources in the hands of a ruling minority.

The allocation of tools, artifacts, and techniques used in production varies in accordance with the same pattern. Where the technology is primitive, proprietary rights are typically determined on the basis of kinship ties and need. As the technology becomes more complex and its component aspects become more interdependent, rights of ownership over major productive goods—factories, power plants, waterworks, transportation systems—tend to become centrally controlled by private entrepreneurs or by the state.

The organized allocation of labor resources is also affected by patterns of technoenvironmental adaptation, by recruitment criteria based on sex, age, and kinship affiliation, and by the structure of the larger economic, social, and political systems of which work organization is a component part.

Work organized on the basis of coercion can take at least seven different forms: (1) forced labor, (2) the corvée, (3) tenancy, (4) peonage, (5) serfdom, (6) slavery, and (7) total mobilization. Work may also be organized on the basis of voluntary associations, especially where centralized authority is weak, absent, or irrelevant to the local organization of work.

In stratified societies positions ranked hierarchically on the basis of caste, class, or ethnicity are invariably primal determinants of work organization.

All forms of work organization entail contract in the sense that there is general agreement on the conditions of work. However, it is only in industrialized (or industrializing) societies that contract—stated explicitly, established independently of other social relationships, and entailing recruitment based primarily on ability to do the job—tends to become the dominant principle in organizing the allocation of available labor resources.

With the advent of advanced farming and industrialization the traditional, domestically oriented systems of production for local consumption tend to be replaced by modern modes of production in which resources are too often allocated to maximize the profits of a relative few rather than to satisfy the basic material needs of the human majority, and in which the objective of achieving implicitly limitless economic "growth" raises tough questions concerning technological feasibility, ecological impact, and ethical justification.

Suggested Readings

For several overviews of the fast-growing literature in economic anthropology see Cook's "Economic Anthropology: Problems in Theory, Method and Analysis," Dalton's *Studies in Economic Anthropology,* Hatch's "The Growth of Economic, Subsistence, and Ecological Studies in American Anthropology," Salisbury's "Economics," and Schneider's *Economic Man.* For an innovative perspective try Meillassoux's "From Reproduction to Production: A Marxist Approach to Economic Anthropology." Sahlins's critical *Stone Age Economics* is a major work. Also of importance is Asad's "The Concept of Rationality in Economic Anthropology."

Examples of what anthropologists have written on the allocation of natural resources, especially land, and of other productive goods are provided by Asad's "Property Control and Social Strategies: Settlers on a Middle Eastern Plain"; the Bohannans' "Land Rights: Social Relations in Terrestrial Space"; Dowling's "Property Relations and Productive Strategies in Pastoral Societies"; Huntingford's important *The Land Charters of Northern Ethiopia; Land Tenure in Oceania,* edited by Lundsgaarde; and Snow's "Wabanaki 'Family Hunting Territories'."

The standard comparative study of labor allocation and organization among nonindustrialized peoples, and one that greatly influenced the content of this chapter, is Udy's *Organization of Work.* On sex and age as the basis of work organization see Brown's "Economic Organization and the Position of Women Among the Iroquois" and her "A Note on the Division of Labor by Sex"; Harrison's "The Political Economy of Housework"; Hiatt's "Woman the Gatherer"; the Johnsons' "Male/Female Relations and the Organization of Work in a Machiguenga Community"; Morren's "Woman the Hunter"; Sacks's "Engels Revisited: Women, the Organization of Production, and Private Property"; Boserup's important study, *Woman's Role in Economic Development,* and Spradley and Mann's interesting *The Cocktail Waitress: Woman's Work in a Man's World.*

Some aspects of kinship as the basis for allocating labor are included in the Suggested Readings for Chapters 6 and 7. See also the two chapters on the domestic mode of production in Sahlins's *Stone Age Economics,* Stauder's "The Domestic Group: Labour and Property," and Lee's "Work Effort, Group Structure and Land Use in Contemporary Hunter-Gatherers."

References to the voluntary organization of work are included in the Suggested Readings for Chapter 8. Rank as a basis for labor allocation is covered in the Suggested Readings for Chapter 9. Most references to work organized on the basis of coercion are contained in the text, but see also Fogel and Engerman's *Time on the Cross: The Economics of Slavery in the Antebellum South,* Genovese's *The Political Economy of Slavery: Studies in the Economy and Society of the Slave South,* and Yetman's *Life Under the "Peculiar Institution": Selections from the Slave Narrative Collection.* On the increasingly important subject of migratory labor see Berger's *The Seventh Man,* Friedland and Nelkin's *Migrant: Agricultural Workers in America's Northeast,* and Wilson's *Migrant Labour in South Africa.*

There is a vast anthropological literature on what is generally termed economic "development." For some good examples see Dalton's collection *Economic Development and Social Change: The Modernization of Village Communities,* and Epstein and Penny's *Opportunity and Response: Case Studies in Economic Development.* For some further cautionary ideas on the subject as it has been dealt with in this chapter, see Davidson's *Can Africa Survive? Arguments Against Growth Without Development,* Frank's "The Development of Underdevelopment," Jacob's *Modernization Without Development: Thailand As a Modern Case Study,* and Mencher's "Socioeconomic Constraints to Development: The Case of South India." For a complementary perspective from economics see Boserup's important *The Conditions of Agricultural Growth: The Economics of Agrarian Change Under Population Pressure.*

Examples of two important new forms of production organization are offered by Abarbanel's *The Cooperative Farmer and the Welfare State: Economic Change in an*

Israeli Moshav; and by Clegg's *Workers' Self-management in Algeria.* Wallerstein's "The Rise and Future Demise of the World Capitalist System: Concepts for Comparative Analysis" provides a politically oriented overview of present and possible future changes in production organization. See also Cook's "Production, Ecology, and Economic Anthropology: Notes Toward an Integrated Frame of Reference."

5

Organizing Distribution

THE various ways people organize distribution of the goods and services they produce can be categorically separated and described in terms of three structurally different systems: reciprocity, redistribution, and market exchange (see Polanyi 1953, 1968; Dalton 1965). Although all three may operate as component aspects of a single economic system, it is usual for one or another of them to be dominant in structuring the processes by which most consumer goods and services are moved within a particular society.

Among peoples with very simple technologies reciprocity and redistribution are always the more important distributive systems; market exchange, except where it results from contact with technologically more advanced groups, is totally lacking. Redistribution is often the dominant process among primitive farming peoples and pastoralists; market exchange is still generally peripheral. Market exchange becomes more important in societies based on advanced agriculture (and among pastoralists in close contact with advanced farmers). In industrial societies both market exchange and redistribution are characteristically prominent; reciprocity has only a limited effect on the distribution of consumer goods and services.

Reciprocity

As a distributive system, reciprocity takes three principal forms (Gouldner 1960; Sahlins 1972a; Service 1966). Among close kinspeople there is an ongoing, diffuse, and generalized exchange of goods and services that reinforces economic interdependence and societal solidarity but does not necessarily entail the short-term expectation of equivalent return: nurturance of the very young, the infirm, and aged members of the family, for example. Such a system may be extended to assure that all kinspeople within a local area are provisioned. Where the environment is marginal, productivity is low, and periods of scarcity are frequent, reciprocity of this sort perpetuates a kind of mutual indebtedness that assures both individual and group survival. The pooling of goods and services among nonrelated persons that occurs within a community during periods of acute stress or disaster is also an instance of generalized reciprocity. However, its duration is generally brief.

Balanced reciprocity is marked by the more intermittent exchange of goods, usually gifts that are culturally defined as appropriate to particular occasions and to the degree of closeness between giver and receiver—presents given to a nephew at his graduation, to a second cousin at her marriage, to friends at the birth of a child, to a hospitalized fellow worker, or to the family of a deceased acquaintance. In all these instances equivalent reciprocity is expected. That is, goods of commensurate worth should be given in return at whatever future time is culturally defined as proper.

The negative reciprocity found in some societies is characterized by competitive gift-giving and counter-gift-giving rituals in

	Transactional Mode		
	Reciprocity	*Redistribution*	*Market Exchange*
Underlying social relationship expressed by the transaction	Friendship, kinship, status, hierarchy	Political or religious affiliation	None

"The various ways people organize distribution of the goods and services they produce can be categorically separated and described. . . ."

Figure 5-1. Schematic representation of the three fundamental transactional modes and the social relationships characteristically associated with each of them. (After Polanyi and Dalton 1968.)

". . . market exchange, except where it results from contact with technologically more advanced groups . . ."
Figure 5-2. Inuk mother shopping with her children in Igloolik, Northwest Territories, Canada. (National Film Board of Canada.)

". . . a kind of mutual indebtedness that assures both individual and group survival."
Figure 5-3. East African lion hunters after the kill. (Courtesy of the American Museum of Natural History.)

which socially distant participants (often members of different societies) try to enhance their own status and esteem and to diminish, by besting or shaming, the status of those to whom their gifts are given. Participants endeavor to maximize their own material and social benefits in the transaction and to minimize the advantages of the others.

"Obligatory gifts may take the form of goods, services. . . ."

Figure 5-4. House building at a cooperative farm, Benin, West Africa. (United Nations.)

In every instance reciprocity functions to create and/or to sustain alliances that extend the participants' field of security. Obligatory gifts may take the form of goods, services, or money. Reciprocal exchange usually occurs in a somewhat public context. As there are witnesses to what is given, the memory of observers serves as a record of what is owed in return. Typically, this social pressure is the principal means of assuring that a gift will be reciprocated—for such exchange most often occurs between parties who do not share allegiance to any common political authority that might otherwise enforce the obligations of each to the other.

Usually reciprocal exchanges occur between persons and groups whose roughly equal social status is a reflection of their equivalent economic position and their capacity to reciprocate with gifts of equal value (Malinowski 1920; Mauss 1954; Polanyi 1944). Typically, participants cannot use the threat of force to compel such reciprocity. Either the relationship exists outside the bounds of the centralized political system ("among friends," for example), or, as is more frequently the case where reciprocity is the dominant mode of exchange, no centralized authority system exists. Assurance that the donor will receive in return goods of approximately equal value is provided by mutual awareness of the usefulness of perpetuating such exchange and by fear of shaming. The person who fails to reciprocate is sooner or later excluded from the exchange relationship and becomes the object of public scorn; his or her credibility is damaged and chances of future sharing are likely to be jeopardized.

Reciprocal exchange is familiar in U.S. society. Most people are involved in gift-giving exchanges with some of their kinspeople, close friends, and other associates in the community. However, such relations are always peripheral, or complementary, to the basic processes by which most goods and services are moved in U.S. society. Gift giving functions most significantly as a means of cementing social relationships that provide the context for other forms of economic, social, and political interaction.

In contrast, in most nonindustrialized societies, reciprocal exchange relations provide the basic mechanism, sometimes almost the only one, for the distribution of goods and services. Such relations are especially important among hunter-gatherers and primitive farmers. More people are involved in exchanging goods and services more often, the gifts they give and receive are more impor-

"However, such relations are always peripheral . . . to the basic processes by which most goods and services are moved in U.S. society."

Figure 5-5. And in Canadian society as well. A Chinese-Canadian market in Vancouver. (National Film Board of Canada.)

tant to their social security and as a means of meeting their material needs, and the sanctions on those who fail to reciprocate are stronger than in societies where gift exchange is of peripheral economic importance.

Among people living close to the level of subsistence the perpetuation of a variety of reciprocal exchange relations can be vital to the maintenance of economic and social well-being. At this level of technological development a man is more dependent for material security on the number of individuals on whom he can rely for economic assistance, if he should be too sick to hunt or if his crop should fail, than he is on his own individual productive endeavor. No matter how hard he works, his technology is simply not sufficiently productive to enable him to meet all his material needs unaided. Sharing is mandatory for material survival. Damas (1972), for example, lists fourteen types of sharing partners among the eastern Copper Eskimo.

A Mossi farmer could not survive independent of the generalized reciprocal exchanges that reinforce his kinship ties and his relations with others in his community (Hammond 1966). During the course of a single season a man may need extra seed for planting, help with cultivation, millet to feed his family during the hunger season that sometimes precedes the harvest, the loan of a burro or a bicycle to visit a market in a neighboring village, the use of another's knife to cut some thatch to repair the roof of his granary, or cash to buy some aspirin for his ailing wife or to pay his tax. Usually he cannot produce unaided enough to provide for all these needs.

Often the most rational means of protecting his material well-being is by reacting with speed and generosity to requests from others for assistance in the form of labor or material goods. By responding as fully as he is able, he is behaving not unselfishly but in accordance with his own economic best interest. Consequently, the wise Mossi farmer maintains his network of reciprocal ties intact, not only volunteering his labor when called on, but also making frequent unsolicited gifts of food, other goods, and labor.

In the same way, he works carefully to perpetuate his reciprocal ties with others whose services he may need: by making small presents of kola nuts to the local earth priest when he meets him in the market, by assisting the leader of his village sector in repairing the crumbling mud wall of his granary, by helping the sons of the village chief in clearing a new field for planting. The point in such reciprocal exchanges is not to pay up and terminate them, but to keep them going, the more the better, for as long as possible.

An important function of any system of distribution is the provision of a means whereby producers can exchange their surplus goods for others in short supply. Surpluses and shortages may result from technological specialization, from environmental variation, or from differences in capability and efficiency that distinguish particular producers in any society. The Mbuti Pygmies (Schebesta 1941), hunters in the Congo, often catch more game than they need. They give the surplus to their Bantu neighbors. In return the Bantu, who are farmers, give the Pygmies a portion of their surplus farm products—rice, cassava, plantains—and iron projectile points for the hunters' spears and arrows. The Arunta of Australia obtain the iron diorite used to make their cutting tools through a network of reciprocal exchange relations that links them with other hunting and gathering groups in areas where this stone is available in greater abundance.

What has become the classic illustration of the organization and operation of a balanced reciprocal system of distribution was first provided by Malinowski's description of

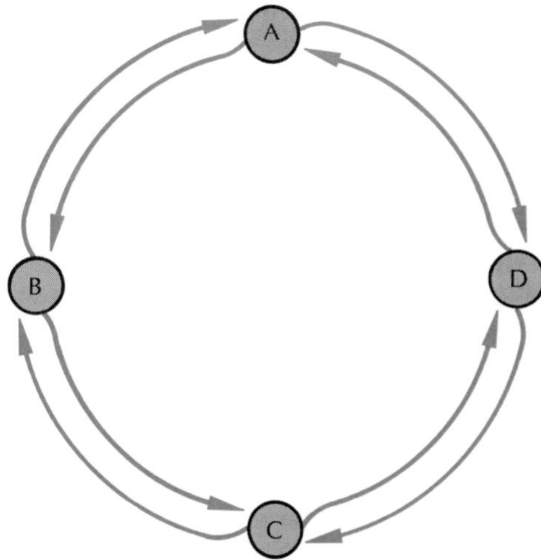

". . . the classic illustration of the organization and operation of a balanced reciprocal system of distribution . . ."

Figure 5-6. A simplified schematic representation of the Kula ring. Each letter represents a community participating in the reciprocal exchange with other communities of ritual objects, food, and other goods. Curved arrows represent intercommunity lines of contact between the Kula partners through whom the exchange is carried on. (After Beals and Hoijer 1965.)

the Kula ring of the Trobriand Islanders (Malinowski 1920, 1922).

Throughout Melanesia reciprocal exchange relationships involve the participation of individuals and groups who are often hundreds of miles apart, separated from one another by language and cultural differences and by the open sea. In eastern New Guinea (Malinowski 1920, 1922) and in the Trobriands, a group of islands off the coast, each local community is separated from others both by some degree of environmental difference affecting the availability of raw materials and by technological specialization. Each has a surplus of some commodities and suffers, at least potentially, from the scarcity of certain others.

Their reciprocal exchange system provides for the intercommunity and interisland distribution of such surplus or scarce goods. Like all reciprocal exchange relations, it is part of a larger network of social ties and is marked by rigid rules of etiquette governing almost all aspects of the participant's conduct, usages that function to provide the individual with a means of acquiring prestige and high status and, if he should fail to reciprocate, of losing them.

Within the family, among members of the local community, and between neighboring communities such exchanges are engaged in on a small scale more or less continuously by all Trobriand Islanders. This same sort of exchange is also conducted between partners more widely separated, both socially and spatially.

Among such partners the exchange of material goods occurs within the context of a system called Kula, which entails the highly ritualized reciprocal exchange of nonutilitarian but valuable goods, principally red spondylus shell necklaces and shell armbands. The largest and most valuable of these continuously circulated objects become well known for their beauty and worth and are given names. Stories become attached to them about the high status and valorous deeds of their former owners: the great distances they have traveled and the perilous experiences they have undergone in the course of their gift-giving expeditions.

The exchange of these well-known objects is economically most important as a symbol of the reciprocal relations that link particular partners in the Kula system. Partnerships are often maintained for years. A commoner may have five or six such relationships, a chief as many as seventy. Each partner serves as the other's host and protector during their respective visits. The ceremonial exchange of objects of ritual value cements the bonds of an economic relation of great practical value. Each partner, and often those who accompany him, also exchanges material goods with the other—

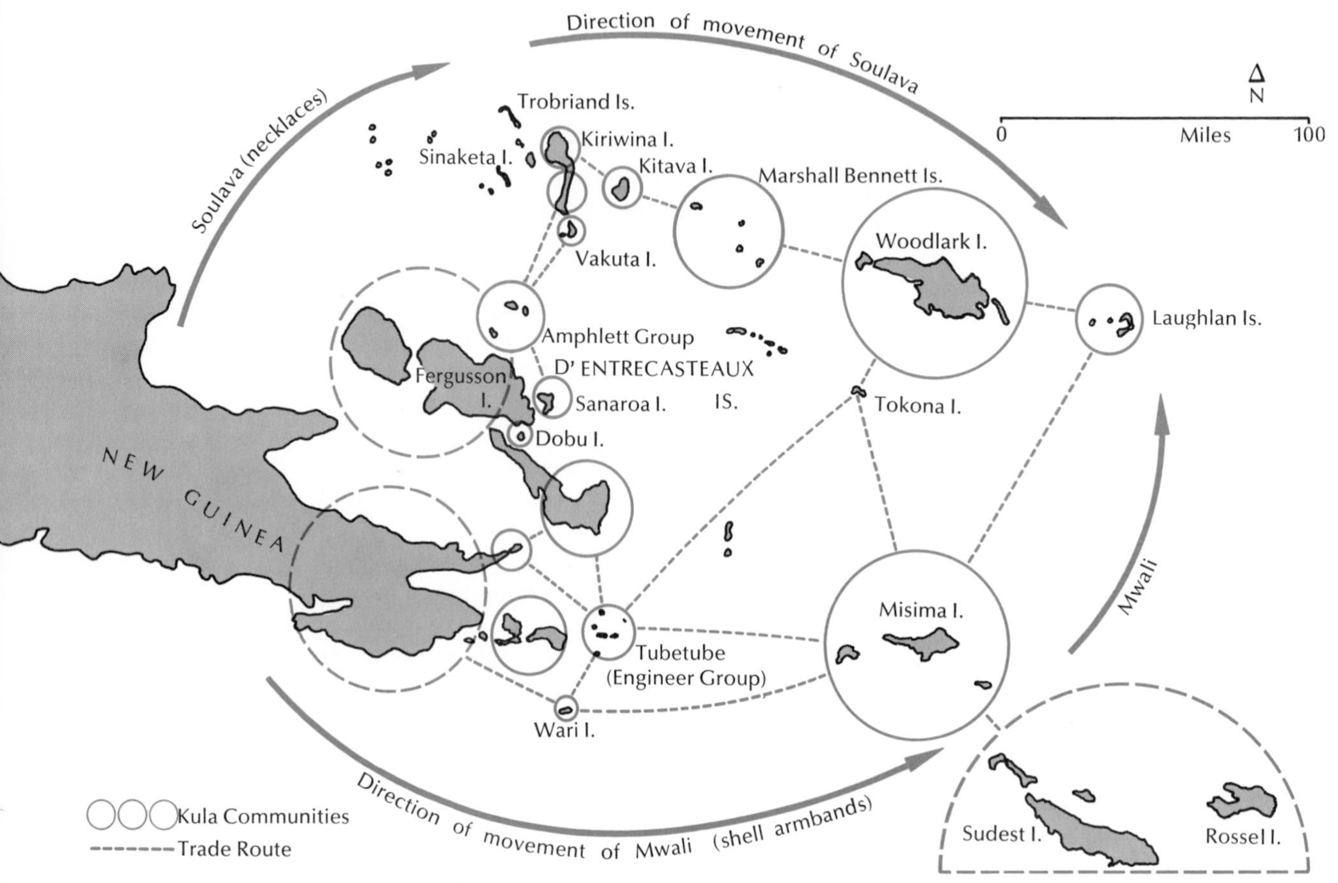

"The movement of goods in the Kula 'ring' is circular in the sense that necklaces move clockwise and shell armbands counterclockwise. . . ."

Figure 5-7. Map of the area in which Kula exchange occurs. Solid circles indicate Kula communities; dotted circles enclose communities indirectly affected by Kula exchange. (After Malinowski.)

pigs, fish, bananas, and other garden crops, as well as the products of local craftsmen in their respective communities. The importance of maintaining a reputation for generosity and honor with one's trading partners in the Kula ring, plus the fact that all exchanges occur publicly, assures that the Trobriand Islander who receives generous presents will reciprocate. Were he to fail to do so, he would be the object of scandalized gossip and painful scorn, and he would be dropped by his Kula partner.

The movement of goods in the Kula "ring" is circular in the sense that necklaces move clockwise and shell armbands counterclockwise throughout all the islands linked in the system. A man on the Trobriand island of Kiriwina gives red spondylus shell necklaces to his partner on the island of Kitava, which lies just to the east. In return, sooner or later, his partner will reciprocate with the gift of a pair of shell armbands, which will ultimately move on in the opposite direction from the necklaces. The man on Kitava will later give the necklace to a partner of his own on one of the still more easterly islands of the Marshall Bennett Archipelago. From there the necklace will be passed even farther east to an island in the Woodlark group, and so on around. The Trobriand Islander who first gave a necklace to his partner in the east, receiving a shell armband in return, will ultimately pass the armband on in the other direction, south to Dobu, perhaps, in the d'Entrecasteaux Islands, and from there it may be passed on further south to Tubetube, moving counterclockwise to make of the Kula ring a double circle.

This ceremonial giving of valuables is maintained steadily. By means of less rigidly formalized reciprocal exchanges a particular trading partner in a particular community assembles the goods—foodstuffs and artifacts—that are the specialty of his area and likely to be welcomed by a particular one of his several distant partners. When he and the others in his community have assembled enough goods, they set off on a gift-giving expedition. In addition to the valuables each member of the party presents to his particular Kula partner and any other presents they make to them, the visitors are also free to bargain with their hosts' neighbors in exchanging the other goods they have brought along.

The highly ritualized reciprocal bond between Kula trading partners provides a context of amity, confidence, and appreciation, and the mutual benefits of economic interdependence, cooperation, and exchange between otherwise alien and potentially hostile groups.

In many societies the emphasis on institutionalized reciprocal exchange relations not only functions to provide a mechanism for the distribution of goods and services but also is a sort of economic leveler, a means of equalizing property holdings by exerting social pressure on any temporarily affluent individual to share with others the goods he holds in excess of his own subsistence needs. Paradoxically, such action temporarily dissipates the wealth on which the donor's high status is based. But the prestige he acquires by such conspicuous, even "wasteful," displays of generosity is more valuable, because it assures perpetuation of the reciprocal relationships on which his material security and social position are most dependent.

However, high esteem and/or diminution of the risk of socially disruptive jealousy may be the generous donor's only reward. Admiration is often all a skilled Bushman hunter receives in return for sharing his kill with others habitually less successful than he. By placing a high value on prowess and generosity, Bushmen society encourages the overproductive striving and munificence that often are necessary to compensate for those who do less than their share. Plains Indians once gave away horses to increase their social status. To this same end Melanesian farmers allow a portion of their yam harvests to rot publicly, and American millionaires give their daughters hundred-thousand-dollar weddings.

The Potlatch of the Indians of the northwestern coast of North America (see Drucker and Heizer 1967; McFeat 1966) illustrates dramatically how negative reciprocity can be institutionalized to enhance the donor's status, to challenge the rank of others, and to provide a system of distribution.

The Indians of the Northwest Pacific coast were exceptional among nonfarming peoples in their ability to accumulate surplus goods. Although they were dependent entirely on wild foods, the unusual richness of their natural environment, especially the abundance of fish in the rivers and the nearby sea, made possible the accumulation of considerable surplus goods. Among them the Potlatch functioned as a means of validating high social status and, ironically, of weakening its economic base.

As is typical of all such institutionalized reciprocal exchanges, the giving of presents was included within the context of a larger, more diffuse relationship, one with both political and supernatural ramifications. The Potlatch was usually held by a chief to solemnify publicly some event of social importance: a marriage, the acquisition of some new honorary title, the ransom of a kinsman captured in war, or the death of a prominent person. Every aspect of the ceremony was conducted with great formality

"The Potlatch of the Indians of the northwestern coast of North America . . . illustrates dramatically how negative reciprocity can be institutionalized to enhance the donor's status. . . ."

Figure 5-8. A Kwakiutl chief ostentatiously gives away blankets at a Potlatch, Fort Rupert, British Columbia, where the Potlatch was developed to an extreme as the result of new sources of wealth made available through trade with the whites. (Courtesy of the American Museum of Natural History.)

and scrupulous attention to the special honors appropriate to the rank of each guest. After much boastful speechmaking and the display of the wealth of the Potlatch giver and his followers, gifts were ostentatiously presented to the visiting chief and his retinue: goat wool robes (later, trade blankets from the Hudson's Bay Company), nuggets of pure copper and beaten copper plates, canoes, animal skins, and other riches so lavish and distributed in such profusion that it generally had taken years for the giver of a Potlatch and his kinsmen to accumulate them. This assistance from kinsmen was also reciprocal; ultimately, the Potlatch organizer was expected to return to his relatives goods slightly more valuable than those he had received.

In quite recent times, during the late 1800s and in the early 1900s, when Kwakiutl population was decreasing and their subsistence technology was becoming more productive (both as consequences of white contact), there was increased emphasis on the aggressively ostentatious aspects of the Potlatch. Reciprocity as a means of distributing goods was transformed. Great quantities of goods were given away or destroyed before the visitors' eyes, oil and money were thrown into the fire, canoes were smashed, blankets were ripped up, copper plates were destroyed (in earlier centuries slaves were killed), as part of a show of wealth intended to bolster the prestige of the Potlatch giver, to challenge his guests' assertions of high status, and to shame them into reciprocating with even more lavish displays of "generosity" and conspicuous waste. Competitive gift giving of this negative sort often went on intermittently for years, as each collected goods for a retaliatory feast and a boastful display of affluence, until one or the other could no longer assemble the wealth necessary to continue. The victor then retained his claim to prestige until he was ultimately bested by some other aspirant to the high esteem accorded to those who could outdo others in the ostentatious distribution of riches.

Redistribution

When the distribution of material goods is organized on the basis of a system of redistribution, provisions (and sometimes money) are obligatorily moved toward an allocative center from which they are then dispersed (Dalton 1962, 1973; Polanyi 1953, 1968; Sahlins 1972a). In its simplest form, such a flow of goods to the center and out again is structurally similar to kinship-based systems of reciprocity, as when a farmer stores the harvested product of the joint labor of himself and his dependents, redistributing portions of it to them individually as they need it; or when a work group pools the product of its collective efforts, redistributing it as needed to meet individual and group needs. But when a ruler receives tribute from his subjects, holding it to draw against to meet their future needs, or when a government taxes its citizenry, the structural differences between redistribution and reciprocity are more apparent. For redistribution typically operates within a social unit that transcends the bounds of the kinship system, including all participants in some larger, usually po-

". . . or when a work group pools the product of its collective efforts . . ."
Figure 5-9. Making way through a dangerous surf at the port of Accra, Ghana. (United Nations.)

". . . as in the collection and redistribution of famine relief supplies by the United Nations."
Figure 5-10. Refugee children near Bethlehem receive a supplementary meal at a United Nations relief agency. (United Nations.)

litical unit. Goods are gathered in on a massive scale in accordance with codified obligations and are then passed out again following similarly stipulated criteria of entitlement.

An important distinction is that goods are no longer distributed between individuals or groups outside a formal system of political controls. Rather, by definition, the participants in a redistributive system operate within some single politically bounded context. Redistribution is most prominent as a principle for organizing the movement of goods in societies with some form of centralized political controls. Often the dimensions of the redistributive system's operation (into the political center and out again to its local constituencies) are coterminous with the frontiers of the political units—the village, the chieftainship, or the state. As long as there is an encompassing political structure, redistribution can also operate internationally, as in the collection and redistribution of famine relief supplies by the United Nations.

Implicit in the definition of the redistributive system is the existence of some central source of authority with power to enforce participation in the distributive process and compliance with its rules. The penalty for noncompliance is usually withdrawal of rights to benefit from some or all aspects of the system. An African farmer who fails to pay material tribute to his chief at harvest time may jeopardize his right to a fair hearing in some future property dispute taken before the chief. An Arab oasis dweller who fails to pay tribute to a local sheik may be left unprotected from nomadic marauders. In most modern states the man who refuses to pay his taxes usually faces a fine, seizure of some of his property, curtailment of his rights as a citizen, restrictions on his activities, or imprisonment.

Although reciprocity is often an important aspect of redistributive relationships—in the sense, for example, that tribute or taxes are paid in anticipation of the receipt of something of value in return (leadership, public works, social services, defense)—the structure of the relationship between participants in such exchange systems is typically asymmetrical. Some individuals or groups, generally a minority, have greater power than the others, usually the majority. In practice this means that the former also have the power *not* to redistribute in goods and services all that they might collect, retaining what some might regard as a disproportionate amount for elite consumption or to shore up materially their hold on the political controls.

Redistribution generally functions most prominently in social systems characterized by a degree of social stratification, where individuals are ranked hierarchically on the basis of technological, economic, social, political, and ideological factors. The form taken by the process of redistribution in the Hindu peasant communities of India illustrates this. The system has already been discussed as it provides the basis for the organization of work, each ranked caste being assigned and limited to the performance of one or more specific tasks.

The high-caste landowners of a farming community are called, in Hindi, *jajmans*. The process of redistribution that functions under their politicoreligious aegis is called the *jajmani* system (see Freed 1970; H. Gould 1964; Neale 1957). The members of the inferior caste—the sweepers, latrine cleaners, laundrymen, farm laborers, mat makers,

"The members of the inferior caste . . . have an obligation to contribute their labor or the product of their special skills to the material maintenance of the jajman families."

Caste	Type of Service	Rights Earned Through Service
Khati (carpenter)	To repair agricultural tools	One *maund* of grain per year along with *ori* rights ($2^1/_2$ *sirs* of grain twice a year at each sowing season)
Lohar (blacksmith)	As above	As above
Kumar (potter)	To supply earthenware vessels and to render services of light nature at weddings.	Grain to the value of the vessels. Additional grain at the son's or daughter's marriage, according to status and capacity
Hajjam or Nai (barber)	To shave and cut hair; to attend to guests on their arrival and to render other services of light nature at weddings	At each harvest as much grain as the man can lift by himself. Additional grain at the son's or daughter's marriage, according to status and capacity
Khakvul or Bhangi (sweeper)	To prepare cow-dung cakes; to gather sweepings, to remove dead mules and donkeys; to collect cots for extraordinary needs, and to render services at weddings	Meals and *rabri* [thickened milk] twice a day; at each harvest as much grain as the man can lift by himself and also at the son's or daughter's marriage, according to status and capacity
Camar (leather-worker)	If a man assists in agriculture and gives all kinds of light services	He gets one twentieth of the produce
	If he does *begar* (compulsory labor), renders ordinary service, and removes dead cattle	He gets one fourth of the produce and the skins of dead cattle

Maund: a unit of weight containing 40 *sirs,* or about 80 pounds.

Figure 5-11. Rules of the jajmani system in a North Indian village, specifying the kinds of work to be done by each caste and the nature of their compensation. (Adapted from Lewis 1965. By permission of Random House, Inc.)

weavers, potters, and carpenters—have an obligation to contribute their labor or the product of their special skills to the material maintenance of the jajman families. In turn, the landowners redistribute to the members of all participating subordinate castes a part of the goods they receive.

The same process links all other ranked groups in the community. The sweepers have a right to a carefully calculated share of the goods produced by all those they serve, and so do the barbers, the laundrymen, and the carpenters. Operation of the system is enforced by coercive economic, social, political, and religious sanctions controlled by the jajmans. The individual who fails to make his due contribution not only loses his right to receive goods and services from others but also is subject to scorn, strong political pressures, and the threat of physical punishment. By violating the supernaturally sanctioned rules and regulations of the jajmani system, as these are set down in the sacred books of the Hindus, he risks supernatural retribution as well.

"... the material requirements of each group are defined in terms of religiously defined inequality. . . ."

Figure 5-12. A member of an Indian carpenter caste (Khati) with his drill. (National Archives.)

Ideally, the system is equitable. As long as everyone meets his obligations, his just needs, as defined by custom in accordance with his caste status, will be met. In fact, however, differences in the relative economic, social, political, and religious positions of the participants inevitably result in gross inequities, for the material requirements of each group are designated in terms of religiously defined inequality, not on the basis of common biologically determined material needs for survival.

In somewhat different form redistribution has been a dominant organizing principle in the economic systems of most feudal societies: for example, during the Tokugawa period in Japan (1600–1868), in some of the kingdoms of West Africa up until the late nineteenth century, and in medieval Europe. In European feudalism (see Bloch 1961) authority for the allocation of almost all goods and services was vested in the local representative of a usually weak central government, the rural lord of the manor or estate. The relative political autonomy characteristic of the medieval estate, particularly from the ninth century on, was paralleled by its economic self-sufficiency. All those who lived on it, from serfs to lords, made their living there. They produced the food they consumed, built their houses and castles from locally available materials, spun the thread and wove the cloth they tailored to make their garments, and made for themselves most of the simple farm tools and weapons they used. This was necessary because as centralized political authority weakened and kingdoms fell apart, trade and the market towns it supported diminished also. Unable to acquire many of the goods it needed through the market, and unable to sell much of its surplus, each estate took on the characteristics of a highly localized, self-sufficient economic system, one in which redistribution served as the principal mechanism for the movement of both productive and consumer goods and services.

Although markets continued to exist, they were important only for the regional distribution of the small farm surpluses of the local peasantry. The other goods that moved through the markets, or, more correctly, were purveyed by traveling merchants from castle to castle, were nonutilitarian luxuries: spices, incense, jewels, silks, and rich brocades imported from Asia and the Middle East, all sold only to the few wealthy churchmen and landholders who could afford them. In neither instance did the markets function as a significant locus for the movement of goods and services basic to the satisfaction of the majority's material needs.

Subsistence needs were provided for within the context of the redistributive system structured by the organization of the estates, each of which was comprised of a scattering of local landholdings containing small farms worked by serfs or by laborers whose status was almost equally subordinate. Although most of the people worked the land, turning over the larger part of what they produced to the landlord, others were employed as herdsmen, as servants, and as laborers in the shops attached to the manor house: the smithy, the weaver, the tailor, the ale maker, the wheelwright, and the shoemaker. All workers paid tribute to the lord in labor and in the goods they produced. He, in turn, drew from the stores of goods he received to meet their needs, providing them land to farm, food, and clothing. As judge he served as the arbitrator of their disputes and the protector of his property rights. As soldier he led them in defense against the attacks of other noblemen. As donor of the land for the local parish church and nominator of its cleric he also assumed responsibility for the religious well-being of all those who lived on his estate. As with the jajmani system, this distribution system was asymmetrical. The concentration of coercive power in the hands of the landlords functioned inevitably (and, it was believed, rightly) to favor those on top. In control of the system of distribution, they manipulated it to their own material advantage. For the times, they lived in luxury. The peasants who supported them were allocated just enough to keep alive.

In many parts of Europe, particularly in the eastern regions, in most of Latin America, on the plantations of the southern United States, and in many parts of Asia and the Pacific variant near-feudal forms of redistribution persisted into the twentieth century, giving way only gradually before the growing importance of the market.

Market Exchange

Market exchange is the third basic process by which goods and services can be distributed (see Polanyi 1953; Bohannan and Dalton 1965). Among peoples with the simplest technologies markets tend to be absent. Or, if present, they are invariably of peripheral importance, usually because the technology is simply not productive enough. After the producers' consumption needs are met, the remaining surpluses are too small, transport and storage are too difficult—and neighboring peoples' surplus produce is too similar—to require or to support the development of a market system. The little that is left after the subsistence needs of a domestic productive unit are met can be more easily moved by the processes of reciprocity and redistribution. For example, meat and most fresh fruit and vegetables usually cannot be preserved and must be quickly consumed. If the temporary surplus is large there is often feasting. Extras in smaller quantities are passed around as gifts.

In the ancient world, markets first became

"Market exchange is the third basic process by which goods and services can be distributed. . . ."

Figure 5-13. Bargainers in the San Jacinto market, El Salvador. (Inter-American Development Bank.)

". . . food producers had a surplus they could exchange for other goods . . ."

Figure 5-14. Bananas for sale, Saigon. (Library of Congress.)

important as food-growing technologies became more productive, as primitive farming evolved into agriculture. Because more food could be produced per hour of human labor expended, a part of the work force could provide enough for all. The twofold result was that food producers had a surplus they could exchange for other goods and that a segment of the labor force could be released from food production to specialize part or full time in craft manufactures and in the provision of special services they could exchange in the market, both for foodstuffs and for the products of other specialists. As technological complexity increased and people's productive activities became more specialized, their reliance on the market tended to grow.

Probably the earliest exchanges between specialists were made on the basis of barter,

". . . that particular process of exchange relying on the use of money that is called marketing."

	Subsistence Economies		**Peasant Economies**
	Marketless	*Peripheral Markets Only*	*Market-Dominated*
Principal source of subsistence livelihood	Self-production and use; reciprocity; redistribution	Self-production and use; reciprocity; redistribution	Production for sale; factor resources for sale; marketing and trading as occupations
Price formulation for goods and services changing hands	Equivalency ratios; gift exchange	Supply and demand forces qualified by idiosyncratic social influences and controls; absence of factor markets	Supply and demand forces; market principle transacts factor ingredients as well as outputs
Money and money uses	Noncommercial transactions use special-purpose monies for bridewealth, bloodwealth, etc. (e.g., means of reciprocal payment); moneyless transactions may be present	Noncommercial transactions use special-purpose monies for bridewealth, bloodwealth, etc. If medium of market exchange is used in market-place transactions, its use is restricted outside markets; moneyless transactions may be present	One, all-purpose money (i.e., European type) is used for commercial and noncommercial transactions
External trade	Reciprocity; administered trade (redistribution)	Reciprocity; administered trade (redistribution); market haggling (e.g., *gimwali)*	Market trade dominates; if gift or administered trade is present, it is peripheral
Technology	Traditional	Traditional	Mostly traditional (or mixed traditional and machine-using)
Cultural practices	Traditional	Traditional	Mostly traditional (beginnings of literacy, etc.)

Figure 5-15. Correlation of subsistence activities, systems of distribution, and other aspects of African culture. (Adapted from Dalton and Bohannan 1965.)

the direct interchange of one good for another through bargaining, but without the use of money. As technological specialization increased in complexity and volume, so did the economic importance of such exchange. As producers' goals shifted from domestic consumption to surplus production and specialization, this new system of distribution, the market, became increasingly critical to organizing all phases of the economic system. One of the important consequences was the gradual development of something called money, and of that particular process of exchange relying on the use of money that is called marketing.

In the economic systems of many modern European nations, and in a significant sector of the economic systems of nearly all the nations of the Americas, the marketplace is now the primary locus and marketing the primary process by which most goods and services are distributed. Through market exchange in the United States, for example, one can acquire almost anything. General-purpose money is in use at this point—money that is negotiable in any exchange (Bohannan 1959; Dalton 1965). Marketing is the dominant process, affecting what is produced, in what quantity, and how it is distributed. Redistribution is of secondary but perhaps growing importance, and reciprocity has become peripheral, limited almost exclusively to the exchange of gifts between kinspeople, friends, and business associates (as payoffs to assure sales, lollipops and balloons for the kiddies, or the

". . . different kinds of money are used in the exchange of different kinds of goods."

Figure 5-16. Stone disks used as special-purpose money on the island of Yap, Micronesia. (United Nations.)

loan of corporate-owned jets to Pentagon purchasing agents).

Where market exchange is peripheral to the main processes by which goods and services move in a society, money takes a different form and fulfills different functions. Usually, under such circumstances, different kinds of money are used in the exchange of different kinds of goods. For example, the Tiv of Nigeria traditionally used brass rods as a medium of exchange only in acquiring slaves, cattle, medicine, magic charms, and white cloth (Bohannan 1959). On Rossel Island in the Pacific several types of shells served as separate types of special-purpose money called ndap, each negotiable only in a special type of transaction (Armstrong 1924). Thin, polished bits of shell ranging in size from an inch to almost a foot across were ascribed values on the basis of differences in their dimensions, color, and patina. Each kind of ndap was limited as a medium of exchange to a particular category of goods. Lime sticks, lime pots, and baskets, for example, could be purchased only with shells of relatively low value, which could not under any circumstances be used for the purchase of other goods. Assuming that a small pig was estimated to be worth four times as much as a lime pot (an estimate a Rossel Islander would never have made because he would not think in terms of all-purpose money equivalencies), one could not give four shells each "worth" a single lime pot and get a pig. Conversely, a more valuable type of shell suitable as exchange for a pig could not be broken up into four parts in order to acquire four lime pots. In other words, the islanders' shells were not general-purpose money. They functioned not so much as media of exchange but as items of equivalent value, as special-purpose money good only within a particular sphere of the Rossel Island distribution system.

As with the Tiv, most subsistence goods on Rossel Island were distributed by reciprocity and redistribution or by barter. In both instances money was not importantly related to the process by which subsistence needs were met. Neither Tiv brass rods nor Rossel Island shells had or needed to have the attributes of the general-purpose money characteristic of market exchange systems.

In contrast, a dollar moving in a market exchange system is a measure of abstract value that can be ascribed to anything. It can be exchanged, in amounts principally determined by supply and demand, for anything else. A dollar is portable and divisible. All these attributes are essential where market exchange is the primary distributive process.

Among many nonindustrialized peoples a kind of market system prevails that is called peripheral, to distinguish it from commercial markets central to the systems of distribution in societies based on advanced agriculture and industrialization. (Some socialist societies, in which peasants are permitted to sell the produce from their private gardens, might also be regarded as having peripheral markets.) The role of the market among primitive farmers in West Africa provides a good example of what is meant by such peripheral markets, markets that, although present—and sometimes quite noisy and colorful—are not basic to the system by which most services and subsistence goods are distributed.

Traditionally, most West African farmers enter the market after their basic subsistence needs have been met through the productive activities of the domestic work group. First a family produces and puts aside the amount of goods necessary to meet its basic needs until the next harvest. Then a part of the remaining surplus may be sold in the local market, often by the women. They may also take along some of the vegetables they have grown in their kitchen gardens, and possibly a few spools of thread spun from their stores

"These goods the women sell for money . . ."
Figure 5-17. Mossi market women, Ouagadougou, Upper Volta. (United Nations.)

of cotton balls. These goods the women sell for money, at prices determined by supply and demand but controlled by custom and by the fact that they personally know most of their purchasers, both as customers and as kinsmen and neighbors with whom they are involved in a variety of economically and socially valuable "nonmarket" relations. Some of the money profits may be saved to make a larger purchase at a later time: material for a new head scarf, a copper bracelet, or a pair of plastic sandals. A woman may spend a small amount on the spot, to buy a few matches, a handful of kola nuts, or a European-made needle. The rest she will turn over to her husband (especially if her garden is planted on land lent to her by his kinspeople). He will save some of what she gives him to pay his taxes and will put the rest aside to spend later: to purchase a cow at some future time when the price is right or to buy himself a Dacron shirt, some sunglasses, or a new part for his aging bicycle.

Once one or another of these relatively limited goals has been reached and the household's marketable surplus has been exhausted, its members may lose interest in market participation until they must again pay their taxes or satisfy once more one of their modest needs for other market goods. The market is thus peripheral to the means by which such a domestic group acquires most of the basic commodities necessary for its material survival. Outside a few major urban centers market participation is sporadic. Price set in the market affects only minimally the movement of most subsistence goods and is even less significant in determining the allocation of productive resources. At this level of socioeconomic development the nondistributive functions of the market are often of almost equal importance: useful information is exchanged in the marketplace, plans are made and agreements reached, potential brides meet possible husbands, and most people have a good time. Where market transactions are overseen by priests or local political figures (often the case where government is not centralized) the economically still peripheral market often provides the occasion for important ritual and political observances.

The markets characteristic of communities based on advanced farming mark a step toward the development of a distributive system in which market exchange is of more fundamental economic importance.

Among most peasant farmers goods in greater amount move through the market, and labor is often purchasable there. Many markets are organized on a regional basis. Although most participants are still basically cultivators and produce more or less the same foodstuffs, there may be some local, environmentally determined specialization in particular food crops, because of the suitability of the soil for growing grapes or for the cultivation of fruit trees, cotton, or tobacco, or simply because of varying local custom. In addition, each community is likely to engage in some craft specialization, to hold a traditionally sanctioned monopoly on the manufacture of particular goods—pottery, basketry, a special kind of cloth—that are distributed by means of a regional network of local markets, bringing separate rural communities into ecologically and economically adaptive interaction and often integrating the rural hinterland with nearby urban centers. Peasant markets of this sort are well developed in the highlands of southern Mexico, in Guatemala, in the Andes, in many parts of Southeast Asia, in North Africa, and in the more remote farming areas of Europe.

In southern Mexico each local community, sometimes each village, has as an aspect of its distinctive subculture a craft specialty that is marketed in a centrally located town (see Beals 1975; Cook and Diskin 1975; Pozas 1959). Sellers set up shop in sections of the market specifically designated for each commodity. There are rows of stalls where shoes are sold. Saddlery and other leather goods are usually available in booths nearby. Beyond there will be a few blanket sellers and next to them some tradesmen selling factory-made cloth, cheap

"The markets characteristic of communities based on advanced farming . . ."

Figure 5-18. Floating market, Bangok, Thailand. (Embassy of Thailand.)

". . . each local community . . . has . . . a craft specialty that is marketed in a centrally located town. . . ."

Figure 5-19. Trying it on for size in the market at Oaxaca, Mexico. (OAS Photo.)

cotton fabrics dyed in locally popular colors. In another part of the market potters display their wares. Next to them will be the several small merchants handling factory-made cutlery, pots, pans, and knives, a brass bedstead or two, some kerosene lanterns, and tin cooking implements crudely cut, shaped, and soldered together by hand.

Elsewhere in the market farm and garden products will be sold. Some women will have set up small kitchens with a bit of kindling, some charcoal in a small brazier, and a piece or two of cooking ware, and will be serving hot food. Someone is likely to be vending his services as a letter writer. A few children may be standing about ready to help purchasers carry home their loads (for a tip). In the shadow of a building nearby the village prostitute may be discreetly soliciting. Coca-Cola, razor blades, cigarettes singly and in tiny clusters, buttons, pencils, herbs, a rich variety of inexpensive patent medicines, pictures of the Holy Family, of the bleeding Sacred Heart, and of favorite local saints, a few cheap magazines: all will be on sale. Purchases are small. Although land is rarely if ever for sale in peasant markets, some land-poor peasant workers may be offered money to sell their labor. Profit margins are small, and every centavo counts. But many buyers and sellers know one another personally and are often bound by other valued ties, a factor that may affect the price at which goods are exchanged.

Although prices vary throughout the day and by the season, each village has a monopoly on production of a particular good, and such price shifts are unlikely to have a profound effect on the allocation of productive resources. If the demand for black glazed pottery falls off, its makers will probably cut their rate of production until the price rises. Perhaps some of their free time will be spent working more intensively on their farms. But if their surplus is adequate they may direct their time instead to other nonproductive but still instrumental activities, visiting kinsmen in other villages, spending more time solidifying valuable socioeconomic bonds by chatting in the shade with other temporarily unemployed pottery makers. But most potters will not be likely to switch to the production of leather goods, bird cages, or serapes, because they lack the

necessary skills, the needed materials (or the capital to purchase them), the necessary information to analyze and predict market trends, or the tradition of engaging in such work—and also because the market is already well supplied with these different commodities by others. Peasant craftworkers in southern Mexico still produce for themselves the largest part of the goods they consume. If the market for their craft specialty crashes, usually they can still survive as long as their corn lasts. What they produce for sale is still determined less by market price and more by tradition, by their lack of "venture capital," by problems of transport, by the poverty of local natural resources, and by their few alternative skills.

However, as such markets grow in size and importance, community craft monopolies become less significant. Some people settled in or near the market town become wholly dependent on it as a means of making a living, as producers of cash crops, as merchants, as middlemen and sellers of professional services, and—a few—as speculators. Gradually control of the distributive system passes out of the hands of the small supplier. And the larger the part of a farmer's land he puts into a cash crop, the smaller are his chances of remaining independent of the market, self-sufficient in the goods necessary to meet his household's basic needs. The more dependent he becomes on market exchange, the more price becomes a determinant in the allocation of his productive resources. If the price of guavas falls, he may grow more bananas (assuming he is among the fortunate few

"Some people settled in or near the market town become wholly dependent on it as a means of making a living. . . ."

Figure 5-20. The artisans' sector of the market at Marrakech, Morocco. (United Nations.)

with enough capital reserves to tide him over until his banana trees begin to bear). If too many bananas begin to enter the market, he may try to put more of his land into sugar cane or the cultivation of hemp. Obviously only the most productive farmers

"... market exchange at money price becomes the basic process in organizing the society's economy."

Figure 5-21. Behind the counter at a Greek-Canadian grocer's, Montreal. (National Film Board of Canada.)

have the capital resources or the credit to manage such costly adaptive "retooling." The rest are often forced to leave their own land and sell their labor to others. Often they are forced to sell the land itself. In contrast to the relative economic independence of the hunter-gatherers, primitive farmers, and many technologically more advanced farmers as well, the man who produces primarily for market distribution (expecting to meet his subsistence needs with the cash he receives) can be ruined by a dip in São Paulo coffee prices, by a rise in French tariffs on sugar cane, or by a crash in Chicago wheat futures.

At this point, as technology becomes more complex and an urbanizing state society emerges, market exchange is no longer peripheral to the factors that affect the allocation of productive resources or the distribution of consumer provisions and services. Commercial relationships become impersonal, and competitive bargaining between anonymous buyers and sellers takes over. Sharp practices are no longer perceived as disruptive to the sellers' network of supportive socioeconomic ties, and it is up to the buyer to beware. Price becomes paramount in organizing the distribution of nearly all goods. And nearly all things become goods available for a price. All-purpose money—portable, divisible, storable, a universally acceptable measure of value and means of payment—comes into its own. Reciprocity and redistribution recede, and market exchange at money price becomes the basic process in organizing the society's economy.

Economic Inequity and the Reorganization of Distribution

At this critical point in humankind's economic history, anthropologists usually turn the task of further exposition and analysis over to the economists. Perhaps this is because the reputation of economists for practicality, statistical wizardry, and competence with computers is perceived as making them better suited to the analysis of free commercial markets. But the fact is that a politically regulated, global trade network now unites almost all industrialized nations and Third World producers of raw materials in what is essentially a single world organization of distribution. The workings of this new world system affect every aspect of people's material existence from the price of oil in Amsterdam to the cost of rice in the remotest rural areas of Bangladesh. Inequities in this exchange system seem to be growing, and projections of a tragic future famine are increasingly frightening.

If it is correct that prevailing patterns of distribution deliver the most to those least in need, perhaps it is time that the attention given to technological means of increasing productivity be matched by an equal effort to rectify those aspects of a world system of distribution whose present inequities threaten possible political explosion.

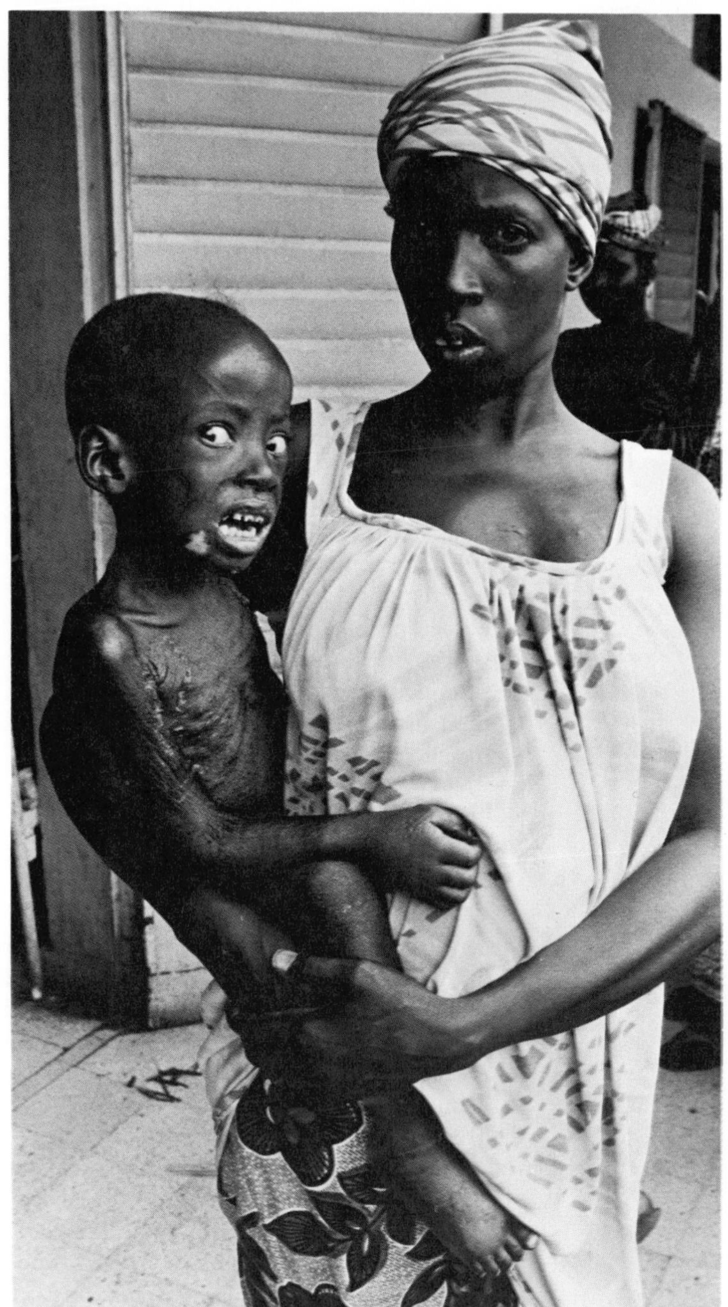

". . . projections of a tragic future famine are increasingly frightening."
Figure 5-22. A child near death from malnutrition during the Sahelian famine, Bamako, Mali. (United Nations.)

Summary

The three fundamentally distinctive systems by which goods and services can be distributed within a society are reciprocity, redistribution, and market exchange.

Reciprocal exchange is usually characterized by the movement of goods between individuals and groups of approximately equal status. It often takes the familiar form of gift exchange. Generally occurring in public, it is also frequently ritualized as a means of assuring that all participants meet their mutual obligations. This is important because reciprocity is not often regulated by political means. Although reciprocity functions as an aspect of most systems of distribution, it is most important among hunter-gatherers and primitive farmers.

The term *redistribution* refers to the movement of goods and services toward an allocative center and then out again. Among foragers and primitive farmers redistribution is marked by the central role of the family head, the leader of the domestic work group, in controlling the allocation among kin group members of both productive and consumption goods—land, tools, labor, food, and other basic material goods. Among technologically more advanced peoples redistribution often takes the form of politically regulated systems of tribute or taxation.

Like reciprocity, redistribution operates in societies at all levels of technological development. Usually complemented by reciprocity, it is found among hunter-gatherers, primitive farmers, and pastoralists. It is the predominant mode of distribution in all socialist societies and in the "public sectors" of the economic systems of all modern nations.

The peripheral markets present in technologically less advanced societies function primarily as a means of reallocating small surpluses. Typically, they are providing for the flow of most of the subsistence goods basic to people's material survival. Societies where the market and the price stated in terms of all-purpose money provide the locus and the process by which most goods are moved are characteristically based on advanced agriculture and/or the early stages of industrialization.

Today, as industrialization progresses and nearly all people are affected by market exchange, a single world system of distribution is emerging. The way it has worked so far—to widen the gap between rich nations and poor—suggests that coping with material want by increasing the production of goods needs to be balanced by at least equal attention to the more equitable organization of their distribution.

Suggested Readings

In addition to the several general works and anthologies suggested at the conclusion of Chapter 4, Sahlins's "On the Sociology of Primitive Exchange" in his *Stone Age Economics* complements the concepts presented here.

The analytic distinctions among reciprocity, redistribution, and market exchange are developed at length in several of the selections by Polanyi collected in *Primitive, Archaic and Modern Economics,* edited by Dalton; see also Dalton's "The Economic System" and Edel's critique; "Karl Polanyi's Concept of Non-market Trade."

The classic source on gift exchange is Mauss's *The Gift.* An excellent contemporary account is C. Johnson's "Gift Giving and Reciprocity Among the Japanese Americans of Honolulu." See also Damas's "Central Eskimo Systems of Food Sharing" and Laughlin's "Deprivation and Reciprocity." On the Kula ring see Malinowski, "Kula: The Circulating Exchange of Goods in the Archipelagoes of Eastern New Guinea" and also his *Argonaughts of the Western Pacific.* For more recent account of variants on this widespread system see Harding's *Voyagers of the Vitiaz Straits;* Strathern's *The Rope of Moka: Big Men and Ceremonial Exchange in Mount Hagen, New Guinea;* Uberoi's *Politics of the Kula Ring;* and Young's *Fighting with Food.* Good recent examples of the now vast literature on the Potlatch, which rectify earlier errors in the interpretation of this system, are Drucker and Heizer's *To Make My Name Good: A Reexamination of the Kwakiutl Potlatch,* Vayda's "A Re-examination of North West Coast Economic Systems," and Rosman and Rubel's "The Potlatch: A Structural Analysis."

In addition to the references already cited in the text on redistributive systems, consult Epstein's "Productive Efficiency and Customary Systems of Rewards in Rural South India," Heale's "Reciprocity and Redistribution in Rural India," and Tiffany's "Giving and Receiving: Participation in Chiefly Redistribution Activities in Samoa."

On markets, try Belshaw's *Traditional Exchange and Modern Markets;* Brookfield's *Pacific Market-Places: A Collection of Essays;* Cancian's *Change and Uncertainty in a Peasant Economy: The Mayan Corn Farmers of Zincantan;* Dalton's "Peasant Markets"; Ortiz's "Colombian Rural Market Organization: An Exploratory Model"; and *Markets in Africa,* edited by Bohannan and Dalton. Davis's *Social Relations in a Philippine Market: Self-interest and Subjectivity* does a good job of analyzing market exchange in cultural context. See also Forman and Riegelhaupt's "Market Place and Marketing Systems: Towards a Theory of Peasant Economic Integration"; Kurtz's "Peripheral and Transitional Markets: The Aztec Case"; Meillassoux's *The Development of Indigenous Trade and Markets in West Africa;* and Richards, Sturrock, and Fortt's *Subsistence to Commercial Farming in Present-day Buganda.* On the specific issue of money, see Dalton's "Primitive Money," Melitz's critical "The Polanyi School of Anthropology on Money: An Economist's View," Watson's important *Tribal Cohesion in a Money Economy,* and Yusuf's "Capital Formation and Management Among the Muslim Hausa Traders of Kano."

Reorganization of the world system of distribution is dealt with in several of the sources on economic "development" cited in the Suggested Readings for Chapter 4. Also try Adelman and Morris's *Economic Growth and Social Equity in Developing Areas,* Beckford's *Persistent Poverty: Underdevelopment in Plantation Economies of the Third World,* Boorstein's *The Economic Transformation of Cuba,* Brown's *The Economics of Imperialism,* Frank's *Capitalism and Underdevelopment in Latin America* and his "The Development of Underdevelopment," Jacobs's *Modernization Without Development: Thailand As an Asian Case Study,* Meier's *Leading Issues in Economic Development in International Poverty,* Myrdal's *The Challenge of World Poverty: A World Anti-Poverty Program in Outline,* Emmanuel's *Unequal Exchange,* and Wallerstein's seminal work, *The Modern World System.*

Part Four

Social Organization

Social organization appears no longer as a category sui generis, *opposed to categories like material culture or ideology, but as a complex process by which groups of people within societies relate themselves to each other or differentiate themselves from each other in the setting of available resources.*

WOLF (1964:55)

Because of their reliance on cooperation with others for survival, people everywhere are organized into groups. For all humans the first and most important group is founded on kinship. Some kin groups are based primarily on the combined criteria of consanguinity and affinity; others are structured in accordance with rules of descent. In most societies kin groups are complemented by associations of various sorts. In many societies still larger groups are organized and related to one another, usually hierarchically, on the basis of differences in economic and social position, ethnicity, and sex.

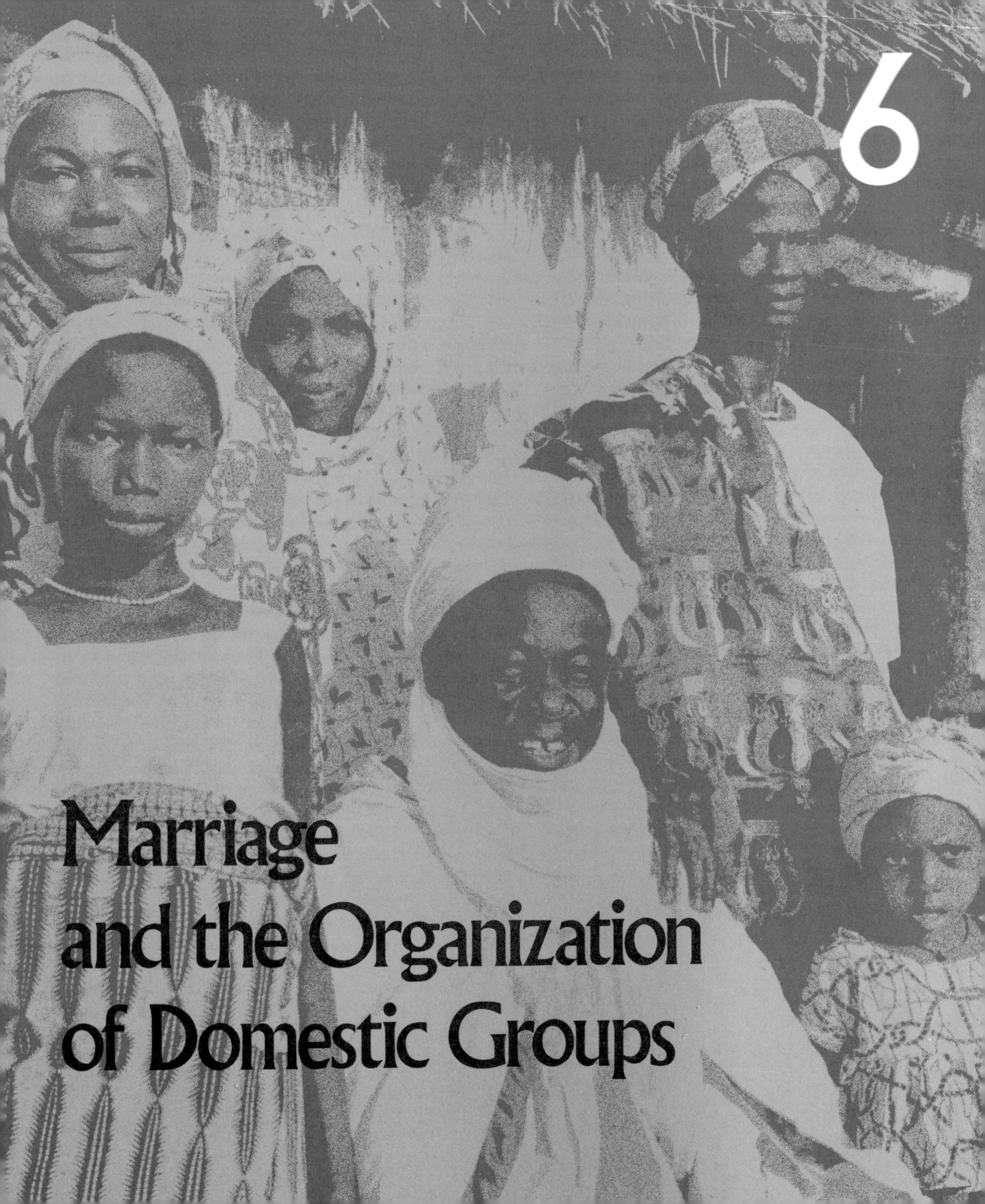

6

Marriage and the Organization of Domestic Groups

THE majority in every society live most of their lives in domestic groups formed and maintained in response to the fundamental human need to cooperate sexually, economically, and socially in bearing and raising children. The most elementary and widespread of these residential kin groups is the nuclear family, composed of a husband and wife and their children. Where polygamy (plural marriage) is practiced, the polygamous family results, and the domestic group is composed of more than one nuclear family linked through the common spouse. Where two or more nuclear or polygamous families are joined by a biological tie to form a still more complex residential unit, the domestic group that results is called an extended family.

Despite their exoticism, these variations in marriage and in the organization of domestic groups are never the random consequence of cultural whims. Rather, they manifest how specific peoples, responding to differing adaptive pressures, have found it best to set up their households to meet a universal human need: for family.

The Nuclear Family

Incest and Exogamy

Because of the universality of a general prohibition against sexual intercourse between parent and child and between brother and sister, the nuclear family and all other domestic kin groups are always composed of some persons primarily related by one form or another of marriage—by affinity—and of some others primarily related by a socially recognized biological tie—by consanguinity. Such households may of course also contain other persons who are only very distantly related, or not at all, but the core members of the group are always bound by kinship ties.

Despite disagreement on the precise origins and functions of the incest prohibition—whether it is the result of inherited

"The most elementary and widespread of these . . . groups is the nuclear family."
Figure 6-1. A French family entering the Paris subway. (United Nations, Rick Grunbaum.)

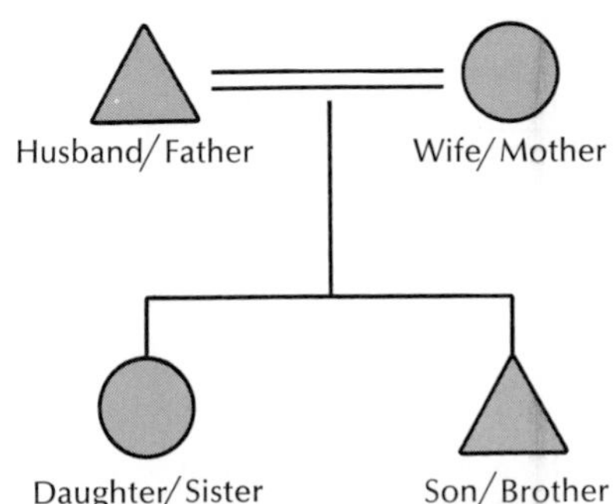

". . . composed of a husband and wife and their children."

Figure 6-2. In kinship charts circles represent females, triangles represent males. Double horizontal lines indicate the marriage relationship; a single horizontal line indicates siblings. A single vertical line separates the generations.

"instinctive abhorrence" or subtle, subliminal learning and whether it reduces or increases intrafamilial conflict—there is general agreement that for the evolution of people and culture the prohibition against mating between certain members of the nuclear family has been both biologically and culturally adaptive: diminishing the chances of genetically harmful inbreeding and fostering the extension to other groups of valuable bonds of reciprocity (see Aberle and others 1964).

In addition to the universal prohibition against sexual intercourse between parent and child and between brother and sister, most societies forbid sexual relations and marriage between certain other culturally recognized biological kinsmen. Often the prohibition of marriage between persons who are members of the same kin group is complemented by prohibition of marriage within other social groups as well: among members of the same age group, for example, or among members of the same community. This rule is called exogamy. It requires that people marry outside certain designated social groups to which they belong.

Endogamy is an opposite rule. It requires that people marry within some usually larger unit such as their descent group, an association to which they belong, or their

". . . a system for designating . . . those persons with whom marriage is preferred."

Figure 6-3. The Crown Prince of Japan and his bride, carefully selected from among eligible members of the Japanese aristocracy. (Embassy of Japan.)

class, caste, or ethnic group. Thus, every society requires a system for designating those persons with whom mating is prohibited and, at least implicitly, those persons with whom marriage is preferred.

Marriage Rules and Residence Rules

Although these systems for prohibiting or encouraging the choice of a mate are referred to as marriage rules, this does not mean that everyone obeys them or that people who violate them are necessarily punished. Sometimes they are and sometimes they are not, usually depending on the extent to which such violation is perceived as a threat to others. Most so-called rules concerning marriage and the formation of domestic groups (and other aspects of social organization as well) are best understood as idealized models to which people tend to conform. There are always some people, often many, who do not. Allowance for such variance is generally as critical for individual survival and societal stability as are the rules themselves, especially during periods of rapid sociocultural change.

In the technologically most highly developed societies the nuclear family formed at marriage is usually economically and socially independent of the kin groups of both partners, and relatively greater freedom is allowed in choosing a mate. In the majority of societies, however, each new marriage functions to establish or reinforce a link in a valuable network of reciprocal ties between kin groups, ties that provide an often critical source of supplementary material and social support. Marriage rules in most societies thus tend to be explicitly stated, and compliance with them is sternly enforced—because the interests of so many people are involved.

As it affects the organization of the domestic group, each rule appears to have adaptive advantages under particular circumstances. Exogamy is almost universally valued as a means of extending outward from the nuclear family to other groups kinship-based alliances that foster intergroup economic and social cooperation and the maintenance of peace. Endogamy tends to assure that these ties will be established only with other groups able and willing to participate in such cooperation and with whom peace is worth keeping.

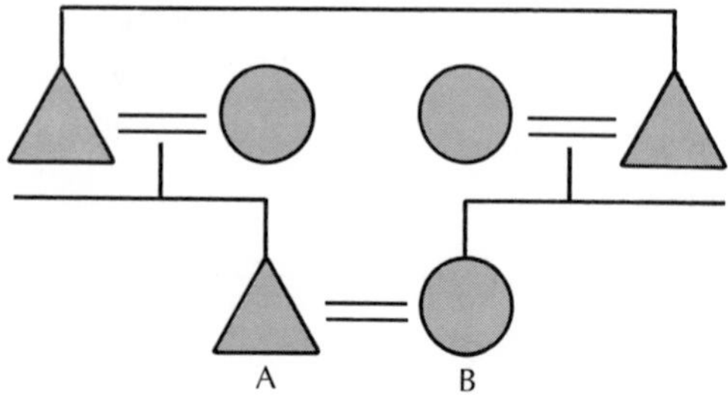

"Parallel cousin marriage, that is, marriage between children of siblings of the same sex. . . ."

Figure 6-4. A man (*A*) marries his father's brother's daughter (*B*), who belongs to his own descent group. (Adapted from Murphy and Kasdan.)

For example, the pastoral nomadic peoples in most of the Middle East practice nuclear family exogamy (as do all people) and endogamy within the male descent group. A man must marry a woman outside his own nuclear family but within his lineage. Parallel cousin marriage—that is, marriage between children of siblings of the same sex—is the preferred form. A man ought to marry his father's brother's daughter, for at least several reasons: to consolidate manpower and property within the descent group, to reinforce the patriarchal authority system, and because parallel cousin marriage is preferred in the Koran. It is also a good way to retain at least some control over married daughters and to assure that they will be well cared for.

Among truly pastoral nomadic Moslems in the Middle East, parallel cousin marriage is actually prescribed. A man who fails to comply threatens the survival of the entire semiautonomous kin group by jeopardizing the organizational cohesiveness these pastoralists require to maintain their fragile technological adjustment to a harsh natural environment amid chronically unstable political conditions. He is likely to be severely punished (see Murphy and Kasdan 1959).

In contrast, among Moslem pastoralists who have settled down in villages to farm under the protection of a relatively stable central government, parallel cousin marriage is still regarded as commendable, but those who marry outside the descent group are rarely chastised. As the nature of the prospective couple's relevant community changes, the rule of lineage endogamy is gradually replaced by the more adaptive preference for village endogamy (see Barth 1953, 1954).

In societies where groups are ranked hierarchically on a caste basis, caste endogamy is invariably the rule. Those who jeopardize the privileged status of their caste by marrying lower-caste persons or who try to improve their socioeconomic position by marrying into a higher caste risk serious opposition. The same tendency is apparent in societies with rigid social class or ethnic divisions. In a society like that of the United States, with groups ranked on the basis of both social class and ethnicity, rules of both class and ethnic endogamy affect the choice of marriage partners. That those who violate these rules suffer societal pressure is reflected in their higher rate of divorce.

Cross-cousin marriage, that between the children of siblings of opposite sex, is a more common form of preferred marriage than parallel cousin marriage; it is derived from

"In a society such as the United States, with groups ranked on the basis of both social class and ethnicity, rules of both class and ethnic endogamy affect the choice of marriage partners."

Figure 6-5. A rural farm family, Georgia. (Courtesy of the Library of Congress.)

the obverse rule, exogamy. Where the rule of bilateral (or symmetrical) cross-cousin marriage prevails, a young man can marry either his mother's brother's daughter or his father's sister's daughter. In either instance such a marriage appears to function to foster cohesion within the domestic group through the selection of a mate from another kin group with which amity and viable reciprocal relations have already been successfully tested in the ascendent generation (for example, when the groom's father married the bride's father's sister. Where cross-cousin marriage is asymmetrical, restricted to just one type of cousin, matrilateral (mother's side) cross-cousin marriage is the more frequent form. It is preferred that a man marry his mother's brother's daughter. The rule occurs in societies where descent is reckoned through the male line. Preference for this form of cross-cousin marriage has been explained as a consequence of the extension to mother's brother's daughter of the affectionate permissiveness characteristic of a man's relationship to his mother's brother in a society where descent is traced through the father's side of the family (Homans and Schneider 1955:38; see also Radcliffe-Brown 1924).

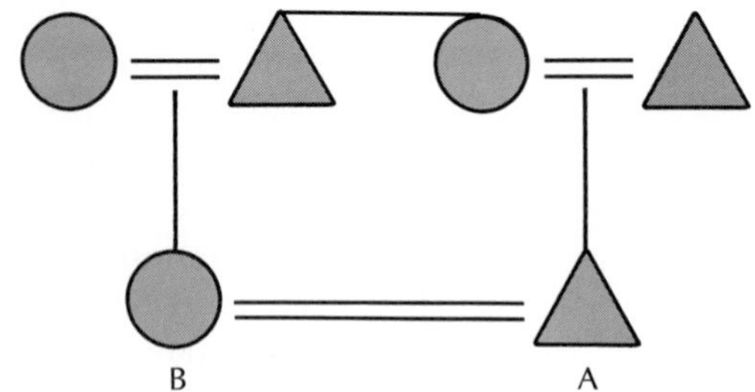

"... cross-cousin marriage. ... It is preferred that a man marry his mother's brother's daughter."

Figure 6-6. A man (*A*) marries his mother's brother's daughter (*B*). As descent is traced through the male line, his wife is not a member of his own descent group.

Formalization of marriage frequently requires an exchange of property. Goods given by the groom's kinsmen to the family of the bride, called bridewealth (or, occasionally and inaccurately, bride price), have been explained by some anthropologists, and by some of the people who follow this custom, as a compensation to the family of the bride for the loss of her services. After being carefully raised by them, she is taken away just at the time she might begin to be most fully productive, both economically, working to support the household materially, and biologically, producing new members for it. Others emphasize the stabilizing effect of bridewealth payments: as functioning to exert pressure on the bride to meet her marital responsibilities. For often, if a young woman does not fulfill her wifely duties, her husband's kinsmen may complain and request the return of the property given to her relatives at the time the marriage was arranged. Reluctant to give up the portion they have received of the bridewealth payment, her kinsmen are likely to put pressure on her to mend her ways. This is especially likely to occur if, as among many marketless East African herding peoples, the property exchanges that occur at marriage are a major aspect of the distribution system.

With some important exceptions, divorce is generally less frequent in societies with a strong system of patrilineages and in which bridewealth payments are large. Where bridewealth payments are lower, women are less thoroughly absorbed into their husband's kin group and divorce is easier and more frequent.

In some instances bridewealth payments are replaced by bride service. Rather than compensating his intended wife's family with goods, the prospective groom among the Copper Eskimo gives his labor instead, residing with his future father-in-law for three or four years, assisting him with his work and demonstrating his ability as provider (Damas 1975). The term *dowry* is used to describe the passage of goods from the family of the bride to the groom and his kinsmen. Typically dowries are given in peasant societies based on advanced agriculture, where the woman's role in the subsistence technology is less valuable. Her economic value must, as a consequence, be augumented by offering her husband and his family a money present. Dowry is also often used as a means of achieving upward social mobility. Greek peasants, for example, try to accumulate a sufficient dowry to be able to acquire for their daughters' better-educated, town-dwelling husbands (Friedl 1959).

Usually the exchange of goods and services between prospective in-laws is, at least to some extent, reciprocal. It may be perceived as a sort of dramatic opening gesture, as a demonstration of each group's capacity to meet the other's expectations in fulfilling the obligations of the valued cooperative alliance that usually unites the kin groups of marriage partners. Failure to be generous in exchange of goods is usually regarded as a literal indication of the families' unwillingness to invest in the marriage. When such obligations are not adequately met, the marriage frequently gets off to a prophetically unstable start.

Once the marriage has been contracted—the actual ceremony may be elaborate or nearly nonexistent, may take a few minutes or be strung out through a series of stages that begin with betrothal in infancy and continue over several decades—the new couple usually establishes its conjugal household in accordance with the rule of postnuptial residence favored in the society. In every culture there is a preferred place for marriage partners to live. Again, the rules are idealized; not all people in a society always obey them. Probably it would be safer to say that most try to conform and are generally successful. The exceptions are useful clues to the patterning of adaptive variance necessary whenever men and women endeavor to live according to any of their culture's rules.

Where the residence rule is *virilocal* (literally, "place of the male"; sometimes the near synonym *patrilocal* is used), the bride generally joins her husband in or near his natal residence. If the rule is *uxorilocal* ("place of the wife"; *matrilocal* is sometimes used as a synonym), the couple customarily attaches its new household to that of the domestic group into which the wife was born. Where the new husband and wife attach their residence to that of the husband's mother's brother or his matrilineal kinsmen, the rule is called *avunculocal* ("mother's brother's place"). In societies where a newly established nuclear family is simply expected to reside in or near the parental home of one partner or the other the rule of residence is called *bilocal.* Where the new nuclear family is domiciled separately from (or without reference to) the place of residence of either partner's kin group the rule of postnuptial residence is called *neolocal.*

Although still-serious flaws in the accuracy with which data on residence rules have been collected and interpreted make reliable generalizations rather hazardous (see Goodenough 1955; Fischer 1958), some correspondences between rules of residence and particular patterns of technoenvironmental adaptation can be confidently stated. (The correlation of residence rules with systems of descent is given more attention in the next chapter.)

Patrilocal (or virilocal) residence is most often the preferred rule in societies where solidarity of the male group is of primary significance: in hunting, herding, doing the harder work usually associated with advanced farming; in organizing and administering a complex system of distribution; in maintaining internal social order; and in protecting the group from hostile outsiders.

Conversely, matrilocal (or uxorilocal) residence is associated with primitive farming, a level of technological development that chronologically follows hunting and gathering and precedes advanced farming. Where residence is matrilocal, women do most of the farm work, probably as a holdover from their more prominent role in gathering wild foods. There is a consequent emphasis on the solidarity of the female work group and on systems of allocation and distribution in which the results of female productivity on the land, and the land itself, tend to be transmitted through the female line. Where the household is uxorilocal these circumstances are usually complemented by relatively stable relations with neighboring groups that make masculine solidarity (for offense or defense) less essential. Uxorilocal residence is also often found in societies under extreme economic stress, such as those of the Caribbean, in which many adult males can find work only by migrating to other areas, leaving their wives at home to care for the household alone or with the assistance of the maternal grandparents. In the United States, uxorilocal residence occurs frequently in urban centers where chronic unemployment weakens the husband/father's link to the domestic group.

Avunculocal residence seems to represent an adaptive accommodation of a previous matrilocal residence rule to the consequences of an increase in the productivity of a horticultural technology. As such productivity increases, the importance of the role of men in administering what typically becomes a more complex economic system also increases; at this point, male-dominated but still matrilineally based systems of political centralization also begin to emerge. Property increases. A young man attaches his nuclear family residence to that of his mother's brother in preparation for the time when he will inherit goods and status from him.

Bilocal residence appears to be correlated either with an unstable technological base that gives adaptive value to a rule allowing for maximum mobility (in severely disrupted societies residence rules often become wildly randomized) and/or with a pattern of technoenvironmental adaptation that requires seasonal shifts from matrilocal to patrilocal residence.

Neolocal residence is most frequent in societies where the technology and the economic system tend to foster separation of the nuclear family from the parental domestic groups of both marriage partners, as is the case in industrializing societies, for example. Although most familiar to Americans, this rule is still atypical for most of humankind. The separation of the new nuclear family from the kinsmen of both husband and wife and the fact that they often find themselves largely surrounded by strangers both increase the pressure on each spouse to meet alone a larger part of the other's needs and decrease the possibility of their kinsmen's restorative intervention if the marriage should threaten to come apart. In our own society, the neolocal residence rule may be one of several related factors contributing to our rising rate of divorce.

The Dissolution of the Marriage Bond

The nuclear family is always characterized by the fulfillment of certain apparently necessary functions. Husband and wife always divide the work and responsibility for the maintenance of the nuclear family household and in preparing their offspring for adulthood. Their economic and social cooperation is paralleled by a sexual relation that provides both with a legitimate (but not necessarily exclusive) channel for sexual gratification and for the production of children. Fulfillment of each of these several interrelated functions reinforces dependence on the others. Reciprocal sexual satisfaction

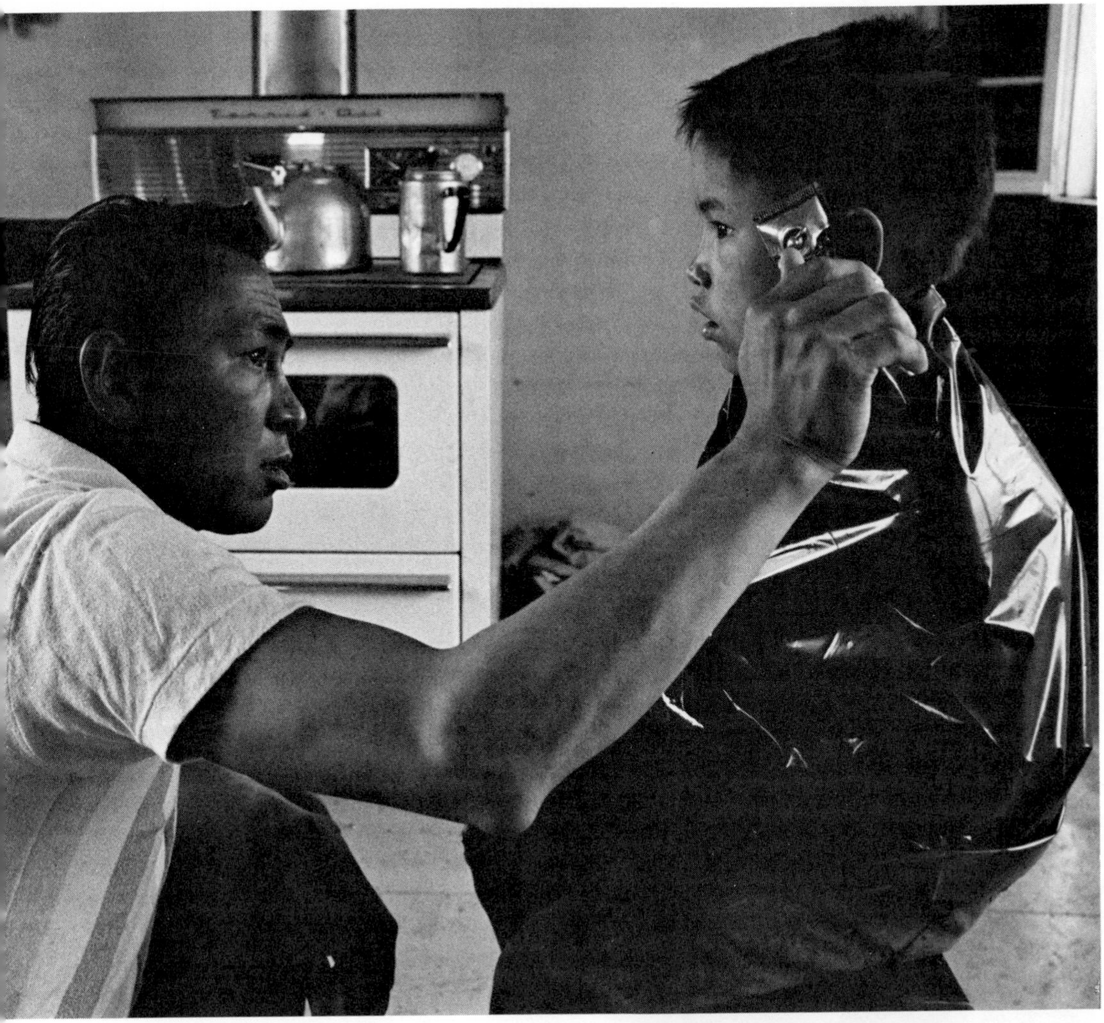

"Husband and wife always divide the work and responsibility for the maintenance of the nuclear family household. . . ." **Figure 6-7.** An Inuk father gives his son a trim (Inuvik, Northwest Territories, Canada). (National Film Board of Canada.)

increases the readiness of husband and wife to cooperate with one another in other ways. Although overt sexuality is universally prohibited as a means of reinforcing parent-child and sibling relations, other rewarding emotions can be fostered. Parental and filial love, especially the feeling of a mother for her child (possibly the strongest and least ambivalent of parent-child emotional bonds), are steadily reinforced as the child's need for maternal attention is gratified. Ties of affection and mutual dependence between siblings may be similarly strength-

"Ties of affection and dependence between siblings. . . ." **Figure 6-8.** French Canadian sisters, Quebec. (National Film Board of Canada.)

ened as they support and cooperate with one another.

Failure of either marriage partner to fulfill any basic aspect of his or her culturally defined responsibility to the other partner (so far, in most societies, a woman's failure to meet these responsibilities is regarded as more serious), to the nuclear family, or to the other's kin group is almost universally grounds for dissolution of the marriage. Even if divorce is forbidden, coresidence and/or cohabitation may be ended.

Nuclear families are dissolved, or their structure and functions are radically altered, by separation, annulment, divorce, or death. Of these processes, separation is usually the least explicitly structured. As it exists in most societies (some contemporary American and European societies excepted), separation is probably better described as the first step toward a more permanent dissolution of the marriage bond. Annulment involves legal or ritual establishment of the fact that a marriage previously regarded as valid has not occurred. Evidence is usually required that one of the essential aspects of the marriage contract or the nuclear family relationship has not been complied with: payment of bridewealth, or failure to consummate the marriage sexually. If there is no question that a valid marriage has taken place, then divorce is required to terminate it and to structure a new relationship between the ex-marriage partners, between each of them and their children, and between all of them and whomever either (or both of them) marries next.

". . . that one of the essential aspects of the marriage contract or the nuclear family relationship has not been complied with. . . ."

Figure 6-9. Peruvian Indian nuclear family group posing for their picture. (OAS Photo.)

Somewhat paradoxically, when the structure and functions of the nuclear family are interrupted by death of the husband or wife, the breach of order and continuity in the domestic group is less severe. Many societies provide a means of minimizing disruption of the household and keeping intact the contractual link established at the time of the original marriage by prescribing a rule for the substitution of the deceased mate by one of two forms of affinal marriage, that is marriage between in-laws.

In societies with a rule called the levirate, the remarriage of a widow to her deceased husband's brother is favored by custom. Practiced most frequently in societies where marriage is cemented by the payment of bridewealth, the levirate has several adaptive advantages: the dead man's descent group retains contractual right to his widow's biological and material productivity; disruption to the continuity of the widow's household, of her relationship to her children, and of the children's relationship to their kinsmen in the male line is reduced; the obligations of the widow's husband's kinsmen to her descent group remain in force; her kinsmen need not return the bridewealth payments they have received.

In societies that observe a rule called the sororate, it is customarily preferred that a man marry his deceased wife's sister. Again, disruption to the domestic group is minimized by replacing the dead wife and mother with her sister. By providing a substitute to fulfill the functions of their deceased kinswoman, her descent group keeps its part of the contractual bargain established at the time of the original marriage, and the valuable reciprocal alliance between the two descent groups is perpetuated.

Perhaps because of the near universality of the somewhat subordinate status of women (traditionally ascribed to their greater dependency and vulnerability when pregnant, when they have young children, and especially during periods of social instability), the culturally prescribed treatment of widows almost always involves a more radical alteration in status than is the case for men. In a few rare instances widows are expected to cope with the problem their continued existence poses by doing away with themselves: throwing themselves on their husbands' funeral pyres, as high-caste Hindu women were once expected to do, or according to Bohannan (1963:119), allowing themselves to be strangled, as he says was once done in Fiji. In most instances, however, the retirement of a still potentially productive widow from the social scene is less violent and only temporary, limited to a culturally designated period of mourning, after which she is usually expected to remarry, thus reintegrating herself in society by establishing with another man her status as a wife and mother within what becomes a new nuclear family.

". . . the retirement of a still potentially productive widow from the social scene is less violent and only temporary. . . ."
Figure 6-10. Dressed in mourning, New Guinea. (Courtesy of the Library of Congress.)

When widowhood is the result of divorce, the cultural rules in most societies also usually allow for the adaptive reassimilation of both partners—often more easily elsewhere than in the United States. As millions of divorcees know, the proper status of no-longer married persons (especially women) is not yet clearly set forth in American culture. Their correct future role is equally ill defined. And their economic position is generally precarious. The societal reintegration of what remains of their already isolated, neolocal, and now also definably "broken" nuclear family households is thus an almost invariably confusing, costly, and emotionally shattering process.

Polygamy

In most societies the nuclear family is linked by polygamy, plural marriage, to a larger kin group. Usually, this larger domestic group is composed of a man and his several wives and his children by each of them. Occasionally, it is composed of a woman and her several co-husbands. In either instance the nuclear family almost always persists as a distinctive unit. The spouse with several mates always maintains a separate relationship with each partner and forms with each and with their offspring a structurally and functionally distinct familial unit within the larger context of the polygamous family.

Societies are classed as polygamous because of the culturally stated preference for this form of marriage, because it is aspired to by the majority. In most societies, however, regardless of the preference for polygamy, most domestic groups are monogamous simply because of the sex ratio: there are usually about as many males as females. If some men have several wives or some women have more than one husband, others will not have any mates at all. Where polygamy is not a mechanism to compensate for an unnatural imbalance in the sex ratio—as the result of warfare, for example—but is, rather, a means of exerting, displaying, and increasing social dominance by collecting women, its potentially disruptive effects may be somewhat muted by permitting females to marry much earlier than males and by providing unmarried persons with other culturally acceptable channels for sexual gratification. But even so, for the majority to marry, the majority of marriages must be monogamous—no matter what the preferred marriage form.

"When women produce a surplus, men try to collect them."

Figure 6-11. A Togolese chief with several of his wives and one daughter. (United Nations.)

Polygyny

Polygyny, the marriage of one man to more than one wife at the same time, is by far the most frequent form of plural marriage and thus most frequently provides the basis for the establishment of the polygamous residential kin group. This preference for polygyny is often correlated with the importance of women's role in the subsistence technology. Where women produce a surplus, men try to collect them. They are most likely to be able to get away with this in societies where the status of women is most successfully kept subordinate.

Polygyny is distinguished from concubinage by the fact that the marriage relationships with all participating females are regarded as equally legitimate, although the first or senior wife sometimes has higher status and a certain measure of authority over the other wives her husband takes later.

Where polygyny is preferred, there often also exists a preferred means of taking additional wives. Sometimes the desirability of a man's marrying his wife's sister is stressed; this is called sororal polygyny. This preference is explained as a means of reducing co-wife friction, as the two women, raised in the same nuclear family household, are more likely to have worked out a means of getting along with one another and are less likely to quarrel. If a man's relations with his first wife's kin group have been satisfactory, contracting with them for another marriage is likely to be relatively easy and rewarding, as it serves to strengthen an already valuable affinal kinship tie.

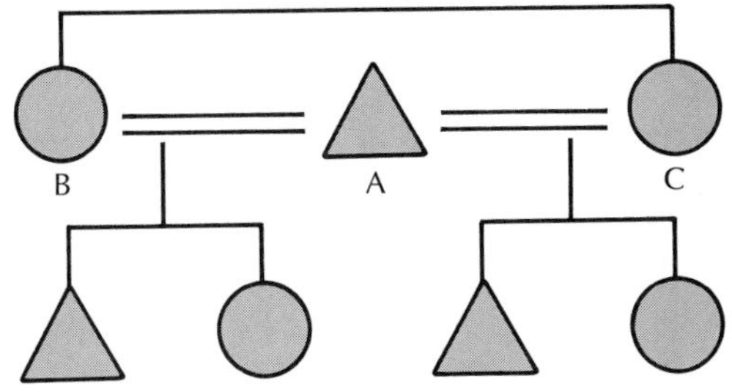

"Sometimes the desirability of a man's marrying his wife's sister is stressed; this is called sororal polygyny."
Figure 6-12. A man (*A*) and the two sisters (*B* and *C*) to whom he is married. Vertical lines link him to his children by each wife.

Unless they are sisters, it is usual for a man's wives in a polygynous family each to have a place set apart for her and her own household, where she sleeps, cooks, cares for her children, and keeps her personal property. This may be a separate room, house, tent, or other shelter. Her husband either visits her there or calls her to join him in his own separate quarters. This spatial separation of each unit within the polygynous household both reinforces the structural and functional distinctiveness of each such unit and reduces the potential for co-wife conflict.

Although jealousy is often a problem in plural marriage, the potential for this disruptive emotion is less than might be expected; for the criteria of what constitutes an emotionally satisfactory marital relationship vary from culture to culture. Love, in the romantic and exclusive sense familiar in contemporary American and European societies, is not demonstrably a universal need. Furthermore, custom usually requires that a man distribute his attentions, sexual and otherwise, equally among all his wives. Where this is so, polygyny does not necessarily result in the withdrawal of love or other forms of support. Thus jealousy generated by fear of the loss of love may be less a problem. Also, where the culture defines such a marriage form as preferred, women are not conditioned to expect exclusiveness and thus have less to lose; there may even be compensatory gains.

If co-wives are not jealous and can get along in other ways, they can provide one another with agreeable companionship and valued assistance and support in the performance of their household tasks and in other work, in childbirth and child care, and in pressuring their husband to meet his conjugal obligations.

Polygyny is often associated with a custom that requires women to abstain from having sexual intercourse for several years after the birth of a child, frequently for as long as the child is nursing. This functions to allow a woman to recover from what is often an arduous delivery and provides a means of spacing children so that they can be adequately fed until they can adjust to a diet of solid food. If a man has several wives this enforced abstinence is less likely to threaten the stability of the household by discouraging the husband from establishing sexual attachments outside the domestic group.

When a nuclear family becomes part of a larger polygynous family grouping, two more social relationships are created in addition to the delicate one of co-wives: the relationship of half siblings (children of the same man by different women) and the relationship of children to their father's other wives. Each co-wife's concern for the protection of her children's rights to such things as the inheritance of their father's status and property is usually a more frequent cause of conflict in polygynous households than is sexual jealousy.

Polygyny is most widespread where it is most adaptively advantageous: among primitive farmers, where infant mortality rates are high, where a man needs assistance in working his land by hand, where his children are likely to be his principal support in old age, and where the importance of many children is reinforced by the belief that a man's descendants must look after his spirit when he dies. Under these conditions polygyny may enhance the chances of both individual and societal survival. A man with only one wife may not have as many children as he needs for help with his work. Or, if he does, his wife may be so worn out from childbearing that she is unable to care for them properly or to do her own heavy share of farming.

Among herding peoples, primitive farmers, and others who make their living by means of a relatively primitive technology under unstable social conditions, the death rate for men is sometimes higher than it is for women, principally as the result of warfare or other forms of strife. In such circumstances, where the work necessary to maintain the household is physically hard, and where there is the frequent threat of violence, it is difficult for a widow alone to survive, especially if she has dependent children. Polygyny serves as a means of protecting and providing for her and her children, and of reestablishing her as a sexually and economically productive member of her community.

". . . it is difficult for a widow alone to survive, especially if she has dependent children."
Figure 6-13. A Mishimi mother and child, northeastern India. (Embassy of India.)

Polygyny occurs infrequently among hunter-gatherers, and usually is practiced only in the instance of widows. In contrast, it is widespread among horticultural and herding peoples, especially in Africa and the Middle East. It is rare among advanced farmers, where it is traditionally practiced only by a wealthy elite as a means of displaying their riches, and it is never the preferred marriage form in industrialized societies. Indeed, the outlawing of plural marriage is frequently one of the first legislative steps taken as a mark of modernization in newly developing nations.

Polyandry

The domestic group made up of the several nuclear families created by polyandry, the marriage of one woman to more than one man at the same time, occurs very rarely as the preferred type of plural family organization (see Fischer 1952; Leach 1961; Peter 1963).

The Todas of southern India practice what is called fraternal polyandry (Peter 1948; Rivers 1906). When a girl is married, often at the age of two or three, she automatically becomes the wife of her husband's brothers also. Each has the right to sexual relations with her when she reaches puberty, and with each she is involved at least to some degree in a separate set of social and

"When a girl is married . . . she automatically becomes the wife of her husband's brothers."
Figure 6-14. A woman (A) marries two brothers (B) and (C).

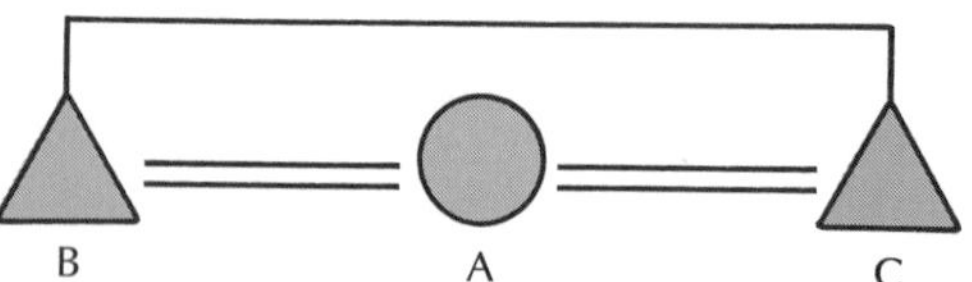

economic relationships. In a simple rite performed during her first pregnancy, one of her husbands presents her with a small toy bow and arrow, and they spend the night alone together away from the settlement. By this observance he assumes the role of father to her expected child and to any further children she bears until the ritual is observed again, by another of her husbands, who then becomes the father of her next several children, and so on.

Fraternal polyandry is the generally preferred form. In those fairly rare instances in which a woman's husbands are not brothers, they are usually related within some larger kin grouping. As with sororal polygyny, the fact that a woman's husbands are brothers may lessen the likelihood of friction between them. Husbands reside together only when they are related. Otherwise they live apart, often in different villages, and their wife travels around among them. The practice of polyandry appears to be adaptively advantageous under a number of interconnected circumstances: where a shortage of women is correlated with the material importance of providing every man with a conjugal household, where fraternal solidarity is necessary to maximize the usefulness of limited land resources, and where it is desirable to keep landholdings intact by limiting the number of heirs.

Among land-poor Tibetan farmers who practice fraternal polyandry (Peter 1955), a group of brothers take a single wife, reside together, and work cooperatively their small inheritance of arable land. The farm is passed on collectively to the male offspring, who rely on the same form of marriage to keep the land in the family and to retain it as a single holding large enough to be worked economically. Good farmland is so scarce among the Tibetan poor that if the usually small allotment of a family were divided up among the male heirs, none would be able to support himself.

If such a polyandrous domestic group fails to produce male offspring, the same form of marriage may be used to perpetuate the family holding: a daughter remains on the farm and takes several husbands. The Tibetans also practice female infanticide, probably to keep down the size of the population and keep the ratio of working adults to dependent children high by limiting the number of childbearing women.

Descriptions of polyandry in the western Himalayas (Berreman 1962a, 1972a, 1975; Majumdar 1955, 1962) further point up the validity of understanding this form of plural marriage as an adaptive strategy. For whereas many of the farming peoples of this region live in fraternally polyandrous households during some phase of their lives, shifts to other forms of marriage and domestic group organization regularly occur as circumstances change. For example, if one of a woman's two husbands dies, a monogamous household results. If the remaining brother later acquires more land and needs supplementary help with the farm work, he may marry a second wife, thus establishing a polygynous household. If, instead, he increases his available labor force by later taking in a younger brother, polyandry reemerges (for custom requires that brothers living and working together must share).

Or if additional wives marry into a fraternally polyandrous household, in order to increase its labor pool or the number of women of childbearing age, the sexuality of the new wives, like their labor and all other domestic resources, is shared by the brothers, and a sort of group marriage, "polygyndry," results. All brothers share paternity; maternity is individually reckoned.

Thus whereas fraternal polyandry is widely practiced and can even be described as the preferred marriage form in parts of the western Himalayas, the cultural rules of the region allow for other marriage forms as well, thereby maximizing the capacity of the domestic group to adjust to changing material circumstances.

But however persuasive the adaptive advantages of polyandry may seem, it is important to point out that such explanations are more logical than "proven." Historical circumstances that may have precipitated the development of polyandry, such as the reasons for the initial imbalance in the ratio of males to females, are not sufficiently well known. And not all peoples with limited land, an emphasis on fraternal solidarity in the work group, and a shortage of women practice polyandry. As with explanations concerning the organization of the other forms of the domestic group, evidence for the apparent survival value of polyandrous family organization is, so far, most suggestive of significant correlations between particular material conditions and this form of marriage and household arrangement. The interesting but noncrucial question of ultimate causality must be deferred.

". . . the sharing of various economic and social responsibilities."
Figure 6-15. Members of an Indian household at work, Guatemala. (OAS Photo.)

The Extended Family

Probably because of its adaptive advantages, especially as an organizational basis for pooling productive resources (particularly land and labor), the extended family is the most widespread of all forms of domestic group organization. The extended family can be defined as a residential kin group organized by joining two or more monogamous or polygamous families through a biological tie. Although each component nuclear and polygamous family typically maintains a functionally separate household within the extended family residence—eating, sleeping, working, and so on as a distinguishable unit—common residence is always importantly complemented by the sharing of various economic and social responsibilities.

In the life experience of the individual and in the organization of the local community, the functions of the extended family—especially socialization of the young, allocation of productive goods, organization of work, and distribution—often become more important than those of the nuclear family units of which the extended family is composed.

The specific organization of the extended family is usually based on a kinship link in either the male or female line; occasionally, it is based on some links through both lines. It can take any one of the following four fundamental forms, each of which is generated by the combined rules of extended family exogamy and a particular rule of postnuptial residence: the patrilocal extended family, the matrilocal extended family, the avunculocal extended family, and the bilocal extended family.

The Patrilocal Extended Family

Where the rule of residence is virilocal and the formation of the extended family is adaptively advantageous, it is the sons of the

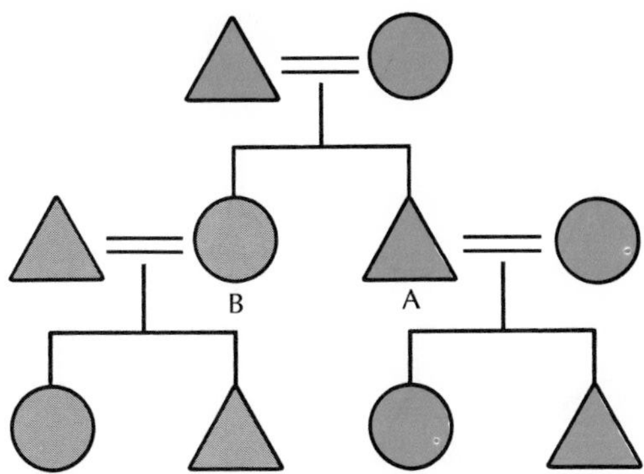

"... it is the sons of the family who remain in their natal extended family residence and are joined there by their wives."

Figure 6-16. Minimal structure of the patrilocal extended family. All shaded kinsmen live together in the same compound household. When a man (*A*) marries he attaches the new household unit formed by himself and his wife and children to that of his father. His sister (*B*) leaves at marriage to join her husband as part of his patrilocal extended family.

family who remain in their natal extended family residence, the household of the father, and are joined there by their wives. The result is the patrilocal extended family, which, in its most elementary form, is composed of a man and his wife, his unmarried daughters, his sons, and their wives and children. The prevalence of the patrilocal extended family is explainable as an extension of the reasons that account for the greater frequency of the virilocal residence rule. Patrilocality fosters the male solidarity that almost all hunter-gatherers (coordination of the work of male hunters requires more delicate balance than the work of female gatherers), most horticulturalists, nearly all pastoral nomads, and most advanced farming peoples are dependent on—both to maintain their particular patterns of technoenvironmental adaptation and to administer their economic systems and the organization of their systems of offense and defense.

Among the Mossi (Hammond 1966), the house of the head of the patrilocal extended family and the separate dwellings of his wives are surrounded by the several smaller residential clusters formed by the individual houses of his married sons and their wives and children. Within each component nuclear or polygynous family, the husband/father is the authority. An older married son has more authority than his younger brother, and their father has authority over them both. Similarly, the older women have authority over their husbands' younger wives. The highest-status female, the one with the final word in regulating relations between all other women in the patrilocal extended family household, is the eldest wife of the extended family head. Compliance with this system of authority is reinforced by the economic, social, and religious dependence of all younger members of the family on their elders. A man must be obedient to his father to assure that his right to use some of the family farmland will be respected, to have help in assembling the goods presented to his intended wife's family as bridewealth, and to have a father's assistance as intermediary in negotiating his marriage and keeping peace with his in-laws once the marriage is contracted. His father gives him support in dealing with the elders of the other, still larger kin groupings of which the Mossi patrilocal extended family is a part. And finally, it is through his father's ritual intercession that a son maintains a secure relationship with the powerful spirits of his ancestors and, indirectly, with the deities of nature that affect his success as a farmer.

Occasionally, extended family organization takes a different and usually temporary form: that of the fraternal joint family. The component nuclear and polygynous families are linked laterally, through brothers: for example, when several brothers, each with his respective wives and children, reside together as one spatially and socially separate composite family group. Often this family form develops when a patrilocal extended family becomes too large to be able to provide adequately for the economic needs, especially the need for land, of all of its members. When this occurs several brothers may move away, together with their wives and children, to establish a new composite family household in another part of the local community, or in another community altogether where land is more readily available. There they live and work together under the authority of the eldest brother. When, within a generation, the sons of the eldest brother marry and bring home their wives, the form of the patrilocal extended family reemerges.

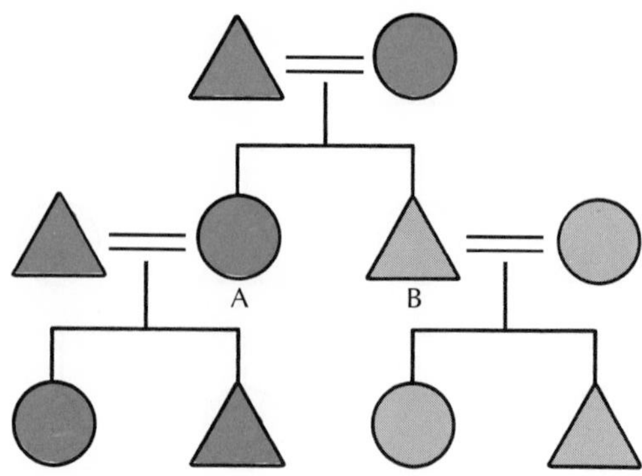

"The matrilocal extended family is composed of a woman and her husband, her unmarried sons, her daughters, and their husbands and children."

Figure 6-17. Minimal structure of a matrilocal extended family. All shaded kinspeople live together. When the daughter (*A*) marries she attaches the new household unit formed by herself and her husband and children to that of her mother. The son (*B*) leaves at marriage to join his wife as part of her matrilocal extended family.

The Matrilocal Extended Family

Where the rule of postnuptial residence is uxorilocal and conditions favor the development of extended families, the bride remains in her natal extended family residence and is joined there by her new husband. The matrilocal extended family is composed of a woman and her husband, her unmarried sons, her daughters, and their husbands and children. Again, as with the rule of postnuptial residence on which it is based, the matrilocal extended family occurs most frequently among primitive farmers, where the solidarity of the female work group appears to be most critical to the people's technoenvironmental adaptation. The productive unit among the Iroquois, primitive farmers in what is now New York, as among many other Indians of North America (see Driver 1971; Morgan 1962), was the matrilocal extended family formed around a core of females related through the mother-daughter tie. All the members of a single matrilocal extended family lived in one long house that was partitioned off into rooms, each occupied by a separate uxorilocal nuclear family—a woman, her husband, and their children. As often occurs with the extended family, the link between the biologically related core members—the mothers, their daughters, and the daughters' children, especially the girls—was especially strong. In contrast, the ties uniting them to their husbands were relatively tenuous. The eldest matron was the authority in all household affairs. She directed farm work, settled family quarrels, and appointed the man who represented the family on the community council. Among the Mandan, sedentary hoe horticulturalists on the edge of the North American Prairies, a single earth lodge served as the residence for a matrilocal extended family that might contain as many as forty members (see Spencer and others 1965).

The Avunculocal Extended Family

Where the rule of residence is avunculocal, the resulting avunculocal extended family is typically composed of a man and his wife, his young sons and unmarried daughters, and a sister's son (who is the uncle's principal heir) and his wife and children. It is the uncle-nephew link that connects the associated nuclear families of adjacent generations to form a single domestic group. Like the postnuptial residence rule on which it is based, the avunculocal extended family enhances solidarity among males in the female descent group by concentrating them in a single residence. This, to us, unfamiliar household form is usually explained as the result of an adaptive shift from a chronologically earlier rule favoring matrilocal residence. The transition to residence in the separate extended family household of a mother's brother enhances the possibilities for male solidarity. This factor of male cohesiveness grows in importance as an increasingly productive system of primitive farming allows for the accumulation of wealth and power, which in turn make necessary the centralization of authority (for administration and protection) in the hands of related males. That avunculocal extended families are not more widespread may be due in part to the tension created within a boy's natal residence, especially in his relations with his father, either when he leaves home to join the household of his mother's brother or when his father's sister's son moves in and establishes himself as a principal heir.

Often a young Ashanti of Ghana resides during the early years of his life in his father's household (Fortes 1950; Rattray 1923). Before or soon after he marries, he moves into the house of his mother's brother, for as the Ashanti trace descent through the female line, his mother's brother, not his father, is his closest male relative. His uncle then becomes the head of an avunculocal extended family. Often the younger men residing in the avunculocal extended family, those less likely to be their uncle's principal heirs, later move off again to establish separate households that they themselves head. Soon afterward they are likely to be joined by their own sisters' sons, and thus the structure of the avunculocal extended family reemerges.

The Bilocal Extended Family

Where the rule of residence is bilocal a newly married couple can join the natal domestic group of either husband or wife, depending on which is the most advantageous in terms of available land and other resources. A bilocal extended family is composed of a man and his wife and usually includes the nuclear or polygamous families of some but not all of their married sons, some but not all of their married daughters, and some but not all of their grandchildren. The structural variability of this form of the extended family is reflective of the unstable technoenvironmental and/or socioeconomic conditions of the peoples among whom it is found.

Toward New Forms of Marriage and Domestic Grouping

Now, seen in a cross-cultural perspective that points up the variability of forms associated with marriage and the establishment of conjugal households, some of the new types of marriage and domestic group organization that are on the rapid increase in industrializing societies seem less startling. They simply represent a new point on the sociocultural continuum, one at which again—as so often before in human history—traditional forms of social organization and cultural behavior become maladaptive under quickly changing conditions.

Although such changes are no longer surprising, they are often revolutionary. Some of the new forms suggest that what we have complacently taken for granted—for example, the husband-wife-offspring model of the domestic group—may be losing cultural ground, particularly among the young. Both smaller and larger and more flexibly structured domestic groupings are emerging, at least experimentally. Increasingly, people are setting up and maintaining households of no more than one adult, or of two sexually relating persons of the same gender, or of groups whose precise size, composition, and specific membership are in a state of ongoing adaptive flux. Old definitions of marriage must be rethought. Equally striking is the extent to which larger numbers of people are turning away from marriage and the residential kin group and toward their friends as a major source of economic, social, and emotional support. And when or if their friends are not enough, they are purchasing professional "family services" or turning to the state for help in coping with needs that most of humankind has so far sought to satisfy within the family household.

There are few historical precedents for this; it is happening fast. The causes seem clearly related to a level of technological development that strips the kin group of its cohesive functions as a productive unit. The cultural consequences of these attempts to develop new and more adaptive forms of relating are still difficult to foresee, but they are certain to be interesting.

"... households of no more than one adult. . . ."
Figure 6-18. Mother and child form a household of two. (National Film Board of Canada.)

Summary

In every society the majority of domestic groups are residential kin groups formed on the basis of the combined principles of consanguinity (socially recognized shared biological descent) and affinity (relationship established by marriage). The most elementary form of the residential kin group is the nuclear family, composed of a wife and her husband and their children.

Beyond the almost universal prohibition against sexual relations between parent and child and between siblings, most definitions of incestuous and preferred marriage forms are most immediately determined by the society's system for reckoning descent. Whatever its origins (which are disputed), the universal incest prohibition is both biologically and socially adaptive. The rule that forbids marriage within a certain socially defined group is called exogamy. The rule that designates the typically larger group within which marriage is culturally preferred is called endogamy.

In most societies marriage provides the connecting link in a larger network of economically and socially valuable reciprocal ties. For this reason neither the establishment of a new marriage nor the dissolution of an old one is considered a private affair. Formalization of the marriage requires recognition of the alliance that binds the two kin groups involved. This usually takes the form of an exchange of goods marking the first step in what is generally perceived as an ongoing relationship of mutual rights and obligations. Presentations made by the family of the groom to the kinsmen of the bride are called bridewealth; such gifts may take the form of commodities or services. Similar gifts given by the bride's parents to the groom and his kinsmen are called dowry.

In nearly every society there is a preferred pattern of postnuptial residence. The rule is called patrilocal where residence is preferred in or near the residence of the groom's father and matrilocal when the new nuclear family establishes its abode within or near the household of the bride's mother. Where a man and his bride take up residence with the groom's maternal uncle, the residence rule is called avunculocal. Where the rule is bilocal, the new family is expected to reside near the paternal household of one partner or the other, but there is no strongly expressed preference for which.

In most societies the nuclear family is embedded within the matrix of some larger residential kin group. Where there is polygyny, the marriage of one man to several women simultaneously, the result is a polygynous household composed of the economically, sexually, and socially distinct units formed by the relationship between the husband and each of his several wives and their respective children. The polyandrous household is usually composed of a woman and her several husbands.

The extended family is a still larger residential kin group composed of the several nuclear or polygynous families organized through the male or female line. Common residence is complemented and reinforced by valuable reciprocal economic, social, and ritual ties. The patrilocal extended family composed of a man and his several wives, his unmarried daughters, and his sons and their wives and children is the most prevalent form. The extended family may also be matrilocal or avunculocal depending on the rule of residence. When the nuclear or polygynous households of several brothers share a residence, the domestic group that results is called a fraternal joint family.

It is generally assumed that particular patterns of marriage, rules of residence, and the forms and processes of family life are most importantly affected by the requirements of technoenvironmental and technoeconomic adaptation, within the context of particular sociocultural settings, especially as these factors govern the allocation of productive goods, the organization of work, and the regulation of social relations people require everywhere in order to make a living. The new forms of marriage and domestic group organization now emerging in parts of Europe and the United States—including the increased incidence of divorce and the maintenance of single-person households—appear to be significantly related to the diminished importance of the kin group as a productive unit in industrializing societies.

Suggested Readings

For a more extensive exploration of some of the aspects of domestic group structure discussed in this chapter see both "The Nuclear Family" and "Composite Forms of the Family" in Murdock's pioneering *Social Structure.* The title of Service's *Primitive Social Organization: An Evolutionary Perspective* speaks for itself, as does Goody's *Comparative Studies in Kinship.* See also Fox's *Kinship and Marriage: An Anthropological Perspective;* Bohannan and Middleton's collection *Marriage, Family, and Residence;* Engels's *The Origin of the Family, Private Property, and the State; Marriage in Tribal Societies,* edited by Fortes; and the important *Household and Family in Past Time,* edited by Laslett and Wall.

For several good case studies of domestic group organization in other cultures see, in addition to the references already cited in the text, Briggs's *Never in Anger: Portrait of an Eskimo Family,* Colson's *Marriage and the Family Among the Plateau Thonga,* Harner's "The Jívaro Household," Kitaoji's "Japanese Family Structure," Langness's "Marriage in Bena Bena," and Wolf's *The House of Lin: A Study of a Chinese Farm Family.*

For a couple of cases closer to home see Fleming's "The Politics of Marriage Among Non-Catholic European Royalty" and Schneider's *American Kinship.* A dynamic perspective on household organization is provided in Goody's *The Developmental Cycle in Domestic Groups.*

For three approaches to the subject of incest see "The Incest Taboo and the Mating Patterns of Animals" by Aberle and others, Livingstone's "Genetics, Ecology, and the Origins of Incest and Exogamy," Wagner's "Incest and Identity: A Critique and Theory on the Subject of Exogamy and Incest Prohibition," Wolf's "Childhood Association and Sexual Attraction: A Further Test of the Westermarck Hypothesis," Goody's "A Comparative Approach to Incest and Adultery," and White's "The Definition and Prohibition of Incest."

In addition to *Bridewealth and Dowry* by Goody and Tambiah, see Chidwick's "Some Ideas Concerning the Origins of Dowry in East Africa," Evans-Pritchard's "Zande Bridewealth," Goldschmidt's "The Economics of Brideprice Among the Sebei in East Africa," and Singer's "Marriage Payments and the Exchange of People."

On the dissolution of marriage see Burch's "Marriage and Divorce Among the North Alaskan Eskimos" and other essays in Bohannan's thoughtful collection *Divorce and After.* See also Cohen's important *Dominance and Defiance: A Study of Marital Instability in an Islamic Society,* Gomm's "Harlots and Bachelors: Marital Instability Among the Coastal Digo of Kenya," and Maher's "Divorce and Property in the Middle Atlas of Morocco."

In addition to several selections contained in the collections suggested above, examples of polygynous family organization will be found in the classic *African Systems of Kinship and Marriage,* edited by Radcliffe-Brown and Forde. Among the many more recent studies see Clignet's *Many Wives, Many Powers: Authority and Power in Polygynous Families* and Goody's "Polygyny, Economy and the Role of Women."

On polyandry, in addition to the references to Berreman and Majumdar in the text, see *A Study of Polyandry* by Prince Peter of Greece and Denmark; and Goldstein's "Stratification, Polyandry, and Family Structure in Central Tibet."

For several related perspectives on one of the several new directions marriage and the organization of domestic groups are taking in response to rapid cultural change and/or socioeconomic stress see Kriesberg's *Mothers in Poverty: A Study of Fatherless Families,* Gonzalez's *Black Carib Household Structure: A Study of Migration and Modernization,* Otterbein's "The Developmental Cycle of the Andros Household: A Diachronic Analysis," Price's "Saramaka Emigration and Marriage: A Case Study of Social Change," and Stack's *All Our Kin: Strategies for Survival in a Black Community.*

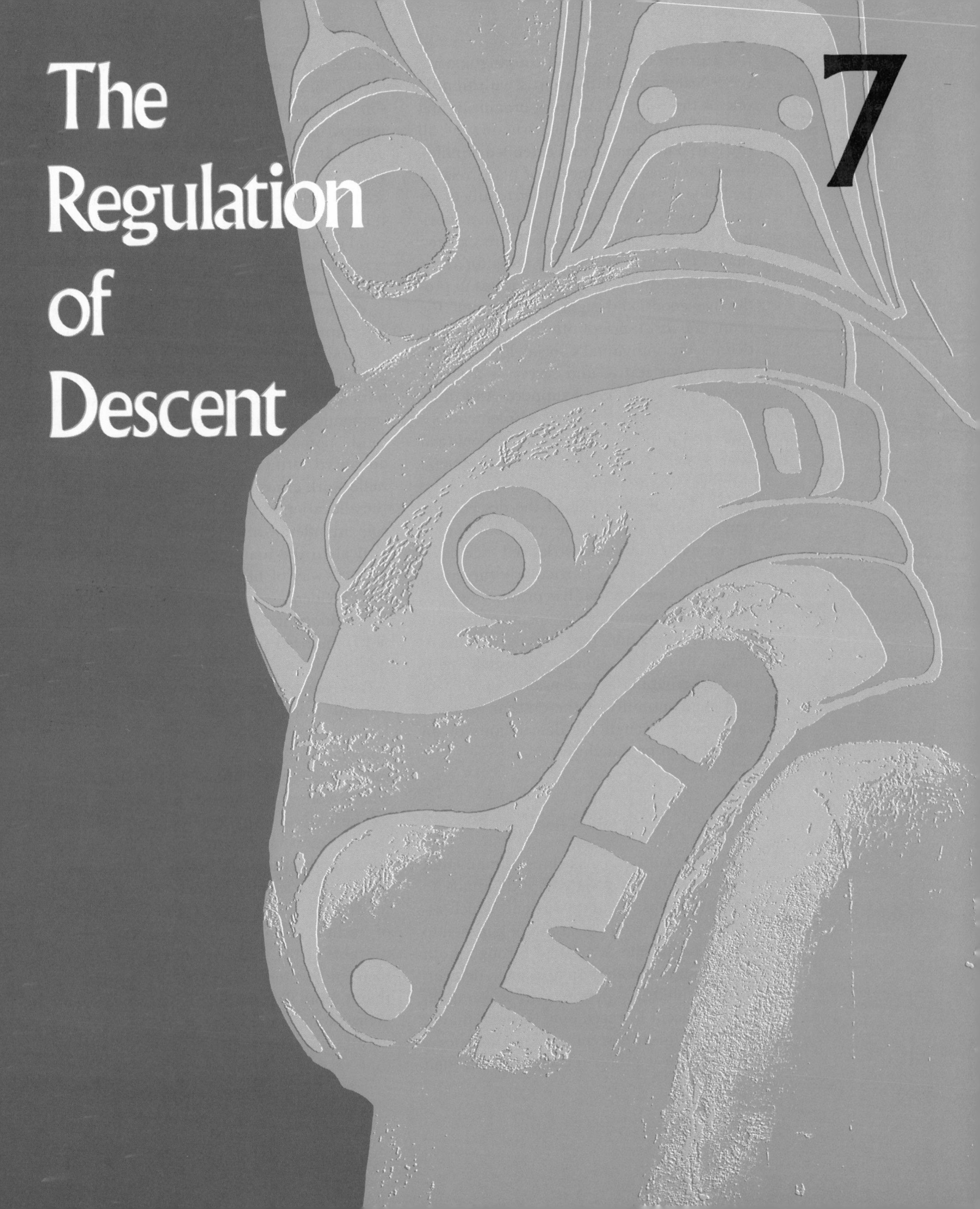

7

The Regulation of Descent

THE cultural recognition of consanguineous, (or genealogical) relationship is, with affinity, one of the two fundamental organizational principles underlying the structure of all nuclear, polygamous, and extended families. In all societies this concept of being related by "blood" is extended further to ally every person with a still larger group of kinspeople. This bond of socially recognized shared descent serves as the basis for regulating the individual's right of access to productive goods and right to call upon the economic assistance of others. Frequently it defines the individual's social identity, determines his status, and serves as a major source of his emotional support. And often the lineage system either supplements or functions in place of a centralized political system, serving as a major source of societal stability. In most industrializing societies many of these functions of the descent system are taken over by the state. But among the majority in nonindustrialized societies it is still the kin group, particularly the group related by descent, that has primary responsibility for providing the social order and political protection that people require to make a living. Occasionally the societal need for such groupings is underscored by the fact that the continuity of the descent group is carried on through the descendants of an adopted son or daughter.

Three Descent Rules

In every culture one of three fundamental rules prevails for assigning individuals to descent groups: bilateral descent, which assigns a person to a close group of kinsmen to whom he or she is related through both males and females; patrilineal descent, which affiliates a person with a group in which descent is traced only through males; and matrilineal descent, which associates a person with a group related only through females. In societies with double descent, two of these rules are combined and a person is assigned simultaneously to two groups, one patrilineal and the other matrilineal. It is not possible to prove which of these three basic systems of reckoning descent developed first in human history, but it is possible to identify some of the sociocultural circumstances with which each system is recurrently associated, thereby suggesting a significant causal correlation.

We saw in the last chapter that the rule of postnuptial residence that designates the culturally preferred place for a new couple to establish its household is primarily determined by the patterns of a people's technoeconomic adaptation. For hunters, for pastoral nomadic peoples, and for most advanced farmers it is the solidarity of the male work group, as seen in their control of the allocation of productive goods and their role in offense and defense, that is most critical to the maintenance and protection of their way of life. This is reflected in the high incidence of the virilocal residence rule (in Latin, *vir* means "man") that locates the newly married pairs in or near the household of the husband's father.

The much rarer rule of uxorilocal postnuptial residence (*uxor* means "wife" in Latin) places the married pair in or near the household of the wife's mother. It occurs most frequently among horticulturalists, where women do most of the farming and solidarity in the female work group is consequently most important, and where the absence of the threat of warfare makes male cohesiveness less critical. The residence rule tends to be bilocal where either the pattern of technoenvironmental adaptation is so unstable or the technoeconomic positions of men and women are so nearly equivalent that a more flexible rule of postnuptial residence is most adaptive.

Intersocietal competition over resources that takes the form of raiding and war-

". . . often the lineage system either supplements or functions in place of a centralized political system. . . ."

Figure 7-1. Lineage elders discuss community affairs in northern India. (National Archives.)

fare—and the consequent need to mobilize for offense and defense—appears to be a major catalyst in the development of descent systems, especially where centralized government is absent or weak. But the specific rules for reckoning descent are most immediately determined by rules of residence. Both residence rules and descent rules reflect the patterns of a people's technoenvironmental and technoeconomic adaptation. Once formed and reinforced by tradition and by other aspects of culture, particularly by the authority system and by the ideology, they may act back on those patterns, sometimes inhibiting or directing their further development—as in the instance of needed changes in work organization that are resisted because they threaten to disrupt traditional farming systems. But sometimes the rules of residence and descent themselves give way to the pressures for technological innovation and economic change and they too begin to change. Despite their apparent rigidity, especially as they are formally described by their adherents, all such descent systems necessarily allow for some bending of the rules to accommodate those whose life situations do not fit the idealized pattern. And, observed over the span of several generations, most such rules are actually in a state of ongoing adaptive flux. In a sense, the descent system in any society can be seen as a sort of ideal, a guide that most of the people are usually able to follow most of the time.

Bilateral Descent

Bilateral (or cognatic) descent is traced through both parents. Where it is symmetrical the individual is associated equally with all four grandparents. Potentially, the principle can be further extended laterally and multiplied geometrically in each ascending generation, relating him or her to all third and fourth cousins, all eight great-grandparents, and so on. In practice, this potentially enormous aggregation is too inclusive to be socially useful and is pared down, usually to a small group of close kinsmen to whom the individual can accurately trace a genealogical tie.

"... a small group of close kinsmen to whom the individual can accurately trace a genealogical tie."

Figure 7-2. Part of a cognatic descent group gathers for Christmas dinner in Rossville, Georgia. (Appalachian Regional Commission.)

Because the bilateral reckoning of descent most closely parallels the genealogical facts, one might assume that it would be widespread, but it is not. Unilineal descent (sometimes called unilateral) is considerably more prevalent. The reason for this seems to be that under the conditions of life characteristic of most technologically less developed peoples bilateral descent is much less adaptive. It works best as a means of keeping track of consanguineous kinsmen only where the group related by a socially recognized biological tie is very small, either because the entire society is small and endogamous and there is no need for a more satisfactorily expandable descent system or because the system of non-kinship-based social groupings, especially in a society established on a more advanced level of technological development, tends to treat descent as a less important basis for individual affiliation and community organization.

In either instance, the small group of cognatic kinsmen produced by the bilateral reckoning of descent is sufficient. This is the case in industrialized societies, where the same factors that foster neolocal residence and the separation of the nuclear family from larger domestic groups also inhibit reliance on descent as an important basis for group organization. The social recognition of biological relationship is both bilateral and limited because the adaptation of the individual and his or her nuclear family is more importantly reliant on alternative types of groups organized on the basis of principles other than kinship.

So far what has been said relates primarily to societies in which the bilateral descent system is the only system for recognizing consanguineous kin. But the bilateral tracing of descent, at least as far as the four grandparents, occurs in all societies. It is frequently overlooked, or its social significance is submerged, because most societies also have more extended and organizationally more important systems for tracing descent, usually unilineally—through only one parental "line."

The significant variable is the relative weighting a society gives to bilateral descent as a means of assigning the individual to a group in which membership is important in the organization of his or her life and in the organization of the community. In some societies with a very strong unilineal bias, bilateral descent reckoning is functionally almost entirely irrelevant, and the small group of close consanguineous kinsmen it forms has no important functions. In other societies these functions are of considerable importance. And in some, as we have said, the bilateral descent system is the only system there is, and the cognatic kin group it produces plays a major role in organizing the life of the individual, in structuring his or her relations with others, in getting things done, and in holding society together.

The Kindred

The group, or quasi-group, produced by the bilateral reckoning of descent is called the kindred. It can be defined as the usually small group of consanguineous kinsmen to whom the individual, or "ego," can trace a genealogical tie through both his or her parents and with whom he or she is associ-

"The . . . quasi-group . . . produced by the bilateral reckoning of descent . . . can be defined as the usually small group of consanguineous kinsmen to whom the individual, or "ego," can trace a genealogical tie through both his or her parents and with whom he or she is associated in a system of reciprocal claims and obligations."

Figure 7-3. The ego-focused kindred. Not all members are related to each other. They are all related to ego. (They have a relative, rather than an ancestor, in common.) Neutral squares are used to represent persons of either sex. *A* and *B* are ego's mother and father, *C* and *D* ego's paternal grandparents, *E* and *F* ego's maternal grandparents, *G* and *H* and *I* and *J* ego's four paternal great-grandparents, *K* and *L* and *M* and *N* ego's four maternal great-grandparents; *O* through *T* are first and second cousins, and so on.

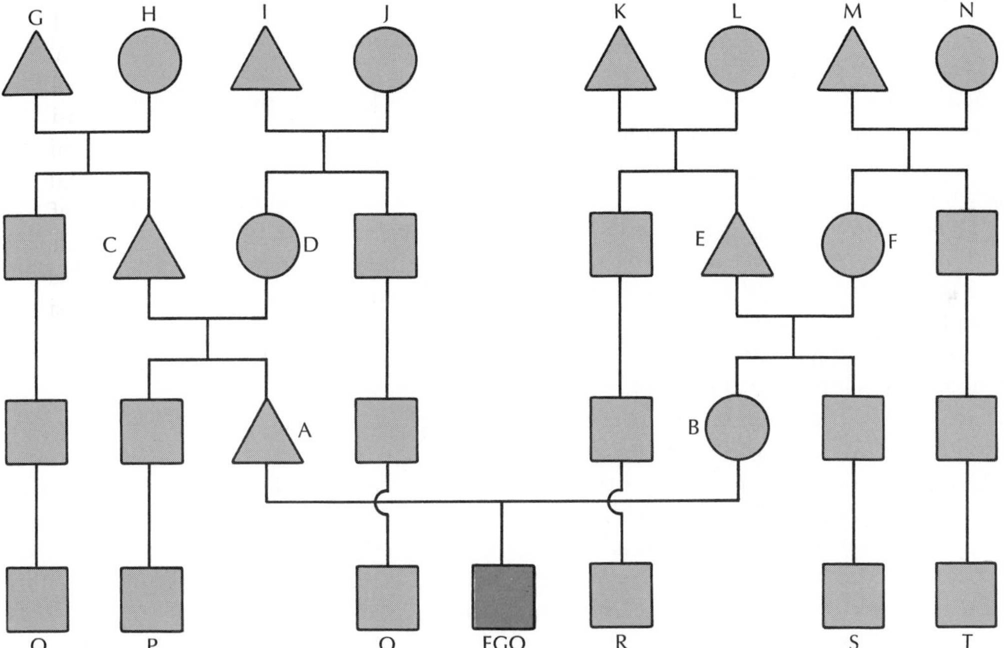

ated in a system of reciprocal claims and obligations.

In U.S. society the group of bilaterally related kinsmen we sometimes call kinfolk or, more vaguely, relatives is a kindred. Most of us can identify the members of our kindreds "up to" second cousins; beyond that we become uncertain (and beyond that we do not really need to be certain). In most societies, as in our own, the kindred includes all those close kinsmen with whom social interaction is obligatory and affection is expected. Several special attributes of the kindred are relevant to understanding why its social role is frequently limited.

The kindred is "ego focused": that is, its membership is different for every person; it is composed not of people who have an ancestor in common, but of people who have a relative (ego) in common. Every person belongs to a kindred, but the composition of every kindred is unique (except for full siblings). Even in relation to ego, the composition of the kindred is constantly changing as the individual moves through the life cycle. When he or she is young it consists primarily of parents, siblings, and a cluster of other close consanguineous, mostly senior kinsmen. When he or she grows old it is composed mostly of descendants and a few remaining relatives of his or her own generation.

These attributes—especially the fact that its boundaries are different for any person and are constantly shifting through time—sharply limit the collective action the kindred can take. What action it can undertake is necessarily short range. It cannot function as a group except in relation to ego, for except in relation to ego, it is not a group; when the individual dies, it ceases to exist entirely. Typically, it lacks a leader. It cannot easily provide the organizational basis for holding and allocating property, for organizing work or warfare, or for ascribing and transmitting status. Its adaptive value is greatest as a basis for recruiting close kinsmen to respond to an urgent but temporary need: to assist with preparations for a wedding or a funeral, or to cooperate in some other important but short-term activity, such as a hunt or a trading expedition.

Where bilateral descent and the kindred are found among a people who also make a strong unilineal emphasis in the reckoning of descent, the "balance" of the kindred, the bilateral equality of obligation, is often skewed. Although ego may feel close to all immediate consanguineous kinsmen, he or she will probably feel closest to those who are members of his or her own unilineal descent group, among whom the inheritance of more property and status can be expected. Where residence is unilocal (that is, patrilocal, matrilocal, or avunculocal) and descent is also traced unilineally, the structural significance of bilateral descent and the functions of the consanguineous kin group it produces are even more muted.

It is through ego's membership in a unilineal descent group based on unilocal residence that the majority of his or her most fundamental needs for group affiliation are met. It is the unilineal descent group, rather than the kindred, that structures the individual's life—that is basic to the organization of subsistence activities, to the maintenance of social and political controls, and to the rituals that reify the patterns of the group's adaptation to its natural and cultural environment.

Unilineal Descent

Unilineal (or unilateral) descent is traced through only one parent, the father or the mother. Heavy social significance is attached to ego's biological tie through this single parent; genealogical relationships through the other parent are given much

". . . ego is automatically assigned membership at birth in a particular consanguineous kin group."
Figure 7-4. New member of a Mexican unilineal descent group (her father's). (National Archives.)

less social importance and may be almost entirely ignored. As this system operates, ego is automatically assigned membership at birth in a particular consanguineous kin group. Where descent is traced unilineally through the father, ego is affiliated with a consanguineous kin group through the male (or agnatic) line, and the descent rule is patrilineal. Where descent is traced unilineally through the mother, ego is affiliated with a consanguineous kin group through the female (or uterine) line, and the rule of descent is matrilineal.

The Lineage

The unilineal descent group composed of all those consanguineous kin to whom ego can trace an actual genealogical tie is called the lineage. Where descent is reckoned patrilineally, the resulting consanguineous descent group is called a patrilineage. Where descent is matrilineal, the resulting consanguineous descent group is called a matrilineage. Typically, both patrilineages and matrilineages are exogamous: ego must find a spouse outside the lineage.

The three major group, or corporate, functions of the kin groups produced by unilineal descent, either patrilineal or matrilineal, are the organization of technoenvironmental relationships, the ordering of internal technoeconomic and social relations, and the regulation of relations with other groups. Typically, it is the unilineal descent group that structures the allocation of productive goods—hunting territory, pasturage or farmland, weapons, tools, special skills, and manpower—and the distribution of consumption goods. Leaders (usually males), whose authority is sanctioned by their seniority, assure compliance with the rules of the system of distribution and oversee the inheritance of goods and status, enforce the residence and marriage rules, arbitrate internal conflicts, and work to protect the territory, property, and membership of the lineage from outside aggressors.

"The unilineal descent group composed of all those consanguineous kin to whom ego can trace an actual genealogical tie is called the lineage."

Figure 7-5. Part of a Northwest Pacific coast Indian totem pole representing a supernatural being mystically associated with the lineage ancestors and their living descendants. (National Film Board of Canada.)

The sanctity of the kin group's technological adaptation to the environment—the propriety of its economic system, of the patterning of social relations, and of the lineage-based authority system—is reinforced by the kinship-connected religious system. Often this takes the form of ancestor worship, which provides both a means of maintaining contact with the supernatural forces believed to affect the group's livelihood and a way of ritually reinforcing kin group solidarity.

In any particular society the relative intensity and extensiveness of each of these major functions of the lineage will be mediated by the absence, presence, or relative importance of other regulatory systems external to the kin group. Among these may be economic systems that provide for reciprocal exchange between nonkinsmen, politically centered redistributive systems, or market exchange or alternative authority systems based on nonkinship criteria, such as associations or centralized government. The significance of the religious functions of the descent group as a corporate entity may also be mediated by the presence of other systems of belief based on principles independent of kinship.

Patrilineal Descent

The adaptive advantages of unilineal descent derive from certain of the structural attributes of the consanguineous kin group it produces. These are seen most clearly when they are compared with the characteristics of the kindred, the group produced by the alternative rule of bilateral descent.

In contrast to the "ego focus" of the kindred, the kin group formed by unilineal descent is "ancestor focused." This means that group membership is defined in relationship to an ancestor who remains as a fixed point of reference; members are related to one another because they all share descent from this common ancestor. Although individual kinsmen come and go—as new ones are born into the group and old members die—the group goes on. Because of this structural continuity through time, because of its expandability, and because it typically has a built-in basis for sanctioning access to authority (for legitimizing leadership), it can more readily take corporate action: organizing productive activities; allocating goods, labor power, and status; and responding effectively to the need for long-range collective action to maintain internal solidarity and to regulate relations with other groups.

Each of these attributes contrasts with the shifting boundaries of group membership, the temporal impermanence, and the leaderlessness that make the ego-focused kindred produced by bilateral descent less effective as a basis for long-range group or corporate action, and may explain the more limited distribution of bilateral groups as a major aspect of social organization, especially in societies where the political system is weak.

The advantages provided by unilineal descent are well illustrated with an example of the operation of patrilineal descent (the more widespread of the two fundamental systems of unilineal descent) within the type of society where its functions are particularly apparent, one based on primitive farming.

Again the kinship system of the Mossi, millet cultivators in the West African Sahel, provides a useful example (Hammond 1966). From the moment of birth the Mossi infant is affiliated closely with all its father's other children, its father's brothers and their children, its father's sisters, and so on. The male members of the descent group, the patrilineage, comprise the core membership of the domestic group, the patrilocal extended family. Typically, the several extended family dwellings of men closely related within the patrilineage are constructed adjacent to one another to form a small neighborhood group all of whose adult male residents are related through the male line.

"From the moment of birth the Mossi infant is affiliated closely with all its father's other children, its father's brothers and their children, its father's sisters, and so on."

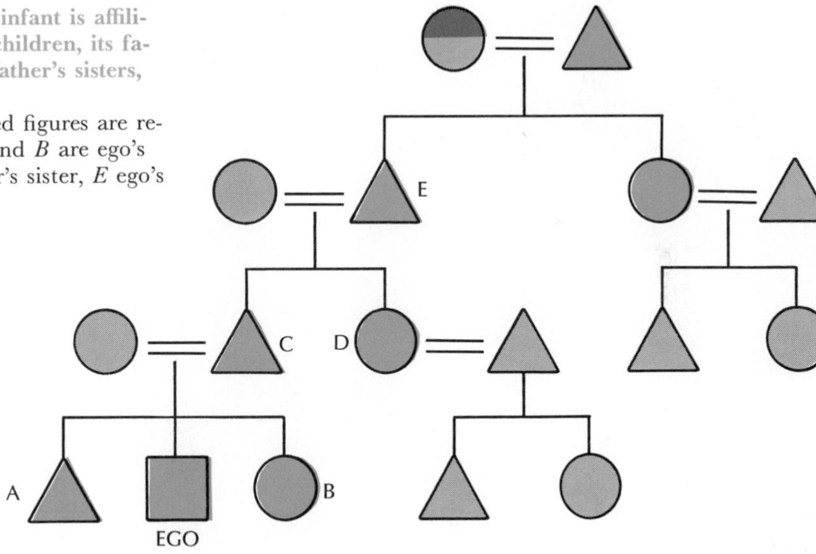

Figure 7-6. A simplified model. Shaded figures are related to ego through the male line. *A* and *B* are ego's siblings, *C* is ego's father, *D* ego's father's sister, *E* ego's father's father, and so on.

Because of the rule of lineage exogamy, the female members of the patrilineage remain in the extended family only until they marry; then they move out and into the residences of their husbands. However, wherever lineage members reside, they act as a single corporate group in their relations with one another and in their relations with other patrilineages and with the rest of the local community.

"The ancestral spirits of the patrilineage protect him, protect his farmlands, and look out for his health, as long as he observes the rules sanctioned by the ancestors' own example. . . ."

Figure 7-7. Mossi woman holding a chicken to be sacrificed to the ancestral spirits of her patrilineage, Yatenga, Upper Volta. (Hammond 1966.)

As a group, the Mossi patrilineage holds all farmland and allocates the right to its use in accordance with individual need. Women married to the men of the patrilineage receive the right to use particular fields from their husbands or other members of the patrilineage. All other goods—tools, granaries, utensils used in processing millet for consumption, and houses—are allocated on the basis of need within the patrilineage. Property is passed on from generation to generation through males in the paternal line, from father to son in some instances, sometimes from senior to younger brother. Women receive the right to use land from their husbands and from other members of their husbands' lineage. Compliance with this system for the allocation of productive goods is required of all lineage members. As long as they conform, their individual economic security is assured.

Social status is also determined on the basis of the person's position within the patrilineage. The right to authority, to succession to the role of patrilineage elder, is ascribed on the basis of patrilineage membership and transmitted generationally. A man inherits the position of elder from his deceased senior brother; when the younger man dies he is succeeded by a still younger brother or, if he has no remaining brothers, by his own eldest son, and so on. If the right to political position, such as that of chief, is held by the patrilineage, it is transmitted in the same way; Mossi chief's are usually the oldest responsible men in their respective patrilineages. The right to succeed to positions of religious leadership is always held by particular descent groups and transmitted by the same process.

In short, for the Mossi his patrilineage is the major source of his material support, the group on which he is dependent to make a living. His position in the patrilineage is the principal factor in determining his social status, his right to hold political office, and his right to succeed to a position of importance in the traditional religious hierarchy. The ancestral spirits of the patrilineage protect him, protect his farmlands, and look out for his health, as long as he observes the rules sanctioned by the ancestors' own example, rules concerning proper land use, residence, and marriage. If he violates them he not only is ostracized from the one group that can provide him with a means of making a living and achieving social status, but also is subject to punishment by these spirits—violation of the rule of exogamy, for example, is defined as incest and is punished by death.

The Mossi patrilineage provides the organizational basis for the farmers' right to use the land and sanctions its use by traditional means, regulates the allocation of other productive goods and the distribution of what is produced, enforces compliance with residence rules and rules of marriage with the threat of disinheritance and supernatural punishment, arbitrates disputes among lineage members, oversees succession, serves as a major structural component of the local community, previously acted as a major structural basis for military organization, and provides a series of rituals that both strengthen the Mossi farmers' relationship to the supernatural and deepen their awareness of dependence on lineage solidarity.

The connection between the patrilocal residence rule, the resultant formation of patrilocal domestic groups, and patrilineal descent serves to keep together the male work group essential among many hunter-gatherers, all pastoral nomads, and most primitive and advanced farming peoples, not only for hunting and herding and farming but also for the maintenance of social order, the control of ceremonial activities, and group protection.

Matrilineal Descent

Where the opposite and less frequent rule prevails—where residence is matrilocal (uxorilocal), the household is matrilocal, and descent is reckoned matrilineally—the major adaptive advantage appears to be maintenance of female solidarity within the work group. Matrilineal descent is most

"Matrilineal descent is most often associated with primitive farming, in which most of the work is done by women."

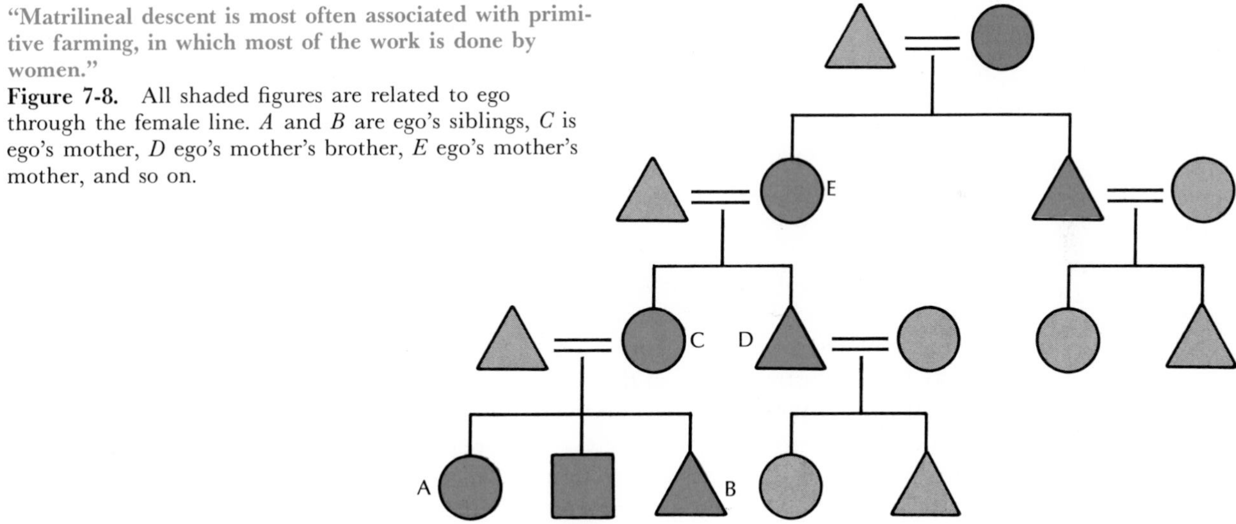

Figure 7-8. All shaded figures are related to ego through the female line. *A* and *B* are ego's siblings, *C* is ego's mother, *D* ego's mother's brother, *E* ego's mother's mother, and so on.

often associated with primitive farming, in which most of the work is done by women. As this is the activity that is most critical to the material maintenance of the household, matrilocal residence is the rule, and descent is matrilineal. As long as male solidarity is only intermittently necessary for offense and defense, the residence rule and the rule of descent both reflect the greater adaptive importance of residence and inheritance through the group whose solidarity is more continuously important. During periods of persistent external threat—of warfare, for example—the rules of residence and descent often begin gradually to shift.

The major nonadaptive feature of matrilineal descent has already been mentioned: the tension it creates within the matrilocal domestic group. Although the males are in authority, it is the mother's brother rather than the husband/father who is the authority in allocating most goods, organizing work, administering disputes, overseeing inheritance and succession, supervising rituals, and so on. The husband has authority also, although not in his "own" domicile but rather in the household of his sister. The result is a potential for conflict between a woman's husband and her brother, a pull toward brother-sister solidarity. The bond between husband and wife is comparatively weak. Further domestic group tension may be generated by the conflict between the strong tie of affection between father and son and the fact that a father's property and status are inherited by his sister's male offspring.

The function of matrilineal descent among the Ashanti, horticulturalists in the tropical rainforest of Ghana (Fortes 1950; Rattray 1923), illustrates some of these conflicts and some of the adjustments that may be made to minimize them.

The Ashanti matrilineage is headed by an elder male member chosen by consensus among all the mature men and women of the descent group. With the assistance and advice of the other senior members of the lineage it is his responsibility to oversee the economic, social, and ritual activities of the entire group, to administer the allocation of individual rights to use lineage-owned property, to arbitrate disputes between members, to approve all marriages, remarriages, and divorces involving members of the matrilineage, to supervise funeral preparations and the enforcement of inheritance rules, and to represent the descent group in its economic, social, and political relations with other groups in the community.

The authority of the matrilineage elder in overseeing the fulfillment of the Ashanti descent group's corporate functions is sanctioned and reinforced by his possession of male ancestral stools (wooden stools used by his predecessors) that serve as shrines for sacrifice to enlist the assistance of their deceased owners' spirits. The Ashanti say the matrilineage is "one blood," a belief that symbolically sanctions the rule of exogamy. They also say the matrilineage is "one person," a metaphorical statement of the corporate status of the entire group in its relations with others.

Despite the strong matrilineal emphasis of the Ashanti in reckoning descent, they by no means ignore the relation between a child and its father. Such a relation is simply regarded as qualitatively different, receives less emphasis, and is less important in affecting the life experience of the individual and the organization of the Ashanti community. This lesser emphasis is rationalized by their beliefs about the physiology of conception: the child is thought to be created by the mingling of the mother's blood and the father's spirit. Consequently, the child is regarded as being biologically closer to its mother. But an intimate personal bond of affection always unites a man with his child.

He gives it its name. And the maintenance of a benevolent relationship between father and child is believed to be essential to its achievement of a physiologically and psychologically sound maturity. A variety of ritual observances reinforce the paternal tie, and a child is prohibited from marrying a close patrilateral relative.

However, the patrilineal kin group has no corporate status among the Ashanti. It holds no property and takes no social or political action as a group. A child can inherit neither goods nor status from its father. A man has no legal authority over his offspring. Like all people with unilineal descent systems, the Ashanti do not ignore the genealogical link to the parent who is not a member of the consanguineous kin group to which the child is culturally assigned; they simply regard the relationship—accurately—as less important to the child's material and social survival and less critical to the organization of the society.

In many societies the principle of unilineal descent that produces the patrilineage and the matrilineage extends still further to provide the basis for alliance among groups whose reciprocal bonds are similarly sanctioned by a tradition of descent from a common ancestor, but one so remote that the genealogical ties among all members can no longer be accurately traced.

Clans

The most widespread of these more extended consanguineous kin groups is called the clan. Patrilineal descent produces a patriclan; matrilineal descent, a matriclan.

Clans most often develop out of lineages when the latter have so expanded and productive resources, especially land, have become so overtaxed that all members can no longer reside in the same locality. As some move off to settle elsewhere, either in the vicinity or at a considerable distance, they retain their traditions of origin and continue to rely on the parent lineage for political and ritual support. But as they have begun to make their living independently in a new

"Patrilineal descent produces a patriclan. . . ."
Figure 7-9. All figures in color believe they are descended from a remote (often mythical) common ancestor through the male line.

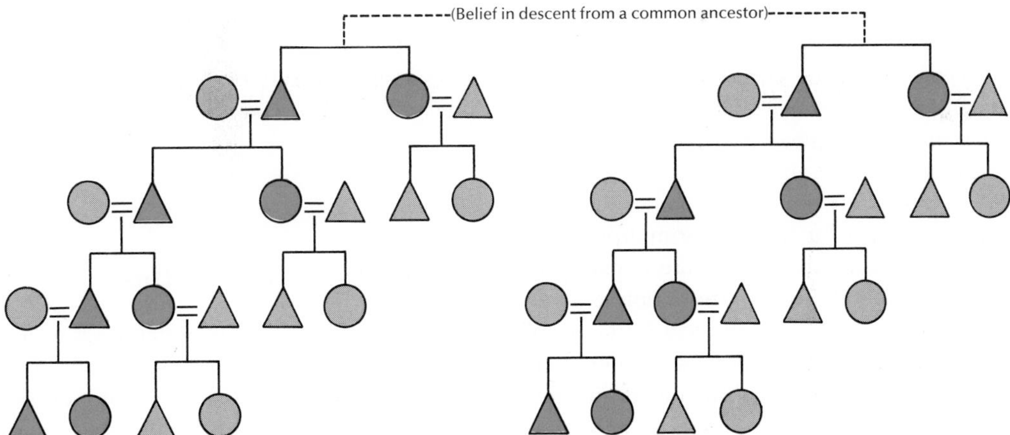

area they are necessarily cut off from the opportunity or the need for intensive collaboration in economic activities characteristic of lineage members residing in the same locale. Interaction diminishes in proportion to the degree of spatial separation, its duration, and the genealogical remoteness of the common ancestor from which the now several lineages are descended. As technoeconomic and social interaction diminish, so does familiarity. In many instances a member of one of several component lineages of a clan may not even know the names of all his or her kinsmen in the other local lineages of the clan. He or she may never have knowingly encountered members of the clan who live in other communities.

Under these circumstances continued awareness of clan membership is facilitated by the use of a name to designate all clan members, often a name taken from some aspect of the locale of the founding lineage or from some animal or natural object associated with the clan's myth of origin, frequently a totem whose ritual veneration further reinforces awareness of the reciprocal obligations of shared descent. As clans are characteristically exogamous, these various means of maintaining the identity of the unilineal descent groups are frequently referred to and relied on as a means of assuring that the prohibition against marriage within the clan is not violated.

Typically, those corporate functions related to subsistence are taken care of within the component lineages of the clan. It is as a residual source of authority in the regulation of disputes between its component lineages and as a basis for mobilizing manpower to resist external threats that the capacity of the clan to take corporate action is most often activated. These political functions of the clan, in widening alliances through marriage with other groups, in mediating disputes, and in organizing for war, as well as its role in structuring the local authority system, are discussed more fully in Chapter 10.

The number of lineages that compose the clan is increased by the process of segmentation just described. Conversely, the number of lineages that compose the clan is sometimes decreased, and the number of separate clans increased, by the breaking off of these segments to form new consanguineous kin groups that, with time, replicate the structure of the parent group. Typically, the process is set in motion when some of the lineage mates who comprise a part of the core membership of a local domestic group, often an extended family, move away to establish a new residence in another locality. As new members are born into this new lineage-based residential kin group, it gradually assumes the structure and takes over the functions of the larger domestic grouping from which it separated. As a new extended family emerges, so does a new segment of the lineage, made up of the consanguineously related core membership of the new residential kin group. If relations within the parent lineage and within other lineages in the clan are friendly, a new lineage is added. But if, for some reason, relations are hostile, the dissatisfied lineage segment may separate itself socially, politically, and ritually from the parent lineage and from the clan of which it is a part. It ceases to participate as a segment of the parent descent group and becomes the founding lineage of a new clan.

Phratries and Moieties

In some societies two or more clans are united in even larger groups, all of whose members share a tradition of common descent more tenuous than the one that unites clan members but that still serves to set its component clans apart from other similarly organized groupings and from the rest of society. A consanguineous group of this type is called a phratry.

The usually vague genealogical link between phratry members is often in contrast with the precision of the formal organization of the political power they exert. All Aztec freemen, for example, belonged to one of twenty clans that were grouped into four phratries. Each phratry constituted a major, semiautonomous tribal subdivision within the Aztec state (Monzón 1952). Collectively the six phratries of the Crow Indians of the Western Plains, each composed of two or more matriclans, were coterminous with the tribe (Lowie 1935). Conversely, the phratry

". . . all members of a person's own moiety are treated as consanguineous kin, as persons he or she is bound to support and respect. . . ."

Figure 7-10. Moiety organization is particularly well developed among Australian Aborigines. (National Archives.)

organization of the Kalmuk herdsmen of Central Asia was exceedingly loose, forming or dissolving in response to temporary amity or enmity, conflict or mutual interest, among the chiefs of the structurally more stable Kalmuk clans.

Where an entire society is divided into two major groups, either clans or phratries, each is called a moiety, from the French word *moitié* for "half." When such dual groupings are based on descent, which is usually but not invariably the case, they may be either matrilineal or patrilineal, depending on the rule of descent in the phratries or clans of which they are composed. Typically, each moiety is named, often after some totemic figure. The matrilineal exogamus moieties of some of the Indians of the Northwest Pacific coast were called Raven and Wolf, for example (Murdock 1934; Swanton 1905). Other American Indian moieties were frequently named after natural dualities, such as Winter and Summer, Sky and Earth, or other entities that symbolized the structural opposition and reciprocity that usually characterized the relations of one moiety with the other. Where moieties are based on descent and are exogamous, they serve as a useful means both of organizing the society and of guiding the individual in his or her relations with it. Among many Australian Aborigines (see Elkin 1964; Meggitt 1962) all members of a person's own moiety are treated as consanguineous kin, as persons whom he or she is bound to support and respect but must not marry. All members of the opposite moiety, the group from which a spouse must be taken, are treated in accordance with the Australian Aboriginal etiquette appropriate to dealing with in-laws. The moiety provides for the reciprocal exchange of women between exogamous unilineal descent groups. This broadens greatly the network of affinal kinship ties that assure the friendliness and cooperation with neighboring groups necessary to hunter-gatherers who must often penetrate the territory of others in pursuit of game or in search of water.

Double Unilineal Descent

In some societies descent is traced both matrilineally and patrilineally. Ego may belong to a pair of such groups. He or she is affiliated through the agnatic (male) line with consanguineous kinsmen who share descent from a common male ancestor. And at the same time, he or she is affiliated through the uterine (female) line with a group of consanguineous kinsmen who share descent from a common ancestress. The result is a society in which ego belongs to two, rather than one, consanguineous kin groups, one patrilineal and the other matrilineal. Typically, each descent group takes corporate action with regard to a separate sphere of activities. The Yako of eastern Nigeria, for example, allocate farmland and the right to hold political office through the patrilineage (Forde 1950). Movable property and the right to hold certain religious offices are transmitted matrilineally.

Among the neighboring Afikpo Ibo (Ottenberg 1960) every individual is a member of two consanguineous kin groups. The patrilineage provides the consanguineously related males and unmarried females who are the core membership of the patrilocal extended family, which typically resides in a single compound residence. Leadership in patrilineage affairs is assumed collectively by all senior male members. Rights to land use, house sites, and access to the groves where raffia palm and oil palm grow are also determined within the patrilineage. In contrast, the membership of the Afikpo Ibo matrilineage is dispersed, usually through several neighboring villages. All members, wherever they live, are related by a strong sentimental tie and are expected to cooperate with one another and assist each other in disputes (especially to come to the defense of female members in marital difficulty), to contribute to the funeral preparations of deceased matrilineal kinsmen, and to oversee the distribution of their property. In the cases of the Yako and of the Afikpo Ibo, and probably generally, such a system might be more precisely described as one of double unilineal descent.

The Future of Descent Systems

Because of the important economic and political functions of descent systems in societies with comparatively weak central governments, it is tempting to assume that with the growth of authority vested in the state, lineage organization will atrophy. With new governments and/or non-kinship-based organizations (such as corporations and unions) taking over the allocation of productive goods, systems of distribution, and military organization, the presumably diminished societal role of descent groups might be expected to result in their disappearance. Eventually this may occur, but it has not yet.

In much of the Middle East political authority is still often organized in accordance with principles that derive from patrilineality. Saudi Arabia and Morocco are two especially vivid examples. In neither nation do lineage systems show much evidence of fading away as means of consolidating wealth and allocating political power. Despite the growing importance of non-kin bonds as a basis for access to strategic resources, lineage organization continues to be important on Formosa and in Hong Kong (Ahern 1976; Freedman 1972; Potter 1970), just as it is in overseas Chinese communities, elsewhere (see Crissman 1967), where ties based on descent provide a basis for cohesion, communication, and cooperation in commercial enterprises that spread from Singapore across the Pacific to San Francisco and beyond.

"In much of the Middle East. . . ."
Figure 7-11. An Algerian herdsmen; patrilineality is a fundamental organizing principle throughout all of the countries of North Africa. (National Archives.)

In China itself lineage organization is reportedly discouraged and is effectively on the wane. In Japan its importance also appears to be decreasing, except among the wealthy, who (like their counterparts in Thailand, Iran, and the upper reaches of U.S. society) continue to find in a selective genealogical reckoning of descent a profitable means of maintaining and circulating among themselves much of the wealth, high status, and special privilege first amassed by their ancestors.

Kinship Terminology

Accompanying every system for organizing domestic groups and for tracing descent is a particular kinship terminology, an often complex set of terms or labels for designating the individual's position within the domestic and descent groups to which he or she is assigned by the society's rules of marriage, residence, and descent.

Each term refers to a status. Use of a term identifies the relationship between the speaker and the person addressed and evokes the behavior—relaxed friendliness, careful deference, the obligation to cooperate—that is culturally defined as appropriate.

Two major sets of criteria are used for distinguishing various types of kinship terminology: (1) the degree of merging (the "lumping" together of a number of relatives under one term) and bifurcation (the separation of kinsmen into two groups) of lineal and collateral kin in the parental generation; and (2) the degree of merging and bifurcation of kin in ego's own generation.

Four analytically different types result. In generational terminology, all relatives of the same generation and sex are referred to by the same term; there is a single term for father, father's brother, and mother's brother, for example. This does not mean that ego cannot distinguish between father and father's brother or mother's brother. Rather, it reflects the absence of any strong unilineal bias in the reckoning of descent, the social fact that father, father's brother, and mother's brother all have a qualitatively similar relation to ego, as senior males within the kindred. As would be expected, generational terminology is associated with bilateral descent.

In *lineal* terminology, the lineal kinsmen in the ascendant generation are distinguished from collateral kinsmen. For example, father, a direct lineal kinsmen in the ascendant generation, is distinguished from father's brother, mother is distinguished from mother's sister and father's sister, and so on. Lineal terminology is also associated with bilateral descent.

The somewhat cumbersome term *bifurcate merging* refers to a type of kinship terminology in which all members of the unilineal descent group of the same generation and sex are terminologically merged: referred to by a single term that also distinguishes them from all affinally related kinsmen of the same generation. If the descent system is patrilineal, for example, father and father's brother (both members of the ascendant generation of ego's own descent group) are referred to by a single term, but mother's brother (a member of mother's patrilineage) is referred to by a different term. Similarly, a single term is used for mother and mother's sister, but father's sister is referred to by a separate term.

These terminological distinctions are reflective of the structural distinctions between consanguineous and affinal kin groups produced by a unilineal descent system, either patrilineal or matrilineal, and they facilitate the extension to genealogically distant kinsmen of the valuable reciprocal bonds that unite biologically "closer" kinsmen within the descent group.

Bifurcate collateral is the label for kinship terminology that is highly particularizing: all collateral kinsmen of the parental generation are differentiated; there is a separate term for father, for father's brother, for mother's brother, and so on.

Using the criterion of merging versus the particularizing of terms for siblings, cross-cousins, and parallel cousins, Murdock (1949) has developed an even more refined six-part typology of kinship systems based on distinctions made in the use of cousin

Society	*Terminology*
Stage I	
A small, isolated kindred.	*Egocentric-Familistic Terminology Alone* This is merely the usual egocentered "kinship system."
Stage II	
This stage may be thought of as including societies like the average primitive "tribe." It has in it not only domestic families but greater families in some number. They are tied together by broad familistic bonds conceived in terms of individual relationships and also in terms of the relationship of groups, segments, and categories of the society. Corporate groups such as sodalities have appeared in addition to kinship segments of society (moieties, clans, etc.), and classes of persons (those who share some particular characteristic, such as married men, generations, etc.) are now larger and more objectively and impersonally defined.	*Sociocentric-Familistic Terminology* Gross familistic categories such as in-law groups, generations, marital statuses, clans, moieties, lineages, and various combinations of these are named and added to the previous system of egocentric-familistic terminology.
Stage III	
Society is the nonindustrialized civil type, standing between tribal society and urban-industrial nations. "Feudal" society could be included. . . . All, or many, of the elements making up the societies of the first two stages may be present, but the society is now larger and more complex and has certain new elements such as socioeconomic classes, political or bureaucratic offices, clearly delineated rich and poor, and other new kinds of criteria of social position.	*Egocentric-Nonfamilistic Terminology* This stage has terminology which is egocentric, but for the first time, nonfamilistic. "(My, his, so-and-so's) Lord, vassal, page, maid, cook," . . . are examples. Titles which refer to hereditary bureaucratic positions and/or positions in relation to other persons are frequent. In reference, titles are often sociocentric, but in address are more frequently egocentric ("My," "your," etc. being understood if not actually stated).
Stage IV	
With modern industrialism, society expanded rapidly—exploded—with the increased size and density accompanied by much greater complexity. The number of social positions based on economic specialization and membership in corporate groups increased commensurately. . . .	*Sociocentric-Nonfamilistic Terminology* The number of possible status terms of this sort in modern industrial society is tremendous. There are titles ("Doctor," "Mister," "Professor") now which do not refer to personal ties; names of economic, social, and political categories of people, as well as specific gradations within them; named professional specialties; and great numbers of corporate groups having special purposes like clubs, labor unions, and organizations in general. None of these terms are familistic and obviously they are all sociocentric.

"So far the expository elegance with which these types of kinship terminology have been delineated has not been accompanied by the development of a clear picture of their relative adaptive value under the different sets of cultural circumstances in which they occur."

Figure 7-12. An exception: Steward's suggested correlations among four kinds of kin terms—(1) Egocentric-familistic, (2) Sociocentric-familistic, (3) Egocentric-nonfamilistic, and (4) Sociocentric-nonfamilistic—and four levels of sociocultural development, presented in simplified form. At each successive stage anterior kinds of terminology are retained but are usually modified in form in response to changed cultural circumstances.

terms, each of which tends to be associated with a particular type of descent system.

So far the expository elegance with which these types of kinship terminology have been delineated has not been accompanied by the development of a clear picture of their relative adaptive value under the different sets of cultural circumstances in which they occur. For the present, understanding of kinship as a mechanism for technoenvironmental, technoeconomic, social and political adaptation can be more readily derived from study of the factors that affect domestic group formation and the development of descent systems, and from study of the other kinds of social groups discussed in the next two chapters: associations and systems of social stratification, both of which often cross-cut and occasionally replace kin groups as major factors in the organization of society.

Summary

Every society provides a systematized set of criteria for assigning social significance to certain biological relationships, for ascribing various kinds of importance to certain genealogical ties, and for deemphasizing or ignoring others.

For the individual, such systems function most importantly as a means of defining his or her primary group membership and for legitimizing his or her access to strategic goods such as land and the rights to particular status. For the community they provide the structural basis for the corporate action of its component groupings as these provide for allocation of productive goods, for distribution, for the assignment and transmission of status, for waging war, and for keeping the peace.

Where a person is socially allocated to membership in a group of close kinsmen through both parents, the descent system is bilateral; the kin group is generically termed a kindred.

When descent is reckoned principally through the agnatic, or male, line, the resulting group, composed usually of all localized persons who share descent from a common male ancestor, is termed a patrilineage. Where descent is traced through the uterine, or female, line, the resulting descent group is called a matrilineage. A system of double descent is one in which the individual is related matrilineally (on mother's side) to her matrilineage and patrilineally (on father's side) to his patrilineage. Each system of descent is associated with particular rules of residence that reflect the society's pattern of technoenvironmental adaptation, its economic system, and the need to group together those kinsmen whose collaboration is most critical to societal survival, particularly during periods of intersocietal (or intrasocietal) competition.

Although every society attaches greater social significance to certain biological ties than to others, this rarely means that relationships to other close biological kin are ignored.

Where the principle of unilineal descent is extended beyond the localized descent group to encompass other lineages with whom there is a shared belief in some more remote common ancestor that provides the basis for less frequent but still important corporate action, this larger descent group is termed a clan. Where two or more clans are categorized together on the basis of what is generally an even more remote unilineal connection, they are collectively referred to as a phratry. Where an entire local community is divided into only two such phratries, each is called a moiety.

Every system for reckoning descent is accompanied by a system of kinship terminology that serves to designate, with varying degrees of precision, the relationship of the individual to all others to whom he or she is related, consanguineously and affinally, and as a guide to the accompanying patterns of behavior that the society defines as appropriate to each such relationship. Typically, descent systems become most critical as a basis for individual affiliation and community organization among primitive farmers and pastoral nomadic peoples. Lineages are rarely found among hunter-gatherers. And, with the exception of the aristocracy and those members of the upper class who still control a large measure of productive wealth, descent groups rarely retain important functions in industrialized societies. Other types of social groups take over, based on associations of various sorts: on caste, class, or ethnic or sexual distinctions.

Suggested Readings

Many of the titles suggested as readings for Chapter 6 contain materials relevant to the subject of Chapter 7. Some useful sources have also been mentioned in the text. Each of the following general works or collections gives extensive attention to the study and analysis of descent: Barnes's *Three Styles in the Study of Kinship;* Bohannan's *Social Anthropology;* Fox's *Kinship and Marriage: An Anthropological Perspective;* Goody's *Comparative Studies in Kinship; The Character of Kinship,* edited by Goody; Graburn's *Readings in Kinship and Social Structure;* Hsu's *Kinship and Culture;* Mair's *An Introduction to Social Anthropology;* and Pasternak's *Introduction to Kinship and Social Organization.* See also Scheffler's "Kinship, Descent, and Alliance."

On the groups formed by bilateral descent see Mitchell's "Theoretical Problems in the Concept of the Kindred." Stack's "The Kindred of Viola Jackson: Residence and Family Organization of an Urban Black Family" describes such a group in action.

See Ember and others' "On the Development of Unilineal Descent" and also Befu and Plotnicov's "Types of Corporate Unilineal Descent Groups." For a seminal analysis of lineage organization outside Africa see Langness's "Some Problems in the Conceptualization of Highlands Social Structure" and Strathern's detailed *One Father, One Blood: Descent and Group Structure Among the Melpa People.*

The reckoning of descent through the female line is well covered in *Matrilineal Kinship,* edited by Schneider and Gough; see particularly Aberle's article "Matrilineal Descent in Cross-Cultural Perspective." On double descent see Goody's "The Classification of Double Descent Systems" and Ottenberg's *Double Descent in an African Society: The Afkibo Village Group.*

In addition to frequent references to the subject contained in the sources already suggested see Service's "Kinship Terminology and Evolution" and Wallace and Atkins's "The Meaning of Kinship Terms," Schusky's *Manual for Kinship Analysis* offers a practical introduction.

As a supplement to the several valuable references cited in the text on lineage structure in China see Anderson's important "Lineage Atrophy in Chinese Society." A useful contrast is provided by Befu's "Corporate Emphasis and Patterns of Descent in the Japanese Family."

Associations 8

In all but the smallest and most simply organized societies, the network of social ties based on kinship is complemented by other systems for forming alliances and grouping people, usually on the basis of friendship, age, sex, mutual interest, or a combination of these criteria. Such groupings are called associations. The term is loose, for the specific structural principles on which associations are organized, the effects they have on their members, and their functions within the societies of which they are a part are extremely diverse.

Associations can most readily be distinguished from other social groups in negative terms: by reference to what they are not. They are not usually based on kinship, for example; or, if they are, it is only one of several equally basic nonkinship criteria for membership. They are hardly ever present in small-scale societies based on hunting and gathering. They occur often in preindustrial states. And fostering cooperation and restraining disruptive behavior as they do, they tend to become more important during periods in which political organization is weakened. Associations with a predominantly or exclusively male membership are more widespread and are almost always more powerful in their social impact—a reflection, in large part, of the continued subordination of women in all cultures.

Several attributes are common to most associations. Although unmarried members may sometimes reside in a club house, they are rarely residential groups. Their membership is often dispersed, through several kin groups, throughout a local community or territory, even across ethnic and political frontiers. Membership may be either ascribed or volitional. Joining may be expected or required of all persons belonging to a certain age category, for example, or members may be forcibly inducted, as occasionally happens in guerilla bands. Either way, once membership is attained, compliance with the association's rules is expected and enforced. Typically, associations are special-purpose groups, perceived by their members as existing for the fulfillment of particular objectives, the pursuit or protection of particular economic interests or social or political goals. Although some appear to be purely "recreational," a closer look usually reveals that they are fulfilling other important functions as well.

". . . systems for forming alliances and grouping people, usually on the basis of friendship, age, sex, mutual interest. . . ."

Figure 8-1. Close friends, Northwest Territories, Canada. (National Film Board of Canada.)

"Some associations . . . have a conservative cultural effect." **Figure 8-2.** Join the Klan? (Michael Smith, Black Star.)

"Still other associations . . . seek change through the overt exertion of pressure on the prevailing organization of society." **Figure 8-3.** Black Power advocate. (Doug Wilson, Black Star.)

Most associations are organized to act as corporate groups in the fulfillment of their goals. Many are internally stratified by rank, with access to leadership roles clearly defined and staunchly supported economically and politically by a disciplined membership.

All associations are similar in providing both their individual members and the societies of which they are a part with a valuable source of flexibility by offering alternatives or complements to kinship as a basis of affiliation and institutionally patterned interaction. Some associations serve principally to maintain the existing social order and thus have a conservative cultural effect. Others facilitate the achievement of or orderly adjustment to new roles to replace ones lost, and cope in other ways with the many problems of adapting to shifting social and cultural circumstances. Still other associations, often those that are highly politicized, seek change through the overt exertion of pressure on the prevailing organization of society.

It appears that wherever an industrially based technology develops, the traditional relationship between associations and kin groups is reversed. In advanced industrial societies clubs, unions, private corporations,

". . . all provide their members with important social roles and alternative bases for group affiliation. . . ."

Figure 8-4. Bull roarer. Twirled by the members of a men's association in New Guinea to make a frightening noise that dramatizes the secret rituals in which only members may participate. (Courtesy of the Museum of Primitive Art.)

political parties, and other special-interest groups tend to replace all kin groups but the nuclear family as primary bases of group affiliation; often even the functions of the nuclear family are diminished. In most nonindustrialized societies it works the other way around. Associations and kinship groups usually are so interlocked that the organization and social effect of each is dependent on the action of the other. But with the first efforts at industrialization the shift begins. In newly industrializing societies like Japan, for example, it is already well under way. In the industrialized sectors of other "developing" areas, in China and to a lesser extent in India and in Latin America, the same trend is apparent. Associations that previously functioned to complement or supplement traditional kinship systems are gradually replacing them.

So far these are the most significant generalizations that can be made about associations: all are based on agreements with which compliance is usually compulsory; members are rarely recruited on the basis of kinship affiliation alone; all provide their members with important social roles and alternative bases for group affiliation; many play a significant part in maintaining community cohesion; many serve as useful sources of social structural flexibility and of individual adaptation; and finally, the relative importance of associations in relation to the kinship system generally increases as the technoenvironmental base of the society becomes progressively more industrialized and the traditional role of kinship groupings is diminished.

Bond Friendship

Bond friendship is a reciprocal association between two persons of the same age and sex whose economic and social positions, and therefore the capacity to meet their mutual obligations, are typically equivalent. Generally, the relationship is established voluntarily on the basis of shared recognition of the potential usefulness of such a tie. Frequently a person has several such relationships simultaneously. Although friendship and affection are useful for establishment of the mutual trust necessary to bond friendship, the association, once formed, is more importantly held together by the steady, ongoing reinforcement of the reciprocal tie through the giving of property, time, attention, interest, and support, both emotional and social.

Although there are often formal rituals that function to cement the relationship, it is fundamentally maintained by the participants' awareness of its mutual advantageousness. When one partner persistently fails to do his or her share, the relationship is seen as exploitative by the other and is likely to atrophy or to be formally terminated.

As an alternative or adjunct to kinship as a primary basis of affiliation, bond friendship is widespread in Africa. It appears to be particularly valuable to the herding peoples of East Africa, among whom a frequently shifting and often precarious balance in the relations between people and the natural resources they need to make a living maximizes the value of a system of social groupings that allows for the maintenance of a widespread network of cooperative alliances. Associational ties often cross-cut and complement the kinship system in providing the structure for such networks.

The Jie of Uganda (Gulliver 1955) are a people whose technoenvironmental adaptation combines both primitive farming and pastoralism. Wealth and status are largely dependent on, and represented by, the ownership of cattle and the capacity to participate in an extended field of reciprocal exchange relationships in which cattle are the principal medium. With the Jie bond friendship functions as a major organizational base for the receipt and reallocation of the cattle and other goods by means of which a man seeks both to maximize his efficiency as a herdsmen and to maintain his status as a man of wealth: a man to be admired and, if possible, to be related to.

Jie bond friendship provides the context of trust, cooperation, and realistic appraisal of mutual advantage that allows for the fulfillment of several valuable technoeconomic functions. It enables a man to disperse his herds in several cattle camps in order to diminish the risk of loss from disease or raids. He can adjust to the temporary depletion of pasturage or water in his own herding territory by requesting access to the land and water resources of bond friends in other areas where such goods are at least temporarily more abundant. Bond friends serve as trading partners in market exchange and, more importantly, as friendly intermediaries in bartering. A man can ask for the assistance of his bond friend in collecting the cattle necessary to make bridewealth payments—he may have to collect as many as fifty head of cattle, and many men take several wives—or to pay a fine. He retains these valuable rights as long as he reciprocates in kind. If his harvest was poor he can beg for grain from a bond friend whose crop was more abundant.

The major social function of the bond friend relationship is closely allied to its economic benefits: a man's bond friends are expected to support him in litigation. Most Jie litigation concerns disputed rights to cattle and is settled by the payment of cattle. A man's bond friends' responsibility to back him in a dispute with others is motivated both by loyalty and by appreciation of the fact that if he wins a settlement, they may share in it. If he loses, they will have to help pay his fine. The economic and social advantages of an enduring bond friend relationship are often extended to the kin groups of the principals as well, thus widening still further the network of valuable alliances.

The association is initially formed between two Jie men on the basis of personal liking. This provides the context of amity necessary to the effective functioning of a relationship in which mutual trust and economic and social interdependence are important. Establishment of the association is initially formalized by the exchange of cattle, an action that symbolizes their agreement to assist one another materially. No other ritual is observed. But this exchange occurs publicly, and acceptance of the agreement is witnessed, a factor of importance in assuring that both live up to its terms. It is the mutual interest of both Jie participants to see that the relationship retains its balance, that neither asks for or receives more gifts of cattle, labor assistance, or other goods than he can in the long run give in return. Although such an association can be terminated at any time, it is more often maintained for life and passed on from father to son, continuing as long as it is mutually rewarding.

In many instances bond friendship may be valued less as a useful means of extending kinship ties than as a valuable alternative to them. When the maintenance of close bonds of kinship becomes irksome as the result of a family quarrel or because a man's individual good fortune makes it less advantageous for him to perpetuate a reciprocal tie with less affluent kinsmen, he may seek to strengthen the network of his associational ties based on bond friendship and endeavor to decrease economic and social interaction with the members of his family.

In West Africa this often occurs as the

"By cooperating with bond friends rather than with members of their families in endeavors involving the money economy, they increase their chances of keeping their gains secret from kinsmen. . . ."
Figure 8-5. West African bond friends who have left their rural homeland together to find work in the city, Mopti, Mali. (Hammond 1966.)

economic system changes. Among the Mossi of Yatenga, for example, young men who have begun to sell their labor for cash or to work in the markets as traders frequently seek release from the obligation to share with their poorer relations (Hammond 1966). By cooperating with bond friends rather than with members of their families in endeavors involving the money economy, they increase their chances of keeping their gains secret from kinsmen with whom their responsibility to share would soon leave their small profits depleted—so soon and so completely as to make market ventures unprofitable.

As with many groups with institutionalized friendship of a similar sort, Mossi bond friendship is often extended to the kin groups of both participants. The entire extended family and patrilineage of a Mossi man can benefit from the tie of amity and the agreement to render mutual aid that unites him with his bond friend and his bond friend's kin group, but such an extension is neither automatic nor so rigidly enforced as the requirement to share with kinsmen.

Frequently among the Mossi the associational link is reinforced with the establishment of a kinship tie: when a man marries one of his bond friend's sisters, for example. But this rarely occurs among the Jie. For them the extension of reciprocal ties is so critical that to marry the kinswoman of a bond friend would be to "waste" the opportunity to use the marriage as the basis for establishing an alliance with still another group.

When the term *blood brotherhood* is applied to bond friend relationships, reference is usually to the ritual that serves to establish this association in some societies (see Tegnaeus 1952). Sometimes participants literally drink each other's blood. Among the Zande of Equatorial Africa the two men who join in such an alliance seal their pact by imbibing each other's blood as it oozes out onto sticks of wood or bits of nutshell held up to cuts made in one another's chests (Evans-Pritchard 1964). Once this ritual has been observed, either man, or his kinsmen, would risk severe supernatural punishment if he were to fail to abide by the terms of the agreement uniting them.

That the expectation for mutual cooperation and the responsibility to come to one another's defense extend to the kin groups of the Zande principals is reflected in the requirement that each man considering the establishment of such a tie must first secure the consent of his kinsmen. In order to travel peaceably outside their own territory, especially among their hostile neighbors the Aberambo and Mangbetu, the Zande often endeavor to exchange blood with members of these tribes. For blood brothers must assure protection and safe passage through one another's territory. As compliance with the requirements of the pact for cooperation and mutual aid is considered sacred by the neighbors of the Zande as well, the association functions valuably to facilitate trade and travel across tribal frontiers.

Ritual Kinship

An analogous extension of reciprocal bonds to nonkinsmen occurs in ritual co-parenthood, or compadrazgo, as it is called in Spain and in the Spanish-speaking countries of the New World, where it is particularly widespread as a means of enlarging the individual's supportive social network (Coy 1974; Foster 1969; Ingham 1970; Middleton 1975; Mintz and Wolf 1950).

Strengthened by the sacraments of the Catholic Church, the association of persons who share this relationship is usually established when a man and a woman, often but not necessarily man and wife, agree to sponsor the newborn child of a friend. The agreement is ritually formalized at the time of the infant's baptism, when they promise to assure its religious education and its guidance in the Catholic faith. Assumption of this obligation is usually complemented by the acceptance of some measure of responsibility for the child's economic support and for its public conduct, an agreement represented symbolically by the presentation of a gift to the newly baptized baby and by the prominent presence of the compadres (co-parents) at other ceremonials marking the child's passage through the life cycle: at first communion, at confirmation, at marriage, and often at birthday parties.

In Brazil the ties of ritual co-parenthood are often further extended at the time of a wedding, by asking one man and one woman to serve as godparents (padrinhos) at the church wedding and another set at the civil ceremony (Wagley 1948). Each of the two marriage ceremonies thus increases the network of ritually reinforced reciprocity by the addition of eight new members. In the instance of both types of ritual kinship sometimes those selected to serve as co-parents or godparents are also kinsmen. If so, the association serves to strengthen an existing relationship rather than to establish a new one outside the kin group.

As with the association that unites bond friends, the ritually sanctified agreement (*compadrazgo*) between co-parents and godparents to cooperate economically and socially is useful to others as well, providing a sort of social insurance not only to the godchild and to his or her parents, but by extension also to their other close kinsmen. In effect, a friendship network is grafted onto the kinship system. Again, reliance on this association as a source of trust and assistance is sometimes preferred to dependence on the kin group. Where the socioeconomic status of kinsmen is not equivalent, more affluent members of the kin group may find the obligations of compadrazgo onerous, being reluctant to aid less well-off members of their family for fear that the goods, money, or labor assistance they provide a relative in need will not be reciprocated. If a symmetrical relationship is sought, compadres who are nonkinsmen are often a better risk.

Where the society is stratified—that is, divided into groups ranked on the basis of differences in socioeconomic status—people often try to establish ritual kinship ties with others whose position is somewhat superior to their own. In such an association the lower-status participants can anticipate not only social and economic assistance in "getting ahead" but sometimes political protection and sponsorship as well. Although the status of the parties in such an association is not equivalent, benefits can be reciprocal: a following of such dependents strengthens the superior social position and may enhance the political power of the more affluent compadre or padrinho.

As with other forms of association, the adaptive value of ritual kinship ties appears to increase sharply during the early stages of accelerated culture change resulting from drastic changes in the pattern of a people's means of making a living. Compadrazgo and the padrinho relationships are likely to be especially valuable to urban migrants newly arrived from the countryside who are cut off from the support of their kinsmen at home and are often isolated among strangers in an unfamiliar city, required to adjust to new jobs with which they have no past experience and to participate in an alienating money-based economy that is new to them. Today in the cities of Latin America, working-class strangers from whom assistance is sought are often addressed as "compadre" in an effort to elicit from them the friendly and cooperative response appropriate to persons who share in this traditionally sanctioned, economically and socially valuable association.

"Age is a universal determinant of individual status. . . ."
Figure 8-6. Navaho couple. (Courtesy of the American Museum of Natural History.)

Age Groups

Age is a universal determinant of individual status and serves widely as a means of assigning people to groups in which members' similar position in the life cycle results in their having common interests that are conducive to pleasurable and often productive interaction.

However, despite the apparent logic of organizing groups on the basis of age, in most societies age groups are structurally and functionally subordinate to other forms of basic social grouping. As with the role of other kinds of associations in technologically less developed societies, age group organization is almost invariably less important than kinship as a basis for organizing groups. It provides a basis for the extension of kinship ties or for complementing them, but rarely takes their place.

At the point in technological development where technoeconomic specialization increases and systems of social stratification begin to emerge, differences in skills, in work, and in socioeconomic status become more important than age as determinants of group membership; the social role of age groups is generally subordinate. Because of the size of society and the degree of internal socioeconomic diversification, age-based groupings will probably be either so small that they are socially ineffective or, if they are large, so loosely structured that their impact on the organization of society is minimal.

There are, as usual, exceptions, notably in East Africa and among the Indians of the North American prairies. Among many peoples in both areas the prominence of age groups appears to have been causally associated with the need of politically noncentralized, often widely dispersed peoples for community, territorial, or "tribal" solidarity—for a unifying bond that cuts across kinship and territorial differences. People divided by other loyalties were often united by age group membership. Discipline, bravery, competitiveness, and respect for senior authority were fostered among groups of young men—warriors and police—whose age-related capacity for physical strength and endurance was critical to their society's survival, both for offense and defense and for the maintenance of internal order under the guidance of a senior age group of judges, administrators, and ritual leaders.

The Karimojong Age System

In East Africa, associations based on age are frequently still central to the organization of community life and to the structure and function of the political system. Among the Karimojong cattle herdsmen of Uganda all adult males who have been initiated into manhood within a single period of from five to six years belong to a single age set (Dyson-Hudson 1963, 1966). Five adjacent age sets are combined to form a single, named generation set composed of all men who have been initiated within a period of from twenty-five to thirty years.

Two of these generation sets are always in "recognized corporate existence." The junior generation set, the adult males who serve as warriors and police, is still open, continuing to recruit its full complement of five adjacent age sets. The senior generation set, the older males who are the judges, administrators, and priests, is closed; its membership is complete. When the junior generation set is fully formed and closed, it replaces the senior generation set, which is retired. In all, the system is composed of four named generation sets that replace each other cyclically through time: (1) the yet to be fully formed generation set of young males socially designated as too immature for initiation; (2) the junior generation set of adult males, still in the process of acquiring its full complement of age sets; (3) the senior generation set of elders; and (4) the generation set of old men

". . . in most societies age groups are structurally and functionally subordinate to other forms of basic social grouping. . . ."

Figure 8-7. The Kikuyu are an exception. Boys dancing at their initiation into the first Kikuyu age grade. (Courtesy of the American Museum of Natural History.)

"In East Africa, associations based on age are frequently still central to the organization of community life and to the structure and function of the political system."

Figure 8-8. Nandi spearmen, members of a warrior age set, Kenya. (Courtesy of the American Museum of Natural History.)

who have been retired. Only the junior and senior generation sets can take corporate action. Of the other two, that of the young men is still being formed, and that of the old men is in the process of actual physical dissolution as its retired members become enfeebled and gradually die off.

In a variation on the common practice of expressing associational relationships in the idiom of kinship, the two adjacent generation sets in operation at any one time are realistically perceived by the Karimojong as standing in relation to each other as fathers and sons. Alternate generation sets are related as grandfathers to grandsons. In fact a man's father is likely to be a member of the adjacent senior generation set, and his sons will belong to the adjacent junior, still-forming generation set of immature young males. The tradition of obedience and respect between adjacent generations in the kin group (between father and son) and of permissiveness between alternate generations (between grandfather and grandson) is paralleled in the behavior of all members of adjacent and alternate generation sets toward those "above" or "below" them in the system.

For the Karimojong youth, affiliation with the age set to which he will belong for life begins with his initiation. Such rituals are an almost universal aspect of the induction of new members into associations. Typically, they function to internalize—by instruction that frequently involves reliance on dramatic, frightening, or painful means—the initiate's awareness of the rights and obligations of his new status and to make this change in his status and these new rights and obligations known to the community.

The first phase of the Karimojong age set initiation ritual is called "spearing the ox." All boys to be initiated gather at the local ceremonial ground. There, under the supervision of a member of the senior age generation, each youth spears a beast belonging to his family. The slaughtered animals are dismembered; their heads and necks are carried off by the women to be used in a later phase of the ceremony. The stomach sacks of the dead animals are carefully laid out and slit with spears. The semidigested food that spills out is smeared on the head, shoulders, and abdomen of each initiate as blessings are called out: "Be well. Become wealthy in stock. Grow old. Become an elder." Other blessings are invoked upon the initiates' age set, upon adjacent sets, upon the generation set to which it will belong, upon the other major institutions of the Karimojong social system, and upon the cattle that support it, thus sanctioning ritually the newly forming relationships of the initiate to his age set, and of the age set to the larger context of Karimojong society and culture. Here and in the several further phases of the initiatory ritual that follow the rightness and sanctity of all these societal forms and of the techno-economic base on which they rest are ritually restated, reinforced, and perpetuated.

At the conclusion of his initiation the boy has become a man. He marks symbolically the achievement of his new status by allowing his hair to grow and weaving into it a sisal string that will remain until his locks are long enough to be done up with mud into the headdress of a full-fledged age set member.

Other important functions are fulfilled by the Karimojong age set initiation ritual. The authority of the elders is symbolically reinforced by their supervision of the ritual, a demonstration of the fact that it is only they who have the right to officiate at the ceremony through which every male must pass to achieve his place as an adult in Karimojong society. The superior-subordinate relation of father to son, as it provides the basis for structuring relations between all Karimojong age groups and their members, is publicly demonstrated by the fact that the men of the fathers' generation set act as the sponsors for their sons' initiation.

The establishment of each of the five age sets that ultimately compose a generation set is marked by a similar ceremony until, finally, the generation set is closed. When this occurs, at the conclusion of a process that takes approximately twenty-five years, the generation set is ready to assume fully the functions of a corporate group. The adjacent generation set is promoted to senior status, and the alternate generation set, that of the grandfathers, is retired, all to the accompaniment of ceremonies organized to restate symbolically the structure and the functions of the age system as they relate to the other major aspects of Karimojong society and culture.

Like most institutions that provide for societal stability, the Karimojong age group system also creates a certain amount of intergenerational tension and pressure for change. As members of the senior generation set grow older, the men of the junior generation set complain increasingly of their elders' senility and incompetence. As the younger men become more impatient and more restless to assume senior status themselves, pressure grows for promotion of their generation set and for the retirement of the senior set. Finally, the old men agree. Again there is a gathering at the ceremonial ground, an oxen is speared, and its flesh is roasted and distributed by the eldest members of the senior generation set to members of the junior group. Akuj, the Karimojong creator deity, is asked to bless the members of the junior generation set who are about to be pro-

"When this occurs, at the conclusion of a process that takes approximately twenty-five years, the generation set is ready to assume fully the functions of a corporate group."

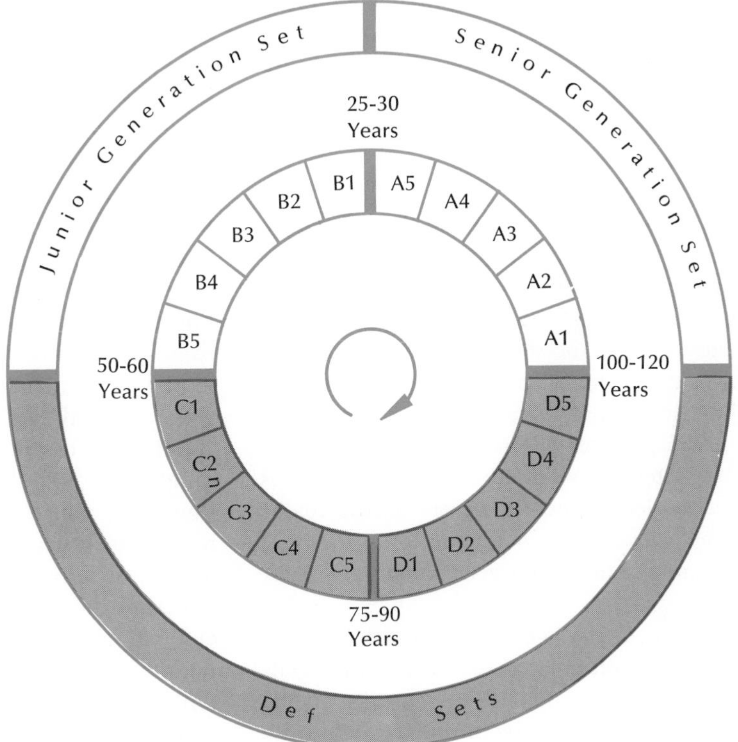

Figure 8-9. Each generation set encompasses five age sets. Age sets *B5* through *B1* belong to the junior generation set. Age sets *A5* through *A1* belong to the senior generation set. The two generation sets in operation at any one time are part of a total series of four specifically named sets that succeed each other cyclically and continuously through time. It takes from one hundred to one hundred and twenty years to complete the cycle. (Adapted from Dyson-Hudson.)

moted to senior status and to the role of guardians of the country. More animals are sacrificed, and all those succeeding to senior status are smeared with their entrails and exhorted by the retiring elders in their new responsibilities as community leaders. At the conclusion of the ceremony the members of the old senior generation set are formally retired, and a new senior generation set is established. Now the young boys, the sons of the new junior generation set, can begin to be initiated. And so the cycle goes on as new age sets are established, gradually grow into generation sets, are first promoted to junior status and then to senior status, and finally are retired.

For the individual the Karimojong age system is the source of status. Knowledge of the behavior appropriate to his position serves him as a valuable guideline to proper comportment. Each knows how he should behave toward all others and how all others should behave toward him. His position in his age set and the status of his age set within its generation set combine to determine the role he is expected to play in almost all social situations.

Economically, age set membership is probably most important to the individual because it provides a group of persons outside his kin group with whom he can cooperate in the expectation of reciprocity and trust. He has the right to move his animals over their lands. Occasionally, he may even be permitted to graze them on his agemates' pastures. Of equal importance, the age system provides the organizational basis for cattle raiding. Members of the senior generation set approve plans for a raid, and the men of the junior generation set carry it out.

Status in the age system also determines political position. Age sets within each generation set are ranked hierarchically on the basis of priority of recruitment, with those more recently initiated always required to defer to the authority of members of the older age sets. Among strangers the behavior appropriate to their relative status in the age system is indicated by the ornaments they wear. The right to exercise authority in community affairs is reserved to the senior members of the senior generation set and involves both the maintenance of order within the community and leadership in defending it from attack by outsiders. Their authority is sanctioned by their age, by the tradition of deference of younger men to their fathers and to the men of their fathers' generation, by the fact that men of both generations share common values, and by the supernatural power of the members of the senior generation set, whose closeness to Akuj, the Karimojong deity, enables them to curse those who defy their authority and to withhold from them the benevolent supernatural support that the Karimojong believe is the basic source of their material prosperity.

In every society people are categorized on the basis of age and are expected to conform to the behavior culturally defined as appropriate to their age category. Everywhere the young grow restless to achieve the higher status and to enjoy the greater authority of their elders. Almost everywhere the older generation resists the loss of power and position that comes with aging. The East Africans' age systems are exceptional principally in their organizational complexity, in the precision with which they determine the social status of the individual and mark his progress through the life cycle, in the explicitness with which they reify and reflect economic, social, and political relationships, and, most importantly, in their capacity to structure the corporate action necessary to enforce compliance with the rules that maintain internal order and provide the authority to mobilize manpower both for defense against attackers and for raids on others.

Associations Based on Sex

Sex as well as age is a criterion for membership in most social groupings based on age. In some societies sex rather than age is the principal qualification for group membership. The system of associations based on sex is probably nowhere more highly developed than among the peoples of Melanesia, the inhabitants of New Guinea and the surrounding islands, where men's clubs provide a valued refuge from female society and a means of reinforcing male solidarity and maintaining male dominance (see Meggitt 1964; Oliver 1955; Read 1965). As a rationale for this male exclusiveness, much is made by the Melanesians of the dangers of the female's supernaturally derived and potentially dangerous sexuality. Little boys are gravely warned by their older brothers and fathers to avoid the company of their mothers and sisters and are encouraged to engage in exclusively male activities. Women are barred from many of the ritual activities connected with the men's associations. Many men live permanently in their club houses, and women are often excluded from the premises, just as they are often barred from men's clubs in Europe and the United States. In Melanesia and in the Americas, and wherever else they are found, such sex-based associations also provide a valued alternative to kin group affiliation, whether it be temporary escape from the responsibilities of life in the nuclear family, respite from a more complex network of kinship ties, or the opportunity to extend the members' field of alliances.

In the United States the greater proliferation of such groupings, as well as of "clubs" that are not necessarily monosexual, may be explained by the diminishing effect of kin group membership on the life of the individual and the need to reinforce reliance on the many non-kinship-based relations that life in U.S. society imposes. They also fulfill a valuable psychological function in a society where the individual often feels anonymous, isolated, and in need of an alternative to the social and emotional support no longer provided by the family. Among the middle class such functions are often first fulfilled by the Brownies, Cubs, Boy and Girl Scouts, then by fraternities and sororities. Still later there are other sexually exclusive organizations: men's and women's associations that range, in the specifics of their organization, in the formal definitions

". . . men's clubs provide a valued refuge from female society. . . ."

Figure 8-10. Exterior of men's house, Asmat, New Guinea. (Courtesy of the Museum of Primitive Art.)

". . . the opportunity to extend the members' field of alliances."
Figure 8-11. Motorcycle gang, Haight Ashbury. (Eugene Anthony, Black Star.)

of their goals, and in the criteria of membership, from clubs in which membership is determined not only by sex, but also by the results of a careful examination of the prospective member's ethnic, social, and economic credentials, to other associations like Kiwanis, the Rotarians, and the Lions Club in which membership qualifications are merely sexist.

The cohesiveness of such groups is often reinforced by the members' participation in regular meetings closed to outsiders, the wearing of special insignia and costumes, the use of secret signals, a hierarchy of ranked grades that determines the allocation of authority, and elaborate secret rituals from which nonaffiliates are barred. In most cultures these groups, in which recruitment is based primarily on sex and an effort is made to conceal members' activities from outsiders, are often more accurately categorized as secret societies.

Secret Societies

Although the economic, social, and political functions they fulfill and many aspects of their organization and activities are quite similar to those of associations based primarily on age or sex, secret societies can usually be distinguished by the fact that their membership is limited to only a segment of the total eligible population and by the focal attention to protection of the secrecy surrounding society rituals, secret rites that are believed to increase the supernatural powers of either individual society members or the entire association. Noninitiates are usually permitted to learn just enough about such covert observances to be frightened and impressed.

Secret societies are widespread, especially in Africa. They were once of great importance in the culture of many Native Americans. Among American Indians of the Northwest Pacific coast secret society organization was particularly highly developed by the Kwakiutl of British Columbia, hunter-gatherers whose exceptionally rich habitat allowed for a degree of population density, sedentarization, and socioeconomic differentiation rare among nonagricultural peoples (Boas 1895; Drucker 1965; McFeat 1966; Spencer and others 1965).

With the Kwakiutl secret society membership provided a means of achieving or increasing high social status as well as increasing supernatural power. Mystery was associated both with initiation and with the ceremonial practices intended to achieve particular supernatural purposes. Noninitiates' fear of the societies and of the power of their members was induced by having them witness carefully staged, terrifying illusory rituals performed, for example, by cannibal dancers who were supposed to be so thoroughly possessed by the cannibal spirit that they could scarcely resist the temptation to kill and eat members of the audience. To restrain them, it was explained to the onlookers, the dancers had to be appeased with human corpses that would be consumed before the audience's eyes. To achieve this effect, the carcasses of small black bears, smoked and treated to resemble human forms, were partially devoured in front of the horrified spectators gathered to witness the dimly lit ceremony. Sometimes, still unappeased, a dancer would appear to lose all control and rush wildly into the audience to cut off and eat a small piece of someone's skin before he could be restrained. Those attacked were, of course, notified in advance

"... secret rites that are believed to increase the supernatural powers ... of society members. ..."

Figure 8-12. Kachina dance among the Hopi. The dancers' masks represent the spirits of the underworld who bring rain. (Courtesy of the American Museum of Natural History.)

of the ceremony and afterwards received special gifts as a reward for their forbearance.

The mystery and terror surrounding secret society activities such as those of the Kwakiutl contribute to the development of a sense of fear and awe among the larger community that often functions importantly to strengthen the members' social and political power. By using terror to enforce traditional norms, secret societies frequently serve as an important aspect of community organization and as significant adjuncts to an often commensurately weak central political system.

The political functions of secret societies are especially well developed in West Africa. Among the Kpelle of Liberia (Fulton 1972; Gibbs 1962, 1965; Welmers 1949) the secular political authority of the chiefs is strongly supplemented by their position within the internal hierarchy of grades of the secret Poro society, an association that is also a fundamental aspect of traditional social and political organization in neighboring Sierra Leone (Little 1965/1966). In addition to serving as a potent "advisory" body to the holders of secular political office, Poro acts as a policing agent, as a secret judiciary, and as a covert channel for diplomatic negotiations between tribal groups in potential conflict. As in many secret societies the corporate identity of the group is personified by representations of a powerful supernatural being, known in Kpelle as Aleka, the "Forest Thing," which in public takes the form of an impressively masked dancer, entirely covered by an elaborate raffia or cloth costume. Only the initiated can look on Aleka. To announce his arrival in a village, usually for the purpose of calling a meeting of the Poro society, the voice of the Forest Thing is represented by a distinctive type of music. At the sound of it all females and uninitiated boys must rush indoors and shut themselves tightly in their houses. Women who catch sight of the Forest Thing will reportedly die. Uninitiated boys who see it are removed from the community at once to begin Poro initiation.

The purpose of this terrifying public display is to reinforce fear and respect for the Forest Thing and for the secret society identified with it. This in turn strengthens the role of Poro as an agency for social control closely linked to the Kpelle political system. Those who violate the rules of Kpelle society, by committing incest, for example, know that they risk trial before a Poro court with the Forest Thing itself sitting as judge.

In Sierra Leone the authority of the elders in the Poro society is strengthened by their control of powerful "medicines" or charms, which they can manipulate to bring prosperity or disaster, sickness, and death, and by their closeness to the spirits of deceased members of Poro, who are believed to be intermediaries between people and God. In both Liberia and Sierra Leone Poro fulfills a dual political function: membership in the society reinforces the power of political leaders, and at the same time reliance on the secret society for the punishment of deviant behavior deflects resentment from secular political officeholders.

Initiation into Poro follows the pattern almost universally characteristic of the ritual by which new members are inducted into secret societies, one in which the initiate abandons his former status and assumes a new social identity. First, the Kpelle initiate is removed from the community at the impressionable time of early adolescence. Boys used to be secluded for several years in "bush schools" located in remote forest clearings; now the period of initiation has been shortened. Noninitiates, including the members of a boy's own family, are led to believe literally that he dies and is reborn, being first devoured by Aleka and then disgorged as an initiate with a new status in the community, new obligations and rights.

Scars cut into his back, explained as marks of the teeth of the Forest Thing as the initiate is disgorged at his rebirth, identify him to the community as a member of Poro.

This period of seclusion is important not only for training the initiate in the secrets (all initiates learn a sign language, for example) and responsibilities of Poro membership but also for preparing him to assume the role of an adult member of his society. While in the forest he is instructed in farming and craft work, in warmaking, in sexual technique and the proper way to treat women, in the deferential comportment appropriate when he is in the presence of a chief or other person of high status, in tribal history, and in the supernatural significance that the Kpelle attach to nearly all aspects of their culture.

Although women's secret societies are, generally, a less widespread phenomenon, probably because of women's subordinate social position and usually more demanding household responsibilities, the women of the Kpelle and of neighboring ethnic groups in West Africa also have a secret society, called Sande. The process of a girl's admission into Sande parallels that of the boys' initiation ritual. Young girls are secluded. Instruction in their sexual, economic, and social responsibilities as adult females is also combined with ritual observances that function to endow their cuturally ascribed activities with an aura of sanctity. The process by which members are recruited into both Kpelle secret societies, the ritual means by which such associations reinforce awareness of traditional social norms, and the capacity of the societies to punish those who defy those norms serve as a powerful source of conservatism in nearly all aspects of Kpelle culture. Whoever challenges the rules set by tradition risks unimaginably terrifying supernatural punishment. As a part of Poro initiation in Sierra Leone initiates were forced to witness the excruciatingly brutal slaughter of fowl as an object lesson of what might happen to them if they defied Poro.

The influence of secret societies on the traditional political systems of West Africa is well documented. They have served as a basis of traditional political stability, for organizing warfare (and later, for mobilizing resistance to colonialist domination). Where societies like Poro retain their power, it will be interesting to observe their impact on the structure and function of the new national governments of the region.

In the United States the effect of secret societies on community organization and on the political system has often been equally evident. The Ku Klux Klan provides a recent vivid example (see Chalmers 1965; Randel 1965). The secrecy surrounding membership, the efforts to inspire fear and awe through reliance on dramatic rituals, the burning of fiery crosses, and the wearing of flowing white robes and pointed hoods all function—as does the KKK's reputation for violence—to create an environment of fear that contributes to the power of the organization as an extralegal agency for social control. Political figures in the U.S. South and in other parts of the country have often drawn added strength from their member-

"In the United States the effect of secret societies on community organization and on the political system has often been equally evident."

Figure 8-13. An eight-week-old child being "christened" by members of the Ku Klux Klan. (Courtesy of the Library of Congress.)

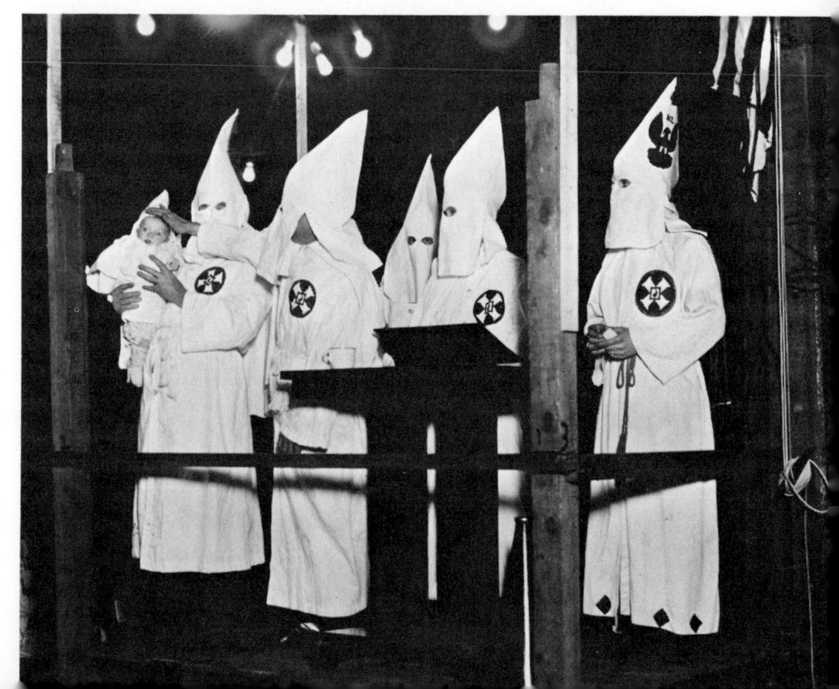

ship in the Klan. Actions threatening to white supremacy—to the whites' economic, social, and political domination—have been punished with beatings and killings carried out by disguised, night-riding Klansmen.

Associations like the Klan and other secret societies in the United States, such as the Masons, the Odd Fellows, and the Shriners—all similar to the Klan in their reliance on ritual secrecy, occult symbols, and fancy costuming but generally more benign in their intended social effect—are not conventionally regarded as aspects of the formal political structure. But their activities, and those of secret societies almost everywhere, must always be taken into account if power relationships in the cultures where they exist are to be accurately understood.

The Role of Associations in Culture Change

Often a rapid increase in reliance on associations as a basis for relationship occurs in situations of accelerated culture change precipitated by radical technological innovations and drastic changes in traditional economic organization. Such innovations frequently cause social changes that make it either undesirable or impossible to rely on kinsmen and other more accustomed sources of support.

Again, Africa provides a good illustration (Little 1957, 1965, 1967, 1972; Soen and De Comarmond 1972). For the last half century or so labor migration in West Africa has been increasing. To acquire the money necessary to pay taxes and to meet their needs for cash to purchase the growing number of goods, especially foreign merchandise available in the market, young West Africans from the more arid north have been leaving their rural homes to seek employment farther south as wage laborers on the plantations that have been established in many of

"... increase in reliance on associations as a basis for relationship occurs in situations of accelerated culture change...."

Figure 8-14. Feminists organize for change. Bella Abzug and Gloria Steinem at the Democratic National Convention. (Stephen Shames, Black Star.)

the forest areas, and as domestic and clerical workers in the growing urban centers. Others travel widely as merchants.

This movement separates the migrants not only geographically but also economically, socially, politically, and emotionally from their families and their home communities. Their kinsmen are no longer available to provide them with material assistance, companionship, and guidance. Familiar sources of supernatural support, ancestral spirits, and other localized deities are also left behind. The resulting sense of alienation and loss is felt especially keenly by Africans accustomed to rely strongly on their kin groups who suddenly find themselves living and working among Europeans and members of other tribal groups with whom they share no common sense of identity and no traditionally sanctioned basis of support. In West Africa, and in other newly developing areas of the world, particularly in Latin America (see Mangin 1965), the result of this absence of traditional organizations and of the need to mobilize for adjustment to rapid cultural change has been an increased dependence on voluntary associations. Often these take the form of mutual aid societies, which serve both temporary migrants and those who have left their homelands permanently.

Frequently, associations are organized on the basis of tribal membership, uniting all those in the vicinity who share a common ethnic identity. Prior to the recent Nigerian civil war the Ibo (Little 1957, 1965; Ottenberg 1955), an ethnic group from the eastern region of the country, had formed tribal unions to protect themselves from harassment and discrimination when they migrated to other parts of Nigeria to work. Members of the unions welcomed new arrivals from the east, assisted them in finding employment and lodging, and gave them counseling, financial aid, and sympathy when they fell ill or lost their jobs. For Ibo who died away from home the tribal association looked after funeral arrangements and the repatriation of their remains. Association meetings were held regularly. Ibo songs and dances were performed, and all members were provided an occasion to maintain and strengthen their close social ties with their fellow tribesmen. Their children, often born far from their parents' homeland, had an opportunity to develop an awareness of their cultural origins and an appreciation of the richness of Ibo traditions and of the importance of keeping alive a sense of their separate tribal identity.

Many of the larger of these tribal associations in Nigeria have become wealthy. They lend money to individual members to start businesses, set up group-owned enterprises, build schools, and provide scholarships for their younger members, often to study abroad. Politically, such associations are also powerful. In many parts of Nigeria they provide the basis for town council organization and function as political pressure groups as well, pressing the government for more schools and roads, improved sanitary facilities, better medical services, and other public works.

The purpose of some voluntary associations is specifically economic. In West Africa truck and bus drivers, dock and plantation workers, and market women all have associations that function primarily to protect their members' economic interests. Yoruba market women's associations in Nigeria try to control the supply of the commodities in which their members deal and to discourage competition in order to keep prices steady and high. Most laborers' associations try to exert control over their members' conditions of work, especially the wages they receive. Equally specific in their economic intent are the savings associations set up in West Africa to help their members to accumulate capital for investment. Often their membership is composed of all persons working in the same office or factory or attending the same school. Sometimes all are related, usually as members of the same clan in the rural area from which they have come. All make fixed contributions to the association's fund at regular intervals. Those who do not comply are fined. Then the total amount is pooled and made available to each individual member in rotation.

Other associations are formed in West Africa, mostly in urban areas, to fulfill what are overtly defined as essentially recreational functions (see Little 1967). Entertainments are organized to raise funds that are used to provide still further entertainment and recreation. But beyond their formally stated goals, these associations often provide their members with important economic, social, and emotional support, serving as a protected context for acquiring new economic behaviors—saving, budgeting, punctuality, adjustment to new routines, and other habits necessary for adaptation to an urban economic scene based on a market economy—providing a means of making useful contacts and establishing and regulating new close interpersonal ties to replace those the migrants have left behind in the rural areas from which they have come and serving generally to facilitate their members' cultural adaptation to urban ways.

Comparisons between West Africa and the United States are apt because of the similarity of the cultural conditions that appear to foster the development of voluntary associations in both places, and wherever else they occur: changes in traditional patterns for making a living and consequent changes in habitat—peasants from the rural areas of West Africa going to new jobs in unfamiliar, rapidly changing cultural settings near or in the new West African cities; people from the farms of Europe and from the rural United States moving to the industrialized urban centers of the Northeast, Midwest, and West. In each instance migration and new kinds of work in a new setting have resulted in a breakdown of traditional groupings based on kinship and homogeneous community and the isolation of the individual or of the nuclear family group in an unfamiliar society, often in an alien culture. Alternatives to the support no longer provided by traditional social groups must be found. Voluntary associations often provide them, offering economic and political protection, companionship and entertainment, freedom from loneliness and boredom, "useful contacts," and perhaps most important a sheltered context for experimentation with the innovations in traditional behavior—new economic practices, new social forms, and new means of political and religious expression—that are necessary for adjustment to a new cultural setting.

"... establishing and regulating new close interpersonal ties to replace those the migrants have left behind. . . ."

Figure 8-15. Cesar Chavez has successfully used similar techniques in assisting farm workers in their struggle to unionize. (George Ballis, Black Star.)

Summary

The various social groupings based on kinship that typically provide the basic organizing principle in the life of the individual and in the organization of the community are frequently complemented by various sorts of associations, based principally on recognition of common interests and an agreement to cooperate, which provide the individual with useful alternative sources of relationship and the community with a significant aspect of its social, economic, and political organization.

The smallest associations are those formed between bond friends or on the basis of ritual kinship. Associations based on age categories are loosely formed in many societies. Among the herding peoples of East Africa, however, the various component groups within a complex system of age grades are paramount in structuring the movement of males through the life cycle and are a major element in the structuring and operation of the political system.

Typically, the rituals that accompany entry into such associations provide a means of dramatizing to the initiates and to the community the responsibilities attendant on the new status they have acquired and serve as a useful means of internalizing both the rules of the association and the norms of the larger society.

Voluntary associations point up the complementary role of associations to those based on kinship and illustrate the particular value of such alternate bases for group affiliation when changing technoeconomic and social conditions diminish the role of the kinship system as a primary determinant of the individual's status and of community organization. More than substitutes for something lost, such associations are often valuable agents of cultural adaptation.

Suggested Readings

There is no single readily accessible general work on associations; Bradfield's two-volume *A Natural History of Associations* is prohibitively expensive, for example. However, Anderson's "Voluntary Associations in History" does an excellent job of placing this important form of social grouping in the perspective of sociocultural evolution. Thompson's "A Theory of Instrumental Social Networks" is also useful. See also Ross's "Toward a Reconstruction of Voluntary Association Theory." For a summary analysis from the standpoint of a prominent social anthropologist see Chapter 10 of Bohannan's *Social Anthropology.*

The most general work on bond friendship is Tegnaeus's somewhat inaccessible *Blood-Brothers.* In addition to the several important sources already cited in the text see Freeman's *Neighbors: The Social Contract in a Castillian Hamlet,* Gilmore's "Friendship in Fuenmayor: Patterns of Integration in an Atomistic Society," and Stricken and Greenfield's *Structure and Process in Latin American Patronage, Clientage, and Power Systems.* Boissevain's *Friends of Friends: Networks, Manipulators, and Coalitions* is also valuable.

On age-based associations see Bischofberger's *The Generation Classes of the Zanaki,* Hamer's "Sidame Generational Class Cycles, a Political Gerontocracy," and Wilson's *Good Company: A Study of Nyakyusa Age Villages.* For a classic account of the workings of an East African age-grade system see Chapter 6 of Evans-Pritchard's *The Nuer.*

Initiation as a form of ritual behavior is considered in Chapter 12. For more detailed analysis of the functions of initiatory rites see Gluckman's "Les Rites de Passage" in his *Essays in the Ritual of Social Relations.* See also Kloos's "Female Initiation Among the Maroni River Caribs," Young's *Initiation Ceremonies: A Cross Cultural Study of Status Dramatization,* Strathern's "Male Initiation in New Guinea Highlands Society," and a classic by Van Gennep, *The Rites of Passage.*

Unfortunately, many of the sources in the literature on secret societies are also not readily available. For more on secret societies in Africa see Watkins's "The West African 'Bush School'" and Morton-Williams's "The Yoruba Ogboni Cult in Oyo." A good recent account of the structure and function of a secret society in the United States is Chalmers's *Hooded Americanism: The First Century of the Ku Klux Klan, 1865–1965.*

Voluntary associations have been extensively studied in Africa, particularly by Little; see especially his *West African Urbanization: A Study of Voluntary Associations in Social Change,* "Voluntary Associations in Urban Life: A Case Study of Adaptation," "Voluntary Associations and Social Mobility Among West African Women," and "Urbanization and Regional Associations: Their Paradoxical Function." Another important source on Africa is Soen and De Comarmond's "Savings Associations Among the Bamilèkè: Traditional and Modern Cooperation in South West Cameroon." For some comparisons from other areas see Bruner's "Batak Ethnic Associations in Three Indonesian Cities," Wu's fascinating "To Kill Three Birds with One Stone: The Rotating Credit Associations of the Papua New Guinea Chinese," and Mangin's "The Role of Regional Associations in the Adaptation of Rural Migrants to Cities in Peru."

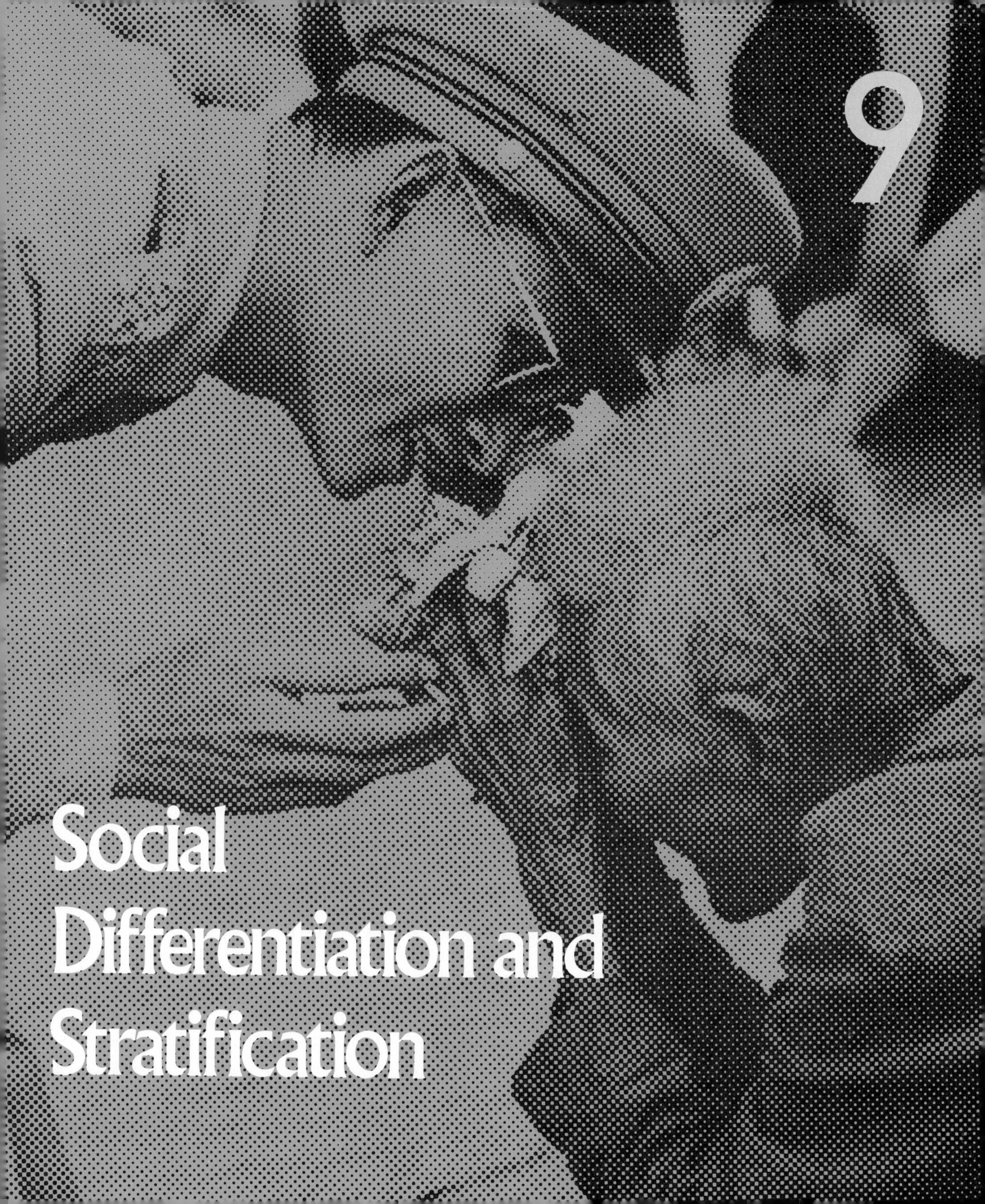

9

Social Differentiation and Stratification

PEOPLE in every culture are socially differentiated and categorized on the basis of such things as physical appearance, personality, or skill in particular technological, economic, social, political, or ideological roles. Those who are more skilled or who possess some other admired attribute are treated as more important or socially valuable and are granted a larger share of available rewards.

In most technologically less-developed societies—among nearly all hunter-gatherers and most primitive farmers, wherever there is lacking the technoeconomic specialization that results in the formation of groups set apart by differences in their productive roles—social relations are egalitarian; all work and whatever is produced are shared equally. Such status differentiation as there is is limited to individuals or, occasionally, to a few kin groups. If degrees of social superiority are recognized, a system of ranking prevails.

Ranking

Most of the peoples of Polynesia, for example, have elaborate systems for ranking individuals in terms of differences in their social position. Every family in Samoa has the right to claim a hereditary title. Those who hold such titles are spoken to in a special language of respect appropriate to their position. If they are of very high rank they are shown elaborate deference on certain ritual occasions. The etiquette of passing around the kava can be as complex as the protocol for the seating chart of a White House dinner. But there are no Samoan social classes, no groups of families whose control of productive resources permits them to dominate the flow of goods and privilege in their favor. Rather, there are ranked categories of individuals principally distinguishable from one another by their relative prestige. The prerogatives of status differences are largely ceremonial.

In such societies high-status persons have limited exploitative power, and the often impressive trappings of their position are rarely accompanied by significant differences in wealth. In fact, a notable attribute of such forms of ranking is that high-status persons can often achieve, maintain, or enhance their social position only by giving away the goods they are able to mobilize, thus regularly depleting the accumulated wealth that might otherwise serve as the material base for the greater and more lasting distinctions in economic position that could evolve into a more permanent system of social stratification.

Among the Indians of the North Pacific coast of North America, for example, individual gradations in rank were based on both descent and possession of the "spirit power" to accumulate valuable exchange goods. A man's claim to retain the privileges of his high social status—special titles, a claim to a show of deference and respect from others, a place of honor at feasts, the right to receive valuable gifts, and so on—was periodically tested in status-asserting, or status-validating, intervillage ceremonial feasts called Potlatches (see Chapter 5), at which he was expected to bestow on his guests or publicly destroy large quantities of property (see McFeat 1966). When, for instance, two chiefs claimed the same honorary title, one would give a Potlatch to assert his claim. His rival from another settlement would then be obliged to try to outdo him by reciprocating with an even more lavish ceremonial display of his ability to accumulate wealth. Finally, one or the other would have assembled and given away or destroyed more property than his competitor could possibly equal. Then the one who was outdone had no alternative but to withdraw his assertion of high status until he could

"... individual gradations in rank were based on both descent and possession of the 'spirit power'. . . ."

Figure 9-1. Among Indians of the Northwest Pacific coast the right to display totem poles was a privilege of rank. (Bureau of Indian Affairs.)

again acquire the wealth necessary to back it up.

In contrast, in more clearly stratified societies high-status persons and groups need not dissipate such a large portion of their wealth to maintain their prestige. Rather, by continuously accumulating wealth they consolidate their superior social position and use their control over productive resources as a means of both exerting and reinforcing their political power. Frequently such ruling groups are also in charge of the religious system. By manipulating access to supernatural resources, they can usually assure that the prevailing ideology sanctions both their privileged status and the system of stratification that maintains it.

The Emergence of Social Stratification

The emergence of a system of social stratification nearly always follows the attainment of a level of technological development sufficiently productive to allow for the accumulation of a surplus of subsistence goods, which in turn permits greater technoeconomic specialization and diversification. Social groups develop whose differences from one another are initially determined by their distinctive roles in the system of production. Some groups are farmers. Others are full-time craft workers—carpenters, potters, or workers of stone, metal, leather, and other materials. Still others are tradespeople. Some are political leaders, public, and private administrators, police, and warriors. Some are religious specialists. Those figuratively at the top are mostly those with the power to control the

"Those figuratively at the top are mostly those with the power to control the society's technology and economic system. . . ."
Figure 9-2. The King of Thailand receives the homage of a subject literally beneath him. (Embassy of Thailand.)

". . . as land, waterworks. . . ."
Figure 9-3. Irrigated rice fields, Java. (National Archives.)

society's technology and economic system through the ownership or right to regulate the allocation of such productive goods as land, waterworks, or industry, or who dominate the economic organization, especially that aspect of the system that allows for the differential distribution of excess wealth—by such means as slavery, plunder, or the manipulation of systems of rents and taxation, market exchange, and usury.

In many ancient societies, systems of stratification ranged down from aristocracy through several strata of commoners to freedmen, serfs, and slaves; with each group in the hierarchy enjoying inferior life chances to all the groups ranked above it. Often, as with caste systems, differences in economic position were reinforced by religious concepts of purity and pollution (or of greater or lesser physical, social, psychological, or moral worth) associated with different occupations, thus rigidifying the ranked separation between groups. Through warfare the same system, with the conquerors politically and militarily dominant, was extended to other peoples as well.

With the partial exception of systems of sexual stratification, differences in stratum ranking are manifested, and group solidarity is strengthened, by the avoidance of marriage, of sharing food, and of other behaviors indicative of status equality between persons culturally assigned to inferior ranks. Although most close social contact occurs only between members of each ranked group, some social climbing is occasionally allowed; but only on an individual basis. In other words, a few people move up or down, but the system holds steady. An equally important attribute of all such ranked systems is that those culturally assigned an inferior social position generally perceive themselves as exploited. And they resist—in ways that range from stealing or running away to organized struggle for revolutionary societal reorganization.

Once set in motion, a system of stratification is usually fundamental to the organization of all technoenvironmental and technoeconomic relationships (by controlling the differential access to productive resources and the unequal distribution of wealth); to the structure and function of all other social groups, particularly kin groups; to the operation of the political system, especially because position in a ranked hierarchy of groups is a determinant of access to power; and to the religious system. (Those at the top of the status heap are also usually in charge at the apex of the ecclesiastical hierarchy.) For the individual, membership in a particular social stratum has a most profound effect on his or her life chances, ascribing a position of relatively privileged access to, or exclusion from, the opportunity to share in the wealth, prestige, and power available in the society.

Today most systems of stratification are based on one of four principal forms: caste ranking, social class, ethnic identity, or sex.

"For the individual, membership in a particular social stratum has a most profound effect on his or her life chances. . . ."

Figure 9-4. A working-class street scene, Montreal. (National Film Board of Canada.)

Caste

Of all systems of social stratification, those based on caste are both most complex and most rigid. A caste system can be defined as an all-encompassing organization of birth-ascribed, hierarchically ranked, closed corporate groups, each set apart from all others in the system on the basis of technoeconomic, social, political, and ideological criteria. Although caste is present in a number of societies, it is particularly prominent in India, where it is the traditional basis of organization of the entire society of the Hindu majority.

Caste systems are characterized by the following five fundamental and interrelated attributes:

1. Caste status determines the differential relationship of group members to the technology and to the economic system. This means that one or more high-caste groups control the characteristically inequitable allocation of the major productive goods, especially farmland. The work performed by the members of all other castes—farm labor, transport, marketing, house building, pottery making, scavenging, street cleaning, and so on—is also determined by lopsided workloads that favor those higher up in the caste hierarchy. The goods and services produced by each caste are exchanged for the products of other castes on an asymmetrical redistributive basis. Those lower down get less.

2. As a consequence of their shared technoeconomic position all the members of each caste share a generally similar social position within the larger system of hierarchically ranked castes. This shared, separate, ranked social identity is reinforced by caste endogamy, by residential separation, and by distinctive social behavior and "life-style."

3. The common technoeconomic and social position of all members is complemented by their participation in a common political system that regulates relations between members and represents the caste in its relations with others.

4. All the distinctive features that set each caste apart within the overall ranked order of the caste system are sanctioned by an ideology that assigns to each caste a separate ritual position, and by a series of ritual observances that intensify awareness of separate group identity. Central to these beliefs and practices are concepts of ritual purity and the fear that violation of the rules of the system will result in punishment by the supernatural.

5. Those of higher caste are generally more enthusiastic about the system than are those of lower caste, whom it exploits.

Caste	Percent of Total Population
Bhumihar Brahman	16.3
Funeral Brahman	0.2
Vaishnava	2.8
Confectioner	3.0
Herdsman	11.4
Garland-maker	2.8
Barber	8.2
Potter	3.1
Hindu weaver	7.8
Carpenter	11.5
Goldsmith	1.9
Merchant	4.2
Jugi weaver	0.9
Oil presser	3.7
Rajbanshi	2.2
Chandal fisherman	5.5
Patuni boatman	0.6
Scavenger	9.0
Leatherworker	4.9
	100

"Caste status determines the differential relationship of group members to the technology and to the economic system."

Figure 9-5. A simplified model of caste stratification in a Bengal village. Eleven distinct ranks further crosscut the elaborate caste hierarchy of this Indian village. (After Nichols.)

Although the origins of caste systems are not precisely clear, their association with a level of technological development that allows for the concentration of control of productive goods in the hands of politicoreligious leaders is invariable. Often this domination appears to have been achieved by warfare, as in the conquest of South India by high-caste Hindus from the north, the conquest and subordination of Bantu farmers and Pygmy hunters by some East African herdsmen, and the conquest of American Indians and West Africans that has resulted in the castelike organization of parts of society in the United States, where the whites' control of the technology, their superior economic and social position, their domination of the political system, and the concept of their racial superiority sanction their superior "caste" status and prohibit equal-status interaction with nonwhites.

Wherever the higher castes' control of the technology and economy holds, as it does in rural India and in the rural U.S. South and elsewhere in the United States, the other aspects of the system also remain intact. Once changes in the fundamental technoeconomic arrangements begin, the attendant differences in the rank ordering of groups with regard to social position, access to political power, and ritual status also begin to change.

Caste in India

In the Hindu caste system all persons are relegated to one of four hierarchically ranked social categories, castes or varnas, each of which is principally identified with a particular occupation. Those "outside" the system, as it is ideally conceived (as opposed to the real situation in which all groups are functionally integrated), are the "outcastes," the more than eighty-five million untouchables. Certain of the still tribally organized aboriginal peoples are also outside the caste hierarchy. The highest-ranking caste is that of the Brahmans, a status associated with the priesthood, although in fact the majority have traditionally been landlords. Then come the Kshatryias, or warriors; the Vaishyas, who are tradesmen; the Shudras, servants; and finally, at the bottom of the hierarchy, the still mostly landless descendants of slaves, the "outcaste" untouchables—or Harijans (God's people), to use Gandhi's euphemism (Gough 1971, 1973; Mahar 1972; Mencher 1974a).

As an idealized construct, all of Hindu society is organized into this single ranked set of interdependent divisions. In practice

"Wherever the higher castes' control of the technology and economy holds. . . ."

Figure 9-6. Low-caste Indian laborers unloading wheat. (Government of India Information Services.)

all castes are internally stratified and territorially circumscribed, usually limited to a particular stratum within the local population and composed of a cluster of extended families related on the basis of common occupation and shared descent. It is these smaller groups, or subcastes, that function most often as corporate groups, providing the continuously operating units within the local caste-based technoeconomic, social, political, and religious system.

Because all technoeconomic roles are ascribed on the basis of caste affiliation, usually (and despite the Indian constitution's prohibition against caste discrimination) the individual quite literally cannot survive except by complying with the requirements of his or her caste status. Although most caste members no longer fill the specific technological roles hereditarily defined as appropriate to their caste, they are still usually engaged in activities defined as appropriately analogous to those roles. Thus, for example, an untouchable may no longer be working as a farm laborer, digging graves, or cleaning the streets of his native village but may have become a latrine attendant in Bombay. Or a family of Brahmans may have leased out their rural landholdings and given up their ritually sanctioned priestly occupation for banking.

In addition to the external manifestations of caste identity that are often a direct result of the caste's ascribed technoeconomic position—not only occupation, but also residential location and the quality of household furnishings, dress (in some areas untouchables were not permitted to wear sandals or shirts in the presence of high-caste Hindus), and other material clues to caste status—the perpetuation of each caste as an integral group separate from all others is reinforced by a series of highly formalized, ritually sanctioned, and carefully observed patterns of action and avoidance. These involve, first, egalitarian interaction among members of the same caste or, more accurately, the same subcaste, and, second, the strict prohibition of equal-status contacts with the members of other castes. This dichotomy is most strikingly represented by avoidances concerning the sharing of food (commensality) and the observance of caste endogamy.

To accept food from or to eat with a person of inferior caste ranking is symbolically to jeopardize the superior social and ritual position of the entire caste—with all that such superiority implies in terms of greater economic advantages, social prestige, favorable political position, and more exalted ritual status. Everything that assures the superior life chances of members of the higher caste is threatened. As the lower-caste person and the food he or she touches are both "unclean," the greater ritual purity of the higher caste is also endangered. If such polluting contact occurs accidentally, the higher-caste person who has been defiled must be ritually cleansed, usually by dousing with water. Objects handled by an untouchable, even a well on which his shadow has fallen, may be regarded as defiled. The observance of caste endogamy functions even more strongly to reinforce differences in caste ranking. Marrying within the caste emphasizes the equal-status relationship of all members (and for the Brahman it assures a united aristocracy). Conversely, the avoidance of marriage with members of all other castes reinforces caste apartness and functions to consolidate caste-held economic advantages and to prevent loss of social status, the literal contamination of the caste's ancestry, and ritual pollution.

There is a significant distinction between this rigid adherence to the rule of caste endogamy and the traditionally weak prohibition against sexual relations between higher-caste men and lower-caste women. In this instance, as paternity cannot be proved and it is the woman who has the baby, no risk to the higher caste is incurred. Furthermore, the sexual exploitation of lower-caste women by higher-caste men symbolically reinforces the dominance of the males' caste status and emphasizes the obligatory submissiveness of members of the lower caste in economic and political (as well as sexual) affairs. In contrast, higher-caste women are rigidly protected from sexual relations with lower-caste men. Any challenge to this prohibition is characteristically perceived as a grave threat to the social superiority and ritual purity of the higher caste and is countered swiftly and violently.

Thus, caste identity is continuously underscored both by egalitarian internal economic, social, political, and ritual interaction and by the careful avoidance of all equal-status contact with the members of other castes, with heaviest emphasis, of course, on the avoidance of social and ritual contamination from castes lower in the hierarchy. Observance of these rules constantly revalidates every person's caste status. Violation of the rules may be met with shaming, physical punishment, "outcasting," or even death, depending on the seriousness of the threat to the caste's position. In 1968 forty-two untouchables in the South Indian state of Tamil Nadu defied the authority of their high-caste Hindu landlords over a wage raise. They were burned alive. Their murderers were later acquitted by a Brahman-dominated court (Gamre 1975; Shivaraman 1973).

Within each caste economic, social, moral, and ceremonial relations between members are regulated by the caste panchayat, a council of acknowledged caste leaders who serve as the guardians of caste rules. The panchayat is usually linked structurally to the larger, community-wide authority system.

Hindu theology sanctions the caste system and provides guidance in the actions to maintain it (see Weber 1946 and 1958). Those of high caste are believed (especially by other high-caste Hindus) to be religiously most pure and must remain so by avoiding contamination through contact with the members of lower castes. Lower-caste persons should know and keep their place, refraining from polluting their next reincarnation (see DeVos 1967; Isaacs 1965). As already indicated, avoidance of such contamination is most typically expressed by the refusal to accept food from those of inferior caste.

For example, ideas on pollution in Rampura, a Hindu village in South India (Srinivas 1959), are related both to occupa-

In consequence of many sinful acts committed with his body, a man becomes in the next birth something inanimate, in consequence of sins committed by speech, a bird, and in consequence of mental sins he is reborn in a low caste....Those who committed mortal sins, having passed during large numbers of years through dreadful hells, obtain, after the expiration of that term of punishment, the following births. The slayer of a Brahmin enters the womb of a dog, a pig, an ass, a camel, a cow, a goat, a sheep, a deer, a bird, a Kandala, and a Pukhasa. . . . A Brahmin who steals the gold of a Brahmin shall pass a thousand times through the bodies of spiders, snakes, lizards, of aquatic animals and of destructive Pukhasas. . . . Men who delight in doing hurt become carnivorous animals; those who eat forbidden food, worms; thieves, creatures consuming their own kind. . . . For stealing grain a man becomes a rat; . . . for stealing a horse, a tiger; for stealing fruits and roots, a monkey; for stealing a woman, a bear; for stealing cattle, a he-goat.

"Hindu theology sanctions the caste system. . . ."

Figure 9-7. The Law of Karma. Past, present, and future existence is determined by the Law. The caste status of individuals is determined by their acts in former incarnations. Present acts determine caste status in the next reincarnation. (From *The Laws of Manu,* cited in Noss 1970:107.)

tional specialization and to caste differences in dietary customs. Both are closely linked with Hindu religion. In Rampura, members of the Besta caste, fishermen, are contaminated because they kill fish. The Korana, who are swineherds, are polluted because they come into close contact with a dirty animal. The Agasa washermen are ritually unclean because they handle soiled clothes, including articles contaminated with menstrual blood. The barber's touch is defiling because he touches hair and nails after they have been separated from the body.

Because killing is a sin, vegetable food is superior to all meats. Brahmans are vegetarians; they are therefore ritually cleaner than all others. Among meats beef is ritually the most contaminated because the cow is a sacred animal that no Hindu must harm. Therefore among meat eaters those who eat beef are considered to be the most unclean. As cattle are never killed by Hindus, already dead cows are used as food only by untouchables, who are thus further despised both as beef eaters and as consumers of carrion. Pork is unclean because pigs sometimes eat human excrement, people who eat pork are still less contaminated than those who eat beef, and so on.

A high-caste person contaminated by contact with someone of inferior caste can and must cleanse himself ritually. After being shaved by his barber, for example, the Rampura Brahman must purify the spot where he has sat by washing it with a solution of cow dung. Then he must himself be thoroughly doused with water, clothes and all.

Growing numbers, especially among the most disadvantaged—the still poorly organized untouchables in particular—seek to eradicate the caste system entirely. Those better off frequently try only to improve their own position within it. The almost ever-present, but always slight, possibility of change probably contributes to the perpetuation of caste as a successful exploitative system.

For although the Indian caste system is extraordinarily rigid (absolutely so, as it is idealized by Brahmanic writers), it is not wholly without flexibility. Although caste and caste subdivisions are ranked hierarchically, few Hindus are ever agreed on all specifics of the ranking system. The precise hierarchical status of particular castes is frequently in dispute. Those who wish to avoid further exploitation and/or to improve their socioeconomic position by participating in activities not traditionally regarded as appropriate to their caste can almost always argue that a really proper interpretation of the history of their caste would reveal that they are legitimately entitled to the higher ranking they seek to acquire by altering their behavior.

To gain the right to engage in materially more rewarding occupations, to enhance their prestige, and to enlarge on their political rights, caste members frequently try to change their status in the hierarchy by imitating their superiors, altering their dietary habits, reinterpreting their myths of origin, and trying to get higher-caste persons to recognize the ritual significance of these changes by accepting food from them or in other ways responding with greater respect, or at least with less abhorrence. Occasionally, such protests are successful. But change occurs slowly; the improvement achieved in caste position is usually minor and is only gradually and grudgingly recognized by persons of higher caste.

For the untouchables, achieving social mobility is most difficult of all. For example, several years ago the Camars, an outcaste group of leatherworkers living in a village in Uttar Pradesh, North India, tried to improve their caste status—with good reasons (Cohn 1955; Lewis 1965). Traditionally, the

Camars are excluded from the right to own land, to hold political office, or even to participate in the political system. They must step off the road, bow, and salute when a higher-caste landowner passes. They should speak to a higher-caste person only when spoken to. They must always seat themselves at a lower level than a person of higher caste; they cannot share food with higher-caste persons; they must even use separate eating and drinking utensils. Some high-caste people believe Camars should be prohibited from drawing water from the local well.

In an effort to improve their position the Camars tried to change their name, which had come to have abusive connotations: "dirty as a Camar," "black as a Camar," and so on. Camar men refused to carry manure. They persuaded their wives to give up preparing dung cakes for their landlord's kitchen fires. To impress their higher-caste neighbors they announced publicly that they had outlawed the eating of beef. They tried to form a political action group.

They were not very successful. Camar who announced they would no longer carry manure were chased from the village. People refused to believe they had really stopped eating beef. Most refused to call them by their new name. Their efforts to exercise their political rights were repressed when they were unable to meet the court costs necessary to defend them. Their landlords and employers threatened them with economic reprisals. One of their leaders was murdered.

Later the men who had been driven out of the village were allowed to return, and their wives were permitted to give up making dung cakes. By great effort they finally attained very little: a slight reinterpretation of their ascribed occupational status that may in time make them seem somewhat less ritually repugnant but will do little to improve the material conditions of their lives. And as a system caste in Uttar Pradesh has remained intact.

For the vast majority of Indians who will continue to live in rural villages far from the few slowly industrializing centers, the caste system is likely to persist as the major determinant of individual and community organization. As population growth continues to outdistance the increase in agricultural productivity, competitiveness may increase. It seems likely that the unequal access to productive resources, consumption goods, and other rewards that is fostered by the Indian caste system will be intensified. If antagonism between low-caste Hindus and untouchables can be effectively manipulated by the Brahmans at the top, the divisiveness necessary to the function of caste as an ex-

"As population growth continues to outdistance the increase in agricultural productivity. . . ."

Figure 9-8. Explaining an intrauterine contraceptive device, Aurangabad, India. (United Nations.)

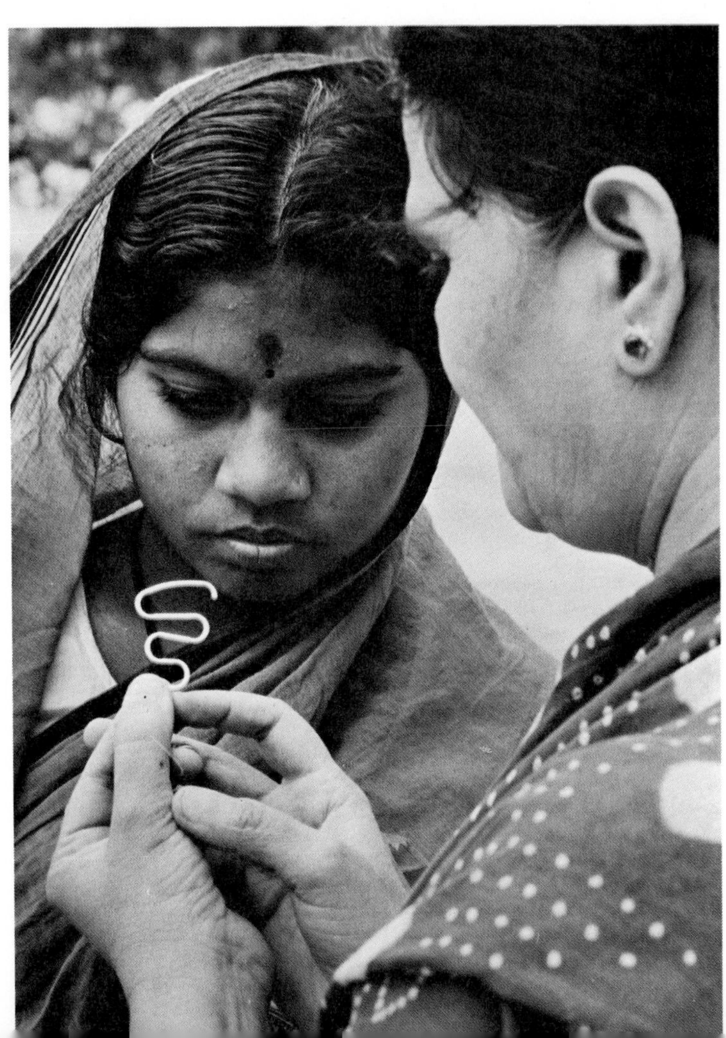

"Although most people die as members of the same class into which they were born. . . ."
Figure 9-9. American family living in the hills of Garrett County, Maryland. (Courtesy of the Library of Congress.)

ploitative system may be sustained. As caste continues to foster separation among those it oppresses, and as Indian population size continues to outdistance increases in the food supply, competition for diminishing resources is likely to increase. If so, caste-based barriers to economic, political, and social mobility may become even more rigid.

Class

Stratified systems based on class are similar to caste systems in the prominence of technoeconomic position as a determinant of social status, group rank, and access to political power. They contrast with caste systems in that membership is not solely birth ascribed, or based on descent. Although most people die as members of the same class into which they were born, some move down or up in the class hierarchy, and either way such movement is generally regarded as legitimate. Losing class status causes nothing more than sympathy; moving up is acceptable as long as those who do so are quiet about it and don't "push."

An improvement in economic position, that is, an increase by whatever means of ownership or control of productive goods, is an almost invariable prerequisite to upward mobility in the class system. Conversely, people who have lost the economic position that supports their class status usually begin to slip in the class hierarchy as well, principally because they can no longer afford the life-style that validates their claim to high status and makes association with them economically, socially, and politically rewarding.

The generalization that class systems differ from those based on caste in that only the latter possess corporate structure should not be overemphasized. Although it is true that classes usually lack the formal internal organization particularly characteristic of localized Hindu subcastes with their regularly designated leaders, caste courts, and so on, all of which facilitate collective group action, the difference is still relative. Classes, especially elites, also often have acknowledged leaders who take action—by exerting economic or political pressure, for example—in defense of what they interpret as the special interests (or privileges) of their class.

Class systems are most highly developed and most rigid among advanced farming peoples, where the level of productivity is sufficiently high to allow for the emergence of significant inequalities in the distribution of goods and services, and thus of differences in economic and political power. The early agriculturally based societies of parts of East Asia, the Middle East, North Africa, and the Americas all had quite rigidly structured class systems. And so, of course, did preindustrial Europe.

In those parts of Europe where the technology is still based primarily on agriculture—in Spain, southern Italy, and Greece, for example—rural class systems in which high social status is based primarily on the ownership of farmland have remained quite inflexible.

Elsewhere on the continent, and elsewhere in the world for that matter, there tends to be a general correlation between the extent to which a nation has shifted or is shifting from an agricultural to an industrial base and the rigidity and "shape" of the class system. In countries where the class system is still closely linked to ownership of land, the system typically takes the form of a pyramid, with a large lower class, much of it landless; a small middle class; and a miniscule ruling elite or upper class, whose members not only are owners of most of the land but also control the majority of other productive resources.

". . . principally because they can no longer afford the life-style that validates their claim to high status. . . ."

Figure 9-10. An ivy-covered mansion in Toronto's exclusive Rosedale section. (National Film Board of Canada.)

Class Stratification in Southern Spain

The system of social class stratification found in a rural area of southern Spain provides a good example of how a society-wide system of class stratification based on land ownership works at the local level, and of the economic, social, political, and ideological forces that contribute to the relative rigidity of such a system. In Alcalá de la Sierra, a farming community in the mountains of Andalusia, almost everyone gets a living directly or almost directly from working the land, or that part of it that is arable (Pitt-Rivers 1961).

Olive trees grow on the terraced hillsides. Where the topography is too rocky for terracing, sheep, goats, and cows are grazed, wild grasses are gathered, and cork is periodically cut from the trees. The more level land, where irrigation is possible, is used for the intensive cultivation of fruits, walnuts, vegetables, and corn.

All farmland is divided into holdings that range in size from two-acre plots to single properties of more than a thousand acres. There are about four hundred families in Alcalá. In accordance with a pattern that still prevails throughout the Spanish social class system (see Lisoń-Tolosana 1966) stratification within the community is based principally on the amount of land owned. In Alcalá de la Sierra twenty families own two thirds of all the usable land. Those with the most extensive holdings frequently live elsewhere, away from Alcalá, and let their lands entirely to tenants. Some landowners work their own farms. The smaller properties of the majority are inadequate to support even their owners, who must work as laborers on the farms of their more affluent neighbors or in the local town, where a few jobs are available at the small textile factory, at several mills, and at the two olive presses. A few land-poor farmers supplement their income by working as carpenters and at other small craft occupations, by helping out in the village shops, or by serving as domestics in the households of the few "ricos" who still live in the community.

At the bottom of the ranked hierarchy of social classes in Alcalá are the propertyless beggars. Slightly above them are those who either are without land or own so little of it that they must work as domestic servants, as farm laborers, or in the mills. Next up in the social class system are the tenant farmers who work for absentee landlords. Then come the small landowners who work their own lands. In addition to the few moderately well-to-do farmers, the small middle class in Alcalá is composed of the shopkeepers, the physician, the veterinarian, a few minor civil functionaries—the secretary of justice, the postmaster, the teacher—and the priest.

Above this small middle class is an even smaller group of upper-class landowners whose property holdings are so extensive and productive that some can live without working at all, supported entirely by the rents they receive from their tenants.

Although extensive landholdings are traditionally the prime requisite for membership in the small upper class of Alcalá, it is the ownership of substantial productive goods of any form that appears to be the more essential criterion. The owners of the mills, the olive presses, and the textile factory are also members of the upper class; many of them have transferred a portion of their wealth into the traditionally more prestigious ownership of farmland.

The association of each social class in Alcalá with a different technoeconomic position is paralleled by those differences in social status and life-style, power, and access to positions of legitimate authority that are always the distinguishing characteristics of hierarchically ranked societies.

The inferior economic position of the lower classes is manifested in their disproportionate share of the hardest work, in the materially inferior quality of their dwellings, their sparser household furnishings, and their dress, in their more limited access to educational and medical facilities—limitations that affect their life chances physically, economically, and socially—and in their lack of opportunity to participate in making the political decisions that affect the organization of community life.

Not only do all members of the lower classes share an essentially similar disadvantageous status, but also that status tends to be fixed. The opportunities for upward mobility in the class system are sharply limited, both by the economic, social, political, ideological, and psychological correlates of their inferior class position and by the tendency of those above them in the class system to guard their more advantageous position.

The landless and land poor are prevented from improving their class status by the near total impossibility within a relatively stagnant, essentially agricultural technoeconomic system of improving their material position. They cannot seek other work locally because that for which they have the skills is scarce or nonexistent. Labor migration, often to industrial areas outside Spain, is the major alternative. The necessity for poor children to leave school early to help support their families and the low level of aspiration of many peasants conditioned by tradition and economic repression to resign themselves to remaining subordinate, combined with the inadequacy of the local schools, inhibit the rural poor of Alcalá from acquiring the skills needed to improve their economic position.

The middle class in Alcalá is almost as frozen in its position as is the lower class. Most of the farmers to whom the middle-class tradesmen and professionals sell their goods and services live close to the level of subsistence and have little cash. The tradesmen's profits, and those of the professionals, are correspondingly meager. Wealthier farmers can afford to purchase what they cannot produce outside Alcalá in the larger towns where prices are lower and quality and selection are better.

The precariousness of the superior position of the middle class is reflected in the jealousy with which they guard their few privileges. They are careful to maintain close equal-status contacts and to marry only with the members of their own class or, when possible, with persons on the lower fringes of the upper class. The middle-class people in Alcalá are distinguishable from lower-class persons by their superior economic position, by the somewhat less arduous work they do, and by perceptible differences in life-style that are both the consequence of their relatively greater prosperity and the means of perpetuating it by validating their separate and superior social position: slightly more comfortable homes, town clothes and carefully polished shoes worn every day, better-dressed children, more varied diet. The members of the middle class also enjoy a superior level of education and familiarity with the world outside Alcalá, and more active participation in the local political system.

Persons who belong to the still smaller upper class of Alcalá de la Sierra are set apart on the basis of the same criteria: the lightest share of the workload (many do not engage in any productive labor at all), even more elevated economic position and a higher material standard of living and the opportunity to satisfy their more cosmopolitan tastes, greatest prestige, control of the political system, and easiest access to the centers of power in the religious hierarchy.

Only the larger landowners can accumulate the money profits sufficient to improve still further the economic base of their higher social position by purchasing land elsewhere in Andalusia and by investing in industries in Spain and abroad. Many members of the upper class live away from Alcalá entirely, in the larger cities of Málaga and Jerez, and visit the town only in the summer to supervise the harvest and to collect their land rents. They send their children away to school and are themselves cosmopolitan in their educational background. Theirs is the most powerful role in community affairs, in the activities of the church, in local charities, and in politics. They also have greatest access to the sources of political power outside Alcalá, at the headquarters of the provincial government.

This highest local class guards its privileged economic, social, and political position by the careful avoidance of equal-status social contacts with persons of inferior class and by insistence on the show of deference and respect that their superior social position traditionally entitles them to. The people of Alcalá know their social "betters"; the terms of address *Don* and *Doña* are reserved for mature upper-class persons, the use of the term *Señorito* for younger men of the upper class, and so on. Members of the upper class also exhibit concern for protecting, consolidating, and improving their social standing by taking precautions concerning the social status of those whom they marry. They rarely marry "beneath" themselves and try, whenever possible, to marry into the still more elevated strata of provincial aristocracy with whom they come into contact outside Alcalá.

"... those who know and accept their inferior position...."

Figure 9-11. Members of two strata of Thai society meet. (Embassy of Thailand.)

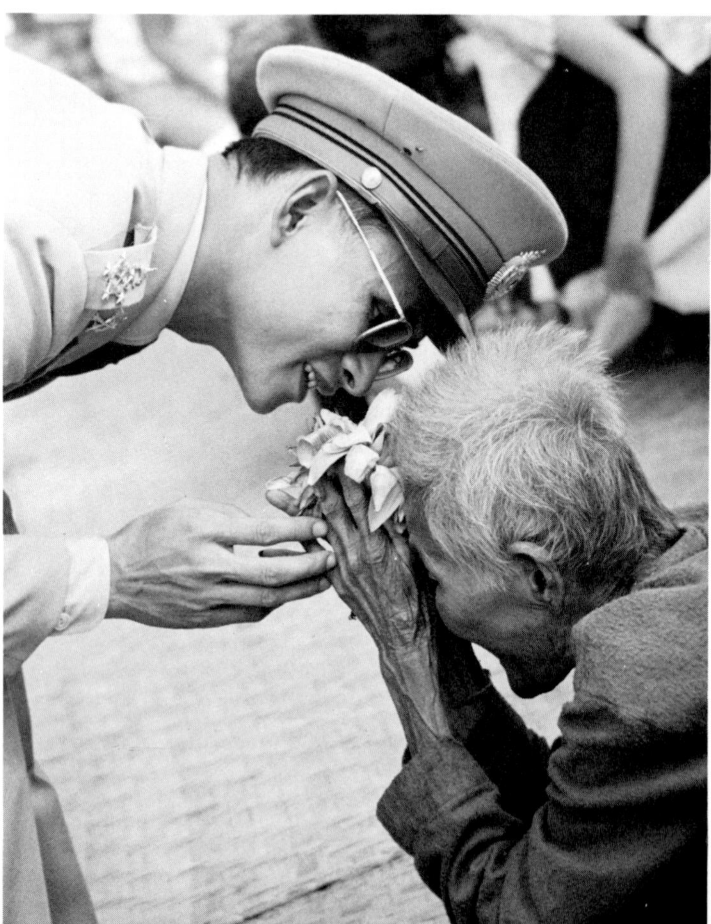

Although it is understood that members of the upper class should keep their social distance, they are also expected to behave with kindness and generosity toward their social inferiors on a highly personalistic basis. The help of an upper-class patron may be available in finding employment, in solving legal problems, in keeping a young son out of the army. For the lower class of Alcalá subservient reliance on the paternalism of the upper class serves as a tenuous form of social security (and as a safety valve against the buildup of pressure for more fundamental social change). Conversely, noblesse oblige functions as a means of solidifying and validating upper-class persons' superior social position. Their higher class status is both emphasized and justified by the conspicuous display of genteel condescension and charity toward those securely ranked beneath them in the social hierarchy.

The social class system of Alcalá and of all of Spain, and in all societies where the chances of social mobility are sharply limited, is supported by a formal ideology that emphasizes in doctrine and ritual the greater virtues of the lower social orders, especially of those who know and accept their inferior position and willingly defer their rewards until some unspecified future time, preferably when they get to heaven. The supposedly more eternal values of obedience, spirituality, and devoutness are sanctimoniously contrasted with the crass materialism of those who can afford inside plumbing or a better education for their children and who seek with success the putatively ephemeral rewards of political power. Privately this pious ideology is generally complemented by repetitious assertions of the lower class's childlike need for the strong leadership of its upper-class superiors.

Frequently the supernaturally sanctioned values that support the class system are complemented by an ethic that emphasizes personal initiative and hard work as the keys to material and social success, with the implication that those who fail to improve their social class position lack ambition and ability (or are "happy as they are")—a strategy that protects the existing order by deflecting dissatisfaction with the unequal distribution of material, social, political, and psychic rewards from "the system" and placing the blame for failure on the individual.

Despite the relative rigidity of the social class system in Alcalá, some mobility is occasionally possible. One of the olive press owners, for example, is the son of a tenant farmer. However, his elevation in social class status was achieved by his extraordinary contribution to the maintenance of the traditional stratified social order. During the Spanish Civil War he had an opportunity to demonstrate his leadership ability in fighting against the "Reds." After the Fascist victory he became mayor. Now he is one of the chiefs of the government-controlled farmers' union. In addition to his olive press, he has acquired extensive landholdings.

But in Alcalá, as elsewhere, the occasional despite-the-odds achievement of superior economic position does not assure instant elevation in the social class hierarchy. First the life-style of the superior class must be learned, and patterns of lower-class behavior must be discarded. Those in Alcalá who cannot learn the new behavior necessary to conceal their socially inferior origins, who cannot overcome the common knowledge of their former "humble" status or successfully avoid the embarrassment of contact with lower-class kinsmen and former associates, must be content to see their sons, raised from birth as Señoritos, attain full recognition as members of the upper class.

As long as agriculture remains the base of the Spanish pattern of technoenvironmental adaptation, there is little likelihood of any decrease, at least by peaceful means, in the relative inflexibility of the class structure in Alcalá de la Sierra and elsewhere in Spain. The members of the lower class are immobilized in the inferiority of their technoeconomic position by the impossibility of bargaining to sell their labor at a higher price because of the lack of sufficient alternatives to farm work as a source of employment. The landowners cooperate to keep wages for farm work low in order to protect the level of their profits.

Migration to the cities to seek other work is costly, often prohibitively so. Workers with few nonagricultural skills, whose small cash wages are almost entirely used up in meeting their daily subsistence needs, have little money left to meet the costs of travel and of supporting themselves while they seek work in an unfamiliar environment. Spain has relatively few industries, anyway, and the poor wages they pay and the harsh political repression and ideological condemnation of independent workers' organizations, combined with the higher costs of city living, make the chances of the labor migrant from Alcalá slight indeed; especially if he stays in Spain.

As the only traditional means of acquiring capital in southern Spain has been through the possession of large landholdings, the owners of the few small factories in Alcalá are necessarily the same people who own the land, or their descendants. In either instance they are members of the same upper class. Many of those who have made money from the land prefer to invest it outside Alcalá, even outside Spain, especially if the investment is to be in industrialization. This practice slows down the rate of innovation in Spanish technology and thus serves to perpetuate the privileged economic position, high social status, and political power of the land-owning aristocracy. Those with the capital necessary to finance technological innovation and economic diversification have little motivation in supporting change that threatens the stability of a traditional social class system that operates to their continuing benefit. Given the marked concentration of power in the hands of the upper class of wealthy landowners, the coming of significant change to Alcalá—as it has come recently to the even poorer rural population of southern Portugal—seems unlikely to be entirely peaceful.

Ethnic Stratification

A third major form of social differentiation and stratification is distinguishable from others so far described principally by the importance attached to ethnic distinctions as a basis for categorizing social groups. Where groups within a society are stratified on the basis of ethnicity, socially assigned "racial" identity and cultural attributes or origins are added to (and usually reinforce) the system of hierarchical ranking based on differences in technoeconomic position, social prestige, life-style and life chances, and access to political power.

"Where groups within a society are stratified on the basis of ethnicity. . . ."

Figure 9-12. Sign in a restaurant window, Ohio, 1938. (Courtesy of the Library of Congress.)

Like systems based on caste and class, both of which can operate in the same society, ethnic stratification is frequently only one of several concurrently operating systems for differentially categorizing people and assigning them to hierarchically ranked groups. In the sense that such systems function to maintain the advantageous status of high-ranking groups and to protect the position of each group from competition from all groups ranked beneath it, the role of ethnic stratification as a system for limiting individual and group mobility and for protecting the privilege of those "on top" further divides and thus further rigidifies the system of stratification.

In modern India, for example, the caste system that categorizes all segments of the Hindu population is cut across by exceedingly important differences based on ethnic criteria. The Sikhs, Moslems, Parsis, and Anglo-Indians are only the culturally and numerically more prominent of myriad non-Hindu ethnic minorities that make the structure of Indian society so complex. Like castes, most ethnic groups in India are internally differentiated on the basis of differences in technoeconomic role, in relative social prestige, in life-style, in dialect or standard of speech, and in political position. Many are further differentiated internally on the basis of violent religious schisms, such as those that separate various Moslem sects, for example.

The historical processes that have precipitated the emergence of systems of ethnic stratification are suggestive of certain causal relationships that were probably important in the formation of systems of caste and class. Three factors appear to be fundamental to the existence of a system of ethnic stratification: (1) a level of technoeconomic development that allows for the centralization of political power, (2) the use of that power to maintain internal systems of stratification based on a continuum from extraordinary privilege to abject exploitation, and (3) the extension of this system to other peoples through military conquest, settlement, and administrative domination.

The colonial expansion of European peoples is the best recent case of a process that has been occurring, but on a much smaller scale, ever since the time of the first ancient states based on advanced agriculture. In every part of the world that Europeans have conquered and subsequently settled since the beginning of the era of exploration and colonial expansion, systems have emerged in which group differences in physical appearance and in cultural origins constitute a major basis for social differentiation and for maintaining the ranked stratification of groups.

With the arrival of the first white settlers, the often diverse ethnic groups living in a particular region—frequently one that included culturally distinct peoples with long histories of hostile relations—found themselves arbitrarily enclosed within the borders of a single colony. Where the aboriginal society was already stratified, as it was in India, Mexico, and the Andean region of South America, and in parts of Africa, traditional high-status indigenous groups—the Brahmans, some African aristocraties, some American Indian elites—were permitted to retain their rank as long as they cooperated with the whites.

Where local population density was low and additional labor was needed to most efficiently exploit the resources of the colony, dependent peoples from other colonized regions were often brought in to work in the mines, on the plantations and ranches, at road building and canal digging, and occasionally as police or as petty functionaries in the colonial administration. By this process East Indians were resettled in Africa, the Caribbean, Fiji, and the islands of the Indian ocean, Mauritius and Réunion. The peoples of French Indochina were dispersed throughout the French-controlled islands of the Pacific; Papuans from New Guinea were kidnapped and taken to work the sugar plantations of northern Australia; West Africans were enslaved by the millions and forcibly resettled in South, Central, and North America and in the Caribbean.

In colonial Indonesia the varied cultural background of the indigenous population had superimposed on it three ethnically alien groups: the Dutch, the Chinese, and in time the Dutch-Indonesians, a separate population resulting from "racial mixing" between the Dutch and the native Indonesians. The lowest stratum in this multiethnic society was occupied by the Indonesian ma-

"In every part of the world that Europeans have conquered and subsequently settled . . ."

Figure 9-13. For "Non-Europeans Only," a bus stop in the Republic of South Africa. (United Nations.)

jority, the culturally and linguistically diverse aboriginal peoples, most of whom worked on the plantations (with the exception of a few Javanese princes and other members of the indigenous aristocracy, who were accorded superior rank for cooperating with the colonial regime). Then, occupying a somewhat higher stratum, came the Chinese, who were to become the commercial middlemen in the Indonesian economy. In a separate but roughly equivalent intermediate stratum but one economically less well off were the Dutch-Indonesians, most of whom served as clerks, plantation overseers, and minor officials in the Dutch administration. The Dutch were on top but were separated among themselves by differences in social class.

In numerically different proportions the Dutch colonies of the Caribbean were marked by an analogous system of ethnic stratification. In Surinam, for example, the tiny Dutch minority, in cooperation with other white-owned corporations, still controls the majority of the nation's exploitable natural resources and is thus able to manipulate the political system. Whites occupy the position of highest social status. Immediately beneath them are three small groups of Middle Eastern, Indian, and Chinese traders, followed by a "colored" elite of mixed European-African ancestry. There is a separate community of Indonesian origin. Beneath them are two strata of blacks: Bush Negroes descended from escaped African slaves and the black majority who work the coastal plantations. And finally, there are the indigenous American Indians, divided into several tribes. To complicate the picture further, most of the endogamous ethnic groups—the Dutch, the Asians, the "colored" people, and the black population of the coast—are internally stratified on the basis of class differences as well.

With specifically different ethnic groups intermixed in differing proportions, the same process was repeated throughout the colonized areas of Asia, the Pacific, Africa,

"... the same process was repeated throughout the colonized areas of Asia, the Pacific, Africa, and the Americas."

Figure 9-14. A British missionary arrives in New Zealand to preach the gospel to the Maori, 1814. From a woodcut. (Courtesy of the Embassy of New Zealand.)

and the Americas. Where the natural environment was suitable to the importation and adaptation of European technology—in Australia, New Zealand, the temperate regions of the Americas, and northern, eastern, and southern Africa—Europeans settled, often in large numbers, and continue today to dominate the ethnically stratified societies that developed in response to the whites' efforts to maintain their economic and political domination. In some areas, such as Australia, many parts of North America, and the Caribbean, the relatively sparse aboriginal populations have largely disappeared, having been killed, forcibly resettled on reservations, or assimilated. In ex-colonies such as the United States where industrialization has decreased the need for unskilled labor, many of the descendants of forcibly imported workers have become economically expendable. Some among them, pushed off the land and crowded into deteriorating ghettoes, have become a nonproductive, almost powerless "under class," so far down in the system of stratification that they are almost out of it.

In South Africa more than eighteen million indigenous blacks have been crowded into "native" reserves covering 13 per cent of the land, most of it so poor that the two million whites do not want it. Elsewhere, in parts of Central and South America, the indigenous population has survived to constitute a socially subordinate majority. Nearly everywhere in the postcolonial world where whites have settled permanently, regardless of the relative numerical size of the different ethnic groups involved and despite specifics of local usage, the same patterns of ethnic stratification are generally found: the indigenous peoples in the inferior, most easily exploited position, the "mixed blood" groups and other nonindigenous minorities assigned an intermediate social status, and the descendants of the foreign conquerors (and those who resemble them closely

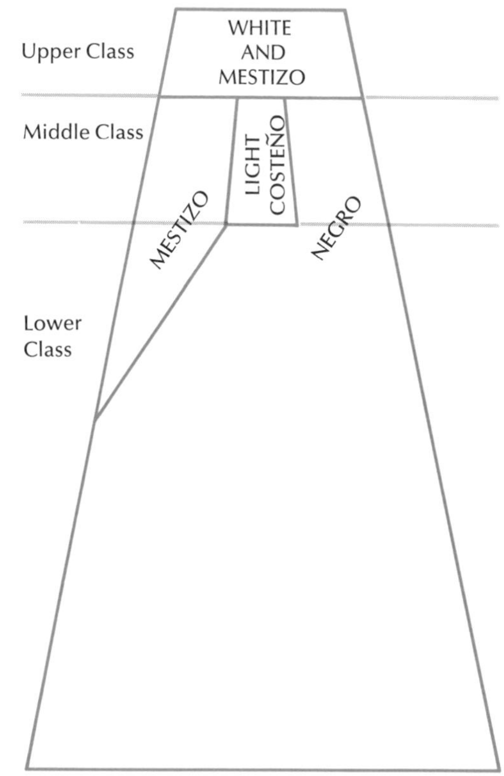

". . . the same patterns of ethnic stratification are generally found. . . ."
Figure 9-15. A variation on this fundamental theme, the major ethnic and social class divisions of San Lorenzo, Ecuador. (Adapted from Whitten.)

enough to be assimilated) in the superior position, owning or controlling most of the wealth, largely in command at the power centers of the political system, having the highest social status—speaking the most "correct" dialect of the language, behaving in the most prestigious manner (driving the right kind of car to the best type of housing in the nicest sort of neighborhood)—and generally enjoying superior chances of acquiring whatever their culture defines as good.

Escape from the punishment of a stigmatized ethnic status can be achieved in two ways: through individual mobility, which usually entails losing those ethnic attributes (family connections, appearance, speech, and behavior) that result in the ascription of inferior ethnic status (such "passing" keeps the system intact), or by abolishing those power relationships that protect the privileges of certain ethnic groups at the cost of others—often the majority.

Sexual Stratification

People in every society are differentiated on the basis of sex. Usually this differentiation is reinforced by ranking, with females as a group subordinated to males. As with other systems of stratification based on caste or ethnicity, membership in the subordinate female stratum is obviously birth ascribed. It is also similar in that it entails less than equal access to productive resources, and women generally have less control over the product of their labor: the services they provide and the wealth they produce. Because their "energy output" is so often unaccompanied by control over the resulting product, women usually lack the economic clout

"... with females as a group subordinated to males."
Figure 9-16. As they are in Afghanistan, where even young girls are expected to cover their faces in the presence of men. (Peace Corps Photo.)

". . . and women generally have less control over the product of their labor. . . ."
Figure 9-17. Afghani women harvesting a crop grown in fields owned by their fathers, brothers, and husbands. (National Archives.)

necessary to acquire political power. To continue with this by now familiar listing of sociocultural consequences, the system of sexual stratification is invariably sanctioned by the prevailing ideology—both by ideas of women's biologically determined incapacity to fulfill certain roles and by faith in the religious rightness of female submission to male dominance. Further, whatever roles are assigned to women within established hierarchies are almost always subordinate. (This is not to say that women do not participate in such religious systems. They do; often with marked ardor and enthusiasm. It is only equal access to power positions that is denied them.)

Also, like castes and ethnic groups, the separate and usually subordinate category of the population to which women are assigned on the basis of their sex is always distinguished by differences in cultural behavior and language. Women are taught to act and speak in a way culturally defined as appropriate to their gender. And, like the members of all other low-status groups—from Indian and Japanese untouchables to American and South African blacks—those females who forget their place and act in "unwomanly" ways risk opposition from those whose privileged status is threatened by feminine insubordination. Mildly "pushy" women may get off with a half joking accusation of latent lesbianism. Those who organize to defy the male-dominated power structure have often been jailed.

In addition to the fact that women's membership in a birth-ascribed inferior category is the result of their sex rather than their ancestry, the position of women in sexually stratified societies differs from that of other oppressed groups in one important sense. Despite the inferiority of women's economic position and the obstacles placed in the way of their full participation in the political system, they often have high prestige. Significantly, such prestige is usually

"Women are taught to act and speak in a way culturally defined as appropriate to their gender."

Figure 9-18. Appropriately dressed for going out in public, women shoppers in Morocco. (United Nations.)

". . . as daughters, sisters, or wives of high-status men."

Figure 9-19. Ladies, Toronto, Ontario. (National Film Board of Canada.)

ascribed through their relationship to males, as daughters, sisters, or wives of high-status men. Even in matrilineal societies, where rank is inherited through the female line, it is still the male members of both domestic and descent groups who allocate the productive goods, control the flow of most wealth, and reserve for themselves the right to assume positions of political and religious power.

In the past those few anthropologists who have not taken sexual stratification as much for granted in other societies as in their own have explained women's economically and politically inferior position as the result of constraints imposed by their role as mothers. In certain technoenvironmental contexts this explanation may have some validity. In hunting and herding societies and among advanced farming peoples, for example, women are often unable to participate as productively as males in the subsistence technology. The products of their labor—domestic services and, of course, babies—generally are not culturally recognized as economic goods. Producing less negotiable wealth, women have less power. Or so the analysis goes.

For this argument to hold up, it ought to follow that where women are engaged more actively in those aspects of the subsistence technology culturally defined as "productive" their status should rise. But this does not automatically happen. In societies based on primitive farming, for example, women often do as much of the productive labor as men. However, the readier and more constant availability of males to participate in administration and warfare has usually meant that women's collective position remains economically and politically inferior.

When such societies begin to "develop" economically—that is, to diversify and increase the productivity of their technology—opportunities to acquire new skills and thus to earn more as wage laborers, clerical workers, government officials, and professionals is largely limited to men. Usually far fewer women are recruited to participate in the modernizing sector. Their traditional productive activities in the home and on the farm continue to bring in little or no pay and the female-male status gap may actually widen.

In a few more highly industrialized societies the beginnings of a revolutionary shift in the until now universally subordinate status of women may be occurring. Women without children and those who are provided with an alternative to assuming major responsibility for child care are beginning to organize to win equal access to both productive resources and to control over the product of their labor. They are increasingly able to accumulate wealth in their own name. Eventually this may provide them with the economic strength necessary to acquire more political power. Even religious hierarchies are being pressured to open at least a few top, possibly token, spots for women.

All this is very new in human history. The shift has not yet occurred in most of the societies that anthropologists have traditionally studied. How anthropologists can best analyze the impact of predicted changes in women's so far subordinate status is a fresh and interesting issue. It is no less pressing than the more fundamental question of how much longer all peoples oppressed by systems of stratification will continue to tolerate forms of social organization that inevitably offer them less than an equal chance.

Summary

In most societies with technologies sufficiently productive to allow economic specialization and accumulation of extensive surpluses, groups are hierarchically stratified on the basis of differences in their relationship to the technology and the economy. These differences designate the social position of their members, determine their access to political power, and often affect their place within the religious system. Such differences are frequently reinforced by differences in physical type and in cultural or historical origins. Systems of stratification are invariably sanctioned by the prevailing ideology and supported by the dominant political system.

Typically, the entire society is composed of a number of such groups ranked hierarchically within an overall structure that is relatively rigid, although some individual mobility and even some group mobility always occur.

The most rigid of these systems are exemplified by the hierarchically ranked, closed corporate groups that constitute the caste system of India. Class systems, based on most of the same criteria, differ principally in that they tend to be somewhat less rigid. Although technoeconomic barriers to social mobility may be nearly as great, those persons who succeed in elevating their status receive at least formal support.

In many parts of the world, particularly during the centuries since the beginnings of European colonial expansion and the conquest of much of Asia and Africa and all of aboriginal America, older systems of stratification have been overlaid with systems based on ethnic identity, with the descendants of the conquered indigenous peoples at the bottom of the status hierarchy, varied "mixed race" and "other nonwhite" groups in intermediary positions, and persons of "pure" European origin at the top, still in control of the technology and the economic system, enjoying greatest prestige and the best available life chances, and dominating the power structure.

Systems of social differentiation and stratification based on sex resemble most closely systems of caste and ethnic stratification. The subordinate economic and politi-

". . . no less pressing than the more fundamental question of how much longer all peoples oppressed by systems of stratification will continue to tolerate forms of social organization that inevitably offer them less than an equal chance.

Figure 9-20. Congresswoman Barbara Jordan in thought. (Dennis Brack from Black Star.)

cal position of women is also supported by an ideology of innate, biologically determined differences that serves to justify female submission. And those who challenge what they perceive as a sexist social order are often as strongly resisted as are the members of any other subordinate group who openly defy a system of social differentiation and stratification that restricts their life opportunities.

Suggested Readings

Several good introductions to the field are provided by Eisenstadt's *Social Differentiation and Stratification,* Fallers's *Inequality: Social Stratification Reconsidered,* Heller's *Structured Social Inequality,* Lenski's *Power and Privilege,* and Tumin's *Social Stratification: The Forms and Functions of Inequality.* The collections edited by Plotnicov and Tuden, *Essays in Comparative Social Stratification,* and by Tumin, *Readings on Social Stratification,* are both valuable. See also Berreman's "Race, Caste, and Other Invidious Distinctions in Social Stratification."

Ranking is analyzed as it operated on the Northwest Pacific coast in Elmendorf's "Coast Salish Status Ranking and Intergroup Ties," and in Ruyle's excellent "Slavery, Surplus, and Stratification on the Northwest Coast: The Ethnoenergetics of an Incipient Stratification System." For Oceania, see Brandwie's "The Place of the Big Man in Traditional Hagen Society in the Central Highlands of New Guinea" and Kaeppler's "Rank in Tonga."

The literature on caste is extensive. As a system caste is insightfully analyzed in Mencher's "The Caste System Upside Down, Or the Not So Mysterious East." See also Gough's "Caste in a Tanjore Village" and Berreman's "Social Categories and Social Interaction in Urban India," as well as his *Hindus of the Himalayas.* Leach's *Aspects of Caste in South India, Ceylon, and Northwest Pakistan* and Yalman's *Under the Bo Tree* are both of value. See as well the important collection edited by DeVos and Wagatsuma, *Japan's Invisible Race: Caste in Culture and Personality;* and, for Africa, Vaughn's "Caste Systems in the Western Sudan."

The critical issue of flexibility in the caste system is dealt with extensively in Mahar's *The Untouchables in Contemporary India;* Isaacs's *India's Ex-Untouchables; Structure and Change in Indian Society,* edited by Singer and Cohn; and *Social Mobility in the Caste System in India,* edited by Silverberg.

So far most studies of class have been undertaken by sociologists. Warner's classic *Social Class in America* continues to have an important effect on the thinking of many anthropologists. See also Blumberg's *The Impact of Social Class;* Domhoff's *The Bohemian Grove and Other Retreats: A Study of Ruling Class Cohesiveness;* Kornblum's *Blue Collar Community;* and *The Hidden Injuries of Class* by Sennett and Cobb. For two good cross-cultural cases see Barrett's "Social Hierarchy and Intimacy in a Spanish Town," and Vogel's *Japan's New Middle Class.*

Shibutani and Kwan's *Ethnic Stratification* contains a still useful bibliography on the subject. *Ethnic Groups and Boundaries* by Barth is a major work. So is Despres's *Ethnicity and Resource Competition in Plural Societies.* See also *Ethnic Identity* by DeVos and Romanucci-Rose; LeVine and Campbell's *Ethnocentrism;* Nikolinako's "Note on an Economic Theory of Racism"; Schermerhorn's *Comparative*

Ethnic Relations; Safa and DuToit's *Migration and Development: Implications for Ethnic Identity and Political Conflict;* and Tumin's *Comparative Perspectives on Race Relations.*

Patterns of ethnic stratification in other societies are the subject of Adam's *Modernizing Racial Domination: The Dynamics of South African Politics;* Barth's "Social Organization of a Pariah Group in Norway"; and both Whitten's "The Ecology of Race Relations in Northwest Ecuador" and "Blackness in northern South America: Ethnic Dimensions." The subject is also dealt with in Cole and Wolf's *The Hidden Frontier: Ecology and Ethnicity in an Alpine Village,* in Morner's *Race and Class in Latin America,* and in Levine's *Greater Ethiopia: The Evolution of a Multiethnic Society.*

Closer to home, the literature on ethnic stratification in the United States is vast. For some good examples see Hannerz's "Ethnicity and Opportunity in Urban America," Simpson and Yinger's standard *Racial and Cultural Minorities,* and Tabb's *The Political Economy of the Black Ghetto.* See also Endo's "Japanese Americans: The 'Model Minority' in Perspective"; Wagner and Haug's *Chicanos; The Mexican American People,* by Grebler and others; and finally Cohen's collection, *Urban Ethnicity.* For an intriguing case illustrating the theoretical borderland between "racial" and religious differences see Rhee's "Jewish Assimilation: The Case of the Chinese Jews."

For two excellent collections that deal with aspects of the newly discovered subject of sexual stratification see Mathiasson's *Many Sisters: Women in Cross-Cultural Perspective* and Tax's *Women Cross-Culturally.* See also Jacobs's *Women in Perspective: A Guide for Cross Cultural Studies,* Friedl's *Women and Men,* and Schlegel's *Male Dominance and Female Autonomy.* On the central issue of women's power see Draper and Cashdan's "!Kung Women: Contrasts in Sex Egalitarianism in the Foraging and Sedentary Contexts," Michaelson and Goldschmidt's "Female Roles and Male Dominance Among Peasants," Nelson's "Public and Private Politics: Women in the Middle Eastern World," and Rogers's "Female Forms of Power and the Myth of Male Dominance: A Model of Female/Male Interaction in a Peasant Society." See as well Strathern's *Women In Between.* Important theoretical questions related to the changing position of women are developed in Bossen's "Women in Modernizing Societies" and Sanday's "Toward a Theory of the Status of Women."

Part Five

Political Organization

It seems probable to us that three types of political system can be distinguished. Firstly, there are those very small scale societies . . . in which even the largest political unit embraces a group of people all of whom are united to one another by ties of kinship, so that political relations are co-terminous with kinship relations and the political structure and kinship organization are completely fused. Secondly, there are societies in which lineage structure is the framework of the political system, there being a precise coordination between the two, so that they are consistent with each other, though each remains distinct and autonomous in its own sphere. Thirdly, there are societies in which an administrative organization is the framework of the political structure.

FORTES AND EVANS-PRITCHARD (1940:6–7)

The essence of the political problem faced by any society entails (1) the maintenance of internal social order—by development of structures and processes for legitimizing authority and for making and enforcing laws, and (2) the regulation of relations with other societies—usually through reliance on an asymmetrical mixture of diplomacy and organized aggression.

Authority Systems

10

DESPITE great variation in the specific ways particular peoples meet the universal need for a system for maintaining internal societal order and regulating external relations, it is possible to identify three structurally distinct forms that authority systems take. From what is known of the factors that have affected their development, each form and the dynamic patterns of political behavior it engenders appears to be causally associated with a particular type of technoenvironmental adaptation.

The oldest and structurally the simplest of these three types is the band, in which almost all processes entailed in organizing relations between individuals and groups within the society are based on kinship. The political system operates through, rather than apart from, the kinship system. Most nomadic hunter-gatherers are organized into bands.

Structurally somewhat more complex are the diffuse or multicentric authority systems characteristic of most primitive farmers and pastoral nomads. Here the localized family group is usually still politically semiautonomous, but the development of lineal descent systems and the increased importance of associational ties provide a basis for occasional larger-scale political unification.

In contrast, the third principal form, the centralized authority system, is marked by the concentration of coercive power in the hands of a single group whose authority is usually relatively stable and permanent. Advanced farmers living in settled communities tend to develop centralized authority systems, and the form is characteristic of all industrialized societies.

"... almost all processes entailed in organizing relations between individuals and groups within the society are based on kinship."

Figure 10-1. Two members of an Australian band painting up for a special ritual occasion. (Courtesy of the American Museum of Natural History.)

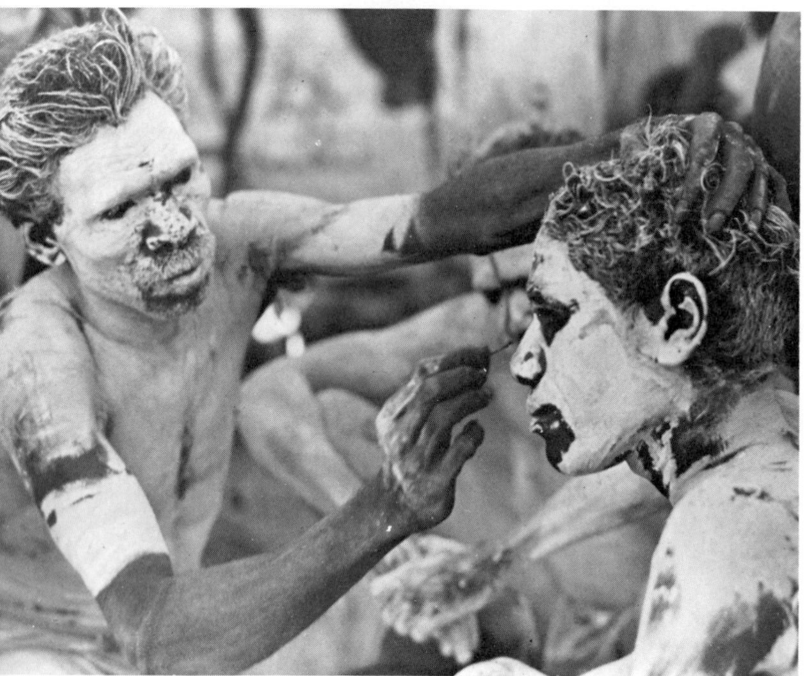

The Band

The band, typically composed of a small, autonomous, exogamous territorial group of related nuclear or extended families, with a total population that usually ranges between twenty and fifty persons, provides the structural basis for the simplest and chronologically the oldest of all known forms of political organization.

Once (in fact, for most of human history), when all humans were nomadic or seminomadic, hunter-gatherers most probably had political systems quite similar to those of contemporary peoples who still make their living by this ancient means. Foraging as a technological base appears to place comparatively stringent limitations on the forms that the political system can take. The only major variable is the relative richness of the natural environment. Up until the relatively recent discovery of plant and animal

domestication, bands of hunter-gatherers undoubtedly lived in a far wider range of natural settings than they do today, when most survive only in marginal environments—deserts, jungles, tundra—that their technologically superior neighbors have not yet found sufficiently valuable to expropriate. Prior to the extinction of hunter-gatherers in richer natural settings, the greater abundance of wild food resources available to them probably resulted in greater population density, which in turn might have increased the necessity for somewhat more centralized authority.

But from what is known of the political systems of foragers who lived on into recent historical times in naturally food-rich settings—the Indians of the Northwest Pacific coast are the prime example (see Drucker 1951, 1965)—it appears that prior to contact with technologically more advanced outsiders the tendency toward the technoeconomic semiautonomy of the local group, communal access to natural resources, and emphasis on reciprocity in the exchange of goods lessened the tendency toward wealth accumulation. The consequent absence of social stratification limited the need for centralized

"Here the localized family group is usually still politically semiautonomous. . . ." **Figure 10-2.** As it is in the Libyan desert. (National Archives.)

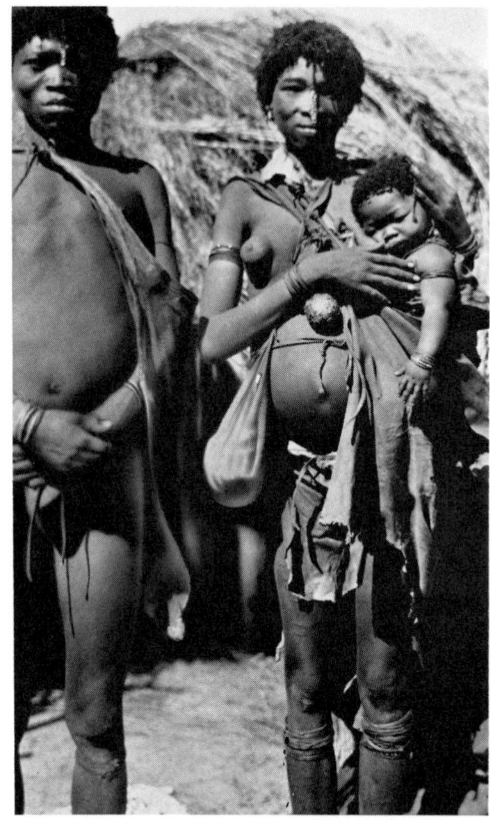

"Typically all core members of the band are closely related by descent or marriage."
Figure 10-3. Three members of a Bushman band, southern Africa. (Courtesy of the Library of Congress.)

"... they cannot produce ... much in the way of material goods beyond the tools and weapons they need to make a living. ..."
Figure 10-4. Eskimo hunter's work. Stone carving from Hudson Bay. (National Film Board of Canada.)

authority and inhibited growth of the coercive economic power to back it up.

Because of their dependence on wild foods, almost all hunter-gatherers must move about frequently in search of provisions; usually their techniques for processing and preserving surpluses are meager. If their habitat is difficult and wild food resources are scattered and sparse, this movement may be almost incessant. To exploit the habitat efficiently, it is usually necessary that the group remain small, that it operate at a considerable distance from other groups, and that it remain structurally flexible enough so that its members can maintain a mixed strategy to best exploit both stable and shifting resources, breaking up temporarily into smaller groups and later reforming in order to adapt to shifts in the availability of particular food resources. Precisely how small the bands should remain, how widely dispersed, and how flexible appear to be principally dependent on the pattern of distribution and the relative abundance of wild foods. But it may also be affected by their need to muster a defense force and by the extent of their reliance on fission, the splitting off of small family groups as a means of controlling conflict.

Typically, all core members of the band are closely related by descent or marriage. Most often the band takes its form from the patrilocal extended family (Eggan 1968; Service 1966, 1971; Steward 1938, 1955c, 1970; Williams 1968). Because of the technological and economic factors that limit the accumulation of wealth in the band, status distinctions are generally based only on sex, age, kinship, and personal attributes such as strength of character or skill.

As a result of the relative primitivism of their technology, they cannot produce (nor would they be able to transport) much in the way of material goods beyond the tools and weapons they need to make a living; thus, the potential for intraband conflict over property is reduced. In comparison to conditions in technologically more advanced societies, the likelihood of conflict resulting from competition for access to productive goods, of aggression resulting from jealousy over the greater affluence of some individuals or groups, of disputes over rights to "private property" or inheritance, or of theft is minimized. Sexual jealousy, particularly conflict over women, remains as the major potential source of intraband discord. Often this potential for disruption is reduced by band exogamy: men cannot compete for mates within the family cluster because the incest prohibition requires that they take their wives from neighboring groups.

When one of the rules of the band is broken, the group response often takes the form of social pressure that can escalate in severity from public scolding, shaming, ridicule, and social isolation to banishment (a punishment more often threatened than carried out). Among people intensely dependent on group cooperation for individual survival, the threat of isolation or ostracism is frequently enough to bring a deviant quickly back into line or, more often, to prevent him or her from misbehaving in the first place.

In the patrilocal band authority to make decisions when necessary and to direct the activities of the group when this is required is usually vested in the eldest responsible male members of the family band. Often there is a headman, the "first among equals," who serves as the central reference point in band organization. However, most of the time his leadership role is largely symbolic, because most of the time people know what to do and do what they should do without direction. All have been similarly enculturated, follow the same customs, know one another well enough to be able to predict each other's responses and avoid disputes (if they want to), and are keenly aware of the survival value of cooperating and remaining friendly.

It is rare that decisions in the band are

"All have been similarly enculturated. . . ."
Figure 10-5. Young Karaja Indian practicing a skill vital to the survival of his group, Brazil. (Courtesy of the American Museum of Natural History.)

made arbitrarily. Usually they arise out of discussion with all adult members of the group in which the leader acts as a catalyst in achieving group consensus. Guidelines to proper action are provided by reference to precedents recalled by the elders, who, as long as they are mentally alert, are valued for their store of useful experience. Once arrived at in this public way, decisions require minimal formal administration. An authoritative word from some senior member of the group whose judgment is respected is usually sufficient to set in motion the appropriate response from all others.

Opportunities for leadership in the band are usually transient. The band headman or the elders are required to lead only during a temporarily critical period to meet an internal or external emergency, such as the threat of an enemy raid, through the intensive short-term coordination of the actions of all members. The need for political consolidation beyond the level of the local band—to organize a communal hunt or a large ceremonial involving the members of several neighboring bands—occurs more frequently. When such leadership entails a special skill, such as hunting prowess, authority often shifts from the headman to some other member of the band. In either instance authority within the band is characteristically accompanied by little in the way of coercive power. The leader is followed because of his demonstrated leadership ability, not because he can punish—physically, economically, or socially—those who do not obey him. If he does not lead them well, they may simply fail to follow.

!Kung Bands

Among contemporary peoples who make their living by hunting and gathering the !Kung (the exclamation mark in *!Kung* represents an implosive click sound made with the tongue; such clicks are a distinctive feature of all Bushman languages) Bushmen of southern Africa are exceptional in the extent to which their traditional way of life has been retained, and with it an authority system that illustrates well how political processes operate in the family band. The !Kung term for the band translates simply as "people who live together" (Marshall 1960, 1961). All those who live and work together at hunting and gathering within a particular territory (the average !Kung band has a few more than twenty members) are related by blood or marriage. The entire !Kung population still living according to traditional patterns, approximately four hundred fifty persons, is dispersed in seventeen or eighteen such bands. The separate territory of each is large enough to allow for efficient exploitation by nomadic hunting and gathering, and every territory contains at least one waterhole.

As each group is patrilocal (although young men live initially with their wive's families) and exogamous, young girls marry out and into other bands, usually ones located in adjacent territories. Consequently, each band is related to most of its neighbors by marriage. Boundaries between territories are not rigidly demarcated but are generally known and respected. !Kung hunters can move freely in and out of the territories of neighboring bands to which they are related. Within their own territory game and other wild foods are free goods until they are killed or collected. The first hunter whose arrow strikes a giraffe or other large animal hunted by a group has the right to dispose of its meat, overseeing its distribution among his fellow hunters and other members of the band.

The headman, usually the senior responsible male member of the band, is regarded as the custodian of the land and of all food resources within the territory. All those who are related to him—his wife or wives, his brothers and sisters, his children, and his children's children—have the right of access

"... game and other wild foods are free goods until they are killed or collected."
Figure 10-6. Indian hunter with his catch, Brazil. (OAS Photo.)

to the territory and to the use of its resources by virtue of this kinship tie. Implicitly, to retain this right they must conform to the rules of the group under the headman's authority.

The stability and continuity of the !Kung authority system are provided for by making the role hereditary, passing it on from father to son. There are few advantages to being a headman, and those who hold or inherit the role are not envied. They receive no tribute or any other special honors or favors. In fact, wise headmen avoid privilege for fear of incurring the envy or resentment of those they must lead. The authority of the headman is analogous to that of the father in each of the component nuclear families of the band. Usually it is only when action must be taken that affects the entire group that he is formally called on to make a decision: in selecting a new campsite, in coordinating the dispersal of several small groups of hunters, in granting permission to members of a distant band to drink from the local waterhole.

When a dispute arises between band members, the word of the headman is usually accepted in settling it. Although his coercive power is actually very limited, everyone has a keen appreciation of the danger to group solidarity of resentment and hostility. Strong social pressure is exerted on the disputants to accept the headman's suggested settlement. But he cannot use force against a wrongdoer or insist on compliance with his request that a dispute be ended. Once a disagreement becomes heated, he cannot prevent the principals from fighting or even trying to kill each other. No person in the Bushman band has the right or the power to command another. General appreciation of the dangers of conflict, rather than any political mechanism for resolving it, appears to be the main source of social control.

The relations of a !Kung band with other bands are limited largely to contact with neighboring groups with whom close bonds of kinship are shared. When circumstances bring them into contact with more distant groups with whom no definite kinship ties can be identified, they rely on a system of name relationships to provide the basis for friendly interaction. When !Kung strangers meet, for example, the elder of the two ascertains the name of the other and then addresses him by the kin term he uses for one of his relatives who bears the same name. If the younger man's name is Gau, for example, he may be addressed as "Uncle" after the older man's father's brother whose name is Gau, for every man has or has had at least one kinsman with each of the limited number of names the !Kung employ. With this cue the younger man returns the greeting, addressing the older man as "Nephew." Use of these specific kin terms activates the behavior appropriate to the particular kinship relation that serves each as a guide, providing a basis for friendliness and feelings of familiarity and security.

"... their numbers and the extent of their territory have been diminishing steadily for centuries."

The political system of the !Kung band works well in regulating internal relations and ordering contacts with neighboring groups whose similarly primitive technology is accompanied by similarly organized means of maintaining law and order. The !Kung system is viable as long as they remain isolated among others like themselves, but it leaves them vulnerable when they come into competition with technologically more advanced, politically more highly organized groups, for they have no effective means of organization and unification beyond the band, no adequate political basis for uniting to resist the incursions of outsiders. For this reason their numbers and the extent of their territory have been diminishing steadily for centuries. Once the ancestors of the !Kung and of other Bushman groups were far more widespread throughout eastern and southern Africa. Now most have disappeared having been slaughtered or assimilated as technologically superior peoples with more complex political systems entered and took over their territories. The !Kung and a few other Bushman populations continue to live independently only in remote areas where natural obstacles, principally the undesirability of the habitat, provide the protection that their technology and political system cannot.

Figure 10-7. Young member of a shrinking band of Bushmen, southern Africa. (Courtesy of the American Museum of Natural History.)

Shoshone Bands

The absence of the need and material basis for any permanent centralization of authority beyond the level of the semiautonomous local band is also illustrated by what is presently known of the interrelationship of the natural environment, the technology, the economic organization, and the political system of nomadic hunter-gatherers who once lived in the arid Great Basin drainage region formed by the Wasatch Mountains of Utah and the Sierra Nevada range of California and Oregon. The Shoshonean-speaking Indians of this area—Ute, Western Shoshoni, and Northern Paiute—made their living by foraging for seed-bearing plants, roots, and pine nuts (Steward 1938, 1955d, 1970; Thomas 1974). From time to time their food supply was augmented by the addition of small game, such as rats, mice, and gophers, and by insects, ants and ant eggs, and fly larvae. Occasionally they hunted for rabbits or antelope.

Their habitat was harsh; rainfall varied unpredictably in abundance and locale from season to season and so, as a consequence, did the distribution of wild plants and the insects and animals that fed on them. As the availability of wild foods shifted it was necessary for the Indians to move about also. During the spring and summer they migrated in separate, small family bands, camping in a single place only as long as the supply of wild foods lasted, then moving on. In the late fall several family bands often converged in a single region to gather pine nuts. By common understanding they worked some distance from one another. Each family band working alone in its own area gathered as many nuts as possible and stored them in the earth. Then the several bands often settled down to pass the winter near one another. If the pine nut harvest had been good each family could hope to survive comfortably until spring, when it would again be necessary to move off separately to forage for fresh sources of wild food.

All during the time it was working at making a living each band operated independently of all others. Because of the sparseness of the wild food supply and its scattered and unpredictable distribution, working in groups larger than the patrilocal extended family would have been inefficient. As a consequence, there was usually neither need nor material basis for the centralization of authority beyond the level of the autonomous family band, in each of which the eldest responsible male member provided all the leadership ordinarily required. Although the Shoshone were gathered together to form a larger aggregation during the winter months, the members of the loose, thinly populated neighborhood thus formed (the camp of each band was from several hundred yards to a mile or more distant from others) were not usually engaged in any group activity that required coordination or the prevention of conflict beyond the organizational level of the component groups.

In the spring, when the family bands moved off from their winter camp, each went its separate way in search of freshly sprouted greens, small game, and whatever else could be found to eat. The following year the time of the pine nut harvest might come when the band was in a different part of the mountain range. There they would settle down amid a new cluster of family bands. Just where they settled depended on the weather, on that season's variations in the distribution of wild foods, and on the particular pattern of migration decided on by the leader of each separate band. As a consequence, not only was there no permanent centralization of authority beyond the level of the band, but also, if there had been, there would have been no way of maintaining it for more than a single season.

There was, however, one activity that required coordination of the otherwise autonomous bands: the communal hunt, usually for rabbits or antelope. These hunts required direction. For their duration an incipient system of centralized authority emerged. Just where and precisely when a hunt was held and the particular bands that participated varied from year to year as a consequence of seasonal changes in the distribution of the wild plants on which the rabbits and antelope fed.

In the communal rabbit drive mesh nets, each several hundred yards long, were attached end to end to form a huge half circle. Then men, women, and children moved out over the surrounding area. At a signal they began to close slowly back in toward the net, frightening the rabbits with their shouts, gradually surrounding them, driving rabbits and other small game back before them into the nets, where, trapped and entangled, the animals were clubbed to death.

All this required coordination: the decision to hold the rabbit drive, selection of a location, deployment of the nets, direction of the beaters, and supervision of the distri-

"... the often important role of magic and religion in legitimizing temporary political control."
Figure 10-8. Bark painting of a totemic figure used to unite members of an Australian Aboriginal band. (Courtesy of the Museum of Primitive Art.)

bution of the game. Temporarily some leadership was needed. As no family band had a status that was in any significant way superior to that of any other, and as no band headman's authority extended beyond his own group, no one had the automatically legitimate right to assume such leadership. Rather, the leader or leaders, sometimes aptly called "rabbit bosses," were selected on the basis of personal qualities—strength of character, experience, and demonstrably superior skill at the task at hand.

The authority of the Shoshone rabbit boss lasted only for the duration of the rabbit drive. When it was over, each band returned to its separate pursuits, activities that required no direction beyond the level of the now once again autonomous band. The ties of command briefly established between the rabbit boss and the several participating bands were dissolved. Once a communal hunt was held in a particular region, the wild animal population was likely to be so depleted that the hunters would not assemble there again for several seasons. As it was improbable that the same bands would ever all meet again in the same place at the right time, it was unlikely that the temporary leader's role would ever be reactivated among the same following.

The Shoshone antelope hunt was similarly organized. The way it was led, by the Antelope Shaman, illustrates both the necessary impermanence of centralized authority among nomadic hunters and the often important role of magic and religion in legitimizing temporary political control. The seed of the development of such a supporting concept, the most familiar variant being the idea of the "divine right" to rule, was evident in Shoshone beliefs about the Antelope Shaman's special powers. For the hunt a corral toward which the frightened animals were to be driven was constructed by piling up brush or stones. During the hunt the shaman stood in the center of this corral.

The curiosity of the antelope, apparently a peculiarity of their species, drew them toward the stockade to get a better look. This was interpreted as evidence of the shaman's ability to capture the animals' souls. His right to authority over all those participating in the communal hunt was thus made legitimate not only by his ability as a leader but also by the Indian's awareness of the material value of the special supernatural power he possessed, a power that, in a sense, set him above ordinary people and provided them with a rationale for following him. But, like that of the rabbit boss, the shaman's leadership ended with the conclusion of the hunt. And it was unlikely ever to be required again by that particular group of otherwise independent nomadic family bands which then once more went their separate ways in search of the smaller wild game and wild plants that were the steadier source of their food supply.

Because of the particular character of their environment and their specific technological adaptation to it, the Shoshone Indians had no need most of the time for centralization of authority beyond the organizational level of the band, and so most of the time they did not have it; when they needed it temporarily, they had a means for developing it temporarily.

Variation in Band Organization

As a type of political system, bands vary both in organizational specifics and in size. Where the natural habitat is poor in usable material resources, where the wild food supply fluctuates unpredictably from season to season and region to region, bands are small, scattered, and economically and politically almost entirely autonomous—for maximum adaptive flexibility. Where the environment is richer or the hunting and gathering technology is more efficient in exploiting it, the band is often larger. Several bands dwell closer together. Their internal authority systems may become structurally more highly differentiated, with an increased tendency toward lineality in the reckoning of descent and in the assignment of leadership roles. The extent and importance of interband social and economic contacts and of occasions requiring coordination of the activities of more than one band—thus requiring more frequent reliance on some incipient form of centralized authority—tend to increase also. But such leadership always remains comparatively weak. At the band level of development the kin group persists as the primary locus for almost all political processes.

Multicentric Authority Systems

Structurally somewhat more complex than bands are the diffuse or multicentric authority systems characteristic of those who make their living by primitive farming or herding, people whose more productive technologies often make possible the emergence of larger population in continuous, close socioeconomic interaction, living together either in settled farming communities or on the move as seminomadic or nomadic pastoralists. The political system of such peoples can best be described in terms of the familiar aspects of "government" that they lack: They have no single centralized authority system, no legislative body, no permanent judicial institutions, and no formal administrative machinery. Internal social stability and relations with neighboring groups are maintained by means of alternative, more diffuse political processes—by what has been aptly termed a system of "ordered anarchy." The fluid multicentric political systems of these larger population aggregates can be perceived as typologically intermediate between the simple band level of political development characteristic of

"The political system of such peoples can best be described in terms of the familiar aspects of "government" that they lack. . . ."

Figure 10-9. Desert dweller, Libya. (National Archives.)

most foragers and the complex political systems of technologically more advanced societies in which authority is permanently centralized in such forms as chiefdoms, states, and empires.

Where a multicentric authority system prevails, the entire society is typically composed of small, unstratified, semiautonomous units of roughly equivalent size and socioeconomic status. Their social system is egalitarian and classless. No one group or local community is subordinate or superior to any other. Each is independent in the ordering of its internal affairs. Usually, the technoeconomic systems on which such societies are based explain this lack of significant stratification. Either the technology is so unproductive that the material surpluses necessary for societal hierarchies are lacking, or the social and economic systems are so organized that no permanent differential accumulation of wealth is possible—thus impeding the differential concentration of political power.

Usually, life among peoples with multicentric political systems is such that there is no need for the permanent centralization of authority even if it were materially and structurally possible to achieve and sustain. Situations requiring intragroup political unification may arise; frequently they do, but they are transitory, and the particular groups whose activities require centralized coordination differ in each situation. Such unification rarely encompasses the entire population.

Analytically, there are four major types of multicentric authority systems: (1) Authority is based on status within a unilineal descent system. The best documented and best understood of these authority systems are based on segmentary lineages. Characteristically, most decisions are made within each of the lineages that constitute the local community. Interlineage relations are regulated on the basis of cooperative alliances between descent groups that are established and maintained through marriage. When dissension arises or a decision must be made that cannot be handled through the lineage-based authority system, that is, by the descent group elders, it is typically referred to an outside arbitrator, perceived to be neutral, whose right to act as mediator is legitimized by the special supernatural forces he is thought to control. (2) Authority is based on positions ascribed within nonunilineal descent groups. (3) In a well-studied but comparatively rare type of system, most authority is vested in individuals and groups on the basis of their position within a system of age groups. Although descent groups are present in such societies, their role in the allocation of authority and in the maintenance of order is secondary. (4) Most internal and external political relations are organized on the basis of leadership within associations, councils, and secret societies of various sorts that cut across, complement, or override the political functions of groups based on locality.

In multicentric political systems of the

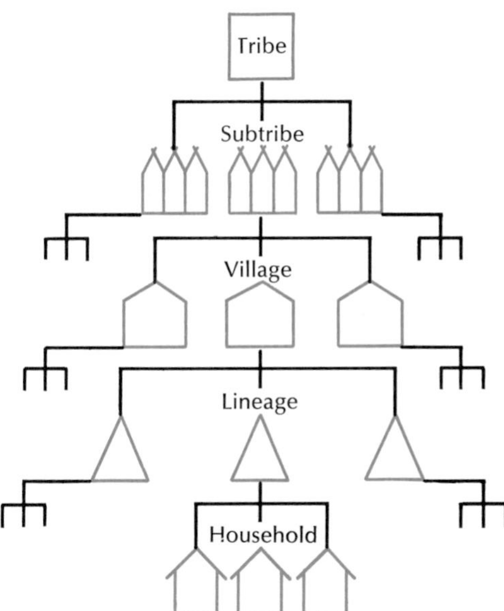

". . . most decisions that affect the maintenance of order within the local community are made by the elder male members of the localized descent groups. The authority of these lineage elders is backed by their control over productive goods . . . , work organization, and . . . their closeness to the powerful spirits of their ancestors."

Figure 10-10. The smaller the segmentary unit, the greater its cohesiveness. (Adapted from Sahlins.)

first type, those that derive their structure from a segmentary lineage system, most decisions that affect the maintenance of order within the local community are made by the elder male members of the localized descent groups. The authority of these lineage elders is backed by their control over productive goods (especially land), work organization, and the allocation of what is produced. It is further strengthened by their closeness to the powerful spirits of their ancestors. Unification for action beyond the level of the local lineage most frequently occurs in response to some external crisis, as when several neighboring but otherwise autonomous communities linked principally by ties of consanguinity unite to resist some common enemy.

Often each community is composed of a core of unilineally related adult males and their wives and children that represents the localized membership of some larger descent grouping, frequently a clan. When a crisis occurs, this larger lineal segment of the kinship system is activated to provide the structural context for coalition and concerted action. When the crisis passes, so does the need for political unification. The next external threat may come from a different direction and require the mobilization for resistance of a different cluster of communities or lineage segments.

The Segmentary System of the Tiv

The multicentric political organization of the Tiv, Nigerian primitive farmers, provides a good example of how a system based on lineage segmentation can operate (L. Bohannan 1958; P. Bohannan 1954, 1957; see also references to the Tiv political system in Sahlins 1961). Each Tiv lineage is identified with a particular territory. All Tiv males living in a single region are descended from a common male ancestor. Groups formed around a core of agnates, male kinsmen living in neighboring areas, are usually descended from brothers of a single, still more remote founding ancestor. Ordinarily, lineages residing in adjacent territories are structurally opposed; that is, each inhabits a specifically separate region and traces its descent to a specifically different ancestral progenitor. But these several neighboring lineages are united in structural opposition to other socially and spatially more distant groups. It is on the basis of this sort of shifting structure that the Tiv are politically organized. In the conduct of day-to-day affairs, each local lineage is independent. The direction of local activities requires no higher authority than that of the lineage headman. In their relations with neighboring lineages they are often opposed. It is only in conflict with some spatially and

". . . in the settlement of disputes between local residents."
Figure 10-11. In contrast government intervention is often necessary to settle local disputes in India. Here an official listens to one side of the case. (National Archives.)

genealogically more remote group that several local communities may be temporarily united.

Under peaceful conditions, when a society such as that of the Tiv is neither threatened from without nor in need of expanding its territory, increasing its supply of goods, or seeking vengeance for some wrong by attacking its neighbors, each local community—representative of a single segment within the larger lineage system—is politically autonomous.

Ordinarily political unification beyond the level of this local community occurs only in response to a crisis; with the termination of the crisis the need for unification ceases also. When crisis persists, the system of temporary political consolidation may evolve into a more permanently centralized type of political organization, initially often in the form of a somewhat loose confederation. Only if crisis continues is such a system likely to hold together and become permanently centralized. Otherwise it has no reason for being and is soon pulled apart by disputes among its component but still structurally distinguishable segments.

Political Authority and the Economy of the Ila

Frequent shifts in the loci of temporarily centralized authority are often a structural characteristic of multicentric political systems. The segmentation and fission of political units in the lineage system of the Tiv have been used to illustrate one aspect of this phenomenon. Another is exemplified by the Ila, a Zambian cattle-keeping people among whom a redistributive economic system functions importantly to impede the permanent consolidation of political power in the hands of any single individual or group (Tuden 1966a and 1966b). Political leaders arise among the Ila, but their authority is never lasting. Competition for status and power is incessant; political allegiance shifts constantly.

The economically semiautonomous Ila village community has a core of about fifteen to twenty patrilineally related men, their wives, and their children. Kinship is the guiding principle in the organization of nearly all aspects of their local affairs: in determination of rights to use farmland, in the allocation of other important productive goods such as cattle, in organizing work, in the distribution of most consumption goods, and in the settlement of disputes between local residents.

External relations are also taken care of under the organizational aegis of the kinship system. As the Ila practice lineage exogamy, the young girls of the village marry into the families of Ila residing in neighboring communities. Consequently, the inhabitants of each village are allied matrilaterally with most of the residents of neighboring settlements, that is, with most of those Ila outside their own village with whom they are likely to come into contact or be involved in relations requiring coordination.

Each small patrilocal family settlement is united with neighboring villages to form a territorial division in which all members are related on the basis of more remote lineal ties. Ila society comprises some eighty such territorial divisions. Some contain as many as fifteen to twenty separate kin groups; others as few as four. Beyond the level of the local communities of which these territorial divisions are composed, the Ila lack any permanently centralized political structure. As is characteristic of all multicentric political systems, no component kinship-based unit has a fixed status subordinate or superior to that of any other.

What centralized authority there is among the Ila shifts about constantly as the fortunes of particular leaders wax and wane. Leadership status is achieved by a show of intelligence and strength of character, by demonstrated skill and diplomacy in the arbitration of disputes, by ability and willingness to provide material assistance to others in need—and others are often in need among the Ila, in need of help in paying the fines that are a characteristic outcome of dispute settlement, in need of assistance in accumulating the goods necessary to negotiate a marriage contract or for some other particular purpose. All these criteria for political leadership are openly accessible to and potentially achievable by all adult males. Although seniority in the kin group sometimes gives a man a slight advantage, the lack of such status is by no means a serious obstacle to the accumulation of political power. But just as access to leadership status is open to all males, so can it be readily lost. There is neither any means by which a leader can permanently consolidate his position nor any legitimate way he can exclude others from competing for it.

Ironically, one of the principal means of acquiring political power among the Ila leads almost automatically to its dissolution. To achieve leadership status a man must be generous to his followers, assisting them financially and entertaining them at elaborate feasts where the principal source of his wealth, his cattle, are destroyed by slaughter. Consequently, the strong social pressure that compels a leader to redistribute his wealth to keep his power can and often does result in the dissipation of the material base on which his power rests. Not that an Ila leader can dispose of his wealth as he wishes. Those to whom he is expected to make gifts, and the quality and amount of such gifts, are rigidly controlled by the rules that regulate his economic obligations to the members of his kin group. It is only by the successful manipulation of these obligations that he is able to accumulate the wealth necessary to make a bid for political power in the first place. Those who have assisted him expect to be remembered. And so, to maintain his position he must sooner or later give away much of the wealth on which it rests. This requirement both weakens his ability to hold onto his position of political leadership and makes it nearly impossible for him to pass on to his heirs the accumulated property that might allow them to retain control of the political authority he has acquired.

A similar check on the centralization of

". . . associations often fulfill an important function in providing a mechanism for maintaining order beyond the level of the kin group."

Figure 10-12. Members of a Lumbwa age grade discuss the organization of a lion hunt, Tanzania. (Courtesy of the American Museum of Natural History.)

political power operates as a significant aspect of the multicentric systems characteristic of many of the pastoral nomadic peoples of the Middle East (see Barth 1959; Evans-Pritchard 1949; Gellner 1969). There, also, leaders competing for the exercise of political power can maintain their unstable following only by redistributing the tribute and other forms of wealth they might otherwise retain as a means of more permanently consolidating their political control.

Age Groups and Authority: The Karimojong Again

In societies with multicentric political systems associations often fulfill an important function in providing a mechanism for maintaining order beyond the level of the kin group. By so doing they frequently eliminate the need for a more permanent form of political centralization. Among the cattle-keeping Karimojong of East Africa (Dyson-Hudson 1963, 1966), for example, it is the age grade system that determines who shall have the right to make decisions that affect public matters and the general welfare.

The component corporate units of the age grade system, the age generations, are activated only when an issue arises that is critical to the well-being of the Karimojong as a single social entity: when an enemy attack is threatened, a large-scale raid on some other group is to be organized, the time comes to coordinate the movement of cattle away from the home pastures, there is drought or an invasion of locusts to be dealt with, or a ritual must be performed that requires the participation of all generation set members. Otherwise, each local neighborhood is politically, as it is technoeconomically and socially, autonomous. The elders resident in each locality arbitrate and adjudicate disputes (after lengthy discussion with all those involved) and provide advice and guidance for the younger men of the local community.

Although the Karimojong and other peoples with multicentric, nonstate authority systems recognize themselves as distinct societies occupying a demarcated territory, there is no single group that can make or enforce decisions that affect them all; there are no governmental institutions to organize and control their internal and external relations as a single people.

Political Centralization

From what we know of the technoenvironmental, economic, and social factors that affect the structure and function of authority systems among hunter-gatherers, primitive farmers, and herdsmen, a similarly significant causal linkage should be found between the centralization of authority on a more permanent basis—the development of chiefdoms, the gradual transition to true government, and the emergence of the state—and a still more complex level of technological adaptation to the environment.

Useful insights into the processes of political centralization are provided by a look at what the archeological record reveals of the cluster of natural and cultural circumstances that have been repeatedly associated with the emergence of more highly centralized forms of political organization in the Middle East (see Braidwood and Wiley 1962; Childe 1968; Wittfogel 1964), in the Americas (Sanders 1972), in China (Chang 1963), and on the Indian subcontinent (Fairservis 1971). This evidence from the past, combined with what anthropologists have learned from the study of contemporary peoples in the process of developing more centralized political institutions, provide a good general picture of the factors that appear most important in precipitating such centralization.

The emergence of centralized authority is invariably associated with the achievement of a more complex, diversified, and productive system of technoenvironmental adaptation that makes possible a larger, denser, more permanently settled population. Such a technology fosters the development of significant differences in the socioeconomic

". . . the emergence of more highly centralized forms of political organization in the Middle East . . . , in the Americas . . . , and in China. . . ."

Figure 10-13. Part of the Great Wall near Chuyungkuan, China. (United Nations, T. Chen.)

status of groups within these larger societies. Those with favored access to productive goods—those who own the land, control water resources and other valued minerals, and can muster the labor of others—can accumulate or control more wealth, which in turn can be translated into greater political power. Often this power is used both to further tighten control over allocation of the goods essential to the society's material base and to protect the privileged socioeconomic position of those in authority.

Usually politically controlled redistributive systems provide for the movement of most strategic goods and services toward one or more administrative centers and out again, and thus allow those in command of the process of allocation—the tax and tribute collectors and those whose interests they represent—to translate their control over the technology and economy into political power, control of what generally becomes at this developmental point some form of centralized government.

Increased technological complexity and productivity resulting in the proliferation of task specialization and in differentiation in the socioeconomic status of groups within the society are often complemented by ecological variability and regional specialization. The resultant diversity of the society's productive base increases the need for administrative coordination. New problems of integration and cooperation arise.

Often external societal threats foster the mobilization of a military force that can be used, as well, to police the society internally and to bolster the position of those in authority. Population growth that outdistances the acquisition of new territory can also

". . . a military force that can be used, as well, to police the society internally. . . ."
Figure 10-14. Mounties. (National Film Board of Canada.)

encourage political centralization—by increasing the need to control mounting dissension resulting from intensified competition and to assure the more efficient allocation of shrinking resources; or to mobilize authority for war in order to obtain additional territory. When all or most of these circumstances converge, the result is often the more or less stable, relatively permanent centralization of political authority, which has as its major function the maintenance of internal order (by means of a thriving bureaucracy composed of legislative, administrative, judicial, and military sectors) among asymmetrically related groups in what has invariably become a stratified society. Authority based primarily on kinship or diffuse associational ties is largely transcended, and coercive power is increasingly concentrated in the hands of those in control of what ultimately become the separate political structures and processes of "the state."

The institutions of politically centralized government can, of course, also be borrowed from other societies. But they will "take" only if internal technoenvironmental, economic, and social conditions allow for their adoption; more is required than mere proximity.

The critical processes by which the right to exercise centralized authority is legitimized are often strengthened by the persistence of crises, internal (resulting from dissension inherent in a system that fosters unequal rights of access to productive resources and material rewards) or external (resulting from competition with other, usually neighboring societies). Generally, this essential legitimacy is further reinforced by reliance on belief in the greater magical and/or religious powers of those in political control.

Initially, the assignment of authority in a newly unified political system is often contingent on special competence in dealing with the particular task requiring coordination: skill as a leader or prowess as a warrior. Or selection may be based on belief in a man's capacity to control by supernatural means certain environmental conditions on which the successful operation of the technology is dependent, such as rainfall, soil fertility, or the health of the working populace. Because possession of these valuable supernatural powers is believed vital to societal survival and because it typically overrides internal social divisions (especially during periods of intense social stress and anxiety), such religious authority is readily translatable into social and political power.

Whatever the initial criterion of his selection, once he acquires control over access to strategic productive resources and the allocation of a significant portion of consumption goods through manipulation of the redistributive system, the leader (or the leadership) has acquired an essential source of support for the continued exercise of political authority. At this stage in the process

". . . religious authority is readily translatable into social and political power."

Figure 10-15. Priest and king in a ritual exchange of "ecclesiastical fans," Thailand. (Embassy of Thailand.)

of political centralization some means is usually devised for further legitimizing the power of the now permanently necessary leader and for providing for continuity in the societal locus of decision-making authority. In this process the supernatural often plays an important part, especially during the early phases of political consolidation. These days the initial stages in the development of political centralization among a people previously lacking such a system are hard to observe. Most have now been dominated for at least a century by colonialist outsiders. Few contemporary peoples are still sufficiently isolated to allow the gradual process of political centralization to develop independently of the strong influence of other already more centrally organized societies.

Incipient Centralization and the Supernatural Sanctioning of Authority Among the Nuer

However a good idea of one way the process of political centralization may occur and of the important role of ideology (in this instance in the form of special supernatural status) in the initial stages of sanctioning the concentration of authority is provided by what is known of circumstances associated with the very early phases of political centralization among the cattle-keeping Nuer of the southern Sudan (Evans-Pritchard 1940, 1968; Greuel 1971; Howell 1954).

The traditional authority system of the Nuer was diffuse and multicentric. Each economically and socially autonomous local community was bound together both by patrilineal kinship ties and by a network of associational links that derived their structure from the Nuer age grade system. These ties were strongest within the local community, which was formed around a core of agnatically related males. There no system of authority external to the lineage was necessary. Also, in accordance with a by now familiar pattern—through marital alliances with neighboring groups resulting from the practice of local lineage exogamy, and the network of associational ties created by the age grade system—most relations with neighboring communities could be regulated without recourse to any centralized system of authority. All the Nuer within each area of "Nuer land" were loosely united within the context of a segmentary lineage system that extended over the several territorial divisions that collectively encompassed all of Nuer society.

Most activities requiring coordination and most conflicts requiring resolution involved Nuer who came into frequent contact with one another as the result of common residence in a single lineage-based local community. The greater their proximity, the greater the likelihood of their being related. Either kinship or associational ties could be activated to provide a means for resolving their differences and for coping with most problems of interpersonal relations that might arise. It was only in those less frequent instances—perhaps a cattle theft or a quarrel in which a Nuer came into conflict with someone from a socially and spatially more distant settlement—that neither the kinship system nor the age grade organization was adequate to provide a structural basis for conflict resolution.

In such cases an alternative means of settlement was necessary. The Nuer often turned to the "leopardskin chief," a neutral arbitrator, usually the member of a minor lineage, whose right to intercede was sanctioned by his power to curse those who failed to comply with the terms of a dispute settlement. When a murder occurred, for example, it was his responsibility to compel the kinspeople of the injured party to accept payment of a given number of cattle as a compensation for the wrong they had suffered. He also contributed to the restoration of order by providing the means of achiev-

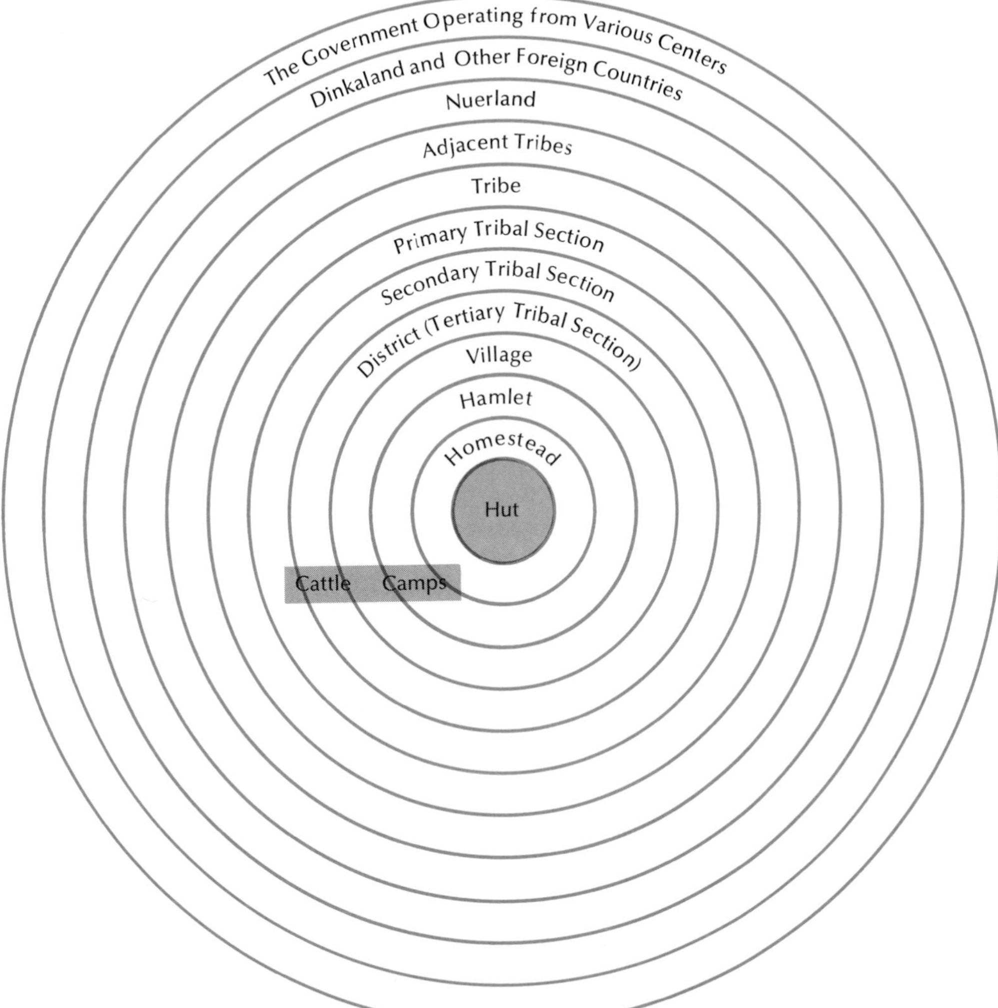

"The greater their proximity, the greater the likelihood of their being related."
Figure 10-16. Schematic representation of the traditional segmentary system of the Nuer, indicating the structure of political relationships with neighboring peoples and with other political systems. (After Evans-Pritchard 1940. By permission of Oxford University Press.)

ing ritual atonement for the disruptive act that had occurred. Under traditional circumstances this was the nearest thing to political leadership known to the Nuer, and it was all they needed.

Only when the Nuer were faced with a permanent crisis, prolonged Arab pressure at their northern tribal frontier, did the permanent centralization of authority emerge as a significant structural aspect of what had until then been a multicentric political system.

The new leaders were prophets, men whose right to lead was sanctioned and made legitimate not by their senior status in the lineage system or by their prominence in the age grade organization but by their special relation to the supernatural. As the Arab pressure persisted and the need for the maintenance of tribal solidarity continued, the Nuer developed the belief that the special supernatural power that legitimized a prophet's right to political control was transmitted to his heirs. With acceptance of this concept, a means of perpetuating their new system of centralized authority was achieved.

At about this point the British intervened, and the efforts of the Nuer to sustain political unification in defense of their tribal independence were brought to an end. If it had not been for this interference, it seems likely that the diffuse, multicentric political system of the Nuer might have been permanently transformed, that they would have found themselves catapulted by their response to prolonged external crisis to a new level of political development under the centralized leadership of a prophet-chief, a ruler by "divine right," the founder of a political dynasty.

Chiefdoms

Of the several developmental levels that have in the past marked the progressive increase in the internal differentiation of political roles and political processes that increasingly override authority based on kinship or associational relationships, the first and simplest level is represented by the chiefdom. The degree of centralization of authority in a chiefdom and the extent of a chief's power are likely to reflect the extent to which the redistributive system he controls affects the allocation of productive resources and is thus critical to the functioning of the subsistence technology and to the distribution of most needed goods.

If, for example, the part of the redistributive system under political control is only one of the society's several systems for the allocation of goods, if there is a considerable network of reciprocal and redistributive ties operating within the context of the kinship system or under the aegis of associational links, then the coercive power of the titular political leadership may be relatively weak. But if, on the other hand, the politically dominated aspect of the redistributive system is central to the operation of the subsistence technology and the economy, then the real power of those in authority is likely to be considerably greater.

Among many African peoples with formally centralized political systems of the sort ordinarily termed chiefdoms, the primitive farming technology that supports the society is often accompanied by an economic organization that operates principally on the basis of reciprocal and redistributive processes that function primarily within the context of the kinship system (see Hammond 1966). Those aspects of the redistributive system under the control of the chief, taxation and tribute, are still peripheral to the working of the basic technoeconomic system. The role of market exchange in the movement of most essential subsistence goods is often equally weak and, in any case, largely independent of the chief's control.

Most other forms of social interaction are still coordinated principally by the interlocking systems of kinship and associational controls. Where these conditions exist, the status of the chief most of the time is essentially ritual. Reliance on his right to mobilize the community in times of societal stress, the principal channel for the assertion of his political authority, is only occasionally necessary. In the day-to-day conduct of community affairs the political functions of such "chiefs" are necessarily of limited importance.

The State and Some of the Seeds of Empire

In contrast, where those with authority control a redistributive system that is vital to conduct of the people's daily lives, the centralization of political power is likely to be far more absolute and far more decisive in the ordering of all community activities. Such a situation is well illustrated by instances in which a ruler and the group that supports him control access to strategic resources, farmland, or a particularly critical scarce good such as the water supply. Where those in authority have the power to provide or deny access to drainage channels that make possible the cultivation of terraced land, or to permit or refuse rights of access to irrigation works necessary to the advanced agricultural pursuits on which entire populations are dependent, the opportunity for the concentration of their political power is greatly enhanced.

Where the environment is such that it is feasible to extend such systems over very wide areas (Steward 1955b; Wittfogel 1964)—as it was long ago in the Tigris-Euphrates Valley of Mesopotamia, along the banks of the Lower Nile, out over the alluvial plain of the Indus in what is now Pakistan, in the Chinese valley of the Huang Ho, in coastal Peru, and in the huge drainage basin that forms the Valley of Mexico—the ultimate result has often been the extension of wide networks of interconnected canals.

In the past, the enormous political task of administering these waterworks both created the need for more complex systems of centralized government and provided such governments with the principal source of their power: control over the distribution of a scarce good on which the entire populace was dependent, either directly, as were the farmers, or indirectly, as was the growing segment of the population released by the more productive farming system to pursue other specialized tasks—full-time craftworkers, traders, warriors, administrators, scholars, artists, and priests.

As this process continued in many parts of the ancient world, the antecedent chiefdoms, representative of an earlier stage in the centralization of political power, were destroyed or assimilated by the emergent states whose more complex systems of government were to serve as the political prototypes for the development of most forms of modern nationhood.

This process by which less centralized political systems have been gradually or suddenly obliterated by societies in which

". . . the enormous political task of administering these waterworks. . . ."
Figure 10-17. Camel crossing at the Indus Basin waterworks, Pakistan. (United Nations.)

"... or where such traditional leaders have so cooperated with politically more powerful states that their destruction and replacement by more direct means of outside political domination have been unnecessary."
Figure 10-18. One of the last of the sultans of Zanzibar seated on a throne provided by the British colonial administration. (Courtesy of the Library of Congress.)

political power was more highly concentrated has gone on more or less steadily ever since. Today chiefdoms, like bands and multicentric political systems, continue to exist only in isolation in those remote parts of the world where natural barriers or an inefficient or indifferent central government has allowed them to persist (or where such traditional leaders have so cooperated with politically more powerful states that their destruction and replacement by more direct means of outside political domination have been unnecessary). Either way, the process by which such traditional chiefdoms might ultimately have developed into states on their own has long since been interrupted by contact with—and direct or indirect domination, by—the technologically more advanced and thus politically more powerful societies of Europe, America, and parts of the Far East.

Political Change: The End of Indigenous Autonomy

Although much can be learned from the study of the political systems so far described, their future as viable autonomous political entities is clearly limited. All are under ever-increasing pressure to accept external domination from nation-states, old and new, concerned with bringing all their citizens under greater centralized political control in order that their productive energies can be more effectively harnessed and directed to the task of national unification.

In the poorer countries of the Third World where most such peoples live a major new national objective is the achievement of "economic growth." Inevitably, this entails an effort to increase the productivity of all tribal peoples by encouraging them to reorganize their productive strategies from subsistence to the production of marketable surpluses that will increase the new nations' capital resources and thus strengthen their economic base so that they can gain at least some semblance of independence from foreign economic and political intervention.

In the course of this effort it seems inevitable that most of the traditional political forms anthropologists have customarily studied will be replaced or co-opted and that local control over those productive resources essential for maintenance of most indigenous peoples' political autonomy will continue to pass steadily into alien control, either to local representatives of often re-

". . . the struggle of aboriginal peoples to retain—or regain—their political autonomy is just beginning. . . ."

Figure 10-19. Angolans celebrating the first day of their independence from Portugal. (United Nations.)

mote and unresponsive new government bureaucracies or to the management offices of even more inaccessible and/or indifferent multinational corporations.

So far anthropologists have generally remained neutral as this process has occurred. Or they have carefully recorded its progress as a variation on the old theme of culture contact. Only a small minority have identified themselves with those indigenous peoples who are resisting the neocolonialist usurpation of native rights to control their lands and the products of their labor. Like the impact of international power blocs and multinational corporations, the struggle of newly organizing aboriginal peoples to retain—or regain—their political autonomy, and thus to direct their future political development themselves, is just beginning to be perceived as a legitimate subject for anthropological inquiry.

Summary

Among the most fundamental functions of any political system are the maintenance of internal societal order through the legitimization of authority and the regulation of intersocietal relations by means of a strategy that, beyond the reach of bonds based on kinship or associational ties, usually mixes diplomacy with the threat of force.

In societies that are economically and socially semiautonomous and based on a relatively primitive level of technological development, the minimal exercise of authority necessary to keep order within what is usually a small band of closely related kinspeople is founded almost entirely on seniority within the family system.

At a more advanced level of technological development, multicentric authority systems emerge in which authority based on kinship is still the principal source of legitimate power. Authority based on seniority within the descent system provides the structural basis for maintaining order. As long as most members of the local community and of neighboring communities are united by ties of kinship, and as long as each kin group and each local community remain economically and socially autonomous, the system works.

In those comparatively rare instances in which conflict develops between persons unrelated to one another, or when the entire community is threatened by a crisis that requires total mobilization, some more centralized form of leadership may emerge, one that typically lasts only until the crisis is past, after which the power of those temporarily in positions of centralized authority is no longer needed and tends to atrophy.

As in the band, cultural homogeneity, the commonly recognized value of local-level cooperation, and various supernatural sanctions often function as useful adjuncts to authority in such "stateless" societies.

In advanced farming societies when there is an attendant increase in population size and in the degree of differentiation between the economic and social status of groups within the society, in societies where reliance on herding has led to the establishment of predatory political domination of subject peoples, and in industrialized societies, authority systems tend to emerge that transcend kinship as a primary locus of power and incorporate or replace authority based on associational ties. The power to regulate internal and external relations is increasingly concentrated in the hands of a small segment of the total population. At this level of political development the traditional authority systems customarily studied by anthropologists have usually been incorporated into or simply replaced by the bureaucracies of the nation-states of the modern world. Control over strategic productive resources is rapidly passing out of the hands of most indigenous peoples, and with it is going the last vestige of their political autonomy.

Suggested Readings

Several good general theoretical sources on political anthropology are Fried's *The Evolution of Political Society,* Colson's *Tradition and Contract: The Problem of Order,* and Balandier's *Political Anthropology.* For two useful reviews of the field see Cohen's "The Political System" and Winkler's "Political Anthropology." Among the best of a number of collections containing useful introductory essays as well as varied descriptive accounts are *Comparative Political Systems: Studies in the Politics of Pre-industrial Societies,* edited by Cohen and Middleton; the now classic *African Political Systems,* edited by Fortes and Evans-Pritchard; and the more recent *Political Anthropology,* edited by Swartz, Turner, and Tuden.

The band level of political development is described and analyzed in *Contributions to Anthropology: Band Societies,* edited by Damas; Service's *The Hunters;* and Steward's "The Patrilineal Band." Current theoretical controversies over the proper understanding of this form of political organization are well summarized in "Part Three: Social and Territorial Organization" of *Man the Hunter,* edited by Lee and DeVore. See also Basehart's "Mescalero Apache Band Organization and Leadership" and Wilmsen's "Interaction, Spacing Behavior, and the Organization of Hunting Bands."

Multicentric political systems are dealt with both theoretically and substantively in *Tribes Without Rulers,* edited by Middleton and Tait, and in Sahlins's *Tribesmen.* Specific types of such systems are described in detail in Dyson-Hudson's *Karimojong Politics,* in Fernea's *Shaykh and Effendi: Changing Patterns of Authority Among the El Shabana of Iraq,* in Jones's *Men of Influence in Nuristan,* in Stauder's "Anarchy and Ecology: Political Society Among the Majangir," and in Leach's *Political Systems of Highland Burma.*

In addition to the general sources listed above, many of which deal extensively with the centralization of authority, the relationship of political centralization to the early development of advanced agriculture is presented in archeological perspective in Adams's *The Evolution of Urban Society: Early Mesopotamia to Prehispanic Mexico* and Ribeiro's *The Civilizational Process.* See also Carneiro's "A Theory of the Organization of the State," Dumond's "Population Growth and Centralization," Kottak's "Ecological Variables in the Origin and Evolution of African States: The Buganda Example," Krader's *Formation of the State,* Service's *Origins of the State and Civilization: The Process of Cultural Evolution,* Wolf's *Peasants,* and Wittfogel's *Oriental Despotism: A Comparative Study of Total Power.* Several good specialized accounts are Carter's *Elite Politics in Rural India: Political Stratification and Alliances in Western Maharashtra,* Fallers's *Bantu Bureaucracy,* Paden's *Religion and Political Culture in Kano,* Beattie's *The Nyoro State,* and Winans's *Shambala: The*

Constitution of an African State. Also important are Bujra's *The Politics of Stratification,* Burling's *The Passage of Power: Studies in Political Succession,* Goody's *Succession to High Office,* and Hammel's *Power in Ica.*

For a sampling of the growing literature on the problems of political modernization in traditional societies see Antoun and Harick's *Rural Politics and Social Change in the Middle East: The Passing of Tribal Man in Africa,* edited by Gutkind; both Fallers's *The Social Anthropology of the Nation State;* and Sathyamurthy's "Social Anthropology in the Study of New Nation States."

11

Law and Organized Aggression

NEITHER law nor the organized exercise of force can be fully understood apart from the subject of authority systems or outside the natural context of problems of preserving order, providing justice, and resolving conflicts within and between societies. What follows in this chapter should be read as an extension of the subject of authority, and especially of the interrelation of authority and coercion, both within a society—to enforce norms, back up adjudication, and oversee dispute settlements—and between societies as they compete to protect their interests, sometimes peacefully and sometimes by resorting to force.

Law: Defining Rights and Redressing Wrongs

Although the authority system can be perceived as coterminous with the processes by which law is established and order is maintained within and between societies, it is useful to try to separate out for analysis a certain patterned process of action and reaction that can be defined as explicitly "legal": the articulation of a law and the response to the breach of law.

A parallelism between the complexity of the legal process and that of the authority system within which it is encompassed is to be expected. Where the political system is largely coterminous with the structure of the kinship system and the complementary operation of associations, and where the rate of culture change is relatively slow, law and custom are generally so closely linked as to be almost indistinguishable. Almost everyone knows almost all the rules and can recognize the difference between a socially harmless, idiosyncratic deviation from custom and the breach of a law that is fundamental to the maintenance of societal order. Because almost everyone knows everyone else, a serious violation of the law is usually readily recognized. And most breaches of law can be settled within the context of the societal unit in which they occur, usually by recourse to the mediating role of senior kinsmen. As population grows and its social organization becomes more complex, the legal system, like the larger system of authority of which it is a part, becomes increasingly distinguishable as a structural entity.

It is at the band level of political development that the system by which laws are made and enforced is most difficult to extricate for analysis, because it is almost entirely embedded within the matrix of the kinship-based authority system. Where the rate of culture change is relatively slow, as it is in bands living in isolation from technologically more advanced peoples, tradition is usually an adequate guide to action. Standards of reasonable behavior are generally agreed on, and when a new but not wholly unfamiliar situation arises, tradition usually serves as an adequate precedent for modifying an old rule or making a new one—a principle that holds, under comparatively stable cultural conditions, at all levels of development of the legal system. (The principle of precedent works much less well where culture change is rapid, especially when it is the result of contact with politically more powerful alien peoples with different norms. Then the old ways of coping with societal disruption often do not work well at all.)

However, the capacity of band society to force compliance with the rules, new or old, is comparatively limited. This is primarily because of the absence of coercive power, but is also because reliance on coercion in a small group whose members are continuously interdependent is nonadaptive: It is too serious a threat to group solidarity. If at all possible, the use of force is avoided.

Despite the lack of very powerful leaders and their frequent reluctance to use their

"Neither law nor the organized exercise of force can be fully understood apart from the subject of authority systems or outside the natural context of . . . conflicts within and between societies."

Figure 11-1. Masai warriors, one with a lion mane headdress, Kenya. (Courtesy of the American Museum of Natural History.)

limited coercive power (see Marshall 1960), and despite the absence of such separate institutions as legislatures, courts, police, 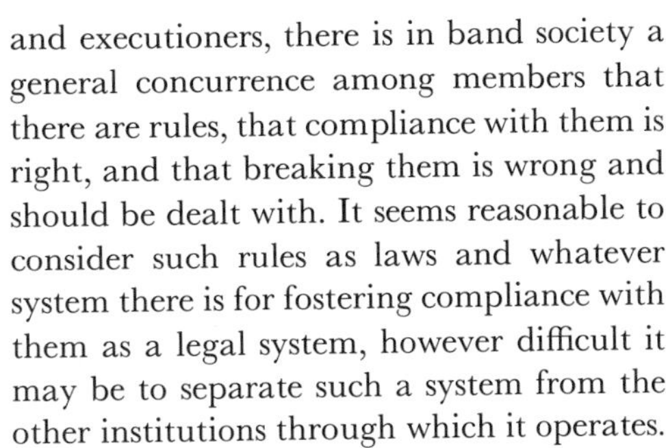

and executioners, there is in band society a general concurrence among members that there are rules, that compliance with them is right, and that breaking them is wrong and should be dealt with. It seems reasonable to consider such rules as laws and whatever system there is for fostering compliance with them as a legal system, however difficult it may be to separate such a system from the other institutions through which it operates.

Differences in the role of law and of the legal system in band societies are more than structural. Law in the band is qualitatively distinct in ways that reflect the conditions necessary for the maintenance of social life among peoples living at the hunting and gathering level of technological development with which the band is recurrently associated.

". . . the legal system, like the larger system of authority of which it is a part, becomes increasingly distinguishable as a structural entity."

Figure 11-2. A San Francisco attorney consults with her client. (Action Photo by Susan Biddle.)

One of the most fundamentally different circumstances characteristic of law and its enforcement in societies based on band organization concerns the sources of the conflicts that lead to disputes requiring settlement. For example, there is comparatively little competition for access to productive resources; they are shared. And private property is insignificant, limited to possession of a few tools and weapons, clothing, and articles of adornment. Theft is virtually unknown because it would be useless. Disputes over property rights and inheritance are resultingly rare. Physical assaults are very uncommon and murder is often almost unheard of. The value of avoiding conflict in a group of people so dependent on each other is another factor of fundamental significance. In comparison with more complex, larger societies, there are fewer material sources of serious intrasociety conflict, more critical economic and social reasons to avoid such conflict, and perhaps resultantly, less definitive means of either settling disputes once they have arisen or keeping them from escalating (which provides still another good reason for avoiding them).

Typically, the processes by which conflict is dealt with in band societies emphasize the reduction of frustration with minimum permanent societal disruption and the simultaneous fostering of reconciliation. When dissension arises between band members, it can usually be mediated by an elder person who, as a senior kinsman to both disputants, has authority that both must accept. Often no such formal judgment is necessary. As everyone knows the rules of the band, and as few infractions can occur without witnesses, the facts of a breach of customary law are soon widely known, and the case can be dealt with by informal public discussion that continues until consensus is reached on a proper means of settlement, usually one that entails compensation to whomever is adjudged the injured party.

In less serious conflicts, disputants often settle their cases themselves. One or the other of the principals to a potentially disruptive disagreement may just decide to go off for a few days to stay with kinsmen or friends in another band, a further example of the usefulness of band exogamy (see Turnbull 1968). When the heat of the dispute is cooled, the aggrieved person may return, and peace is restored, although the initial issue may never have been formally resolved.

"Self-help" and Song Singing

Although breaking the law may be publicly recognized, sometimes it must be privately settled. Where interpersonal conflict is not dealt with by the intervention and arbitration of a senior member of some kin group to which both disputants belong, and where neither disputant can or will just go away for awhile, frequently those in conflict are allowed to "work out"—argue out or fight out—their differences. Such a means of coping with conflict permits the principals to forcefully express their frustration, to protest the wrong that has been done them (and thus to solicit public support for their side of the dispute), and to reduce the tension and anger they feel, even if no one necessarily comes out the absolute winner.

One of the best-known and most formally structured techniques for fulfilling these several hostility-reducing functions is the famous song duel of the Eskimo. As an alternative to seeking legal redress by more violent means, each party to a disagreement composes and loudly sings insulting songs about the other (Hoebel 1954). These songs, as humorously scurrilous as their composers can make them, serve each litigant both as a means of noisy advocacy and as a catharsis. In the course of the witty musical exchange of abuse, much of the hostility that might otherwise drive them to some more violent means of conflict resolution is harmlessly dissipated. The system provides both persons with a means for making for themselves the strongest and literally the most exhaustive case possible. Afterward, both feel relieved. Their frustrations are abated, their dispute has been fully aired, if not entirely "settled," and they are expected to be reconciled. Among Greenland Eskimo the singer who gets the most enthusiastic support from the audience finally silences the other singer and is considered the victor. To acknowledge settlement of their dispute and the end of hard feelings, the singers exchange gifts.

Wife Stealing

Where mediation, singing contests, and other more benign alternatives to direct confrontation fail or are not available, stronger measures to right a wrong may be socially recognized as appropriate by the Eskimo band. Still it is often left up to the individual.

The Eskimo expect a man against whom a serious crime has been committed to seek redress on his own (Birket-Smith 1929; Hoebel 1954; Rasmussen 1929; Service 1966). If his wife is stolen, for example—a fairly common occurrence among certain Eskimo groups—the aggrieved husband, furious by this challenge to his rights, to the integrity of his household, and to his status as household head, and inconvenienced by having to get along without a helpmate, has the tacit permission of his society to kill his wife's abductor. If he does so, he will not be punished, an indication that his society recognizes the legality of his act, for otherwise killing is a crime among the Eskimo. But, again, responsibility for rectification rests with the kin group; an Eskimo murdered must be killed by his own kinsmen, so they can avoid a feud with his victim's family. By not pressing his kinsmen to kill him when he slays his wife's abductor, the members of the dead man's band confirm the husband's right to retribution for wife stealing. Social order is restored and the case is formally closed, although resentment may linger on.

"If his wife is stolen, for example. . . ."
Figure 11-3. An Eskimo woman carved in stone. (National Film Board of Canada.)

Law Where Authority Is Diffused

In multicentric authority systems the structure of the kinship system is characteristically more complex. It is usually based on the more extensive tracing of descent and the elaborate reckoning of affinal ties. Typically, the local members of the descent group collectively own the productive goods (land or rights of access to pasturage and watering places), and nearly all those who work collaboratively are kinsmen. Because the size of the local population is typically larger, the field within which disputes are likely to occur is generally more widely extended, especially if a redistributive system is in operation and if the inherited right to use increasingly scarce farmland and the transmission of ownership in such goods as cattle occur on an individual basis. Although there are now both more things to be in conflict about and more people likely to be involved, dissension is still most likely to occur between persons who are related. For most persons with whom the individual comes into contact, and thus with whom he may come into conflict, are likely to be kinsmen, either members of the same descent group or in-laws. If not, they are at least likely to belong to the same associations, as in the instance of East African cattle-keeping peoples.

Again, most conflict can be resolved through reliance on the authority of some senior person or persons within either the kin group or an association. Where this fails, a diviner, a prophet or saint, or some other neutral outsider whose authority is derived from a supernatural source usually serves as the intermediary, sorting out the conflicting claims, evoking relevant legal principles, and—often—checking on the size and strength of each litigant's supporters before negotiating a final settlement (see Barth 1959; Evans-Pritchard 1940).

In comparatively rare instances neither kinship nor cross-cutting associational ties may be relied on as a source of authority strong enough for adjudication and settlement based on a combination of social pressure, threats of punishment by the supernatural, and a self-interested appraisal of the possible merits of *not* pressing suit. Then, although the society may recognize that the law has been broken, the absence of any centralized authority system usually means that those who believe they have been wronged must right their grievances themselves.

Among the pastoral Turkana of northern Kenya (Gulliver 1951), a people with a multicentric political system, a man injured by another man who is neither related by kinship nor closely allied within the age grade system is expected to seek redress himself, usually by forcibly taking cattle from the wrongdoer's herd until he feels that he has been adequately compensated for the offense. If this escalates the dissension and the two come to blows there is little means of stopping them. Ultimately, they may tire of fighting, give up temporarily, and go home to nurse their wounds, but later the struggle may be resumed. Intervention is impossible because the Turkana have no courts, no means of formally accusing a person, trying him, deciding on a conviction or an acquittal, or enforcing the terms of either such settlement. The only apparent reason that such fighting does not go on interminably once it has started is that the herds of adversaries are soon likely to use up all the locally available pasture and must be moved off. If they are wise, the disputants depart in different directions.

Law and the Concentration of Coercive Power

The concentration of coercive power, the power to force obedience to legal decisions, is coterminous with the centralization of authority that is part of the political systems of most settled farming peoples and many pastoral nomadic groups, especially in the Middle East. But despite the presence of chiefs in chiefdoms, despite the often elaborate paraphernalia of their office, and despite the presence of an active court system, the way that disputes are settled there and the number of cases that are still dealt with by alternative means reflect the persistence,

"... the power to force obedience to legal decisions. . . ."
Figure 11-4. Honor America Day, Washington, D.C. (Michael Abramson, Black Star.)

even at this somewhat more complex level of societal development, of kin groups and associations as primary contexts for most interactions and thereby as structures of continuing major importance in coping with conflict. When and if disputes do reach the courts, the emphasis in judicial procedures is still on mediation for compensation and conciliation rather than punishment, and reliance is on catharsis and consensus building rather than on arbitrary decision making.

Traditional African societies provide examples of some of the most developed

"... emphasis in judicial procedures . . . on mediation for compensation and conciliation rather than punishment. . . ."
Figure 11-5. Sleeping cages in a convict camp, 1941, Georgia. (Courtesy of the Library of Congress.)

systems of law outside the nation-states of the modern world. Yet the operation of the legal process within the court system of most African chiefdoms still provides as generously for discussion leading to settlement by consensus as it does for judgment based on an impartial legal authority that hears the dispute, decides who is right and who is wrong, and dictates and enforces the terms of settlement.

This emphasis on decision by consensus and settlement by reconciliation is importantly related to the need of primitive farmers and stock raisers, who usually live in small, settled communities (even if such communities are part of some larger, politically centralized system), to protect the solidarity, friendliness, and cohesiveness of the local community, the community peace they all depend on to assure that their neighbors will help them if the need arises. In the small-scale communities characteristic of most of the primitive farming peoples of Africa, those who come into conflict are most often close neighbors who must continue to live near one another after their differences are settled. It is in their interest and in the interest of all those to whom they are related by valued kinship and associational ties that a dispute be settled in a way that is as nearly satisfactory to all parties as possible. Otherwise, the persistence of bad feeling may seriously disrupt the orderly life of the community for a long time to come.

People's social relations in such communities are not only close but also diffuse (see Gluckman 1955). Frequently they are related to one another in a variety of interdependent ways. The neighbor with whom a farmer comes into conflict over the boundaries of a particular plot of farmland, for example, may also be an earth priest on whose intercession with the spirits of the earth the farmer is dependent for the success of his crop. The same man may also be a member of the village chief's council, the farmer's brother's father-in-law, the paternal uncle of a young woman the farmer's son is thinking of marrying, and a good friend of the farmer's trading partner in another village. If the conflict between the disputants is not settled to the satisfaction of both, or at least in such a way as to leave them both feeling they have been treated justly, their rancor may have a domino effect, seriously disrupting a whole series of social relationships and drawing so many others into the dispute that the peace and well-being of the entire community are threatened.

The danger of such disruption is reflected in the conduct of African court proceedings. Often to the outsider they seem to drag on interminably. In fact, they frequently continue until every one who wants to testify has been patiently heard out. In the process every aspect of the case is openly argued over and thrashed out, the applicable cultural norms are publicly restated, and much hostility is verbally dissipated. A general consensus on the proper disposition of the case gradually takes form as witnesses both testify and express their judgment and the judge or judges and their advisors listen on until everyone involved has fully had a say. Gradually, the dispute is settled, to almost everyone's satisfaction and relief. There has been a public investigation, everyone interested has had a chance to hear what the problem is, and it has been resolved in a manner that maximizes the chances for reconciliation and minimizes the potential for lingering resentment that would continue to threaten social peace (see Gibbs 1963).

All this is in marked contrast to the social context in which conflicts are legally resolved in large-scale societies based on advanced agriculture or, especially, on modern industry. There disputants can rarely settle their differences legally on their own. Indeed, in most instances "taking the law into your own hands" may itself be the basis for a court case. The principals and their supporters in a court dispute, the lawmakers, the judges, and the police may all be either unknown to one another or related only through the litigation. Once the case is closed, all can part, bad feeling and all, with the reasonable expectation that they may never have to come into contact with one another again, and with the near certainty that they will never have to cooperate. Settlements are often correspondingly harsher and punishments more severe. Deterrence and restraint through imprisonment or execution frequently become more important in the law enforcement process. Efforts to achieve reconciliation and rehabilitation are minimized, or, if they are considered, it is as something daringly and possibly dangerously new in the evolution of the law.

With the important exception of the often despotic early nation-states based on advanced agriculture, the emphasis in the judicial process of most nonindustrialized societies on consensus and restoration of amity rather than on coercion reflects both the more fragile, less productive technologies on which these necessarily smaller interdependent societies are based and the consequent weakness of centralized political authority therein.

In looking at these so-called simpler legal systems one can regard them as merely antique means of coping with conflict—appealing perhaps, but obviously irrelevant to the resolution of conflict in more complex societies. Or one may seek in them some possibly useful alternatives to the seemingly ever harsher, more impersonal, more brittley binding, and more socially disruptive procedures of many modern legal systems. In these increasing conflict may often result in decreasing reliance on law as an agent of social reconciliation. And law may be interpreted instead as a legitimate source of societal repression.

Organized Aggression

There are three principal ways conflict between politically separate peoples can be dealt with: (1) by diplomacy, the ongoing adjustment of different interests through negotiation and efforts at reconciliation; (2) by isolation, using avoidance as a means of minimizing the potential for conflict; or (3) by aggression, the organized use of force as a means of settlement. Of these three, diplomacy and aggression are necessarily relied on more frequently. Avoidance works as a means of coping with conflict only between peoples who are so isolated from one another that they have little basis for contact anyway.

Competition for control over scarce resources—land and other goods—is a major cause of the conflict that may lead to armed aggression, particularly during periods when population growth is outdistancing increase in the productive capacity of a people's technology. Such armed aggression then results either from the absence of those political institutions that allow for peaceful negotiations to resolve competitive tensions or from the failure of such institutions to do their job. Armed combat is often seen as the only alternative. Killing the enemy is not culturally categorized as murder. Economically motivated, armed aggression becomes socially, politically, and ideologically sanctioned as necessary and even honorable.

Feuding and Raiding

At the band level of political development relations with most other groups with which there is occasion to come into contact can

". . . diplomacy and aggression are necessarily relied on more frequently."

Figure 11-6. United Nations patrol, Cyprus. (National Film Board of Canada.)

usually be handled under the aegis of the kinship ties that link neighboring groups, providing a context of friendliness, respect, and appreciation of mutual interest that allows for the settlement of most disputes by peaceful political means, usually after long discussion with all those involved.

Where such efforts at diplomacy fail, fighting often breaks out in the form of sporadic feuding in which those members of each group most involved in the dispute attack one another physically, often turning their tools into lethal weapons and applying their hunting techniques to bringing down their enemies. Typically, the feud does not actively involve the entire community or even all able-bodied fighting men, but only the principals and those most closely allied with them by kinship.

However, because there is no central leadership that can take the responsibility for negotiating a truce and working out the terms of a peace settlement, feuds can easily escalate, becoming more bloody and protracted than anyone really wants. As vengeance is sought for each new act of aggression the cycle of terror and retaliation goes on; the "score" remains endlessly uneven. Neither side is ever entirely satisfied. Rarely can either put the other completely and permanently out of action. Each retires from the field only to lick its wounds (or harvest its crops) and build up strength for a new attack. If there is no figure who can legitimately intervene and impose a settlement, hostile skirmishing can drag on for years, and may even be passed on to the next generation.

Feuding as a characteristic means of dealing with intergroup tensions resulting from property disputes or conflict over women (who are in such instances regarded as property) is observable in its most intractable form among hunter-gatherers and those primitive farmers and pastoral peoples who lack either a centralized authority system (that could otherwise restore peace by unifying contending factions) or associations (whose membership frequently cross-cuts and counteracts divisive factionalism).

An example of what can happen when feuding cannot be politically controlled is provided by a look at the state of affairs among the Jíbaro Indians of Ecuador (Karsten 1923). There intergroup hostility has become endemic. The Jíbaro themselves recognize their feuding as a curse, but lacking any unifying political system, they have no satisfactory means of putting a stop to it. Each Jíbaro family group lives separately in a single compound surrounded by its banana groves and manioc gardens. Most houses are built on hills so that approaching enemies can readily be sighted. Gardens are enclosed with fences made of strong poles. Often the pathways leading to the family settlement are boobytrapped as a means of further protection. All of this is because most Jíbaro families live in a state of open or temporarily suspended feud with their neighbors. A feud may grow out of any conflict between two politically independent family groups. Pigs belonging to one may enter the garden of another, rooting it up and ruining the manioc crop. The irate proprietor of the garden may then demand compensation that the pigs' owner refuses to pay. A bloody fight may ensue, resulting in severe bodily injury and even greater hostility. Later a member of one of the families may fall ill with one of the many diseases that the Jíbaro ascribe to workers of evil magic. Divination usually reveals that the enemy family has caused the malady. If the sick person dies it is the duty of his kinsmen to kill the suspected sorcerer. Then the murdered man's family must retaliate, and so the blood feud begins. In the absence of any means of bringing it to an end, it may go on for years. Jíbaro fathers who still harbor hatred and a desire for vengeance against old enemies indoctrinate their sons with their enmity to assure that the feud will be carried on by their descendants.

As long as people are nomadic, their mobility may serve as a sort of control on such feuding. For then it is often difficult for both parties to a dispute to stay together in a single place long enough for the fight between them to become too serious. Once separated, each group migrates independently, and there is a good chance they will meet again only infrequently.

The impossibility of relying on any centralized system of authority for the settlement of a feud becomes more serious once a people, like the Jíbaro, have settled down. Then the likelihood of conflict increases both because contact between the same groups occurs more often and because they are all competing for access to the same usually limited resources. As the sedentary population grows, competition for farmland is especially likely to accelerate the potential for conflict. If no institutions are available that provide the basis for peace negotiations—either political or religious leaders who could act as intermediaries—the consequent reliance on force as a means of settling disputes can easily get out of control. Once the network of hostile relationships spreads and feuding is elaborated and is institutionalized as a means of "settlement," chances are diminished of developing an alternative, less violent means of coping with conflict.

Raiding

Raiding is usually a somewhat more contained and controllable process of conflict adjustment by aggression. Again competition for scarce resources is the trigger. Usually the emphasis is on the highly organized, short-term exercise of force to achieve a particular, limited goal, the expropriation of goods, land, animals, occasionally women, or other forms of wealth belonging to a neighboring group. Raiding is probably most highly developed among herding peoples, especially those who use their animals for transport and thus have developed refined techniques for the quick deployment of their forces—into the attack, out, and quickly off with the spoils. This is the classic strategy of nomadic Arab camel raiders. With the introduction of the horse it was a form used widely by Indians on the North American plains and on the South American pampas.

Raiding is often associated with a multicentric political system, one in which authority is shifting, unstable, and impermanent. The traditional political systems of Middle Eastern pastoral nomadic peoples are often of this type (see Barth 1953). The only permanent political units are the component corporate patrilineages. In a situation of crisis—to organize a raid or to organize defense against other raiders—the usually autonomous groups, each formed around a core of agnatically related males, can be temporarily unified under a "chief," the head of some larger, more all-encompassing lineal grouping through which all trace their descent back to a distant common ancestor. As is usually the case among people so organized, the chief is primarily a coordinator, charged with leading the alliance only as long as the brief battle lasts, after which it is his task to supervise the redistribution of the loot. Then, depending on the success of the raid and on other circumstances, the temporarily mobilized raiders may settle down and camp together for a while, or their temporary cohesion may be allowed to lapse as they break up into their component lineage segments and move off separately, each with its own portion of the spoils and each now once more politically independent of the others.

In contrast to those who rely on open-ended feuding as a way of adjusting their relations with others, among raiders there is usually some commonly accepted means of bringing hostilities to an end. Raiders have

"... emphasis is on the highly organized, short-term exercise of force to achieve a particular, limited goal. . . ."

Figure 11-7. Scene outside the men's ceremonial house, often the center for organizing raids against neighboring peoples, New Guinea. (Courtesy of the Museum of Primitive Art.)

leaders, and leaders can make and enforce a truce. However, raiding is often profitable. In the absence of a peaceful political means of coping with competition, it is frequently perceived as a necessary and honorable means of ecological and economic adjustment, especially among people whose technological adaptation to a harsh, unpredictable environment like the desert is fragile. Consequently, the truce among raiders, although rigorously complied with, is most often only temporary.

In many parts of the Middle East and in North Africa, nomadic herdsmen have frequently used their skills as raiders to establish permanent political domination and an exploitative economic relation over isolated settled communities (see Briggs 1960; Coon 1958; Miner 1963; Musil 1928; Nicolaisen 1963). Often oasis-dwelling farmers have been required to pay tribute in the form of foodstuffs, craft goods, and labor to nomadic raiders, who provide them in return with protection from other desert predators. With this development the raid, a usually small-scale short-term act of aggression to achieve a limited goal, becomes a war of conquest in microcosm.

Warfare and Revolution

Ordinarily, large-scale warfare is possible only among peoples with a sufficiently developed technology, usually based on advanced farming or industrialization, to support a centralized authority system that includes full-time military specialists, war leaders, strategists, and warriors and that is able to provide them with often costly armaments. At this higher level of technological development long-term, large-scale warfare also becomes materially more profitable, especially if the enemy's technology is sufficiently productive or the natural resources they control are sufficiently rich to allow for their occupation and long-term economic exploitation. Aggression on this considerably larger, more lethal scale—and for this considerably more valuable economic objective—first developed as an aspect of the political growth of the early, agriculturally based nation-states of Asia, the Middle East, and the Americas. Armies maintained with a portion of the surplus produced by the farming population served both to back up the internal political control of the central government and as a means of extending and maintaining by force and the threat of force political domination over the territory and productive resources of neighboring peoples.

As the scattered communities of settled farmers became first city-states, then nations, and finally empires, the techniques of organized aggression, including an elaborately ranked hierarchy of full-time military specialists in charge of permanently mobi-

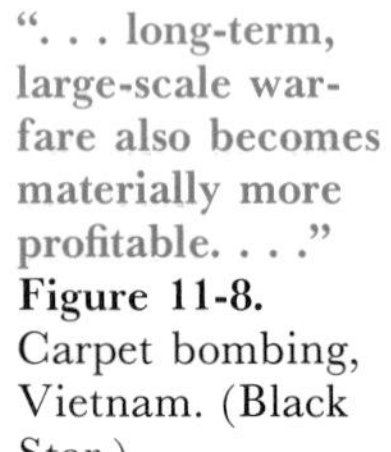

"... long-term, large-scale warfare also becomes materially more profitable. . . ."

Figure 11-8. Carpet bombing, Vietnam. (Black Star.)

lized armed forces, developed into powerful, sometimes dominant, adjuncts of the permanently centralized political systems of which they had initially been only a subordinate, supporting part. Making war became an industry. When this occurred, the techniques of diplomacy and peacemaking fell into disuse, occasionally even disrepute.

Those of these wars that were imperialistic, that had as their objective the political domination and economic exploitation of technologically less developed indigenous peoples, produced, with time, rebellions that often became armed revolts. Starting out as necessarily small-scale guerilla wars of liberation, they have frequently developed into full-scale revolutionary warfare.

Summary

Legal systems, like other aspects of culture, can be arranged on an analytic continuum from the simple to the complex. In band societies, where what centralized authority there is is usually in the hands of the elders of the kin group, and where maintenance of group solidarity is critical to societal survival, rules are derived from tradition, and the value of compliance with them is usually self-evident. Because of the communally shared rights of access to productive goods and the relative lack of private property, economic competition is rarely a source of conflict requiring legal intervention. When conflicts do arise, efforts at their resolution generally emphasize compensation and the restoration of friendly relations rather than punishment.

In some food-growing societies, and among some herding peoples with multicentric authority systems, the larger field of social interaction is accompanied by a more extended network of bonds based on kinship or associational ties. Despite the increased potential for conflict over property, most disputes can still be settled without coercion. When a mediator is required, the person who fulfills this role is usually a neutral outsider whose power is supernaturally, rather than politically, backed. In other farming societies, where growing population and the increase in socioeconomic specialization and differentiation make conflict resulting from competition over productive resources more likely, the potential for dissension is kept in check by systems of adjudication. These permit the achievement of consensus, often through purposefully long-drawn-out debate that allows for the socially harmless dissipation of hostility and assures that the final judgment will be publicly supported and social peace maintained.

It is in societies based on advanced agriculture and industrialization that the emphasis on consensus building and on reconciliation tends to diminish, its place taken by increasing reliance on formal legislative bodies, courts, prisons, and police as the principal institutions for making and enforcing the law.

The regulation of conflict resulting from competition between societies can be dealt with by diplomacy, by avoidance, or by reliance on a variety of forms of organized force: from feuds, which typically involve only the principals and their close associates, to raiding and warfare. Raiding is generally a more highly organized enterprise than feuding. Alleged wrongs provide the rationale for sporadically acquiring property through armed attack and pillage. Large-scale, prolonged warfare can be managed only by societies based on a sufficiently productive pattern of technoenvironmental adaptation to provide extended support for full-time specialists in making war. Once the armed forces have been developed and once they are victorious, however, a portion of the material support for further warmaking is often exacted from conquered peoples, and continued political domination and economic exploitation becomes increasingly profitable. At this point, the armed forces, characteristically controlled by the leaders of the necessarily centralized authority system, may use their power both as a major means of dominating and exploiting other societies and as a way of maintaining their version of internal law and order. If the resulting oppression cannot be peaceably dealt with by political means, the revolt of those who are exploited may escalate into armed rebellion, and what are initially guerilla wars may develop into widespread revolution.

Suggested Readings

The only source that also uses law and organized aggression as categories analytically separable from political organization is *Law and Warfare: Studies in the Anthropology of Armed Aggression*, edited by Bohannan.

On law the most recent collection that takes an anthropological perspective is *Law in Culture and Society*, edited by Nader; see also her *The Ethnography of Law* and "On Studying the Ethnography of Law and Its Consequences" by Nader and Yngvesson. Pospisil's *Anthropology of Law* is another useful source. Two excellent review articles are Koch's "Law and Anthropology: Notes on Interdisciplinary Research" and Moore's "Law and Anthropology." Also of general value are Diamond's "The Rule of Law Versus the Order of Custom" and Gulliver's "Negotiations As a Model of Dispute Settlement: Towards a General Model." Also see Barjun's *Law Without Sanctions.*

Fallers's *Law Without Precedent,* Gluckman's *Politics, Law and Ritual in Tribal Societies,* and Hoebel's *The Law of Primitive Man* are classic works.

Of importance among recent studies of law within the context of particular cultures are Deng's *Tradition and Modernization: A Challenge for Law Among the Dinka of the Sudan*, Epstein's *Contention and Dispute: Aspects of Law and Social Control in Melanesia*, Gluckman's *Ideas and Procedures in African Customary Law,* Reid's *A Law of Blood: The Primitive Law of the Cherokee Nation*, and Schlegel's *Tiruray Justice: Traditional Tirunay Law and Morality.* See also Bohannan's *Justice and Judgment Among the Tiv* and Goldschmidt's *Sebei Law.*

There are now several excellent sources on a subject that anthropologists too long have ignored: Divale's *Warfare in Primitive Societies: A Bibliography; War: The Anthropology of Armed Conflict and Aggression,* edited by Fried, Harris, and Murphy; Harrison's *Warfare;* Otterbein's *The Evolution of War;* Tax's *War: Its Causes and Correlates;* and Vayda's *War in Ecological Perspective.* Turney-High's *Primitive Warfare* provides a useful bibliography on the earlier literature. See also Hallpike's "Functionalist Interpretations of Primitive Warfare"; Harris's "The Human Strategy, Warfare Old and New"; and Otterbein's "Anthropology of War."

Some good analytic case studies are Gardner and Heider's *Gardens of War: Life and Death in the New Guinea Stone Age,* Goodwin's *Western Apache Raiding and Warfare,* Kiefer's *Tausug Armed Conflict,* Koch's *War and Peace in Jalemo,* McNitt's *Navajo Wars,* Netting's "Kofyar Armed Conflict: Social Causes and Consequences," and Vayda's "Phases of the Process of War and Peace Among the Marings of New Guinea."

On the increasingly compelling subject of rebellion and revolution see Friedrich's *Agrarian Revolt in a Mexican Village; Imperialism and Revolution in South Asia,* edited by Gough and Sharma; Kohl and Litt's *Urban Guerilla Warfare in Latin America;* Mack's "Sharpening the Contradictions: Guerilla Strategy in Imperialist Wars"; Miller and Aya's *National Liberation: Revolution in the Third World;* Russell's *Rebellion, Revolution, and Armed Force: A Comparative Study of Fifteen Countries with Special Emphasis on Cuba and South Africa;* Wolf's *Peasant Wars of the Twentieth Century;* and also his "Peasant Rebellion and Revolution."

Part Six
Ideology

At the root of ideology is explication: ideologies explain to man why he is, whence he came, what he should be. Ideologies explain how the universe operates, how the environment may be dealt with, and the end to which culture struggles.

FRIED (1968:615–616)

The word *ideology* is used here to refer collectively to the several component aspects of all peoples' systems of beliefs about themselves and the reasons for their being: about their relation to others, to the world, and to the universe as they perceive it. Such explanations both provide a means of comprehending people's relation to their environment and serve as guides to the actions necessary to maintain or secure their place within it.

Ideology as a universal aspect of culture will be developed here with particular attention to the supernaturally based systems of belief and observance—religious and magical systems—that still predominate among most of the world's peoples. However, it is important to bear in mind that it is ideology, that is, *some* system of beliefs—not necessarily supernaturally based—that is demonstrably universal.

Here the term *ideology* is intended to encompass also secular beliefs, values, and ethical and moral systems that frequently fulfill functions parallel to those of supernaturally based belief systems, and sometimes replace them.

12
Belief and Ritual

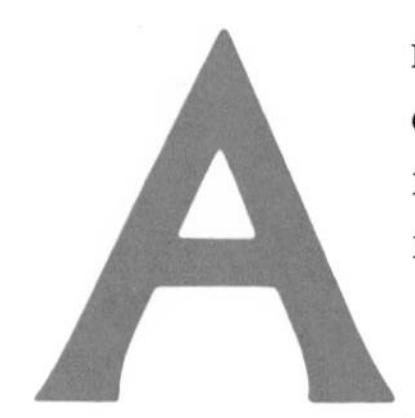

NALYTICALLY, every people's ideology can be separated into two essential components: a system of beliefs and an accompanying set of actions or ritual observances.

Myths of Origin

Fundamental to nearly every ideology is a system of beliefs concerning the origins of the world and people's relation to it. Often such beliefs take the form of myths of origin, or creation myths. Usually these myths describe the origins of various supernatural beings and the means by which they in turn created the universe, the world, and humankind. These myths often emphasize descriptions of the ways people received those things that are fundamental to the material maintenance of their culture and those skills by which they make a living, such as fire, rainfall, wildlife, and a knowledge of hunting and farming.

The creation myths of many of the peoples of the Pacific are particularly elaborate and lovely. Although they are usually familiar to all believers, they are frequently retold for the reassurance that plausible explanations of reality always provide.

For each island, and often for each kin group, the creation myth may vary. According to a recorded version of the story of the origins of the Gilbertese lineage Karangoa-of-the Kings, for example, the universe was created by Naareau the Elder, who was "the First of All":

> Not a man, not a beast, not a fish, not a thing was before him. He slept not, for there was no sleep; he ate not, for there was no hunger. He was in the void. Long he sat, and there was none but he. Then Naareau said in his heart, "I will make a woman." Behold! A woman grew out of the void: Nei Teakea. He said again, "I will make a man." Behold! A man grew out of his thought: Na Atibu, the rock. And Na Atibu lay with Nei Teakea. Behold! their child was born: Naareau the Younger, And Naareau the Elder said to Naareau the Younger, "All knowledge is whole in thee. I will make a thing for thee to work upon." So he made that thing in the void. It was called the Darkness and the Cleaving Together, the sky, and the earth, and the sea were within it; but the sky and the earth clove together, and the darkness was between them, for as yet there was no separation. And when his work was done, Naareau the Elder said, "Enough! It is ready. I go never to return."
>
> [Grimble 1951:622]

The account continues with Naareau the Younger's lifting the sky up from the earth and awakening the animals and people he found sleeping there. The islands were created, and finally "all the lands of the earth."

Usually myths of creation such as the one just described or the somewhat different version familiar to most Europeans, Americans, and Middle Easterners, that begins, ". . . God created the heaven and earth. And the earth was without form, and void; and darkness *was* upon the face of the deep . . ." provide more than an explanation of the origins of the world and of humankind. The events and the people they describe, the things that happened in the mythical past, serve believers as a sort of allegorical code for living in the present. In this way, a people's belief system is always importantly related to their values, to the particular ethical and moral concepts that give them a basis for making judgments and taking action. For the anthropologist this is perhaps the most significant function of ideology: its role as a guide to behavior, to defining right and wrong, to choosing between good and evil, and in sanctioning both individual behavior and cultural institutions—economic morality, the right form of marriage, the proper organization of society, the best type of political system, and, of course, the "right" ideology itself. The study of ideology is also important to the student of culture because it illuminates the concepts fundamental to people's ways of thinking, to their perception of reality, and to understanding the world as they see it.

The Functions of Ritual

The actions that accompany a given system of beliefs are invariably objectified in ceremonial observances, ritual actions that both reinforce belief itself and provide participants with what they perceive as a means of controlling, or at least affecting, their relations with others, with the world, and with the powers, supernatural or natural, that they believe determine the destiny of all things. Usually, participation in ritual observances is intended to perpetuate or improve the believer's relation to such powers; supplication is frequently explicit.

The ritual of sacrifice, for example, is based on the belief that a particular source of power, usually a specific supernatural being, shares people's evaluation of a particular object, action, or thought. The believer's sacrifice consists of giving up, denying, even destroying the thing that is valued in order to please the supernatural being, and thus maintain or enhance the believer's status in relation to it. Animals are often sacrificed for this purpose. The lives of human beings have also been offered as a means of favorably influencing the forces of the supernatural. Sometimes particular foods or some form of pleasurable activity is given up.

Moslems abstain from all food and drink, from sexual intercourse, and from smoking during the daylight hours of Ramadan, the month (in 610 A.D.) in which they believe that the Koran was sent down from heaven and the word of Allah was revealed to Mohammad. Many Christians give up specific foods during ritual periods such as Lent. Orthodox Jews avoid at all times certain foods, such as pork, or the combination of certain foods believed to be offensive to the particular supernatural being in which they believe.

Avoidance of activities prohibited by supernatural beings often takes the form of ritual abstentions called tabus, or taboos, from the Polynesian word *tapu,* which refers to a variety of both sacred and secular prohibitions—avoidance of marriage within certain categories of kinship, for example, or of fishing in certain lagoons. In turn, the observance of taboos is often associated with totemism, belief in the existence of a sacred symbiotic partnership between particular human groups and some particular animal or plant species.

Totemism is widespread in the world, but it is developed with unusual elaborateness among the native peoples of Australia (see Elkin 1964; Meggitt 1962). Among the Aboriginal Walbiri a particular descent group may, for example, trace its ancestry to an original progenitor symbolically identified with a certain insect, such as the honey ant or wichety grub, an animal such as the dingo, kangaroo, or wallaby, or a natural

"The actions that accompany a given system of beliefs are invariably objectified in ceremonial observances. . . ."
Figure 12-1. Baptism, Mineola, Texas. (Courtesy of the Library of Congress.)

"Prayer is another ritual means by which people try to influence . . . the supernatural being or beings in which they believe."
Figure 12-2. Praying for the dead, Mexico. (OAS Photo.)

object, for example, a hill, a species of plant, or the moon.

Among the Arunta, another Australian people, it is believed that an animal of the tabooed species saved the life of the founding ancestor of a particular descent group. To show his gratitude he is believed to have admonished his descendants never to harm his savior, whose spirit will continue to be their protector so long as it is not harmed. All those mystically linked to the kangaroo, for example, are regarded as being of one flesh and are normally prohibited from harming their kangaroo totem and also from marrying one another: sharing one ritual prohibition, they must also observe the other.

Prayer is another ritual means by which people try to influence the action or attitude of the supernatural being or beings in which they believe. The supplicant assumes a particular posture, attitude, and voice culturally defined as appropriate for communication with the supernatural. Some prayers are rigidly formulaic in their content and in the time, place, and means of their delivery. Others may be improvised to fit the exigencies of the occasion. But whether spontaneous or elaborately formalized and automatically repeated, the intent of prayer is always the same, to induce from a particular supernatural being (or beings) a desired response.

In Java, for example, a distinction is made between *doa,* voluntary personal prayers that can be modified in form and content to fit the supplicant's need, and *solar,* elaborate and precisely worded incantations in which word content, tone of utterance, time, and place are all set with a precision regarded as essential to their efficacy (Geertz 1960). Such prayers are used rather like magical formulas. In Javanese Islam the repetition thirty-three, sixty-six, or ninety-nine times of certain prayer phrases such as "Allahu Akbar" ("God is greatest") is believed to improve more or less mechanically a person's status with the supernatural.

For Catholics the prayerful recitation of the Rosary, a formalized set of devotions to the Virgin Mary consisting of sets of ten "Ave Marias," or "Hail Marys," each preceded by an "Our Father" and terminated with a "Gloria Patri," is also believed to have an almost automatically beneficial effect. Tibetan Buddhist rosaries serve also as

a means of counting prayers. As with prayer "wheels," barrel-shaped receptacles containing written prayers and other sacred Buddhist formulas that are turned by hand with a crank, the worshiper's relationship to the supernatural is further enhanced with each repetition (Ekvall 1964).

Priests As Intermediaries with the Supernatural

Among most peoples there are religious specialists, priests of one sort or another, who serve as intermediaries between ordinary humans and the supernatural beings they believe in. This kind of occupational specialization occurs most often in technologically more advanced, larger-scale societies.

In very small societies full-time religious specialists are lacking. There may not even be any part-time priests. Among the !Kung Bushmen of southern Africa everyone prays for himself or herself anytime, any place, composing the prayer to fit the occasion (Marshall 1962:246–247). One may "think" a prayer, state it aloud, or address the gods

"Some prayers are rigidly formulaic in their content and in the time, place, and means of their delivery."

Figure 12-3. Friday prayers at the Grand Mosque, Dakar, Senegal. (United Nations.)

directly, as one might in begging the deity to spare the life of a loved one: "Goa! Na [the great god], why have you made me grieve so? Favor me. Let this person live . . ."; or when asking for supernatural assistance with the hunt: "Gauwa [a lesser god] . . . help us that we kill an animal"; or when starvation threatens: "Gauwa, help us. We are dying of hunger. . ." (Marshall 1962:224–247).

In contrast, the prayers of Burmese Buddhists are highly formalized (Spiro 1967). The good Buddhist says the Augatha "wheel of life," a rigidly patterned, essentially formulaic prayer, at least once a day before the household altar or at the village shrine: ". . . To the Buddha I am offering respect with hands clasped, bowing, adoring, humble, in devotion to the Buddha. As I have adored, spare me the fourth level [of hell, in which rebirth is in the form of a monster], spare me famine, killing, disease. . . ."

The orthodox Jewish worshiper prays to the Lord God, King of the universe. Praise for the deity is often mixed with requests for assistance, for oneself and others. At Passover such prayers used to be accompanied by the sacrifice of a lamb. Now only a dwindling sect of Samaritans in Palestine continues to observe this ancient rite, which illustrates the similar intent of prayer and sacrifice as varying forms of supplication.

Other Means of Achieving Closeness to the Supernatural

Frequently ritual efforts to affect the worshiper's relationship to the supernatural involve reliance on techniques intended to bring the believer "closer" to or even to achieve "oneness" with the object of worship, by inducing changes in the believer's normal physiological and psychological condition that are identified as heightened states of "spirituality." The dervish among the Middle Eastern Naqshabandi induces an ecstatic state by shutting his eyes and mouth, clenching his teeth, and holding his breath, while with "great force" he recites "with the heart" the declaration of belief in

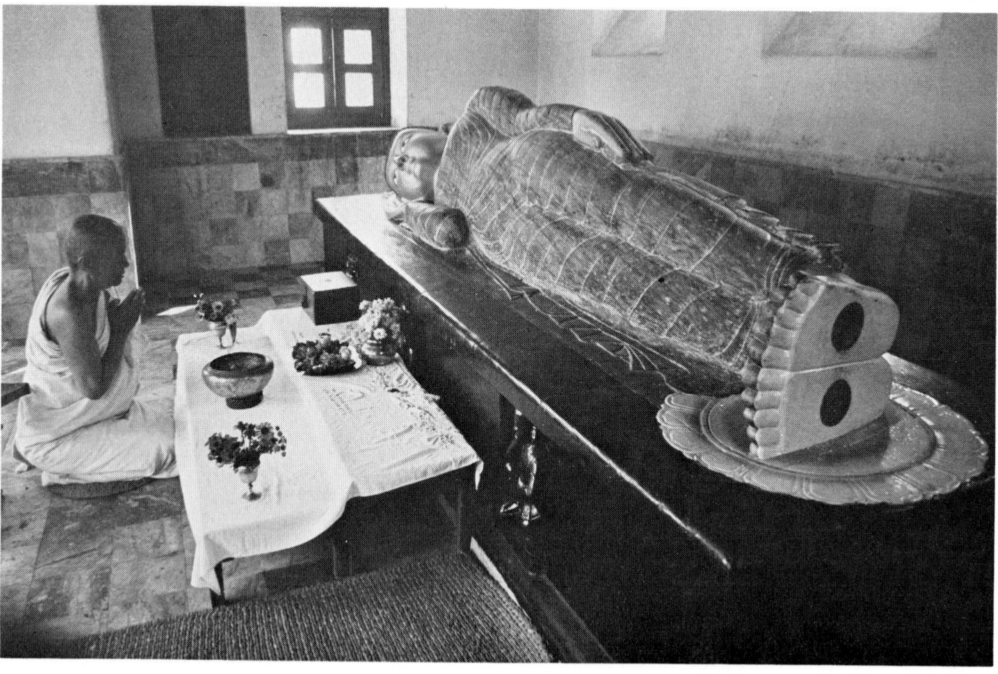

"'To the Buddha I am offering respect with hands clasped. . . .'" **Figure 12-4.** Praying before the reclining Buddha at Ananda Koti, Katmandu, Nepal. (United Nations.)

Allah and his prophet, repeating the declaration three times with each single respiration (Guillaume 1961:152). In western Iran, dervishes of the Ahl-I-Haaq sect enter a trance-like state induced by the repetitious reading of sacred texts to the accompaniment of rhythmic music and then walk on red-hot coals, grabbing them up in their hands (Tritton 1954).

Members of the Mulawiya sect of Moslem dervishes achieve release from "the prison of their bodies" and greater closeness with the deity by whirling until they are dizzy and exhausted. Followers of other Islamic sects induce a condition of intensified spiritual awareness (and of hyperventilation) through patterned changes in breathing accompanied by repetition in unison of the name of God, "Al-lah, Al-lah," exhaling on the first syllable and inhaling on the second to the accompaniment of rhythmic hand clapping and carefully prescribed body movements, until gradually the worshipers go into a trance and begin to cry out the name of God ecstatically. As others join them, tension mounts until, released by a word from the priest, the worshipers' trance is broken and they emerge from the spiritual experience relaxed, refreshed, and with a renewed sense of spirituality and closeness to God (Coon 1958).

Elsewhere in the Middle East, in Asia, and in the Americas drugs are frequently used as an important adjunct to the ritual means by which worshipers achieve an altered state of consciousness. In the southwestern United States the Indians chew the flesh and roots of the peyote, a small cactus, to induce both physical changes—euphoria, nausea, and "heightened sensitivity to nuances of sound, color, form and texture"—and hallucinations, "ranging from fairly elaborate scotomata [dark spots in the visual field] to quite detailed pictures," in a few cases "full-fledged visions, including what are evidently major distortions of visual and auditory stimuli" (Aberle 1966:5). Elsewhere in the United States marijuana, derivatives of opium, and LSD are often employed in order to achieve an analogous heightening of "spiritual experience."

In West Africa and in many New World communities settled by the descendants of West Africans, the rituals by which people achieve a closer relation to the forces of the supernatural frequently involve the use of syncopated drumbeats, group singing, and rhythmic body movements, which, preceded by the necessary liturgical preparations and with prolonged repetition, actually induce the worshipers' possession by the deities in which they believe. Among the Yoruba of Nigeria spirits called orishas regularly possess communicants by this means.

Belief in these same supernatural beings, often still called by their West African names, has been retained among Voodoo devotees in Haiti, Brazil, and elsewhere in Afro-American communities in the New World (see Herskovits 1966). In Voodoo possession, as in the culturally related phenomenon by which members of various Fundamentalist and Pentecostal sects induce possession by the Holy Ghost, the worshipers identify their altered physiological and psychological state as the achievement of true oneness with the deity. Such experience is psychologically satisfying both in

"... actually induce the worshipers' possession by the deities in which they believe."

Figure 12-5. Possession by orishas in an Afro-Brazilian religious ceremony, Bahia, Brazil. (OAS Photo.)

providing a sense of control and power over the forces believed to affect the worshiper's fate—a sense that is often at dramatic variance with the believer's usual feelings of relative helplessness in an environment he or she is powerless to affect—and in providing, physiologically and psychologically, for a temporary reduction of tension and anxiety.

In every instance the intended function of ritual is to affect, or control, the relation of the believer to the supernatural powers in which he or she believes. Each time the ritual is performed, the beliefs themselves are reaffirmed and strengthened. Where circumstances make participation in such rituals impossible, the intensity of belief itself tends gradually to be weakened.

Nature Worship

People's use of ritual to control their relations with the powers they believe affect their destiny is particularly well illustrated by a type of religious belief and action usually referred to as nature worship.

"A priest specially charged with the maintenance of good relations between people and the earth. . . ."
Figure 12-6. A Mossi earth priest with an offering of money before him on the altar, a clay vessel supported by stone, Yatenga, Upper Volta. (Hammond 1966.)

Systems of belief and observance that provide this sense of control are most prominent among peoples whose intense dependence on nature is unaccompanied by any very efficient technological means of controlling it. Nature worship is usually an important aspect of the ideologies of hunting and gathering peoples and of primitive farmers. Usually their beliefs about nature and the ritual observances that accompany them provide a means to maintain or increase the supply of natural resources they depend on for material survival. Throughout northern North America, for example, there were important beliefs and rituals concerning bears, the Indian hunters' particularly valuable but dangerous quarry. In some regions a special group of priests was charged with propitiating the Great Bear Being (see Driver 1971:81, 408), who was the guardian of bear as game and on whose good will the hunters' success depended. To assure the continued benevolence of this powerful spirit a variety of ritual precautions were taken to avoid offending him. Bears were ceremonially warned in advance that they were to be killed and after they had been slain were apologized to and mourned. Their inedible remains were placed in trees so that dogs and other scavengers could not defile them.

Among primitive farming peoples rituals intended to control people's relation to the supernatural forces of nature often take the form of a ceremonial cycle marking each new phase in the annual round of activities involved in food production. Among the Mossi of Upper Volta (Hammond 1966) this cycle begins late in the dry season with a rainmaking ceremonial called Tengana. Although the growing season is still several months away, Tengana is the first step in the long series of rituals by which the Mossi farmers endeavor each year to reaffirm and perpetuate a reciprocal relation with the forces of nature. A priest specially charged with the maintenance of good relations between people and the earth receives, from all kin groups in the local community, offerings of ground millet grains mixed with water. These are poured out over the altar to the earth to the accompaniment of prayers in which the deity is both thanked for the heavy rains and good growing conditions of the past year and thanked in advance for benevolence during the new season just beginning.

In the next phase of the ceremonial cycle—Tido Wende—the aspect of the Mossi supreme being specifically identified with the fertility of plants also receives an offering. For seven nights following these sacrifices young girls gather in the evening in each village to clap their hands and describe in song the conditions that sacrifice to Tido Wende is intended to bring about:

This year is sweet.
Next year will be sweeter still.

The household head will be there where the earth is moist.

His children will be abundant, as the cotton bush is covered with flowers.

There will be no end to harvesting them.

The rains will fall,
The water will rush through the valleys,
The parched earth will be drenched, the lowlands white with water.

Children will run joyously in the rain.

And

I need someone to shake the heavy branches of my shea tree

I have already seen the branches are full of fruit,
But I cannot gather them alone. . . .
[Hammond 1966:189–190]

At the conclusion of Tido Wende Mossi farmers go to their fields to clear and clean them in preparation for the planting that will begin soon after the first light rains. Later ceremonies mark each stage in cultivation, the first and second weedings of the new millet plants, and preparations for the harvest. When the first ripe millet stalks are cut in the early fall, a further series of rituals of thanksgiving is observed. At the conclusion of the rituals all the forces, natural and social, that the farmers believe their well-being to depend on have been identified, rewarded ritually for their support during the past growing season, and encouraged by the generosity of their supplicants to continue their benevolence in future seasons.

Although primary emphasis in the Mossi ceremonial cycle centers on the farmers' dependence on the supernatural forces they believe control their natural environment, such ritual observances also underscore belief in and dependence on the supernatural beings that sanction the authority of their religious and secular leaders—the earth priests, the king, the village chiefs, the lineage elders, all those who may on one occasion or another intercede between people and the supernatural forces of nature. To be assured of the cooperation of these intermediary figures in their relations with the supernatural the Mossi must show respect for and deference to their authority in the conduct of secular affairs. In this way, supernatural power and social and political authority are closely linked.

As among many worshipers of nature, the Mossi annual cycle of ceremonials, intended to assure the continuing renewal of nature and perpetuation of those natural conditions people depend on for survival, is complemented by other rituals reserved for crises. Not performed calendrically, they are enacted in emergencies, to bring rain to end a summer drought, to ward off a threatened attack of locusts, or to control the spread of some plant disease.

In this emphasis on the modification of

natural conditions by supernatural means the reliance of the Mossi on the supernatural is analogous to others' reliance on science. Among peoples whose scientific understanding of nature is meager and whose technologies are rudimentary, it is to religion rather than to science that people turn in their efforts to control their environment, and considerable energy is allocated to ritual efforts at control. For those who perceive most cause-and-effect relationships in religious and magical terms, sacrifice, the observance of ritual prohibitions, praying, and participation in often elaborate, costly, and time-consuming ceremonials are an integral aspect of the subsistence technology. Such activities are generally believed to be quite as important to the success of people's endeavors as planting properly, working hard, and keeping their weapons and tools in repair. Conversely, as their scientific understanding of how to operate their technology increases, people's reliance on supernatural means of control tends to diminish.

Those who use scientific rather than magically and religiously based methods to increase their technological productivity tend usually to be materially more successful. "All other things being equal," the Mossi farmer who tries to increase the fertility of his fields by sacrificing a chicken to the earth deity is likely to have a less abundant harvest than his neighbor who tries to get the same result by collecting and spreading manure. The possibly greater spiritual benefits of one form of action over another cannot be objectively measured, only the greater material efficacy of the action that is scientifically based.

Ancestor Worship

The tendency of people to perceive the supernatural "world" as being organized in a way analogous to that of their own society and culture is strikingly illustrated by a form of religion generally termed ancestor worship. The way people represent the spirits of their ancestors—the activities, attitudes, and values they ascribe to them—is generally a modified projection of their own activities, attitudes, and values.

The spirits of ancestors are usually regarded as still being members of the kin group, with personalities like those they possessed in life, retaining a keen interest in family affairs and a strong sense of responsibility for family welfare. If properly taken care of ceremonially, ancestral spirits may serve their descendants as protectors and guides. If angered, usually by their descendants' failure to live by the social and ritual rules they have set, the ancestral spirits can be terrible in their punishing wrath. They can disrupt their living kinsmen's affairs, cause them serious accidents, make them sick, and even kill them.

People who believe their dead continue to be active and useful members of the kin group and the community often have feelings about dying that are quite different, and frequently less terrifying, than those of people who regard death as an irrevocably final breach, the end to contact with the living and the termination of conscious existence. Death is probably always hard for the living to cope with, but its inevitability may be accepted somewhat more easily if the separation between the living and the dead is perceived only as a difference in status, the attainment of which may offer such attractive compensations as reunion with deceased loved ones, veneration by future generations, continued authority, and considerable supernatural power.

When ancestor worship is an important aspect of a people's ideology, the kin group, particularly the descent group, is usually of major importance in the life experience of the individual and in the organization of the community. In China the concept of the ancestor as protector of the living is an ancient one and has always been closely related to the importance of the descent group and the family household as the primary sources of the individual's status and material and social support (see Freedman 1972; Hsu 1948). This tradition is now most actively maintained among the Chinese living on Taiwan or elsewhere outside mainland China. The emphasis placed by the living on filial piety and acceptance of the authority of family elders is extended into the supernatural to include the deceased family members as well.

Before the development of Confucianism out of Buddhism and prior to the invention of writing, Chinese family ancestors were probably represented by idols of stone or clay (Laufer 1913). Later, with the Confucian suppresseion of Buddhist idolatry in the third century B.C., the practice of using images to represent ancestors was replaced by the use of a more abstract symbolic form. These are rectangular pieces of wood inserted vertically into pedestals and covered on both sides with black ink inscriptions giving the special posthumous name of the deceased, his rank and title, the dates of his birth and death, and the name of the eldest son who has erected the tablet. Traditionally, for the first hundred days after burial daily offerings of food and drink are presented to the tablet, and it is treated with great respect as an animate representative of the deceased. Afterward it is placed in the ancestral shrine. There it remains as a symbolic reminder to the dead man's wife and children and especially to his eldest son of their continuing responsibility to respect their deceased elder kinsman and to conduct their lives in accordance with standards he would approve, especially as such standards relate to the survivor's obligations to their lineage. It is believed that from time to time the soul of the dead man will reenter the tablet to receive the devotions of his family and to partake of the essence of their sacrificial offerings of incense, food, drink, and flowers.

As in most relationships between people and the supernatural beings they worship, the traditional relationship of the Chinese to

"Death is probably always hard for the living to cope with. . . ."

Figure 12-7. Funeral after a mine disaster, Kentucky. (Appalachian Regional Commission.)

the spirits of their ancestors is symbiotic. The ancestors provide their descendants with protection; their descendants reciprocate with sacrificial offerings, respect, and compliance with the ancestors' rules of propriety. With each sacrifice at the ancestral shrine the living are freshly reminded of this relationship and of their responsibility to maintain it.

In Africa, also, the kin group traditionally has been both the principal source of the individual's security and the organization of greatest importance in the structuring of local society. There, too, relationships between the living and the dead parallel relationships among the living. Both are based on reciprocity.

Among the LoDagaa of northern Ghana (Goody 1962) it is also the eldest son who takes the initiative in providing for the worship of the spirit of his deceased father. Each known ancestor is represented by a forked "spirit stick" placed in a shrine located in a corner of the burial vault used by all closely related members of the patrilineal descent group. There sacrifices to the ancestors are made both during ritual observances that are part of the regular LoDagaa ceremonial calendar and on special occasions. When a woman bears a child, for example, a chicken is sacrificed at the shrine of her patrilineal ancestors to assure that her milk will flow. Whenever a LoDagaa enjoys good fortune—if his harvest is abundant, if he is successful in the hunt, if he has been well paid as a wage laborer—thanks are due the spirits of his ancestors, especially the spirit of the particular ancestor, often a deceased paternal grandfather, who is regarded as his special protector. If he fails to acknowledge this dependence and to reward his ancestors for their benevolence, he may be punished. A serious accident may befall him. He may become ill, or one of his children may die. To remain on good terms with the ancestors and to avoid the risk of their punishment, a man must meet his obligation to them both by sharing his goods, in the form of sacrifices to them, and by following the rules of proper behavior they have set down for their descendants to follow.

Like most ancestral spirits, those of the LoDagaa are particularly concerned with the correct conduct of relations within the kin group. The obligation of lineage members to cooperate with one another, to avoid disputes, and to accept the mediation of a senior kinsmen when disputes occur is required of all family members who want to remain on good terms with the spirits of their dead.

Incest and adultery are punished by the ancestral spirits of the LoDagaa. Expiation can be achieved only by making them a special sacrifice. Under some circumstances, as when a man allows a friend to sleep with his wife, the wrath of the ancestors can be bought off with a chicken sacrificed to them before the woman and her husband's friend have intercourse.

In some societies people live in affectionate harmony with the ghosts of their ancestors. Others assume that the personalities of the deceased undergo transformation, that the dead are envious of the living and likely to be malevolent. Where the spirits of the dead are thought to be jealous of the living, funeral observances are usually marked by great attention to the ritual separation of the deceased and to measures intended to assure that they will not return.

The Mapuche Indians of central Argentina believe that after death spirits go to the world of the dead, where they dwell in eternal tranquility but remain available to come to the assistance of their descendants if they are formally called on (Faron 1961). It is important among the Mapuche that the transition from life to death be satisfactorily made. Spirits that linger on after death and are not ritually attended to, although not evil in themselves, can be captured by sor-

"Like most ancestral spirits. . . ."
Figure 12-8. Asmat ancestral figure, Irian Jaya. (Courtesy of the Museum of Primitive Art.)

cerers and used for malicious purposes. During a funeral the ancestral spirits of the Mapuche kin group are always called upon and reminded that it is their responsibility to protect the newly released spirit of the deceased and to prevent it from being captured by workers of evil. Cooperative ancestral spirits are compensated for their services with sacrificial libations of wine and other alcoholic drinks.

As Mapuche spirits of the dead are believed to retain the social status they possessed when living, the spirits of deceased chiefs are regarded as particularly powerful. Because they watch over Mapuche community affairs, their return is welcomed. But the return of other spirits is feared, because it is believed they reappear only when they have been captured by sorcerers who intend to do other people harm, materializing in the dark of the night to lurk about, causing trouble for the living. Such ghosts are the ones who cause mishaps that occur for no apparent reason. It is they who are responsible when disaster strikes an innocent person. For the Mapuche the contrast between the benign spirits of the ancestors and the evil ghosts created by sorcerers from captured souls is an explicit symbolic representation of their perception of the forces that govern human life, good and evil powers forever in opposition, among which people must warily make their way, relying on their priests for guidance and aid.

For the Mapuche, as for many peoples, the belief in ancestral spirits provides a means of explaining the otherwise unexplainable, the things that go wrong without evident cause and despite everyone's best efforts. Adversity always creates anxiety. Finding an explanation reduces people's sense of helplessness and vulnerability by plausibly identifying the cause of misfortune and, often, by providing some basis for taking action believed to prevent its future recurrence.

The inhabitants of Ifaluk, a small Micronesian atoll in the South Pacific, attribute most misfortune to the malevolent spirits of particular ancestors, alus, whose disagreeable personalities and obviously antisocial tendencies persist after death, making their descendants' lives difficult, spreading immorality and aggressiveness, possessing people, and causing them physical and mental illness and endless anxiety (Spiro 1952). Everyone on Ifaluk would like to be rid of such ghosts, and people are very frequently engaged in efforts to enlist the cooperation of friendly ghosts (the spirits of friendly people) and the assistance of the priests in exorcising the malevolent beings that cause them so much trouble.

Although the people of Ifaluk perceive these spirits as the source of nothing but adversity, their fear of the ghosts of the malevolent dead fulfills several important functions (Spiro 1952). Belief in them provides a theory of disease, offering both an explanation of cause (the action of malevolent ancestral spirits) and a means of prevention (enlistment of the cooperation of friendly spirits and a good priest). In the absence of any effective medical means of coping with disease, such belief and the course of action it calls for may reduce the pain of helplessness and bewilderment that would otherwise add to the distress that the people of Ifaluk, like all peoples, experience when faced with serious illness, death, or some other calamity.

Hatred of malevolent spirits also provides a socially acceptable channel to express aggression. In a small society like that of Ifaluk, where the interdependence of community members is great but political centralization is weak, aggression that is not deflected could lead to seriously disruptive quarreling, violent physical combat, and even murder. Because of the importance of cooperation, the small size of the society, and its sharply delimited territory, withdrawal as a means of reducing the threat of overt aggression is difficult. Because the people of Ifaluk have no liquor that is genuinely intoxicating, they cannot drown their frustrations, anxieties, or hostilities in drink. If they were to repress their aggression, turning it inward on themselves, their personality integration would be threatened, probably making them sick. As Spiro puts it (1952:502), aggressive drives "demand expression; if they are not permitted expression they are deflected from their original goal and are either inverted or displaced. . . . This has not happened in Ifaluk, because the Ifaluk have a socially acceptable channel for the expression of aggression—the alus." The people of Ifaluk are, as they need to be, generally relaxed, friendly, and helpful, except for their fear and loathing of the evil ancestral spirits who serve both as a focus for their anxieties and as a socially harmless target for their aggressions.

In this sense the belief of the Ifaluk in the malevolent spirits of their dead can be perceived not as a needlessly terrifying superstition they ought to rid themselves of but rather as a belief well integrated with many other aspects of their culture and useful to its orderly function.

Monotheism, Polytheism, and Nontheism

Like the often too rigidly drawn distinction between religion and magic, more is frequently made of the distinction between monotheistic and polytheistic ideologies than is warranted by the real differences between them. In theory, monotheism means one or another of several varieties of belief in a single supernatural being who is usually thought to be the source or creator of the universe and the originator of all within it. Judaism, Islam, and Christianity are usually regarded as monotheistic ideologies; so is Hinduism, and there are of course many others. Usually each is presumed to involve belief in a single supernatural entity, a god or "supreme being." Typically, each entails formal opposition to idolatry and to any other practices or beliefs regarded as magical or "superstitious."

In contrast, polytheism is usually defined as belief in and worship of a variety of sources of supernatural power: ghosts, spirits, gods, and many other sorts of nonnatural beings, as well as various inanimate supernatural forces. Such ideologies frequently include belief in a so-called high god and in other, lesser gods as well.

The distinction between monotheism and polytheism is overdrawn when stated in absolute terms. In fact most people who profess

"... polytheism is usually defined as a belief in and worship of a variety of sources of supernatural power...."

Figure 12-9. Buddha resisting the temptation of Mara, the god of desire and death, and a host of other demons. (Information Office, Government of India.)

adherence to a monotheistic belief system believe also in other supernatural powers—fortune tellers, astrologers, curers, witches and demons, saints and spirits, and such inanimate forces as luck. In practice as well as in belief the religious behavior of monotheistic peoples frequently includes observances that are markedly similar to those ordinarily defined as polytheistic. Like the so-called fetishists whose idolatry they scorn, they often represent the beings they revere symbolically in sculpture and in charms and talismans. Many monotheists practice sacrifice. Many become possessed, sometimes by devils or by such supposedly benevolent beings as the Holy Ghost himself.

Although anthropologists and some theologians emphasize the distinctions between "folk" beliefs and practices and orthodox dogma, both patterns of behavior are usually parts of what functions for a people as a single system of beliefs and practices. The distinction between theistic and nontheistic (the latter referring to secular ideologies, that is, systems of belief that do not formally deify persons or things) must also be made with caution. Again the differences are relative rather than absolute. What is apparent is not the universality of people's need for religion in the theistic sense, but their need for ideology, in the sense that all people apparently require some system of beliefs that rationalizes their relation to the world and provides them with a guide to the necessary actions to maintain a secure place within it. Such an ideology may or may not include belief in a deity or deities. Although most ideologies are theistic, the existence of individuals and even very large human groups whose belief systems specifically deny the existence of supernatural power indicates that it is ideology, not religion, that is the universal.

Most contemporary communist ideologies illustrate this distinction. All are explicitly nontheistic but invariably include an elaborate system of beliefs about the origins of the world and the nature of people's relation to

"... belief in the edifying effects of a pilgrimage to Lenin's tomb. ..."

Figure 12-10. A line of visitors stretches across Red Square waiting to enter the Tomb of Lenin. (Novosti Press Agency, Moscow.)

it. All provide detailed guides to right action that include strong elements of ritual: the veneration of Lenin, Mao, and "Che," for example, and of their works and of relics related to their lives; belief in the edifying effects of a pilgrimage to Lenin's tomb or in the benefits of a sing-song incantation of Mao's thoughts. All such observances serve functions analogous to those of theistic rituals in using symbolism to reinforce belief, in building societal cohesion, and in giving the committed an exalted sense of the rightness of their creed and of the actions required of true believers.

Ideological Change

As people's life experience is altered by changing natural and cultural circumstances, the systems of belief that give meaning to life and provide them with a means of coping with it must be altered also. In the past, ideological change has usually occurred so gradually as to go almost unperceived by the majority of believers. It was by such a centuries-long process that Christianity developed out of the teachings of a series of prophets, finally taking shape as a separate ideology with the advent of Jesus, and then spreading around the eastern Mediterranean and into Europe—and finally throughout the world—everywhere it was adopted adjusting to local conditions and incorporating in the process such aspects of indigenous, non-Christian belief and observance as Greek philosophy and such elements of "barbarian" nature worship as Easter and Christmas.

Sometimes the need for ideological change resulted in modification within the context of orthodox Christian dogma. In other instances the changes required were too drastic, schisms resulted, and a variety of distinctive bodies of doctrine and practice emerged, each with a separate church organization and a group of followers strongly convinced of the essential rightness of their particular interpretation of the basic tenets of Christian belief and practice.

Although ideological change is necessarily an ever-present phenomenon, it is rarely achieved easily. Theistic ideologies tend to be particularly conservative, frequently because creed and ritual are regarded as having been divinely revealed to a prophet or some other figure associated with the founding of the religion. To justify a fundamental change in belief and action, further prophecy, a new interpretation of divinely revealed truth, is frequently needed. Usually this takes time, sometimes more than is available.

Where ideological change is required to provide men with a system of beliefs meaningful and usable in dealing with swiftly changing sociocultural circumstances, old ideologies may be either altered or abandoned, depending on their flexibility and on the immediacy and extent of the need for ideological change.

Often under such circumstances new prophets arise to provide supernaturally sanctioned reinterpretations of traditional doctrine. Sometimes they become the founders of new sects within the context of traditional religious systems, as has often occurred within Christianity. Sometimes they establish new and separate religions, as did Jesus and Mohammad. But "new" religions are never so pristine as their prophets and followers contend. Inevitably, they are the product of a reworking of many aspects of traditional belief combined with new elements either invented or borrowed from other cultures.

The processes of ideological change and the cultural circumstances that precipitate it can be observed in dramatic form as they are occurring today in parts of the world where the traditional ways of life of many peoples are subject to increasing stress from

"Sometimes they establish new and separate religions, as did Jesus and Mohammad."

Figure 12-11. A follower of the Prophet Mohammad kneels in prayer, Iran. (United Nations.)

the threat of encroachment and domination by technologically more advanced peoples. Several instances of this phenomenon are provided by the historical record of the American Indian's efforts to adjust to cultural takeover by advancing white settlers. Within the contemporary United States as well, Indians and other culturally subordinated peoples, particularly black Americans, are developing new ideologies in an effort to understand their subjugation and exploitation so that they can struggle against it more effectively.

The term *revitalization,* first used by Wallace in 1956, is now frequently applied by anthropologists to the often radical movements for ideological innovation that develop to deal with the stress members of simpler, smaller-scale societies experience when their traditional way of life is threatened by outsiders (see Lanternari 1960; Wallace 1958, 1961a, 1966; Worsley 1957). Such movements to achieve an ideologically effective response to the stress of rapidly shifting circumstances are also sometimes described as nativistic, messianic, or millenarian.

However they may vary in specifics of form and content from place to place and time to time, revitalization movements typically emerge when suddenly and radically altered circumstances threaten people's sense of cultural autonomy and worth, rendering their traditional beliefs about the world and their relation to it irrelevant or inadequate to their need to explain the oppressive events affecting them and to define how they ought to respond. The stress, ideological confusion, and doubt resulting from sudden contact and conflict between peoples with greatly differing cultural traditions has frequently served as a stimulus to ideological disequilibrium. This stress probably increases in proportion to the differences between the cultures in contact and to the oppressiveness of the dominant culture.

The incidence of contact between peoples with radically different ways of life was greatly accelerated during the period of European exploration and colonial and neocolonial conquest that began in the fifteenth century and is still going on. Native Americans were among the first to feel its effects.

The Word of God As Revealed to Handsome Lake

What happened to the Iroquois during the early phases of white contact is illustrative of a widespread phenomenon (Deardorff 1951; Oswalt 1966; Parker 1913; Wallace 1966). When the European settlers were newly arrived in the northern part of what was to become the state of New York, the Iroquois were able to protect their territorial rights and maintain their traditional way of life by playing the French colonists off against the English. Life in the small, scattered Iroquois communities went on much as it always had. The Indians continued to make their living by growing corn, squash, and beans and by hunting.

Toward the end of the eighteenth century the old balance of relations between the Iroquois and the whites began to break down. During the French and Indian Wars many Iroquois settlements were destroyed. Then the Indians sided with the British in the American Revolution, and lost. Justifying their action as punishment for the Iroquois "treason," the newly independent Americans seized the Indians' farmlands and hunting territories. Soon the Iroquois found themselves crowded into small, rural reservations dispersed among the spreading settlements of prosperous white farmers.

Iroquois culture began to fall apart. The traditional technology and the tribal economic system were disrupted by the loss of land. Having lost their traditional material base, the Iroquois' social and political systems quickly deteriorated under mounting dissension, external repression, and the

"Then a prophet appeared, a Seneca chief named Handsome Lake. . . ."

Figure 12-12. The founder of the Handsome Lake religion standing before some of his followers. (Photograph courtesy of Museum of the American Indian, Heye Foundation.)

demoralization of the Iroquois' conquered war leaders. To the Indians it seemed that their traditions were failing them. The old ways no longer worked. Poverty, drunkenness, violence, apathy, and despair were widespread.

Then a prophet appeared, a Seneca chief named Handsome Lake, who said he was a messenger sent by God to tell the Iroquois they would be destroyed unless they changed their ways. In a series of visions God revealed to Handsome Lake the actions the Indians would have to take to avoid punishment for their sins. According to Wallace (1966:32), "Heavenly messengers had told him that unless he and his fellows became new men, they were doomed to be destroyed in an apocalyptic world destruction." They should adopt the whites' agricultural methods. Iroquois husbands should help their wives with farm work. Traditional family organization, based on matrilineal descent and matrilocal residence, should be discarded for a household organization built around the married couple and their children. Everyone should learn English. Men were to give up drinking and live sober lives.

The word of the deity as revealed to Handsome Lake became the bible of the Handsome Lake religion. Following its tenets, the Indians abandoned many of the old, no longer practicable aspects of their traditional culture for new usages that provided for a more efficient adjustment to the changed circumstances of their lives. Iroquois farmers prospered. Family and community life and community organization on the reservations were stabilized. Conversion to the Handsome Lake religion, or the New Religion, as it was called, seemed to offer a new means of achieving a life of dignity and stability, an ideological justification for the abandonment of traditionally sanctioned but no longer adaptive behaviors and for adoption of those aspects of the white people's ways that enhanced the Indians' chances of surviving. The reputation of the Iroquois for thrift and industriousness spread widely.

A Paiute Messiah

Elsewhere in North America the Indians' efforts to revitalize their threatened ways of life by taking on new ideologies or reinterpreting old ones were often less successful. The Paiute of Nevada sought to escape from white encroachment and return to the glories of their traditional culture by means of the Ghost Dance, a new religion derived, as most new ideologies are, from a reinterpretation of traditional beliefs and practices

(Mooney 1965). Under the guidance of Wovoka, the Paiute Messiah, converts sought by ritual means to bring back, almost literally to dance back, the good old days, to obliterate the stressful present, and to bring to reality their nostalgic image of the past.

The Ghost Dance religion first appeared in 1870 as the white settlers were pushing west across Nevada and into California. As the white population spread so did the Indians' new religion, from the Paiute to many other Indian groups faced with the same threat. It was taken up by the Indians of the Plains. By 1890 the Ghost Dance had spread even to the Navaho of Arizona and New Mexico. Prophets brought word from the Great Spirit that the world was soon to be transformed. Paradise would come to earth in the form of a return to the Glorious Age of aboriginal Indian culture. The intruding whites and their evil ways would be driven out forever. There would be no more sickness or death, and the buffalo would return.

To prepare for this great event the Indians were instructed by Wovoka and by other Ghost Dance prophets to purify themselves of all foreign habits and to live strictly according to the rules of their traditional culture. By conducting themselves as if the millennium had arrived, they would speed its coming. More formal rituals involved ceremonial bathing and marathon dancing that induced possession. All who gave themselves wholeheartedly to the new religion would be rewarded with salvation.

In contrast to Handsome Lake, the prophets of the Ghost Dance religion did not sanction adaptive changes in the Indians' cultural behavior that might have enhanced their chances of competing successfully with the invading whites. Rather, emphasis was on the obsessive retention of functionally outdated behaviors and the reduction of social tensions through fantasy and the cathartic effects of exhausting dances and possession. None of these observances offered any practical means of rectifying the real sources of the Indians' distress, their incapacity to effectively resist or adjust to the cultural changes brought about by contact with the technologically and numerically more powerful whites. And so the Ghost Dance failed.

". . . their incapacity to effectively resist or adjust to the cultural changes brought about by contact with the technologically and numerically more powerful whites."

Figure 12-13. An Eskimo convert stands among the graves of his dead. (National Film Board of Canada.)

Cargo Cults

Emphasis on the ritual achievement of a wished-for millennium as a means of reducing the stress of culture contact and alien domination has also marked the response of many of the peoples of Melanesia to European colonization (see Worsley 1957; Lawrence 1964). On many different South Pacific islands culturally separate groups not in contact with one another have responded similarly to the same crisis brought about by the islanders' traumatic confrontation with technologically superior, materially vastly more prosperous communities of European settlers. Melanesians have observed the higher standard of material well-being the Europeans enjoy but have generally lacked any means of achieving such a life-style for themselves. Their traditional technologies are too rudimentary, and opportunities to acquire the Europeans' skills and to obtain power to participate in the European-controlled sector of the economy have been largely denied them by Europeans determined to maintain their privileged position.

Action to reduce the islanders' resultant frustration and sense of relative deprivation has repeatedly taken the form of revitalization movements called cargo cults, after the pidgin word *kago* for the European manufactured goods, wealth that the Melanesians covet but cannot acquire and that they regard as evidence of the Europeans' greater power. Prophets have arisen among them promising a sort of salvation and an end to the stressful inequities of the present, and describing a millennium when present circumstances will be reversed: the whites will be economically and politically subordinate to the Melanesians, who will receive the "cargo" really intended for them but somehow diverted by the whites by sorcery.

One of the early cargo cult movements occurred in 1913 on the Torres Straits island of Saibai (Belshaw 1950), where a prophet promised his converts they would be rewarded when the spirits of the dead, the traditional guardians of people's material prosperity, would return on a steamship laden with manufactured "cargo." In Papua during the early 1920s prophets exorted their followers to engage in European-style close-order military drill, an otherwise apparently useless activity the Melanesians reasonably assumed to be some sort of ritual the whites used to control the supernatural sources of their material wealth. Flagpoles were used to communicate with the spirits of deceased relatives who would soon return on a cargo-laden boat. On the island of Espirito Santo a prophet urged his followers to kill all the Europeans so that the dead would rise from the grave with white faces. During World War II the apparently miraculous arrival of enormous quantities of European weapons, construction materials and machinery, trucks and jeeps, and great stores of food heightened the Melanesians' sense of relative powerlessness and deprivation and resulted in intensified ritual efforts to get at and control the supernatural sources of the whites' seemingly unlimited wealth.

The actions advocated by the prophets of the various new ideologies that sprang up throughout Melanesia called for ritual preparations involving both a return to traditional patterns of cultural behavior and the magical manipulation of objects believed somehow to be the source of the Europeans' evidently greater supernatural power. Old customs such as polygyny and kava drinking were revived at the same time that superficial aspects of the whites' behavior—their clothing styles and house types and other of their artifacts such as airfields and bamboo "radio receiving" towers—were all ritually copied in an effort to capture the secret supernatural power it was assumed they contained. With time the Americans came to be perceived as the liberators of the natives from their greedy European colonial oppressors. On the island of Tana an airstrip was cleared to receive them. Prophets on Guadalcanal directed the construction of warehouses to store the cargo it was believed the American military would soon bring.

In the Mamberamo area of West Irian the goddess of the afterworld, accompanied by spirits of the dead all dressed in European clothes, appeared before the people and instructed them to spread the word of her advent among the tribes: "We will return again with ships full of clothing, axes, tobacco, matches, out-board motors, and other cargo," she said (Oosterwall 1963). No one would ever lack for anything again. There would be pigs, sago, and other foods for all, she promised. There would be no more sickness or death, and everyone would be as rich as the Europeans, who had been keeping "all these riches to themselves."

In those parts of Melanesia where emphasis on the reduction of individual and group frustration by purely ritual means has continued—in some instances prophets have advised their followers to destroy their homes and not bother to plant their farms in order to be ready for the coming of the cargo—relief from the stresses of culture contact and subordination to alien outsiders is obviously only temporary. The underlying sources of tension have persisted or increased. In other areas, especially in the Solomon Islands, changes in cultural behavior advocated by prophets, like the innovations Handsome Lake urged upon the Iroquois, frequently have been adaptive. Laborers have been forbidden to work for Europeans unless their wages were increased, for example. On the island of Malaita, where more extensive contact with European culture has enabled the Melanesians to acquire a more accurate understanding of the European behaviors that do in fact contribute to their greater material well-being, thousands of islanders were instructed by their religious leaders to demonstrate before the buildings of the colonial government for more education, better working conditions, and the placement of Melanesians in jobs previously reserved for whites.

But lacking both the scientific understanding and the technological skills necessary for the improvement of their material conditions by empirical means, many Melanesians continue to try to reduce the stress they experience and bring about the changes they seek by the only means they know: through reliance on new means of manipulating the supernatural. When their efforts fail, this does not cause them to abandon their faith but only intensifies their frustration and stimulates them to seek all the more ardently for a new and better messiah whose prophecies will be fulfilled.

The Black Muslims

The several phases that have marked the development of the World Community of al-Islam in the West (WCIW) (see Essien-Udom 1962; Lincoln 1961) as a new American religion are structurally and functionally quite similar to the processes that have characterized the development of revitalization movements among other peoples reacting to the pressures of economic, social, and political subordination and exploitation. The cultural context in which the Muslim movements among black Americans began—the early mid-twentieth-century United States—was marked by increasing tension resulting from blacks' growing sense of frustration and increased awareness both of the inequities of their material and political position and of the obstacles to overcoming them. Many of those most frustrated and least equipped to improve their status because they lacked the required skills and were discriminated against in both acquiring and using them turned away from traditional religious tension-reducing techniques—from participation in fundamentalist Christian sects that provided only temporary release from a sense of oppression through emotion-laden rituals, syncopated singing and shouting, and promises of heavenly rewards for those who accepted their downtrodden lot on earth—to new prophets and a new ideology that offered a fresher and more immediate promise of deliverance.

One of the first of these New Muslim leaders was a black man from Detroit named Timothy Drew. As Noble Drew Ali, he preached that black Americans were the lost tribe of Islam (Fauset 1944). Gradually the new ideology he helped to found was expanded and altered under the guidance of a later prophet, the son of a Southern Baptist minister who, as The Honorable Elijah Muhammad, proclaimed himself the latter-day Messenger of Allah. Still later, Malcolm X, a disciple of Elijah Muhammad, broke away from the Black Muslims to establish a separate sect in which the early

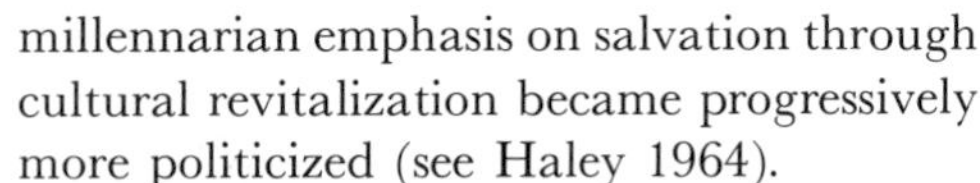

millennarian emphasis on salvation through cultural revitalization became progressively more politicized (see Haley 1964).

The new version of Islam initially offered a proud new cultural heritage to black Americans. They were not "so-called Negroes" at all, but really Asiatics, descendants of devout and cultivated Muslims who were tricked by the evil whites, sold into slavery, robbed of their true names and real identity, and forced to abandon their religion and to give up their native language, which was Arabic. Salvation rested on the reassertion of their original identity, the rejection of the sinful influences of the culture of the "blue-eyed devils," and abandonment of all efforts to achieve integration and racial or cultural assimilation.

By indignantly denying every symbol of the subordinate status forced on them by the whites, they could become a new people. Their rightful identity was reclaimed: they were strong, courageous, black sons and daughters of Islam, most of whose faults could be blamed on the debasing influences of the culture imposed on them by the whites. Black people were given a new homeland to seek; as with most promised lands, its exact location and just when they were to get there were left vague. But sooner or later they were assured a glorious future, when the new Nation of Islam would be established and a righteous and vengeful Allah would give the white oppressors the punishment they deserved. In the interim they were to lead sober lives, work hard, protect their women, their homes, and their communities, lead other blacks into the fold, and steadfastly and together resist the whites' efforts to deny black people their rights.

As with the development of the Handsome Lake religion, the Ghost Dance, and the many cargo cults of the Melanesians, the new religion of the black Muslims offers both an explanation of the causes of frustra-

". . . increasing tension resulting from the blacks' growing sense of frustration. . . ."
Figure 12-14. Malcolm X shortly before his break with Elijah Muhammad and his subsequent assassination. (Wide World Photos.)

tion and a ritual means of reducing them—by reversing the roles of oppressor and oppressed.

The development of the WCIW has been marked by a series of circumstances that may be representative of the conditions under which new ideologies appear in societies or among groups within a society that are experiencing intense stress as a result of economic exploitation, social discrimination, and political domination. First, their traditional supernatural beliefs and practices appear to fail them. Accustomed to trying to control their environment and cope with stress by reliance on the supernatural, they seek and find a prophet who promises deliverance to those who accept his supernaturally derived guidance. A group of disciples is formed to protect the prophet and to serve as the administrators and the priests of the new ideology and as guardians of its orthodoxy. Mass conversions follow. Gradually the new system of beliefs is routinized and gains wide acceptance.

If it fails to provide the promised relief, or if its opponents are powerful enough to repress it, the new belief system may die. Otherwise, if the actions it advocates are truly adaptive, if it reduces frustrations and gives its adherents a new sense of life's meaning, it will persist—until, like all other particular ideologies, it too ultimately becomes culturally outmoded and gives way to some still newer system of beliefs, the product of people's so far ceaseless search for fuller and more effective understanding of themselves, their world, and the best way of dealing with the dilemmas of human existence.

". . . until, like all other particular ideologies, it too ultimately becomes culturally outmoded and gives way to some still newer system of beliefs. . . ."

Figure 12-15. The Panthers, another ideological variation on the theme of black redemption. (Wide World Photos.)

Summary

The ideology of every people provides a guiding system of beliefs that explains the nature of the universe and of its relationship to humankind. Among most peoples such systems of belief are based on supernaturalism. However, it is people's need for *some* system of beliefs, not necessarily supernaturally based, that is demonstrably universal. For many, secular ideologies appear to function just as well.

Invariably, an ideology encompasses a system of rituals, actions that function both to reinforce belief and to provide people with a sense that they can in some measure control the forces they believe affect them. Prayer, ritual abstention from certain foods, the ingestion of others, the observance of taboos associated with totemism, sacrifice, and possession are prominent among the means by which people seek to take action intended in some measure to control—usually to improve—their relation to the forces they believe dominate their lives.

The significance of ideology as a system for explaining the world and for providing people with a means of controlling their relation to it is especially well illustrated by the beliefs and practices characteristic of nature worship. The sense in which people's social experience affects the structuring of their perception of the supernatural is strikingly exemplified by the worship of ancestral spirits.

Ideology, like all other aspects of culture, is constantly changing, as the changing circumstances of human lives render older patterns of cultural behavior impracticable and require the development of new beliefs and practices that sanction the changes in conduct necessary to adjust to new conditions.

Where culture change is slow, there is usually time for the gradual modification of traditional ideologies, a process that often entails the expeditious occurrence of new divine revelations that sanction adaptive changes in cultural behavior.

However, for some peoples undergoing more rapid cultural change, traditional ideologies may not be amenable to fast modification. Among groups whose traditional beliefs and practices seem to be failing them in their efforts to adjust to rapid culture change resulting from the competitive encroachment of more powerful peoples, revitalization movements often develop in which the deprived group seeks to redeem its status by combining aspects of the oppressors' apparently more efficacious ideology and actions with elements of their own traditional beliefs. Sometimes this works, and a new religion is born, to last until it too becomes adaptively irrelevant as a guide to coping with the ever-changing circumstances of human life.

Suggested Readings

Because religious ideologies have been among the most extensively studied of all aspects of culture, there are many good introductory works on religion in anthropological perspective. Among the most recent and best are Eister's *Changing Perspectives in the Scientific Study of Religion,* Evans-Pritchard's *Theories of Primitive Religion,* Hahn's "Understanding Beliefs: An Essay on the Methodology of the Statement and Analysis of Belief Systems," Hill's *Symbols and Society: Essays on Belief Systems in Action,* Malefijt's *Religion and Culture,* Norbeck's *Religion in Primitive Society,* van Baal's *Symbols for Communication: An Introduction to the Anthropological Study of Religion,* and Wallace's *Religion: An Anthropological Perspective.*

Also useful are the anthologies: *Anthropological Approaches to the Study of Religion,* edited by Banton; the excellent *A Reader in Comparative Religion,* edited by Lessa and Vogt, and their *On New Approaches to the Study of Religion;* see also *Gods and Rituals,* edited by Middleton.

On myth and world view see Campbell's *The Masks of God; Primitive Views of the World,* edited by Diamond; Freud's *Myths of Creation, African Worlds,* edited by Forde; *Myth, Symbol, and Culture,* edited by Geertz; Jones's "World Views: Their

Nature and Their Function"; *Myth and Cosmos,* edited by Middleton; *Making of Myth,* edited by Ohmann; and *Myth: A Symposium,* edited by Sebeok.

Nearly all of the general works listed here deal extensively with ritual, but see also Beattie's "On Understanding Ritual," Barth's *Ritual and Knowledge Among the Baktaman of New Guinea,* Goody's "Religion and Ritual: The Definitional Problem," La Fontaine's *The Interpretation of Ritual: Essays in Honour of A. J. Richards,* Turner's *The Ritual Process* and his *The Forest of Symbols,* Arinze's *Sacrifice in Ibo Religion,* Firth's *Tikopia: Ritual and Belief,* Rappaport's "Ritual, Sanctity, and Cybernetics" and his *Pigs for the Ancestors: Ritual in the Ecology of a New Guinea People,* and Shack's "Hunger, Anxiety and Ritual: Deprivation and Spirit Possession Among the Gurage of Ethiopia." For a classic source on sacrifice see the recently reprinted *Sacrifice: Its Nature and Function* by Hubert and Mauss.

On totemism and taboo see Sections 4 and 5 of Lessa and Vogt's *A Reader in Comparative Religion,* also *Totemism* by Lévi-Strauss. For an account of nature worship see the chapter on religion in Hammond's *Yatenga,* Coursey's "The Yam Festivals of West Africa," Rappaport's "Ritual Regulation of Environmental Relations Among A New Guinea People," and Schapera's *Rainmaking Rites of the Tswana Tribes.*

Ancestor worship is also given extended attention in many of the sources already cited; see especially Colson's "Ancestral Spirits and Social Structure Among the Plateau Tonga," Ahern's *The Cult of the Dead in a Chinese Village,* Bloch's *Placing the Dead: Tombs, Ancestral Villages and Kinship Organization in Madagascar,* and Curley's *Elders, Shades, and Women.* See also Kopytoff's "Ancestors as Elders in Africa," Nash's *In the Eyes of the Ancestors,* Nelson's "Ancestor Worship and Burial Practices," Freedman's "Ancestor Worship: Two Facets of the Chinese Case," Goody's *Death, Property and the Ancestors,* and Smith's *Ancestor Worship in Contemporary Japan.*

Ideological change, especially revitalization movements, receives extended attention in Wallace's *Religion: An Anthropological View.* See also Aberle's "A Note on Relative Deprivation Theory as Applied to Millennial and Other Cult Movements"; Barkun's *Disaster and the Millennium; Religion, Altered States of Consciousness and Social Change,* edited by Bourgignon; Burridge's *New Heaven, New Earth: A Study of Millenarian Activities;* Errington's "Indigenous Ideas of Order, Time, and Transition in a New Guinea Cargo Movement"; Fernandez's "Zulu Zionism"; Horton's two-part article "On the Rationality of Conversion"; Jorgensen's *The Sun Dance Religion: Power for the Powerless;* La Barre's *The Ghost Dance Religion and the Sioux Outbreak;* and also La Barre's "Materials for a History of Studies of Crises Cults: A Bibliographic Essay" and Wilson's *Religion and the Transformation of Society: A Study of Social Change in Africa.* See as well Deshen's "On Religious Change: The Situational Analysis of Symbolic Action." Also of value are Lanternari's *The Religions of the Oppressed: A Study of Modern Messianic Cults; Millennial Dreams in Action,* edited by Thrupp; Worsley's *The Trumpet Shall Sound: A Study of Cargo Cults in Melanesia;* Lawrence's *Road Belong Cargo,* Wallace's *The Death and Rebirth of the Seneca;* and Wilson's *Magic and Millennialism: A Sociological Study of Religious Movements of Protest Among Third World Peoples. When Prophecy Fails* is the subject of a book by Festinger, Reicken, and Schacter.

Several good studies of the religions of particular peoples are Benítez's *In the Magic Land of Peyote,* Evans-Pritchard's *Nuer Religion,* Geertz's *The Religion of Java,* Judah's *Hare Krishna and the Counter Culture,* Métraux's *Voodoo in Haiti,* Norbeck's *Religion and Society in Modern Japan: Continuity and Change;* Paden's excellent *Religion and Political Culture in Kano,* Simpson's *Religious Cults of the Caribbean: Trinidad, Jamaica, and Haiti,* Spiro's *Burmese Supernaturalism: A Study in the Explanation and Reduction of Suffering,* Yang's *Religion in Chinese Society,* and Zaretsky and Leone's *Religious Movements in Contemporary America.*

13

Magic, Witchcraft, Divination, and Curing

There was a time when anthropologists used the distinction between belief in supernatural beings, a practice traditionally called animism, and the attribution of supernatural power to inanimate objects, called animatism, as the basis for distinguishing religion from magic. It was asserted that religion involved the supposedly more "highly evolved" and more "civilized" belief in such supernatural beings as souls, ghosts, devils, demons, and gods of various sorts (see Tylor 1958). Magic, on the other hand, entailed the presumably more "primitive" belief in—and "heathenish" tendency to invoke the power of—idols, spells, incantations, and other awesome inanimate forms; it was also contended that practitioners of magic were ignorant of the concept of soul (Marett 1909). In fact, the effort to make absolute distinctions between religion and magic probably obscures more than it clarifies. Most modern anthropologists agree that a sharp differentiation between magic and religion cannot be sustained by the ethnographic facts.

Magic

Magic is often further distinguished from other forms of religious belief and practice by the greater emphasis given to manipulation rather than supplication as a means of controlling the supernatural. Magical beliefs and actions are defined as characteristically giving greater attention to the induction of more or less automatic supernatural responses, usually by means of a particular combination of actions. In accordance with this somewhat forced distinction, magic is

"... greater emphasis given to manipulation. . . ."

Figure 13-1. Sacred festoons hung over the entrance to a Japanese house at the New Year are believed to bring good fortune to its inhabitants. (Information Section, Embassy of Japan.)

formalistic; it "consists of a variety of ritual methods whereby events can be automatically or mechanistically influenced by supernatural means" (Lessa and Vogt 1970:245). In contrast, religious efforts at supernatural control typically entail a request, supplication in the form of such rituals as prayer and sacrifice, addressed to a specific supernatural being whose response is determined by its independent will.

Although it may in some instances be analytically useful, the distinction between religion and magic should not be overstated. Essentially similar metaphysical premises underlie both magical and religious beliefs and practices. An effort at mechanical manipulation is frequently involved in religious rituals, particularly those that entail an elaborate liturgy, the almost mechanical repetition of formulaic prayer, the observance of ritual avoidances, the wearing of protective talismans, and the like. Both religion and magic are turned to with increased ardor in times of stress and crisis when empirical means of coping appear to fail. As with many conceptually useful distinctions, that between magic and religion is one of emphasis, on automatic manipulation in the case of magic as opposed to conciliatory supplication in the case of religion.

Magic can be used for either benign or malevolent ends. It can be employed to bring good luck, to assist a person in foretelling the future, to cure an illness. Or it can be used destructively, to ruin a farm crop, to cause a rival's misfortune, or to kill an enemy. Well-intentioned magic is usually performed openly, evil magic in secret. Either way, magical practices typically involve the ritual manipulation of objects such as charms, amulets, potions, or concoctions of various supernaturally endowed materials; the use of word formulas; and reliance on a wide variety of actions such as dancing, meditation, fasting, narcotics use, deep breathing, hypnosis, and other techniques intended to modify normal physiological and psychological functioning as a means of increasing the practitioner's magical powers. But again many of these behaviors are often a part of religious observances as well.

In addition to the difference between good and evil magic, a descriptively useful distinction can be made between imitative (or homeopathic) magic and contagious magic (see Frazer 1922). The classic example of imitative magic is the voodoo doll, prepared to resemble the intended victim and then ritually mistreated: stuck with pins, burned, buried, or exposed to the weather and allowed to rot. Wallace (1966) calls this procedure simulation. It may be employed in an effort to control either a supernatural being or an abstract supernatural power and arises from a belief in some sort of mystical link between similar objects, so that what is made to happen to one will happen to the other. In another common form of imitative magic, the wished-for event is made to occur by enacting it ritually. Among the Arunta of Australia, for example, a particular descent group is believed to have the power to increase the supply of witchety grubs—soft, wormlike larvae much prized by other members of the tribe as food. An increase in the witchety grub supply is induced by a ceremonial pantomime in which dancers, their bodies painted to represent the newly emergent larva, mimic the movements of the insect as it emerges from its chrysalis. The kangaroo supply is increased by means of a similar ritual performance.

Contagious magic, based on the belief that things that have once been in contact will continue to act on each other, is exemplified by such ritual acts as the cannibal's consumption of the heart of an enemy in order to gain the dead man's strength or intelligence. It is fear of contagious magic that causes many people to dispose cautiously of their nail cuttings and hair clippings, the navel strings of newborn infants,

"It is fear of contagious magic. . . ."

Figure 13-2. Desecrated grave. (National Film Board of Canada.)

or the afterbirth. All of these are sometimes thought to be collected by workers of evil magic, who inflict on these parts, still mystically associated with the person from whom they were taken, a variety of punishments: burning, stabbing, or strangling them to induce the sensation or effect of such suffering on the body of their intended victim.

The term *sorcerer* is usually used to describe persons who use their knowledge of magic for malevolent ends. The effectiveness of sorcerers' practices generally requires that the person who is the object of their maliciousness know that evil magic is being worked against him or her. Such knowledge can kill. Intense anxiety, for example, can result in a loss of appetite, which in turn debilitates an intended victim and causes symptoms that—if the victim is suggestible—may convince him or her that a sorcerer's magic is taking effect. This creates still greater anxiety and continued lack of appetite, which, combined with mounting terror and hopelessness, can send a person into a steady decline ending in death.

The real efficacy of the sorcerers' magic lies in their capacity literally to frighten the victim to death. A man knows evil magic is being worked against him. He and all his fellows believe in the inevitability of such magic's effectiveness. He thinks he is going to die, and so does everyone else. So his friends treat him accordingly, often further intensifying his anxiety by beginning to make preparations for his funeral. Unless he is quickly able to obtain a strong magical antidote, he will die, not from sorcery, but from the lethal effects of fear.

As Cannon (1942) has chronicled such a decline in his classic article "Voodoo Death," the victim's sympathetic nervous system responds to the stress he or she feels by inducing the production of quantities of sugar and adrenalin and by contracting certain blood vessels. If such stress continues, shock results, blood pressure drops, body temperature falls, normal heart function ceases, plasma escapes into the tissues, morbidity progresses, and death soon follows.

Australian Aborigines are reported to have died in this way from the effects of having a sorcerer point at them with a bone (Basedow 1925; see also Warner 1964). People who discover they are being "boned" by someone trying to kill them become so terrified they can neither speak nor move. They begin to froth at the mouth, their muscles twitch involuntarily, and finally they faint and fall to the ground. When aroused they first writhe, horror-stricken, in the dust, moaning in anguish. Then, slowly, they regain control of themselves, crawl off hopelessly to shelter, to lie totally listless, refusing food and drink, unwilling to communicate, taking no further interest in life around them, and within a few days, dying.

Frequently the morbidity of people who believe themselves to be victims of sorcery is intensified by the evident helplessness and despair of those around them. Death is the only escape from the agony of their badly weakened physical condition, anxiety, and hopelessness.

Inanimate Power

Just as supernatural power is often ascribed to particular animate beings—spirits and deities of various sorts—so are inanimate objects frequently believed to be endowed with supernatural force.

Mana

The concept of inanimate supernatural power was first explicitly identified by anthropologists studying the religious ideas and practices of the peoples of Melanesia, where belief in such power, locally called mana after the Polynesian term, is widespread. According to the interpretation of those who have studied it, mana is perceived by believers as an intangible, invisible power, a supernaturally derived force that may be embodied either in animate or inanimate objects or in events. People who touch an object so endowed may receive some of its power to serve them for a specific purpose, as when a worshiper touches a sacred relic to be cured of some disease, a traveler carries an amulet or medal for protection away from home, or a gambler strokes a rabbit's foot before throwing the dice.

In contrast to reliance for supernatural assistance on ancestral spirits or other animate beings who are presumed to have a will of their own and who may or may not respond to the believer's request for help, the transfer of power that results from touching an object that has mana is generally believed to be automatic and thus "magical." Mana itself is neutral and can be manipulated for benign or malevolent purposes.

Although belief in manalike power is an attribute of the belief systems of many peoples, it is, as just indicated, a markedly dominant theme in Melanesia (see Firth 1940). There most events that occur as the result of some apparently "nonnatural" cause are explained as consequences of the power of mana, a force believed to be contained most often in unusual natural objects, such as peculiarly shaped stones, or in mysterious events, such as a death by witchcraft or an occurrence of unexpectedly good

". . . belief in manalike power is an attribute of the belief systems of many peoples. . . ."

Figure 13-3. A bone suspended from the branch of a tree warns potential thieves that if they enter this field they will sicken and die, Yatenga, Upper Volta. (Hammond.)

fortune. The presence of mana can be ascertained by testing. If, for example, a person comes across an oddly formed stone suspected to contain mana, it can be buried in a newly planted yam garden. If the harvest from this garden is unusually abundant, the finder was right—the stone contained mana.

Just as an exceptionally abundant garden is evidence that the stones buried in it contain mana, so is a person who possesses unusual qualities—good luck, a strong personality, the ability to lead—often believed to derive these special attributes from mana. For mana functions in a way that is literally supernatural, outside, beyond, or transcending the powers of nature. Ordinary yam gardens, like ordinary people and everyday events, are thought to develop by natural processes. It is only the extraordinary aspect of otherwise ordinary objects, beings, and circumstances that reveals the presence of the mana that Melanesian believers try to acquire as a means of enhancing their capacities, improving the nature of their possessions, and bettering the quality of their activities.

. . ."a force believed to be most often embodied in people who are extraordinarily devout. . . ."
Figure 13-4. Veiled Moslem women outside a mosque in the Casbah at Fes, Morocco. (United Nations.)

The concept of an impersonal power is by no means limited to Melanesia. It was also widely found among American Indians. The exceptional prowess of particular war leaders among the Fox, Indians of the prairies, was ascribed to the possession of manitu, an impersonal power acquired during the course of a vision. In fact this was the principal means by which a temporary leader could legitimize his right to authority over his fellows. Such power was transitory. Manitu lasted only for the duration of a single battle and thus could not be used to sanction the permanent centralization of political power in the hands of any particular leader. The Siouan word *wakan* and the Iroquois word *orenda* refer apparently to the same concept (Underhill 1957:128).

Baraka

The concept of a dynamic, impersonal power as the vitalizing force behind people, objects, and actions is also well known in the Middle East and Africa. Among North African Moslems, for example, it is called baraka, or holiness, a force believed to be most often embodied in people who are extraordinarily devout or saintly. Mohammad, the messenger of Allah, is popularly believed to have been endowed with an abundance of baraka. Although he emphasized his human nature, he did not deny that he possessed baraka, and he made "no objection when his companions fought for his spittle or the water with which he had washed and when they gathered up and kept his hair" (von Gruenebaum 1961:92).

Like mana, baraka may be transmitted by contact. Consequently, the clothes worn by a holy man, the earth he has walked on, any object he has used may contain baraka and may be collected by the devout as a means of acquiring for themselves some of the special supernatural power that sets such a person apart.

The Christian veneration of relics, the bones of martyrs and saints, or of the places holy women and men are known to have inhabited or of the objects they have used is an analogous phenomenon. Something similar is apparent also in the reverential attitude taken toward places and things known to have come into contact with charismatic secular personalities—political heroes and martyrs, philosophers, and great artists. The respectful preservation of their places of birth, even of beds in which they slept, and the sense of worthiness and inspiration, the psychological "lift," associated with visiting such places, seem to be functionally similar to the baraka that Moslems can automatically acquire by making the pilgrimage to Mecca and that others can obtain from touching them on their return, or the spiritual benefit Jews and Christians derive from visits to the shrines of the Holy Land.

Witchcraft

Witches as workers of evil are usually distinguished from sorcerers by the belief that anyone can acquire the magical knowledge to be a sorcerer, whereas the supernatural power of witches is innate. It may, however, lie dormant, and a witch may even be unaware of his or her special powers. Belief in witchcraft is ancient, worldwide, and remarkably tenacious, perhaps because it is so useful. Certain of the essential aspects of witchcraft are almost universal, such as the idea that witches are in league with the forces of evil, often represented as a devil.

Also widespread is the belief that witches enhance or reinforce their supernatural powers by preparing concoctions of despised ingredients and by participating in culturally prohibited acts.

In some European countries such rituals are believed to have entailed the repulsively distorted enactment of rites associated with prevailing religious practice. One of these was the "Black Mass," a travesty of the Catholic Mass in which sacred objects and symbols were purportedly used in intentionally blasphemous ways, often to the supposed accompaniment of a rich variety of orgiastic sexual practices, apparently in the belief that the power of such desecrations could in some way be captured and utilized by the communicants. All such terrifying ritual practices deepen the participants' sense of involvement with the evil forces with which it is assumed they are already, whether they like it or not, in league.

In addition to reliance on the preparation of "hideous" potions and alleged participation in "ghastly" rituals as a means of maintaining or increasing their magic powers, witches can also cause harm by purely psychic means, by willing someone to suffer misfortune, or they can bring mischief with a glance, as they do with the "evil eye."

Belief in witches and the fear of witchcraft are generally most intense in times of suddenly increased social tension and crisis that a society is unable to reduce by reliance on alternative institutional means. As witches are believed to cause misfortune, when misfortune strikes—especially if it strikes suddenly, inexplicably, and with widespread effect—witches are frequently believed to be at work, and a witch hunt gets under way.

Belief in witchcraft is conveniently accompanied by belief in various means of witch detection and in techniques for counteracting their evil purposes, bringing to an end the crisis they are thought to have created and restoring social peace.

The relationship among witchcraft beliefs, witch hunting, and societal stress resulting from conflict and competition is well illustrated by the role of witchcraft among the Gusii of Kenya and their neighbors. Among many of the peoples of Kenya, and elsewhere in East Africa, witches are thought to be jealous individuals who use their evil powers for vengeance or to harm their rivals or those they envy. Accusations of witchcraft tend to occur particularly often among people in competition over territory, property, or other culturally valued goods in limited supply. A relationship in which the potential for competitive jealousy is particularly great is that between co-wives in a polygynous household. The Gusii have a special word, *engareka,* for "hatred between co-wives," and it is expected that a man's several wives will practice witchcraft and accuse one another of it. To minimize such conflict and maximize household harmony a Gusii husband builds the houses of his wives as far apart as possible.

"... witches are thought to be jealous. ..."

Figure 13-5. In southern Africa tension between co-wives often results in witchcraft accusations. Zulu co-wives with their husband between them. (Courtesy of the American Museum of Natural History.)

Comparative anthropological fieldwork conducted by LeVine among neighboring tribal groups, the Luo and the Kipsigi, who are also polygynous and also believe in and practice witchcraft, has revealed what appears to be a direct correlation between co-wife proximity and the frequency of witchcraft accusations. Co-wives among the Luo live in adjacent houses, share a common courtyard, and are constantly preoccupied with witchcraft. The houses of Gusii co-wives are spaced as far apart as possible by their husbands, and witchcraft accusations occur less often. Kipsigi co-wives live miles apart and go for days without seeing each other, and accusations of witchcraft are even rarer.

In each of these three instances jealousy resulting from co-wives' intense competition for the sexual and economic attentions of a shared husband is the specific cause of witchcraft accusations. The greater the intensity of such competition, the greater the potential for frustration and aggression, and the greater the likelihood of reliance on witchcraft as a means of expressing it. In those parts of Gusiiland where population increase has made it necessary to crowd the houses of co-wives closer together, both jealousy and accusations of witchcraft have increased.

Among the Gusii, Luo, and Kipsigi of Kenya—as was the case among the seventeenth-century inhabitants of Salem, Massachusetts—witches are culturally defined as a principal cause of otherwise unexplainable trouble. So, when there is trouble, the way to cope with it is to find the witch who is responsible. To rid themselves of witches, and thus end the social disorder witches were believed to be causing, New Englanders hanged them (Davies 1947).

The problem with such magical means of coping with crisis is that relief is never more than temporary. It comes only from belief that the source of disruption and stress has been accurately identified and adequately dealt with. But because witches never are, and never were, the real cause of trouble, hunting them down and punishing them cannot do any lasting good. Despite the temporary catharsis it may provide, witch hunting has no direct effect on the real causes of frustration, anxiety, and social tension. In southwestern Kenya polygyny, population increase, and a shortage of living space, rather than co-wives who are witches, are the basic causes of social disequilibrium and neurotic response. Until these real causes are rectified, tensions will inevitably rise again, setting off a new search for the witches mistakenly believed to be the cause of it all.

Divination

In divination techniques are employed to obtain the additional, otherwise unavailable information necessary to decide wisely between alternative courses of action. By the ritual manipulation of a system of signs and symbols, such as tea leaf patterns or the sequence of playing cards within a deck, or by examination of the lines in the palm of the hand and omens of various sorts, people believe they can learn about things that are otherwise unknowable.

Where means of acquiring crucial information are otherwise limited, often because of the relative simplicity of a people's technology, reliance on divination is most likely to be culturally valued. Hunter-gatherers use divination to find game. For agriculturalists locating subsurface water sources is often an important problem. Even in the United States, farmers who cannot obtain geological advice or do not wish to accept the geologist's discouraging conclusions rely on "water witching" (Vogt 1952). A wand, often made from the forked branch of a willow tree, is held by the diviner as he or she walks back and forth across the field where the client wants to dig a well. Because a magical bond is believed to exist between willows and water—willow trees often grow along riverbanks and beside ponds—it is thought that a willow branch passed over a place where water lies beneath the surface will dip downward.

Divination is also frequently used to foretell what will happen in the future and to ascertain what has occurred in the past—to extend comprehension in time as well as space.

In the traditional culture of Tibet, in which nearly every facet of people's experience is believed to be permeated with supernaturalism, diviners are consulted for guidance on all life problems: to determine the most efficient scheduling of daily and seasonal economic activities; for assistance in deciding wisely on the conduct of family affairs, marriage arrangements, the naming of newborn children, and funeral preparations; and for advice in diagnosing and treating sickness (Ekvall 1963).

The guidance the Tibetans seek from the supernatural reflects both the universality of people's need for some means of coping with the discomfort and inconvenience of uncertainty and the peculiarly precarious circumstances of Tibetan life, where nearly every aspect of the natural setting seems antagonistic to human survival. Tibetan topography is bleak and austere. The climate is often catastrophic: violent storms of wind, snow, and sand threaten the crops, the herds, and the people. It is believed that a host of malevolent spirits and angry demons are constantly causing misfortune, precipitating accidents, and sending sickness. Until recently the threat of raids and of robbery and frequent feuding was almost incessantly disruptive to the orderly conduct of life and often made life itself precarious.

Anxiety resulting from the threat of one or more of these several sources of disaster is compounded by most Tibetans' inability either to control such conditions or to obtain

"Where means of acquiring crucial information are otherwise limited. . . ."

Figure 13-6. As they are for West African farmers in Benin. (United Nations.)

the information that might at least assist them in anticipating, preparing for, or avoiding the hardship they cause. Until the last few years there were no meteorological stations to broadcast weather predictions, no health service to warn of epidemics or to provide advice on disease prevention, no market reports to serve as guides to commercial transactions, no police patrols to warn of storm damage on the roads or information on the movements of outlaw bands. Traditionally it has been principally through reliance on divination that Tibetans could acquire information on these circumstances that could so drastically affect the course of their lives. Such divination has taken many forms.

In Tibetan rosary divination, for example, a selected length of prayer beads is counted off by threes. If the number remaining is odd, a favorable or positive response is indicated. An even number indicates a negative answer. If the question put to a diviner concerns the auspiciousness of a particular date for beginning spring planting, for starting a trip, or for a wedding, and if seven rosary beads remain uncounted, the questioner can confidently proceed. If an even number are left the questioner would know to alter the arrangements. Other Tibetan systems for knowing the otherwise unknowable entail throwing dice, scattering pebbles and determining the signs indicated by the patterns into which they fall, and opening a book, spotting a word or phrase at random, and then carefully studying it for the revelation of a sign. Dreams also serve as a source of guidance. Omens are sought everywhere: in the appearance of animals, the color of foods, changes in the weather. All can be analyzed for warnings and signs that provide the Tibetans with the comforting sense that they are able to foresee the innumerable circumstances of their lives.

A special category of Tibetan lamas, or monks, serve as diviners. If their forecasts are correct, they are rewarded financially and accorded high status and authority as men whose closer relation to the sources of supernatural power makes them valuable allies and dangerous opponents.

Often diviners are believed to be inspired by supernatural beings of various sorts, as in the case of mediums or shamans, who can discover previously unknown information by entering a trancelike state believed to place them in contact with the spirit world. Frequently reliance on such purely mechanical techniques as throwing the dice is combined with dependence on supernatural revelations, inspiration, or intervention for the proper interpretation of magically revealed signs, another instance of the frequent overlapping of "magical" and "religious" behavior.

Curing

The magical and/or religious treatment of illness illustrates even more strongly the many ways in which "religious" as opposed to "magical" systems for controlling the supernatural actually run together. Citing Clement, Wallace (1966:116) refers to five widespread theories of disease and treatment based on belief in religious or magical causation: (1) "imitative and contagious magic"; (2) "disease-object intrusion," in which some foreign object is supposed to have been magically introduced into the victim's body; (3) "soul loss," in which the

". . . curing practices often include medically effective methods. . . ."

Figure 13-7. Acupuncture, a case in point. (National Film Board of Canada.)

victim's soul is thought to have been stolen and he or she is left to fall ill and die; (4) "spirit intrusion," as when a person is believed to be possessed by a spirit; and (5) "breach of taboo."

In addition to considerable emphasis on ritual observances that lack any empirically verifiable efficacy, curing practices often include medically effective methods such as the use of minerals, herbs, roots, leaves, and berries with pharmaceutical value as well as massage, bloodletting, surgery, and a variety of sound psychotherapeutic techniques.

"... chewing up and swallowing carefully written out passages from the Koran."
Figure 13-8. Moslems in West Africa sometimes treat disease by washing off and drinking ink used in writing out passages from the Koran. Here a young boy studies a Koranic passage written out on a wooden slate. (United Nations.)

The frequent success of curers is to be explained not only by the real effectiveness of their medicinal and psychological treatment but also by the fact that most sick people recover from their maladies anyway, frequently despite the therapy they receive. Like belief in divination, the widespread reliance on supernaturally based systems for curing probably derives partially from the universality of people's need to decrease their anxiety in crisis situations by taking what they believe to be instrumental action, by *doing* something.

The Javanese Dukun

In Java there are specialists in curing by nearly every means (Geertz 1960). Some administer herbs, others insert golden needles under the skin, still others cure with spells. To be a Javanese dukun, or curer, usually requires both practical training and spiritual preparation. Many believe their curative powers derive from their closeness to God. The techniques by which they achieve this closeness range from meditation and extended fasting to chewing up and swallowing carefully written out passages from the Koran.

Frequently the Javanese curer's diagnosis is based on numerology. By taking the sick person's birth date in connection with the date on which he or she fell ill, elaborate calculations are used to arrive at a number that represents a particular method of treatment, often one involving the use of herbs. Diagnosis and a decision on the appropriate therapy may also be arrived at through meditation. Or the patient's symptoms can be "medically" analyzed. Most dukuns probably combine all three approaches. The treatment they prescribe may involve taking herb remedies and aspirin, wearing amulets and charms, changing surroundings and life habits, avoiding emotional stress, swallowing ground iron filings, being massaged, rubbing glass on the skin, having bones set, reciting spells, and drinking tea mixed with the curer's spittle. But finally it is the spiritual power of the curer, rather than the specifics of the therapy, that is believed to be the most critical determinant of the patient's chances for recovery.

In addition to the services of professional curers, the Javanese use a number of "home remedies" that do not require the assistance of a curer such as pebble necklaces, amulets containing Arabic verses from the Koran, ground dragon's tongue, polliwogs, and a variety of concoctions whose potency seems somehow related to their repulsiveness: feces, hair clippings, the stub of the patient's umbilical cord (taken with bananas to make it go down more easily). If somewhat more imaginative, such remedies are no more irrational than those prescribed by quacks in more "modern" societies. In parts of the United States various folk remedies, such as the proverbial "snake oil," were until quite recently accepted panaceas for everything from acute appendicitis to nervousness. The affluence of contemporary physicians who treat terminal cancer patients with computerlike gadgets covered with impressive ranks of flashing lights or with regimens of carrot juice, wheat germ, and prayer suggests that sufferers in every society will accept almost any treatment that promises a release from pain and the fear of death.

Ethiopian Psychotherapy and the Zar Cult

In some places in Ethiopia people who are accident prone, listless, apathetic, melancholy, or alcoholic are believed to be possessed by a spirit, or zar, that they must recognize and come to terms with in order to be cured (Messing 1958). In a process functionally analogous to that by which the patient undergoing modern psychoanalytic therapy is encouraged to confront the anomalies in his or her behavior, to try to understand their causes, and thus to cope with them more efficiently—often learning new and alternative ways of dealing with the situations that cause the stress—the Ethiopian patient in a zar cult is first placed in a trance in order that the unknown spirit that is causing the problems will manifest itself. The demands of the zar are made known to the troubled person, who may thereafter try to control his or her neurotic or psychotic symptoms through worship of the zar spirits, and regular donations to the congregation, which is composed largely of others similarly afflicted by troublesome spirits.

Most zar cult members are persons whose deprived social situation is a principal source of their stress: unhappily married women, ex-slaves who are discriminated against, lonely foreigners, lower-class Moslems shunned by Christians. In cult membership they find a legitimate channel for the expression of their frustration, and they also find warmth, sympathy, a measure of social acceptance not available to them in other relationships, and an opportunity for social contacts across class and religious lines. Probably most important for the remission of their symptoms, members are provided an accepting social context in which they are permitted to describe their complaints to a compassionate audience, to "act out" in the course of zar possession the violent emotions that are making them ill, and to indicate while in trance the therapy they require; often the promise of presents and the assurance of better treatment by their kinsmen are all that is needed.

During the ritual in which possession takes place the patients both indicate their frustration and identify and apologize for their weakness and shortcomings. The violent behavior expected during active possession by the zar provides for the cathartic but temporary reduction of emotional tension.

Afterward the patients are instructed in the means by which in future they can better control their morbid symptoms. For mildly disturbed patients one visit to the zar cult may be enough. For the more deeply troubled, prolonged group therapy, as active members of the zar cult, may be required to hold their mental illness in check.

Summary

The major distinction between magic and religion is generally made on the basis of the greater emphasis on manipulating inanimate supernatural power that is assumed to be characteristic of magic, whereas religion is supposedly typified by greater efforts at supplicating various sorts of animate supernatural beings with minds of their own. Most anthropologists now agree that the distinction between magic and religion cannot be sharply drawn.

Magic has often been analytically categorized as either imitative or contagious. The frequent effectiveness of magic is probably best explained by the believers' profound faith in its efficacy and by the various ways in which the sorcerer dramatizes his or her activities and their intent, sometimes so terrorizing the victim that radical physiological changes precipitated by anxiety do in fact cause death.

Magic constitutes another variation of supernaturalism as a fundamental system of beliefs and accompanying actions relied on by people who lack scientific means to achieve a sense of understanding and control over the powerful forces that always affect, and often disrupt, their lives.

The Melanesian concept of mana, the Middle Eastern belief in baraka, the powers sometimes ascribed by Christians to medals and religious relics, and the concept of luck are various manifestations of belief in the more impersonal supernatural power generally associated with magical, as opposed to religious, beliefs and practices.

The accusation of witchcraft is recurrently used as a means to cope with societal disharmony and crisis by designating a culprit and so both explaining what is wrong and making it right and restoring social order—if only temporarily. Divination, still another variation on the same fundamental theme of controlling powerful forces that are otherwise uncontrollable, is most important among people who lack any other reliable means of foretelling the critical events that can affect their lives. Curing fulfills analogous functions in meeting the crises of illness and the threat of death.

Suggested Readings

Many of the general sources cited in the preceding chapter also deal with the topics covered here. See especially the sections on "Mana and Taboo," "Magic, Witchcraft, and Divination," and "The Magical Treatment of Illness" in Lessa and Vogt's *A Reader in Comparative Religion.* Also see the anthology edited by Middleton, *Magic, Witchcraft, and Curing.*

On the specific topic of magic see Hammond's "Magic: A Problem in Semantics," Philsooph's "Primitive Magic and Mana," and the Waxes' "The Notion of Magic."

The literature on witchcraft is extensive. For some good examples see Caro Baroja's *The World of the Witches; Witchcraft Confessions and Accusations,* edited by Douglas; Lester's "Voodoo Death: Some New Thoughts on an Old Phenomenon"; Lewis's "A Structural Approach to Witchcraft and Spirit Possession"; Lex's "Voodoo Death: New Thoughts on an Old Explanation"; Lindenbaum's "Sorcery and Structure in Fore Society"; Macfarlane's *Witchcraft in Tudor and Stuart England: A Comparative Study;* Mair's *Witchcraft;* Marwick's "The Study of Witchcraft" and his *Witchcraft and Sorcery;* Middleton's "Witchcraft and Sorcery in Lugbara"; Obeyeskere's "Sorcery, Premeditated Murder and the Canalization of Aggression in Sri Lanka"; Rush's *Witchcraft and Sorcery: An Anthropological Perspective on the Occult;* and Thomas's "The Relevance of Social Anthropology to the Historical Study of English Witchcraft."

In addition to the several references to divination contained in the works already cited see Aberle's "Religio-magical Phenomena and Power, Prediction, and Control," Beattie's "Consulting a Nyoro Diviner: The Ethnologist as Client," Middleton's "Oracles and Divination Among the Lugbara," Turner's *Revelation and Divination in Ndembu Ritual,* and Vansina's "The Bushong Poison Ordeal."

Curing is the subject of Buxton's excellent *Religion and Healing in Mandari.* See also Davidson and Day's *Symbol and Realization: A Contribution to the Study of Magic and Healing;* Dobkin de Rios's *Visionary Vine: Psychedelic Healing in the Peruvian Amazon;* Edgerton's "A Traditional African Psychiatrist"; *Hallucinogens and Shamanism,* edited by Harner; Kiev's *Magic, Faith, and Healing: Studies in Primitive Psychiatry Today;* Landy's "Role Adaptation: Traditional Curers under the Impact of Western Medicine"; and *Cultural Illness and Health,* edited by Nader and Maretzki. See also Young's "Magic as a 'Quasi-Profession': The Organization of Magic and Magical Healing Among Amhara."

Several book-length monographs that provide extensive detailed coverage on many of the subjects touched on this chapter are Beyer's *The Cult of Tārā: Magic and Ritual in Tibet,* Endicott's *An Analysis of Malay Magic,* Evans-Pritchard's classic *Witchcraft, Oracles, and Magic Among the Azande,* Fortune's *Sorcerers of Dobu,* Lieban's *Cebuano Sorcery: Malign Magic in the Philippines,* and Reynold's *Magic, Divination, and Witchcraft Among the Barotse of Rhodesia.* Of general interest is Keith's *Religion and the Decline of Magic.*

Part Seven

The Arts

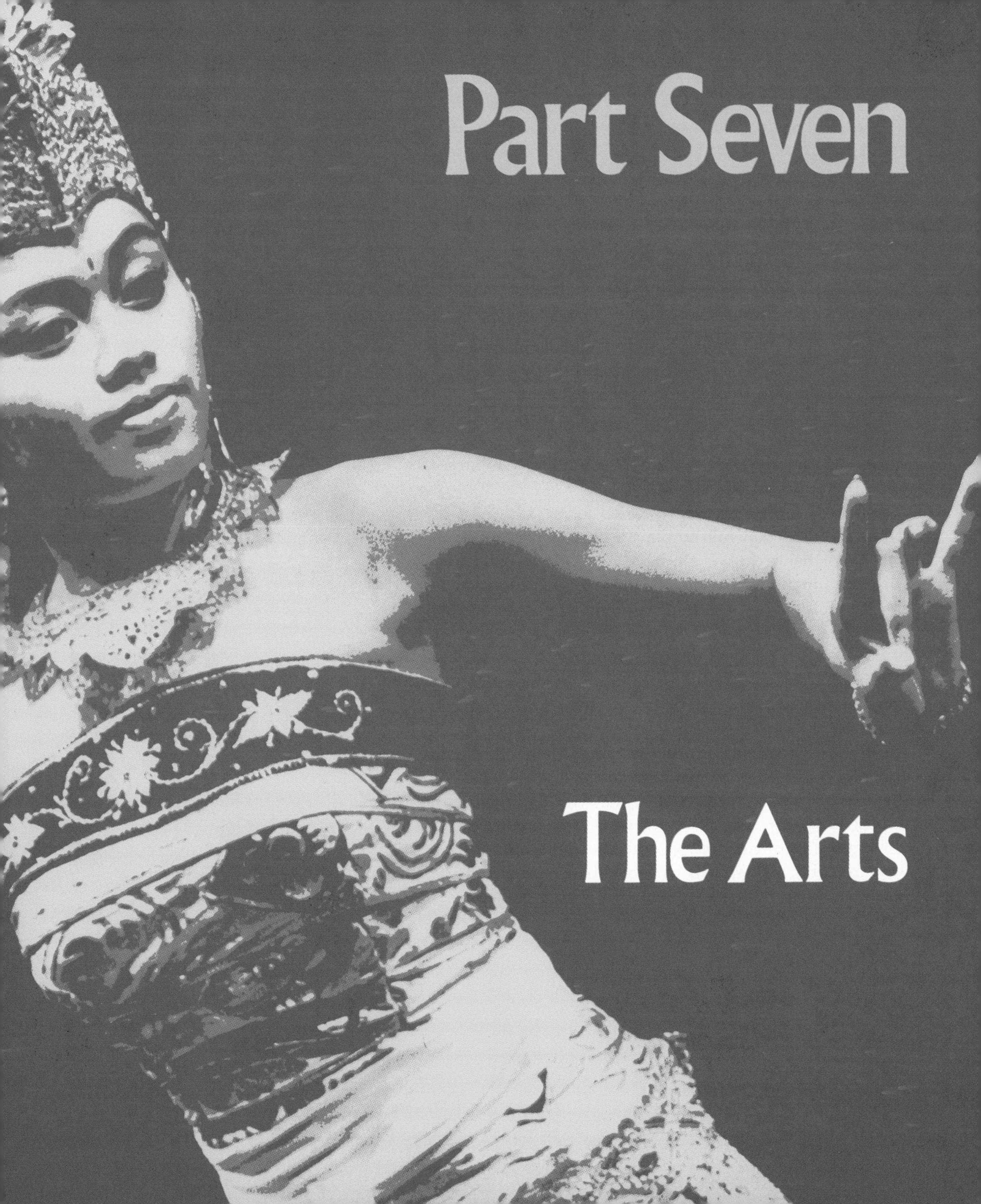

. . . The primitive artist is first and foremost a craftsman, from whom art flows as an extension of his craft activity. By this is meant that he is essentially the constructor of things for use which are also regarded as giving enjoyment. He does not make things simply for the aesthetic satisfaction to be got out of looking at them. Even songs as a rule are not composed to be listened to for pleasure. They have work to do. . . .

FIRTH (1956:171)

Art for art's sake alone is rarely found among the peoples whose forms of aesthetic expression anthropologists have traditionally studied. Probably this is because among most such people the struggle for existence is too critical to allow for the extensive allocation of materials, work, and time to activities not fundamentally related to individual and societal survival.

Art there is, in abundantly varied forms, but most of it has an important role to play. The non-Western artist and his or her creations are often centrally associated with the functioning of major cultural institutions—with the people's means of making a living, the structure of their social and economic relationships, and the control of power, both political and supernatural.

Much of the traditional art of many of the smaller non-Western societies was destroyed at or soon after contact with the first Europeans, either as the people themselves were wiped out or absorbed or as their art was literally wrecked by missionaries eager to destroy what they often correctly perceived as the symbolic representation of ideologies they were determined to eradicate.

Despite the tragedy of all that was irrevocably lost, what remains and what is currently being produced in many areas (in both traditional and contemporary forms) is still an immensely rich treasure.

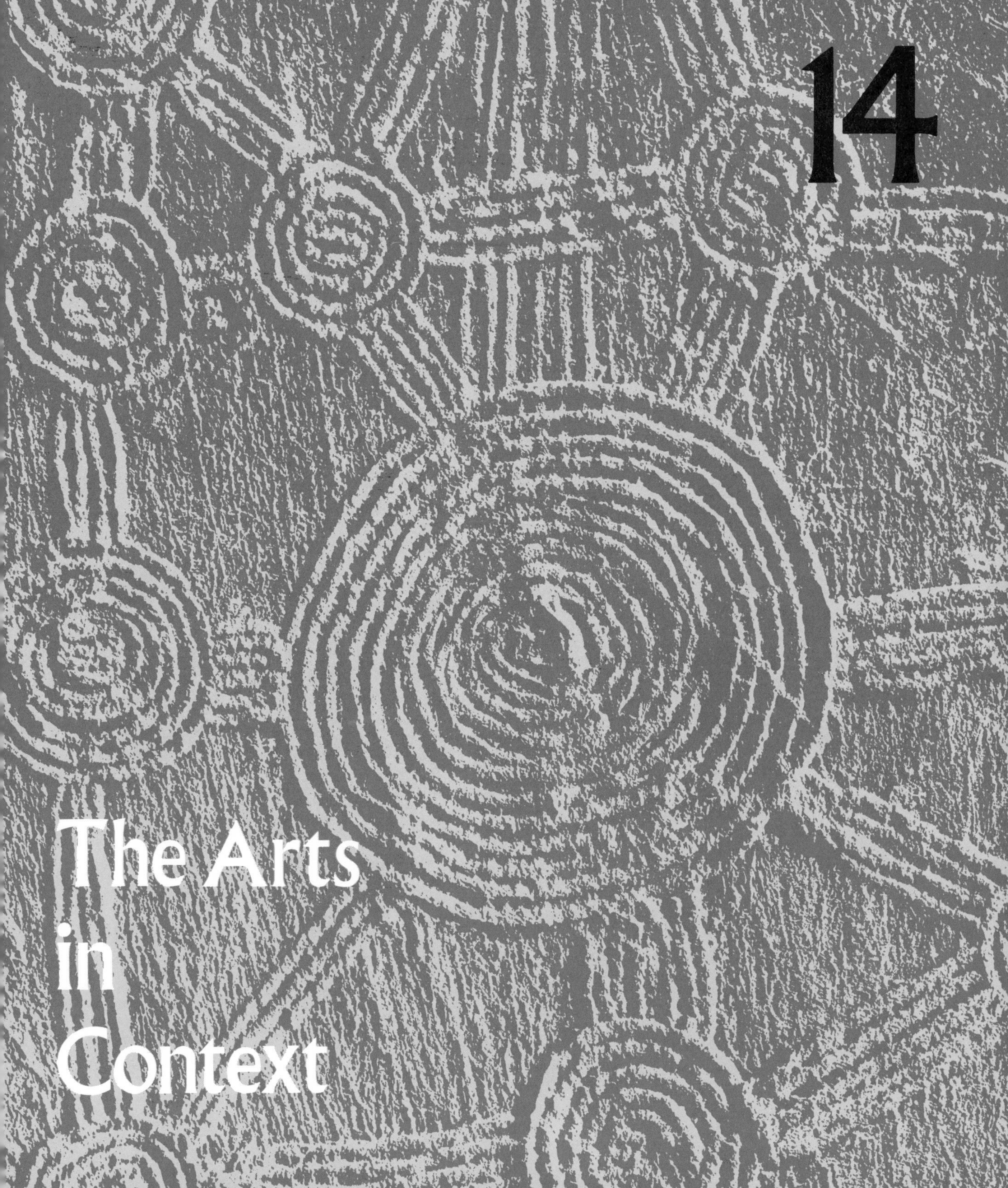

14

The Arts in Context

ART for the anthropologist can be partially defined as the formal product of any activity "whether it be a performance in sound or movement, any combination of visual, auditory, tactile, olfactory, or other sense impressions conveyed through a permanent or impermanent medium": written or oral literature, plastic or graphic representation, "drama, dance, architecture or other form" in which one or more people purposefully create an affective expression of some aspect of their experience (d'Azevedo 1958:712). A concluding part to the definition, linking art to the other aspects of culture within the context of a scientifically usable theory, largely remains to be made.

"... art forms that are persistently and inaccurately called primitive."

Study of the arts by anthropologists has been limited mostly to the traditional arts of Africa, the Pacific, and the Americas, art forms that are persistently and inaccurately called primitive. The tremendously varied forms indiscriminately labeled primitive are, in fact, rarely crude, unless that is part of the artist's intention; typically their meaning is even more complex than their form.

Beyond the convincingly documented contention that the term *primitive* is a misnomer, specialists in the field have so far failed to provide us with a ready means of relating their findings to the general body of theory in cultural and social anthropology. A satisfactory synthesis of the scientific and humanistic traditions in anthropology has not yet been made. As Kavolis has noted, scientifically oriented (cultural) anthropologists have been wary of the apparent imprecision and subjectivity of artistic expression—and of those who have attempted to study it. In contrast, humanists have limited their concern to the "sensitive analysis of particular styles and periods" and have so far failed to develop a theoretical "framework of neces-

Figure 14-1. A Tlingit wood panel, Northwest Pacific coast. (U.S. Department of the Interior.)

sarily gross generalization that might be applied to a cross cultural range of forms of expression" and so be tested (Kavolis 1968:1).

Creativity and Cultural Constraint

Despite the lack of a unified theory that might be readily summarized here, a few generalizations about the relationship of art to the other aspects of culture can be made as a means of suggesting the direction in which such a theoretical synthesis might be developed.

One of the most fundamental questions relates to the dynamic interplay between cultural conditioning and individual creativity, a variation on the still more fundamental issue of freedom of expression versus cultural constraints. The "answer" has implications that go beyond comprehension of the process of artistic creativity to the major question of the causal relations between humankind and culture and the extent to which people can ever be considered "free" of the processes that make them human—that is, cultured—animals.

To what extent is the artist (or any innovator or inventor) really free, his or her expression limited only by the bounds of personal creativity? The other way around the question concerns the extent to which *what* and *how* the artist creates are unavoidably affected by culturally determined circumstances beyond his or her control, beginning with where and when he or she was born. Had Beethoven been born to a BaMbuti hunter in Zäire instead of into a family of eighteenth-century German musicians, would he still have composed the *Eroica?* Obviously not. Even an artistic genius is limited to the creative reworking of culturally available forms.

The materials and techniques available to the artist and the conditions under which he or she can use them all sharply limit, if they do not actually foreordain, the ways in which his or her creativity takes form. Deveraux sees this interplay between the creative artist and his or her culture—the effort to reconcile inner drive to externally imposed rules, "the straining of pure affect against pure [culturally structured] discipline" (1961:362)—as central to the creation of any art form.

The combination of a relatively primitive technology and its usual consequence, a small-scale society, limits the alternatives available to the artist in ways that illustrate concretely both how art can be affected by and can, in turn, affect the culture in which it is created.

Among hunter-gatherers limitations resulting from the rudimentary character of their technology are apparent in two fundamental ways. First the artists' materials

"The materials and techniques available to the artist and the conditions under which he or she can use them all sharply limit . . . the ways in which his or her creativity takes form."

Figure 14-2. Gonroku Matsuda, a master of Japanese lacquer work. (Information Section, Embassy of Japan.)

". . . the artists' materials themselves are largely limited to articles readily available in nature that require a minimum of modification for use . . . ."

Figure 14-3. An Australian artist paints the wall of a rock shelter, western Australia. (Courtesy of the American Museum of Natural History.)

themselves are largely limited to articles readily available in nature that require a minimum of modification for use: stone, the walls of caves and rock shelters, sand and clay, the earth's surface itself, shells, tree bark, sticks, flowers, the bones, skin, feathers, teeth, blood, and other parts of animals and other people, the juice of berries and roots, charcoal and lime, red and yellow ochre. Skin, feathers, and flowers excluded, most of these materials are readily available for use and quite durable.

Graphic and Plastic Forms

Paintings made on the walls of caves by prehistoric Europeans endure still. Among the oldest remains of human artistic endeavor are the cave paintings of Southern Europe, the rock paintings of East Africa, and the primitive clay sculptures of the ancient Middle East. Undoubtedly, these very early artists worked in other, more fragile materials as well, but these have not lasted. In both materials and subject matter the artwork of these ancient foragers is strikingly similar to the work of many contemporary groups who make their living in the same way.

In the artworks of most of hunter-gatherers, ancient and modern, the link between art, technology, and ideology is marked: not only in the use of many of the same materials—rock, bone, and rough wood, and colors made from roots and berries—but also in the artists' themes, which project repeatedly the dominance of material concerns over the availability of wild food resources, the natural conditions necessary to assure their continued abundance, the fertility and increase of wild game, and the growth and renewal of wild plants. All are statements in graphic and plastic form of the artists' concern with the material circumstances essential to their survival.

Among contemporary hunter-gatherers this linkage between art, ideology, and technology is particularly notable in the graphic and plastic arts of the Aborigines of Australia (see Elkin 1964; M. H. Levine 1957; Meggitt 1962; Warner 1964). The quality of the Australians' art also illustrates the importance of the semantic distinction between the relative crudeness of some technical aspects of the so-called primitive artists' rendering (most Australian painting and engraving are done on the walls of caves and rock shelters and on rough wood surfaces, using a few ochres and other pigments easily obtainable in nature) and the subtlety and refinement of their use of symbolism, color, and line to achieve their ideological and aesthetic purposes: the increase by ritual means of a species of plant or animal, or the retelling of a myth.

In addition to painting on rocks, shells, sheets of bark, and crude shields made from strips of wood, the Australians paint themselves, using clays and powders to create abstract designs that are further elaborated by adding leaves, feathers, and blood. Most of this painting entails the symbolic representation of totemic figures: animals, insects, and natural objects associated with the Aboriginal system of nature worship.

Art among the Australian Aborigines, and among most peoples, does not exist for "art's sake" alone, but is usually closely related to their most compelling concerns: the renewal of nature, the maintenance of life, the perpetuation of traditional social institutions, and the avoidance of misfortune and death.

Australian artists engrave stone surfaces, shell, and wood. They create geometric representations of natural objects by pecking and cutting into the exposed portions of outcropping rock formations and the walls of caves and rock shelters. Often the relief of incised surfaces is heightened by rubbing red ochre, charcoal, and other colored pigments into the grooves and crevices to create an impression of greater depth. Such designs may appear to the unfamiliar observer as abstractions. But to the Australians conditioned by their culture to understand the symbolic content of this artwork—which

"Such designs may appear to the unfamiliar observer as abstractions."

Figure 14-4. An incised, painted stone, an Australian ceremonial object. (Courtesy of the Museum of Primitive Art.)

usually contains an intermingling of purely decorative motifs, forms symbolizing totemic protectors and other beings from the Australian supernatural, and stylized representations of people, animals, and plants—the objects depicted and the message such depiction is intended to convey are usually readily apparent.

Eskimo Art

Among other contemporary foragers similarly highly stylized, symbolic representations of the patterned interrelations of technology, economy, and ideology frequently recur. Because societies based on this level of technoenvironmental adaptation are almost invariably small and culturally homogeneous, most members share a common symbolic vocabulary, unlike the artist and his "public" in technologically more developed societies, especially those based on industrialization. The work of the Eskimo artists, for example, is often highly abstract, yet is readily understood by their audience. As with the Australians working within the domain of an elaborate system of symbols representing the forces of the supernatural, the Eskimo have the task not of "creating" a wholly new work of art but of producing an original and pleasing variation on a culturally accepted form, in which the criteria of aesthetic excellence and ideological acceptability are inextricably linked.

"Study of the art of the Eskimo . . . ."

Figure 14-5. Eskimo woman carved in stone. (National Film Board of Canada.)

Many Eskimo masks are carved and painted to be used as a means of propitiating or driving off evil spirits. Others are designed specifically to be worn by priests seeking communication with some more benign supernatural being in order to foretell the outcome of a future hunting expedition or to cure an illness. Eskimo masks as they were used in the context of traditional Eskimo culture were a reflection of many aspects of Eskimo cosmology, depicting "good and bad mythological beings that created man, his livelihood, and his ceremonies or, conversely, tried to destroy them; deities, especially sun and moon, which controlled certain aspects of men's lives; and . . . an array of spirits that could be manipulated for various purposes" (Ray 1967:6–7).

As a means of increasing the dramatic and ritual impact of such masks, their makers often purposefully distort the natural features of the face, creating an effect of humorous or grotesque asymmetry. Frequently the sense of motion is heightened by the attachment of smaller decorative pieces: bits of bone or leather, feathers, and other materials that quiver and shake as the wearer moves.

Study of the art of the Eskimo, like study

of the aesthetic traditions and techniques of any people, provides more than an insight into the connections between their art and other aspects of their culture. Used with proper caution, it may also reveal important clues to their cultural and historical origins. Comparative analysis of the decorative styles of some present-day Eskimo groups with artifacts found by Soviet archeologists working several-thousand-year-old sites in eastern Asia is used by Fraser, for example, to support the argument, developed through the convergence of several lines of inquiry, that the traditional way of life of the contemporary Eskimo represents a variant form of an aquatic culture that originated somewhere along the Northeast Pacific coast of Asia and spread from there across the Bering Straits and into the Americas (Fraser 1962:307*ff*). Similar stylistic comparisons of Eskimo masks with those of other groups make it possible to relate the Eskimo's culture history to that of such other old American groups as the Nootka of the Pacific Northwest and the peoples of the Aleutian Islands and suggest that the Eskimo's distinctive art styles developed independently (Ray 1967:90).

By extension of the same techniques of comparison, art historians and archeologists can plot the hypothetical course of cultural contact between these relatively recently arrived North American groups and Indians elsewhere in the Americas. In many aboriginal American societies the same motifs—fanged animals and human figures wearing caps or masks topped with fierce, long-tongued monsters—appear repeatedly. Recurrence throughout the hemisphere of these same motifs, combined with other evidence, supports the argument that all "indigenous" Americans came originally from Asia. Present differences in aesthetic tradition from one American Indian group to another, differences in specifics of form and content, result from the interaction in relative isolation of unique circumstances: the availability of particular raw materials, distinctive technologies, the role of individual innovators, and locally differentiated aesthetic and ideological traditions, all historically explainable as elaborations on a series of ancient artistic themes possibly common to all the Americas.

Pacific Art and Island Migrations

The comparison of styles of graphic and plastic forms of aesthetic expression, and of art styles in general, has also been used as an aid in reconstructing the culture history of the peoples who inhabit the islands of the Pacific, most of whose ancestors also came originally from mainland Asia. Migrating slowly, for thousands and thousands of years, they were ultimately spread out over nearly every habitable island of the South Seas. So long did the migrations last, so different were the island environments where the people settled—from the temperate regions of Tasmania and southern New Zealand through a variety of desert island ecologies to the humid tropical environments of much of Melanesia—so various were the specific cultural traditions of the migrant groups, and so long were the periods of geographic and cultural isolation of many of them, once settled and once the influx of Asiatic migrants had ceased, that innumerable regional cultures and art traditions were developed. The art of Pacific peoples is now enormously varied. But evidence of common origins is still strong, and in some areas frequent interisland contacts have made for a wide distribution of regional ideas and art forms.

Again there are the same parallels not only in the fundamental stylistic similarities that mark all Pacific art objects but also in the close interconnections between the island peoples' art and the patterns of their technoeconomic adaptation, beliefs, and rituals.

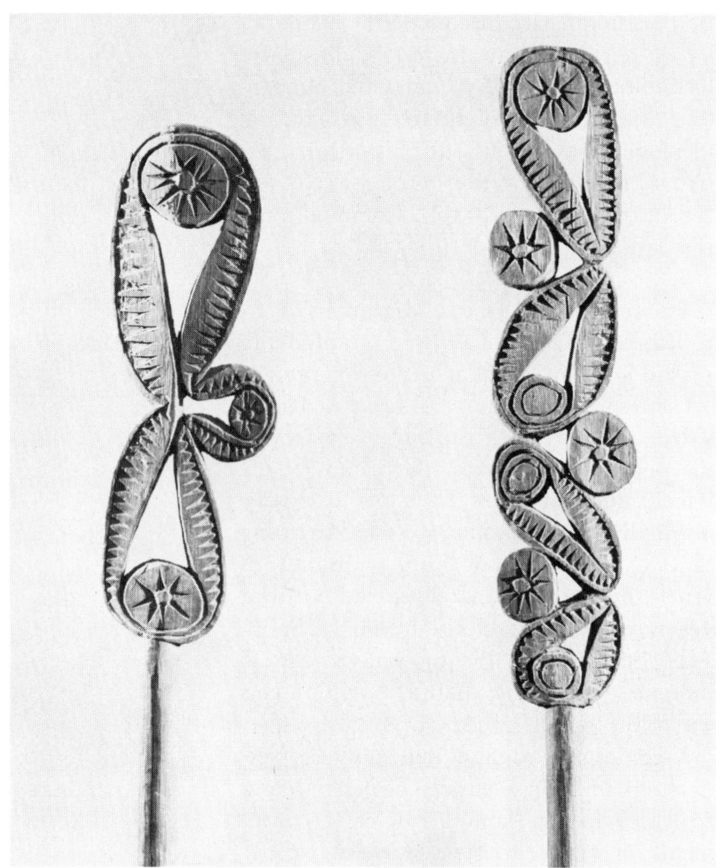

"... innumerable regional cultures and art traditions were developed."
Figure 14-6. Two wooden paddles from the upper Sepik region, New Guinea. (Courtesy of the Museum of Primitive Art.)

Among the earliest migrants to the Pacific were the ancestors of the Australians and the peoples of that geographic and cultural area known as Melanesia, which includes all of New Guinea and the surrounding islands as far north as Fiji.

In New Guinea the wooden masks of the coastal Sepik region, carved with stone tools to create powerful images of part human, part animal beings are utilized as an adjunct to ceremonials relating to worship of the ancestors, to crises in the life cycle, and to observances that sanctify important stages in the economic cycle, especially the harvest festivals.

Stylistically the art of the Sepik region is distinctive within New Guinea, the art of New Guinea is distinctive within Melanesia, and Melanesian art is distinctive within the Pacific. The art style or styles of each Pacific people, and of every people, invariably involve the repeated use in varying, traditionally set ways of an always limited number of materials, motifs, and design of features. Within these constraints, by working and reworking a naturally limited number of raw materials and a culturally limited number of motifs that the prevailing art style makes available, the artist in any culture must find a means of being creative.

It is by the systematic analysis of such stylistic differences that what may otherwise

"Stylistically the art of the Sepik region is distinctive within New Guinea, the art of New Guinea is distinctive within Melanesia . . . ."

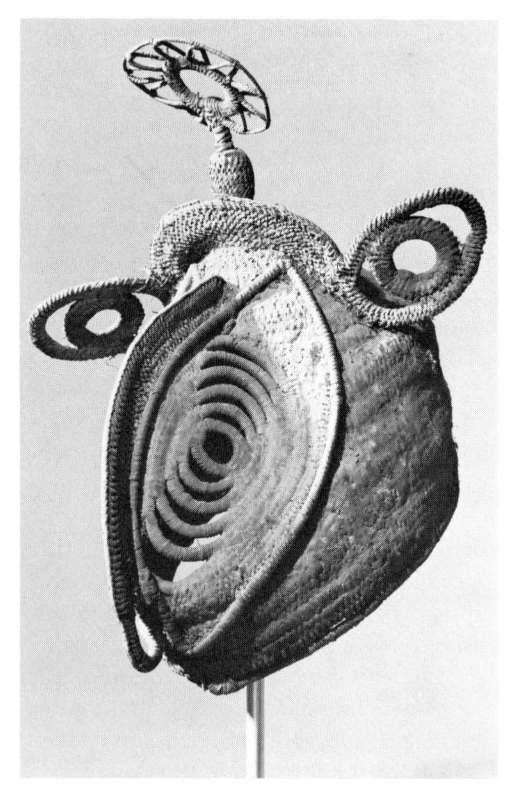

Figure 14-7. Helmet mask from the northern part of the Sepik region, New Guinea. (Courtesy of the Museum of Primitive Art.)

appear as an incomprehensible jumble of art forms from what may seem superficially to be a single geographic region can be sorted out, and their respective cultural origins correctly identified. To take a specific aspect of the graphic and plastic aesthetic traditions of the coastal Sepik (Fraser 1962:170*ff*) as an example, the prevailing style of mask making features elongated, monochromatic, predominantly reddish masks. Among a neighboring group bark cloth masks for use in spirit visitation rites are a recurrent and dominant theme. And so on around and throughout New Guinea: in the western Torres Straits area turtle shell masks are the most representative form; just to the east a basically similar mask type is embellished by the addition of human hair attachments, and representations of the human face are marked by a style of carving that emphasizes the frontal ridge of the forehead.

African Art and Culture History

The study of African graphic and plastic art also illustrates the recurrent interrelation of technology, economy, and art, and especially the relation between art and ideology. It underscores also the potentially productive role of studies of style. In Africa similarities and differences in the art styles of particular regions again provide useful clues to the reconstruction of the continent's culture history.

African artists with the most rudimentary technologies—that of the Bushmen hunter-gatherers of southern Africa being the notable example—are, like nearly all people living at a similar level of technological development, largely limited to easily accessible materials ready for use as they are. Most Bushmen painting and engraving are done on exposed rocky surfaces, on bone, on ostrich eggshell, on wood, on the surface of roughly tanned skins, or on shell. Themes that have been common to hunter-gatherers since Paleolithic times persist: highly stylized representations of animals and men engaged in hunting activities or in rituals intended to increase the supply of wild foods.

More complex techniques and more intricate forms of aesthetic expression are found among technologically more advanced African peoples. Plastic forms, particularly sculpture, are especially highly developed

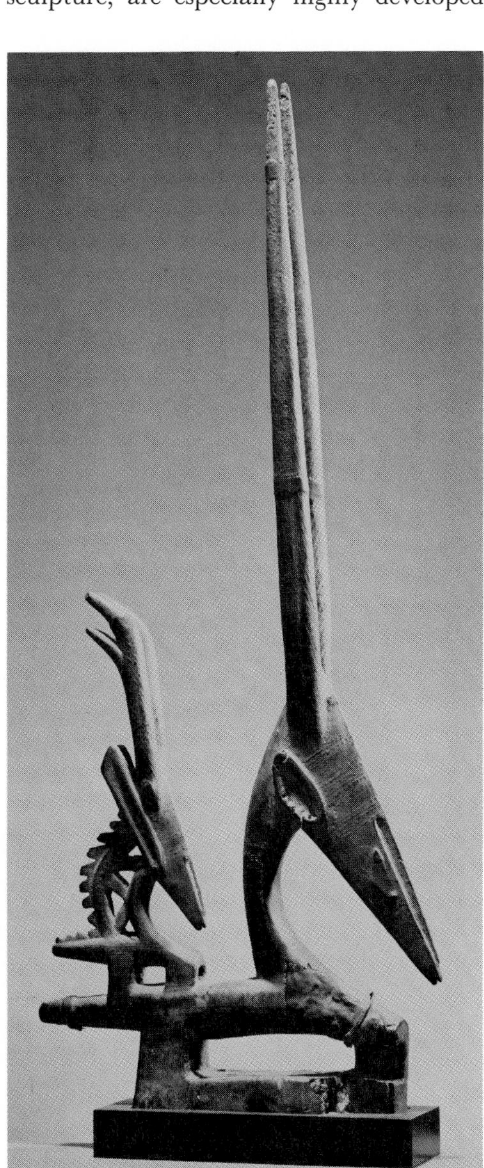

". . . and of other supernatural beings associated with the renewal of nature . . . ."
Figure 14-8. Antelope headpiece, Mali. (Courtesy of the Museum of Primitive Art.)

among the farming groups of West and West Central Africa. Sculptors work not only in wood and terra-cotta but also in metal. Brass casting, usually by the lost wax process, and the work in iron and gold of the peoples of the forest region of West Africa reached their peak during the late Middle Ages and were fully comparable in technical proficiency and aesthetic refinement to the work of European artists during the same period.

Much of the art of West Africa was, and still is, reflective of people's concern with ritual systems of control. Representations of ancestral deities and of other supernatural beings associated with the renewal of nature are recurrent and dominant themes.

Traditional forms also reflect other aspects of indigenous culture, particularly the incipient sociopolitical stratification made possible by farming and by some of the rulers' share in the slave trade.

"Works commissioned by West African kings and their courtiers—bas reliefs . . . ."

Figure 14-9. Bronze plaque of a Benin king and his attendants, late sixteenth century, Nigeria. (Courtesy of the Museum of Primitive Art.)

The prominence of sumptuary art is an example. Works commissioned by West African kings and their courtiers—bas reliefs, sculpture-in-the-round, gold weights, carved ivories, elaborate jewelry, various forms of regalia—were all designed to embellish the surroundings and glorify the image of the court figures who were the artists' patrons. Like the work of European painters of the same period, the West African artists' efforts to enhance the image of their rulers offer the cultural historian rich insights into the social and political life of the society in which the artists worked.

The variety of devices used to represent symbolically the exalted status of the rulers reflect, for example, a system of social stratification in which important status differences between the ruling elite and the common folk were beginning to emerge. At the court of Benin in what is now Nigeria, and also in ancient Egypt, divine rulers were always shown by their sculptors as larger than their subjects. The reduced size and more rigid pose of the royal retainers were literally expressive of their lesser status and of the ritual decorum they were required to observe in the presence of their ruler.

Plastic art forms, particularly carved wooden masks, have traditionally been related to, and reflective of, the social system in other ways.

In West Africa masks are widely employed as a means of social control, by representing and thus reinforcing belief in and fear of the supernatural beings, ancestral spirits, deities, and various demons that both symbolize traditional values and in themselves possess the power to punish those whose behavior deviates from traditionally sanctioned norms. In a sense the masks are perceived as the embodiment of the supernatural beings (spirit or spirits—ancestral, natural, totemic, or divine) they represent; the person of the wearer unites with the spirit of the mask when he puts it on.

". . . gold weights . . . ."

Figure 14-10. Ashanti gold weight in the form of a chameleon, Ghana. (Courtesy of the Museum of Primitive Art.)

Much of the effectiveness of masks is dependent on the forcefulness of the West African sculptors' depiction of the supernaturally powerful beings their carvings represent. Dramatic impact is heightened by a stylized representation of human features in which the scale of parts is deliberately distorted: the mouth and eyes are reproduced oversize, the dome of the forehead is enlarged, the curve of the lips is exaggerated, and the volume of the flaring nostrils is increased, whereas other features are made to recede. In sculptured figures body lines are often contracted or elongated to create an impression of sudden or slow and sinuous motion.

The masks used by secret societies in many parts of West Africa (see Chapter 8) exemplify the merging of artistic technique, ideology, and social function. Among the Kpelle and Mano of Liberia, judges presiding at secret society tribunals wear masks that both symbolize and embody the powerful, potentially wrathful beings of the spirit world who are the ultimate source of authority, punishing wrongdoers and rewarding the right-living, sanctioning the secular administration of society, and reinforcing their will through carved wooden masks that represent the spirits' power and confer it on those who wear them.

West African sculpture is also related to disease control. In West Africa, as elsewhere among most of the peoples of the world, the cause and prevention, treatment and cure of sickness are still traditionally understood in supernatural terms and are be-

"Although the relationship between art and ideology usually is and generally always has been more specifically a relationship between art and religion . . . ."
Figure 14-11. One thousand and one images of the Buddhist goddess of mercy, Kyoto. (Information Section, Embassy of Japan.)

lieved to be amenable to supernatural intervention.

To increase their healing power curers wear masks depicting the spirits believed to cause the disease they want to cure. Carvers among the Dan and Guere, neighboring West African tribal groups, often alter the features on their masks to depict the symptoms of the malady the spirit of the mask is believed able to cure. A mask used to treat facial paralysis, for example, may show the features lopsided. Others represent the effects of smallpox, yaws, and leprosy. In all such forms of art, aesthetic and instrumental considerations are closely linked.

For art as an adjunct to ideology liturgical correctness is as important as "beauty." The connection between ritual efficacy and aesthetic worth is generally very close. As people usually assume that the gods share, if they do not indeed dictate, their artistic values, it seems reasonable to assume that the deities will be better pleased by and more responsive to an artist's creation that is aesthetically pleasing as well as religiously correct.

Art and Ideology

Although the relationship between art and ideology usually is and generally always has been more specifically a relationship between art and religion, it is the association between art and ideas that is the more profound, more indissoluble connection. Many forms of aesthetic expression can be quite free of religious connotations—every people has artistic traditions that are separate from its systems of belief and observance concerning the supernatural—but art cannot exist independently of ideology. It is also true that even the most determinedly nonrepresentational painter can never escape from the conceptual system that is the source of his or her inspiration. Even in denying that a work has symbolic content, the artist reveals the idea that motivates him or her.

". . . the nonreligious but strongly ideological use of aesthetics . . . ."

Figure 14-12. Beating a sword into a plowshare, sculpture by Eugene Vuchetich. (Novosti Press Agency, Moscow, U.S.S.R.)

Currently, one of the most conspicuous instances of the nonreligious but strongly ideological use of aesthetics to project and promote an ideologically conditioned perception of reality is the widespread use of all artistic media—graphic and plastic forms, music, literature, and drama—to represent and reinforce commitment to various systems of political belief. The sixteenth-century icon painted by a Russian Orthodox artist was intended to fix the worshipful attention of the viewer on the religious subject of the painting in the same way that bobbing, heroically scaled placard portraits of Marx and Lenin massed in a sea of red banners are intended to represent and to reinforce belief in an alternative system of beliefs.

The Pleasure Principle

A pleasure principle is often, if not invariably, involved in artistic expression. Observing the universality of people's efforts to elaborate or embellish certain objects and actions beyond the requirements of function, some anthropologists have suggested that an aesthetic drive is basic to human nature. The Formosan boat builder works on after he has fashioned a well-made oar to create a finished product so shaped and decorated that it is aesthetically pleasing as well. The way people use clothing is a universal instance of the same phenomenon.

Play, creativity, exhibitionism, and a variety of other pleasure-impelled motivations, as well as reflections of and attempts to control their environment and efforts to enhance their chances of survival, are also undoubtedly involved when people express themselves in art. Perhaps the precise components of the mixture of drives and emotions involved will one day be sufficiently understood to be more usefully analyzed. Then we will better understand not only artistry but also the complex motivations and skills integral to all forms of cultural creativity.

"Clothing is obviously only one aspect of the larger subject of personal adornment. . . ."

Figure 14-13. A young man from the Marquesas Islands, not completely tattooed. (Courtesy of the American Museum of Natural History.)

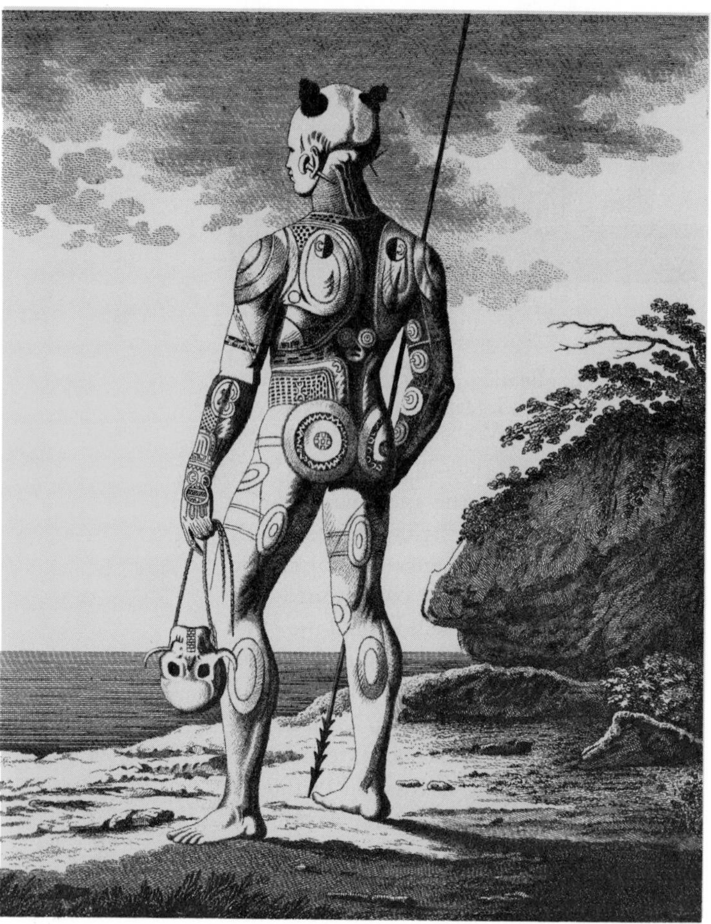

Personal Adornment

The arts as a manifestation and reflection of the more fundamental aspects of culture are universally represented in what is probably the most widely practiced of all forms of aesthetic expression, dress and personal decoration.

The relation of clothing to technology has already been dealt with, especially as the technology determines in large part the materials available for dress and self decoration. Clothing is obviously only one aspect of the larger subject of personal adornment, only one of the several means by which people attempt to modify or embellish their appearance. Beyond the mundane function of dress as a means of keeping warm, keeping cool, or covering delicate body parts, three concerns are paramount in guiding the way people adorn themselves: work, sex, and social status.

People usually wear clothing that is functionally appropriate to the work they are doing and that often indicates the productive activity in which they are engaged—hunting, farming, mining, house building, supervising the work of others, or performing some ritual or political service. They also designate certain forms of dress as appropriate to such activities as sleeping and playing. They dress to indicate the rituals they are engaged in, such as marrying or mourning. They dress in a special way for making war or to show that they have returned from making war. They dress to indicate group affiliation. In each instance the pattern of their attire is also affected by their sex and age.

People dress both to conceal and to reveal their sexual attributes. In most societies the genitals are covered in accordance with prevailing attitudes concerning modesty and cleanliness. Psychologically, concealment of the sex organs seems to emphasize their importance, to heighten interest in them and in the always special circumstances under which they are fully exposed. Clothing worn to conceal the wearer's sex is invariably designed to indicate it in other ways. If people are culturally defined as being of mating age, what they wear is often designed specifically to increase both their body awareness and their sexual attractiveness.

If the society is stratified, occupationally linked differences in what is considered appropriate attire are cross-cut by dress differences linked with distinctions of rank, class, or caste. Within a stratified society a young bride from a social class in which premarital chastity is valued is dressed differently for her wedding than is an older widow who is taking her third husband. A rich man burying a first-born son is likely to be dressed differently than a man of moderate means attending the funeral of a second cousin. In most societies these rules about dress and adornment and the intricacies of their relationship to distinctions in social position are generally known and closely followed. The apparently important social functions of these regulations are revealed by the shock and disapproval frequently expressed when a person breaks the rules and appears "inappropriately" attired. Like any other particular way of doing things, once people have been conditioned by their culture to adorn themselves in a way defined as correct, deviation in their appearance or in the appearance of others may be deeply distressing. Even in industrial societies, where technological capacity, anonymity, and rapidly changing styles generally allow for greater variation in dress, conflicting interpretations of such correctness can lead to violence.

In U.S. society from time to time, earlier during the era of the bloomer girls and more recently as the dress of the beatniks gave way to the styles of hippies, yippies, Aquarians, and others, resentment over deviations from the middle-class code has been expressed in physical attacks on those whose costume and hair style was perceived as defying the rules—presumably not because different forms of dress and adornment were aesthetically so offensive but because they symbolized a challenge to the existing order: assertion of minority rights, criticism of the Vietnam War, or rejection of the "Establishment's" materialism.

But despite the rigidity of every culture's approved patterns of personal adornment, some variation is always allowed. It is this opportunity for choice within a usually narrow range that provides for individual aesthetic expression: for a display of both creativity and "taste."

Techniques employed in personal adornment range from recoloring body parts through reshaping them (adding to some, removing others) to changing their

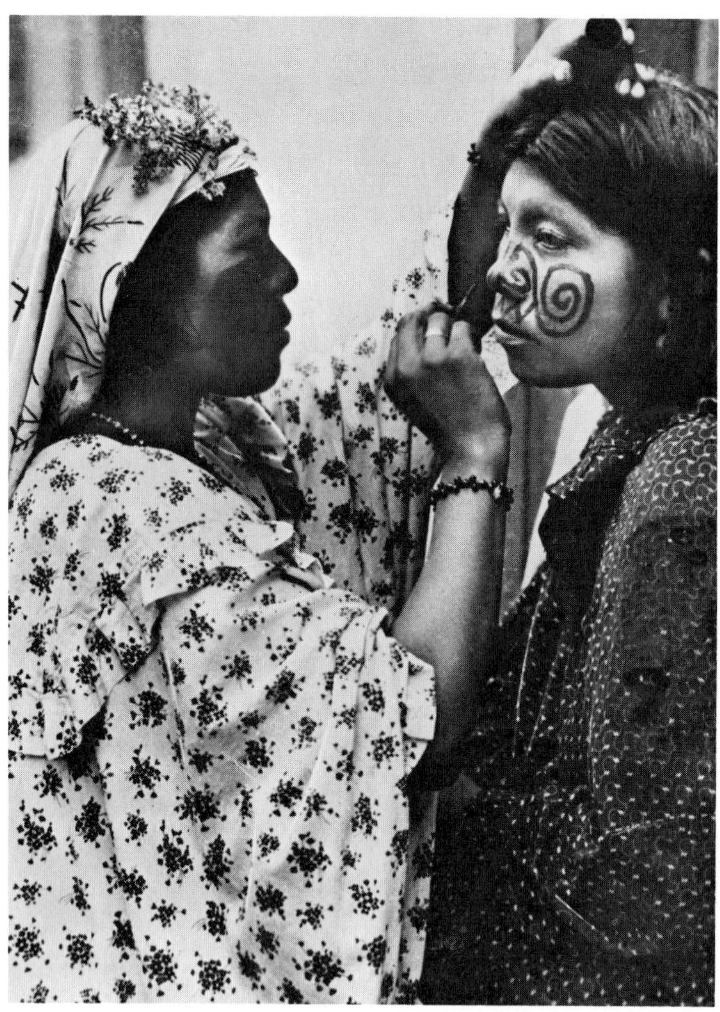

". . . from recoloring body parts . . . ."
Figure 14-14. Panamanian Indian face painting. (OAS Photo.)

smell. People paint, dye, and tattoo their skin and recolor their teeth, nails, and hair. They alter the shape of their heads, torsos, and feet. They stick out, add on to, or pad out some body parts and constrict or cut off others. They incise designs in their flesh and cut or pull out their hair. They knock out, replace, file, and polish their teeth. They deodorize and perfume themselves.

Several East African herding peoples remove their front teeth in order to more closely resemble their cattle. Many South American Indians and some Pacific islanders pluck out all body hair to make themselves more attractive. The removal of at least some portions of male facial hair is now a nearly universal custom.

Scarification, cutting designs into the skin of the face and body, is an especially widespread cosmetic technique in Africa. Frequently such designs also indicate tribal identity. Differences in the patterning of markings may indicate differences in social position. Men and women are usually scarified differently. High-status persons may have particular kinds of designs cut into their skin as marks of their rank. Willingness to submit to the pain involved in scarification may provide a young man with a conspicuous means of demonstrating his bravery. Young women who submit to the ordeal may be admired for their willingness to suffer to please. Circumcision is also always regarded as a means of enhancing body image.

Body parts are sometimes re-formed as a way of increasing their beauty. Several Central American Indian and Central African groups used to bind the heads of infants to reshape them in a way judged to be aesthetically more pleasing. The Mangebetu of Central Africa use loops of copper wire to elongate and thus beautify the necks of young girls. Until recently the feet of upper-class Chinese girls were bound to enhance their beauty by inhibiting their growth, causing a malformation of the arch called the "lotus foot." Because only a lady of wealth could survive with nearly useless feet, such deformation was a mark of high status. The many variants of the corset, past and present, are another example of the efforts people almost everywhere expend to alter the shape of their bodies in accordance with some culturally defined aesthetic ideal.

Shrinking, usually by dieting, steaming, or exercising, is a beautification technique limited largely to materially more advanced societies (although sweat baths have a somewhat wider distribution). Peoples who have

"Because only a lady of wealth could survive with nearly useless feet . . . ."
Figure 14-15. Feet of an upper-class Chinese woman bound in the traditional way. (Courtesy of the Library of Congress.)

limited amounts of food available to them frequently regard fat as pleasing, probably because it is evidence of the heavier person's greater access to a valuable scarce good. Fat women may also be admired because their obesity is a sign of the somewhat higher social status that can mean freedom from the hard work that, combined with a meager diet, keeps most of their fellow women thin.

Padding or adding on extra body parts is another means of personal embellishment widely practiced. Breasts and buttocks are often artificially built up by this means. The

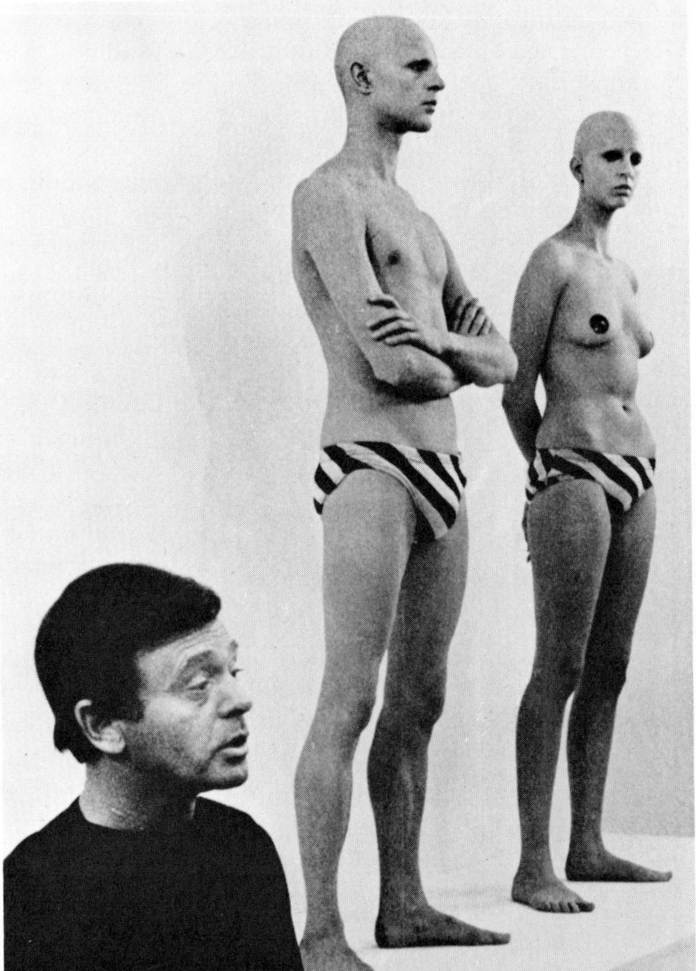

"No matter how grotesque the results may seem to an outsider . . . ."
Figure 14-16. Designer Rudi Gernreich's "Statement for the 70's." (AP Wirephoto.)

addition of false hair—wigs and eyelashes—is common throughout the middle and upper social strata of the Euroamerican cultural sphere as means of increasing personal attractiveness.

In many cultures people decorate their skin to improve their appearance. Sometimes, as in the widespread customs of tattooing, hair dying or bleaching, and application of henna or other pigments to the hands and feet, the colors or colored designs are added permanently. More often they are painted on. Berber women in North Africa tattoo or paint delicate, abstract designs on their cheeks, foreheads, and chins. Several Brazilian Indian groups paint themselves almost all over. Elite ladies in ancient Egypt gilded their breasts and applied blue paint to their nipples; in Europe and America women put the blue on their eyelids. Men in Papua use various shades of blue to recolor their chins. Skin is also often tanned or bleached to make it appear more attractive. No matter how grotesque the results may seem to an observer from another place or time, personal adornment is always an art.

But as this necessarily cursory survey indicates, like most of the arts, personal adornment is still difficult to analyze in terms that reveal it as more than a reflection of other more fundamental aspects of culture. Much remains to be learned before we can identify the aesthetic drive and the aesthetic act as major keys to understanding the processes of cultural creativity and change.

Summary

Specialists in the subject inappropriately called primitive art have not yet successfully related the results of their studies to the major theoretical issues in cultural and social anthropology, partly because most work on the art of non-Western peoples is still necessarily descriptive and partly because the synthesis of humanistic anthropology with the work of those who use a more scientific model is still imperfect.

So far, one of the more productive approaches to the study of art as an aspect of culture has focused on hypotheses suggesting causal relationships between patterns of technoenvironmental adaptation and art forms as the latter are influenced by the materials, tools, and techniques that the artists' culture makes available and as the resultant forms reflect people's concerns with material survival and their use of art as a means of ritual control over both the natural and cultural dimensions of their environment.

At more complex levels of technological development art is one of the many activities in which full-time specialization becomes possible. With the emergence of social stratification art forms are often reflective of the larger cultural scene in several ways; for example, sumptuary forms serve as a means of display, of accumulating wealth, and of symbolically representing status inequality and the structure of power relationships.

Examples of the use of art as a means of exerting social and political control range from the role of masks in West African secret societies to the use of posters for political indoctrination in China, the U.S., and the U.S.S.R.

Of almost all aesthetic forms, the art of personal adornment has received the least descriptive and theoretical attention, despite the universality of dress and other forms of personal decoration as a means of artistic expression, of sexual display, of status signaling, and—as in the fashion industry—of creating demand by wastefulness.

Where art is considered in cultural context it is typically treated as a reflection of other aspects of culture, particularly—in what has become almost a truism—as an adjunct to ideology. Equally important questions related to the understanding of artistic endeavor as a creative process, particularly as it entails the critical interplay between pressure for change and cultural sources of constraint, require more attention.

Suggested Readings

The principal problem with most general books on the subject of so-called primitive art is that the texts accompanying the usually beautiful illustrations are either banal or wildly misleading (another drawback is that they cost too much). Several collections for which these criticisms do not hold are *Art and Anthropology,* edited by Beardsley; *Tradition and Creativity in Tribal Art,* edited by Biebuyck; *Essays on the Verbal and Visual Arts,* edited by Helm; and *Art and Aesthetics in Primitive Societies,* edited by Jopling. See also *Primitive Art and Society,* edited by Forge; Maquet's *Introduction to Aesthetic Anthropology;* and *Anthropology and Art,* edited by Otten.

Fischer's "Art Styles As Cultural Cognitive Maps" is a major work of analysis. Also see Sieber's "The Arts and Their Changing Social Function" and Wolfe's "Social Structural Bases of Art."

For some useful theoretical speculations on various aspects of the creative process see d'Azevedo's "Sources of Gola Artistry," Fernandez's "Exposition and Imposition of Order: Artistic Expression in Fang Culture," and Goodale and Koss's "The Cultural Context of Creativity Among Tiwi."

Of all forms of non-Western art sculpture has probably received the most attention, but of very uneven quality. For some exceptions to this generalization see d'Azevedo's "Mask Makers and Myth in Western Liberia," Messenger's "The Role of the Carver in Anang Society," Thompson's "Abâtàn: A Master Potter of the Egbáde Yorùbá," and Weil's "The Masked Figure and Social Control: The Mandinka Case." See also Price's important "Saramaka Woodcarving: The Development of an Afro-American Art." Wingert's *Art of the South Pacific Islands* and Gerbrand's *Wow-ipits: Eight Asmat Woodcarvers of New Guinea* deal with aspects of sculpture in the Pacific. Linton and Wingert's *Arts of the South Seas* is still a good source on this same region. See also Errington's *Karavar: Masks and Power in a Melanesian Ritual.*

On the much neglected subject of architecture as an art form in non-Western societies see Current and Scully's *Pueblo Architecture of the Southwest,* Oliver's *Shelter in Africa,* Prussin's *Architecture in Northern Ghana,* and Wenzel's *House Decoration in Nubia.*

On graphic forms of aesthetic expression see Grant's *Rock Art of the American Indian,* Harvey's *Ritual in Pueblo Art: Hopi Life in Hopi Painting,* Hatcher's *Visual Metaphors: A Formal Analysis of Navajo Art,* Munn's *Walbiri Iconography: Graphic Representation and Cultural Symbolism in a Central Australian Society,* Rudner and Rudner's *The Hunter and his Art: A Survey of Rock Art in South Africa,* and, for an important time perspective, *Paleolithic Cave Art* by Ucko and Rosenfeld.

Fortunately the literature on self-adornment is beginning to grow. For some good recent examples see Faris's *Nuba Personal Art;* the Stratherns' *Self Decoration in Mt. Hagen;* and *Dress, Adornment, and the Social Order,* edited by Roach and Eicker. See also Bogatyrev's *The Functions of Folk Costume in Moravian Slovakia,* Lincoln's "The Religious Significance of Women's Scarification Among the Tiv," Seeger's "The Meaning of Body Ornaments: A Suya Example," and Turner's "Tchikrin: A Central Brazilian Tribe and Its Symbolic Language of Bodily Adornment."

15
Verbal Art,
Music,
Dance,
and Drama

VERBAL art, music, dance, and drama viewed in cultural context are marked by the recurrence of familiar themes. These forms of aesthetic expression are also affected by technological limitations on the materials available to the artist, and by his society's material concerns. The economic system structures the allocation of labor power and other goods used in the production of works of art, often encouraging some forms of artistic expression and effectively impeding others. Aspects of the social system, particularly current sources of social conflict and culturally sanctioned means of coping with it, are frequently the subject of oral literary forms, song texts, dance, and drama. Political history and political issues, especially past and present struggles for power, may be challenged or reinforced through the same forms. The role of ideology in aesthetics is manifested not only in the expectable connections between art and ritual but also in the values, philosophical positions, and differing perceptions of the world that are expressed through art. Language is a central element in nearly all of these forms.

"... current sources of social conflict ... are frequently the subject of oral literary forms, song texts ...."

Figure 15-1. Dylan in concert. (Dave Repp, Black Star.)

Finally, the "art scene" in any culture often provides a particularly telling perspective on what is perhaps the most critical issue of all: the status of the ever-present conflict between the sources of cultural conservatism and the forces of creativity and change.

These are some of the things that can be learned from a people's art. They are things we need to know.

Verbal Art

Of all the forms of aesthetic expression, verbal art—such forms as prose narratives, poetry, riddles, and proverbs, all of which once were (or still are) primarily transmitted orally—is the one to which anthropologists have given most attention. Some have made the broader subject of folklore their principal professional occupation; folklore includes the study of everything from myths and legends to jokes and limericks, from street vendors' cries and latrinalia to quilting patterns and gravestone markings.

Understanding of a people's orally transmitted literary traditions can be important to the anthropologist for at least three major reasons: because the content of verbal art frequently reflects important aspects of their culture; because it complements and can facilitate comprehension of the workings of their language; and because it is often useful in reconstructing their culture history.

Verbal art, sometimes called oral literature, is usually divided into several basic, cross-culturally recurrent types: myths and legends, proverbs, riddles and jokes, and poetry. Although there is some disagreement among anthropologists and folklorists on the precise definition of these categories, there is general consensus that myth is a major form.

Myth and Legends

The term *myth* usually designates traditionally based, dramatic narratives on themes that emphasize the nature of humankind's relationship to nature and to the supernatural. The tales people tell about the origins of the world and of animals and humans are generally most closely linked to their ideologies, particularly their religious beliefs. In contrast, legends are usually defined as tales concerning other times and places that do not give the same extensive emphasis to supernatural themes. Legends, more often than myths, are retold purely as entertainment. But the specifics of audience response are difficult to assess; a tale listened to primarily for its religious content by one person may be regarded by another as no more than an entertaining narrative, and its supernatural content may be largely ignored.

As an accompaniment to the theme of human creation and the creation of the world, myths of origin also often provide explanations of the origin, reason for being, and relevance to people of the other significant aspects of their environment and of their cultural means of adapting to it.

The mythological repertoire of many of the Aborigines of Australia includes both general accounts of human origins (usually people are described as descendants of mysterious ancestral beings, part animal and part human) and quite specific narratives that account for the origins of particular wild plants, particular natural regions, and other particular natural phenomena. Collectively, such a body of myths provides an all-encompassing, coherent view of the world, a definition of people's place in it, and a guide to the right actions necessary to keep that place and to predict and plan for the future.

For the Mescalero Apache of the American Southwest a collection of myths with a Coyote and a Divine Creator as the principal actors provide them with the sense that they understand their origins, their relationship to other creatures and other things, and the likely outcome of future events, both here and in the hereafter. The mythology of the neighboring Navaho divides all personalities into Earth Surface people, who are living men and women and the spirits of their dead, and Holy People, supernatural beings, the gods, spirits, and demons who abide on sunbeams, in the rainbow, and in the lightning's flash, and who are both the protectors of humankind and a major cause of its trouble.

Because they are usually concerned with characters and events of dramatic importance to those who tell them, myths, legends, and other tales constitute for the anthropologist a potentially rich source of insights into the principal preoccupations of a particular group of people: their major fears and chief pleasures, the situations regarded as most rewarding, most dangerous, most amusing, and most tragic. In this sense the tales people tell, whether "original" with them or received, adapted, and reinterpreted from the traditions of other peoples, are likely to be a symbolic projection of what is on their

"In this sense the tales people tell . . . are likely to be a symbolic projection of what is on their minds."
Figure 15-2. Telling a story, Afghanistan. (United Nations.)

minds. And what is on their minds is their way of life, and their response to it.

Proverbs

Like myths and legends, proverbs frequently have an important moralizing function. Myths serve as guides to correct action in the present by providing examples of ethically approved behavior taken from the past or from other places; occasionally mythical figures may point the moral by behaving in ways diametrically opposed to the rules of propriety. Proverbs often work similarly. In West Africa proverbs function both as a repository, in symbolic form, of predominant cultural values and as a means of restating these values in order to induce compliance. Rather than directly rebuking a person who has behaved badly, for example, courteous West Africans cultivated in the oral literary traditions of their culture can cite a proverb that serves as an admonishment of such subtlety and wit that the critical message is transmitted without offense.

Retention of both the structure and the function of proverbs and other traditional literary forms among the descendants of West Africans brought as slaves to the Americas illustrates the possible usefulness of the study of oral literary forms both as an adjunct to the study of culture contact and culture history and as a means of gaining insights into prevailing, culturally conditioned attitudes and responses. The Haitian peasant proverb, "A cockroach is never in the right when it is up against a hen," is used to sum up cynically poor people's perception of their status in relation to the exploitative Haitian elite. That the powerless peasant must conceal resentment of an oppressive ruler is expressed by the proverb, "He who strikes the blow forgets. He who bears the mark remembers": a saying that serves as a means of expressing guarded resentment and covertly counseling vengeance.

In addition to serving as veiled criticism of social and political circumstances, proverbs are often used more openly in Haiti to draw participants' attention to the relevant moral and legalistic principles involved in conflict situations. By hearing these proverbs often, the young are instructed in the attitudes and actions that their culture defines as appropriate. In a more casual context proverbs are frequently used among both West Africans and Afro-Americans as jocular means of cautioning impulsive persons against being too trusting of those who surround them. "The fish trusts the water," the Haitians say, "and it is in the water that he is cooked."

Riddles

Riddles, another recurrent type of verbal aesthetic expression, appear to function principally as a form of entertainment and as means of exercising wit. Their analysis can be useful to the anthropologist interested in acquiring insight into the characteristics of a particular people's mental processes: the symbols that dominate the people's thought, the manner in which they categorize aspects of reality, and the patterned ways in which they perceive relationships, especially the analogies that hold the key to answering the enigmatic questions that riddles always pose.

Poetry

Agreement on the status of poetry as a separate category of verbal art is complicated by the problem of settling on a cross-culturally valid definition of just what poetry is and of how it is to be categorically separated from prose. Myths, songs, and prayers include components of expression that seem clearly poetic but are so intermixed with other literary forms that it is difficult to separate them out. Poetic elements can nonetheless be examined whenever they occur, independently or intermingled, in terms of the several relationships that poetry may have both to language and to culture: Linguists, for example, have examined poetry as a form of verbal play (see Hymes 1964). Study of the processes of poetic composition can provide a useful perspective on the dynamics of aesthetic creativity in general.

All that is entailed in the anthropological study of poetry illustrates the variety of data that generally must be recorded whenever an art form is examined in terms of its function in cultural context. Patterned variations in the manner of poetic delivery and in anticipated audience response are to be noted. Oral literary traditions as a source of conservatism in the development of new poetic forms need to be considered. The role of spontaneity in poetic expression has to be accounted for. What is the sociocultural context in which poetry is composed and recited? Is every person a poet? Or is formal poetic expression the exclusive prerogative of specialists? As one might expect, the role of poet tends to be more highly elaborated as a specialist skill in stratified societies. Poets are often retained to recite in elegantly rhymed sequence the distinguished genealogies, courageous deeds, and sterling attributes of their wealthy patrons. In such instances poetry as an art form is also clearly an instrument of political propaganda, a publicly staged argument for the legitimacy of the claims to high status of the poet's patron.

Distributional Studies

Until the last twenty-five years or so most comparative studies of verbal art were historically oriented. Emphasis was on determination of the historical processes by which such forms were distributed from people to people around the world. To this end specialists tended to concentrate on the formal content of verbal art. Tale typologies and plot and motif indexes were developed in order to reconstruct the processes of their spread. From the perspective of most anthropologists this has been a useful but essentially preliminary analytic exercise.

Now less static units of analysis have been added to the collectors' repertoire. More effort has been made to develop typologies of social relationships, of distinctive actor-personality types, of the play of elements of humor, cosmology, world view, ideology, and values as these attributes make of verbal art a richly elaborated projection of the structure of a people's society and way of life. The recording of these factors is more appropriate to the anthropologists' goal of studying peoples' verbal literary traditions within the context of the cultures from which such traditions derive their meaning, and in which they frequently play an active role in initiating cultural change.

Oral Literature and Exploration of the Unconscious

Some anthropologists have become interested in the application of psychoanalytic theory to the study of verbal art. Initially, much of their study was focused on the widespread recurrence of a number of common themes—the wayward child, the devouring mother, the vengeful father—that, it was thought, might be explained in terms of certain dreams, drives, or wishes assumed to be manifestations of some vaguely defined cosmic unconscious.

Recently the interest of psychoanalytically oriented students of folklore has shifted from speculation on such amorphous subjects as primal urges and universal dreams to the considerably more concrete question of the interrelationship between the structure and content of particular types of social relationships—problems of social organization and disorganization, cultural crises—and the way a people's culturally conditioned response to such situations may be projected into the content of their verbal art.

The precision recording of oral traditions has been greatly facilitated by the availability of high-quality recording devices. This makes possible much fuller and more usable documentation than results from simply writing down a tale, poem, joke, or riddle. Recording oral literary forms within the context of the cultural situation preserves more of the components of the total aesthetic happening. In addition to the myth, proverb, riddle, or poem itself, the style of delivery, the musical or other accompaniment, and the audience's response can all be collected intact, ready to be analyzed by the anthropologist, turned over to a specialist, or stored away for study in the future.

Music

Despite the universal importance of music as an aspect of culture—as a significant adjunct to most important rituals, as a channel for aesthetic creativity, as a means of communication, as a mechanism for the achievement of emotional release, and as a source of pleasure for composer, performer, and listener alike—the study of music has until recently been badly neglected by many anthropologists.

As with many of the scholars who have studied the other arts, anthropologists whose principal work has been in musicology have generally taken a humanistic approach that has failed to provide data of the sort that would help to relate the arts to the rest of culture in theoretically productive ways. As a result, many of the conceptual bridges linking music to the other aspects of culture and to the development of a scientific theory of culture either remain to be built or stand on relatively weak foundations.

So far, only a very small sampling of the

music of the contemporary peoples of the world has even been recorded. And, of course, nearly all of the music created by people in the past, except for the last few centuries in Europe and America, was never recorded at all and is now irrevocably lost, as now nearly everywhere older forms of musical expression have been replaced by newer styles.

As any Western listener to a traditional Chinese opera can quickly attest, music is not a universal language. The forms of musical expression that particular people pronounce as aesthetically acceptable are usually defined quite as narrowly as any of the other forms they are willing to designate as art. The ear of the listener, like the eye of the beholder, is precisely conditioned by his or her culture. Although outsiders may experience pleasure in listening to a Ghanaian drum recital, a Javanese gong ensemble, or a Hopi chant, their capacity for full apprecia-

". . . and as a source of pleasure for composer, performer, and listener alike . . . ."

Figure 15-3. Peruvian boy with flute. (OAS Photo.)

". . . only a very small sampling of the music of the contemporary peoples of the world has even been recorded."

Figure 15-4. Fiddler at work. (National Film Board of Canada.)

". . . there is probably no such thing as 'primitive music.'"

Figure 15-5. Drummer, Benin. (Courtesy of the Library of Congress.)

tion is sharply limited by their cultural conditioning, by either their formal musical training or their more casual absorption of their culture's canons of what is and what is not music.

Like most other forms of aesthetic expression, techniques for making music are affected by the general level of a people's technology. A group that makes its living by hunting and gathering obviously could not support a full-sized symphony orchestra. But it is less certain that such technologically limiting factors have a significant effect on the complexity or content of the music itself. In this sense, there is probably no such thing as "primitive music." Scaling and melody and rhythm, harmony, polyphony, and song style often are just as complex among "simple" hunter-gatherers as they are among technologically more advanced peoples. In fact, the general audience may be considerably more sophisticated in its appreciation of the subtle use of symbolism and abstraction and in its appreciation of the musicians' artistry than are all but the most cultivated music lovers in any "civilized" society.

Description and the Development of Taxonomies

Analysis in the anthropological study of music, or ethnomusicology, begins, reasonably enough, with the instruments used to make music and with differences in the structure of the music itself: in scaling, rhythm, melody, vocal technique and song style, harmony, and polyphony.

The instruments available to a people affect its music in several obvious ways. If the instruments are structurally simple this may limit the possibility of developing instrumental melodies of very great complexity. For example, American Indians lacked stringed instruments almost entirely. Consequently, elaborate melodic expression was confined largely to vocal music. In contrast, in Asia, Africa, and Europe the various stringed instruments that developed once a taut string was first stretched over a resonator facilitated the development of traditions of complex melodic expression in which instrumentation replaced the voice as a principal medium of melodic expression.

Patterned differences in scale are important to the anthropologist in determining or classifying a particular people's musical style. To make such a determination he or she notes the number of tones in a scale, measures the intervals between them, and identifies those tones that recur most frequently in terminal positions. Without extensive musicological training this is difficult, for there is always the danger that the outside listener's inappropriately trained ear may erroneously perceive as monotony or too much scale flexibility what native musicians and their audiences appreciate as complexly structured relationships between tonal units. Differences in melodic movement—whether melody tends to be level, ascending, or descending—provide a further means of objectively defining the characteristic structure of a particular musical system. Rhythmic structure, the patterned recurrence of beats or stresses, is also a factor that varies markedly from group to group. In some musical systems the arrangement into bars and measures is quite free. In others the typical beat is rigidly uniform and repetitive.

Such culturally determined differences in patterned rhythmic structure further illustrate the futility of classifying musical systems on any sort of scale from "primitive" to "advanced." Classical European music, for example, is marked by a relatively simple rhythmic structure. European folk music and the music of many non-European peoples are rhythmically more complicated. A judgment based on a comparison between levels of relative rhythmic "primitivism" would lead to the conclusion that the rhythmically simple European classics are more primitive than the complicated, rhythmically asymmetrical music of the Eskimo or the Pueblo Indians. Conversely, a judgment based on relative complexity of melodic structure would have to be made in favor of the music written by the classical composers of Europe.

"The instruments available to a people affect its music in several obvious ways."

Figure 15-6. Playing on a conch shell flute, Peru. (OAS Photo.)

The Functions of Music

As an aspect of culture, music functions in many ways. It is universally an accompaniment and an accessory to a variety of social, political, and religious ceremonies. It also often serves as a source of pure pleasure, and as a means of achieving both intellectual stimulation and emotional release for composer, performer, and audience.

Among American Indians, as among all non-European people, music was an indispensable aspect of most ceremonial and ritual observances (see W. Driver 1961). In some Indian cultures the efficacy of music as a means of capturing magical or religious

"Universally it is an accompaniment and an accessory to a variety of social, political, and religious ceremonies."

Figure 15-7. Ritual drumming and singing inside a men's ceremonial house, Asmat, New Guinea. (Courtesy of the Museum of Primitive Art.)

power—to ensure the success of a rainmaking ritual or to cure an illness—was as important as its essentially aesthetic aspect.

In most societies music tends to be less "compartmentalized" as an aspect of culture, less the preserve of professionals, than it is in Euro-American culture. Not only is music more intimately related to more aspects of culture, but also more people are competent music makers and make music more often. The distinctions between musician and audience, between professional performer and amateur, are often made, but rarely so strictly as in highly "specialized" societies such as ours.

Once one thinks about it, the role of music as an integral aspect of nearly all other cultural institutions, from work and play to politics and warfare, religion and death rituals, is clearly evident. But how to get beyond hopeful assertions that its presence indicates its importance? Our data are still crude. For instance, it is still not certain how far our understanding of the emotional functions of music can be extended beyond trite allusions to the varieties of "pleasure" it provides.

We need to know more about who the musicians in a society are, and of the relationship of music to the social structure, for example. Is musicianship reserved for the elite? Or is it a role set aside only for low-status persons, or, even more specifically, for people with certain kinds of infirmities? In parts of West Africa, for example, blind children are frequently taught to sing and to accompany themselves on the gourd fiddle (or bowed lute) in order to earn their living as entertainers. How are musicians trained and treated in various other cultures? Where do they "fit" in the societies of which they are a part?

In what ways can study of people's music assist in understanding other aspects of their ways of life, their perception of reality and of the problems of human life?

Song texts, like the content of other forms of verbal art, are an index of people's deep-seated feelings: their aspirations, their troubles, their style of life, and the life issues that concern them most deeply (see Keil on the Blues 1966). Singing songs deeply felt may have multiple functions, providing for some a sort of catharsis, for others a sense of solidarity, shared goals, and urgency for action. The "folk" songs sung so widely in the United States are an important and familiar instance of the ways in which music, as a vehicle for social pressure and satire, as political statement and ethical plea, can be related to the most fundamental of human concerns.

Dance

Dance is almost as automatically associated with the stereotype of non-Western peoples as is their naively alleged "natural sense of rhythm." Although the association between rhythm and dance has nothing directly to do with a people's physical type or "race," it may have something to do with the kinds of musical instruments that are used. Just as musical systems marked by rhythmic complexity occur most often among peoples with percussion instruments, it seems likely that music with a strong beat may be especially well suited to the development of the patterned, usually pleasing, carefully coordinated succession of body movements defined as dance. The causal relationship between dance forms and instrument types probably works both ways.

Dance is as closely associated with other aspects of culture as music is. Often it plays a part at every stage in the life cycle. For children dance may be an important part of

"... the patterned, usually pleasing, carefully coordinated succession of body movements defined as dance."

Figure 15-8. Country dancing, Virginia. (Appalachian Regional Commission.)

"People also dance during periods of crisis and anxiety . . . ."
Figure 15-9. Kwakiutl Indians dancing to restore an eclipsed moon. (Courtesy of the American Museum of Natural History.)

play. At adolescence it provides a means of sexual display, stimulation, or sublimation. Marriage ceremonies often involve dancing. Many people dance to celebrate other welcome events: a successful harvest, a victory in battle, the initiation of boys and girls at puberty, the accession to power of a new political or religious leader. People also dance during periods of crisis and anxiety, to cure sickness, to drive out evil spirits, and to placate angry gods. Frequently, dancing is a part of the death ritual. Considering how much dancing goes on in most people's lives, and considering the prominence of dance as an aspect of so many important occasions, it is unfortunate that anthropologists have not given the subject more theoretical attention.

Again, as with music, the subject of dance is most readily discussed in terms of what we do not know and need to find out. To begin to fill in the gaps in our knowledge dancing and dance-related behavior should be extensively recorded on film, particularly among those non-Western people for whom dance is a part of cultural institutions now rapidly changing. Analytic techniques need to be developed that will help to achieve a more precise understanding of the symbolism involved in dance and of the functions of such symbolism. The dynamics of dance composition and dance performance as creative processes need also to be better understood.

Like music, dance is far from the universal language it is sometimes described as

"Like music, dance is far from the universal language it is sometimes described as being."
Figure 15-10. Acoma Hoop Dancer, New Mexico. (Bureau of Indian Affairs.)

being. Frequently it is a highly abstract art form that must be studied by performer and audience alike, and one that involves such subtle use of symbols that an unfamiliar audience may be unable to perceive any but the most obvious forms and not able to understand even them.

Many of the peoples of the Pacific have developed dancing to an extraordinary point of refinement, as a means of both aesthetic expression and communication, by the use of highly abstract movements full of symbolic subtleties, as in the storytelling dances of Polynesia, of which the popular Hawaiian hula is a vulgarized but familiar instance, and the elaborately stylized dance of the Javanese. In the intricate, often almost brittle stylization of the dances of the peoples of Southeast Asia a slight arm motion, a quivering eyebrow in an otherwise masklike face, and a half-bent knee must often convey both the dancer's many-faceted emotional response and the elements of the equally complex dramatic situation to which he or she is responding.

The Dances of Java

Dances, like forms of music, are usually categorized according to the specifics of their style, meaning, and cultural function. Sometimes they take the form of a highly refined, stylistically distilled representation of the prevailing social structure; as in categories of traditional Javanese dance set apart on the basis of the social status of the performers and the social position of the audience permitted to witness them. On Java dancing is divided into two principal types: Putri, a set of ancient "princess dances" performed only by young girls, and Wajang Wong, more recently developed dances in which real dancers take the parts traditionally played by puppets in dramatizing the plots of the Javanese shadow play (Geertz 1960).

Putri dances are further separated into two categories, Srimpi and Bedaja. Srimpi consists of four dance sets, Bedaja of nine. Performance of both dance types requires extensive training and elaborate costuming and staging. Traditionally, the right to perform Putri dances and the opportunity to witness them were the exclusive prerogative of the Javanese aristocracy. Srimpi dancers were recruited only from the nobility. Bedaja dancers, drawn from the commoner

"... the intricate, often almost brittle stylization of the dances of the peoples of Southeast Asia ...."

Figure 15-11. Javanese Wajang Wong dancers. (Courtesy of the Cultural and Educational Division, Embassy of the Republic of Indonesia.)

"... her face set stiffly in a trancelike expression of inner concentration."
Figure 15-12. The Javanese dancer Sukarni. (Courtesy of the Cultural and Educational Division, Embassy of the Republic of Indonesia.)

class, were incorporated into court society as concubines.

Most classical Javanese dances enact traditionally set story motifs by means of starkly symbolic, precisely prescribed, almost ritualistically disciplined motions of the head and body, as in the gravity- and anatomy-defying "waves of the sea," a hypnotic rocking movement made in one spot, with the dancer's eyes cast down and to the side, her face set stiffly in a trancelike expression of inner concentration. As the dance progresses, the mood of introspection may be broken suddenly with a single, sharp gesture as the sarong is kicked back and the body begins to turn slowly, the shoulders moving with such controlled liquidity that the arms and shoulders appear boneless; breathing must be imperceptible. The repertoire of precisely defined symbolic movements is so exacting that court dancers must begin their conditioning early in childhood. By mid-adolescence dancers have reached the peak of their careers. Soon after twenty they retire.

Like most art forms patronized by the aristocracy in a rigidly stratified society, the Putri and Wajang Wong dances of the tradition-oriented Javanese court have been limited and popularized by performers from the Indonesian commoner classes, who have developed a "proletarian" dance drama that both mirrors the working people's considerably different traditions and, as a more flexible art form, reflects and guides the economic, social, political, and ideological changes occurring in contemporary Indonesia. As with many radical artistic innovations, particularly those that symbolize or symbolically advocate social changes that threaten the position of an elite fearful of losing its prerogatives, the resulting changes in story content, production style, and dance technique are regarded by those conditioned to the aristocratic standards of Javanese court dance as vulgar and debased (see Peacock 1968a). A more objective appraisal would require that such dances be judged on the basis of their distinctive merits as the products of that popularizing process by which any art form restrained by tradition and accessible only to an elite minority is reinterpreted to meet a larger society's changing needs.

Dance As an Adjunct to Ideology

Where dance is related to religion, usually as an aspect of ritual, attention to precision performance is likely to be especially great. A poorly executed movement may not only shame the performer and create an adverse audience reaction but also literally ruin the ritual of which it is a part by displeasing the supernatural beings whose favor it is meant to elicit.

In many societies dance is as important as music in religious observances. Throughout sub-Saharan Africa dance to the accompaniment of music with a strong beat is a principal ritual means of making contact with and attempting to control the forces of the supernatural—ancestral spirits, nature deities, and other beings. Often the motions of individual dancers are intended to be representational or abstract imitations of activities or attitudes associated with the particular supernatural being with whom the dancer seeks contact. Yoruba dancers in Nigeria imitate the movements of their gods in order to induce possession by them. Dancers among the neighboring peoples of Benin do the same, as do many of the descendants of these West African peoples who have resettled throughout the Americas.

Separation of the Dead: The LoDagaba Funeral Dance

Among the LoDagaba of the Ivory Coast dance is an important aspect of the funeral ritual intended to assure the separation of the dead from the living (Goody 1962). Funeral participants enact in dance form activities associated with a deceased man's role in the kin group, both memorializing his contribution to his kinsmen and separating him from them by ritually relegating him and the events connected with his life to the hereafter.

Like most art forms used as an adjunct to important rituals, the LoDagaba funeral dance dramatically reinforces the participants' awareness of the permanent change in status that the deceased has undergone, and by recounting in dance form his contributions to the kin group, the responsibilities that all people bear to their kin are ritually restated.

Still other aspects of the same dance provide a structured outlet for the mourners' grief. Those most bereaved, a dead man's closest kinsmen, are expected to run about distractedly during the funeral observances, breaking suddenly into frenetic dancing to the strong beat of the xylophones that are played steadily for several days. To some extent the form of the mourners' dance is culturally channeled and conditioned; a special style of dancing is considered appropriate to the occasion. But allowance is also made for improvisation, providing the mourners with a means of personally expressing the powerful feelings of pain, loss, fear, and anger that are a common response to the death of a close relative.

The sense of frustration the LoDagaba experience at their helplessness in the face of death is also acted out in dances. Some dancers seize war clubs and bows and arrows and wave them in the air in defiance of those who are believed to have used evil magic to bring about their relative's demise. They also express in dance, and in the accompanying chants, their anger with the dead man himself for having left them so suddenly and without warning—all in all releasing in socially acceptable form powerful feelings whose dissipation is critical both to the distraught mourners' emotional reintegration and to the reestablishment of societal stability.

"The anthropological study of drama . . . illustrates both the potential interrelatedness of all forms of aesthetic expression and the fusion of art with most other aspects of a people's way of life."

Figure 15-13. Devil dancers in a religious pageant, Colombia. (OAS Photo.)

Drama

The anthropological study of drama, more than any other art form, illustrates both the potential interrelatedness of all forms of aesthetic expression and the fusion of art with most other aspects of a people's way of life. During the last few centuries in Europe and the Americas, "the theater" has tended to emerge as a discrete art form. In most societies, although drama is quite evidently an important art form, it is not easily separated from the larger aesthetic matrix of which it is a vital part.

The relationship between drama and religious ideas and practices is particularly close, as it is still by ritual means that the majority of people try to control the circumstances of their lives. Generally such drama takes either the form of reenacting events—the creation of the world, scenes from the lives of the gods and other supernaturally endowed beings—that validate and reinforce the premises basic to the people's system of beliefs or of acting out wished-for events, as if by representing them ritually they could be brought about in fact.

Drama as an aspect of ritual also provides a means of reducing anxiety and tension through such relief-giving patterns as prayer, penance, sacrifice, possession, and other behaviors culturally designated as appropriate for coping with anxiety and the pressure of other strong emotions. Whatever the specific form of dramatic devices, from sanctioned licentiousness through elaborate liturgy to the starkest sense-denying observance of silence, drama enhances ritual by contributing to the assurance of its effectiveness.

The Gururumba Pig Festival: Drama in New Guinea

The potentially many-faceted relationship between dramatic ritual and other aesthetic forms and their frequent fusion with the major aspects of a people's way of life can best be demonstrated with an example.

For many of the peoples of New Guinea and the surrounding islands of Melanesia, ritual dramas are literally a part of life, day in and day out. Some last for months and are only concluded in time to initiate a new series. The preparations such dramas require, the production of costumes and masks, the carving of the towering wood sculptures essential to the ritual setting, the composition and rehearsal of dances, songs, and their instrumental accompaniments can take years.

Carvers in the Papuan Gulf region of New Guinea require as long as twenty years to prepare the huge vertical masks—painted intricately in red, black, and white to represent powerful supernatural beings, deities of the forest and the sea—that are pivotal to the ritual dramas through which the people try to control the powerful supernatural forces they believe govern their destinies.

Among the Gururumba, a group that lives in the Eastern Highlands of New Guinea, the time devoted to the preparation for ritual dramas and their presentation reflects the central place of such productions in their lives (Neuman 1964). The Gururumba Pig Festival, as a dramatic-ritual production involves nearly all people, nearly all the important aspects of their culture, and almost every variety of aesthetic expression in a single, sustained dramatic presentation that requires months of preparation. The central "act" of the entire ritual entails the killing and distribution of pigs, an event that symbolizes the economic success of those who sponsor the Pig Festival, enhances their social status and renown, and serves as a means of settling old social and economic obligations and of establishing new ones. This is accomplished through an assertive display of wealth, intended by the sponsors to demonstrate their worth as members of the community and their value as economic

". . . to the starkest sense-denying observance of silence . . . ."

Figure 15-14. Kabuki actor, Japan. (Information Section, Embassy of Japan.)

associates. It is the function of drama to accomplish this within the context of a single, grandiose spectacle.

Reliance on dramatic techniques underscores every phase of the ritual demonstration. Musicians parade through the community, playing on flutes to announce that preparations for the Pig Festival are under way, to make known to everyone that some men among them have attained the pinnacle of achievement according to Gururumba values: mastery of the powerful and elusive forces that control the growth of plants and animals on which Gururumba material prosperity is dependent.

Every aspect of the dramatic ritual that follows the flutists' parade illustrates the continuing fusion of art and ritual within a

"... all are combined in a single ... lavishly produced, dramatically staged performance ...."

Figure 15-15. The Bison Dance of the Mandan Indians, a dramatization of the creation of the earth, plants, animals, and people, performed to renew the world and to strengthen Mandan society. (Smithsonian Office of Anthropology, Bureau of American Ethnology Collection.)

single cultural matrix. Each element fulfills several functions. The flutes, for example, make music and also make an announcement; as ritual objects, their playing stimulates the regrowth of the depleted pig population (to sustain this capacity the flutes must be "fed" from time to time: bits of food are placed in their open ends). At the conclusion of the Pig Festival the flutes are stored close to the carved wooden house poles of their owners so that the poles will absorb a part of their power. Then later the house poles are buried to enable the power they have accumulated to pass back into the bodies of the men who have sponsored the Pig Festival and whose own personal strength has been dissipated by the distribution and destruction of a major portion of their material wealth.

The flutes and their multiple aesthetic and ritual meanings and functions are just one of numerous ritual-aesthetic devices. Dancing and singing, the preparation and dramatic display of elaborate feather- and shell-covered costumes, the creation of huge, elaborately sculptured wooden boards painted with polychrome geometric designs representing entities from the Gururumba supernatural, myths—all are combined in a single, elaborately plotted, lavishly produced, dramatically staged performance in which the economic, social, political, and religious beliefs of the Gururumba are enacted, incorporating the most compelling themes in Gururumba culture in a massive, "mixed media," multiform dramatic presentation.

Summary

So far, verbal art, or oral tradition, has been the most thoroughly studied of all non-Western art forms. Until recently, most emphasis has been on form and content, either for the purposes of historical reconstruction or as a means of getting at supposedly universal themes that reflect the "psychic unity" of humankind. Currently, more attention is being given to the ways that the various forms of verbal art may reflect important values, a people's attitudes to life crises, a way of seeing the world. Oral traditions serve also as repositories of knowledge and as verbal restatements of codes of ethics, as in the instance of proverbs used as ridicule and as a source of precedent in litigation.

The anthropological study of music has recently received increased attention. A principal obstacle to its unification with the body of data, method, and theory central to contemporary cultural and social anthropology derives in part from the not entirely successful synthesis of the humanistic and scientific approaches in anthropology. Another problem is the still rudimentary status of most ethnomusicological studies, in which major attention is necessarily directed to accumulation of a sample of descriptive materials adequate for the formulation of theory. Fortunately there is increased interest in the study of music as a form of cultural behavior: interest in the roles of the composer and the performer, in the performance, and in the response of the audience as aspects of a total aesthetic experience. This may provide a more comprehensive model for the anthropological study of other art forms.

The study of dance, despite the universally close relation of dance to so many important human activities, is even more seriously hampered by the need for the fundamental recording of a sample of dance in context adequate to generate testable hypotheses concerning its role in culture.

Drama is among the art forms most seriously neglected by anthropologists, perhaps because in so many societies it is not easily separated from its usual context of ritual observances (themselves a symbolic representation of still more fundamental aspects of culture) and perhaps also because its analysis is complicated by the manner in which it typically incorporates nearly all other aesthetic forms—frequently reflecting dominant traditional cultural themes and also providing a context for social criticism and cultural innovation.

Suggested Readings

Verbal art is but a single aspect of folklore, an extensively developed subfield within anthropology. The range of the folklore literature can only be suggested here. See, for example, Bauman's "Verbal Art As Performance"; "Towards a Definition of Folklore in Context" by Ben-Amos; *Folklore: Communication and Performance,* edited by Ben-Amos and Goldstein; and, from the most prominent scholar in the field, Dorson's "Current Folklore Theories" and his *Folklore and Folklife: An Introduction.* See also Dundes's *The Study of Folklore;* Edmonson's *Lore: An Introduction to the Scientific Study of Folklore and Literature;* and *Toward New Perspectives in Folklore,* edited by Paredes and Bauman.

A listing of excellent accounts of folklore within the context of particular cultures would include *Vietnamese Folklore: An Introductory and Annotated Bibliography* by Công-Huyêen-Tôn-Nū, Crowley's *I Could Talk Old Story Good,* Dorson's *America in Legend: Folklore from the Colonial Period to the Present,* Mintz's *Legends of the Hasidim: An Introduction to Hasidic Culture and Oral Traditions in the New World,* Lessa's *Tales from Ulithi Atoll,* Jackson's *Get Your Ass in the Water and Swim Like Me,* Shack and Marcos's *Gods and Heroes: Oral Traditions of the Gurage of Ethiopia,* and Gossen's *Chamulas in the World of the Sun: Time and Space in a Maya Oral Tradition.* See also any issue of the *Journal of American Folklore.*

The anthropological study of music is the subject of a special journal, *Ethnomusicology.* There are also several recent and good introductions to the field: Greenway's *Ethnomusicology,* Hood's *The Ethnomusicologist,* Merriam's *The Anthropology of Music,* and Nettl's *Theory and Method in Ethnomusicology.* For examples of the study of the music of particular non-Western peoples see Carrington's "The Talking Drums of Africa," Deng's *The Dinka and Their Songs,* Ellis's *Aboriginal Music,* Green's *Only a Miner: Stories in Recorded Coal Mining Songs,* McPhee's *Music in Bali,* Merriam's *The Ethnomusicology of the Flathead Indians,* and Whitten's "Personal Networks and Musical Contexts in the Pacific Lowlands of Colombia and Ecuador."

Much of the serious early work on dance was done by Kurath. See her "Panorama of Dance Ethnology" and her *Dance and Song Ritual of Six Nations Reserve.* See also Comstock's *New Dimensions in Dance Research;* Bourgignon's *Trance Dance; Research in Dance: Problems and Possibilities,* edited by Bull; and Thompson's superb *African Art in Motion.*

The anthropological literature on drama is just beginning to grow. Much of it is still descriptive. For an example of some that is not, see Herskovits's still useful "Dramatic Experience Among Primitive People," Turner's *Dramas, Fields, and Metaphors: Symbolic Action in Human Society,* and Crumrine's "Ritual Drama and

Culture Change." For some well-analyzed pieces on the role of drama within particular cultural contexts, see Brandon's *On Thrones of Gold: Three Javanese Shadow Plays,* Hein's *The Miracle Plays of Mathura,* Hill's *The Trinidad Carnival,* Hopkins's "Persuasion and Satire in the Malian Theatre," Messenger's "Ibibio Drama," Nash's "The Passion Play in Maya Indian Communities," and Peacock's excellent *Rites of Modernization: Symbolic and Social Aspects of Indonesian Proletarian Drama.*

Part Eight
Language

. . . certainly for linguistics associated with anthropology the leading questions increasingly concern: How best describe the working of a language in a particular social context? How identify and explain the uniformities and differences between languages in social function?

Hymes (1964b:92)

People's capacity for culture and their capacity to use language are closely linked. Probably the two developed together. Certainly neither could exist without the other, for the ability to use language is essential to the acquisition of culture. As infants first develop into young children and as children continue on to maturity, they learn the culture of their group by a process in which language as a means of cultural transmission becomes increasingly important as their intellects grow. If, because of some impairment, a child cannot readily use spoken language, its acquisition of culture will be seriously interfered with until the impairment is overcome.

Culture is learned. Without language, learning cannot occur, and culture can be neither acquired, used, nor passed on.

The closeness of the relationship between language and culture is now so generally conceded as to be almost a cliché. Yet the processes by which the relationship is sustained are far from adequately understood.

16

Linguistic Anthropology

The Evolution of Language and Culture

Probably the linkage that now exists between language and culture has been present from some very early stage in that several million years long process during which our apelike ancestors little by little came to rely more and more on communication and cooperation as means of survival among hostile competitors and gradually developed the cranial and cortical capacities that were critical to their becoming totally human.

Some idea of what the earliest phases of the development of language among our near-human ancestors might have been like may be derived from observation of the systems of gestural and oral communication evolved by our closest primate kin, the great apes, which use a variety of patterned, apparently learned utterances—roars, cries, growls, calls—for such social purposes as establishing the limits of their territory, beckoning, play, sexual display, warning and scolding their young, signaling anger, and threatening their adversaries (see DeVore 1965). We share with the apes some common but exceedingly ancient ancestors. Although we may never know with certainty what their early attempts at communication were like, we can assume that the earliest forms of near-language must have met needs that were in at least some ways like those that language fulfills among people today. If so, such incipient forms of language would have given our ancestors a tremendous advantage over their speechless competitors. Once fully evolved, the ability to rely on language as a means of adaptation meant that *learning* to adjust to change, rather than dependence on genetic adaptation, was to continue to be for us humans the principal tool in our survival kit (see Hockett and Ascher 1964).

For modern humans, *Homo sapiens,* language fulfills several absolutely crucial functions. In addition to providing a means for acquiring culture, it is the indispensable means for using it: to communicate, to elicit response from others, to respond appropriately in turn, and, what is most important for the ongoing evolution of culture, to accumulate, store, transmit, and speculate on the past and present experience of others.

Language must have evolved coterminously with humans' capacity to use it. There are no human groups whose ability to use language as a means of adaptation is less evolved than others'. All human groups are demonstrably equal in this respect. However, it may be possible to refer—very cautiously—to some languages as being more evolved than certain others.

Such an assertion requires quick qualification, for judged in relationship to the traditional cultures of which languages are a part, some languages cannot be said to be more primitive than others in the sense that they are less adequate to their speakers' needs. On the contrary, all languages are uniquely well adapted to the cultural context of which they are a part. Often their adaptive efficiency is especially marked in the richness of vocabulary describing those particular kinds of phenomena that are most important to a particular people's survival: aspects of the natural environment on which they are dependent for making a living, as in the famous instance of the Eskimo's four separate words for snow or our own vast vocabulary of technical terms for machine parts. Living within the context of their respective traditional cultures, all peoples can probably say equally well whatever they need to say.

In this fundamental sense there are no primitive languages. In one language it may take more words than in another to say the same thing, and there are actual differences in vocabulary size (although not necessarily in the size of the vocabularies of specific speakers). But all peoples have a vocabulary

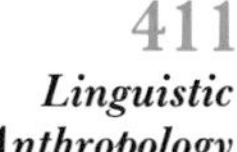

". . . the linkage that now exists between language and culture . . . ."
Figure 16-1. A deaf child watches for guidance from her speech therapist, Kuwait. (United Nations.)

adequate to their needs. And if, in a new situation, they find that they do not, they can always invent or borrow new words. No language is a closed system. Every language includes the capability of adding or altering vocabulary as necessary.

This concept of the absence of primitive languages among contemporary peoples has been a precious tenet among anthropologists interested in languages (especially among those disturbed by the frequent use of the concept of other peoples' primitivism as a justification for colonialism and oppression). Part of their argument against the concept of linguistic primitivism may be justifiably related to past tendencies to correlate what was assumed to be a relative lack of linguistic complexity or apparent adaptive efficiency with a people's intellectual capacity, in a variation of the antiquated equation of "primitive culture" with "primitive mentality."

Now that the absence of correlation be-

". . . to accumulate, store, transmit, and speculate on the past and present experience of others."
Figure 16-2. In the Language Lab, Abidjan, Ivory Coast. (United Nations.)

tween the content of a particular culture and the potential of a people's intellect is a settled issue, the question of the relative adaptive value of particular languages can be reconsidered without prejudice to the firmly established principle that as groups, people in every society are intellectually equally endowed.

With the dangers of such misinterpretations clearly stated it becomes possible to assert that there is a sense in which some languages can be regarded as less evolved with regard to certain specific linguistic features than are others. What is meant is that some languages may not yet have developed (because it has not been necessary) those changes that facilitate their speakers' adaptation to certain kinds of evolutionary sociocultural change. They have not done so because it has been easier to employ another language, such as English, in which such adaptive changes have already taken place. Put another way: there are few books on astrophysics in Urdu, not because Urdu is not potentially able to cope with the scientific concepts and the technical vocabulary of astrophysics, but because it is much easier to employ another language already adapted to the requirements of communicating about supernovae, zero gravity, and the Big Bang. It has been suggested that the Japanese may be the last of modern peoples to evolve their own language of science. Hereafter, most aspiring Urdu-speaking astrophysicists, like their counterparts who speak Amharic, Albanian, or any Austronesian tongue, may have to study in a European language for their advanced degrees. Thus, in the evolutionary perspective in which all peoples must sooner or later come to some kind of terms with industrially based technology and the changed patterns of living it makes necessary, some languages can be regarded as being, at least for the present, evolutionarily more "advanced" than others.

It is true, of course, that the languages of all peoples, like most of the other aspects of

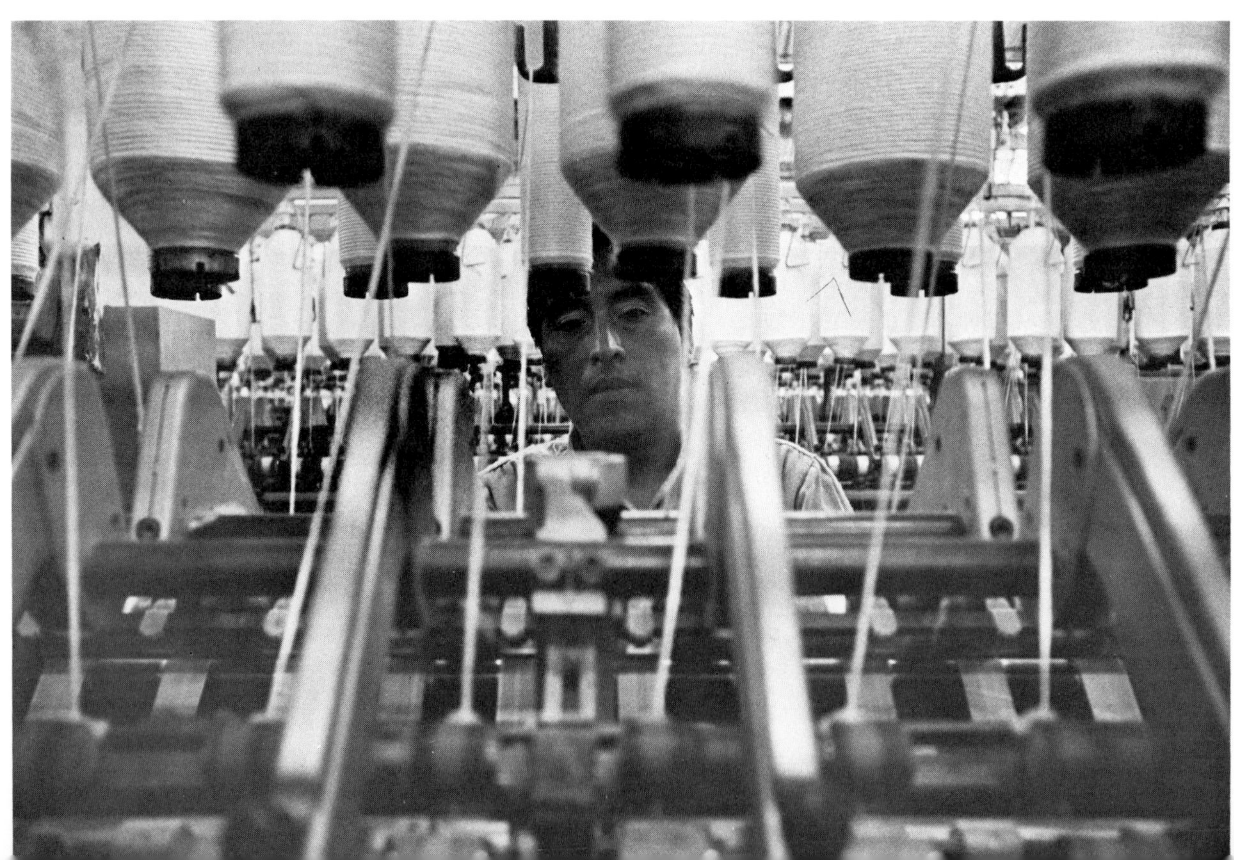

". . . all peoples must sooner or later come to some kind of terms with industrially based technology . . . ."
Figure 16-3. Indian factory worker, Peru. (Inter-American Development Bank.)

"... or as long as those who remember the native language survive."

Figure 16-4. For many Native Americans that time has past. A Coharie chief speaking the English that is now his people's only language. (Azar Hammond.)

their traditional ways of life, could make the changes necessary to adapt. But many may not, simply for the reason already stated: It is less wasteful in energy and time to adopt the language of another people that has already undergone the modifications necessary to efficient communication of new information in a rapidly changing world. Such an assertion implies nothing about the intrinsic worth of other languages under traditional cultural circumstances. Nor does it necessarily follow that those languages that may be considered as less evolved in the strictly scientific or technical sense will, as a result, die out. As long as they are well adapted to dealing with major aspects of their speakers' experience they are likely to persist. Indeed, in providing an efficient means of communicating about most traditional aspects of their users' ways of life, they may be perceived as more "advanced" than the new foreign language adopted for communicating about science. The old ways of talking may persist as long as the old ways of life go on—or as long as those who remember the native language survive. But, barring external preventive intervention, an old language may certainly become extinct, sooner or later. Many younger anthropological linguists now take a position similar to that of Hymes (1964:105), who argues that some languages can indeed be considered to be evolutionarily more advanced than others, "If one accepts a biologist's criterion of advance as 'change in direction and increase in the range and variety of adjustments to environment' (including, for language, sociocultural environment), and if one admits that the oft-mentioned *potential* equivalence of languages . . . is not the same as *actual* equivalence."

Language Description

During the first part of this century linguists generally emphasized the separateness of language from other aspects of human behavior, the autonomy of language structure, and the independence of the processes of language change. Now the interest of linguistic anthropologists is focusing increasingly on the integration of language in sociocultural context. To arrive at testable generalizations about the universal attributes of language that will allow for the formulation of laws explaining language and the processes of language change, it is, of course, first necessary to study an adequate sample of various peoples' patterns of linguistic behavior.

Traditionally, the primary goal of language description has been the development of an economical, complete, and accurate account of the patterned utterances that collectively constitute a particular people's speech at a particular time, a description of the system of rules for organizing sounds and meanings that *is* the language. To obtain this information the anthropologist studying language must first decide on criteria for determining where the language he or she wants to study leaves off and the languages of neighboring peoples begin. There are rarely clear-cut demarcations between languages. Like other aspects of cultural behavior, linguistic patterns at the periphery of any "speech community" tend to blend with those of their neighbors; sometimes the decision on language boundaries must be made arbitrarily. Whereas it is standard, for example, to use "potential mutual intelligibility" as a criterion, the dialects of a single language are often in fact not mutually intelligible. This is likely to be the case wherever the speakers of a "single" language are either regionally dispersed (for example, the rural populations of the various provinces of Italy and Spain) or rigidly separated socially (for example, the black population of urban ghettos in the United States). As a result of relative sociocultural isolation and the greater intensity of interaction and communication within the component groups of society, local communities develop variants of their language adapted to their specific subcultural environment that outsiders, including those who speak the high-prestige dialect designated as "standard" often cannot understand.

In such instances the decision to consider dialects as parts of a single language is usually based on whether or not the speakers share membership in some larger sociocultural unit, such as a tribal federation or a nation-state. By this criterion the linguistically related but often mutually unintelligible ways of speaking of the inhabitants of

". . . local communities develop variants of their language adapted to their specific subcultural environment . . . ."

Figure 16-5. And so between them another language must often be used. This Gabonese surveyor uses French. (United Nations.)

the adjacent Spanish provinces of Andalusia and Murcia, for example, are usually considered as dialect variations of a single language, Spanish, but the closely related way of speaking of peasants living just beyond Spain's frontier, in the province of Portugal called Alentejo, is considered as a dialect of a separate language, Portuguese. Usually geographic separation must be accompanied by relative cultural isolation and a high degree of local socioeconomic autonomy for linguistic diversification to occur.

It is only in isolation that initially common ways of speaking diverge to the point of becoming unintelligible, because it is only isolation that prevents borrowing and diffusion of the linguistic innovations that result in permanent, language-wide changes. Culturally isolating factors that may contribute to the development of marked but less than radical variations in speech among those who share a common language are differences in social class, ethnicity, occupation, age, and sex. Such cultural sources of linguistic diversity among the speakers of a single language are not so much obstacles to be overcome as they are factors to be taken into account in assuring that the sampling taken of a given people's speech behavior is truly reflective of how the people talk.

The scholar concerned with developing an accurate description of a language also faces the task of controlling for differences in speech behavior from speaker to speaker and time to time. For we do not always say things the same way, and we use the same language quite differently when speaking informally to a friend, for example, from the way we use it when speaking to a stranger who is holding a microphone to our face. People whose social status is changing often exhibit marked differences in speech within a relatively short time, or speak quite differently to their old associates from the way they speak to their new, would-be peers.

The dilemma created for linguists by such sources of variation as these is similar to the methodological problems that must be dealt with by anthropologists studying any other aspect of culture. It is manifested concretely in the problems encountered in selecting a sample. Who will be the informants? How can linguists be sure that the utterances they collect from speakers will be truly representative? How, for example, do one's own unfamiliar presence, one's peculiar questions, and the strange recording devices one employs affect an informant's response? How can one be sure of having found a typical speaker? (What *is* a typical speaker?)

Defining linguistic frontiers, deciding how to cope with dialect diversity, and selecting an informant whose speech is "representative" are only part of the problem of sampling entailed in the study of language. Speech behavior, like all cultural behavior, not only varies spatially, socially, and idiosyncratically, it also varies over time. To control for such variability it is desirable if the anthropologist collecting linguistic data can record the speech of persons belonging to all generations, from toddlers just learning to talk to the oldest members of the community, in order to check out the variant usages he or she detects and to determine whether they represent increments to the language or old sounds and meanings on their way out. Bearing such potential sources of distortion in mind, the anthropologist can produce a sample adequate to develop a description of the basic attributes of the language sufficiently accurate to permit formulation of testable generalizations. Such accuracy can be verified by using the description to produce sentences. If they are accepted as correct by native speakers, the anthropologist can assume the description is accurate. If not, something has been left out.

Full description of a language requires attention to three analytically separable aspects of language structure: (1) phonology, the sound system of the language; (2) gram-

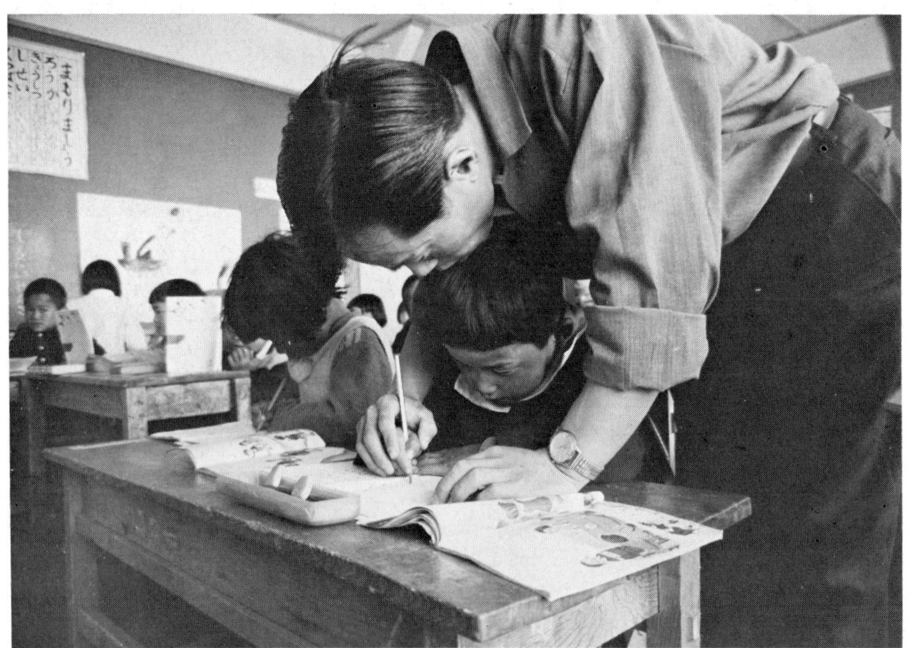

"... all of those meaningful utterances that collectively constitute a people's speech."

Figure 16-6. Japanese speech was first written down in the eighth century A.D. by adapting Chinese ideographs (nonphonetic pictorial symbols) to spoken Japanese. (United Nations.)

mar, the system for organizing sounds into words, phrases, clauses, and sentences; and (3) lexicon, the basic words of the language and their meaning.

Phonology

To describe the phonology of a language it is necessary to determine and describe the distinctive sounds, or phonemes, of the language and the rules that govern their occurrence. The total number of phonemes in any language is always finite and usually relatively small; the range is from about twenty to about sixty (English has approximately thirty-five). These phonemes are combined in various sequences in accordance with set rules to produce all of those meaningful utterances that collectively constitute a people's speech.

The first task in describing the sound system of a language is the collection and transcription of a representative sample of these utterances. In transcription the sounds that produce meaningful utterances are described in terms of "articulatory processes," that is, the positions and movements of the speech organs by means of which the sounds are made and in terms of which all possible speech sounds can be described.

The sounds of a language are produced by the organs of speech. Collectively called the speech tract, the organs of speech comprise "all the movable parts in the oral cavity [mouth], the nasal cavity, the pharynx [throat], and the lungs, together with the muscles that move these parts" (Hockett 1958:63). By observation of the visible motions involved in articulation, by "mimicking and introspective analysis of the sound thus produced," and by the use of X-ray photography and the laboratory construction of such organs as the palate, a system of terminology has been developed for distinguishing the limited number of articulatory processes by which all speech sounds are produced. In this way each sound produced in any of the world's languages can be defined in terms of the positioning of the vocal organs required to make it. For example, in making the initial sound in the English

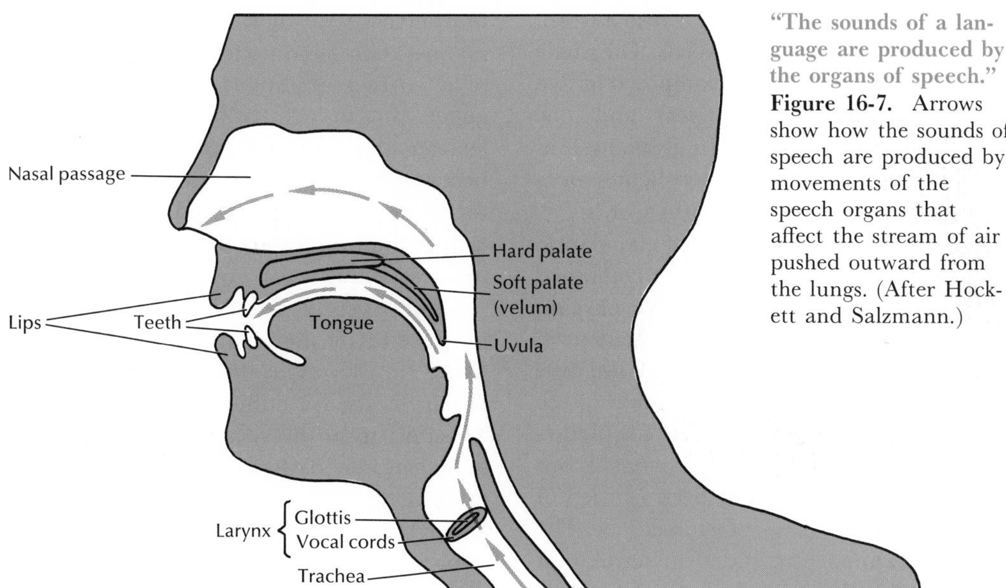

"The sounds of a language are produced by the organs of speech."
Figure 16-7. Arrows show how the sounds of speech are produced by movements of the speech organs that affect the stream of air pushed outward from the lungs. (After Hockett and Salzmann.)

word *box* both lips are closed while the vocal cords are vibrated. In the terminology of anthropological linguistics this initial sound is defined as a bilabial voiced stop: bilabial (both lips), voiced (vibration of the vocal cords), stop (total closing of the oral cavity).

The series of positions taken by the speech organs in the production of meaningful utterances is usually recorded by means of an alphabet developed by the International Phonetic Association to provide for the accurate transcription of every speech sound that could occur in any language. Now the use of highly sensitive recording devices and of mechanical means of acoustic analysis, such as the sound spectrograph, greatly facilitates accurate language description.

A phonetic transcription of a representative sample of utterances is first analyzed to identify the distinctive sounds that signal differences in meaning, the phonemes. Nonmeaningful sound differences are ignored; only those that are semantically significant are listed. Once all the phonemes of a language have been identified, the system that governs their occurrence must be ascertained and described as well, because every language has rules that permit certain kinds of sound combinations and prohibit others. The result is a schematic representation of the sound system of the language: All the sounds that signal differences in meaning, the ways they are produced, and the pattern by which they are organized into understandable sequences.

Grammar

A complete account of the structurally relevant differences that characterize the sound systems of particular languages requires the consideration of grammatical factors as well. Traditionally, and with somewhat static results, the study of grammar has been divided into two principal parts: morphology and syntax.

Morphology refers to study of the internal structure of words. The unit of analysis is the morpheme, a presumably irreducibly minimal unit of meaning, one that cannot be further reduced without altering its meaning. *Man,* for example, is a morpheme.

Because it can stand alone, it is also a word. But not all morphemes are words. The single word *man's,* for example, is composed of two morphemes, one "free" (*man*) and one "bound" (*s*). Morphology entails analysis of the systematic ways the morphemes of a language are combined to form words.

The study of syntax involves elucidation of the rules by which words are combined into longer grammatical structures: phrases, clauses, sentences, and groups of sentences.

Many modern anthropological linguists require that an adequate description of the grammar of a language provide for prediction, a statement not only of what is but also—in terms of what has been learned of the grammatical rules—of what can be. The rules of grammar are stated in terms that make possible the production of a hypothetical infinity of grammatical sentences.

This more dynamic approach is called generative. The particular type of generative grammar that is presently most prominent is termed transformational, in reference to the speaker's capacity to rearrange the basic elements of his or her language in order to express grammatically whatever new utterances are needed (see Chomsky 1957, 1965). Implicit in the emphasis on prediction in generative or transformational grammar is the concept that language differences, like differences in other aspects of culture, are explainable as surface, adaptive variations on deeper, universally shared attributes of the cultured human mind: attributes whose operation can ultimately be discovered and stated as laws. In this perspective language becomes, as Greenberg (1973:57) interprets it, not so much a set of actual sentences as an internalized mechanism of rules for producing sentences.

Lexicon

Traditionally, the principal semantic aspect of language description, the preparation of a lexicon, a dictionary-type listing of morphemes with their definitions, has been an operation separate from the preparation of a written grammar of a people's language. But, in fact, the boundaries between lexicon and grammar are frequently and necessarily blurred. The grammar often lists meanings, for example, and lexicons regularly include notations on such grammatical items as gender.

Until recently most lexicons were prepared using the dictionary as a model. To do this is to risk serious distortion, for the dictionary is itself a culture-bound form, and the effort to fit the vocabulary of an exotic language into its format may lead the anthropologist to distort the image of the language he or she is describing. Some scholars apparently concluded that the risks of such distortion were not worth taking and, purposefully or by omission, tended to exclude semantic material from their descriptive accounts. In recent years this tendency to ignore or underplay the role of meaning in describing languages has begun to be reversed.

Language Comparison

The next step in analyzing languages once they have been adequately described entails their comparison and classification. This is accomplished on the basis of three different kinds of resemblances: (1) those that are genetic, the consequence of their descent from a common ancestral language; (2) those that are diffusional, the result of transmission from one language to another; and (3) those that are the evidence of language universals.

Genetic Comparison

Understanding of the processes by which languages change through time is essential to understanding the rationale of genetic

"... those [resemblances] that are genetic, the consequence of their descent from a common ancestral language ...."

Figure 16-8. The development of the Germanic languages from a common proto-Germanic ancestral language that branched off from an even more ancient Indo-European language. (After Salzmann.)

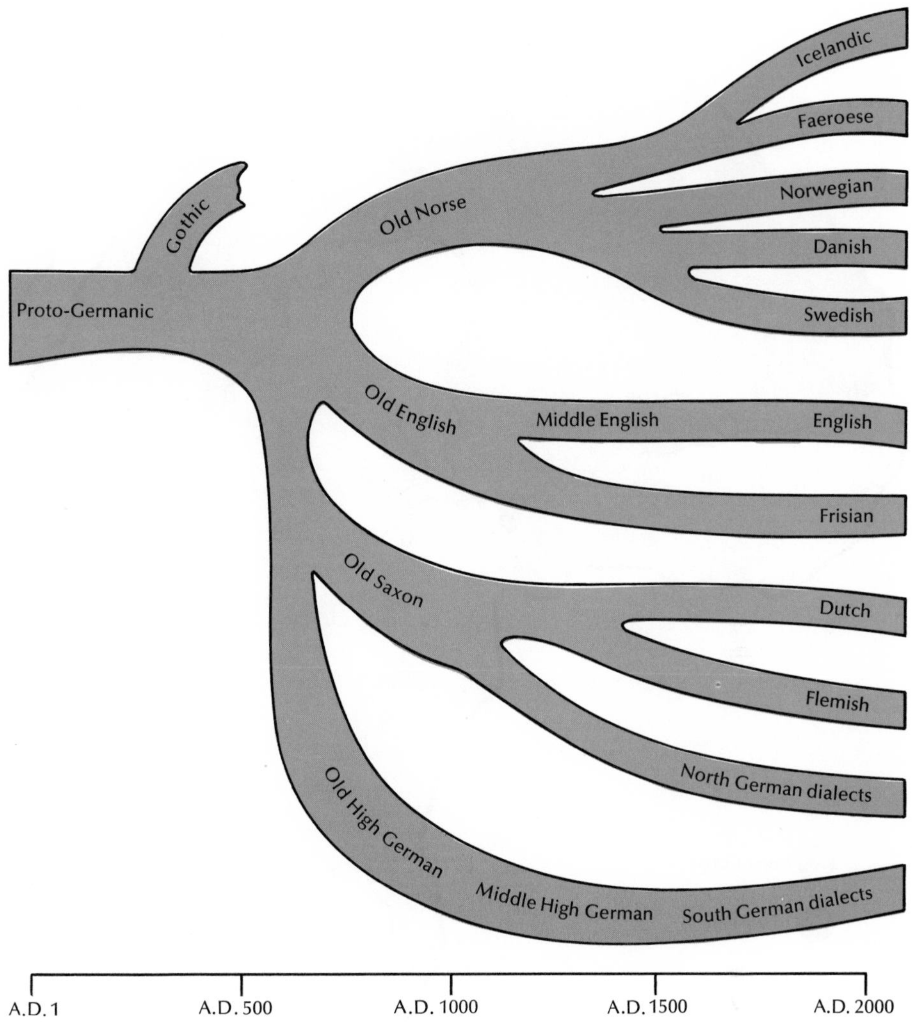

classification. As Greenberg (1968:120) has described this process:

> in a speech community of any considerable geographic extent there develop regional . . . variants (local dialects)—particularly if migration or the intervention of a foreign group splits the community into segments that do not communicate with one another. Eventually, unless linguistic unity is restored by the spread of a single dominant dialect, such dialects become more and more different, until they reach the point at which we can reasonably say that mutual intelligibility no longer exists.

At that point, he continues, "we speak of related but separate languages, rather than of dialects of the same language."

This was the process by which the Romance languages developed gradually from local dialects of Latin into now mutually unintelligible but still obviously closely related (genetically related) languages within the same family. Broadening the range of languages included and extending reconstruction of the process of diversification farther back in time, it is possible to trace the connections of most of the languages of

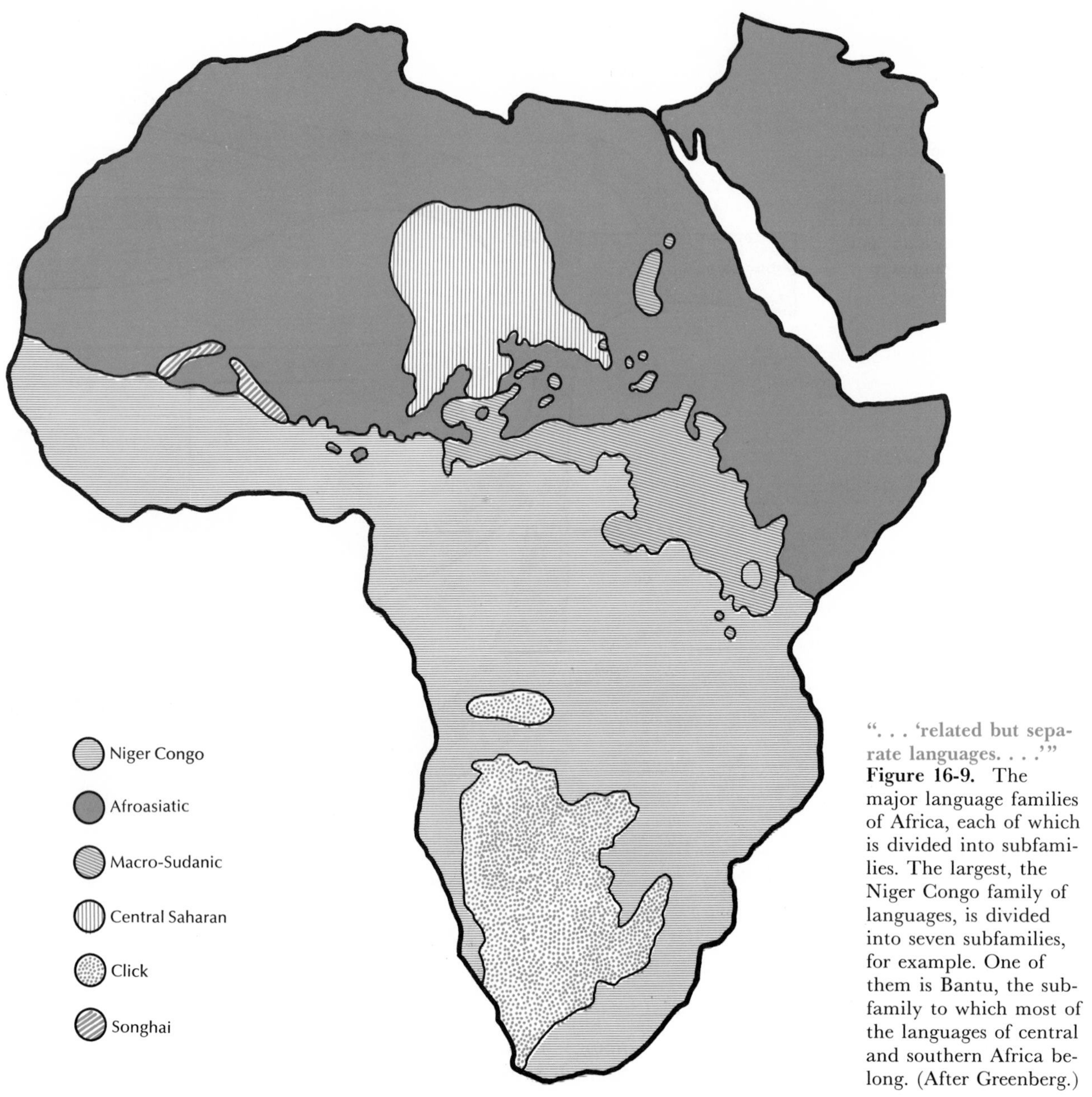

"... 'related but separate languages....'" **Figure 16-9.** The major language families of Africa, each of which is divided into subfamilies. The largest, the Niger Congo family of languages, is divided into seven subfamilies, for example. One of them is Bantu, the subfamily to which most of the languages of central and southern Africa belong. (After Greenberg.)

the Old World—from Persian and Pashto to Portuguese and Norwegian—back to a single proto-Indo-European stock. It is the evidence of this relatedness that justifies the classificatory assignment of all of these languages to a single Indo-European language family. What this ancient language, ancestral to the languages of millions throughout the Old World but no longer spoken, was like can be learned only by rigorous comparison of the languages descended from it, and application to this comparison of what is known of the always regular processes by which languages change.

Understanding of the processes of linguistic change is derived both from analysis of language diversification as it is occurring today and from observation of its results as these are represented in the record of the regular and relentless, consistent and systematic changes in phonology and grammar that occur in all languages and that have marked, for example, the emergence of modern English (about four hundred years ago) from Middle English (spoken from about 1000 to 1500 A.D.) and the development of Middle English out of the even older Anglo-Saxon.

The basic assumption underlying and justifying the analysis of languages for the purpose of establishing their shared descent from some earlier, common prototype is that a resemblance in form and meaning for 5 per cent or more of the vocabularies of two different languages cannot be explained by chance and must be regarded as evidence of historical connection. Essentially, such connections can be of two types. If, for example, both languages show a high incidence of structural resemblance (morphological) and of cognates in their basic vocabularies, whereas they are markedly dissimilar in loan words, this is usually regarded as evidence of an ancient genetic connection followed by a relatively long period of separation. Conversely, if the basic structures and vocabularies of the two languages are radically different but they share a number of loan words (related, for example, to modern technology), no significant genetic relationship is indicated, and such superficial resemblances are assumed to be evidence either of recent direct contact between their speakers or of diffusion, as with the near universality of some form of such words as *tobacco* and *television.*

Glottochronology

The methods first developed to study change in the languages for which there are documents recording their antecedent forms (for example, Old English, Middle English, modern English) have recently been modified to allow for the chronological analysis of change in nonwritten languages as well. This technique, called glottochronology, was first developed by Swadesh in the early 1950s. The fundamental assumption in glottochronology is that the rate at which languages change by the replacement of

"If . . . both languages show a high incidence of structural resemblance . . . ."

Figure 16-10. As do Portuguese and Spanish, for example. Subway scene, São Paulo, Brazil. (Inter-American Development Bank.)

words assumed to represent the "basic vocabulary" (core items of vocabulary: pronouns, numerals, body parts, geographic terms, and so on, all assumed to be less subject to change than other words) is relatively constant for all languages through time. For example, an analysis of thirteen languages for which there are historical records showed an average rate of loss of basic vocabulary of about 19 per cent per thousand years (Lees:1953 118–119).

Using this assumption it is possible to compare the core vocabularies of two related languages on the basis of the extent to which they have diverged from a common ancestral language and estimate the length of time that has elapsed since divergence within the original speech community began. The greater the difference between the languages, the farther back in time this divergence is assumed to have occurred.

Originally developed as a means of applying mathematical precision to the chronological plotting of genetic relationships between languages, the glottochronological approach has recently been modified further by the addition of statistical concepts of probability serving to establish connections between languages that more superficial means of comparison would be unlikely to reveal. This lexicostatistical approach allows both for the reckoning of genetic relationship and for the study of language borrowing. It is used not only to estimate the time of original divergence of two speech communities but also to estimate the duration of contact between genetically unrelated or distantly related languages. A lexicostatistical analysis that reveals similarities between them beyond the range of chance probability suggests past relationships, genetic and/or diffusional, that otherwise might not be perceived.

In response to criticism of both the empirical method and the mathematical theory of glottochronology and lexicostatistics (the two terms are sometimes used interchangeably), most chronological conclusions are now made simply as cautious statements of probability. For one thing, it has been found that the tendency for core vocabulary to change at a constant rate through time is

". . . for the study of language borrowing."

Figure 16-11. Arabic-speaking students in Morocco studying chemistry in French. (Christine and Bill Graham, World Bank.)

not in fact universal (see Bergsland and Vogt 1962). Rather, as one would expect, the rate at which vocabulary is retained or changed appears to be importantly related to the function of particular words in particular sociocultural contexts.

Diffusional Comparison

Languages can also be compared on the basis of resemblances that are the result of diffusion or borrowing. In some instances resemblances between languages within a single geographic area must be explained in terms of both genetic and diffusional factors, as in the linguistic borrowing between two contiguous speech communities: France and Spain, for example, whose now separate languages have emerged from different dialects of a common ancestral tongue. But greatest emphasis in diffusion-based classification is on resemblances between genetically independent speech communities that are the result of contact and diffusion or borrowing.

Classification Based on Universals

The aim of classification based on identification of the universal features of language is to develop a roster of those resemblances between languages that cannot be explained by either common origin or diffusion. The remarkable cross-language similarity of terms for close kinsmen is a striking instance. Such resemblances must be manifestations of the universality of certain basic linguistic forms and processes, reflections of a "deep" logical structure derived from the attributes of mind shared by all humans. Discovery of these universals is fundamental to the building of a generalizing, scientific theory of language. Conversely, the discovery that certain logically possible forms and processes do not exist contributes to the same end: accurate definition of the full range and limits of linguistic variation. The result should be a theory that, no matter how apparently abstract, can be concretely applied to explaining the evolution of all forms of modern speech out of the system of primitive gestures and animal cries of our ancient prehuman ancestors. Ultimately, such a theory should explain the processes of language development in a way that enables us to deal more effectively with the diverse and pressing problems of how to cure speech defects and learning disabilities, how to resolve the issue of dialect differences and social discrimination, and how to communicate more effectively: the last as critical now to the avoidance of danger, to learning, and to cooperation for survival as it was when speech first began to evolve.

Summary

In contrast to some nonanthropological linguists, anthropologists have always regarded language as closely related both historically and contemporaneously to the rest of culture. So close is this relation that neither language nor culture could have evolved alone, and neither could survive without the other. The role of language in abstract, symbolic thinking and as a means of communication and cooperation—of acquiring, storing, and passing on knowledge—is patently fundamental to the function of culture.

No language is more primitive than another, in the sense that all people's languages function equally well in fulfilling their needs within the context of their traditional cultures. At the same time, there is growing acceptance of the concept that some languages may be evolutionarily more advanced than others in having undergone more of those changes in form and content necessary to cope with culture change, especially change resulting from an accelerated evolution of technology.

This being so, people faced with a rapidly changing cultural situation are likely to find it easier to learn a new language already adapted to the requirements of such change. This may reduce the pressure for adaptive change in their traditional language and may lead ultimately to its replacement.

Despite the growing interest of younger anthropological linguists in such relatively new problems as understanding the functions of language in cultural context, traditional fields like descriptive linguistics continue to provide the essential data about phonology, grammar, and lexicon on which sound theory must always be based.

A similarly basic function is fulfilled by comparative linguistics. Languages are compared and classified according to such traditional criteria as genetic relationships, diffusion, and the universality of certain fundamental attributes. The ultimate anthropological objective of all such analysis is to develop a more usable theory of the relationship between language and culture, one that not only can deepen our understanding of all forms of cultural behavior but also can be applied to a spectrum of problems ranging from the treatment of speech defects to improvement of systems of cross-cultural communication.

Suggested Readings

Several collections provide a good introduction to the variety of important issues in anthropological linguistics. Among the best are Blount's *Language, Culture, and Society: A Book of Readings,* Garvin's *Method and Theory in Linguistics,* Greenberg's *Language, Culture and Communication,* especially "The Science of Linguistics" therein, and Hymes's *Language in Culture and Society.* See also Burling's *Man's Many Voices. Themes in Linguistics: The 1970s,* edited by Hamp, is of value; so is Ardener's *Social Anthropology and Language.*

On the origin and evolution of the unique human capacity to use language see Greenberg's "Language and Evolution"; Campbell's "The Evolutionary Emergence of Language"; *Cognition and the Development of Language,* edited by Hayes; Hockett and Ascher's "The Human Revolution"; Hymes's "Functions of Speech: An Evolutionary Theory"; Swadesh's "Out of Animal Cries into Language"; and Washburn and Lancaster's "On Evolution and the Origin of Language." On the related subject of animal communication see Sebeok's *Perspectives in Zoosemiotics.*

Both Gleason's *An Introduction to Descriptive Linguistics* and Lehmann's *Descriptive Linguistics: An Introduction* provide good coverage of this field.

Comparative linguistics is extensively dealt with in several of the general works already listed. See also Sherzer and Bauman's "Areal Studies and Culture History: Language As a Key to the Historical Study of Culture Contact" and, for a classic example of language classification applied to a major geographic region, Greenberg's *Studies in African Linguistic Classification.*

For more on the universal features of language see Greenberg's *Language Universals.* And on other aspects of the "deep structure" of language see Chomsky's *Language and Mind* and *Studies on Semantics in Generative Grammar;* also *Readings in Applied Transformational Grammar,* edited by Lester.

17

Language, Culture, and Society

LINGUISTIC anthropologists are becoming increasingly interested in the interrelations of language, culture, and society, that is, in the functions of language in sociocultural context and in the effects of language and particular patterns of language use on other aspects of culture. Three subfields representative of the new anthropological linguistics and of its concerns with the workings of language in context are ethnolinguistics, ethnosemantics, and the ethnography of speaking.

Ethnolinguistics

In ethnolinguistics the primary questions posed are how language affects the way a people perceives and responds to the environment and, conversely, how the cultural environment may influence the content and structure of language.

The Sapir-Whorf Hypothesis

Much of the early attention to this interrelationship was centered on a formulation that has come to be known as the Sapir-Whorf hypothesis, after the pioneering linguists Edward Sapir and Benjamin Lee Whorf. The essence of the concept as it was initially elaborated by Sapir is contained in his statement, "Language is not merely a more or less systematic inventory of the various items of experience which seem relevant to the individual, as is so often naively assumed." Language is also, he wrote,

> . . . a self-contained, creative symbolic organization, which not only refers to experience largely acquired without its help but actually defines experience for us by reason of its formal completeness and because of our unconscious projection of its implicit expectations into the field of experience. [cited in Hymes 1964:128]

In this view, language is hypothetically seen as standing between people and their environment as a sort of interpretive screen, inducing the observer's perception of certain relationships and facilitating thought about them, and at the same time effectively impeding him or her from alternative ways of perceiving and thinking. Because of its relative stability over time the grammatical structure of language and the ways in which it forces the individual's experience into such structural categories as number, gender, tense, and voice have so far been assigned the most important role in conditioning perception, thought, and action, in determining what Sapir described as "the tyrannical hold that linguistic form has upon our orientation to the world" (Sapir 1931:578).

For the anthropologist studying a particular culture awareness of the relationship between the language and the people's response to what they perceive is vital to developing insight into the way they interpret their world and the way that interpretation affects their behavior and helps to explain it.

Hopi Clouds

To illustrate how linguistic study can lead to the uncovering of a people's way of perceiving, thinking about, and responding to the world, Whorf uses the example of an anthropologist among the Hopi who discovers that the Indians refer to clouds as if they were alive, by speaking of them in the animate plural in their prayers for rain (Whorf 1956).

Having noted this, Whorf's anthropologist would need to find out whether such a usage is a metaphor, possibly a ritual figure of speech, or whether it represents their "ordinary and usual way of thinking about clouds." To get the answer he would turn to the gender system of Hopi to see if a distinc-

". . . the effects of language and particular patterns of language use . . . ."

Figure 17-1. Campaign oratory, for example. (Tiff Ford, Black Star.)

". . . how language affects the way a people perceives and responds to the environment . . . ."

Figure 17-2. Lone house, Harrisonburg, West Virginia. (Appalachian Regional Commission.)

tion is made between living and nonliving things. First, he would find that Hopi grammar has no overt gender system at all, but on deeper analysis he would learn that clouds belong to a class of nouns that are always pluralized in the animate way. The question would then be, "Why?" And this would lead him on into the Hopi view of the world, one in which the ascription of life to clouds may be a clue to other associated beliefs and practices related to the Hopi way of seeing their environment. But, then, is it the structure of their language that modifies their perception and their behavior, or is it their belief system and the behaviors that follow from it, about the animate nature of clouds (and what other things?) that determine the structure of their language?

Other variations of this question of causality concern the relation between language and the perception and response of a people not only to objects but to other aspects of the environment, particularly such fundamental components of reality as space, time, and motion. (Or is it our language that makes these *seem* fundamental?) Almost always the question can be posed both ways: "How does language modify cultural behavior?" or, "Does culture determine the structure of language, and if so, in what ways?"

Navaho Eventings

Hoijer, a specialist in American Indian linguistics who has critically explored the Sapir-Whorf hypothesis, notes, for example, that verb categories in the language of the Navaho—a traditionally nomadic people who live near the Hopi in the Southwest but have a very different culture and language—give marked emphasis to the reporting of events in process, or "eventings," as he terms them. These eventings are divided into "eventings in motion" and "eventings whose stillness is perceived as the withdrawal of motion so that even this neuter category of verbs is relatable to the dominant conception of a universe in motion . . ." (Hoijer 1951:115). Hoijer then discerns in the Navaho's perception of the world—as filled with objects incessantly in the process of becoming and events constantly in the process of occurring—a parallel to the emphasis on movement that is a basic attribute of the Navaho's nomadic life, an interpreta-

". . . verb categories in the language of the Navaho . . . give marked emphasis to the reporting of events in process, or 'eventings' . . . ."

Figure 17-3. A Navaho family. (Bureau of Indian Affairs.)

"... soft, powdery, drifting dangerously ...." **Figure 17-4.** Blizzard at Eskimo Point, Northwest Territories. (National Film Board of Canada.)

tion that suggests that the structure of the Navaho language reflects this quality of ongoing movement that has been a basic part of their experience for centuries.

"Even today," Hoijer writes,

> the Navaho are fundamentally a wandering, nomadic folk, following their flocks from one pasturage to another. Myths and legends reflect this emphasis, both gods and culture heroes move restlessly from one holy place to the next, seeking by their motion to perfect and repair the dynamic flux which is the universe. [Hoijer 1951:115]

Such examples, which strongly suggest that the relation between language and culture works both ways—that the form and content of language may be shaped by culture as well as vice versa—have so far put off "proving" or "disproving" the Sapir-Whorf hypothesis.

It is to be hoped that the continued quest for answers to the questions posed by Sapir and Whorf will carry us forward toward better understanding the linkages between "overt behavior and the numerous symbolic systems that men set up as a screen between themselves and the objective universe in which they live" (Hoijer 1951:120). Such understanding may then assist us in better comprehending and coping with the group differences in perception and cognition that are sometimes the real obstacles behind the so-called language barrier.

Another aspect of the same general question concerns the way the content of language, as opposed to its structure, is affected by the characteristics of the culture of those who speak it. The essential notion is a commonsense one. If language is one of the major means by which people adapt to their environment, it is reasonable to expect that people's language should reflect this, being most efficient at dealing with those aspects of experience that are most critical to survival under a particular set of technoenvironmental circumstances.

Words for Snow in Eskimo and Arabic

Long ago the anthropologist Boas observed that Eskimo languages had several precise terms describing the particular attributes of snow important to their survival in a usually snowy environment: whether the snow was frozen solid and might easily be

"... features of the natural environment that were most relevant ...."

Figure 17-5. Aerial view of the McKenzie River, Northwest Territories, Canada. (National Film Board of Canada.)

traveled over, or whether it was soft, powdery, drifting dangerously, and therefore treacherous, and so on. Such elaboration suggested to Boas the possibility of a correlation between the structure of a people's language and those aspects of the habitat and culture that were of particular concern or interest to them. Implicit was the idea not only that those objects and object relations people regarded as most important would be reflected in the structure of their language (and the language would likely be structured to facilitate the expression of information the culture defined as important), but also that elaboration in some areas of expression might be paralleled by linguistically determined obstacles to the expression of other kinds of information. For example,

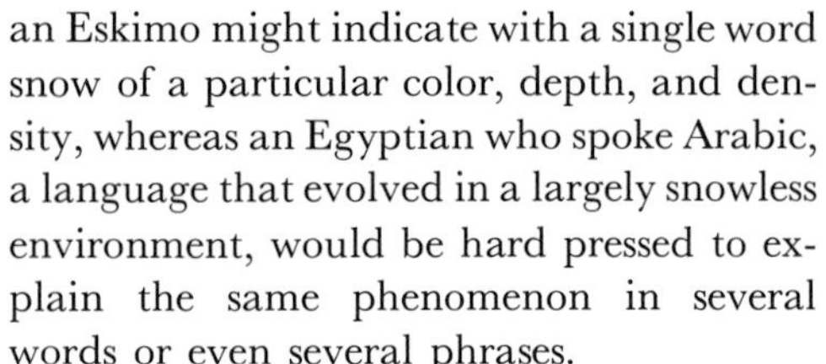

an Eskimo might indicate with a single word snow of a particular color, depth, and density, whereas an Egyptian who spoke Arabic, a language that evolved in a largely snowless environment, would be hard pressed to explain the same phenomenon in several words or even several phrases.

The issue relates, again, to determination of the ways in which language reflects culture, and conversely, to determination of the ways the content of culture can be affected by the structure of language.

Fishing, Foraging, and Place Naming on the Northwest Pacific Coast

In a study of the geographical terminology of the seafaring Kwakiutl Indians of the Pacific Northwest, Boas observed that in aspects of both morphology and lexicon their language reflected their concern "with the forms of land and water," especially with those aspects of the coastal area—the rivers and lakes, the underwater topography, the shoreline and forest—that were critical to the fishing, hunting, and food-gathering activities basic to their material survival (Boas 1934). Places on the water bore such names as "having swells," "breakers at rear end," "having trout," or "having sockeye salmon," all attributes of the environment important to the navigator and fisherman. Names assigned to places on land, "having elderberries" or "having cedar bark," reflected the reliance of the Kwakiutl on the gathering of wild plant material for food and other purposes.

Boas contrasted the Kwakiutl with the "historically minded" Dakota Indians of the North American Plains. In their focusing of cultural interest on the relationship of people to the sea and the surrounding land, the Kwakiutl used names tc designate geographic relationships that underscored those features of the natural environment that were most relevant to their culture (features that might have been quite irrelevant to others who made their living in the same environment by other means). The Dakota Indians in their choice of place names, such as "abandoned site-of-the-Pawnee" and "Four-Bear's-encampment," reflected their particular interest in significant historical events and important people.

Among the Pueblo Indians of the southwestern United States he noted frequent reference in place names to incidents in mythology or aspects of religious ritual, which he interpreted as indications of the Indians' dominant concern with their relation to the supernatural.

In instances such as these an aspect of language is seen to reflect those aspects of the speakers' way of life that, to use Herskovits's terminology, might be within their "cultural focus": aspects that being of greatest interest are likely to be most extensively elaborated (Herskovits 1950:542*ff*).

Can the Structure of Language "Structure" Culture?

There are also instances in which the relationship seems to work the other way, in which aspects of linguistic structure appear to determine the structuring of aspects of culture. An example is provided by Lotz's analysis of the ways in which the numerical system provided by a language affects the setting of "ideal targets" in sports (Lotz 1955). In England and in the United States and Canada, where the language provides for the measurement of distance in miles, running a mile in four minutes or less is set up as an ideal goal, whereas use of the metric system results in the designation of ideal targets in such terms as a hundred meters in ten seconds and twenty kilometers in an hour. In each case an aspect of linguistic structure determines the form of an aspect of culture: the setting of an ideal target or goal.

Our own quite arbitrary system for measuring time appears to have an equally deterministic role in both the form and the internal organization of other aspects of our way of living. For example, "native" peoples often criticized by Westerners for their lack of "any sense of time" may well have quite different perceptions of time relationships, often determined by the time allocated for activities in the daily round or by technologically or ritually significant phases of the seasonal periods we perceive as part of an annual cycle. The "natives" organize their time accordingly.

Causality between language and culture probably works both ways; clear perception of the processes involved is impeded by the fact that language is the medium through which humans learn most of the rest of their culture. In some instances, as with Kwakiutl place names, cultural interests seem to determine linguistic forms. In others, as with "ideal targets" in sports, the "eight-hour day," and the "forty-hour week," aspects of language seem clearly to affect the organization of units of cultural experience. However, it is likely that culture is still the more important initial factor. Linguistic forms

". . . language is the medium through which humans learn most of the rest of their culture . . . ."

Figure 17-6. Indian children learning to read, Bolivia. (United Nations.)

may be deterministic within a limited time frame, but in a longer, historical perspective it is probably the response of language to cultural circumstances that results in the emergence of grammatical (and other) forms. Then these forms, once set in motion, can significantly affect, if not actually determine, the direction of further change in culture.

Where Do We Go from Whorf and Sapir?

That there are correlations among "language, thought, and reality" is now generally accepted. The question is what is the extent of such correlations and what is necessary to record and evaluate them.

That this interesting subfield in anthropological linguistics has not developed faster may be explained by the persistent tendency of an older generation of linguists and anthropologists to treat language as if it were analytically separable from culture and in the process to exclude or give short shrift to meaning, to the semantic aspects of language description. As a theory can be no better than the data on which it is based, it is disappointing but not entirely surprising that linguists have so little to say beyond reelaboration of the now almost quarter-century-old Sapir-Whorf hypothesis. Attention is gradually shifting, however, from study of the relationship between language and thought in homogeneous small-scale societies to analysis of the cognitive consequences of living in the sort of culturally heterogeneous, multilingual societies characteristic of many parts of the contemporary world. The new linguistic anthropology, is marked by an increased interest in the social functions of language and in semantics.

Ethnosemantics

Anthropological linguists and cultural anthropologists interested in the relations between language and culture are increasingly emphasizing the theoretical aspect of language description, using a people's definitions of the significant aspects of reality and system for categorizing these aspects as an approach to understanding the people's "cognitive world." This approach, sometimes called ethnosemantics, strongly emphasizes avoiding the imposition of the outside observer's descriptive categories upon this world. Attention is rather directed to what are termed "native categories" and systems of classification. Students of ethnosemantics share the interest of the ethnolinguists, just described, in discovering how language and perception are related. But their concern goes beyond cultural differences in perception to seek an underlying logical system that may, they argue, be common to all language.

Although the point of departure in taking this approach is linguistic, especially as it suggests that all languages may share a common "deep" structure, inquiry carries over quickly into questions central to current issues in ethnographic method and anthropological theory. For this reason more extended discussion of this subject—critical to many, trivial to some—will be deferred here and included instead in Chapter 18, where it will again be taken up (under another of its confusingly interchangeable rubrics) as "ethnoscience."

The Ethnography of Speaking

Of the several new approaches being taken in anthropological linguistics, one that is most relevant to the rest of the field of cultural and social anthropology entails study of the ways language, particularly speech, functions as a particular kind of cultural activity. Attention is focused not on the description and analysis of language itself but rather on cultural variations and patterns of speaking. Here the central question relates to the ways different patterns of speech use may affect the sociocultural context in which they occur, and again, as always, the converse: the ways in which the sociocultural context can affect how speech is used. The objective of those who seek to answer this question is the development of a theory of speaking that will parallel theories explaining other aspects of cultural behavior. The "speech event," all that is occurring when two or more people interact verbally, is the core unit of analysis.

So far, most study related to this general question has been directed to such things as the role of speech in the development of personality, the use of speech as a means of interacting socially with others, and the processes by which such communicative competence is acquired.

Speech Use as Cultural Behavior

The essence of the question is a variant on a now familiar theme: Given the universality of language—the variability of specific linguistic forms aside—what are the significant differences in the ways speech is used from people to people, and what do we need to know about these variable functions of language in order to better understand the dynamic interrelationship of language and culture? Implicit in asking such a question is the assumption that answering it may help to more efficiently relate the study of language to the resolution of human problems. Political problems resulting from bi- or multilingualism, educational problems resulting from the need to teach such social dialects as Standard English to speakers of nonstandard dialects, problems in fair assessment of the intelligence of dialect speakers—these are only some of the practical difficulties that can be more efficiently dealt with through a scientifically based understanding of speech as a kind of cultural behavior.

The relation of speech forms used in direct address to the structure of social relationships provides a concrete opportunity to observe in operation the cultural rules that always govern the use of language. Here the issue is not one of grammatical correctness but of the culturally defined appropriateness of the speech form to the social situation in which it is used. For example, in English two basic ways of addressing a male stranger are "Excuse me, sir," and "Hey, you." Both are equally faithful to the structural rules of the language. But one expression is culturally designated as polite or deferential, as indi-

"The 'speech event,' all that is occurring when two or more people interact verbally . . . ."
Figure 17-7. Talking together in Rae-Edzo, Northwest Territories, Canada. (National Film Board of Canada.)

cating the equality or superiority of the person so addressed. Depending on the place, time, attitudes, and social values of those who overhear it, the other phrase is defined as rude, insulting, or even challenging, in accordance with a rule that is not linguistic but cultural. That is, a major aspect of the meaning of the words is derived from the cultural interpretation of how, when, where, and by whom to whom they are spoken. From long and careful observation of the speech behavior of a people it becomes possible to identify such rules. To do so is to engage in an aspect of anthropological linguistics that Hymes has defined as "the ethnography of speaking," a new disciplinary field in anthropological linguistics (Hymes 1962, 1964). The object of study of the scholar interested in the ethnography of speaking is designated by Hymes as "the totality of speech habits of a community." Assuming that "all of the speech activity of the linguistic community is subject to patterning," he defines the researcher's task as the discovery and statement of the rules that govern such use, as these are "implicit in appropriate, or ordinary behavior."

"Learning the rules that govern the use of speech . . . ."
Figure 17-8. Study Hall on Ponape Island, Micronesia. (United Nations.)

With the development of the ethnography of speaking we shall have, as a complement of the rules of grammatically correct usage, a statement of the rules that determine which of several grammatically correct utterances is appropriate to the sociocultural context in which it occurs. These rules go beyond considerations of good and bad manners to encompass such variables as the social position of the speaker and the person addressed (differences in age, sex, social, economic, political, religious, and/or ethnic status) and include also attention to the manifest and latent intentions of the speaker (as in a publicly issued multipurpose joking insult that may allow the speaker to express anger and to communicate indirectly the source of frustration, providing him or her a chance to weaken an adversary's position in the eyes of onlookers and to elicit their support).

Learning the rules that govern the use of speech is quite as important as learning the language itself. Without such understanding the speaker who knows only the rules of grammar and phonology will make frequent, serious social errors. To the speech ethnographer the process of acquiring competence in the socially acceptable use of speech is as important as the analytically separate process by which language is learned. Grammatical correctness and social appropriateness are seen as almost equally critical to the mastery of language use.

The link between speech form and cultural context is particularly apparent in the relationship between ways of speaking and ways of structuring social relationships. It is, for example, the person's position in his or her society that frequently determines both the name—more often, the names—he or she bears and the particular rules that dictate which of them will be used by whom, and when, in addressing him or her. Among the cattle-keeping Nuer of the Sudan the names a male accumulates in the course of his progress through the life cycle both reflect his position in the social structure and provide insight into a variety of other aspects of Nuer culture: the technology and economy, the kinship organization, the system of age grades, the patterning of social life, the authority system, and aspects of Nuer attitudes about the supernatural (Evans-Pritchard 1968). A Nuer youth gets his first name, one he keeps throughout life, from his parents. Later his small friends may give him another, derived often from some attribute of the male calf of one of the cows he is assigned to attend, thus formalizing what is for all Nuer a lifelong relationship of symbiosis between men and their cattle. A third personal name is given to him by his maternal grandparents and functions symbolically to link him to the lineage of his mother. Later he assumes also the name of his father's lineage, the social group to which he always owes primary allegiance. At initiation into manhood he receives a name taken from some aspect of the appearance of the ox he is given at that time. Later, if another animal attracts his special favor, he may take a new ox-name inspired by its appearance. Obviously, he is not called by all these names all the time. When he is grown, his "true name" is used only by age-mates and the members of adjacent age sets. The use of his other names is determined by kinship relations. In his mother's home community he may be addressed by members of her lineage by the personal name they have assigned him; others in her community may call him by his mother's lineage name. If a Nuer man is elderly and deserving of respect, a younger man may address him as "son-of," using his father's name. Conversely, if an older man wants to favor and slightly flatter a younger person, he may use this same respectful form in return.

Which particular linguistic form is selected to address a particular person may be affected not only by considerations of the speaker's relation to the addressee in the social structure but also by a variety of psychological variables, such as the specific history of past associations between the two, their present feelings toward one another, and the circumstances of their meeting (the formality or informality of the occasion, the time and place, and so on).

For the anthropologist, understanding the culturally derived rules that underlie such patterns of linguistic usage is critical. For they reflect important aspects of the culture from which they derive and provide valuable clues in understanding other nonlinguistic rules of behavior: deference to senior kinsmen, informal joking with age-mates,

"Later . . . he may take a new ox-name."

Figure 17-9. The Masai herdsmen of Kenya have a similarly close relationship with their cattle. (United Nations.)

guarded politeness with in-laws. The values of a people are also reflected in the patterned application of such usages: showing respect for those who deserve it because they are fulfilling their expected roles, indifference or contempt for those who fail to achieve the goals defined by the culture as worthy, and so on. Or selection of a particular form of address may function as a significant means of stating the speaker's relationship to the person being addressed and thereby of eliciting from him or her a favorable response: friendliness, attention, cooperation. In a less amiable perspective the form of address selected may serve as a means of controlling intimacy, as a way of maintaining formal social distance and thereby avoiding the unwanted obligation to cooperate that use of an intimate form of address often may evoke.

An illustration of the many-faceted cultural function of terms of address is provided by the continuing conflict in U.S. society between those committed to the maintenance of a rigid system of ethnic stratification and those who want to eradicate it, or at least loosen it up. Here, as is so often the case, sharp differences in language use are a manifestation of societal cleavages, instability, and unrest. For example, the persistent use by some whites of the term *boy* in addressing black male adults functions to state symbolically and to reinforce a status and power inequality. Black Americans' refusal to make the acquiescent, deferential response that in some instances has been defined by traditional usage as appropriate constitutes an increasing challenge to a social system structured to keep them in their culturally designated subordinate "place."

". . . the many-faceted cultural functions of terms of address . . . ."

Figure 17-10. Description by a black psychiatrist of his verbal encounter with a white policeman in Jackson, Mississippi. (Poussaint 1967:53, cited in Kochman 1970:147–148. © 1967 by the New York Times Company. Reprinted by permission.)

Once last year as I was leaving my office in Jackson, Miss., with my Negro secretary, a white policeman yelled, "Hey, boy! Come here!" Somewhat bothered, I retorted: "I'm no boy!" He then rushed at me, inflamed, and stood towering over me, snorting, "What d'ja say, boy?" Quickly he frisked me and demanded, "What's your name, boy?" Frightened, I replied, "Dr. Poussaint; I'm a physician." He angrily chuckled and hissed, "What's your first name, boy?" When I hesitated he assumed a threatening stance and clenched his fists. As my heart palpitated, I muttered in profound humiliation, "Alvin."

He continued his psychological brutality, bellowing, "Alvin, the next time I call you, you come right away, you hear? You hear?" I hesitated. "You hear me, boy?" My voice trembling with helplessness, but following my instincts of self-preservation, *I murmured, "Yes, sir." Now fully satisfied that I had performed and acquiesced to my "boy" status, he dismissed me with, "Now boy, go on and get out of here or next time we'll take you for a little ride down to the station house!"*

Summary

A classic and persistently intriguing question in the subfield of anthropological linguistics called ethnolinguistics concerns the causal relations between linguistic and cultural forms: the ways language may condition perception of reality and the ways language structure may reflect culture, especially the pattern of a people's adaptation to a particular set of environmental circumstances.

Closely related problems are the subject of those interested in ethnosemantics, which is the study of the manner in which the people's linguistically expressed categories may provide insight both into their particular cognitive worlds and into the underlying and possibly similar patterns of thinking that are common to all people—a subject that is also of major concern to the ethnoscientists whose work is discussed in Chapter 18.

Another approach that narrows the

methodological gap between the study of language and that of other aspects of culture is the one taken by students of the ethnography of speaking, an approach in which not language alone but the "speech event" and the cultural rules that govern the use of speech as a social instrument are the objects of study.

The linguistic anthropologist's objective, particularly in the ethnography of speaking, is to develop a way of studying the rules of language use that parallels and interrelates with the anthropological study of the sociocultural constraints that shape all other forms of human behavior.

Suggested Readings

Several of the general works cited for Chapter 16 also cover anthropological linguistics. See also Greenberg's *Anthropological Linguistics,* Garvin's *Method and Theory in Linguistics,* and Gumperz's "Linguistic Anthropology in Society."

On the relation between language and perception see "World View and Grammatical Categories" in Hymes's *Language in Culture and Society: A Reader in Linguistics and Anthropology.* The classic source is *Language, Thought, and Reality: Selected Writings of Benjamin Lee Whorf,* edited by Carroll. See also Hoijer's "The Sapir-Whorf Hypothesis" and Henle's "Language, Thought and Culture."

On ethnosemantics see many of the suggested readings on ethnoscience in Chapter 18. In addition, see "Cultural Focus and Semantic Field" in Hymes's *Language in Culture and Society* and particularly the seminal articles "Hanunóo Color Categories" by Conklin and "The Diagnosis of Disease Among the Subanum of Mindinao" by Frake. A more recent major work is Berlin, Bredlove, and Raven's *Studies in Tzeltal Botanical Ethnography: Principles of Classification.* In addition, see *Formal Semantic Analysis,* edited by Hammel, and *Transcultural Studies in Cognition,* edited by Romney and d'Andrade.

On the ethnography of speaking see both *The Ethnography of Speaking,* edited by Gumperz and Hymes, and Hymes's pioneering article "The Ethnography of Speaking." See *Directions in Sociolinguistics: The Ethnography of Communication,* also edited by Gumperz and Hymes; and *Explorations in the Ethnography of Speaking,* edited by Bauman and Sherzer; and their article "The Ethnography of Speaking." Of related interest are Fishman's *The Sociology of Language: An Interdisciplinary Social Science Approach to Language and Society; Language in Its Social Setting,* edited by Gage; *Language and Social Context: Selected Readings,* edited by Giglioli; Gumperz's *Language in Social Groups;* and Labov's *Sociolinguistic Patterns.*

For some excellent illustrations of the application of the ethnography of speaking to the patterns of language use of a population that has been particularly well studied see Abrahams and Szwed's "Black English: An Essay Review"; *Rappin' and Stylin' Out,* edited by Kochman; Kochman's "Toward an Ethnography of Black American Speech Behavior"; Labov's *Language in the Inner City: Studies in the Black English Vernacular;* Mitchell-Kernan's "Speech Acts in a Black Urban Community: Signifying, Loud Talking, and Marking"; and Wolfram and Clark's *Black-White Speech Relations.* Of related interest is Labov's excellent *The Social Stratification of English in New York City.*

Part Nine

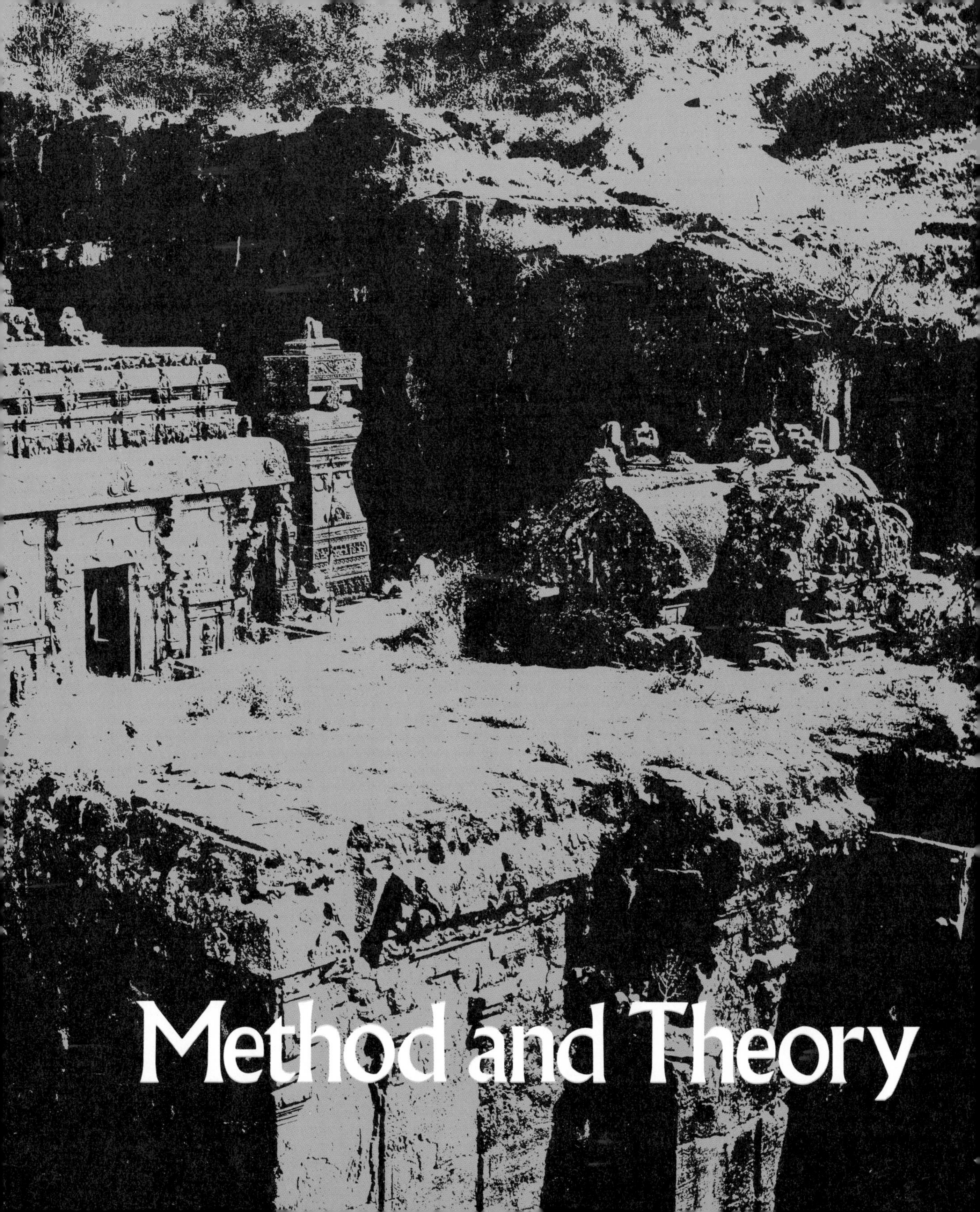
Method and Theory

Unless anthropology is to interest itself mainly in the unique, exotic, and non-recurrent particulars, it is necessary that formulations be attempted no matter how tentative they may be. It is formulations that will enable us to state new kinds of problems and to direct attention to new kinds of data which have been slighted in the past. Fact-collecting of itself is insufficient scientific procedure; facts exist only as they are related to theories, and theories are not destroyed by facts—they are replaced by new theories which better explain the facts.

STEWARD (1955a:209)

By now there are a variety of well-developed methodological and theoretical approaches in cultural and social anthropology. Some of them are so respectably established or so tenaciously protected by the powerful egos of their importantly placed protagonists that they are known as "schools."

What follows is an effort to indicate some of the issues and methods of analysis that are associated with the most prominent of these approaches, in a logical series that is partly chronological, although no history of anthropological theory is attempted. Many of these approaches, regarded as antithetical by their most committed adherents, can be productively combined. This is not to suggest the vacuous sort of theoretical eclecticism that is a frequent cop-out. Rather, it is intended as an argument against the kind of theoretical orthodoxy that can prevent a scholar from making use of whatever combination of methods and theories helps him or her best to understand the problem at hand.

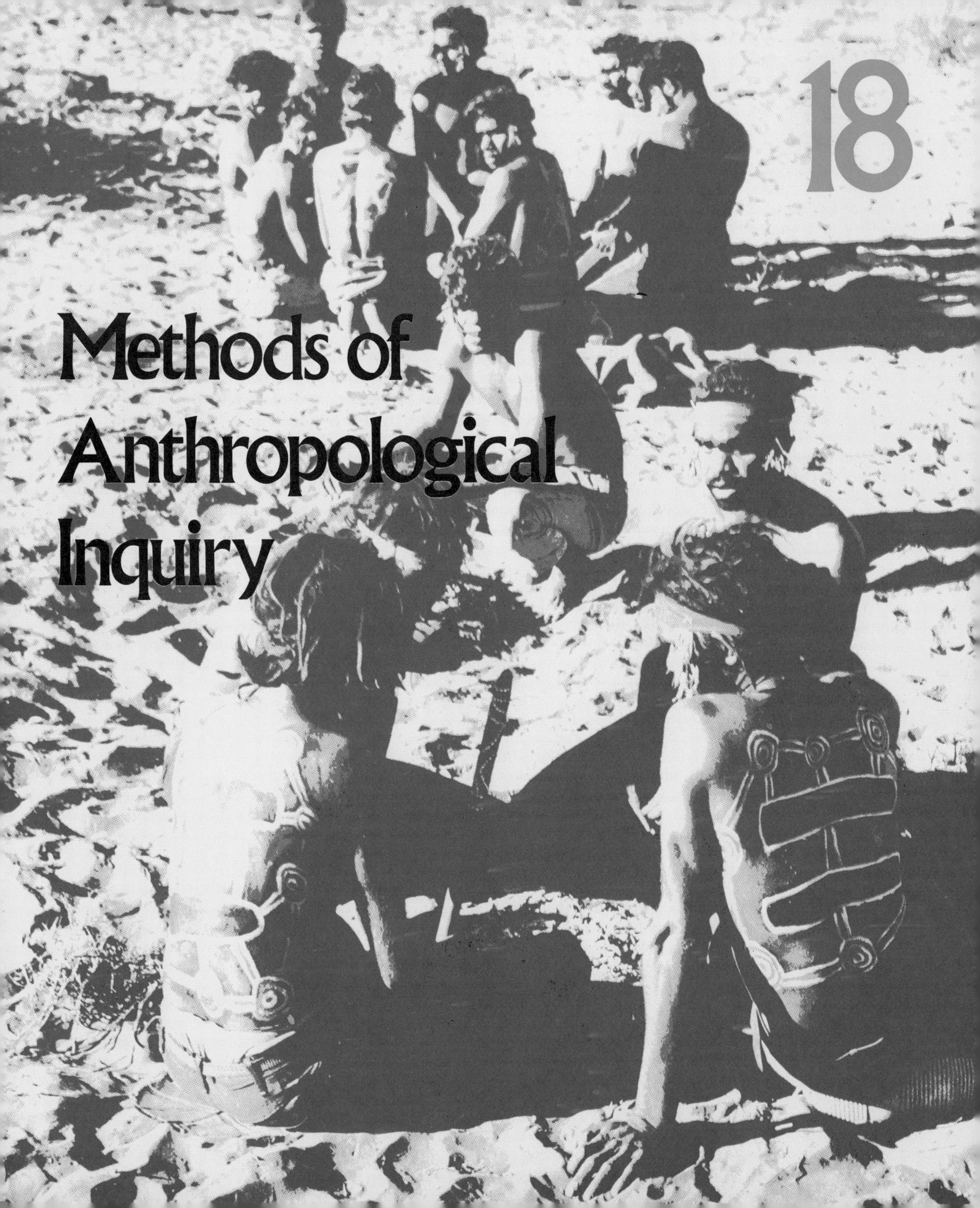

18

Methods of Anthropological Inquiry

At the outset of this book the subject of how and why culture is studied was briefly discussed, with some mention of how anthropologists work in the field and of the ways in which the ethnographic data on which all anthropological theory is based are processed and analyzed. The major aspects of culture studied by the anthropologist in the field and in the library were listed as a means of introducing the parts of the book that followed, beginning with technology and economic organization and continuing through social and political organization and ideology to the arts and language.

The description of these various aspects of culture was never "pure," nor was their sequential organization a decision made at random. From the outset, materials on the fundamental aspects of culture (even, obviously, the decision as to what aspects of culture were and were not "fundamental") have been accompanied by theoretical interpretation—inevitably.

Description must be theoretically structured or one would not know what information to include and how to present it, nor would one know what to leave out. Unavoidably, various aspects of anthropological method have already been considered. Now is the time and here is the place to extend this consideration and make it more explicit, beginning with further consideration of the methods anthropologists use in gathering the data on which theory is later built.

Ethnography, Old and "New"

An ethnography is a descriptive account of the way of life, or culture, of the people living in a particular society. All of cultural and social anthropology is based fundamentally on ethnographic data gathered by anthropologists working "in the field," living among and studying the way of life of particular peoples. The data are the raw material of theory building and testing that make anthropology a science. Beyond the anthropologist's personal problems of getting the grant necessary to get to the field, ideally he or she should be a paragon of personal and professional virtues: adaptable yet disciplined and persistent; compassionate yet able to be a stoic when professional performance requires it; energetic yet capable of patience and restraint; tough enough to withstand physical discomfort yet sufficiently self-aware not to be overconfident; curious yet discreet and respectful of informants' privacy; responsive to the feelings of others yet sufficiently stable and secure to remain psychologically comfortable and capable of functioning among people whose feelings toward him or her are likely to range from overt hostility and suspicion through indifference and guarded tolerance to cooperation and occasional lasting friendship.

In a more strictly professional sense (although all the formal methodological expertise in the world won't do any good if a person can't get along with the people he or she plans to study), the ethnographer must, of course, be well trained, with a command of anthropological method and theory sufficiently extensive to enable him or her to organize research objectives and to proceed systematically toward them, yet always remaining prepared to fall back on alternative methods and theories made necessary by changes in the field situation—drought, an epidemic, the outbreak of war, or the unforeseen discovery of information that irrevocably alters the original research objectives. And despite the best-laid research plans the ethnographer will always make some of his or her most valuable findings by accident.

An investigator must be aware of and capable of coping with the hazards entailed in acquiring an adequate sample of the cultural behavior being recorded as this may be affected by circumstances never entirely

"... although all the formal methodological expertise in the world won't do any good if a person can't get along with the people he or she plans to study ...."

Figure 18-1. A potential informant eyes the anthropologist skeptically, Mali. (Hammond.)

controllable: his or her sex, age, and, inevitably, status as a strange-looking, oddly behaved outsider whose mere presence instantly contaminates the "purity" of whatever cultural event is being observed. To obtain a representative sample of the way of life of the people being studied the ethnographer will try to gather information from persons of both sexes and as many different ages, social positions, and locales as possible. The worker will try to complement observations made in the present by collecting accounts of the past and will check the accuracy of individual informants' accounts by asking the same questions of others. To the extent possible he or she will use the subjects' language. But more than a rough working knowledge of their language is often necessary to verify details and to be certain of having caught all the important nuances in an informant's explanation of the intricacies of pig raising, marketing yams, making a proper marriage, casting a spell, or reciting a prayer. The right interpreter can be a valuable informant and guide to the anthropologist in avoiding serious blunders in learning how to get along in an unfamiliar culture; the wrong one, a low-status person in a stratified society or an unpopular person involved in community factionalism, can be a disaster.

Traditionally, the anthropologist settles for a year or more among the people he or she is studying. By acting as a neutral but

"... from persons of both sexes and as many different ages, social positions, and locales as possible."

Figure 18-2. More potential informants. Haliwa teenagers dressed for a Pow Wow, North Carolina. (Azar Hammond.)

cooperative community member the fieldworker tries gradually to allay his or her new neighbors' natural suspicions that an outsider may be a government spy or may have come to steal their land or to lead an insurrection.

By developing the role of an apparently harmless person who can possibly be of occasional use in providing aspirin or transportation to the dispensary, in floating a small loan or in filling out a money order, and in making gifts from what usually appears to be an abundant store of riches, the anthropologist tries to develop a network of reciprocal ties that will make him or her as socially acceptable as any exotic outsider can ever hope to become. Some such measure of social acceptability must be achieved if a fieldworker is to be able to observe the life of the community and gradually be permitted to participate in some of its affairs. This does not mean that one "goes native" but rather that one tries to assume a role that both is culturally acceptable to the people and allows for the maintenance of one's own sense of identity and integrity. To the impressions gained by these general means—usually termed participant observation—may be added such more formal efforts at data gathering as mapping, census taking, interviewing, filming, recording, collecting genealogies and life histories, keeping a careful journal, and in some instances administering a variety of projective tests.

Most importantly, the anthropologist will be guided by his or her theoretical orientation and by the particular anthropological "problem" that is of interest—the economic and social repercussions of a people's switch from dry farming to wet rice cultivation; the function of puberty rites in internalizing adult sex roles; the effect of kinship on channeling the inheritance of property; the impact of modern medicine on traditional curing practices; the correlation of variations in dance style with differences in ethnic origin—and by the particular body of theory that is used to analyze such problems. The specific subject the anthropologist has selected before going to the field will structure both the research design and the way it should be carried out. For a reminder of data that might otherwise not be recorded the anthropologist may rely on such guides as *Notes and Queries* and G. P. Murdock's *Outline of World Cultures.* But primarily the worker will be guided by his or her own principal theoretical interests, by those questions about society and culture he or she wants most to comprehend and, ultimately, be able to answer. Usually one elects to work among a particular group of people because one already knows enough about their way of life to strongly suspect that studying among them would be helpful in finding answers to some of the questions he or she finds of greatest professional concern.

If a study is successful, after a year or so the result of all this effort will be a reasonably well-organized body of information that usually will require one's leaving the field to analyze and rework until it is ready to be shared with others through the preparation of books, articles, films and recordings, in consulting, and in the classroom.

So far, this is the way most anthropological inquiry has been conducted. There are, however, those anthropologists who argue persuasively for a major innovation in this still standard approach, for a particular way of studying culture that is called by some the "new ethnography."

Ethnoscience

Ethnoscience, as this new ethnography is also called, entails a relatively recent and somewhat controversial perspective on cultural and social anthropology. Major emphasis is on the development of a methodology that will yield data as free as possible of contamination by the observer's own culturally conditioned biases. As already indicated, ethnoscience is closely allied to the study of language, especially to the study of the implicitly common set of meanings that underlie all language. The conceptual model is partially taken from phonemics, the branch of linguistics that seeks an objective, value-free means of recording the basic or significant sound units of language. Ethnoscience also has important links with ethnosemantics. Both entail extensive methodological attention to ascertaining the meanings given to aspects of a culture as these are expressed in the language of native speakers fully participating in their traditional society.

Ethnoscience shares with transformational grammar the goal of developing a descriptive ethnography that can be used to state the rules of appropriate or acceptable cultural behavior in much the same way as a grammar can be used to state and to predict correct linguistic behavior. According to the tenets of ethnoscience, the adequacy of the anthropologist's ethnographic description is measured by the extent to which it provides an accurate and economical basis for correctly anticipating the "natives'" culturally appropriate behavior under all culturally possible circumstances. In other words, what is sought by the ethnoscientist is the full set of rules that guides all facets of behavior in every possible situation within a particular society. What is already known is used to generate further questions about native informants' knowledge of their culture.

Rather than imposing his or her own culturally derived categories on the way of life of the people being studied—collecting data according to the outlined categories of culture suggested by the organization of this book, for example—the ethnoscientifically oriented anthropologist sets out to deal with what is seen as the more basic task: developing a means of ethnographic observation and recording that is as free as possible of interference from the investigator's own culturally conditioned biases. A major part of this task is learning how the people being studied perceive their world and the relationships among its parts. It is intended that this effort to uncover a people's cognitive

". . . to state the rules of appropriate or acceptable cultural behavior . . . ."
Figure 18-3. In ritual seclusion following an initiation ceremony, Australia. (Courtesy of the American Museum of Natural History.)

system—their subjective explanation of the world and how it works—should not only contribute to a universal theory of human cognition but also allow for more efficient ascertainment of whether the aspects of culture the anthropologist abstracts for cross-cultural comparison are in fact truly comparable in meaning as well as form.

So far, work in ethnoscience has strongly emphasized study of cross-cultural differences in people's systems of categorization: their methods for defining the component elements of their reality and for establishing the boundaries between them, and their culturally determined criteria for classifying them. A pioneering application of the ethnoscientific method was developed by Conklin (1955) in reporting on the color-categorizing system of the Hanunóo, a Philippine people whose perceptual judgments of color differences were found to be modified by the nonsensory, cultural significance ascribed to various objects. Such judgments included consideration of attributes that are not at all a part of the category *color* as it is defined in English. Frake has used a study of disease diagnosis among another Philippine people as a means of uncovering their cognitive system. By discovering their culturally determined criteria for ascribing relevance and thus for categorizing the various maladies from which they suffer, he seeks to better understand the way their thought processes affect their perception of and reaction to objective reality.

A major value of the ethnoscientific approach lies in its emphasis on trying to understand the component aspects of a people's culture as the people themselves perceive them, a step defined by those who favor this approach as being of first necessity in raising "the standards of reliability, validity, and exhaustiveness in ethnography" (Sturtevant 1964:123). The ethnoscientific method has been criticized for the emphasis it places on cultural rules, an emphasis that may detract attention from the important process by which people develop new, alternative cultural "rules" in order to adapt to evolving circumstances (Harris 1974). Those who question its utility also reject its idealist orientation and the temptation it offers for the anthropologist to become so absorbed in seeing the culture he or she is studying as the people see it themselves as to risk impairment of the capacity for detachment, abstraction, comparison, and analysis; becoming so engrossed in thinking as the "natives" think that he or she may lose track of the scholar's necessarily culture-bound responsibilities to his discipline (see Berreman 1966; Harris 1968b).

The Historical Approach

To understand the processes that have led to development of a particular way of life, it is always essential to explore a people's past, to uncover as much information as possible about the antecedent circumstances that appear to have led to their living as they do in the present. Historical investigation is a major dimension of anthropological inquiry, one that entails reliance on an approach that raises some particularly complex methodological problems.

Among the nonliterate peoples with whom anthropologists have traditionally worked, historical reconstruction is usually complicated by the lack of written records. Frequently, documentary evidence on the past dates back only as far as their first contact with literate outsiders, usually European colonizers. For parts of sub-Saharan Africa and for many areas of the Pacific and the Americas this record extends back only a few hundred years. For some of the geographically and culturally isolated groups living in the equatorial rainforests of South America and in the still partially unexplored interior of New Guinea, written records go

"... and in the still partially unexplored interior of New Guinea ...."

Figure 18-4. A Melanesian family scene. (Courtesy of the Library of Congress.)

back no more than a decade, and are frequently scanty at that.

By necessity, anthropologists trying to put together a congruent picture of the past of a nonliterate, little-known people usually rely on a variety of nondocumentary sources of historical evidence. Some may be archaeological, based on clues derived from analysis of the material remains of the way of life of a people's forebears. Other evidence is linguistic, derived from analysis of the people's language as this may reveal genetic or diffusional resemblances with the speech of neighbors or more distant peoples, in either case a sure sign of past cultural contact and possibly of shared cultural origins.

Another important source of historical evidence is provided by comparative ethnography. Comparison of the way of life of the group under study with what is known of the culture of other peoples, usually those close by, often reveals similarities that strongly support the possibility of cultural borrowing and the likelihood of an at least partially similar or shared past.

Diffusion and the Transmission of Culture Traits

Study of diffusion, the processes by which culture traits are transmitted from group to group throughout usually wide geographic areas, has, especially in the past, been a useful adjunct to other efforts at historical reconstruction.

". . . similarities that strongly support the possibility of cultural borrowing . . . ."

Figure 18-5. Although still culturally distinctive, the aboriginal peoples of Himachal Pradesh have adopted many of the ways of their Indian compatriots. (Press Information Bureau, Government of India.)

". . . the spread of the use of tobacco is a classic example . . . ."
Figure 18-6. Half way around the world from the place where the use of tobacco originated, a Gujarati farmer smokes his pipe. (Government of India, Information Services.)

Study of the spread of the use of tobacco is a classic example of such cultural borrowing (Linton 1936). The custom of smoking tobacco originated among Indians somewhere in the region of Peru, Bolivia, or Argentina and spread from there throughout most of the Americas. It was first taken to Portugal and Spain in the mid-sixteenth century. From court circles in Madrid and Lisbon smoking spread to the commoner classes throughout the countryside and on through the rest of Europe, around the Mediterranean to the Middle East, on from there to Asia and Africa, and finally to the Pacific islands. At last, about three hundred years later, it had been diffused all the way around the world and was reintroduced to the Americas at Alaska.

Diffusion studies date back to the nineteenth century. There were once several "diffusionist" schools, each with a slightly different approach. But the premises from which they proceeded and the methods of analysis they followed were essentially similar. All of them, for example, tended to disregard or deemphasize independent invention as a process of much significance in understanding the means by which people develop new aspects of culture, contending that it was easier for people to borrow new ways of behaving, new institutions, and new artifacts from others than it was to discover or invent them for themselves. Most diffusionists were similarly inattentive to processes of cultural evolution. It was cultural transmission that most interested them. Unless evidence for independent origins was very strong, similar traits observed in separate cultures were generally assumed to be the result of borrowing by diffusion. The more simplistic of these studies argued that most of the discoveries important to the cultural history of mankind had been made in ancient times, in only a few areas, and principally during a few periods of extraordinary cultural creativity.

The diffusionists' premise that it is usually easier for people to borrow and to adapt new behaviors, institutions, and artifacts from others rather than to invent or discover them for themselves is correct. The error was in overemphasizing this factor. The diffusionists were also careless in determining the similarities they used as evidence to support their ideas. For similarity of form is no sure indicator of similarity of function.

Historical "Particularism"

In the United States a major response to some of the methodological and theoretical excesses of the diffusionists (and to the work of some early cultural evolutionists described in the next chapter) was a strong, often atheoretical, emphasis on the careful reconstruction of the history of particular people, with minimal attention to cultural borrowing. An even more cautious approach was taken to efforts at historical generalizing, that is, to the search for those regularities in culture change through time that may ultimately be stated as laws. Franz Boas, one of the founders of the historical approach in American anthropology and the teacher of more than a dozen of this century's most prominent anthropologists, took the position that before anthropology could engage further in what he saw as grandiose, often unsupportable contentions about the forces shaping the culture history of all humankind, it was necessary to carefully collect far more data on the particular cultures, and the particular culture histories, of particular peoples. The meticulous collection of ethnographic and ethnohistorical data, as opposed to "premature generalizing," was central to Boas's definition of the anthropologist's task.

Where generalization was permitted, it took the cautious form of plotting the spread of culture traits over limited geographic areas, computing them, and drawing general inferences about the similar distinctive features of cultures throughout what was defined, on the basis of these similarities, as a single culture area.

"The meticulous collection of ethnographic and ethnohistorical data . . . ."

Figure 18-7. On the relationship of the age grade system of these Nandi warriors to those of neighboring East African peoples, for example.

The value of the culture area approach derives from the system it provides for clustering together the essentially similar ways of life of neighboring groups into area-wide categories according to an agreed-on set of criteria. Frequently, emphasis has been on the correlation between particular types of natural environment and particular patterns of technological adaptation, although the theoretical importance of such correlations is generally ignored. Driver (1971), for example, has divided the many hundreds of Indian groups in North America into seventeen culture areas stretching from the Arctic to Panama. Herskovits (1945) took a similar approach to classifying the culture areas of Africa.

In contrast to other efforts at historical reconstruction, which are often criticized as hopelessly conjectural because there are none of the documents that some historians consider indispensable to respectable scholarship, the cultural contacts between "Western" and "non-Western" peoples resulting from European conquest and colonization usually are a matter of written record (although such records often have been biased to justify colonialism as bestowing the blessings of civilization and freedom on benighted savages). The study of colonial conquest brought a shift from the examination of cultural borrowing in the distant past to study of the processes of such borrowing as it was occurring contemporaneously, especially among the indigenous peoples of the Americas—and also in other parts of the world where colonialist expansion and its aftermath were having an equally violent impact on the traditional cultures of native peoples. The emphasis in historical studies on borrowing moved from the diffusionists' concentration on the listing of culture traits and the meticulous plotting of their spread to concern with understanding the conditions under which people do and do not borrow from one another: how borrowing occurs and what happens to a culture trait once transmitted, incorporated into the context of another people's way of life, and adapted to their needs.

Acculturation

A distinction developed between the kind of borrowing studied by the diffusionists, which was not necessarily the result of direct contact, and acculturation, defined as the

"Herskovits . . . took a similar approach to classifying the culture areas of Africa."
Figure 18-8. The heavier lines mark "boundaries" between culture areas. Broken lines show political frontiers established under European colonial control. (After Herskovits.)

process of borrowing that occurs between groups with different cultures who are in prolonged face-to-face interaction (Redfield and others 1936). Where, for the first time in modern history, Europeans were coming into direct and prolonged contact with non-European peoples a situation was created that facilitated the study of the transmission of cultural traits from one group to another as it was happening or as it had occurred within the memory of those still living. Study of this kind of cultural borrowing was facilitated by the usually sharp contrast between the two or more cultures so juxtaposed, by the coexistence of sectors in which the traditional culture persisted and of other sectors in which rapid sociocultural change was occurring, by the anthropologists' personal familiarity with the variant of European culture involved, and by the frequent availability of written records describing circumstances at the time of and following initial contact between aboriginal peoples and foreign explorers and would-be settlers.

Identified as a particular variation of the more general process of culture change, acculturation was defined by Herskovits, a pioneer student of the subject, as "the study of cultural transmission in process"; diffusion was distinguished as the study of cultural transmission that had already been achieved (Herskovits 1950:525).

Most acculturation studies are diachronic; that is, attention is given to both past and present events. Herskovits's work in West Africa and among the descendants of West Africans forcibly resettled in the Americas provides a classic illustration of the design that acculturation studies can take. To determine the general character and the specific regional and temporal variations in the culture captive Africans brought with them to the New World, his studies always took as their point of departure what he termed the "historical baseline" (Herskovits 1966:49).

Following this approach, it was first necessary to develop an accurate picture of what the culture of the blacks was like at the time of initial contact with their white captors. Two principal kinds of data were used to construct such a picture. The first were accounts written by witnesses to the early stages of contact. Careful analysis of these amateur but often rich documentary sources was particularly useful in determining the major regional and tribal origins of Africans brought to the New World. Most of these documents are found in libraries, government archives, and the records of European and American slave-trading firms (see Donnan 1965). The second are modern ethnographic accounts, the results of recent anthropological fieldwork in the areas from which the slaves were taken. In many of the rural areas in the interior of West Africa the rate of culture change has been relatively slow, and many of the fundamental aspects of indigenous culture persist, especially the traditional means of making a living and of organizing family and community life. Aspects of traditional religion are also still present, although Islam and Christianity are gaining ground fast in some regions. Many traditional art forms and, of course, indigenous languages have been retained as well.

Combined and carefully analyzed data from these two major sources, one documentary and the other ethnographic, provide the basis for developing a good general picture of what life was like in West Africa when the first Europeans sailed down along the coast in the late fifteenth century. Records kept by the traders at the coastal forts, on the slave ships, and in the slave markets of the Americas by white masters and some slaves (see Curtin 1968) are helpful in developing an equally accurate general picture of the conditions under which contacts and

"... many of the fundamental aspects of indigenous culture persist ...."
Figure 18-9. A traditional chief and his retainers, Accra, Ghana. (United Nations.)

cultural borrowing between the two groups first occurred.

Further understanding of the processes of acculturation operative in this instance is provided by the results of anthropological fieldwork conducted among the descendants of West Africans resettled throughout the Americas: on the islands of the Caribbean and in South, Central, and North America. Herskovits himself worked both in West Africa—in Dahomey, Nigeria, and Ghana—and in black communities in Haiti, Trinidad, Surinam, and Brazil.

Through comparative analysis of the sort done principally by Herskovits and also by some of his students—on Nigerian religious influences in Cuba (see Bascom 1950), on Afro-American music (Waterman 1952), on possession by West African spirits in Trinidad (Simpson 1965), on belief in zombies in

"Many traditional art forms ... have been retained as well."
Figure 18-10. Yoruba helmet mask, Nigeria. (Courtesy of the Museum of Primitive Art.)

". . . and on the Afro-American cultural heritage in general . . . ."
Figure 18-11. Design traced in the sand at the beginning of a voodoo ceremony in Haiti to invoke the West African deity Elegbara, known in Haiti as Papa Legba and as St. Anthony. (After Maximilien n.d.)

Haiti (Bourgignon 1959), on Afro-Colombian religious beliefs (Price 1955), and on the Afro-American cultural heritage in general (see Simpson and Hammond 1960; Hammond 1970)—what is known of the West African past is combined with what is observable in the present in West Africa and in black communities throughout the Americas to develop a dynamic perspective on the ongoing processes of cultural borrowing from the time when West Africans and Europeans first came into contact to the present.

Perhaps partly because of the advantages of having access to written historical records in studying the consequences of culture contact between European and "native" peoples in many parts of the world, the equally important subject of acculturation between non-Western groups—the results of contact between neighboring tribal groups in Africa, in aboriginal America, and among the peoples of Asia and the Pacific—has so far received much less attention. Such an omission tends to perpetuate the ethnocentric implication that the only contacts that have resulted in significant borrowing and sociocultural change among non-Western peoples have been contacts with Europeans and Euroamericans.

Ethnohistory

Partially in an effort to rectify this and to overcome or compensate for difficulties resulting from lack of reliable written records on the history of nonliterate peoples, many anthropologists are becoming interested in developing techniques for the use of such peoples' orally transmitted historical traditions—narratives, legends, sagas, anecdotes, hearsay accounts transmitted by word of mouth—to acquire a time-depth perspective on the past events that have shaped their present way of life (see Vansina 1965, 1973).

Scholars whose work emphasizes the use of such oral traditions as well as written records are often identified with a subfield that overlaps with acculturation studies but has come to have the separate title of ethnohistory. As long as there are controls for the possible distortions that can result from informants' culturally conditioned differences in perception of temporal, spatial, and sequential relationships and in concepts concerning the relative significance of particular events, from each teller's tendency to add to the story his or her own stylistic twist, and from the possibility that some details may be forgotten and that others may be embellished for aesthetic or ideological effect, analysis of such tales is one of the several valuable means by which the anthropologist uses ethnohistorical techniques in trying to put together a picture of a people's past, an important aspect of which is frequently the chronicle of contacts, conflicts, and cultural exchanges with others.

Although such traditions are not often fully accurate in either specific details or

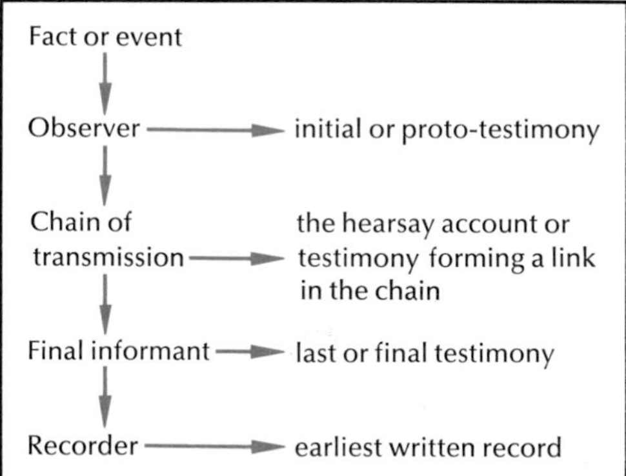

"... analysis of such tales is one of the several valuable means by which the anthropologist uses ethnohistorical techniques in trying to put together a picture of a people's past . . . ."

Figure 18-12. Schematic representation of the chain of transmission by word of mouth from the fact or event observed to the first written record. (Vansina 1965:21.)

precise chronology, they can be combined with other sorts of information—archaeological and linguistic evidence on past migrations and the possibility of cultural borrowing and such "chronological indicators" as genealogies, documented contacts with literate peoples, dated natural phenomena like earthquakes, floods, and eclipses of the sun recalled in the course of telling tales—to help anthropologists fill out a picture of what a people's past way of life was like and to develop an understanding of the historical circumstances and cultural processes that combined to produce the particular patterned way of living the people follow in the present.

Such a history serves anthropologists in two ways. It deepens their understanding of the major antecedent events that have shaped the contemporary culture of a given people. And it provides them with another particular case that may ultimately be used in the cautious collection of historical data that must precede construction of the testable hypotheses about causality that can lead to better explanations of the processes by which all cultures change.

Controlled Cross-Cultural Comparison

An important method in the study of society and culture relies heavily on ethnographic fieldwork as the source of its data yet is usually conducted away from "the field" in libraries, in archives, and at computer centers. It is generally called the comparative method and is used in statistically testing generalizations about culture that are drawn from study of a usually large and always carefully compiled sample of the world's societies. Although based on data acquired through fieldwork, the comparative method is heavily dependent, also, on reliable historical information as a means of validating generalizations about causality—about the cause-and-effect relationship between aspects of culture as they evolve through time.

A primary focus of attention among anthropologists who use the comparative method is the adequacy of the sample of world societies selected for comparison and the accuracy of the quantification, coding, and other procedures imposed on such a sample to yield theoretically useful results.

Comparison of data drawn from a number of historically unrelated cultures as a means to validate generalizations about the causal relationships that appear to exist between the component aspects of culture dates back at least as far as the eighteenth century. In the past it was given most attention by scholars who saw in it a means of hypothetically reconstructing the chronology of earlier stages of cultural evolution. The premise basic to this approach has already been mentioned in referring to the interrelationship of ethnography, archaeology, and technology. Essentially, it is that at any particular level of technological development the structure and function of most other aspects of culture are likely to vary within a fairly limited range, a specific version of the old concept of "limited possibilities."

In applying this method to the analysis of anthropological materials, it might, for example, be assumed that under a given set of environmental and technological conditions only a limited number of cultural forms were possible—only those sufficiently adaptive to provide for the society members' survival. It appears to follow that all people who make their living by hunting and gathering or by primitive farming, for example, are likely, no matter where (allowing for some variation depending on the relative richness of habitat) or when they have lived, to have similarly organized economic and social systems, similarly rudimentary political systems, and similarly structured systems of belief about the supernatural.

Following the logic of this approach it could then be assumed that the comparative study of a representative sample of contemporary peoples with relatively primitive technologies might validate statistically a correlation between a comparatively rudimentary pattern of technoenvironmental adaptation and certain other sociocultural forms—of family organization and economy, for example, or of political organization or ideology. Once established for the present, such a correlation could be tested against historical data to ascertain which came first, the particular means of making a living or the particular family structure, thus strongly suggesting the correct causal linkage between sociocultural forms. Early application of the comparative method, especially by Tylor (1865) and by Keller (1915), was directed to just this sort of effort at reconstructing the cultural evolutionary record.

However, in more recent years those who have contributed most to the elaboration of the comparative method have either disregarded or deemphasized the role of technological factors in determining the cross-cultural regularities revealed by their carefully controlled comparison of data drawn from a sampling of the world's societies.

The most sophisticated approach associated with current interest in the comparative method is based on use of the Human Relations Area Files (HRAF) developed initially by Murdock at Yale as a means of processing ethnographic data in such a way that statistical techniques could be applied to them in order to generate and test hypotheses about causality. Constantly expanded as new information becomes available on the cultures represented, the Human Relations Area Files are available at most major universities in the United States and abroad. They now contain nearly five hundred thousand pages of source materials based on independent studies of several hundred cultures. Ethnographic data drawn from all the major culture areas of the world are categorized and duplicated on slips that are filed in accordance with a sophisticated system of coding. This allows the researcher to locate quickly the specific data he or she needs on any of several hundred aspects of many hundreds of cultures. And the HRAF bank of data is constantly being expanded. A researcher interested in assembling quantitative evidence to support a hypothesis concerning the significance of a correlation between any two or more aspects of culture can readily extract from the files the data necessary for a statistical test of validity.

The principal difficulty encountered by those who rely extensively on the comparative method relates to the adequacy and accuracy of data included in the sample. Obviously no conclusion can be better than the information on which it is based.

There are several dimensions to the problem of accumulating the adequate samples that are the raw material of statistical validation. Many cultures have been studied by only a single anthropologist, who is therefore the only source of data. If there is only one witness, how are the data to be controlled for errors of fact, interpretation, and omission? There is the question of selecting for comparison units that are truly comparable. As Galton put it nearly a century ago in criticizing a pioneering comparative study made by Tylor, it is essential "for the sake of those who wish to study the evidence . . . that full information should be given as to the degree in which the customs of the tribes and races which are compared are independent" (Tylor 1889:270). Much cautious attention is now given to coping with what has come to be known as Galton's Problem, to assuring that cultural comparisons are derived from societies that have developed with maximum independence from one another.

Such aspects of culture must also be truly comparable in function as well as form. This consideration becomes a problem when items are abstracted from the cultural context that defines their meaning. Naroll, for example, has pointed out the pitfalls of a cross-cultural comparison of cannibalism that fails to take into account that human flesh is consumed in some societies to humiliate an enemy, is eaten in others as a means of acquiring an adversary's strength, and among still others is simply regarded as another form of market produce (Naroll 1968:268). Marriage provides another example. Despite the obvious problems of precisely defining such a variable institution in cross-culturally acceptable terms, marriage customs are clearly an aspect of culture that, with appropriate caution, can be usefully compared.

To controls on the accuracy and comparability of ethnographic information must be added attention to the adequacy of coding and the provision of a sufficiently large sample to minimize statistical error.

Murdock used HRAF as his main resource in comparing two hundred and fifty societies from all parts of the world in order to develop and test the important series of hypotheses on kinship that are central to the content of his *Social Structure,* the first major modern work derived from reliance on the comparative method. As we shall see in the next chapter, Whiting and various associates have used the files in the cross-cultural testing of hypotheses about child rearing, often with valuably controversial results (see, for example, Whiting and Child 1953). Young (1965) has used the comparative method in testing a series of hypotheses alternative to those developed by Whiting and others (1958) concerning certain correlations between "the degree of solidarity" characteristic of certain social systems and the prevalence and prominence of initiation rites and other rituals that dramatize status transition and assure the continuity of the existing social order.

Still more recently, Cohen has used the comparative method to check out statistically the cross-cultural recurrence of the often observed correlation (typically described in vague terms of "tendencies" or "trends") between "certain kinds of belief about the afterlife" and certain types of social structure. So far, the results of his comparisons give statistical support to the general proposition that in societies where there is a belief "in the life of the soul after mortal death, the world of the dead is held to be ordered . . . in much the same way as the world of the living." Also supported are such more specific contentions as that there exists a statistically significant correlation between "highly stratified vertically entrenched civil state structures" and the dichotomization of the afterlife into heaven and hell.

Cohen's results indicate that "the promise of an eternal reward of 'heaven'—and the corollary threat of eternal punishment in a 'hell'—is one of the ways in which the ruling classes exact obedience and conformity from the lower classes" (Cohen 1968:414). In each of these instances the generalization that is supported by the comparative method is stated in terms of a statistical probability. A *significant* relationship, presumably *causal* (historical or functional), is strongly suggested. But the concluding statement must still always be made in terms of statistical association, not cause and effect.

For beyond the important discovery that two or more aspects of culture are recurrently associated with a frequency that surpasses chance, we need also to know which came first. The most promising step toward correcting this methodological fault is being taken by those who, like Jorgensen (1966), are suggesting ways of establishing the time relationship between the variables tested for correlation. The problem is difficult to resolve because most reliable ethnographic data on the intangible aspects of culture among nonliterate peoples have been collected only during the last hundred years. That the resultant lack of data with time depth creates a problem for those using the comparative method has been pointed up succinctly by Harris. In contrasting causal factors with ones that are merely predictive, he suggests that the difference between "knowing whether wounds cause gunshots or gunshots cause wounds is not to be taken lightly" (Harris 1968b:621).

As long as the so far unresolved methodological problems in the statistical representation and manipulation of data on so intricately interconnected, symbolically manyfaceted, and volatile a subject as culture are honestly taken into account, the comparative approach can be a highly useful one, particularly when it is employed as an adjunct to other methodological approaches. For although statistical evidence of correlation can never, alone, explain causality, it can indicate to researchers that they are proceeding in a potentially productive direction, that they are on to a possibly significant causal linkage that may then be best further explored using other methods, especially those in which the intellectual energy devoted to statistical precision is complemented by the creativity necessary to generate hypotheses worth testing.

The method of controlled cross-cultural comparison was first developed in anthropology as a means of uncovering those recurrent regularities in culture and in the

". . . a statistically significant correlation between 'highly stratified vertically entrenched civil state structures' and the dichotomization of the afterlife into heaven and hell."

Figure 18-13. Statue of the Buddha at Todaiji Temple, Nara, Japan. In India and throughout Asia Buddhism, with its emphasis on the achievement of nirvana and the avoidance of hell, is recurrently associated with highly stratified social systems. (Information Section, Embassy of Japan.)

processes of culture change that could be hypothesized, tested, and ultimately stated as laws. Although not yet entirely fulfilled, the comparative method still holds promise of providing the solid quantifiable evidence needed for building sound theory.

Summary

Despite many scholars' earnest emphasis on "objective" ethnographic description, methods of anthropological inquiry can never be wholly separated from questions of theory. It is always some theoretical stance that structures the ethnographers' approach to work in the field, what they observe there, and how they record it. Recently the proper conduct of fieldwork has itself become the explicit subject of serious theoretical debate. Innovations in the traditional role of participant observation have been suggested by some anthropologists who propose a more objective "new ethnography," ethnoscience.

Concern for the kind of accurate ethnographic data collection necessary for compilation of cross-culturally comparable data has been an important influence in the development of ethnoscience. To increase the effectiveness of their perceptions, anthropologists working in the field are encouraged to discard their own culturally conditioned system of seeing and categorizing reality in order to perceive the world more nearly as the people being studied see it, thus allowing for less distortion in description.

The historical method of anthropological inquiry encompasses a variety of techniques for reconstructing the cultural past of societies lacking written records. Archaeology, linguistics, comparative ethnography, study of diffusion and acculturation, ethnohistory, and collection and analysis of oral literary traditions may all be programmatically combined to create a picture of the antecedent circumstances, and the processes of their combination, that have produced the pattern of a contemporary people's way of life.

In recent decades generalizations concerning causality that were in the past made in imprecise terms of tendencies and trends have increasingly been tested statistically against a growing sample of carefully coded information on a major portion of the world's cultures. The Human Relations Area Files are a principal source of data for such testing. As remaining problems relating to the adequacy and accuracy of sampling are overcome, especially to assure the independence of the items compared, and as increased attention is given to the collection of data with the time depth essential to statistical support of statements of causality, the contribution of the method of controlled cross-cultural comparison to the status of anthropology as a science is certain to be enhanced.

Suggested Readings

There are now several excellent collections of articles on ethnographic fieldwork. For some good examples see *Marginal Natives: Anthropologists at Work,* edited by Freilich; *Women in the Field: Anthropological Experiences,* edited by Golde; and *Being an Anthropologist: Field Work in Eleven Cultures,* edited by Spindler. See also a number of the selections in *A Handbook of Method in Cultural Anthropology,* edited by Naroll and Cohen; especially "Entree into the Field," by Cohen, Langness, Middleton, Uchendu, and Vanstone. Glazer's *The Research Adventure: Promise and Problems in Field Work* is also of value, as are Hatfield's "Fieldwork: Toward a Model of Mutual Exploitation," Kimball and Watson's *Crossing Cultural Bounda-*

ries, and Wax's excellent *Doing Field Work: Warnings and Advice.* See as well sections of Pelto's *Anthropological Research: The Structure of Inquiry.*

Among the most interesting accounts by anthropologists of doing fieldwork among particular peoples are Chagnon's *Studying the Yanomamo,* Berreman's *Behind Many Masks: Ethnography and Impression Management in a Himalayan Village,* Gearing's *The Face of the Fox,* and McTaggart's *Wolf That I Am: In Search of the Red Earth People.* On the use of life histories as a means of gaining insight into the workings of a people's way of life see Langness's *The Life History in Anthropological Science,* and, as examples of the method applied, Lewis's classic *The Children of Sanchez,* Lurie's *Mountain Wolf Woman,* and Du Bois's *People of Alor: A Social Psychological Study of an East Indian Island.*

On the use of film in the field see Collier's *Visual Anthropology: Photography as a Research Method.*

For a good sampling of the extensive literature on ethnoscience see *Basic Color Terms: Their Universality and Evolution,* by Berlin and Kay; *Principles of Tzeltal Plant Classification,* by Berlin, Breedlove, and Raven; Conklin's "Hanunóo Color Categories" and his *Folk Classification;* Goodenough's *Description and Comparison in Cultural Anthropology; Transcultural Studies in Cognition,* edited by Romney and d'Andrade; Tyler's *Cognitive Anthropology;* and Werner and Fenton's "Method and Theory in Ethnoscience or Ethnoepistemology." For three critiques of the ethnoscientific approach see Berreman's "Anemic and Emetic Analysis in Social Anthropology," Harris's "'Emics,' 'Etics,' and the 'New Ethnography,'" and his "Why a Perfect Knowledge of All the Rules One Must Know to Act Like a Native Cannot Lead to the Knowledge of How Natives Act."

On the historical method in anthropological inquiry see Vansina's "Cultures Through Time"; Sturtevant's "Anthropology, History, and Ethnohistory"; Pitt's *Using Historical Sources in Anthropology and Sociology;* Lewis's *History and Social Anthropology;* Herskovits's *Acculturation: The Study of Culture Contact;* and, on the work of a pioneer, *The Anthropology of Franz Boaz,* edited by Goldschmidt. Four good examples of the application of the historical method are Hickerson's *The Chippewa and Their Neighbors: A Study of Ethnohistory,* Leacock and Levine's *North American Indians in Historical Perspective,* McCall's *Africa in Time Perspective,* and Vansina's *Oral Tradition: A Study in Historical Methodology.*

On controlled cross-cultural comparison see Driver's "Cross Cultural Studies"; *Readings in Cross-Cultural Methodology,* edited by Moore; Driver and Chaney's Cross-Cultural Sampling and Galton's Problem"; Honigmann's "Sampling in Ethnographic Fieldwork"; and Naroll's "Cross-Cultural Sampling." On data collected for cross-cultural comparison see Moore's "The Human Relations Area Files," and Murdock's *Outline of World Cultures,* and his *Ethnographic Atlas.*

Important questions concerning the ethics of anthropological inquiry, particularly as they relate to the anthropologists' responsibility to the mostly Third World peoples among whom they work, is considered at length in many of the articles in *Reinventing Anthropology,* edited by Hymes, and in the section on "The Social Responsibility of the Anthropologist," edited by Berreman as part of Weaver's *To See Ourselves, Anthropology and Modern Social Issues.* See also Wolf's "American Anthropology and American Society."

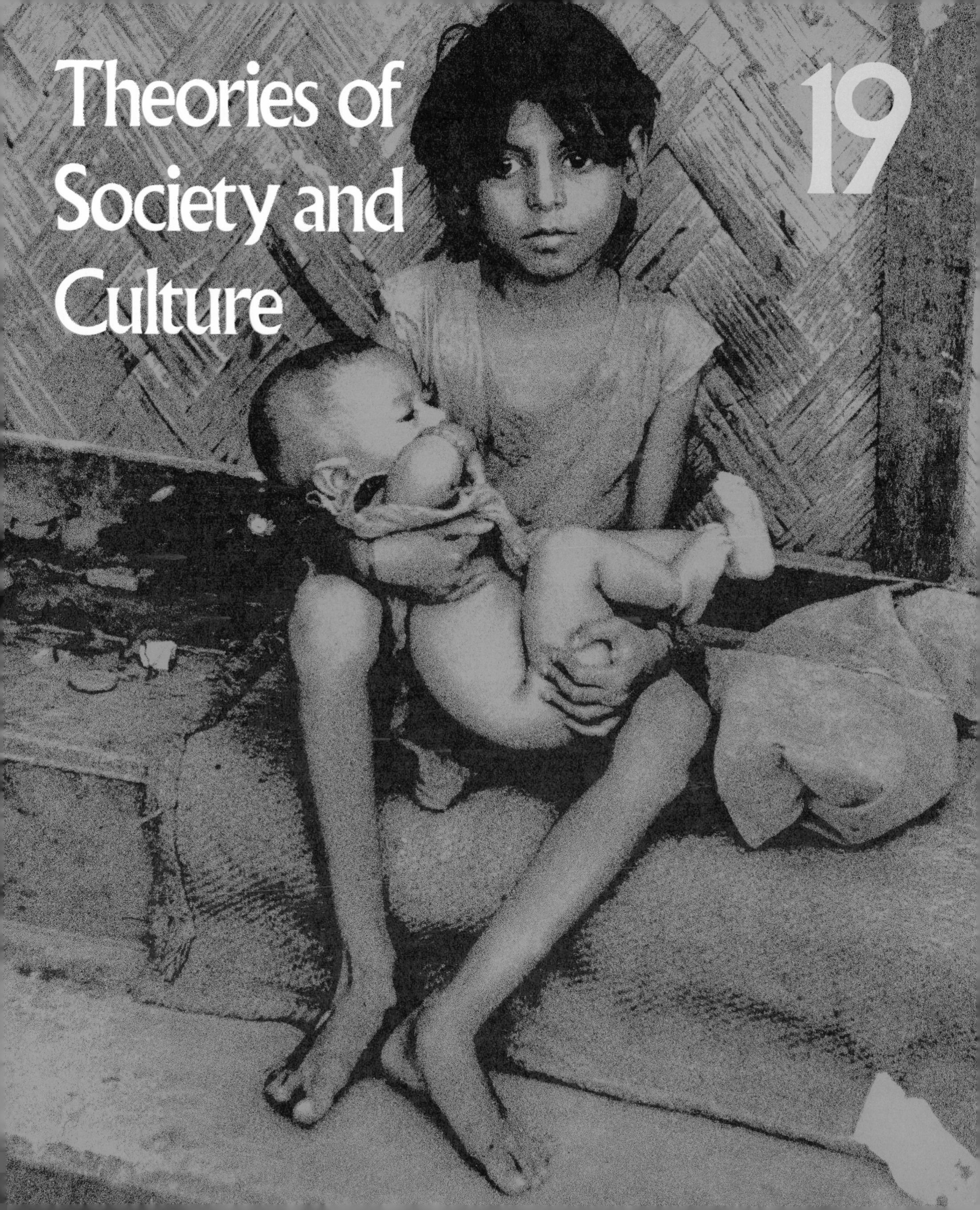
Theories of
Society and
Culture
19

Ever since the eighteenth century, scholars have perceived and have sought to document what appear to be significant parallels between the development of societies and the biological processes by which simply structured organisms evolve into more complex, internally more highly differentiated forms (see Montesquieu 1949; Spencer 1883; Marx 1857–58; Tylor 1889, 1958; Engels 1972; Morgan 1963). It has seemed to many that human societies or cultures might develop in the same way, as systems subject to a similar competitive struggle for survival and to laws just as immutable as those that govern biological evolution.

Cultural Evolution

The material remains of extinct societies and cultures, like the fossil record that provides evidence of the evolution of humankind, has seemed to support such a theory. The farther down the archaeologists dig and the older the remnants of ancient humans they unearth, the simpler are the artifacts they find, from the most sensitively structured and complex nuclear reactors back through time to the oldest and crudest tools of wood, bone, and stone. The generally

"The material remains of extinct societies and cultures . . . ."

Figure 19-1. Eighteenth-century temple at Hyderabad. (Government of India Information Services.)

correct supposition has been that the relative simplicity of the material remnants of the ways of life of our ancient ancestors was paralleled by an equal lack of complexity in the interrelated nonmaterial aspects of their cultures, their economic, social, and political systems, ideologies, artistic traditions, and so on. It has been assumed that there exists a causal link between the level of a people's material culture, particularly the level of their technological development, and the other major aspects of their way of life. As the earliest technologies were the simplest, so, presumably, were the social and cultural forms that accompanied them. And then, as technology evolved, as the tools and techniques people used to meet their physical needs increased in complexity and efficiency, the other aspects of their culture also became more highly differentiated, more specialized, and more complex.

In the course of this evolution the societies able to develop new social and cultural forms that facilitated a more efficient adaptation to changing environmental circumstances had a better chance of competing for survival. Those that did not risked extinction.

Support for this general theoretical approach, based in part on archaeological evidence, was derived from observance of the nonmaterial aspects of the ways of life of some of the technologically less developed people with whom scholars were for the first time beginning to come into extensive contact as a consequence of European exploration and colonial conquest during the eighteenth and nineteenth centuries. The cultures of "native" peoples, especially the ways of life of those whose technologies were relatively primitive, were regarded by European observers as relics, contemporary examples of what the ways of life of all our ancestors had been like at one of the earlier stages of what was generally perceived as a universally operative, more or less unilinear process of evolutionary development from cultural homogeneity and simplicity to cultural heterogeneity and complexity.

"The cultures of 'native' peoples . . . were regarded . . . as relics . . . ."
Figure 19-2. Pehriska-ruhpa, an Hidatsa Indian. (Smithsonian Office of Anthropology, Bureau of American Ethnology Collection.)

Herbert Spencer, building on the work of Montesquieu, Comte, and others and influenced by (and influencing) the parallel development of Darwinian thought, was the principal European protagonist of the evolutionary approach to the understanding of culture and the processes by which it changes. Insisting on a parallel between the evolution of social and cultural forms and the "ever beginning, ever changing" evolution of organic and inorganic forms, Spencer argued that it would be strange indeed "if, in the midst of this universal mutation, man alone were constant, unchangeable," continuing "but it is not so [for man also] obeys the law of indefinite variation. His circumstances are ever changing and he is ever adapting himself to them . . ." (Spencer 1883:46). To Spencer, adaptive social change was synonymous with "progress," and such progressive change was never random or accidental but the manifestation of a law underlying "the whole of organic creation."

Lewis Henry Morgan, an early student of the Iroquois, was the nineteenth-century founder of the evolutionary approach in the United States. Central to Morgan's theory was the concept that cultures develop through a series of progressive stages, each based on a more complex and more efficient level in the evolution of subsistence technology.

From his firsthand experience with the Iroquois and other American Indian groups, and from his analysis of the findings of scholars from around the world with whom he corresponded, Morgan developed a system for classifying cultures in which the presence or absence of particular technological traits determined their appropriate evolutionary niche. Each of the seven stages in Morgan's scheme was defined principally by a more progressive stage in the evolution of technology. This is how he set it up:

1. *Lower Savagery*—the long period during which our ancestors were evolving from the lower apes, gradually becoming fully human, able to use language, and "subsisting upon fruits and nuts."
2. *Middle Savagery*—marked by human mastery of fire making; it began with the discovery of fishing and "ended with the invention of the bow and arrow."
3. *Upper Savagery*—"commenced with the invention of the bow and arrow, and ended with the invention of the art of pottery."
4. *Lower Barbarism*—marked by continued practice of the art of pottery making; this era was thought of as lasting up to the discovery of plant and animal domestication.
5. *Middle Barbarism*—began with the domestication of animals and the development of "cultivation by irrigation."
6. *Upper Barbarism*—began with "the manufacture of iron" and ended with the invention of a phonetic alphabet.
7. *Civilization*—marked by "the use of writing in literary composition" and "the production of written records" (Morgan 1963:*9ff*).

Although aspects of Morgan's ideas and the very similar evolutionary approach taken by Tylor (see 1958) have been criticized as conceptually oversimple and sometimes poorly documented, many of the concepts basic to Morgan's scheme are now widely accepted, even by anthropologists not considered to be "evolutionists."

A particularly strong source of support for evolutionary theory is provided by the archaeological record, which allows for the testing of cultural evolutionary hypotheses against the material evidence of more than a million years of cultural development. The results of such testing are interpreted by many as revealing the operation of a "process leading from Paleolithic bands to industrial civilization," in which the essentials of Morgan's conception are supported, needing only to be enlarged in "scope and refined in detail" (Carneiro 1968).

Culture does appear to evolve in a way that is similar in its process to that of biological evolution. And, over all, the development of human society from most ancient times to the present has been marked by persistent progression from technological and societal simplicity to complexity. It is true that all people were first hunter-gatherers, that the discovery of plant and animal domestication came later, to be followed by the discovery of metalworking and writing. And it was on the material base developed through the confluence of these progressive discoveries and inventions that the first large-scale, internally highly differentiated, structurally complex societies were established—in Mesopotamia, Egypt, the Indus Valley, China, Mesoamerica, and the Andean region.

Among contemporary cultural evolutionary theorists the work of Leslie A. White is widely regarded as adhering most closely to the lines of inquiry and style of analysis established in the nineteenth century. But White and those who have worked with him on the theoretical principles of cultural evolution transmitted from Spencer, Tylor, and Morgan have added some important refinements, particularly in conceptualizing more sharply the fundamental role of tools and energy in the development of culture. Equating the evolution of culture with humankind's progressive harnessing of increased amounts of free energy from the environment, White states the relationship as a law: "Culture advances as the amount of energy per year increases, or as the efficiency or economy of the means of controlling energy is increased, or both" (White 1959:56).

He expresses the essence of this relationship among tools, energy, and the evolution of culture in a simple formula $E \times T = P$, with E representing energy, T the technological means by which people utilize it, and P the product or human-need-serving result (White 1959:40). As the efficiency with which people harness energy to meet their needs progresses, their culture evolves. Revolutionary advances in the evolution of culture are causally associated with the discovery of major new ways of harnessing and utilizing energy: fire making, the discovery of plant and animal domestication, the development of steam-powered engines, the discovery of electricity, and, most recently, the harnessing of atomic energy. When people do not continue to develop or borrow new and more adaptive means of harnessing energy—often because of the successful opposition to change made by those in political power—the evolution of their culture ceases, regresses, or continues only at a rate reduced to that of their sluggishly evolving technology. If such people live in relative geographic or cultural isolation, and are therefore not in competition with others technologically superior to them, they may continue to survive, but usually only until such isolation ends. Then, faced with the need to cope with the encroachment of technologically more advanced outsiders whose "energy-capturing devices" are more efficient, they must either make those innovations necessary to compete or face being taken over, annihilated, or absorbed. This process has been succinctly described by Service:

> As some cultures have successively become larger, more complex, more adaptable and powerful, so also have they increased their dominance over the less advanced. This dominance has taken many forms: destruction or assimilation of the weaker, occupation of its territory (as in "colonialism" in its literal sense), political rule ("imperialism"), or modern "indirect rule" with capital or commercial dominance only. . . . [Service 1971:10]

"It is true that all people were first hunter-gatherers . . . ."
Figure 19-3. As the Tasaday of the Philippines still are. (John Launois, Black Star.)

"... faced with the need to cope with the encroachment of technologically more advanced outsiders ...."
Figure 19-4. This is the dilemma of many herding peoples. Fulani women wait in despair for drought relief, Upper Volta. (United Nations.)

In the contemporary world, Service points out, "this latter indirect aspect of cultural dominance has become increasingly frequent." It is this process of selection, similar to the struggle in biological evolution in which those best adapted prevail, that is used to explain why culture in general continues to evolve, even as particular societies and their specific ways of life become extinct.

Although the role of technology or of technoeconomic arrangements is perceived as always being fundamental to the evolution of culture, proponents of the evolutionary approach are aware of the divergent ways in which the evolution of particular cultures is also affected by specific environmental and historical circumstances (see Service 1968). And they do not contend, as their detractors often intimate, that all societies must proceed through each evolutionary stage. For "a society can always skip stages through which others have passed by learning from those societies how to avoid their mistakes" (Peacock and Kirsch 1970:44) and by borrowing, rather than inventing, new and more efficient means of energy utilization. The important distinction here is between the larger, more general, or "macroevolutionary" view of the processes of the evolution of the way of life of all humankind from prehistoric times to the present—which has proceeded through a marked series of stages—and the equally important narrow, or "microevolutionary" view of the processes of cultural evolution as they are operative within a particular culture at a particular place during a particular time period.

Where the evolutionary approach is applied to understanding the process of selective adaptation that has marked the development of individual cultures, other factors—environmental variations, accidents of history—obviously must also be taken into account.

Structure and Function

The concept of society and culture as systems constantly in the process of adapting to ever-changing circumstances in the surrounding natural and sociocultural environment is shared by the majority of social anthropologists, many of whom are British or British trained. An early tendency to exclude history as a dimension of inquiry and concentration on the contemporary structure and function of what they generally term the "social institutions" of the peoples they study have resulted in their being called structuralists or functionalists.

Traditionally, social anthropologists identified with this approach have given principal attention to study of the formal structure of the major institutions of a particular society and the way these institutions function as component parts of a single integrated system to meet society members' needs, thereby maintaining societal equilibrium and fostering societal survival. (This useful focus on the structural sources of societal order may be partially explained by the fact that many British anthropologists did their fieldwork under the auspices of a Colonial Office interested in maintaining British imperial law and order.)

An analogy has often been made between the structurally and functionally integrated relations of the component institutions of a society and the biological concepts of morphology and physiology (see Radcliffe-Brown 1952). Following from the assumption of functional integration, it is generally assumed that the meaning of any part, any particular institution, within a society can be fully and accurately assessed only by considering it in functional relationship to the other component institutions of that society. Just as there is a sense in which the heart can be most fully understood by taking into account its structural and functional relationship to the other organs with which it works to keep the organism alive, so a single aspect of a social system can also be most effectively understood by studying it in relation to the societal totality of which it is a part. The full significance of any specific social structure, a particularly patterned way of organizing kinship relations, for example, was to be studied as it functioned in conjunction with all other constituent parts of the system to provide for the society's continued survival as an integrated whole.

Gradually developed out of a synthesis of the work of the British anthropologists Bronislaw Malinowski, A. R. Radcliffe-Brown, and those they trained, the fundamental tenets of the structural-functional approach now seem both reasonable and unremarkable. The strength of its impact on anthropology is best appreciated by considering it in contrast to an earlier tradition in which historically oriented anthropologists appeared to be less concerned with comprehending the meaning of other people's cultures than they were with describing them in all their exotic details in order to list and plot their diffusion. With acceptance of the functionalist premise that all human behavior was meaningfully related to all other institutionalized patterns of behavior and to the structure and function of society as an integrated totality, the cultures of "non-Western" peoples could no longer be described (as sometimes they had been in the past) as a tangled mass of alternatively savage and illogically childlike ways that a "civilized" scholar might report on but could never hope to comprehend.

Rather, it became the anthropologist's task—it is now regarded as a very elementary part of that task—to anticipate that every aspect of a people's culture, every behavior, has a potentially discoverable, probably significant reason for being.

Following the structural-functionalists'

"With acceptance of the functionalist premise that all human behavior was meaningfully related . . . ."

Figure 19-5. Bark painting from New Guinea utilizing symbols intimately connected with the people's ceremonial life. (Courtesy of the Museum of Primitive Art.)

biological analogy, and assuming that cultural institutions can most usefully be studied as functionally integrated totalities, some aspects of culture are easier to study than others. Kinship systems and economic and political organization lend themselves particularly well to the diagrammatic plotting that is a fundamental requisite of structural-functional analysis. Other aspects of culture—aesthetics and certain of the more ephemeral components of ideology—have so far proved to be less amenable to analysis in these terms.

Although some members of the founding generation of students of structure and function tended to ignore history out of realistic concern for the risks of error in undertaking historical reconstruction without the aid of written records, this is no longer so. In fact, functionalism is an analytic approach particularly well suited to study of the processes of social and cultural change. Given that all aspects of culture are structurally and functionally interrelated, change in one component aspect of the total system, such as in economic organization or in the structure of kinship relations, is always expected to be both the result of changes occurring elsewhere in the system and the cause of still others. The concept now seems so obvious as to be hardly worth restating, yet it is still widely ignored, especially by those "practical" planners of social and cultural change who repeatedly express surprise and dismay when their programs to "assist" developing nations, to put an end to poverty, eradicate racism, control population growth, or clean up the environment run afoul of the fact that the various component aspects of a people's culture are functionally so interrelated that one cannot be altered or deliberately prevented from changing (especially property or power relationships) without precipitating reaction in other aspects of the system as well.

In recent decades the somewhat simplistic concept of culture or society as composed of functionally integrated parts has usefully been modified by the addition of other concepts, many taken from sociology. (In fact, some slightly critical scholars contend that social anthropology is really "no more" than

Positive Function		Negative Function		Irrelevant	
Manifest	Latent	Manifest	Latent	Manifest	Latent

"It is no longer assumed . . . that all component aspects of a particular social or cultural system necessarily function to benefit one another and to maintain the system in equilibrium."

Figure 19-6. For a functional analysis to be complete, all six functions of any aspect of cultural behavior should be explored. (From Goode 1951:33, cited in Yinger 1970:102.)

a kind of cross-cultural sociology.) It is no longer assumed, for example, that all component aspects of a particular social or cultural system necessarily function to benefit one another and to maintain the system in equilibrium. Although it is justifiable and often useful to assume that each aspect of culture affects all others, such effects may just as well be harmful as beneficial. Actually, a single culture trait or complex almost invariably has multiple functions in relation to the system of which it is a part. It may have a positive effect on some aspects of culture and a negative, or dysfunctional, effect on others. Organized crime, for example, may be positively functional (eufunctional) for the criminal segment of society that profits from it, but it is dysfunctional for most other institutions and individuals in the society. Organized warfare might be analyzed in the same way. Making war fulfills positive functions for those who benefit financially from it or for whom it functions as a means of consolidating or extending political power, but it may be dysfunctional for the society as a whole, for the domestic and foreign institutions that are threatened, and, of course, for all those who are killed.

It is the job of the social anthropologist to take these multiple and frequently conflicting functions into account. He or she may also assess them in considering a particular society's chances of survival, an approach that provides a relatively value-free criterion for making cross-cultural judgments. For in place of scientifically useless evaluations made on the basis of the anthropologist's own likes and dislikes, aspects of culture can be objectively assessed in terms of their functions as these enhance the society's chances of survival or threaten its collapse.

Another useful distinction in structural-functional analysis is made between those functions of a particular institution that are manifest, that is, obvious and intended, and other functions that are latent, unintended and frequently unperceived. For example, in many cultures there is a rule that husbands should avoid or minimize direct face-to-face contact with their mothers-in-law. The manifest function of such avoidance behavior is simply a show of good manners. One of the several latent functions derives from the contribution of such behavior to social stability and cohesiveness by reducing the chances of direct confrontation between persons with a high potential for coming into conflict. Just as a single pattern of behavior can have multiple functions, some positive and some negative, it also can have a variety of manifest and latent functions.

For the anthropologist trying to comprehend the operation of a people's way of life and to determine the effects on the individual and the society of particular patterns of social action, this concept of single behaviors and patterns of behavior having multiple functions—some dysfunctional, others eu-

". . . the household of the aging parents contracts . . . ."
Figure 19-7. A Blackfoot burial site. (Bureau of Indian Affairs.)

functional, both manifest and latent—can be especially helpful in putting together a scientifically usable picture of what a people's way of life is like, for objectively determining what may be wrong with it, and, once these functional relationships can be confidently stated in terms of generalizations, for predicting change.

Concurrent with the development of the structural-functional approach to the study of social organization, a system for classifying social systems, particularly kinship systems, was developed that ultimately made it possible to reduce apparently endlessly variable forms for reckoning descent and affiliation to a limited number of universally recurrent structural types. These were described in Chapter 7. A similar approach, described in Chapter 10, has been taken to the study of authority systems and of law. However, such classification and description are necessary but relatively low-level scientific procedures. Once they are provided, the anthropologist is prepared to explore the more intriguing questions of why and how such systems developed as they did and of how such particular developments are related to general processes of culture change, innovation, borrowing, and ongoing adaptive reintegration that can ultimately be stated as laws.

From the analogy between the structure and function of society and that of the biological organism in which all parts are perceived as working to foster the organism's survival, an exertion toward the maintenance of societal equilibrium, of balance in the relationship between component parts, was initially assumed to be a principal motive force in the ongoing operation of any social system.

This view now has been replaced by one in which the dynamics of interinstitutional structures and functions are seen in a longer perspective: change rather than a state of equilibrium is perceived as the more basic tendency in the operation of social and cultural systems.

The injection of dynamism into the potentially static functionalist model of the social system has been stimulated by concepts such as those of Bohannan (1963), who has added the useful idea of the "event system," which suggests that a given structure of social relationships—a domestic group, a local community, or a larger grouping—should be analyzed in terms of the cycle of human events constantly moving through it. As one example, he uses the new household unit established in the United States when a couple first marries. As they have children and their family needs increase, the structure of the domestic group and its functions are expanded. When the children grow up, marry, and move out, the household of the aging parents contracts, until finally, when they both die, it ceases to exist. In addition, there are the often complex event cycles of the daily routine of the domestic group and the round of annual observances, social, economic, political, and religious, in which household members participate. Emphasis on this concept points up the importance, even for the anthropologist uninterested in history, of achieving time perspective on the cultural behavior he or she is recording and analyzing in order both to see how it works under changing conditions and to avoid the distortion that can result from observing its operation under circumstances that a longer perspective may reveal as nonrepresentative.

Gradually, as earlier concepts are reevaluated, the content of the structural-functional approach has been modified. Employed alone, it is particularly useful as a means of organizing observations in the ethnographic field, providing concrete points of departure in collecting fieldwork data and subjecting them to preliminary categorization. But as a control on functionalism's tendency toward teleology, with everything seen as related to everything else, and with questions of origin and causality sometimes slighted, the structural-functional approach is particularly valuable when it is combined, as it readily can be and often is, with other theories whose advocates are less reluctant to assign greater causal significance to some aspects of culture than to others.

French Structuralism

A somewhat different "structural" approach is currently most characteristic of contemporary anthropology in France. It is now an important influence, and often the subject of heated controversy, in cultural and social anthropology in Britain and the United States. Currently, the most prominent protagonist of French structuralism is Lévi-Strauss. In Britain, Leach takes a similar approach. In the United States this new structuralism is most closely related to the interests of Conklin, Goodenough, and others in native systems of categorization involved in what has already been described as the "new ethnography," or ethnoscience (see Chapter 18).

In French structuralism, emphasis is also on the structure of social systems, particularly on kinship organization and ideological systems (see Lévi-Strauss 1963, 1969a, 1969b). But as in ethnoscience, attention is not so much on these systems as models of social action functioning to meet human needs. Rather, it is on their significance as models of thought, as the surface representation of humankind's underlying collective unconscious presumably made manifest in an elaborate symbolic system that the interested anthropologist must discover in order to get at the deep mental processes that presumably lie beneath and allegedly explain all culturally patterned variations in human behavior.

"... presumably made manifest in an elaborate symbolic system that the interested anthropologist must discover ...."

Figure 19-8. Aztec calendar stone, an example of the mixture of mysticism and science that marked Aztec cosmology. (Courtesy of the American Museum of Natural History.)

Cultural Ecology

Defined broadly, cultural ecology refers to the dynamic interrelationship of people and the natural and cultural components of their environment. The three dimensions of environment relevant to human existence are organic, inorganic, and cultural. The organic aspect of the environment significant to humankind includes all of the surrounding forms of life, from biologically simple, disease-carrying microorganisms to the wild and domesticated varieties of plants and animals on which humans depend for food and for raw materials. The range of potentially germane nonorganic aspects of the environment is equally extensive: from the mineral content of the subsoils to the complex of atmospheric forces that determine climate. The relevant cultural dimension of a people's setting is composed of their own culture and the ways of life of others, both neighboring groups and more distant societies with whom contact may be intermittent or indirect.

So far, most attention has been given to study of the effects of the first two of these three equally important dimensions of our surroundings, the organic and inorganic aspects of the environment.

Dramatically exaggerated interpretations of the role of environment once made by geographers and a few geographically oriented anthropologists may explain the persistence of an untenable position, usually called environmental or geographical determinism, that assigns to the natural environment a determining role in shaping the development of culture (see Huntington 1915). This simplistic notion, now discredited by anthropologists, is most readily refuted by reference to the many instances in which very different cultures are found in natural settings that are a lot alike. California and Australia, for example, both mostly semiarid with mostly dry temperate climates, once had sparse aboriginal populations of technologically primitive hunter-gatherers. Today essentially the same natural settings support large populations whose exceptionally complex technologies support cultures radically different in form and content from those of their indigenous antecedents. Obviously, in these and in all other instances culture and culture history are the significant intervening variables in affecting and explaining the manner in which any particular people adapt to the organic and inorganic attributes of its environment.

As an alternative, contemporary scholars concerned with accurately comprehending the role of environmental factors in cultural development use the more reasonable concept of circumstances in the natural setting as limiting, that is, as facilitating certain kinds of cultural ecological adaptation and inhibiting others. Take as examples two extremes: the coastlands of the Arctic Circle and the fringes of the Sahara. The arctic environment is correctly perceived as having facilitated the emergence of a culture an important aspect of whose technological base was the hunting of sea mammals. Conversely, such an environment would obviously not encourage the development of a culture dependent for subsistence on the cultivation of tropical fruits. Similarly, the arid edges of the Sahara, where distribution of the always sparse grassy cover shifts with each occasional light rain, are relatively well suited to pastoral nomadism. But such an environment would seriously impede the development of horticulture or fishing as a means of getting a living.

It is in these more reasonable terms, as an always significant, sometimes formative, but never narrowly determining factor, that most anthropologists now try to understand the role of environment in relation to culture. And it is this position that is associated in anthropology with the field of study usually termed cultural ecology. Culture itself is defined as coterminous with human adaptation. Each culture is seen as a specific instance of patterned adaptation, one in which the attributes of each particular natural setting, depending on the specifics of a people's culturally conditioned response to them, always have a part to play in explaining the past, in affecting the present, and in setting some likely limits on cultural devel-

". . . to the wild and domesticated varieties of plants and animals on which humans depend for food . . . ."

Figure 19-9. Reindeer, source of their herders' meat, milk, clothing, and transport, Canada. (Northwest Territories, Department of Mines and Resources.)

opment in the future. The relation is perceived as dynamic: as culture modifies the environment, such changes act back upon and affect the further development of culture (for example, the polluted Danube, the overcultivated mountainsides of Haiti, the strip-mined valleys of Appalachia).

"... as when rainfall diminishes in an already semiarid region and farmers are forced to abandon their settlements ...."

Figure 19-10. Plowing the parched earth in anticipation of the first rains, Pakistan. (United Nations.)

The processes of ongoing cultural ecological adaptation are particularly well illustrated by the typically fragile relation of pastoral nomadic peoples to the climatic aspects of their environment. Animals overgraze sparse pasturage, precipitating erosion that makes necessary a shift in population. This creates demographic pressures on neighboring areas that may lead to warfare, the invasion and destruction of adjacent farming regions, and the destruction of people and property all around. Or the chain reaction can begin in the environment itself, as when rainfall diminishes in an already semiarid region and farmers are forced to abandon their settlements, shift to greater reliance on their domesticated animals for food, and ultimately set out to follow their herds in search of water and grazing land, thus gradually shifting from agriculture to pastoral nomadism. Or a single environmental change may affect several peoples living in the same region quite differently, depending on the specifics of their particular patterned means of adaptation. The drop in rainfall will hit settled farmers hardest. If they lack any knowledge of how to make a living by alternative means, such as by making the transition to herding, they may have no choice but to migrate or to stay on the land and face starvation. Pastoralists in the same region may be better able to survive because their technology permits them to adjust more readily to changes in the availability of food resources without moving out entirely. Still others, who make their living by fishing off the nearby seacoast, may not be affected at all by the rainfall drop.

The significance of natural resource distribution within a given environment is similarly modified by cultural circumstances. The mineral resources, mostly copper and uranium, of the forest zone of central Africa had relatively little effect on the traditional way of life of the African farmers of the region. The subterranean presence of gold and diamonds in parts of southern Africa was equally irrelevant to development of the indigenous cultures of the Bantu, the Bushmen, and the Hottentots. Because of the white settlers' quite different patterns of cultural ecological adaptation (essentially an industrial technology brought from Europe), they responded in a radically different way to these same two sets of environmental circumstances.

Often in the past, anthropologists interested in the effect of environment on culture limited themselves largely to consideration of the natural or noncultural aspects of the environment. But for people the presence of other humans culturally adapted to the environment in other ways is obviously always a significant aspect of the total setting. The presence or absence of competitors for scarce resources; of would-be conquerors, persecutors, or religious proselytizers or of opportunities for cultural borrowing and intersocietal cooperation is clearly critical both to any particular people's way of life and to the rate at which it changes.

Although more than mere proximity must be considered in determining the effect of geographically provided chances for borrowing, the ways of life of people living along migratory routes or at trading centers—in Asia Minor or Western Europe, for example—are likely to change more rapidly than those of people living for millennia isolated in such remote regions as Tasmania, the Chilean archipelago, and northern Greenland.

"... of competitors for scarce resources, of would-be conquerors ...."

Figure 19-11. Part of the Indian treasure sought by the Conquistadores, a breastplate of hammered gold, Colombia. (Courtesy of the Museum of Primitive Art.)

Cultural Ecology and Societal Survival

A comparison of cultures based on the relative efficiency or productivity of their cultural ecological adaptation suggests another comparatively value-free basis for making cross-cultural judgments. If culture is seen as an adaptive mechanism, then it may be possible to compare the particular adaptations of differing peoples to the same environment for the purpose of assessing which one appears—at least in the short run, and considerations of "happiness" and the risks of environmental degradation aside—to provide best for society members' material maintenance. It may then be possible to speak of one people's pattern of cultural ecological adjustment as "better" than that of another, in the sense that it both contributes more efficiently to their material well-being and enhances their chances for competing successfully with others, and thus of surviving. In this narrowly materialistic perspective the cultural ecological adaptation achieved by contemporary Californians and nonindigenous Australians might, for example, be assessed as more efficient than those of their aboriginal antecedents.

At this point the analytic style characteristic of the cultural ecological approach converges with that of the cultural evolutionists. For anthropologists who favor either of these two closely related theoretical positions see culture as an adaptive mechanism in which the interrelationship of technology and the natural environment is particularly critical both in affecting other aspects of the pattern of a people's cultural adaptation and in determining their chances for competing successfully against others for social and cultural survival.

The Parallel Operation of Identical Causality

Once some understanding is attained of the ways in which particular patterns of cultural ecological adaptation can affect the development of other aspects of culture, it becomes possible, by collecting and comparing evidence from a number of histori-

". . . culture as an adaptive mechanism in which the interrelationship of technology and the natural environment is particularly critical . . . ."
Figure 19-12. Farmers building an irrigation canal, Java. (United Nations.)

cally unrelated and geographically separate settings, to begin to state as theoretical generalizations some of the principles that appear everywhere to underlie the relationship among people, culture, and environment.

Julian Steward was the pioneering creative force in the development of this approach, one that combines both archaeological and ethnographic data in an effort to identify the processes of cultural ecological adaptation that have recurrently resulted in the development of basically similar patterns of culture at many different times and in many different places.

In outlining the method of cultural ecology Steward (1955a:40*ff*) advocated three fundamental procedures: (1) analysis of "the interrelationship of exploitative or productive technology and environment"; (2) examination of "the behavior patterns involved in the exploitation of a particular area by means of a particular technology"; and (3) determination of "the extent to which the behavior patterns entailed in exploiting the environment affect other aspects of culture." Although Steward's method provides for consideration of the role of "historical influences" in accounting for the particular details of a specific people's cultural ecological adaptation, his principal interest is in the discovery of similarities that allow for generalization. The fundamental problem as he states it "is to determine whether similar adjustments occur in similar environments" and whether accompanying regularities in other aspects of culture can be explained as the consequences of the operation of these "similar adaptive processes."

As a means of accounting for the intervening role of culture in structuring the relationship between people and their natural setting, Steward uses the concept of "levels of sociocultural integration." These are successive, qualitatively distinctive stages that recurrently mark the evolutionary development of historically separate cultures in which similar cultural ecological processes are at work. As a principal case Steward uses the parallel processes of adaptation to a particular set of environmental circumstances that have repeatedly accompanied the development of complex societies: the emergence of agriculturally based civilizations in northern Peru, in Mesoamerica, in Mesopotamia, in Egypt, and in China (Steward 1955a:185*f*). In each of these areas a similar natural setting was similarly exploited by its inhabitants—with similar cultural consequences. Each region was arid or semiarid. Long dry periods were interspersed with spells of moderate rainfall or the flooding of rich alluvial river valleys. Steward contends that in contrast to the forested regions of the tropics and the northerly latitudes and in contrast to plains areas or steppes, these semiarid regions facilitated the development of farming because the earth could be relatively easily tilled by people with a preiron technology. Without iron tools the clearing of forested areas and the breaking up of the earth of the heavily sodded plains would have been more diffi-

". . . these semiarid regions facilitated the development of farming . . . ."
Figure 19-13. A present-day successor to Mexico's ancient cultivators. (United Nations.)

cult. In each region, Steward asserts, the suitability of the natural environment to exploitation by use of the digging stick and incipient irrigation techniques "seems to have entailed similar solutions to similar problems and consequently to have caused similar developmental sequences."

These sequences Steward divides into eras: (1) the Preagricultural Era, (2) the Era of Incipient Agriculture, (3) the Formative Era of Basic Technologies and Folk Culture, (4) the Era of Regional Development and Florescence, and (5) the Era of Cyclical Conquests. For each he suggests a number of "diagnostic features." For example, the Preagricultural Era in each region he describes as having been marked by a number of attributes causally related to this most rudimentary level of cultural ecological adaptation. Social and political systems were based primarily on kinship, age, and sex. Warfare was limited to feuds and occasional retaliatory attacks against trespassers. Basketry, loom weaving, metallurgy, permanent house construction and boat and animal transportation were probably absent; if not, he suggests they were probably borrowed from other, technologically more advanced peoples.

The theoretical significance of such parallelism lies in the observation that in each of the five spatially separate regions identified previously, at a different point in time, the transition from the Preagricultural Era to the Era of Incipient Agriculture, for example, was marked by a similar cluster of cultural consequences that led through a series of intermediate stages of cultural development to the emergence in each region of permanently settled communities supported by the cultivation of plants and the raising of domestic animals.

Steward cites the archaeological record to suggest the continued operation of the parallel process of cultural development in the next period, which he terms the Era of Regional Development and Florescence. Irrigation resulted in an increase in productive land use and the release of a larger portion of the labor force to engage in more specialized tasks: various craft occupations, full-time participation in trade, or work as administrators, religious functionaries, artists, educators, or warriors. The direct or indirect

"Irrigation resulted in an increase in productive land use . . . ."
Figure 19-14. Javanese rice paddy. (United Nations.)

dependence of the entire community on maintenance of the irrigation system that assured the water supply essential for food production resulted in the centralization of authority for control of this system, and thereby in accumulation of extraordinary power by a relatively small group. This power was first centered in the hands of religious leaders. Later, it passed to a ruling class whose right to political authority was supernaturally sanctioned by their relation to the antecedent ruler-priests. Reliance on militarism increased in importance as a support for authority within the multicommunity states, as a means of defending their frontiers and of expanding them in response to the pressures of population growth and increasing demands for food and goods. The priests' traditional concern over control of the forces of nature led to the development of astronomy and mathematics. The need to keep a record of the flow of trade, tribute, and taxes contributed to the development of a system of writing. With regional specialization in the production of subsistence goods and crafts the redistributive and market systems expanded into a network of internal and external trade relationships. Wealth increased, so did socioeconomically based differences in relative social status and access to power. At opposite ends of the socioeconomic spectrum aristocracy and serfdom emerged.

Finally, out of these circumstances the next period, the Era of Cyclical Conquests developed. Large-scale warfare came to be relied on as a means both to extend economic and political domination by exploiting the productive capacities of neighboring peoples and to reduce the pressures created by an expanding population. And so Steward's analysis goes, drawing not only on data collected by archaeologists but also on the theoretical formulations of both historically oriented anthropologists and cultural evolutionists.

"... a sort of chain reaction set off ... by the initial convergence of food gatherers and wild seed-bearing grasses growing near arid or semiarid floodplains."
Figure 19-15. Harvesting rice, India. (United Nations.)

In each instance a similarly patterned cultural ecological adaptation is perceived as having facilitated, if not precipitated, the otherwise independent recurrence of a series of causally linked developments. These similar sequences of developmental events cannot be explained on the basis of borrowing because of their separate occurrence at different times and places among historically unrelated peoples. Such recurrences, Steward strongly suggests, must be regarded as evidence of "the parallel operation of identical causality," a sort of chain reaction set off in each instance by the initial convergence of food gatherers and wild seed-bearing grasses growing near arid or semiarid floodplains.

The results of Steward's approach to identification of those developmental regularities that appear to have marked the early emergence of complex cultures at several different times both in the Old World and in the Americas have implications that transcend the field of cultural ecology alone. For his work represents a successful synthesis of at least three major antecedent approaches in anthropology, combining aspects of the methodology of the culture historians with the theory of the structural-functionalists and the cultural evolutionists.

Steward's critics fault him on the inadequacy of the samples he selected for comparison, on his failure to recognize explicitly the occasionally causal role of factors only secondarily related to the fundamental processes of cultural ecological adaptation (for example, religious or political leaders' frequently successful opposition to technological innovations they perceive as threatening to their power), and on a certain sense of "inevitability" that some read into his work (see Vayda and Rappaport 1968:485*f*). But such criticism does little to diminish the essential theoretical value of Steward's approach as a rich source for the generation of hypotheses to explain the relationship among people, their culture, and the natural environment that surrounds them. It is as it should be in science that a younger generation of anthropologists now sees the theory of cultural ecology not as *the* way to explain correctly a people's relationship to its environment but as one of several fundamental approaches, which are often most productive when they are combined.

Culture and Personality

The study of culture and personality constitutes a subfield within cultural and social anthropology that deals with the ways vari-

"... studying the processes by which the developing personality of the young human being is gradually shaped to assure conformity with his or her culture's expectations."

Figure 19-16. Young girls at play. (Government of India, Information Services.)

ous aspects of culture, and varying patterns of these aspects, affect the development of personality. Secondarily, it involves examination of the ways in which personality, once formed, can affect the further development of culture.

A fundamental task of the student of culture and personality is to identify the particular aspects of culture that appear most significant in shaping personality, to discover the processes by which this shaping occurs, and to relate such findings to the main body of anthropological theory. So far, most attention has been directed to the first two of these three related tasks: to identifying those aspects of culture, such as family organization, child-rearing techniques, and education, that appear to be most immediately (if not necessarily most basically) related to personality development and to studying the processes by which the developing personality of the young human being is gradually shaped to assure conformity with his or her culture's expectations.

Development of the field of culture and personality has been importantly affected by the Freudian and Neo-Freudian emphasis on the primacy of infantile and early childhood experience to the formation of both normal and "abnormal" personality and to the development of neuroses, character disorders, and psychotic states. The cross-cultural study of the processes of psychosexual maturation; the investigation of incest prohibitions and oedipal conflicts, of repression, regression, guilt, anxiety, and depression, of the relation between frustration and aggression; and the analysis of the close relationship between these phenomena and the structure of kinship relations and child-rearing techniques—all are traceable to the influence of Freud and his followers. More recently, interest has increased in relating the cultural patterning of behavior to a general theory that emphasizes personality development as an adaptive mechanism in the ongoing evolution of culture (see LeVine 1973).

To make Freudian theory cross-culturally usable it has been necessary for anthropologists to release it from its culture-bound context, partially derived from the limitations of Freud's firsthand experience (mostly with middle-class, early-twentieth-century Viennese) and his tendency to generalize from this to the psychology of all humankind. His concept of the fundamental significance of experience in infancy and early childhood, especially his emphasis on a connection between interference with infantile drives related to sexual development and the emergence of character disorders and neu-

"... emphasis on the primacy of infantile and early childhood experience ...."

Figure 19-17. Child tending her baby brother, Bangladesh. (United Nations, Philip Teuscher.)

roses, has been retained. What has been largely rejected is his contention that the emotional conflicts generated within the middle-class European nuclear families typical of his patients were necessarily universal. Investigations among peoples who have different types of family organization and use differing child-rearing techniques—by Malinowski among the matrilineal, avunculocal Trobriand Islanders, who, for example, reportedly experience oedipal conflict as "repressed hatred against the maternal uncle" rather than against the father (Malinowski 1923); by Mead in Samoa and New Guinea (1928, 1930); and by Du Bois among the inhabitants of the East Indian island of Alor (1944)—all strongly indicate that differences in family organization and in the patterning of infant and child care are correlated with marked, culturally determined differences in the development of personality.

Out of the effort to enlarge on some of Freud's culture-bound and historically inaccurate generalizations about childhood emotional conflicts there has emerged a cross-culturally more viable theory of personality and culture that draws heavily on his basic psychodynamic principles but has modified them to fit the data drawn from the study of the differing ways personality develops in other cultures.

Much of this early work was highly speculative, but stimulating, and illustrative of the kinds of conceptual problems with which students of culture and personality have been concerned.

". . . allegedly manifested by the contrast between the superficial charm, gentility, and courtesy characteristic of Japanese cultural behavior in some situations . . . ."

Figure 19-18. Flower arranging, Japan. (Courtesy of the American Museum of Natural History.)

National Character

Some of these problems were particularly apparent in studies of national character undertaken in the late 1930s and in the 1940s that sought to establish causal relationships between culturally determined differences in socialization and the patterning of adult personality. During World War II, for example, Gorer (1943) and La Barre (1945) both attempted, separately, to explain the compulsiveness supposedly typical of Japanese national character, allegedly manifested by the contrast between the superficial charm, gentility, and courtesy characteristic of Japanese cultural behavior in some situations and the obsessive concern with order and precision (the ritualistic masking of aggression), fanaticism, arrogance, and sadomasochistic brutality that marked their behavior in other cultural circumstances, particularly during wartime. Following Freud, Gorer and La Barre linked such compulsiveness with the severity of Japanese toilet training.

In *The Chrysanthemum and the Sword,* a book written during World War II and necessarily based entirely on secondary sources, Benedict (1946) affirmed these conclusions and related the capacity of adult Japanese to accept "the subtle compulsions of Japanese culture" to the "inescapable routine implacably insisted upon" by their parents during the formative years of early childhood.

Not long after, in a study of Russian national character, Gorer and Rickman concluded that the custom of swaddling was the source of the impotent rage presumed to cause the manic-depressive mood swings alleged to be characteristic of the Russian personality. From birth onward, they wrote, the Russian baby is "tightly swaddled in long strips of materials holding its legs straight and its arms down to its sides . . . when swaddled the baby is completely rigid . . . it is assumed that this inhibition of movement is felt to be extremely painful and frustrating and is responded to with intensive and destructive rage, which cannot be adequately expressed physically" (Gorer and Rickman 1950:97–99).

The impressionism of such studies—their methodological weaknesses, especially in data collection, and the speculativeness of their analytic assumptions—made them scientifically unacceptable to some anthropologists and vulnerable to strong criticism from many others.

Toward a More Careful Methodology

A later generation of anthropologists retained an interest in the Freudian approach but sought a more scientific means of studying the impact of socialization.

For example, Whiting, in collaboration with Richard Kluckhohn and Albert Anthony, used data in the Human Relations Area Files to test a series of hypotheses concerning the relationship among childhood sleeping arrangements, postpartum sexual taboos, and male initiation ceremonies. According to their principal hypothesis,

> Societies which have sleeping arrangements in which the mother and baby share the same bed for at least a year to the exclusion of the father and societies which have a taboo restricting the mother's sexual behavior for at least a year after childbirth will be more likely to have a ceremony of transition from boyhood to manhood than those societies where these conditions do not occur (or occur for brief periods). [Whiting and others 1958:864]

Testing the hypothesis against information taken from fifty-six societies, they found that over 80 per cent of the cases supported their prediction. Whiting's approach merits attention not because the early results of its application were so successful—in fact they have been seriously questioned (see Young 1962, 1965)—but because it has provided a valuable complement to the necessarily more speculative theories of psychoanalyti-

". . . swaddling was the source of the impotent rage presumed to cause the manic-depressive mood swings alleged to be characteristic of the Russian personality."

Figure 19-19. Nursery scene, Naro-Fominsk, U.S.S.R. (Novosti Press Agency, Moscow, U.S.S.R.)

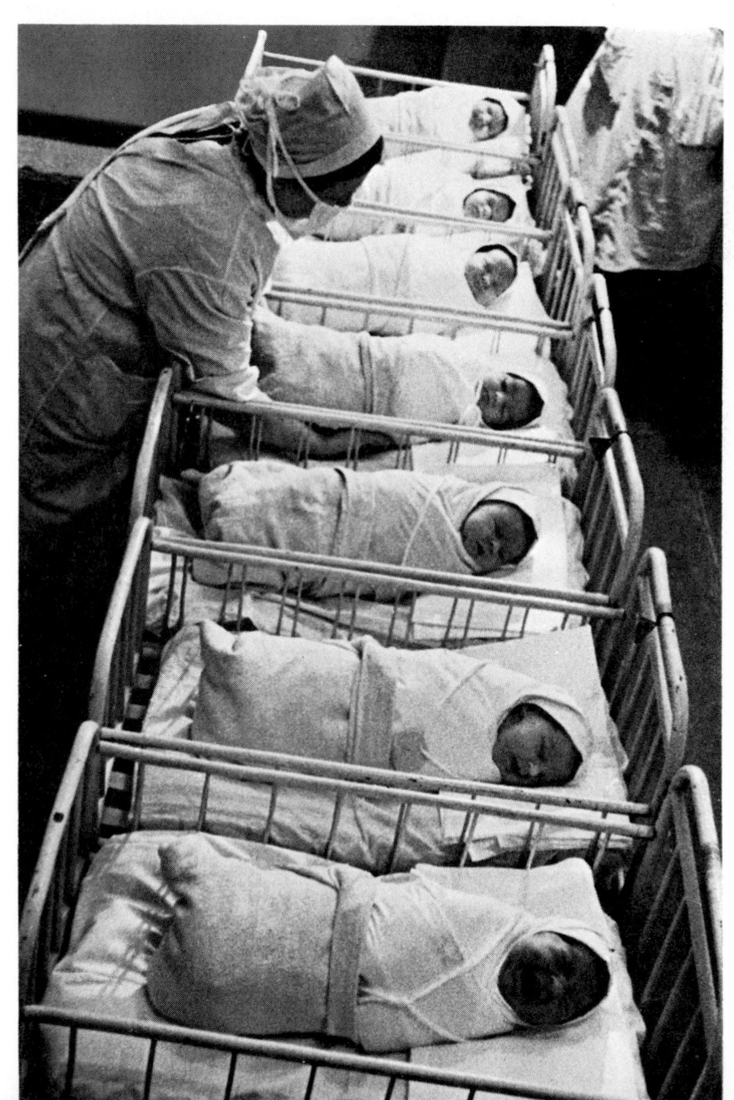

". . . the role of economic factors in determining the pattern of socialization . . . ."
Figure 19-20. A young Pakistani assists his parents in harvesting their sugar cane. (United Nations.)

cally oriented students of culture and personality.

The linkage of such statistically significant correlations between childhood training and personality with other fundamental issues in cultural and social anthropology, although easy to establish, has often been ignored.

It is striking, for example, that anthropologists, with more reason than most other behavioral scientists to be aware of the importance of an often difficult environment and a primitive technology in the life of the peoples they study, have so frequently failed to relate the correlations they have discovered between culture and personality development to the matrix of technoenvironmental circumstances in which the human organism must survive.

There have been exceptions. Aberle has persistently emphasized the role of economic factors in determining the patterning of childhood socialization (see Aberle 1961). Lewis's studies in Latin America and India strongly suggest that poverty breeds a particular configuration of personality traits in whatever culture it is found (see Lewis 1966). And Wallace's analysis (1961b) of the relation between arctic hysteria and protein deficiency disease has important parallels in the attention Whiting has recently given to the interrelation of technoenvironmental factors and those aspects of culture whose effect on personality formation appears to be more immediate (Whiting 1964).

Parker's analytic account of the "wiitiko psychosis," a culturally structured mental illness found among the Ojibwa of northeastern Canada, also provides the basis for clearly analyzing the causal linkage of technoenvironmental factors, nearly all the other major aspects of culture—social and economic organization, ideology, mythology—and the development of a violent psychosis. A condition primarily affecting Ojibwa men, in the wiitiko psychosis the "hallucinating patient sees the people around him turning into delicious looking animals which, unless restrained, he attacks and tries to eat" (Parker 1960).

The links in the chain of causality leading to the development of this mental illness can be hypothetically connected, beginning with the harsh natural environment of the Ojibwa, their hunting and gathering technology that often requires the nuclear family to live isolated in the frozen wilderness for long periods during the trapping season, the frequent threat of starvation, and a pattern of infant nurturance in which the first three years of life are marked by a close and affectionately permissive relationship between mother and infant son. This is followed by a "sudden and drastic" change when her son is between three and five years old, as "the socially shared anxieties and values of the group begin to impinge directly on the youngster."

His parents live so close to the level of subsistence "that the child, in his untrained state, is regarded as a liability both to himself and to the group." It is impressed on him that he must develop self-reliance and be aware that he can no longer truly depend on anyone, that only through reliance on supernatural power can he survive. Overt parental affection is withdrawn. He is forced to bathe in the icy rivers, to run naked in the snow, to fast for weeks at a time. Any hint of disobedience brings threats of further denial of food and parental love. To further assure his compliance with this harsh regime he is told the wiitiko monster, a terrible cannibalistic demon, will "get" him if he is bad.

Parker explains the onset of the wiitiko psychosis in adulthood as a consequence of the Ojibwa child's long-pent-up rage over this systematic frustration of his early dependency needs. In later years it finally boils over in the adult's response to frustration, in which he associates sharp disappointment, usually precipitated by repeated failures in the hunt, with earlier traumatic threats of the withdrawal of love, nurturance, and support.

The first phase of the illness is marked by prolonged melancholic depression and finally develops into "full blown psychotic symptoms involving fixed paranoid delusions and cannibalistic behavior." The victim becomes convinced that he is possessed by the spirit of the cannibalistic wiitiko monster. Parker suggests that

> . . . the *prototype* of the wiitiko monster is the mother figure, who is a major agent of dependency frustration in early life. The basis for the predisposition that later results in the phantasy of a persecuting monster is established in the early socialization process, particularly in the mother-son relationship. It is cultivated and given definite form by the cultural belief in such a monster. In the adult Ojibwa, it is more fruitful, heuristically, to think of the wiitiko monster as a phantasy figure symbolizing the wider circle of significant others who continue to threaten the dependency cravings of the adult and constitute threats to his vulnerable self-esteem (Parker 1960:619).

In support of his analysis Parker cites the observations of Kardiner (1939:224) on the psychoanalytic implications of cannibalistic fantasies in which the individual's incapacity to trust others to satisfy his basic emotional cravings leads to a feeling of being persecuted, "whereupon active steps in the form of aggression are taken." The wish to eat becomes the fear of being eaten. Turning the "nurturing object into the persecuting object," Parker's wiitiko victim, his other neurotic defenses having failed him, wishes to obliterate his persecutor by eating him up. The "dam (constituted by ego defenses) is shattered and the repressed cravings for the expression of dependency and aggressive needs burst forth" (Parker 1960:620). Conflict between the wiitiko victim's rage and his fear is resolved. His psychotic symptoms serve to "allay his dependency cravings (by becoming one with the object of dependency) and to aggress against the frustrating object (by killing and eating it)."

Like many other students of culture and personality, Parker concentrates on the relationship between socialization and personality formation. But if his findings are combined with other ethnographic accounts of the Ojibwa (see Cooper 1933; Hallowell 1949), it is not difficult to link his analysis with the already described fundamental cultural factors that set the causal chain in motion: a difficult natural environment with widely dispersed wild food resources, a technology that makes it necessary for the Ojibwa nuclear family to live isolated in its hunting territory for most of the year, a pattern of socialization intended by parents to provide their children with an adaptive capacity for self-reliance, religious beliefs that project the individual's helpless dependency, a mythology that makes the same point (with recurrent stories of helpless children starved by a mother who ultimately turns into a cannibalistic wiitiko monster and tries to devour them) (Parker 1960; Jones 1919; Schoolcraft 1956)—all leading, finally, to the point where Ojibwa men break down under the onslaught of what they experience as overwhelming misfortune. Depressed and anxious over their failure as hunters, over the failure of their pleas for supernatural help or assistance from their fellows, their defenses against the overt expression of their anger finally give way. The last link in the causal chain connects and they become psychotic.

Such a conclusion is, of course, tentative. Like the more modest psychodynamic hypothesis that Parker proposes, its testing "will have to await more methodologically vigorous research in the comparative study of other societies" in which environmental adaptation, social structure, socialization, religion, mythology, and adult personality—"normal," neurotic, and psychotic—appear to be similarly linked. It is suggested here as an example of the potential for relating even the most individually centered, psychoanalytically oriented analysis of culture and personality to the most fundamental issues in contemporary cultural and social anthropology.

Summary

The premises basic to the cultural evolutionary approach have so influenced the organization and content of this book that they should be familiar enough to require only a minimal restatement. Perspective on the always fundamental role of technological development as a primal factor in determining the form, content, and development—or lack of development—of the other aspects of culture must be modified by the awareness that, once set in motion, the process often results in the emergence of economic, social, political, and ideological systems that are so rigidly structured and so profoundly and powerfully committed to the sociocultural status quo as to make impossible the experimentation with new and alternative forms that is necessary for continued technological innovation and further cultural evolution. The path of human history is littered with the skeletons of societies that were so inflexibly organized that they could not make those adaptations necessary to their continued survival.

The traditional position of those associated with the structural-functional approach has been marked by emphasis on synchronic study of societal form and of the systematic integration of the component aspects of society as a whole, functioning to meet its members' material and psychological needs and to maintain the equilibrium necessary to the society's continued existence. Among a younger generation of scholars this preoccupation with a somewhat static equilibrium model has given way to an increasing emphasis on social change in time perspective. Those social anthropologists who have been influenced by French structuralism share most of their theoretical tenets and objectives with the ethnoscientists described in Chapter 18.

In essential premises, theory, method, and goals, cultural ecology has many similarities to the cultural evolutionary approach. In cultural ecology also it is a people's technological adaptation to their environment—stated, however, in terms of levels of techno-environmental adaptation—that is seen as having a paramount effect on the form and content of the other aspects of their culture. Differences between the two approaches lie in the somewhat more cautiously limited developmental formulations of the cultural ecologists and their more explicit attention to the formative role of the organic, inorganic, and "superorganic" or cultural aspects of the human setting.

Development of a body of theory and method to explain the ways variation in the patterning of culture can affect the conditioning of personality has benefited both from the insights of psychoanalytic theory and from the methodological rigor of controlled comparison. Linked to consideration of the ways in which the more fundamental aspects of culture—technology, economic organization, social and political systems, ideology, and language—can affect the structure of the cultural matrix in which personality is formed, the study of culture and personality delineates the cluster of causal interrelationships within which individual personality is affected by the forces that shape all people into cultured social animals.

Suggested Readings

For a recent analysis of the contribution of one of the earliest scholars to develop the concept of cultural and social evolution see *The Evolution of Society: Selections from Spencer's Principles of Sociology,* edited by Carneiro. See also Carneiro's "Structure, Function and Equilibrium in the Evolutionism of Herbert Spencer" and his "The Four Faces of Evolution: Unilinear, Universal, Multilinear, and Differential." See as well the classic source by Morgan, *Ancient Society,* available in a recent edition prepared by Leacock. The subject as it has been developed by White is extensively covered in his *The Science of Culture* and *The Evolution of Culture;* see also *Evolution and Culture,* edited by Sahlins and Service; and Service's *Cultural Evolutionism: Theory and Practice,* an approach that is criticized by Harris in his "Monistic Determinism: Anti-Service." Also of importance are Ribeiro's *The Civilizational Process* and Ruyle's innovative "Energy and Culture."

In addition to the several important sources already cited in the text see Goody's "Functionalism," Mair's "The Concept of Function," Firth's "An Appraisal of Modern Social Anthropology," and the excellent synthesis of the structural-functionalist approach in Kuper's *Anthropologists and Anthropology: The British School, 1922–1972.* On French structuralism see both *Structural Anthropology* and *The Elementary Structures of Kinship* by Lévi-Strauss. For an American overview see Werner's "Structural Anthropology" and Sahlin's critical summation: *Culture and Practical Reason.*

The literature on cultural ecology is extensive and fascinating. The classic compilation by the founding scholar in this field is Steward's *Theory of Culture Change: The Methodology of Multilinear Evolution.* Among good recent expository reviews of the field are Sahlins's "Culture and Environment: The Study of Cultural Ecology," and Vayda and Rappaport's "Ecology: Cultural and Non-cultural." See also Harris's related "Cultural Materialism: Cultural Ecology"; *Environment and Cultural Behavior: Ecological Studies in Cultural Anthropology,* edited by Vayda; and Rappaport's "Nature, Culture, and Ecological Anthropology."

For an introduction to the field of culture and personality, see the contents and the bibliographies of several excellent collections: LeVine's *Culture and Personality: Contemporary Readings,* Hsu's *Psychological Anthropology,* and Hunt's *Personality and Culture: Readings in Psychological Anthropology.* See also LeVine's "Basic Concepts in an Evolutionary Model," Wallace's *Culture and Personality,* Honigmann's "Personality in Culture," and Edgerton's excellent *The Individual in Cultural Adaptation.*

Glossary

A

Aardvark. A large, nocturnal burrowing animal that feeds on ants and termites; native to Africa.

Aboriginal. Indigenous or native; pertaining to the original inhabitants of a region, country, or continent.

Adz. A tool with a heavy, chisellike end, usually mounted on a wooden handle.

Affinal. Related by marriage.

Age grade. A group whose members' assigned roles are determined by the socially designated age category to which they belong; typically, part of an age organization composed of several such grades.

Agnate. A relative whose connection is exclusively through males; one related by descent through the male line.

Agriculture. In anthropology, cultivation with the use of draft animals, irrigation, and fertilizers; usually distinguished from horticulture by reliance on these generally more productive techniques.

Animatism. The attribution of consciousness to inanimate objects and natural phenomena.

Animism. Belief in spirits and other supernatural beings; Tylor's minimal definition of religion.

Apocryphal. Pertaining to religious writings of uncertain origin or authenticity.

Archaeology. The study of historic or prehistoric peoples, based principally on the material remains of their artifacts.

Assimilation. The merging of the cultural traits of two or more groups with previously distinct cultures.

Association. A social group usually formed on the basis of shared interests and/or attributes.

Asymmetrical. Lacking symmetry; uneven, unbalanced, or unequal.

Autonomous. Independent; self-sufficient.

B

Band. A small, territorially based social group most of whose members are related.

Baraka. In Islam, the popular belief in the supernatural power of events, objects, or actions associated with supernaturally favored persons.

Bifurcate. To divide or fork into two separate branches.

Bilabial stop. A speech sound made by pressing the lips together so that a stream of air from the lungs is temporarily halted.

Bilateral descent. A system for reckoning descent in which the individual is related almost equally to all the close kinsmen of both parents.

Bride service. Labor or other services rendered to a woman's kinsmen by her husband, before or after marriage.

Bridewealth, or bride price. Goods, usually property or money, given by a prospective husband and his relatives to the family of his bride.

Bull roarer. A flat board that makes a loud whirring noise when twirled at the end of a string.

Bustard. Any of several large, chiefly terrestrial birds of the family Otididae; related to the cranes.

C

Caste. A hereditary, endogamous group usually identified with a specific occupation; typically, one of several such groups, all of which are ranked hierarchically.

Charisma. An aura of magnetism or extraordinary power radiated by a person.

Chinampa. In Mexico, an artificial garden island made by filling in a portion of a lake or pond with aquatic vegetation.

Churinga. An object, usually elliptical in shape and decorated with surface designs, made of wood or stone and considered the symbol or repository of supernatural power.

Cicatrization. Scar tissue produced by incising the skin to make decorative or symbolically significant patterns.

Clan. A unilineal descent group whose members claim descent from a remote common ancestor, often a mythical figure; sometimes used to refer to a residential kin group composed of a core of unilineally related persons and their wives or husbands.

Class. A social stratum composed of persons sharing basically similar economic, social, political, and other interests and cultural attributes and having the same social position; one of several such strata within a ranked system.

Coercion. The exercise of force to obtain compliance.

Cognate. A word related to another word by common origin.

Cognition. Knowledge, or a way of perceiving and thinking about reality.

Collateral. Referring to relationship through nondirect or horizontal links, as in the instance of one's "uncles," "aunts," and "cousins."

Compadrazgo. The Spanish term for the institution of ritual co-parenthood.

Conjugal. Pertaining to marriage or marital relations.

Consanguinity. Pertaining to kinship based on common descent; of the same "blood."

Copperbelt. A region of Central Africa rich in copper and other mineral deposits.

Corporate. Pertaining to a group of individuals whose organization and actions are continuous and independent of the existence of individual members.

Cross-cousins. The offspring of siblings of unlike sex; i.e., the children of one's father's sister or one's mother's brother.

Culture area. A geographic region in which the cultures tend to be similar in a number of significant aspects.

Curds. A substance obtained from milk by coagulation; used as a food or made into cheese.

D

Dahomey. A West African nation, now called Benin.

Deleterious. Injurious.

Deme. An endogamous community composed almost entirely of the members of a single kindred.

Dervish. A member of any of various Moslem ascetic orders.

Diachronic. Pertaining to events or phenomena as they change through time.

Diffusion. The transmission of a culture trait from one group to another in the absence of face-to-face contact.

Dingo dog. A wolflike wild dog native to Australia.

Double descent. Pertaining to the coexistence in a single society of patrilateral and matrilateral systems for tracing descent.

Dowry. Property given to a daughter to take with her into marriage.

Dromedary. The single-humped camel of Arabia and North Africa.

Dugong. An aquatic mammal of the Red Sea and Indian Ocean.

Durian. An edible fruit, with a hard, prickly rind, of a tree native to Southeast Asia.

E

Ecology. The study of living systems as integrated complexes.

Ego. The "I" in kinship analysis; designation

for the hypothetical person used as the point of reference in analyzing kinship relations.

Eland. Either of two African antelopes having long, spirally twisted horns.

Empirical. On the basis of verifiable evidence or experience.

Enculturation. The processes by which a person gradually learns and assimilates the patterns of cultural behavior expected by the members of his or her society.

Endogamy. The custom or law requiring or encouraging a person to marry within the particular social group to which he or she belongs.

Ephemeral. Short-lived; transitory.

Esophagus. A tube connecting the mouth cavity with the stomach.

Eta. The derogatory Japanese term for a member of an outcaste group that occupies a subordinate position in Japanese society.

Ethnic. Pertaining to the distinctive social, cultural, linguistic, and physical attributes of a particular group.

Ethnocentric. Pertaining to the learned use of the values of one's own culture as a standard against which other patterns of behavior are invidiously compared.

Ethnography. That aspect of cultural and social anthropology devoted to the objective, firsthand description of a particular culture.

Ethnology. Theoretical analysis and interpretation based on ethnographic data.

Ethnomusicology. The anthropological study of music, particularly the study of the music of nonliterate peoples, with emphasis on the place of music in cultural context.

Etiology. The study of the causes of disease.

Eufunctional. Of positive value; a pattern of cultural behavior that is adaptive.

Exogamy. The socially enforced requirement that a person marry outside the culturally defined group to which he or she belongs.

F

Family, conjugal-natal. A social group composed of spouses and their offspring.

Feud. Bitter, long-lasting, generally overt hostilities between two groups.

Feudal. Pertaining to or like the social and economic system in Europe during the Middle Ages, based on the holding of lands in fief.

Fief. A tenure of land subject to feudal obligations.

Fission. The act of cleaving or splitting into parts.

Forage. A roving search for provisions.

Fulcrum. The support or point of rest on which a lever turns; any prop or support.

G

Genealogy. A record or account of the ancestry of a person or kin group.

Genetic. Of, pertaining to, or produced by genes; pertaining to developmental origins.

Genghis Khan. The Mongol conqueror of most of Asia and Eastern Europe, 1162–1227.

Glottis. The variable space between the vocal chords.

H

Haggle. To bargain in a quarrelsome way.

Herbivore. A plant-eating mammal.

Hierarchy. Organization on the basis of ranked groups of unequal status.

Horticulture. In anthropology, the cultivation of plants without the use of draft animals, fertilizers, irrigation, or the plow; generally a less productive system of cultivation than agriculture (although this is not always true in the tropics).

Hypothesis. A proposition; an explanation asserted as highly probable in the light of established facts.

I

Ideograph. A nonphonetic symbol, drawn, carved, or painted, that represents an object or an idea in the language of its user.

Incest. Sexual relations with a relative with whom such relations are prohibited by custom or law.

Indigenous. Aboriginal or native, pertaining to the original inhabitants of a region, country, or continent.

Institution. An established practice, custom, or organization.

K

Kalahari. A desert region in Southwest Africa, largely in Botswana.

Karma. In Hinduism and Buddhism, an action seen as bringing inevitable results in this life or in the next reincarnation.

Kindred. An "ego-focused" group of close bilaterally related kinsmen.

Koran. The holy book of Islam.

Kudu. A large African antelope.

L

Lapp. Mostly nomadic people living in northern Norway, Sweden, and Finland.

Law. A social norm usually sanctioned by the threat of physical coercion by one or more persons whose right to the exercise of force is socially legitimized.

Levirate. The custom whereby a widow marries her deceased husband's brother; "brother-in-law" marriage.

Lexicon. The vocabulary of a particular language; the total inventory of morphemes in a given language.

Lineage. A group of kinspeople who share unilateral descent from a common known ancestor; such a group usually spans at least three generations.

Litigation. Pertaining to a contest at law; a lawsuit.

M

Machete. A large, heavy knife, used especially in cutting sugar cane and clearing underbrush.

Mana. A Malayo-Polynesian term for an impersonal supernatural force believed to be concentrated in a particular person or object.

Manioc. Cassava; a tropical plant cultivated for its tuberous roots, which yield a nutritious starch.

Matriclan, or matrilineal clan. Usually several descent groups with a tradition of relationship based on the belief that they are all descended through the female line from a common ancestress.

Matrilateral. Pertaining to descent reckoned through the female line.

Matrilineage. A lineage based on descent traced exclusively through females.

Matrilocal, or uxorilocal. Pertaining to postmarital residence of the husband and wife with or near the kinsmen of the wife.

Matrix. That which gives order or form to a thing; the structural core.

Maund. A unit of weight in India, varying from about twenty-five to eighty-two pounds.

Melanesia. A major cultural and geographic area in the South and Southwest Pacific, which includes the Solomon Islands, the New Hebrides, New Caledonia, the Bismarck Archipelago, the Admiralty and Fiji Islands, and New Guinea.

Millenarian. Pertaining to a prophesied millennium.

Mise en scène. A theatrical setting; the setting for a dramatic presentation.

Moiety. Half; the social group formed when a community is divided into halves on the basis of kinship affiliations.

Monogamy. The practice of marriage with but one person at a time.

Monotheism. The belief in or worship of a single god.

Morpheme. One or more phonemes having a unitary meaning.

Morphology. In linguistics, the patterns of word formation in a particular language, including inflection, derivation, and composition.

Multicentric. Many centered.

N

Natal. Pertaining to one's birth.

Nautilus. A spiral-shaped, chambered shellfish.

Neoevolutionary. Referring to contemporary unilinear evolutionary theory.

Neolocal. Pertaining to the establishment of postnuptial residence independent of the location of the parental home of either partner.

Night soil. Human excrement used for fertilizer.

Nomadism. Pertaining to the continuous or regularly intermittent movement of people and their livestock in response to variations in the availability of pasturage.

Nuclear family. The family group composed of one set of parents and their children, and no other relatives.

O

Oedipal. Pertaining to a child's unconscious sexual desire for the parent of opposite sex.

Orisha. A Yoruba term for a particular type of supernatural being.

P

Paddy. A rice field.

Padrinho. The Portuguese term for a ritual co-parent or godparent; in Spanish, *compadre.*

Parallel cousins. The children of one's father's brother or one's mother's sister; cousins whose related parents are of like sex.

Parasitic. Dependent on another for nourishment and shelter.

Pastoralism. A subsistence technology centered about the herding and husbandry of domesticated animals.

Patriclan. A clan based on descent traced exclusively through males.

Patrilateral. Pertaining to descent traced through the father's side.

Patrilineage. A group of kinsmen related exclusively through the male (agnatic) line to a common known male ancestor.

Patrilocal, or virilocal. Pertaining to the establishment of postnuptial residence with or near the kinsmen of the husband.

Pejorative. Deprecating.

Peyote. A variety of cactus (*Lophaphora williamsii*) ingested to induce visions as part of a religious ritual.

Phenomenon. An observed fact, occurrence, or circumstance.

Phone. A speech sound.

Phoneme. A minimal unit of spoken sound, a change of which produces an alternation of meaning in the utterance.

Phonemics. Pertaining to the study of phonemes.

Phonetics. The scientific study of speech sounds.

Phonology. The study of speech sounds with emphasis on the historical and theoretical analysis of sound changes.

Phratry. Two or more clans united by an often mythical belief that they share a remote common ancestor.

Physical anthropology. The branch of anthropology that studies human evolution and physical variation.

Pillage. To strip of goods and money by means of open violence.

Polity. A particular form or system of government.

Polyandry. A form of marriage that allows a woman to have more than one husband at a time.

Polygamy. A form of marriage in which one partner is allowed to have more than one spouse at a time.

Polygyndry. A marital union involving a multiplicity of both husbands and wives (rare).

Polygyny. A form of polygamy that allows a husband to have two or more wives at the same time.

Polynesia. "Many islands," an area of the Central Pacific that falls within a triangle formed by Hawaii, Easter Island, and New Zealand.

Polyphony. Pertaining to a musical composition having two or more voices or parts, each with an independent melody, but all harmonizing.

Polytheism. A religion that entails belief in more than one god.

Poro. A men's secret society in West Africa.

Possession. A ritual state in which the worshiper feels possessed body and soul by some supernatural being.

Postpartum. Pertaining to the period immediately following childbirth.

Potlatch. Ceremonial, often competitive gift giving among the Indians of the Northwest Pacific coast.

Potsherd. A broken pottery fragment.

Prayer. A devout petition to any object of worship, usually to a supernatural being.

Predatory. Habitually preying on other animals.

Primate. Any mammal of the order Primates, including man, the apes, monkeys, lemurs, tarsiers, and marmosets.

Primitive farming. See *Horticulture.*

Primordial. Pertaining to the elementary materials from which the universe evolved.

Progenitor. A biologically or nonbiologically related ancestor.

Projective. The faculty of eliciting a mental conception or idea.

Proletarian. Pertaining to membership in a propertyless class.

Propitiate. To make favorably inclined; to appease or conciliate.

Proto-Indo-European. The ancient language from which the modern Indo-European languages are descended.

Psychosis. An extreme behavior disorder marked by relatively fixed patterns of maladaptive attitudes and responses.

Pueblo. A village composed of compound dwellings constructed of clay (adobe) bricks or of stones, characteristic of the Indians of the U.S. Southwest and Mexico.

Puffin. A North Atlantic seabird.

Putative. Reputed; supposed.

R

Race. A term of disputed scientific utility, used to designate a population whose members' inherited physical appearance tends to reflect their distinctive genetic heritage.

Raid. A sudden, usually small-scale attack upon something intended to be seized or destroyed.

Rank. Pertaining to the position of a number of persons within a graded hierarchy.

Reify. To convert into or regard as a concrete thing.

Revitalize. To give new life to.

Ritual. An established ceremonial procedure, usually religious.

Role. The behavior culturally defined as appropriate to a particular status or position, such as that of father.

S

Sacerdotal. Pertaining to the priestly activities of a religious functionary.

Sacrifice. The propitiatory offering of plant, animal, or human life to some supernatural being.

Sago. A starchy foodstuff derived from the soft inner trunk of a Malayan feather palm.

Sahel. The arid region of Africa bordering the southern edge of the Sahara.

Sanction. A reaction operating to induce conformity to a culturally defined standard of behavior; may be either negative or positive.

Scarification. See *Cicatrization.*

Scythe. A long, curved blade fastened at an angle to a handle, for cutting grass or grain.

Sedentary. Pertaining to human groups that remain more or less permanently settled; not migratory.

Segmentary. A descent group in which internal divisions result in the frequent emergence of new and separate descent groups.

Shaman. One who acts as a ritual intermediary between other persons and the spirit world; generally such a person is assumed to have supernatural power.

Sib. A unilateral descent group, synonymous with clan.

Sibling. One of two or more children of the same parents.

Sickle. A curved or hooklike blade attached to a short handle.

Slag. Fused matter separated during the reduction of a metal from its ore.

Smelt. To fuse or melt ore to separate the metal.

Socialization. The early stages of the learning

process during which the young child internalizes the behaviors required of him or her by society.

Society. A generally large group of people who share a common culture and a sense of common identity; also, the system of interpersonal and intergroup relationships among such a group.

Sorcery. The use of supernatural power for aggressive purposes.

Sororal polygyny. The simultaneous marriage of two or more sisters to one husband.

Sororate. A practice whereby a woman marries the husband of her deceased sister.

Status. The position of an individual in relation to others within a society.

Steppe. One of the vast, comparatively level, and treeless plains of southeastern Europe and Siberia.

Strychnos. A kind of plant that contains the colorless poison stychnine.

Subculture. A significantly distinctive but nonautonomous sector of a larger culture; often based on differences in ethnic identity, class, or caste, and/or on geographic separation.

Supernatural. That which cannot presently be explained as resulting from natural causes.

Symbiosis. The mutually beneficial living together of dissimilar organisms.

Synchronic. Concerned with events within a limited time period, usually ignoring historical processes.

Syncretism. The fusion of two distinct systems of belief and practice.

Syntax. The study of how words and significant features of intonation are arranged in phrases or sentences, and of how sentences relate to each other.

T

Taboo, or tapu. Usually pertaining to a certain kind of ritually prohibited activity punishable by supernatural sanctions.

Tapa. Polynesian bark cloth.

Taro. A tropical plant cultivated for its tuberous, starchy, edible root.

Taxonomy. The systematic classification of things according to scientific principles.

Temper. The degree of hardness and strength imparted to a metal or to other substances such as pottery.

Totem. An object, often an animal, plant, or place, supernaturally related to a particular kin group.

Transhumance. The regular movement of herders and their livestock in response to seasonal shifts in the availability of pasturage.

Travois. A carrying device that has two poles, like the tongues of a buggy, hitched to a draft animal. The free ends drag on the ground.

Tribe. An autonomous but not necessarily "centrally" or politically organized social group with a distinctive culture, a distinctive language or dialect, a recognized territory and a sense of common identity.

Truffle. A subterranean, edible fungus.

U

Unilateral. Referring to descent through one line of relatives only.

Unilineal descent. The tracing of descent through kinsmen of one sex only; that is, a line of descent traced exclusively through males or through females.

Untouchable. An English term for certain members of Hindu society who are categorized as outside the formal structure of the caste system.

Usury. The lending of money at an exorbitant rate of interest.

Uxorilocal, or matrilocal. The practice of establishing postnuptial residence with or near the wife's kinsmen.

V

Varna. Any of the four main Hindu castes.

Virilocal, or patrilocal. Pertaining to the practice of establishing postnuptial residence in or near the household of the husband's family.

Voodoo. The English vernacular for a system of religious beliefs and practices brought to the

Americas, principally to the Circum-Caribbean region, by Africans from Dahomey. *Vodûn* in French, the official language of Haiti.

W

Warp. The parallel-lying foundation threads of a fabric.

Wattle. Stakes or rods interwoven with twigs or tree branches.

Weft. The threads woven at right angles through the parallel-lying foundation thread or warp; also called woof.

World view. A culturally conditioned perception of the total environment shared by the members of a particular culture.

Y

Yak. A shaggy-haired ox.

References Cited

A

Abarbanel, J., 1974, *The Cooperative Farmer and the Welfare State: Economic Change in an Israeli Moshav.* Humanities, Atlantic Highlands, N.J.

Aberle, D. F., 1961, "Matrilineal Descent in Cross-Cultural Perspective," in D. M. Schneider and K. Gough (eds.), *Matrilineal Kinship.* U. of Calif. Press, Berkeley, pp. 655–727.

———, 1966a, *The Peyote Religion Among the Navaho.* Viking Fund Publication in Anthropology 42. Wenner-Gren Foundation for Anthropological Research, New York.

———, 1966b, "Religio-magical Phenomena and Power, Prediction, and Control," *Southwestern Journal of Anthropology,* **22,** 221–230.

———, 1970, "A Note on Relative Deprivation Theory as Applied to Millennial and Other Cult Movements," in S. Thrupp (ed.), *Millennial Dreams in Action.* Schocken, New York, pp. 209–214.

———, and others, 1964, "The Incest Taboo and the Mating Patterns of Animals," *American Anthropologist,* **65,** 253–265.

Abrahams, R. D., and J. F. Szwed, 1975, "Black English: An Essay Review," *American Anthropologist,* **77,** 329–335.

Adam, H., 1971, *Modernizing Racial Domination: The Dynamics of South African Politics.* U. of Calif. Press, Berkeley.

Adams, R. McC., 1966, *The Evolution of Urban Society: Early Mesopotamia to Prehispanic Mexico.* Aldine, Chicago.

Adelman, I., and C. T. Morris, 1974, *Economic Growth and Social Equity in Developing Areas.* Stanford U.P., Stanford.

Aggarwal, P., 1971, *Caste, Religion and Power: An Indian Case Study.* Shri Ram Centre for Industrial Relations, New Delhi.

Ahern, E. M., 1973, *The Cult of the Dead in a Chinese Village.* Stanford U.P., Stanford.

———, 1976, "Segmentation in Chinese Lineages: A View Through Written Genealogies," *American Ethnologist,* **3,** 1–16.

Alland, A. J., Jr., 1973, *Evolution and Human Behavior.* Natural History Press, New York.

Amsbury, C., 1972, "Reply to Anderson's Voluntary Associations in History," *American Anthropologist,* **74,** 770.

Amsden, C. A., 1949, *Navajo Weaving: Its Technique and History.* U. of New Mexico Press, Albuquerque.

Anderson, E. N., 1970, "Lineage Atrophy in Chinese Society." *American Anthropologist,* **72,** 363–367.

Anderson, J. G., 1973, *Children of the Yellow Earth: Studies in Prehistoric China.* M.I.T. Press, Cambridge, Mass.

Anderson, R. T., 1971, "Voluntary Associations in History," *American Anthropologist,* **73,** 209–222.

Antoun, R., and I. Harick (eds.), 1972, *Rural Politics and Social Change in the Middle East.* Indiana U.P., Bloomington.

Ardener, E. (ed.), 1971, *Social Anthropology and Language.* Barnes and Noble, New York.

Arinze, F., 1970, *Sacrifice in Ibo Religion.* Edited by J. S. Boston. Ibadan U.P., Ibadan.

Armstrong, W. E., 1924, "Rossel Island Money: A Unique Monetary System." *The Economic Journal,* **34,** 423–429. Reprinted in Dalton, 1967.

Asad, T., 1974, "The Concept of Rationality in Economic Anthropology," *Economic Studies,* **3,** 211–218.

Aswad, B. C., 1971, *Property Control and Social Strategies: Settlers on a Middle Eastern Plain.* Anthropological Papers 44. U. of Mich. Press, Ann Arbor.

B

Balandier, A., 1970, *Political Anthropology.* Pantheon, New York.

Barth, F., 1953, *Principles of Social Organization in Southern Kurdistan.* Universitets Etnografiske Museum Bulletin 7, Oslo.

———, 1954, "Father's Brother's Daughter Marriage in Kurdistan," *Southwestern Journal of Anthropology,* **10,** 164–171.

———, 1959, *Political Leadership Among Swat Pathans.* London School of Economics Monographs in Social Anthropology 19, London.

——— (ed.), 1969, *Ethnic Groups and Boundaries.* Little, Brown, Boston.

———, 1975a, *Ritual and Knowledge Among the Baktaman of New Guinea.* Yale U.P., New Haven.

———, 1975b, "Social Organization of a Pariah Group in Norway," in F. Rehfisch (ed.), *Gypsies, Tinkers, and Other Travelers.* Academic, New York.

Bascom, W., 1950, "The Focus of Cuban Santería," *Southwestern Journal of Anthropology,* **6,** 64–68.

Basedow, H., 1925, "The Australian Aboriginal," in *The Adelaide Register,* March 4, Adelaide, Australia.

Basehart, H. W., 1970, "Mescalero Apache Band Organization and Leadership," *Southwestern Journal of Anthropology,* **26,** 87–106. Reprinted in Hammond 1975.

Bastide, R., 1958, *Le Candomblé de Bahia.* Mouton, Paris.

Bateman, H., 1970, *The Kung of the Kalahari.* Beacon, Boston.

Bauman, R., 1975, "Verbal Art As Performance," *American Anthropologist,* **77,** 290–311.

———, and J. Sherzer (eds.), 1974, *Explorations in the Ethnography of Speaking.* Cambridge U.P., New York.

———, 1975, "The Ethnography of Speaking," in B. Siegel and others (eds.), *Annual Review of Anthropology.* Annual Reviews, Palo Alto, pp. 95–119.

Beals, R., 1975. *The Peasant Marketing System of Oaxaca, Mexico.* U. of Calif. Press, Los Angeles.

Beals, R., P. Carrasco, and T. McCorkel, 1944, *Houses and House Use of the Sierra Tarascans.* Smithsonian Institution, Washington, D.C.

Beardsley, R., 1973, *Art and Anthropology.* Burgess, Minneapolis.

———, J. W. Hall, and R. E. Ward, 1959, *Village Japan,* Chicago U.P., Chicago.

Beattie, J., 1967, "Consulting a Nyoro Diviner: The Ethnologist as Client," *Ethnology,* **6,** 57–65.

———, 1970, "On Understanding Ritual," in B. Wilson (ed.), *Rationality.* Harper, New York.

———, 1971, *The Nyoro State.* Oxford U.P., New York.

Beckford, G., 1972, *Persistent Poverty: Underdevelopment in Plantation Economies of the Third World.* Oxford U.P., New York.

Befu, H., 1966, "Corporate Emphasis and Patterns of Descent in the Japanese Family," in R. J. Smith and R. K. Beardsley (eds.), *Japanese Culture.* Aldine, Chicago, pp. 34–41.

———, 1971, *Japan: An Anthropological Introduction.* Chandler, San Francisco.

———, and L. Plotnicov, 1962, "Types of Corporate Unilineal Descent Groups," *American Anthropologist,* **64,** 313–327.

Belshaw, C. S., 1950, "The Significance of Modern Cults in Melanesian Development, *The Australian Outlook,* **4,** 116–125. Reprinted in abriged form in Lessa and Vogt 1970.

———, 1965, *Traditional Exchange and Modern Markets.* Prentice-Hall, Englewood Cliffs, N.J.

Ben-Amos, D., 1972, "Towards a Definition of Folklore in Context," in A. Paredes and R. Bauman (eds.), *Toward New Perspectives in Folklore.* U. of Texas Press, Austin, pp. 3–15.

———, and K. Goldstein (eds.), 1975, *Folklore: Communication and Performance.* Mouton, the Hague.

Benedict, R., 1946, *The Chrysanthemum and the Sword.* Houghton, Mifflin, Boston.

Benítez, F., 1975, *In the Magic Land of Peyote.* U. of Texas Press, Austin.

Berg, G., 1935, *Sledges and Wheeled Vehicles.* Levin and Munksgaard, Copenhagen.

BERGER, J., 1975, *The Seventh Man.* Penguin, Baltimore.

BERGSLAND, K. and H. VOGT, 1962, "On the Validity of Glottochronology," *Current Anthropology,* **3,** 115–158.

BERLIN, B., and P. KAY, 1969, *Basic Color Terms: Their Universality and Evolution.* U. of Calif. Press, Berkeley.

———, D. BREEDLOVE, and P. RAVEN, 1973, *Studies in Tzeltal Botanical Ethnography: Principles of Classification.* Seminar, New York.

———, 1974, *Principles of Tzeltal Plant Classification.* Academic, New York.

BERNARD, H., and P. PELTO (eds.), 1972, *Technology and Social Change.* Macmillan, New York.

BERREMAN, G., 1962a, "Pahari Polyandry: A Comparison," *American Anthropologist,* **64,** 60–75.

———, 1962b, *Behind Many Masks: Ethnography and Impression Management in a Himalayan Village.* Society for Applied Anthropology Monograph 4, Ithaca, N.Y.

———, 1966, "Anemic and Emetic Analysis in Social Anthropology," *American Anthropologist,* **68,** 346–354.

———, 1972a, *Hindus of the Himalayas.* U. of Calif. Press, Berkeley.

———, 1972b, "Social Categories and Social Interaction in Urban India," *American Anthropologist,* **74,** 567–587.

———, 1972c, "Race, Caste, and Other Invidious Distinctions in Social Stratification," *Race,* **13,** Reprinted in Hammond 1975.

———, 1975, "Himalayan Polyandry and the Domestic Cycle," *American Ethnologist,* **2,** 127–138.

BEYER, S., 1974, *The Cult of Tārā: Magic and Ritual in Tibet.* U. of Calif. Press, Berkeley.

BICCHIERI, M. (ed.), 1972, *Hunters and Gatherers Today.* Holt, New York.

BIEBUYCK, D. (ed.), 1969, *Tradition and Creativity in Tribal Art.* U. of Calif. Press, Berkeley.

BIRDSELL, J. B., 1972, *Human Evolution: An Introduction to the New Physical Anthropology.* Rand McNally, Chicago.

BIRKET-SMITH, K., 1929, *The Caribou Eskimos: Material and Social Life and Their Cultural Position, Report of the Fifth Thule Expedition.* Gyldendalske Boghandel, Copenhagen.

BIRRELL, V., 1959, *The Textile Arts: A Handbook of Fabric Structure and Design Processes: Ancient and Modern Weaving, Braiding, Printing, and Other Textile Techniques.* Harper, New York.

BISCHOFBERGER, O., 1972, *The Generation Classes of the Zanaki.* Fribourg U.P., Fribourg, Switzerland.

BLACK, C. B., 1974, *All Our Kin.* Harper, New York.

BLASSINGAME, J., 1972, *The Slave Community.* Oxford U.P., New York.

BLAU, P., and O. DUNCAN, 1967, *The American Occupational Structure.* Wiley, New York.

BLOCH, M., 1971, *Placing the Dead: Tombs, Ancestral Villages and Kinship Organization in Madagascar.* Seminar, New York.

BLOUNT, B. (ed.), 1974, *Language, Culture, and Society: A Book of Readings.* Cambridge U.P., New York.

BLUMBERG, P., (ed.), 1972, *The Impact of Social Class.* Crowell, New York.

BOAS, F., 1895, *The Social Organization and Secret Societies of the Kwakiutl Indians.* U.S. National Museum, Washington, D.C.

BOAS, 1934, *Geographical Names of the Kwakiutl Indians.* Columbia University Contributions to Anthropology 20. Columbia U.P., New York. Reprinted in Hymes 1964b.

BODLEY, J. H., 1975, *Victims of Progress.* Cummings, Menlo Park, Calif.

BOGATYREV, P., 1971, *The Functions of Folk Costume in Moravian Slovakia.* Mouton, Paris.

BOHANNAN, L., 1958, "Political Aspects of Tiv Social Organization," in J. Middleton and D. Tait (eds.), *Tribes Without Rulers.* Routledge, London, pp. 33–66.

BOHANNAN, P., 1954, "The Migration and Expansion of the Tiv," *Africa,* **24,** 2–16.

———, 1957, *Justice and Judgment Among the Tiv.* Oxford U.P., Oxford.

———, 1959, "The Impact of Money on an African Subsistence Economy." Journal of Economic History, **19,** 491–503. Reprinted in Hammond 1964.

———, 1963, *Social Anthropology.* Holt, New York.

——— (ed.), 1970, *Divorce and After.* Doubleday, New York.

———, and L. BOHANNAN, 1968, "Land Rights: Social Relations in Terrestrial Space," in their *Tiv Economy.* Northwestern U.P., Evanston, pp. 77–92. Reprinted in Hammond 1975.

———, and G. Dalton (eds.), 1965, *Markets in Africa.* Northwestern U.P., Evanston.

———, and J. Middleton (eds.), 1968a, *Kinship and Social Organization.* Natural History Press, New York.

———, 1968b, *Marriage, Family, and Residence.* Natural History Press, New York.

Boissevain, 1974, *Friends of Friends: Networks, Manipulators, and Coalitions.* Blackwell, Oxford.

Boorstein, E., 1968, *The Economic Transformation of Cuba.* Monthly Review Press, New York.

Boserup, E., 1965, *The Conditions of Agricultural Growth: The Economics of Agrarian Change Under Population Pressure.* Aldine, Chicago.

———, 1970, *Woman's Role in Economic Development.* St. Martin's Press, New York.

Bossen, L., 1975, "Women in Modernizing Societies," *American Ethnologist,* **2,** 587–601.

Bouglé, C., 1971, *Essays on the Caste System.* Cambridge U.P., New York.

Bourgiugnon, E., 1959, "The Persistence of Folk Belief: Some Notes on Cannibalism and Zombis in Haiti," *Journal of American Folklore,* **72,** 36–46.

———, 1968, *Trance Dance.* Dance Perspectives Foundation, No. 35, New York.

——— (ed.), 1972, *Religion, Altered States of Consciousness and Social Change.* Ohio State U.P., Columbus.

Bradfield, R. M., 1974, *A Natural History of Associations,* 2 vol. International Universities Press, New York.

Braidwood, R. J. and G. R. Willey (eds.), 1962, *Courses Toward Urban Life.* Aldine, Chicago.

Brandewie, E., 1971, "The Place of the Big Man in Traditional Hagen Society in the Central Highlands of New Guinea," *Ethnology,* **10,** 194–210.

Brandon, S. (ed.), 1970, *On Thrones of Gold: Three Javanese Shadow Plays.* Harvard U.P., Cambridge, Mass.

Briggs, J. L., 1970, *Never in Anger: Portrait of an Eskimo Family.* Harvard U.P., Cambridge.

Briggs, L. C., 1960. *Tribes of the Sahara.* Oxford U.P., London.

Brigham, W. T., 1911, *Ka Hana Kapa: The Making of Bark Cloth in Hawaii.* Bishop Museum, Honolulu.

Brookfield, H. C., 1969, *Pacific Market-Places: A Collection of Essays.* Australian National U.P., Canberra.

Brown, J., 1970a, "Economic Organization and the Position of Women Among the Iroquois," *Ethnohistory,* **17,** 151–167.

———, 1970b, "A Note on the Division of Labor by Sex," *American Anthropologist,* **72,** 1073–1078.

Brown, M. B., 1974, *The Economics of Imperialism.* Penguin, Baltimore.

Bruner, E., 1972, "Batak Ethnic Associations in Three Indonesian Cities," *Southwestern Journal of Anthropology,* **28,** 207–229.

Bujra, A. S., 1971, *The Politics of Stratification.* Oxford U.P., New York.

Bull, R. (ed.), 1968, *Research in Dance: Problems and Possibilities.* Committee on Research in Dance, New York.

Bunzel, R., 1929, *The Pueblo Potter.* Columbia University Contributions to Anthropology 8. Columbia U.P., New York.

Burch, E. S., Jr., 1970, "Marriage and Divorce Among the North Alaskan Eskimos," in P. Bohannan (ed.), *Divorce and After.* Doubleday, New York, pp. 152–181.

Burling, R., 1970, *Man's Many Voices.* Holt, New York.

———, 1974, *The Passage of Power: Studies in Political Succession.* Academic, New York.

Burridge, K., 1969, *New Heaven, New Earth: A Study of Millenarian Activities.* Schocken, New York.

C

Cambel, H., and R. Braidwood, 1970, "An Early Farming Village in Turkey," *Scientific American,* **222,** 50–56.

Campbell, B., 1976, "The Evolutionary Emergence of Language," in his *Human Evolution: An Introduction to Man's Adaptation.* Aldine, Chicago, pp. 344–357. Reprinted in Hammond 1976.

Cancian, F., 1972, *Change and Uncertainty in a Peasant Economy: The Maya Corn Farmers of Zinacantan.* Stanford U.P., Stanford.

———, 1974, "New Patterns of Stratification in

the Zinacantan Cargo System," *Journal of Anthropological Research,* **30,** 164–173.

Cannon, W. B., 1942, "Voodoo Death," *American Anthropologist,* **44,** 169–181.

Carneiro, R. (ed.), 1968, *The Evolution of Society: Selections from Spencer's Principles of Sociology.* U. of Chicago Press, Chicago.

———, 1970, "A Theory of the Organization of the State," *Science,* **169,** 733–738.

———, 1973a, "The Four Faces of Evolution: Unilinear, Universal, Multilinear, and Differential," in J. Honigmann (ed.), *Handbook of Social and Cultural Anthropology.* McGraw-Hill, New York.

———, 1973b, "Structure, Function, and Equilibrium in the Evolutionism of Herbert Spencer," *Journal of Anthropological Research,* **29,** 77–95.

———, 1974, "A Reappraisal of the Roles of Technology and Organization in the Origins of Civilization," *American Antiquity,* **39,** 179–186.

Caro Baroja, J., 1973, *The World of the Witches.* U. of Chicago Press, Chicago.

Carrington, J., 1971, "The Talking Drums of Africa," *Scientific American,* **225,** 90–94.

Carter, A., 1974, *Elite Politics in Rural India: Political Stratification and Alliances in Western Maharashtra.* Cambridge U.P., New York.

Chagnon, N., 1974, *Studying the Yanomamo.* Holt, New York.

Chalmers, D. M., 1965, *Hooded Americanism: The First Century of the Ku Klux Klan 1865–1965.* Doubleday, New York.

Chance, N., 1966, *The Eskimo of North Alaska.* Holt, New York.

Chaney, R. P., K. Morton, and T. Moore, 1972, "On the Entangled Problems of Selection and Conceptual Organization," *American Anthropologist,* **74,** 221–230.

Chang, K., 1963, *The Archaeology of Ancient China.* Yale U.P., New Haven.

———, 1970, "The Beginnings of Agriculture in the Far East," *Antiquity,* **44,** 175–185.

Chidwick, P., 1970, "Some Ideas Concerning the Origins of Dowry in East Africa," *Journal of Modern African Studies,* **8,** 143–149.

Childe, V., 1968, *New Light on the Most Ancient East.* Praeger, New York.

Chomsky, N., 1957, *Syntactic Structures.* Mouton, The Hague.

———, 1965, *Aspects of the Theory of Syntax,* M.I.T. Press, Cambridge, Mass.

———, 1968, *Language and Mind.* Harcourt, New York.

———, 1972, *Studies on Semantics in Generative Grammar.* Mouton, The Hague.

Clark, G., 1970a, "The Achievement of Civilization in South-West Asia," in his *World Prehistory: A New Outline.* Cambridge U.P., New York, pp. 94–118. Reprinted in Hammond 1976.

———, 1970b, *Aspects of Prehistory.* U. of Calif. Press, Berkeley.

———, and S. Piggott, 1970, *Prehistoric Societies.* Pelican, Baltimore.

Clark, J. D., 1962, "The Spread of Early Farming in Sub-Saharan Africa," *Journal of African History,* **3,** 211–228. Reprinted in Hammond 1976.

———, 1970, *The Prehistory of Africa.* Praeger, New York.

Clegg, J., 1972, *Workers' Self-management in Algeria.* Monthly Review Press, New York.

Clignet, R., 1970, *Many Wives, Many Powers: Authority and Power in Polygynous Families.* Northwestern U.P., Evanston.

Cline, W., 1937, *Mining and Metallurgy in Negro Africa.* George Banta, Manasha, Wis.

Cohen, A. (ed.), 1974, *Urban Ethnicity.* Harper, New York.

Cohen, R., 1970, "The Political System," in R. Naroll and R. Cohen (eds.), *A Handbook of Method in Cultural Anthropology.* Natural History Press, New York, pp. 484–499.

———, 1971, *Dominance and Defiance: A Study of Marital Instability in an Islamic Society.* American Anthropological Association, Washington, D.C.

———, and J. Middleton (eds.), *Comparative Political Systems: Studies in the Politics of Pre-industrial Societies.* Natural History Press, New York.

———, and others, 1973, "Entree into the Field," in R. Naroll and R. Cohen (eds.), *A Handbook of Method in Cultural Anthropology.* Natural History Press, New York, pp. 220–245.

Cohen, Y., 1968, "Macroethnology: Large Scale

Comparative Studies," in J. Clifton (ed.), *Introduction to Cultural Anthropology.* Houghton Mifflin, Boston, pp. 402–448.

Cohn, B. S., 1955, "The Changing Status of a Depressed Caste," in M. Mariott (ed.), Village India. U. of Chicago Press, Chicago, pp. 53–77.

Cole, J. W., and E. Wolf, 1974, *The Hidden Frontier: Ecology and Ethnicity in an Alpine Village.* Academic, New York.

Collier, J. W., 1967, *Visual Anthropology: Photography as a Research Method.* Holt, New York.

Collins, H. B., and others, 1945, *The Aleut Islands: Their People and Natural History.* Smithsonian Institution War Background Studies 21. U.S. Government Printing Office, Washington, D.C.

Colson, E., 1974, *Tradition and Contract: The Problem of Order.* Aldine, Chicago.

Comstock, T. (ed.), *New Dimensions in Dance Research: Anthropology and Dance—The American Indian.* Committee on Research on Dance, New York.

Công-Huyên-Tôn-Nû, N., 1970, *Vietnamese Folklore: An Introductory and Annotated Bibliography.* U. of Calif. Press, Berkeley.

Conklin, H. C., 1955, "Hanunóo Color Categories," *Southwestern Journal of Anthropology,* **11,** 339–344.

______(ed.), 1972, *Folk Classification: A Topically Arranged Bibliography of Contemporary and Background References Through 1971.* Department of Anthropology, Yale University, New Haven, Conn.

Cook, S., 1973a, "Production, Ecology, and Economic Anthropology: Notes Toward an Integrated Frame of Reference," *Social Science Information,* **12,** 25–52.

______, 1973b, "Economic Anthropology: Problems in Theory, Method and Analysis," in J. Honigmann (ed.), *A Handbook of Social and Cultural Anthropology.* Rand McNally, Chicago, pp. 795–860.

Cook, S., and M. Diskin (eds.), 1975, *Markets in Oaxaca.* U. of Texas Press, Austin.

Coon, C., 1958, *Caravan.* Holt, New York.

Cooper, J. M., 1933, "The Northern Algonquian Supreme Being," *Primitive Man,* **6,** 41–111.

Cornell, J. B., and R. J. Smith, 1956, *Two Japanese Villages.* U. of Mich. Press, Ann Arbor.

Coursey, D., and C. Coursey, 1971, "The New Year Festivals of West Africa," *Anthropos,* **66,** 444–84.

Coy, P., 1974, "An Elementary Structure of Ritual Kinship: A Case of Prescription in the Compadrazgo," *Man,* **9,** 470–479.

Crissman, L., 1967, "The Segmentary Structure of Urban Overseas Chinese Communities," *Man,* **2,** 185–204.

Crowley, D., 1966, *I Could Talk Old-Story Good.* U. of California Press, Berkeley.

Crumrine, N., 1970, "Ritual Drama and Culture Change," *Comparative Studies in Society and History,* **12,** 361–372.

Curley, R., 1973, *Elders, Shades, and Women.* U. of Calif. Press, Berkeley.

Current, W., and V. Scully, 1971, *Pueblo Architecture of the Southwest.* U. of Texas Press, Austin.

Curtin, P. (ed.), 1968, *Africa Remembered; Narratives of Africans from the Era of the Slave Trade.* U. of Wisconsin Press, Madison.

D

Dalton, G., 1962, "Traditional Production in Primitive African Economies," *The Quarterly Journal of Economics,* **76,** 360–378. Reprinted in Dalton 1967.

______, 1965, "Primitive Money," *American Anthropologist,* **67,** 44–65.

______(ed.), 1967, *Tribal and Peasant Economies.* Natural History Press, New York.

______, 1970, "The Economic System," in R. Naroll and R. Cohen (eds.), *A Handbook of Method in Cultural Anthropology.* Natural History Press, New York.

______(ed.), 1971a, *Economic Development and Social Change: The Modernization of Village Communities.* Natural History Press, New York.

______, (ed.), 1971b, *Studies in Economic Anthropology.* American Anthropological Association, Washington, D.C.

______, 1974, "Peasant Markets," *The Journal of Peasant Studies,* **1,** 240–243.

Damas, D. (ed.), 1969, *Contributions to Anthropology: Band Societies.* National Museums of Canada Bulletin 228. National Museums of Canada, Ottawa.

______, 1972, "Central Eskimo Systems of Food Sharing," *Ethnology,* **11,** 220–240.

______, 1975, "Demographic Aspects of Central

Eskimo Marriage Practices," *American Ethnologist,* **2,** 409–418.

DANIEL, P., 1972, *The Shadow of Slavery:* U. of Ill. Press, Urbana.

DARLINGTON, C., 1970, "The Origins of Plant Domestication," *Natural History Magazine,* May, 47–56.

DAVIDSON, B., 1975, *Can Africa Survive? Arguments Against Growth Without Development.* Heinemann, London.

DAVIDSON, R., and R. DAY, 1974, *Symbol and Realization: A Contribution to the Study of Magic and Healing.* U. of Calif. Press, Berkeley.

DAVIES, B. T., 1947, *Four Centuries of Witch Beliefs.* Methuen, London.

DAVIS, W. G., 1973, *Social Relations in a Philippine Market: Self Interest and Subjectivity.* U. of Calif. Press, Berkeley.

D'AZEVEDO, W. L., 1958, "A Structural Approach to Esthetics: Toward a Definition of Art in Culture," *American Anthropologist,* **60,** 702–714.

———, 1973a, "Sources of Gola Artistry," in W. L. d'Azevedo (ed.), *The Traditional Artist in African Societies.* Indiana U.P., Bloomington, pp. 282–340.

——— (ed.), 1973b, *The Traditional Artist in African Society.* Indiana U.P., Bloomington.

———, 1973c, "Mask Makers and Myth in Western Liberia," in A. FORGE (ed.), *Primitive Art and Society.* Oxford U.P., New York, pp. 126–150.

DEARDORFF, M., 1951, "The Religion of Handsome Lake: Its Origin and Development," in W. Fenton (ed.), *Symposium on Local Diversity in Iroquois Culture.* Bureau of American Ethnology Bulletin 149. Smithsonian Institution, Washington, D.C., pp. 77–107.

DENG, F. M., 1971, *Tradition and Modernization: A Challenge for Law Among the Dinka of the Sudan.* Yale U.P., New Haven.

———, 1973, *The Dinka and Their Songs.* Oxford U.P., New York.

DESHEN, S., 1970, "On Religious Change: The Situational Analysis of Symbolic Action," *Comparative Studies in Society and History,* **12,** 260–274.

DESPRES, L., 1975, *Ethnicity and Resource Competition in Plural Societies.* Aldine, Chicago.

DEVERAUX, G., 1961, "Art and Mythology, Part 1: A General Theory," in B. Kaplan (ed.), *Studying Personality Cross-Culturally.* Row, Evanston, Ill., pp. 361–386.

DEVORE, I. (ed.), *Primate Behavior.* Holt, New York.

DEVOS, G., 1967, "Psychology of Purity and Pollution as Related to Social Self-Identity & Caste," in A. de Reuck and J. Knight (eds.), *Caste and Race,* Little Brown, Boston, pp. 292–315.

———, and H. WAGATSUMA (eds.), 1967, *Japan's Invisible Race: Caste in Culture and Personality.* U. of Calif. Press, Berkeley.

DIAMOND, S., 1973, The Rule of Law Versus the Order of Custom," in D. Black and M. MILIESKI (eds.), *The Social Organization of Law.* Seminar, New York, pp. 318–343.

———, 1974, *In Search of the Primitive.* Dutton, New York.

DILLARD, J. L., 1972, *Black English; Its History in the United States.* Random House, New York.

DIVALE, W., 1971, *Warfare in Primitive Societies: A Bibliography.* American Bibliographical Center—Clio Press, Santa Barbara, Calif.

DOBKIN DE RIOS, M., 1972, *Visionary Vine: Psychedelic Healing in the Peruvian Amazon.* Chandler, New York.

DOMHOFF, G., 1975, *The Bohemian Grove and Other Retreats: A Study of Ruling Class Cohesiveness.* Harper, New York.

DONNAN, E. (ed.), 1965, *Documents Illustrative of the Slave Trade to America,* 4 vols. Octagon, New York.

DORSON, R. M., 1963, "Current Folklore Theories," *Current Anthropology,* **64,** 93–112.

——— (ed.), 1972, *Folklore and Folklife: An Introduction.* U. of Chicago Press, Chicago.

———, 1973, *America in Legend: Folklore from the Colonial Period to the Present.* Random House, New York.

DOUGLAS, M. (ed.), 1970, *Witchcraft Confessions and Accusations.* Tavistock, London.

DOWLING, J. H., 1975, "Property Relations and Productive Strategies in Pastoral Societies," *American Ethnologist,* **2,** 419–426.

DRAPER, P., and E. CASHDAN, 1975, "!Kung Women: Contrasts in Sex Egalitarianism in the Foraging and Sedentary Contexts," in R. Reiter (ed.), *Toward an Anthropology of Women.* Monthly Review Press, New York, pp. 77–109.

Driver, H. E., 1971, *Indians of North America.* Chicago U.P., Chicago.

———, 1973, "Cross Cultural Studies," in J. Honigmann (ed.), *Handbook of Social and Cultural Anthropology.* Rand McNally, Chicago, pp. 327–367.

———, and R. P., Chaney, 1970, "Cross-Cultural Sampling and Galton's Problem," in R. Naroll and R. Cohen eds.), *A Handbook of Method in Cultural Anthropology.* Natural History Press, New York, pp. 990–1003.

Driver, W., 1961, "Music," in H. E. Driver, *Indians of North America.* Chicago U.P., Chicago, pp. 212–223.

Drucker, P., 1951, *The Northern and Central Nootkan Tribes,* Bureau of American Ethnology, Bulletin 144. Smithsonian Institution, Washington, D.C.

Drucker, P., 1965, *Cultures of the North Pacific Coast.* Chandler, San Francisco.

Drucker, P., and R. F., Heizer, 1967, *To Make My Name Good: A Reexamination of the Kwakiutl Potlatch.* California U.P., Berkeley.

Du Bois, C., 1944, *The People of Alor: A Social Psychological Study of an East Indian Island.* Minnesota U.P., Minneapolis.

Ducret, P., 1901, "Production et Utilisation du 'Tapa' de Tahiti," *Revue Scientifique, Series 4,* **16,** 187–188.

Dumond, D., 1972, "Population Growth and Political Centralization," in B. Spooner (ed.), *Population Growth: Anthropological Perspectives.* M.I.T. Press, Cambridge, Mass., pp. 286–310.

Dundes, A. (ed.), 1965, *The Study of Folklore.* Prentice-Hall, Englewood Cliffs, N.J.

Dyson-Hudson, N., 1963, "Karimojong Age System," *Ethnology,* **3,** 353–401.

———, 1966, *Karimojong Politics.* Oxford U.P., New York.

———, and W. G. Irons (eds.), 1972, *Perspectives on Nomadism.* Brill, Leiden.

Dyson-Hudson, R., and N. Dyson-Hudson, 1969, "Subsistence Herding in Uganda," *Science,* **220,** 76–89.

E

Eckstein, H., 1972, "Towards an Etiology of Internal War," in C. Welch, Jr., and M. Tainter (eds.), *Revolution and Political Change.* Duxbury, North Scituate, Mass.

Edel, M., 1970, "Karl Polanyi's Concept of Non-market Trade," *Journal of Economic History,* **30,** 127–130.

Edgerton, R., 1971a, *The Individual in Cultural Adaptation.* California U.P., Berkeley.

———, 1971b, "A Traditional African Psychiatrist," *Southwestern Journal of Anthropology,* **27,** 259–278. Reprinted in Hammond 1975.

Edmonson, M., 1971, *Lore: An Introduction to the Scientific Study of Folklore and Literature.* Holt, New York.

Edwards, T., 1969, "The Tenant System and Some Changes Since Emancipation," in A. Meir and E. Rudwick (eds.), *The Black Community in Modern America,* Vol. 2. Atheneum, New York, pp. 20–26.

Eggan, F., 1968, "Typology and Reconstruction," in R. B. Lee and I. DeVore (eds.), *Man the Hunter.* Aldine, Chicago, pp. 161–162.

Eisenstadt, S., 1956, *From Generation to Generation.* Free Press, New York.

———, 1971, *Social Differentiation and Stratification.* Scott, Glenview, Ill.

Eister, A. W., 1974, *Changing Perspectives in the Scientific Study of Religion.* Wiley, New York.

Ekvall, R. B., 1963, "Some Aspects of Divination in Tibetan Society," *Ethnology,* **2,** 31–39.

Elkin, A., 1964, *The Australian Aborigines.* Doubleday, Garden City, N.Y. Original edition 1938.

Ellis, C., 1964, *Aboriginal Music Making.* Libraries Board of South Australia, Adelaide.

Elmendorf, W., 1971, "Coast Salish Status Ranking and Intergroup Ties," *Southwestern Journal of Anthropology,* **27,** 353–380.

Ember, C., M. Ember, and B. Pasternak, 1974, "On the Development of Unilineal Descent," *Journal of Anthropological Research,* **30,** 69–94.

Embree, J. F., 1939, *Suye Mura: A Japanese Village.* Chicago U.P., Chicago.

Emery, I., 1966, *The Primary Structures of Fabrics: An Illustrative Classification.* Textile Museum, Washington, D.C.

Emmanuel, A., 1973, *Unequal Exchange.* Monthly Review Press, New York.

Emmerich, A., 1965, *Sweat of the Sun and Tears of the Moon: Gold and Silver in Precolumbian Art.* Washington U.P., Seattle.

ENDICOTT, K., 1970, *An Analysis of Malay Magic.* Oxford U.P., New York.

ENDO, R., 1974, "Japanese Americans: The 'Model Minority' in Perspective," in R. Gomez, C. Cottingham, Jr., R. Endo, and K. Jackson (eds.), 1974, *The Social Reality of Ethnic America.* Heath, Lexington, Mass.

ENGELS, F., 1972, *The Origin of the Family, Private Property, and the State. With an Introduction by E. Leacock.* International, New York.

EPSTEIN, A. (ed.), 1974, *Contention and Dispute: Aspects of Law and Social Control in Melanesia.* Australian National University, Canberra.

EPSTEIN, S., 1967, "Productive Efficiency and Customary Systems of Rewards in Rural South India," in R. Firth (ed.), *Themes in Economic Anthropology.* Tavistock, London, pp. 229–252.

EPSTEIN, T. S., and D. H. PENNY (eds.), 1972, *Opportunity and Response: Case Studies in Economic Development.* Hurst, London.

ERRINGTON, F., 1974, "Indigenous Ideas of Order, Time, and Transition in a New Guinea Cargo Movement," *American Ethnologist,* **1,** 255–267.

———, 1975, *Karavar: Masks and Power in a Melanesian Ritual.* Cornell U.P., Ithaca.

ESSIEN-UDOM, E. V., 1962, *Black Nationalism: A Search for Identity in America.* U. of Chicago Press, Chicago.

EVANS, I. H., 1927, *Papers on the Ethnology and Archaeology of the Malay Peninsula.* Cambridge U.P., Cambridge.

———, 1937, *The Negritos of Malaya.* Cambridge U.P., Cambridge.

EVANS-PRITCHARD, E. E., 1937, *Witchcraft, Oracles, and Magic Among the Azande.* Clarendon, Oxford.

———, 1940, "The Nuer of the Southern Sudan," in M. Fortes and E. E. EVANS-PRITCHARD (eds.), *African Political Systems.* Oxford U.P., New York.

———, 1949, *The Sanusi of Cyrenaica.* Oxford U.P., New York.

———, 1964, *Social Anthropology and Other Essays.* Free Press, New York.

———, 1967, "Zande Iron-Working," *Paideuma,* **13,** 26–31.

———, 1968, *The Nuer.* Clarendon, Oxford. Original edition 1940.

———, 1970, "Zande Bridewealth," *Africa,* **40,** 115–124.

EWERS, J. C., 1955, *The Horse in Blackfoot Indian Culture.* Bureau of American Ethnology Bulletin 159. Smithsonian Institution, Washington, D.C.

F

FAGG, W., and J. PICTON, 1970, *The Potter's Art in Africa.* British Museum Publications, Shenval, London.

FAIRSERVIS, W., 1971, "The Origin of the Harappan Civilization," in his *The Roots of Ancient India.* Macmillan, New York, pp. 217–239. Reprinted as "The Valley of the Indus" in Hammond 1976.

FALLERS, L., 1956, *Bantu Bureaucracy.* Heffer, Cambridge.

———, 1969, *Law Without Precedent.* U. of Chicago Press, Chicago.

———, 1971, *The Social Anthropology of the Nation State.* Aldine, Chicago.

———, 1973, *Inequality: Social Stratification Reconsidered.* U. of Chicago Press, Chicago.

FARIS, J. C., 1972, *Nuba Personal Art.* Toronto U.P., Toronto.

FARON, L., 1961, "On Ancestor Propitiation Among the Mapuche of Central Chile," *American Anthropologist,* **58,** 824–830.

FAUSET, A. H., 1944, *Black Gods of the Metropolis.* U. of Pennsylvania Press, Philadelphia.

FEDER, N., 1967, *North American Indian Painting.* Museum of Primitive Art, New York.

FERNANDEZ, J., 1970, "Exposition and Imposition of Order: Artistic Expression in Fang Culture," in M. C. Albrecht, J. H. Barnett, and M. Griff (eds.), *Sociology of Art and Literature.* Praeger, New York.

———, 1971, "Zulu Zionism," *Natural History,* **80,** 44–51.

FERNEA, R., 1970, *Shaykh and Effendi: Changing Patterns of Authority Among the El Shabana of Iraq.* Harvard U.P., Cambridge, Mass.

FIRTH, R., 1940, "An Analysis of Mana: An Empirical Approach," *Journal of the Polynesian Society,* **58,** 483–510.

———, 1956, *Elements of Social Organization.* Watts, London.

FIRTH, R. (ed.), 1972, *Themes in Economic Anthropology.* Tavistock, London.

———, 1975, "An Appraisal of Modern Social Anthropology," in B. Siegel and others (eds.), *Annual Review of Anthropology.* Annual Reviews, Palo Alto.

FISCHER, H. T., 1952, "Polyandry," *International Archives of Ethnography,* **45,** 106–115.

FISCHER, J., 1958, "The Classification of Residence in Censuses," *American Anthropologist,* **60,** 508–517.

———, 1961, "Art Styles As Cultural Cognitive Maps," *American Anthropologist,* **63,** 79–93.

FISHER, B., 1928, "Irrigation Systems of Persia," *Geographical Review,* **18,** 302–306.

FISHMAN, J., 1972, *The Sociology of Language: An Interdisciplinary Social Science Approach to Language in Society.* Newbury House, Rowley, Mass.

FITCH, J., and D. BRANCH, 1960, "Primitive Architecture and Climate," *Scientific American,* **203,** 134–144.

FITT, R. L., 1953, "Irrigation Development in Central Persia," *Journal of the Royal Central Asian Society,* **40,** 124–133.

FLANNERY, K., 1968, "Archaeological Systems Theory and Early Mesoamerica," in B. Meggers (ed.), *Anthropological Archaeology in the Americas.* Anthropological Society of Washington, Washington, D.C., pp. 67–87. Reprinted as "The Southern Highlands of Mexico" in Hammond 1976.

———, 1969, "Origins and Ecological Effects of Early Domestication in Iran and the Near East," in P. Ucko and G. Dimbleby (eds.), *The Domestication and Exploitation of Plants and Animals.* Aldine, Chicago.

FLEMING, P., 1973, "The Politics of Marriage Among Non-Catholic European Royalty," *Current Anthropology,* **14,** 231–249.

FOGEL, R., and S. L. ENGERMAN, 1974, *Time on the Cross: The Economics of Slavery in the Antebellum South,* 12 vols. Little, Brown, Boston.

FONTANA, B. L., and others, 1962, *Papago Indian Pottery.* U. of Washington Press, Seattle.

FORDE, D., 1950, "Double Descent Among the Yako," in A. R. Radcliffe-Brown and D. Forde (eds.), *African Systems of Kinship and Marriage.* Oxford U.P., London, pp. 285–332.

FORGE, A. (ed.), 1973, *Primitive Art and Society.* Oxford U.P., New York.

FORMAN, S., and J. RIEGELHAUPT, 1970, "Market Place and Marketing Systems: Towards a Theory of Peasant Economic Integration," *Comparative Studies in Society and History,* **12,** 188–212.

FORTES, M., 1950, "Kinship and Marriage Among the Ashanti," in A. R. Radcliffe-Brown and D. Forde (eds.), *African Systems of Kinship and Marriage.* Oxford U.P., London, pp. 252–284.

FORTES, M. (ed.), 1972, *Marriage in Tribal Societies.* Cambridge U.P., New York.

———, and E. E. EVANS-PRITCHARD (eds.), 1940, *African Political Systems,* Oxford U.P., London.

FORTUNE, R. F., 1963, *Sorcerers of Dobu.* Dutton, New York. Original edition 1932.

FOSTER, G., 1969, "Godparents and Social Networks in Tzintzuntzan," *Southwestern Journal of Anthropology,* **25,** 261–278.

———, 1973, *Traditional Societies and Technological Change.* Harper, New York. Original edition 1962.

FOX, R., 1967, *Kinship and Marriage: An Anthropological Perspective.* Penguin, Baltimore.

FRAKE, C. O., 1961, "The Diagnosis of Disease Among the Subanum of Mindinao," *American Anthropologist,* **63,** 113–132.

FRANK, A. G., 1966, "The Development of Underdevelopment," *Monthly Review,* September, 17–31. Reprinted in Hammond 1975.

———, 1969, *Capitalism and Underdevelopment in Latin America.* Modern Reader, New York.

FRASER, D. 1962, *Primitive Art.* Doubleday, New York.

FRAZER, J. G., 1922, *The Golden Bough.* Macmillan, New York.

FREED, S., 1970, "Caste Ranking and the Exchange of Food and Water in a North Indian Village," *Anthropological Quarterly,* **43,** 1–13.

———, and R. FREED, 1972, "Some Attitudes Towards Caste in a North Indian Village," *Journal of Social Research,* **15,** 1–17.

FREEDMAN, M., 1972, *Chinese Lineage and Society.* Humanities, Atlantic Highlands, N.J.

FREEMAN, S. T., 1970, *Neighbors: The Social Contract in a Castillian Hamlet.* U. of Chicago Press, Chicago.

Freilich, M. (ed.), 1970, *Marginal Natives: Anthropologists at Work.* Harper, New York.

Fried, M., 1967, *The Evolution of Political Society.* Random House, New York.

———, (ed.), 1968, *Readings in Anthropology,* vol. 2, Crowell, New York.

———, 1972, *The Study of Anthropology.* Crowell, New York.

Friedl, E., 1959, "Dowry and Inheritance in Modern Greece," *Transactions of the New York Academy of Sciences,* **22,** 49–54.

Friedland, W., and D. Nelkin, 1971, *Migrant: Agricultural Workers in America's Northeast.* Holt, New York.

Friedrich, P., 1970, *Agrarian Revolt in a Mexican Village.* Prentice-Hall, Englewood Cliffs, N.J.

Fukutake, 1967, *Japanese Rural Society.* Oxford U.P., New York.

Fulton, R. M., 1972, "The Political Structure and Functions of Poro in Kpelle Society," *American Anthropologist,* **74,** 1218–1233.

G

Gage, W. W. (ed.), *Language in Its Social Setting.* The Anthropological Society of Washington, Washington, D.C.

Gamre, K., 1975, "International Conference for the Eradication of Untouchability," London, Spring 1975. *Race and Class,* **14,** 311–15.

Gardner, R., and K. Heider, 1968, *Gardens of War: Life and Death in the New Guinea Stone Age.* Random House, New York.

Garvin, P. (ed.), *Method and Theory in Linguistics.* Mouton, The Hague.

Gearing, F., 1970, *The Face of the Fox.* Aldine, Chicago.

Geertz, C., 1960, *The Religion of Java.* Free Press, New York.

———(ed.), 1974, *Myth, Symbol, and Culture.* Norton, New York.

Gellner, E., 1969, *Saints of the Atlas.* Aldine, Chicago.

Genovese, E., 1965, *The Political Economy of Slavery: Studies in the Economy and Society of the Slave South.* Vintage, New York.

———, 1974, *Roll, Jordan, Roll: The World the Slaves Made.* Pantheon, New York.

Gerbrands, A., 1967, *Wow-ipits: Eight Asmat Woodcarvers of New Guinea.* Mouton, the Hague.

Gibbs, J. L., Jr., 1962, "Poro Values and Courtroom Procedures in a Kpelle Chiefdom," *Southwestern Journal of Anthropology,* **4,** 341–350.

———, 1963, "the Kpelle Moot: A Therapeutic Model for the Informal Settlement of Disputes," *Africa,* **33,** 1–10.

———, 1965, "The Kpelle of Liberia," in James L. Gibbs, Jr. (ed.), *Peoples of Africa.* Holt, New York, pp. 197–240.

Giglioli, P. (ed.), 1972, *Language and Social Context: Selected Readings.* Penguin, Baltimore.

Gilmore, D., 1975, "Friendship in Fuenmayor: Patterns of Integration in an Atomistic Society," *Ethnology,* **14,** 311–324.

Gladwin, T., 1970, *East is a Big Bird: Navigation and Logic on Puluwat Atoll.* Harvard U.P., Cambridge, Mass.

Glazer, M., 1972, *The Research Adventure: Promise and Problems of Field Work.* Random House, New York.

Gleason, H. A., Jr., 1961, *An Introduction to Descriptive Linguistics.* Holt, New York.

Gluckman, M., 1958, "The Kingdom of the Zulu in South Africa," in M. Fortes and E. E. Evans-Pritchard (eds.), *African Political Systems,* Oxford U.P., London, pp. 25–55.

Gluckman, M., 1962, *Essays in the Ritual of Social Relations.* Manchester U.P, Manchester.

Golde, P. (ed.), 1970, *Women in the Field: Anthropological Experiences.* Aldine, Chicago.

Goldschmidt, W. (ed.), 1959, *The Anthropology of Franz Boas.* Chandler, San Francisco.

———, 1967, *Sebei Law.* California U.P., Berkeley.

———, 1974, "The Economics of Brideprice Among the Sebei in East Africa," *Ethnology,* **13,** 311–333.

Goldstein, M., 1971a, "Stratification, Polyandry, and Family Structure in Central Tibet," *Southwestern Journal of Anthropology,* **27,** 64–74.

———, 1971b, "Serfdom and Mobility: An Examination of the Institution of 'Human Lease' in Traditional Tibetan Society," *Journal of Asian Studies,* **30,** 521–534.

Gomm, R., 1972, "Harlots and Bachelors: Marital Instability Among the Coastal Digo of Kenya," *Man,* **7,** 95–113.

GONZALEZ, N., 1969, *Black Carib Household Structure: A Study of Migration and Modernization.* U. of Washington Press, Seattle.

———, 1970, "Social Functions of Carnival in a Dominican City," *Southwestern Journal of Anthropology,* **26,** 328–342.

GOOD, P., 1966, "The Thorntons of Mississippi: Peonage on the Plantation," *Atlantic* **218** (September), 95–100.

GOODALE, J. C., and J. D. KOSS, 1967, "The Cultural Context of Creativity Among Tiwi," in J. Helm (ed.), *Essays on the Verbal and Visual Arts.* American Ethnological Society, U. of Washington Press, Seattle.

GOODENOUGH, W., 1955, "Residence Rules," *Southwestern Journal of Anthropology,* **12,** 22–37.

———, 1970, *Description and Comparison in Cultural Anthropology.* Aldine, Chicago.

GOODWIN, G. (ed.), 1971, *Western Apache Raiding and Warfare.* Compiled by K. Basso. U. of Arizona Press, Tucson.

GOODY, J., 1958, *The Developmental Cycle in Domestic Groups.* Cambridge U.P., New York.

———, 1961, "The Classification of Double Descent Systems," *Current Anthropology,* **2,** 3–12.

———, 1962, *Death, Property and the Ancestors.* Stanford U.P., Stanford.

———, 1969, "A Comparative Approach to Incest and Adultery," in *Comparative Studies in Kinship.* Stanford U.P., Stanford, pp. 13–38.

———(ed.), 1971, *Kinship.* Penguin, Baltimore.

———, 1973a, "British Functionalism," in R. Naroll and F. Naroll (eds.), *Main Currents in Cultural Anthropology.* Prentice-Hall, Englewood Cliffs, N.J., pp. 185–215.

———, 1973b, "Polygyny, Economy and the Role of Women," in J. Goody (ed.), *The Character of Kinship.* Cambridge U.P., New York.

———, 1975, *The Myth of the Bagre.* Oxford U.P., Oxford.

———, 1973, and S. TAMBIAH, *Bridewealth and Dowry.* Cambridge U.P., New York.

GORER, G., 1943, "Themes in Japanese Culture," *Transactions of the New York Academy of Sciences, Series 2,* **5,** 106–124.

GORER, G., and J. RICKMAN, 1950, *The People of Great Russia: A Psychological Study.* Chanticleer, New York.

GOSSEN, G. H., 1974, *Chamulas in the World of the Sun: Time and Space in a Maya Oral Tradition.* Harvard U.P., Cambridge, Mass.

GOUGH, K. (ed.), 1971, "Caste in a Tanjore Village," in E. Leach (ed.), *Aspects of Caste in India, Ceylon, and Pakistan.* Cambridge U.P., New York.

———, 1973, "Harijans in Thanjavur," in E. K. Gough and H. P., Sharma (eds.), *Imperialism and Revolution in South Asia.* Monthly Review Press, New York, pp. 22–45.

———, and H. P. SHARMA (eds.), 1973, *Imperialism and Revolution in South Asia.* Monthly Review Press, New York.

GOULD, H. A., 1964, "A Jajmani System of North India: Its Structure, Magnitude, and Meaning." *Ethnology,* **3,** 12–14.

GOULD, R., 1969, *Yiwara: Foragers of the Australian Desert.* Scribners, New York.

GOULDNER, A., 1960, "The Norm of Reciprocity: A Preliminary Statement," *American Sociological Review,* **25,** 161–178.

GRABURN, N., 1971, *Readings in Kinship and Social Structure.* Harper, New York.

GRANT, C., 1967, *Rock Art of the American Indian.* Crowell, New York.

GREBLER, L., and others, 1970, *The Mexican American People.* Macmillan, New York.

GREEN, A., 1972, *Only a Miner: Stories in Recorded Coal Mining Songs.* U. of Illinois Press, Urbana.

GREENBERG, 1955, *Studies in African Linguistic Classification.* Compass, New Haven.

———, 1959, "Language and Evolution," in B. Meggers (ed.), *Evolution and Anthropology: A Centennial Appraisal.* Anthropological Society of Washington, Washington, D.C., pp. 61–75.

———, 1966, *Language Universals.* Mouton, The Hague.

———, 1968, *Anthropological Linguistics.* Random House, New York.

———, 1971a, "The Science of Linguistics," in his *Language, Culture, and Communication.* Stanford U.P., Stanford, pp. 274–294. Reprinted in Hammond 1975.

———, 1971b, *Language, Culture, and Communication.* Stanford U.P., Stanford.

———, 1973, "Linguistics As a Pilot Science," in E. Hamp (ed.), *Themes in Linguistics: The 1970s.* Mouton, The Hague, pp. 45–60.

GREENWAY, J., 1972, *Ethnomusicology.* Burgess, Minneapolis.

GREUEL, P. J., 1971, "The Leopard Skin Chief: An Examination of Political Power Among the Nuer," *American Anthropologist,* **73,** 1115–1120.

GRIMBLE, A., 1951, "A Gilbertese Creation Myth," *The Listener,* **45,** 621–625.

GROSS, D., and B. HARWOOD, 1971, "Technological Change and Caloric Costs: Sisal Agriculture in Northeastern Brazil," *American Anthropologist,* **73,** 725–740.

GUILLAUME, A., 1961, *Islam.* Penguin, Baltimore.

GULICK, J., 1970, "Village and City Fieldwork in Lebanon," in M. Freilich (ed.), *Marginal Natives.* Harper, New York, pp. 123–152.

GULLIVER, P., 1951, *A Preliminary Survey of the Turkana,* Capetown University School of African Studies 26, Capetown.

———, 1955, *The Family Herds.* Routledge, London.

———, 1973, "Negotiations As a Model of Dispute Settlement: Towards a General Model," *Law and Society Review,* **7,** 667–691.

GUMPERZ, J., 1971, *Language in Social Groups,* Stanford U.P., Stanford.

———, 1974, "Linguistic Anthropology in Society," *American Anthropologist,* **76,** 785–798.

———, and D. HYMES (eds.), 1972, *Directions in Sociolinguistics: The Ethnography of Communication.* Holt, New York.

GUTKIND, P. (ed.), 1970, *The Passing of Tribal Man in Africa.* Brill, Leiden.

H

HAAS, W., 1944, *Irrigation Problems and Settlement Problems in Persia.* Studies of Migration and Settlement Memorandum Series M-94. Library of Congress, Washington, D.C.

HADARY, G., 1951, "The Agrarian Problem in Iran," *Middle East Journal,* **5,** 181–196.

HAHN, R., 1973, "Understanding Beliefs: An Essay on the Methodology of the Statement and Analysis of Belief Systems," *Current Anthropology,* **14,** 207–229.

HALEY, A., 1964, *The Autobiography of Malcolm X.* Grove, New York.

HALLOWELL, A. I., 1949, "The Size of Algonkian Hunting Territories: A Function of Ecological Adjustment," *American Anthropologist,* **51,** 35–45.

HALLPIKE, C. R., 1973, "Functionalist Interpretations of Primitive Warfare," *Man,* **8,** 451–470.

HAMER, J., 1970, "Sidamo Generational Class Cycles, a Political Gerontocracy," *Africa,* **40,** 50–70.

HAMMEL, E. (ed.), 1965, *Formal Semantic Analysis.* American Anthropologist Special Publication 67, Part 2, No. 5.

HAMMOND, D., 1970, "Magic: A Definitional Problem in Semantics," *American Anthropologist,* **72,** 1349–1356.

HAMMOND, P. B. (ed.), 1964, *Cultural and Social Anthropology: Selected Readings.* Macmillan, New York.

———, 1966, *Yatenga, Technology in the Culture of a West African Kingdom.* Free Press, New York.

———, 1970, "West Africa and the Afro-Americans," in J. Paden and E. Soja (eds.), *The African Experience.* Northwestern U.P., Evanston, pp. 195–209.

———, (ed.), 1975, *Cultural and Social Anthropology: Introductory Readings in Ethnology.* Macmillan, New York.

———, (ed.), 1976, *Physical Anthropology and Archaeology: Introductory Readings.* Macmillan, New York.

HAMP, E. (ed.), 1973, *Themes in Linguistics: The 1970s.* Mouton, The Hague.

HANNERZ, U., 1974, "Ethnicity and Opportunity in Urban America," in A. Cohen (ed.), *Urban Ethnicity.* Tavistock, London, pp. 37–76.

HARDING, T. G., 1967, *Voyagers of the Vitiaz Straits.* U. of Washington Press, Seattle.

HARLAN, J., 1971, "Agricultural Origins: Centers and Non-centers," *Science,* **174,** 468–474.

———, and J. de Wet, 1973, "On the Quality of Evidence for Origin and Dispersal of Cultivated Plants," *Current Anthropology,* **14,** 51–62.

HARNER, M., 1972a, *The Jívaro: People of the Sacred Waterfalls.* Doubleday, New York.

———, 1972b, "The Jívaro Household," in his *The Jívaro: People of the Sacred Waterfalls.* Doubleday, New York, pp. 78–105. Reprinted in Hammond 1975.

——— (ed.), 1973, *Hallucinogens and Shamanism.* Oxford U.P., New York.

HARRIS, M., 1959, "Labour Emigration Among

the Mozambique Thonga: Cultural and Political Factors, *Africa,* **34,** 50–65.

———, 1968a, "Cultural Materialism: Cultural Ecology," in his *The Rise of Anthropological Theory.* Crowell, New York, pp. 654–687. Reprinted in Hammond 1975.

———, 1968b, *The Rise of Anthropological Theory.* Crowell, New York.

———, 1968c, "'Emics,' 'Etics,' and the 'New Ethnography,'" in his *The Rise of Anthropological Theory.* Crowell, New York, pp. 568–604.

———, 1969, "Monistic Determinism: Anti-Service," *Southwestern Journal of Anthropology,* **25,** 198–206.

———, 1972, "The Human Strategy, Warfare Old and New," *Natural History,* **81,** 18–20.

———, 1974, "Why a Perfect Knowledge of All the Rules One Must Know to Act Like a Native Cannot Lead to the Knowledge of How Natives Act," *Journal of Anthropological Research,* **30,** 242–251.

———, 1975, *Culture, People, Nature.* Crowell, New York.

Harrison, J., 1973, "The Political Economy of Housework," Bulletin of the Conference of Socialist Economists, Winter, 35–52.

Harrison, R., 1973, *Warfare.* Burgess, Minneapolis.

Hart, D., 1959, *The Cebuan Filipino Dwelling in Caticugan: Its Construction and Cultural Aspects.* Yale U.P., New Haven.

Harvey, B., III, 1970, *Ritual in Pueblo Art: Hopi Life in Hopi Painting.* Augustin, Locust Valley, N.Y.

Hatch, E., 1975, "The Growth of Economic, Subsistence, and Ecological Studies in American Anthropology," *Journal of Anthropological Research,* **29,** 221–243.

Hatcher, E. P., 1974, *Visual Metaphors: A Formal Analysis of Navajo Art.* West, St. Paul, Minn.

Hatfield, C., 1973, "Fieldwork: Toward a Model of Mutual Exploitation," *Anthropological Quarterly,* **46,** 15–29.

Hayes, J. R. (ed.), 1970, *Cognition and the Development of Language.* Wiley, New York.

Heider, K., 1969, "Attributes and Categories in the Study of Material Culture: New Guinea Dani Attire," *Man,* **4,** 379–391.

———, 1970, *The Dugum Dani: A Papuan Culture in the Highlands of West New Guinea.* Aldine, Chicago.

Hein, N., 1972, *The Miracle Plays of Mathura.* Yale U.P., New Haven.

Heller, C. (ed.), 1969, *Structured Social Inequality.* Macmillan, New York.

Helm, J. (ed.), 1967, *Essays on the Verbal and Visual Arts.* U. of Washington Press, Seattle.

Henle, P., 1958, "Language, Thought, and Culture," in his *Language, Thought, and Culture.* U. of Michigan Press, Ann Arbor, pp. 398–408. Reprinted in Hammond 1975.

Herskovits, M., 1934, *Rebel Destiny.* McGraw-Hill, New York.

———, 1937, "African Gods and Catholic Saints in New World Negro Belief," *American Anthropologist,* **34,** 635–643.

———, 1944, "Dramatic Experience Among Primitive People," *Yale Review,* **33,** 683–698.

———, 1945, *Backgrounds of African Art.* Denver Art Museum, Denver.

———, 1950, *Man and His Works.* Knopf, New York.

———, 1958, *Acculturation: The Study of Culture Contact.* Smith, Gloucester, Mass.

———, 1964, *Life in a Haitian Valley.* Octagon, New York. Originally published 1937.

Hewes, G., 1973, "Primate Communication and the Gestural Origin of Language," *Current Anthropology,* **14,** 5–24.

———, 1966, *The New World Negro,* (edited by F. S. Herskovits) Indiana U.P., Bloomington.

Hiatt, B., 1970, "Woman the Gatherer," in F. Gale (ed.), *Woman's Role in Aboriginal Society.* Australian Institute of Aboriginal Studies, Canberra.

Hickerson, H., 1970, *The Chippewa and Their Neighbors: A Study in Ethnohistory.* Holt, New York.

Higgs, E., 1972, *Papers in Economic Prehistory.* Cambridge U.P., New York.

Hill, C. E. (ed.), 1975, *Symbols and Society: Essays on Belief Systems in Action.* U. of Georgia Press, Athens.

Hill, E., 1972, *The Trinidad Carnival.* U. of Texas Press, Austin.

Hockett, C. F., 1958, *A Course in Modern Linguistics.* Macmillan, New York.

Hockett, C. F., and R. Ascher, 1964, "The Human Revolution," *Current Anthropology,* **5,** 135–168.

HODGES, H., 1964, *Artifacts: An Introduction to Early Materials and Technology.* Baker, London.

———, 1970, *Technology in the Ancient World.* Knopf, New York.

HOEBEL, E. A., 1954, *The Law of Primitive Man: A Study in Legal Dynamics.* Harvard U.P., Cambridge, Mass.

HOGBIN, I., 1970, *The Island of Menstruating Men: Religion in Wogeo, New Guinea.* Chandler, San Francisco.

HOIJER, H., 1945, "The Sapir-Whorf Hypothesis," in H. Hoijer (ed.), *Language in Culture.* U. of Chicago Press, Chicago, pp. 92–104.

———, 1951, "Cultural Implications of Some Navaho Linguistic Categories," *Language,* **27,** 111–120.

HOLE, F., and R. HEIZER, 1973, *Introduction to Prehistoric Archaeology.* Holt, New York.

HOMANS, G. C., and D. M. SCHNEIDER, 1955, *Marriage, Authority, and Final Causes: A Study of Unilateral Cross-Cousin Marriage.* Free Press, New York.

HONIGMANN, J., 1973a, "Personality in Culture," in R. Naroll and F. Naroll (eds.), *Main Currents in Cultural Anthropology.* Prentice-Hall, Englewood Cliffs, N.J.

———, 1973b, "Sampling in Ethnographic Field Work," in R. Naroll and R. Cohen (eds.), *A Handbook of Method in Cultural Anthropology.* Columbia U.P., New York, pp. 266–281.

HOOD, M., 1971, *The Ethnomusicologist.* McGraw-Hill, New York.

HOPKINS, N., 1972, "Persuasion and Satire in Malian Theatre," *Africa,* **42,** 1217–1228.

HORNELL, J., 1946, *Water Transport: Origins and Early Evolution.* Cambridge U.P., New York.

HORTON, R., 1975, "On the Rationality of Conversion," *Africa,* **45,** 219–235.

HOWELL, P. P., 1954, *A Manual of Nuer Law.* Oxford U.P., New York.

HSU, F. L. K., 1948, *Under the Ancestors' Shadow.* Columbia U.P., New York.

——— (ed.), 1972, *Psychological Anthropology.* Schenkman, Cambridge, Mass.

———, 1975, *Iemoto: The Heart of Japan.* Wiley, New York.

HUNT, R. (ed.), 1967, *Personality in Culture: Readings in Psychological Anthropology.* Natural History Press, New York.

HUNTINGFORD, G., 1965, *The Land Charters of Northern Ethiopia.* Oxford U.P., New York.

HUNTINGTON, E., 1915, *Civilization and Climate.* Yale U.P., New Haven.

HURAULT, J., 1961, *Les Noirs Réfugiés Boni de la Guyane Française.* Institut Français d'Afrique Noire (IFAN), Dakar, Senegal.

HUTCHINSON, H. W., 1957, *Village and Plantation Life in Northeastern Brazil.* U. of Washington Press, Seattle.

HYMES, D. H., 1961, "Functions of Speech: An Evolutionary Approach," in F. Gruber (ed.), *Anthropology and Education,* U. of Pennsylvania Press, Philadelphia, pp. 55–83.

———, 1962, "The Ethnography of Speaking," in T. Gladwin and W. Sturtevant (eds.), *Anthropology and Human Behavior.* Anthropological Society of Washington, Washington, D.C., pp. 13–53.

——— (ed.), 1964a, *Language in Culture and Society: A Reader in Linguistics and Anthropology.* Harper, New York.

———, 1964b, "A Perspective for Linguistic Anthropology," in S. Tax (ed.), *Horizons of Anthropology,* Aldine, Chicago, pp. 92–107.

——— (ed.), 1972, *Reinventing Anthropology.* Pantheon, New York.

I

INGHAM, J., 1970, "The Asymmetrical Aspects of Godparenthood in Tlayacapan, Morelos," *Man,* **5,** 281–289.

INVERARITY, R., 1950, *Art of the Northwest Coast Indians,* U. of Calif. Press, Berkeley.

ISAAC, E., 1970, *Geography of Domestication.* Prentice-Hall, Englewood Cliffs, N.J.

ISAACS, H. R., 1965, *India's Ex-Untouchables.* Day, New York.

ISHIDA, T., 1975, *Japanese Society.* Random House, New York.

ISHINO, I., 1966, "Social and Technological Change in Rural Japan: Continuities and Discontinuities," in R. Firth and R. Beardsley (eds.), *Japanese Culture: Its Development and Characteristics.* Aldine, Chicago, pp. 100–112.

IVANOV, S., 1928, "Aleut Hunting Headgear and Its Ornamentation," *Proceedings of the Twenty-*

Third Congress of Americanists. Science Press, New York, pp. 477–504.

J

JACKSON, B., 1974, *Get Your Ass in the Water and Swim Like Me: Narrative Poetry from Black Oral Tradition.* Harvard U.P., Cambridge, Mass.

JACOBS, N., 1971, *Modernization Without Development: Thailand As an Asian Case Study.* Praeger, New York.

JACOBS, S. E., 1973, *Women in Perspective: A Guide for Cross Cultural Studies.* U. of Illinois Press, Urbana.

JAY, P. C., 1968, *Primates: Studies in Adaptation and Variability.* Holt, New York.

JOHNSON, A., 1971, *Sharecroppers of the Sertão: Economics and Dependence on a Brazilian Plantation.* Stanford U.P., Stanford.

JOHNSON, C., 1974, "Gift Giving and Reciprocity Among the Japanese Americans of Honolulu," *American Ethnologist,* **1,** 295–308.

JOHNSON, D., 1969, *The Nature of Nomadism.* Department of Geography Research Paper 118. U. of Chicago Press, Chicago.

JOHNSON, O., and A. JOHNSON, 1975, "Male/Female Relations and the Organization of Work in a Machiguenga Community," *American Ethnologist,* **4,** 634–648.

JOLLY, A., 1972, *The Evolution of Primate Behavior.* Macmillan, New York.

JONES, J. D. R., and C. M. DOKE (eds.), 1937, "Bushmen of the Southern Kalahari," *Bantu Studies,* Vols. 10 and 11. Reprinted by Wiwaterstrand U.P., Johannesburg.

JONES, S., 1974, *Men of Influence in Nuristan.* Academic, New York.

JONES, W., 1919, *Ojibwa Texts.* Edited by T. Michelson. Steckert, New York.

JONES, W., 1972, "World Views: Their Nature and Their Function," *Current Anthropology,* **13,** 79–91.

JOPLING, C. F. (ed.), 1971, *Art and Aesthetics in Primitive Societies.* Dutton, New York.

JORDAAN, K., 1975, "The Bushmen of Southern Africa: Anthropology and Historical Materialism," *Race and Class,* **17,** 141–160.

JORDAN, D. K., 1972, *Gods, Ghosts, and Ancestors.* U. of Calif. Press, Berkeley.

JORGENSEN, J., 1966, "Addendum: Geographical Clusterings and Functional Explanations of In-Law Avoidances: An Analysis of Comparative Method," *Current Anthropology,* **7,** 167–182.

______, 1972, *The Sun Dance Religion: Power for the Powerless.* U. of Chicago Press, Chicago.

JUDAH, J. S., 1974, *Hare Krishna and the Counter Culture.* Wiley, New York.

K

KAEPPLER, A., 1971, "Rank in Tonga," *Ethnology,* **10,** 174–193.

KAHN, M., 1931, *Djuka: The Bush Negroes of Dutch Guiana.* Viking, New York.

KARDINER, A., 1939, *The Individual and His Society.* Columbia U.P., New York.

KARSTEN, R., 1923, *Blood Revenge, War, and Victory Feasts Among the Jibaro Indians of Eastern Ecuador,* Bureau of American Ethnology Bulletin 179. Smithsonian Institution, Washington, D.C.

KAVOLIS, V., 1968, *Artistic Expression—A Sociological Explanation.* Cornell U.P., Ithaca.

KAWAGUCHI, E., 1909, *Three Years in Tibet.* The Theosophist Office, Adyar, Madras.

KAY, P., 1970, "Some Theoretical Implications of Ethnographic Semantics," *Current Directions in Anthropology, American Anthropological Association Bulletin,* **3 (3),** Part 2, 19–31.

KEESING, R., 1970a, "Shrines, Ancestors, and Cognatic Descent: The Kwaio and Tallensi," *American Anthropologist,* **72,** 755–775.

______, 1970b, "Death, Property, and the Ancestors," *Africa,* **40,** 40–49.

KEIL, C., 1966, *Urban Blues.* U. of Chicago Press, Chicago.

KEITH, T., 1973, *Religion and the Decline of Magic.* Scribners, New York.

KELLER, A. G., 1915, *Societal Evolution.* Macmillan, New York.

KHARE, S., 1970, *The Changing Brahmins: Associations and Elites Among the Kanya-Kubja of North India.* U. of Chicago Press, Chicago.

KIEV, A. (ed.), 1964, *Magic, Faith, and Healing: Studies in Primitive Psychiatry Today.* Free Press, New York.

KIMBALL, S., and J. WATSON, 1972, *Crossing Cultural Boundaries.* Chandler, San Francisco.

KITAOJI, H., 1971, "Japanese Family Structure," *American Anthropologist,* **73,** 1036–1057.

Klima, G., 1970, *The Barabaig: East African Cattle Herders.* Holt, New York.

Kloos, P., 1969, "Female Initiation Among the Maroni River Caribs," *American Anthropologist,* **71,** 889–905.

Kluckhohn, C., W. Hill, and L. Wales, 1971, *Navaho Material Culture.* Harvard U.P., Cambridge, Mass.

Koch, K., 1974, *War and Peace In Jalemo.* Harvard U.P., Cambridge, Mass.

Kochman, T., 1970, "Toward an Ethnography of Black American Speech Behavior," in N. Whitten, Jr., and J. Szwed (eds.), *Afro-American Anthropology.* Free Press, New York, pp. 145–162. Reprinted in Hammond 1975.

——— (ed.), 1972, *Rappin' and Stylin' Out,* U. of Illinois Press, Urbana.

Kogon, E., 1946, *The Theory and Practice of Hell: The German Concentration Camps and the System Behind Them.* Farrar, Straus, New York.

Kohl, J., and J. Litt, 1974, *Urban Guerilla Warfare in Latin America.* M.I.T. Press, Cambridge, Mass.

Kolata, G., 1974, "!Kung Hunter-Gatherers: Feminism, Diet, and Birth Control," *Science,* **185,** 932–934.

Koojiman, S., 1972, *Tapa in Polynesia.* Bishop Museum, Honolulu.

Kopytoff, I., 1971, "Ancestors As Elders in Africa," *Africa,* **41,** 129–142. Reprinted in Hammond 1975.

Kornblum, W., 1975, *Blue Collar Community.* U. of Chicago Press, Chicago.

Kottak, C., 1972, "Ecological Variables in the Origin and Evolution of African States: The Buganda Example," *Comparative Studies in Society and History,* **14,** 351–380.

———, 1974, *Cultural Anthropology.* Random House, New York.

Krader, L., 1955a, "Principles and Structures in the Organization of Asiatic Steppe Pastoralists," *Southwestern Journal of Anthropology,* **11,** 67–92.

———, 1955b, "The Ecology of Central Asian Pastoralism," *Southwestern Journal of Anthropology,* **11,** 801–826.

———, 1968, *Formation of the State.* Prentice-Hall, Englewood Cliffs, N.J.

Kriesberg, L., 1970, *Mothers in Poverty: A Study of Fatherless Families.* Aldine, Chicago.

Kuper, A., 1973, *Anthropologists and Anthropology: The British School, 1922–1972.* Pica, New York.

Kurath, G., 1960, "Panorama of Dance Ethnology," *Current Anthropology,* **1,** 233–241.

———, 1968, *Dance and Song Ritual of Six Nations Reserve.* National Museum of Canada Bulletin 220, Ottawa.

Kurtz, D., 1974, "Peripheral and Transitional Markets: The Aztec Case," *American Ethnologist,* **1,** 685–705.

L

La Barre, W., 1945, "Some Observations on Character Structure in the Orient: The Japanese," *Psychiatry,* **8,** 326–342.

———, 1970, *The Ghost Dance: The Origins of Religion.* Doubleday, New York.

———, 1971, "Materials for a History of Studies of Crisis Cults: A Bibliographic Essay, *Current Anthropology,* **12,** 3–44.

Labov, W., 1966, *The Social Stratification of English in New York City.* Center for Applied Linguistics, Washington, D.C.

———, 1973a, *Sociolinguistic Patterns.* U. of Pennsylvania Press, Philadelphia.

———, 1973b, *Language in the Inner City: Studies in the Black English Vernacular.* U. of Pennsylvania Press, Philadelphia.

La Fontaine, J., 1972, *The Interpretation of Ritual: Essays in Honour of A. J. Richards.* Tavistock, London.

Lambton, A. K. S., 1953, *Landlord and Peasant in Persia.* Oxford U.P., New York.

Landy, D., 1974, "Role Adaptation: Traditional Curers Under the Impact of Western Medicine," *American Ethnologist,* **1,** 103–127.

Langness, L., 1964, "Some Problems in the Conceptualization of Highlands Social Structure," in J. B. Watson (ed.), *New Guinea: The Central Highlands.* American Anthropologist Special Publication, Vol. 66, Part 4, No. 2, 162–182.

———, 1965, *The Life History in Anthropological Science.* Holt, New York.

———, 1969, "Marriage in Bena Bena," in R. Glasse and M. Meggitt (eds.), *Pigs, Pearl-*

shells, and Women: Marriage in the New Guinea Highlands. Prentice-Hall, Englewood Cliffs, N.J.

LANTERNARI, V., 1960, *The Religions of the Oppressed: A Study of Modern Messianic Cults.* Knopf, New York.

LAUBIN, R., and G. LAUBIN, 1970, *The Indian Tipi.* U. of Oklahoma Press, Norman.

LAUFER, B., 1913, "The Development of Ancestral Images in China," *Journal of Religious Psychology,* **6,** 111–123.

LAUGHLIN, C. D., JR., 1974, "Deprivation and Reciprocity," *Man,* **9,** 380–396.

LASLETT, P., and R. WALL (eds.), 1972 *Household and Family in Past Time.* Cambridge U.P., New York.

LATTIMORE, O., 1941, *Mongol Journey.* Doubleday, New York.

LAWRENCE, P., 1964, *Road Belong Cargo.* Manchester U.P., Manchester.

LEACH, E., 1954, *Political Systems of Highland Burma.* Harvard U.P., Cambridge, Mass.

______, 1960, *Aspects of Caste in South India, Ceylon, and North Pakistan.* Cambridge U.P., New York.

______, 1961, "Polyandry, Inheritance and the Definition of Marriage: With Particular Reference to Sinhalese Customary Law" in E. R. Leach, *Rethinking Anthropology.* Athlone, London.

______, and S. MUKHERJEE (eds.), 1970, *Elites in South Asia.* Cambridge U.P., New York.

LEACOCK, E., and N. LEVINE (eds.), 1971, *North American Indians in Historical Perspective.* Random House, New York.

LEACOCK, S., and R. LEACOCK, 1972, *Spirits of the Deep.* Doubleday, Garden City, N.Y.

LEBAR, F., 1963, "Some Aspects of Canoe and House Construction on Truk," *Ethnology,* **2,** 55–69.

LEE, R. B., 1968, "What Hunters Do for a Living," in R. B. Lee and I. DeVore (eds.), *Man the Hunter.* Aldine, Chicago.

______, 1972a, "Population Growth and the Beginnings of Sedentary Life Among the !Kung Bushmen," in B. Spooner (ed.), *Population Growth.* M.I.T. Press, Cambridge, Mass., pp. 329–342.

______, 1972b, "Work Effort, Group Structure and Land Use in Contemporary Hunter-Gatherers," in P. Ucko, R. Trimingham, and G. Dimbleby (eds.), *Man, Settlement, and Urbanism.* Schenkman, Boston, pp. 177–185.

______, and I. DEVORE 1968 (eds.), *Man the Hunter.* Aldine, Chicago.

______ (eds.), 1976, *Kalahari Hunter-Gatherers.* Harvard U.P., Cambridge, Mass.

LEES, R. B., 1953, "The Basis of Glottochronology," *Language,* **29,** 113–127.

LEES, S., 1973, *Sociopolitical Aspects of Canal Irrigation in the Valley of Oaxaca.* U. of Michigan Press, Ann Arbor.

LEGESSE, A., 1973, *Gada, Three Approaches to the Study of African Society.* Free Press, New York.

LEHMAN, W., 1972, *Descriptive Linguistics: An Introduction.* Random House, New York.

LENGYEL, O., 1947, *Five Chimneys: The Story of Auschwitz.* U. of Chicago Press, Chicago.

LESSA, W. A., 1961, *Tales from Ulithi Atoll.* U. of Calif. Press, Berkeley.

______, and E. Z. VOGT (eds.), 1970, *A Reader in Comparative Religion.* Row, Peterson, Evanston.

LESTER, D., 1972, "Voodoo Death: Some New Thoughts on an Old Phenomenon," *American Anthropologist,* **74,** 386–390.

LESTER, M. (ed.), 1970, *Readings in Applied Transformational Grammar.* Holt, New York.

LEVINE, D. N., 1974, *Greater Ethiopia: The Evolution of a Multiethnic Society.* U. of Chicago Press, Chicago.

LEVINE, M. H., 1957, "Prehistoric Art and Ideology," *American Anthropologist,* **59,** 949–962.

LEVINE, R. A., 1973, "Basic Concepts in an Evolutionary Model," in his *Culture, Behavior, and Personality.* Aldine, Chicago, pp. 115–135. Reprinted in Hammond 1975.

______ (ed.), 1974, *Culture and Personality: Contemporary Readings.* Aldine, Chicago.

LÉVI-STRAUSS, C., 1963a, *Structural Anthropology.* Doubleday, Garden City, N.Y.

______, 1963b, *Totemism.* Translated by R. Needhan. Beacon, Boston.

______, 1969a, *The Elementary Structures of Kinship.* Beacon, Boston.

______, 1969b, *The Raw and the Cooked.* Holt, New York.

LEWIS, D., 1972, *We, the Navigators.* U. of Hawaii Press, Honolulu.

LEWIS, I. M., 1963, *A Pastoral Democracy.* Oxford U.P., New York.

———, 1968, *History and Social Anthropology.* Tavistock, London.

———, 1970, "A Structural Approach to Witchcraft and Spirit Possession," in M. Douglas (ed.), *Witchcraft Confessions and Accusations.* Tavistock, London, pp. 293–309.

Lewis, O., 1961, *The Children of Sanchez. Knopf,* New York.

———, 1965, *Village Life in Northern India,* Vintage, New York.

———, 1966, "The Culture of Poverty," *Scientific American,* **215,** 19–25.

Lex, B. M., 1974, "Voodoo Death: New Thoughts on an Old Explanation," *American Anthropologist,* **76,** 818–823.

Lieban, R. W., 1967, *Cebuano Sorcery: Malign Magic in the Philippines.* U. of Calif. Press, Berkeley.

Lincoln, B., 1975, "The Religious Significance of Women's Scarification Among the Tiv," *Africa,* **45,** 316–325.

Lincoln, E., 1961, *The Black Muslims in America.* Beacon, Boston.

Lindenbaum, S., 1971, "Sorcery and Structure in Fore Society," *Oceania,* **41,** 277–287.

Linton, R., 1936, *The Study of Man.* Appleton, New York.

———, and P. Wingert, 1946, *Arts of the South Seas.* Museum of Modern Art, New York.

Lisón-Tolosana, C., 1966, *Belmonte de los Caballeros,* Clarendon Press, Oxford.

Little, K., 1949, "The Role of the Secret Society in Cultural Specialization," *American Anthropologist,* **51,** 199–212.

———, 1957, "The Role of Voluntary Associations in West African Urbanization, "*American Anthropologist,* **59,** 579–596.

———, 1965, *West African Urbanization: A Study of Voluntary Associations in Social Change.* Cambridge U.P., New York.

———, 1965/1966, "The Political Function of the Poro," In Africa Part 1, **35,** 349–365, and Part 2, **36,** 62–71.

———, 1967, "Voluntary Associations in Urban Life: A Case Study of Adaptation," in M. Freedman (ed.), *Social Organization: Essays Presented to Raymond Firth.* Aldine, Chicago, pp. 153–165.

———, 1972, "Voluntary Associations and Social Mobility Among West African Women," *Canadian Journal of African Studies,* **6,** 275–288.

———, 1973, "Urbanization and Regional Associations: Their Paradoxical Functions," in A. Southall (ed.), *Urban Anthropology.* Oxford U.P., New York, pp. 407–423.

Livingstone, F. B., 1971, "Genetics, Ecology, and the Origins of Incest and Exogamy," *Current Anthropology,* **10,** 45–62.

Lotz, J., 1955, "On Language and Culture," *International Journal of American Linguistics,* **21,** 187–189.

Lowie, R. H., 1935, *The Crow Indians.* Rinehart, New York.

Lundsgaarde, H. (ed.), 1974, *Land Tenure in Oceania.* U. of Hawaii Press, Honolulu.

Lurie, N., 1961, *Mountain Wolf Woman.* U. of Michigan Press, Ann Arbor.

Lustig-Areco, V., 1975, *Technology: Strategies for Survival.* Holt, New York.

M

MacDonald, D., 1929, *The Land of the Llama.* Seeley, Service, London.

Macfarlane, A., 1970, *Witchcraft in Tudor and Stuart England: A Regional Comparative Study.* Routledge, London.

Mack, A., 1975, "Sharpening the Contradictions: Guerilla Strategy in Imperialist Wars," *Race and Class,* **17,** 161–178.

MacNeish, R., and others, 1977, *The Prehistory of Tehuacan.* Vol. 6: *The Dawn of Civilization.* U. of Texas Press, Austin.

Mahar, J. M. (ed.), 1972, *The Untouchables in Contemporary India.* U. of Arizona Press, Tucson.

Maher, V., 1974, "Divorce and Property in the Middle Atlas of Morocco," *Man,* **9,** 103–122.

Mair, L., 1962, *Primitive Government.* Penguin, Baltimore.

———, 1965, *An Introduction to Social Anthropology.* Oxford U.P., New York.

———, 1969, *Witchcraft.* McGraw-Hill, New York.

———, 1972, *Marriage.* Universe. New York.

Majumdar, D. N., 1955, "Demographic Structure in a Polyandrous Village," *The Eastern Anthropologist,* **8,** 161–172.

———, 1962, *Himalayan Polyandry: Structure, Function, and Culture Change.* Asia Publishing House, New York.

Malinowski, B., 1920, "Kula: The Circulating Exchange of Goods in the Archipelagoes of Eastern New Guinea," *Man*, **51**, 97–105.

———, 1922, *Argonauts of the Western Pacific.* Routledge, London.

———, 1923, "Psycho-analysis and Anthropology," *Psyche*, **4**, 293–322.

Mangin, W., 1965, "The Role of Regional Associations in the Adaptation of Rural Migrants to Cities in Peru," in D. Heath and R. Adams (eds.), *Contemporary Cultures and Societies of Latin America.* Random House, New York, pp. 311–323.

Manners, R., and D. Kaplan (eds.), 1968, *Theory in Anthropology.* Aldine, Chicago.

Maquet, J., 1971, *Introduction to Aesthetic Anthropology.* Addison/Wesley, Reading, Mass.

Marett, R. R., 1909, *The Threshold of Religion.* Methuen, London.

Marshall, J., 1956, "The Hunters," (16 mm. film). Film Study Center of the Peabody Museum, Harvard University, Cambridge, Mass.

———, 1958, "Man as Hunter," *Natural History*, **67**, 291–309, 376–395.

Marshall, L., 1960, "!Kung Bushman Bands," *Africa*, **30**, 325–355.

———, 1961, "Sharing, Talking, and Giving: Relief of Social Tensions among !Kung Bushmen," *Africa*, **32**, 221–251.

———, 1962, "!Kung Bushman Religious Beliefs," *Africa*, **32**, 221–251.

———, 1965, "The !Kung Bushmen of the Kalahari Desert," in J. L. Gibbs, Jr. (ed.) *Peoples of Africa.* Holt, New York, pp. 241–278.

———, 1969, "The Medicine Dance of the !Kung Bushmen," *Africa*, **39**, 347–381.

Marwick, M., 1967, "The Study of Witchcraft," in A. L. Epstein (ed.), *The Craft of Social Anthropology.* Tavistock, London, pp. 231–244.

——— (ed.), 1970, *Witchcraft and Sorcery.* Penguin, Baltimore.

Marx, K., 1888, *The Communist Manifesto.* W. Reeves, London. Original edition 1848.

———, 1965, *Pre-Capitalist Economic-Formations: Karl Marx.* E. Hobsawn, (ed.), International, New York. Original manuscript 1857–1858.

Mason, O. T., 1904, *Aboriginal American Basketry.* U.S. National Museum Annual Report, Washington, D.C.

Mason, P., 1970, *Patterns of Dominance.* Oxford U.P., London.

Matson, F. R. (ed.), 1965, *Ceramics and Man.* Aldine, Chicago.

Matthiasson, C. (ed.), 1974, *Many Sisters: Women in Cross-Cultural Perspective.* Free Press, New York.

Mauss, M., 1954, *The Gift.* Free Press, New York.

McCall, D. F., 1969, *Africa in Time Perspective.* Oxford U.P., New York.

McFeat, T., (ed.), 1966, *Indians of the North West Coast.* U. of Washington Press, Seattle.

McNitt, F., 1972, *Navajo Wars: Military Campaigns, Slave Raids and Reprisals.* U. of New Mexico Press, Albuquerque.

McPhee, C., 1966, *Music in Bali.* Yale U.P., New Haven.

McTaggart, F., 1975, *Wolf That I Am: In Search of the Red Earth People.* Houghton Mifflin, Boston.

Mead, M., 1928, *Coming of Age in Samoa.* Morrow, New York.

———, 1930, *Growing Up in New Guinea.* Morrow, New York.

Meggers, B. (ed.), Anthropological Archeology in the Americas. The Anthropological Society of Washington, Washington, D.C.

———, 1971, *Amazonia: Man and Culture in a Counterfeit Paradise.* Aldine, Chicago.

Meggitt, M. J., 1962, *Desert People.* U. of Chicago Press, Chicago.

———, 1964, "Male-Female Relationships in the Highlands of Australian New Guinea," *American Anthropologist*, **66**, 204–224.

Meier, G., 1970, *Leading Issues in Economic Development in International Poverty.* Oxford U.P., New York.

Meillassoux, C. (ed.), 1971, *The Development of Indigenous Trade and Markets in West Africa.* Oxford U.P., New York.

———, 1972, "From Reproduction to Production: A Marxist Approach to Economic Anthropology," *Economics and Society*, **1**, 93–105.

Melitz, J., 1970, "The Polanyi School of Anthropology on Money: An Economist's View," *American Anthropologist*, **72**, 1020–1040.

Mencher, J., 1973, "Socio-economic Constraints to Development: The Case of South India," *Annals of the New York Academy of Sciences*, February, 155–167.

———, 1974a, "The Caste System Upside Down, Or the Not So Mysterious East," *Current Anthropology,* **15,** 469–478.

———, 1974b, "Problems in Analysing Rural Class Structure," *Economic and Political Weekly,* **9,** 1495–1503.

MERRIAM, A. P., 1964, *The Anthropology of Music.* Northwestern U.P., Evanston.

———, 1967, *The Ethnomusicology of the Flathead Indians.* Aldine, Chicago.

MESSENGER, J., 1971, "Ibibio Drama," *Africa,* **41,** 208–222.

———, 1973, "The Role of the Carver in Anang Society," in W. d'Azevedo (ed.), *The Traditional Artist in African Societies.* Indiana U.P., Bloomington, pp. 101–127.

MESSING, S., 1958, "Group Therapy and Social Status in the Zar Cult of Ethiopia," *American Anthropologist,* **60,** 1120–1126.

MÉTRAUX, A., 1948, "The Tupinambá," in J. Steward (ed.), *The Tropical Forest Tribes,* Vol. 3 of *Handbook of South American Indians.* Smithsonian Institution, Washington, D.C., pp. 95–133.

MHLONGO, S., 1975, "An Analysis of the Classes in South Africa," *Race and Class,* **16,** 259–294.

MICHAELSON, E., and W. GOLDSCHMIDT, 1971, "Female Roles and Male Dominance Among Peasants," *Southwestern Journal of Anthropology,* **27,** 330–352.

MIDDLETON, D. R., 1975, "Choice and Strategy in an Urban Compadrazgo," *Man,* **2,** 461–475.

MIDDLETON, J., 1963, "Witchcraft and Sorcery in Lugbara," in J. Middleton and E. Winter (eds.), *Witchcraft and Sorcery in East Africa.* Routledge, London.

——— (ed.), 1967, *Magic, Witchcraft, and Curing.* Natural History Press, New York.

———, 1971, "Oracles and Divination Among the Lugbara," in M. Douglas and P. Kayberry (eds.), *Man in Africa.* Doubleday, New York, pp. 262–278.

———, and D. Tait (eds.), 1958, *Tribes Without Rulers.* Routledge, London.

MILLER, N., and R. AYA (eds.), 1971, *National Liberation: Revolution in the Third World.* Free Press, New York.

MINER, H., 1963, *The Primitive City of Timbuctoo.* Princeton U.P., Princeton, N.J.

MINTZ, J., 1974, *Legends of the Hasidim: An Introduction to Hasidic Culture and Oral Traditions in the New World.* U. of Chicago Press, Chicago.

MINTZ, S. W., and E. R. WOLF, 1950, "An Analysis of Ritual Co-parenthood (Compadrazgo)," *Southwestern Journal of Anthropology,* **6,** 341–368.

MITCHELL, W. E., 1963, "Theoretical Problems in the Concept of the Kindred," *American Anthropologist,* **65,** 343–354.

MITCHELL-KERNAN, C., 1972, "Speech Acts in a Black Urban Community: Signifying, Loud Talking, and Marking," in T. Kochman (ed.), *Rappin' and Stylin' Out.* U. of Illinois Press, Urbana, pp. 315–335.

MONOD, T. (ed.), 1975, *Pastoralism in Tropical Africa.* Oxford U.P., New York.

MONTESQUIEU, 1949, *The Spirit of the Laws.* Translated by T. Nugent. Hafner, New York. Original edition 1748.

MONZÓN, A., 1952, *El Calpulli en la Organizacíon Social de los Tenochca.* Institute of Social Anthropology Publication. Smithsonian Institution, Washington, D.C.

MOONEY, J., 1965, *The Ghost Dance Religion and the Sioux Outbreak of 1890,* Edited and abridged by A. F. C. Wallace. U. of Chicago Press, Chicago.

MOORE, F. W. (ed.), 1966, *Readings in Cross-Cultural Methodology.* Human Relations Area Files, New Haven.

———, 1970, "The Human Relations Area Files," in R. Naroll and R. Cohen (eds.), *A Handbook of Method in Cultural Anthropology.* Columbia U.P., New York, pp. 640–648.

MOORE, S., 1970, "Law and Anthropology," B. Siegel (ed.), *Biennial Review of Anthropology, 1969a* Stanford U.P., Stanford, pp. 252–300.

MORAL, P., 1961, *Le Paysan Haitien.* Editions Maisonneuve et Larose, Paris.

MORGAN, E., 1975, *American Slavery, American Freedom: The Ordeal of Colonial Virginia.* Norton, New York.

MORGAN, L. H., 1962, *League of the Iroquois.* Corinth, New York.

———, 1963, *Ancient Society.* Edited by E. Leacock. World, New York. Originally published 1887.

———, 1966, *Houses and House Life of the American*

Aborigines. Chicago U.P., Chicago. Originally published 1881.

Morner, M. (ed.), 1970, *Race and Class in Latin America.* Columbia U.P., New York.

Morren, G., 1974, "Woman the Hunter," *Concerned Demographer,* **4,** 16–20.

Morris, H. S., 1953, *Report on a Melanau Sago Producing Community in Sarawak.* Colonial Research Studies 9. H.M.S.O., London.

Morris, R. B., 1946, *Government and Labor in Early America.* Octagon, New York.

Morton-Williams, P., 1960, "The Yoruba Ogboni Cult in Oyo," *Africa,* **30,** 362–375.

Munn, N., 1973, *Walbiri Iconography: Graphic Representation and Cultural Symbolism in a Central Australian Society.* Cornell U.P., Ithaca.

Murdock, G. P., 1934, "Kinship and Social Behavior Among the Haida," *American Anthropologist,* **36,** 355–385.

———, 1949, *Social Structure.* Macmillan, New York.

———, 1967, *Ethnographic Atlas.* U. of Pittsburgh Press, Pittsburgh.

———, 1969, *Outline of World Cultures.* Human Relations Area Files, New Haven.

Murphy, R. F., and L. Kasdan, 1959, "The Structure of Parallel Cousin Marriage," *American Anthropologist,* **61,** 17–29.

Musil, A., 1928, *Manners and Customs of the Rwala Bedouins.* American Geographical Society, New York.

Myrdal, G., 1970, *The Challenge of World Poverty: A World Anti-Poverty Program in Outline.* Random House, New York.

N

Nader, L., and T. W. Maretzki (eds.), 1973, "Cultural Illness and Health," American Anthropological Association, Washington, D.C.

———, and B. Yngvesson, 1973, "On Studying the Ethnography of Law and Its Consequences," in J. Honigmann (ed.), *Handbook of Social and Cultural Anthropology.* Rand McNally, Chicago, pp. 883–921.

Naroll, R., 1968, "Some Thoughts on Comparative Method in Cultural Anthropology, in H. Blalock and A. Blalock (eds.), *Methodology in Social Research.* McGraw Hill, New York.

Naroll, R., 1970, "Cross-Cultural Sampling," in R. Naroll and R. Cohen (eds.), *A Handbook of Method in Cultural Anthropology.* Natural History Press, New York, pp. 889–927.

———, and R. Cohen (eds.), 1970, *A Handbook of Method in Cultural Anthropology.* Natural History Press, New York.

Nash, J., 1968, "The Passion Play in Maya Indian Communities," *Comparative Studies in Society and History,* **10,** 318–327. Reprinted in Hammond 1975.

———, 1970, *In the Eyes of the Ancestors: Belief and Behavior in a Mayan Community.* Yale U.P., New Haven.

Neale, W., 1957, "Reciprocity and Redistribution in Rural India," in K. Polanyi, C. Arensberg, and H. Pearson (eds.), *Trade and Markets in the Early Empire.* Free Press, New York. Reprinted in Hammond 1975.

Nelson, C. (ed.), 1973, *The Desert and the Town: Nomads in the Great Society.* U. of Calif. Press, Berkeley.

———, 1974, "Public and Private Politics: Women in the Middle Eastern World," *American Ethnologist,* **1,** 551–563.

Nelson, H. C. H., 1974, "Ancestor Worship and Burial Practices," in A. Wolf (ed.), *Religion and Ritual in Chinese Society.* Stanford U.P., Stanford.

Nelson, R., 1973, *Hunters of the Northern Ice: Design for Survival Among the Alaskan Kutchin.* U. of Chicago Press, Chicago.

Netting, R., 1968, "Kofyar Building in Mud and Stone," *Expedition,* **10,** 10–20.

———, 1974, "Kofyar Armed Conflict: Social Causes and Consequences," *Journal of Anthropological Research,* **30,** 139–163.

Nettl, B., 1964, *Theory and Method in Ethnomusicology.* Free Press, New York.

Neuman, P. L., 1964, "Religious Belief and Ritual in a New Guinea Society," *American Anthropologist,* **66,** 257–272.

Nicolaisen, J., 1963, *Ecology and Culture of the Pastoral Tuareg.* National Museum of Copenhagen.

Noel, Col. E., 1944, "Qanats," *Journal of the Royal Central Asian Society,* **31,** 191–202.

Norbeck, E., 1970, *Religion and Society in Modern Japan: Continuity and Change.* Tourmaline, Houston, Tex.

Obeyeskere, G., 1975, "Sorcery, Premeditated Murder and the Canalization of Aggression in Sri Lanka," *Ethnology,* **14,** 1–23.

Oliver, D. L., 1955, *A Solomon Island Society.* Beacon, Boston.

Oliver, P., 1971, *Shelter in Africa.* Praeger, New York.

O'Neale, L., 1949, "Weaving," in J. Steward (ed.), *The Comparative Ethnology of South American Indians.* Vol. 5 of *The Handbook of South American Indians.* Smithsonian Institution, Washington, D.C., pp. 97–138.

Oosterwaal, G., 1963, "A Cargo Cult in the Mamberamo Area," *Ethnology,* **11,** 1–14.

Ortiz, S., 1967, "Colombian Rural Market Organization: An Exploratory Model," *Man,* **2,** 393–412. Reprinted in Hammond 1975.

Osgood, C., 1970, *Ingalik Material Culture.* Taplinger, New York.

Oswalt, W. H., 1966, *This Land Was Theirs: A Study of the North American Indians.* Wiley, New York.

———, 1973, *Habitat and Technology: The Evolution of Hunting.* Holt, New York.

Otten, C. M. (ed.), 1971, *Anthropology and Art.* Natural History Press, New York.

Ottenberg, S., 1955, "Improvement Associations Among the Afikbo Ibo," *Africa,* **25,** 1–25.

———, 1960, "Double Descent in an Ibo Village Group," in A. F. C. Wallace (ed.), *Selected Papers of the Fifth International Congress of Anthropological and Ethnological Sciences.* U. of Pennsylvania Press, Philadelphia, pp. 473–481.

———, 1968, *Double Descent in an African Society: The Afikbo Village Group.* U. of Washington Press, Seattle.

Otterbein, K., 1970a, *The Evolution of War: A Cross Cultural Study.* Human Relations Area Files, New Haven.

———, 1970b, "The Development Cycle of the Andros Household: A Diachronic Analysis," *American Anthropologist,* **72,** 1412–1419.

———, 1973, "Anthropology of War," in J. Honigmann (ed.), *Handbook of Social and Cultural Anthropology,* Rand McNally, Chicago, pp. 923–958.

Paden, J. N., 1973, *Religion and Political Culture in Kano.* U. of Calif. Press, Berkeley.

Paredes, A., and R. Bauman (eds.), 1972, *Toward New Perspectives in Folklore.* U. of Texas Press, Austin.

Parker, A. C., 1913, *The Code of Handsome Lake, the Seneca Prophet.* New York State Museum Bulletin 163, Albany.

Parker, S., 1960, "The Wiitiko Psychosis in the Context of Ojibwa Personality and Culture," *American Anthropologist,* **62,** 603–623.

Pasternak, B., 1976, *Introduction to Kinship and Social Organization.* Prentice-Hall, Englewood Cliffs, N.J.

Patterson, T., 1973, *America's Past: A New World Archaeology,* Scott, Glenview, Ill.

Peacock, J. L., 1968a, *Rites of Modernization: Symbolic and Social Aspects of Indonesian Proletarian Drama.* U. of Chicago Press, Chicago.

———, 1968b, "Ritual, Entertainment and Modernization," *Comparative Studies in Society and History,* **10,** 328–334.

———, and A. T. Kirsch, 1970, "The Evolution of Society and Culture," in their *The Human Direction: An Evolutionary Approach to Social and Cultural Anthropology,* Appleton, New York, pp. 41–71.

Pelto, P., 1970, *Anthropological Research: The Structure of Inquiry.* Harper, New York.

Peter, Prince of Greece and Denmark, 1948, "Tibetan, Toda and Tiya Polyandry: A Report on Field Investigations," *Transactions of the New York Academy of Sciences,* 10, 210–225.

———, 1955, *The Polyandry of Tibet.* Actes du 4ème Congrès des Sciences Anthropologiques et Ethnologiques 2, Vienna, pp. 176–184.

———, 1963, *A Study of Polyandry.* Mouton, The Hague.

Philsooph, H., 1971, "Primitive Magic and Mana," *Man,* **6,** 182–203.

Pitt, D., 1972, *Using Historical Sources in Anthropology and Sociology,* Holt, New York.

Pitt-Rivers, 1961, *The People of the Sierra.* U. of Chicago Press, Chicago.

Plotnicov, L., and A. Tuden (eds.), *Essays in Social Stratification.* U. of Pittsburgh Press, Pittsburgh.

Plumer, C., 1971, *African Textiles: An Outline of*

Handcrafted Subsaharan Fabrics. Michigan State U.P., East Lansing.

Polanyi, K., 1944, *The Great Transformation.* Holt, New York.

———, 1953, *Semantics of General Economic History,* Columbia University Project on the Origins of Economic Institutions. Columbia University, New York.

———, 1968, *Primitive, Archaic and Modern Economies: Essays of Karl Polanyi.* (Edited by G. Dalton. Doubleday, Garden City, N.Y.

Potter, J. M., 1970, "Land and Lineage in Traditional Chinese Society," in M. Freedman (ed.), *Family and Kinship in Chinese Society.* Stanford U.P., Stanford, pp. 121–138.

Pozas, R., 1959, *Chamula: Un Pueblo Indio de los Altos de Chiapas.* Instituto Indigenista, Mexico D. F., Mexico.

Premack, D., 1971, "Language in a Chimpanzee?" *Science,* **172,** 808–822.

Price, R., 1970a, "Saramaka Woodcarving: The Development of an Afro-American Art," *Man,* **5,** 363–378.

———, 1970b, "Saramaka Emigration and Marriage: A Case Study of Social Change," *Southwestern Journal of Anthropology,* **26,** 57–189.

Price, T., 1955, *Saints and Spirits: Differential Acculturation in Colombian Negro Communities.* Unpublished doctoral dissertation, University Microfilms, Ann Arbor.

Prussin, L., 1970, *Architecture in Northern Ghana: A Study of Forms and Functions.* U. of Calif. Press, Berkeley.

R

Radcliffe-Brown, A., 1924, "The Mother's Brother in South Africa," *South African Journal of Science,* **21,** 542–555.

———, 1933, *The Andaman Islanders.* Cambridge U.P., London.

———, 1952, *Structure and Function.* Free Press, New York.

Ramos, A., 1939, *The Negro in Brazil.* Associated, Washington, D.C.

Randel, W., 1942, *A Aculturação Negra No Brasil.* Companhia Editora Nacional, São Paulo.

———, 1965, *The Ku Klux Klan: A Century of Infamy.* Chilton, Philadelphia.

Raper, A., and I. de A. Reid, 1941, *Sharecroppers All.* U. of North Carolina Press, Chapel Hill.

Rappaport, R., 1967, "Ritual Regulation of Environmental Relations Among a New Guinea People," *Ethnology,* **6,** 17–30. Reprinted in Hammond 1975.

———, 1971, "Nature, Culture, and Ecological Anthropology," in H. Shapiro (ed.), *Man, Culture, and Society.* Oxford U.P., New York.

Rasmussen, K., 1929, *Intellectual Culture of the Ingulik Eskimo,* Report of the Fifth Thule Expedition, 1921–1924. Vol. 7, Copenhagen.

Rattray, R. S., 1923, *Ashanti.* Oxford U.P., New York.

Rawick, G. P., 1972, *The American Slave: A Composite Autobiography.* Vol. 1: *From Sundown to Sunup: The Making of the Black Community.* Greenwood, Westport, Conn.

Ray, D. J., 1967, *Eskimo Masks: Art and Ceremony.* U. of Washington Press, Seattle.

Read, K. E., 1965, *The High Valley.* Scribners, New York.

Redfield, R., R. Linton, and M. J. Herskovits, 1936, "Memorandum on the Study of Acculturation," *American Anthropologist,* **37,** 149–152.

Reid, J., 1970, *A Law of Blood: The Primitive Law of the Cherokee Nation.* New York U.P., New York.

Reisenberg, S., 1972, "The Organization of Navigational Knowledge on Puluwat," *Journal of the Polynesian Society,* **81,** 19–56.

Reynolds, B., 1963, *Magic, Divination, and Witchcraft Among the Barotse of Rhodesia.* U. of Calif. Press, Berkeley.

Rhee, S. N., 1973, "Jewish Assimilation: The Case of the Chinese Jews," *Comparative Studies in Society and History,* **15,** 115–126.

Ribeiro, D., 1968a, "The Urban Revolution," in his *The Civilizational Process.* Smithsonian Institution, Washington, D.C., pp. 40–45. Reprinted in Hammond 1976.

———, 1968b, *The Civilizational Process.* Translated by B. J. Meggers. Smithsonian Institution, Washington, D.C.

Richards, A. I., 1950, "Hut-Building Among the Bemba," *Man,* **1,** 134–162.

———, F. Sturrock, and J. Fortt, (eds.), 1974, *Subsistence to Commercial Farming in Present Day Buganda.* Cambridge U.P., New York.

Rivers, W. H. R., 1906, *The Todas.* Macmillan, New York.

Roach, M. E., and J. B. Eicker (eds.), *Dress, Adornment, and the Social Order.* Wiley, New York.

ROCKHILL, W. W., 1895, *Notes on the Ethnology of Tibet.* Report of the U.S. National Museum for 1893. Smithsonian Institution, Washington, D.C.

ROGERS, S., 1975, "Female Forms of Power and the Myth of Male Dominance: A Model of Female/Male Interaction in Peasant Society," *American Ethnologist,* **4,** 727–756.

ROMNEY, K., and R. D'ANDRADE (eds.), 1964, *Transcultural Studies in Cognition.* American Anthropologist Special Publication 66, Part 2, No. 3.

ROOT, W. C., 1949, "Metallurgy," in J. Steward (ed.), *The Handbook of South American Indians,* Vol. 5. Bureau of American Ethnology Bulletin 143. Smithsonian Institution, Washington, D.C.

ROSMAN, A., and P. RUBEL, 1972, "The Potlatch: A Structural Analysis, *American Anthropologist,* **74,** 658–671.

ROSS, J., 1972, "Toward a Reconstruction of Voluntary Association Theory," *The British Journal of Sociology,* **23,** 20–32.

ROWE, J. 1946, "Inca Culture at the Time of the Spanish Conquest," in J. Steward (ed.), *The Andean Civilizations.* Vol. 2 of *The Handbook of South American Indians.* Smithsonian Institution, Washington, D.C., pp. 183–330.

RUDNER, J., and I. RUDNER, 1970, *The Hunter and His Art: A Survey of Rock Art in South Africa.* C. Struik, Capetown.

RUSH, J., 1974, *Witchcraft and Sorcery: An Anthropological Perspective on the Occult.* Thomas, Springfield, Ill.

RUSSELL, D. E. H., 1974, *Rebellion, Revolution, and Armed Force: A Comparative Study of Fifteen Countries with Special Emphasis on Cuba and South Africa.* Academic, New York.

RUYLE, E. E., 1973, "Slavery, Surplus, and Stratification on the Northwest Coast: The Ethnoenergetics of an Incipient Stratification System," *Current Anthropology,* **14,** 603–617.

———, 1976, "Energy and Culture," in B. Bernardi (ed.), *The Concept and Dynamics of Culture.* Aldine, Chicago.

S

SABLOFF, J., and C. C. LAMBERG-KARLOVSKY (eds.), 1974, *The Rise and Fall of Civilizations.* Cummings, Menlo Park, Calif.

SACKS, K., 1974, "Engels Revisited: Women, the Organization of Production, and Private Property," in A. Rosaldo and L. Lamphere (eds.), *Woman, Culture, and Society.* Stanford U.P., Stanford, pp. 207–222.

SAFA, H., and B. DUTOIT, 1975, *Migration and Development: Implications for Ethnic Identity and Political Conflict.* Aldine, Chicago.

SAHLINS, M., 1961, "The Segmentary Lineage: An Organization of Predatory Expansion," *American Anthropologist,* **63,** 322–345.

———, 1964, "Culture and Environment: The Study of Cultural Ecology," in S. Tax (ed.), *Horizons in Anthropology.* Aldine, Chicago, pp. 132–147.

———, 1968, *Tribesmen.* Prentice-Hall, Englewood Cliffs, N.J.

———, 1972a, "On the Sociology of Primitive Exchange," in his *Stone Age Economics.* Aldine, Chicago, pp. 185–275.

———, 1972b, "The Original Affluent Society," in his *Stone Age Economics.* Aldine, Chicago, pp. 1–39.

———, 1972c, *Stone Age Economics,* Aldine, Chicago.

———, 1977, *Culture and Practical Reason.* U. of Chicago Press, Chicago.

———, and E. SERVICE (eds.), 1960, *Evolution and Culture.* U. of Michigan Press, Ann Arbor.

SALISBURY, R., 1970, "Economics," in O. von Mering and L. Kasdan (eds.), *Anthropology and the Behavioral and Health Sciences.* U. of Pittsburgh Press, Pittsburgh, pp. 62–88.

SALZMAN, P., 1971, "Movement and Resource Extraction Among Pastoral Nomads: The Case of the Shah Nawazi Baluch," *Anthropological Quarterly,* **44,** 185–197. Reprinted in Hammond 1975.

SANDAY, P., 1973, "Toward a Theory of the Status of Women," *American Anthropologist,* **75,** 1682–1700.

SANDERS, W., 1972, Population, Agricultural History and Societal Evolution in Mesoamerica," in B. Spooner (ed.), *Population Growth.* Aldine, Chicago, pp. 101–153.

SAPIR, E. H., 1931, "Conceptual Categories in Primitive Language," *Science,* **74,** 578.

SATHYAMURTHY, T. V., 1973, "Social Anthropology in the Study of New Nation States," *Current Anthropology,* **14,** 557–565.

SCHAPERA, I., 1951, *The Khoisan Peoples of South*

Africa: Bushmen and Hottentots. Humanities, New York.

———, 1971, *Rainmaking Rites of Tswana Tribes.* Cambridge U.P., New York.

Schebesta, P. J., 1926a, "The Jungle Tribes of the Malay Peninsula," *Bulletin of the School of Oriental Studies,* **4,** 269–278.

———, 1926b, "The Bow and Arrow of the Semang," *Man,* **26,** Article 5.

———, 1941, *Die Bambuti-Pygmaen von Ituri-Bambuti: Die Wirtschaft der Ituri-Bambuti.* Memoires, Institut Royal Colonial Belge, Coll. 4, Vol. 2, Part 1.

Scheffler, H., 1974, "Kinship, Descent, and Alliance," in J. Honigmann (ed.), *Handbook of Social and Cultural Anthropology.* Rand McNally, Chicago.

Schlegel, A., 1972, *Male Dominance and Female Autonomy.* Human Relations Area Files, New Haven.

Schlegel, S. A., 1970, *Tiruray Justice: Traditional Tiruray Law and Morality,* U. of Calif. Press, Berkeley.

Schneider, D., and K. Gough (eds.), 1961, *Matrilineal Kinship.* U. of Calif. Press, Berkeley.

Schneider, H., 1970, *Wahi Wanyaturu.* Aldine, Chicago.

———, 1974, *Economic Man.* Free Press, New York.

Schoolcraft, H. R., 1956, *Indian Legends from Algic Researches and Historical and Statistical Information Respecting the Indian Tribes of the Eastern United States.* Edited by M. L. Williams. Michigan State U.P., East Lansing.

Schusky, E. L., 1965, *Manual for Kinship Analysis.* Holt, New York.

Sebeok, T., 1955, (ed.), *Myth: A Symposium.* Indiana U.P., Bloomington.

———, 1972, *Perspectives in Zoosemiotics.* Janua Linguarum, Series Minor 122. Mouton, The Hague.

Seeger, A., 1975, "The Meaning of Body Ornaments: A Suya Example," *Ethnology,* **14,** 211–224.

Sennett, R., and J. Cobb, 1973, *The Hidden Injuries of Class.* Knopf.

Service, E. R., 1960, "Kinship Terminology and Evolution," *American Anthropologist,* **62,** 747–763.

———, 1966, *The Hunters.* Prentice-Hall, Englewood Cliffs, N.J.

———, 1968, "The Prime Mover of Cultural Evolution," *Southwestern Journal of Anthropology,* **24,** 396–409.

———, 1970, *Cultural Evolutionism: Theory in Practice.* Holt, New York.

———, 1971, *Primitive Social Organization: An Evolutionary Perspective.* Random House, New York.

———, 1975, *Origins of the State and Civilization: The Process of Cultural Evolution.* Norton, New York.

Shack, W., 1971, "Hunger, Anxiety and Ritual: Deprivation and Spirit Possession Among the Gurage of Ethiopia," *Man,* **6,** 30–43.

———, and H. Marcos, 1974, *Gods and Heroes: Oral Traditions of the Gurage of Ethiopia.* Oxford U.P., New York.

Sharp, A., 1964, *Ancient Voyagers in Polynesia.* U. of Calif. Press, Berkeley.

Sharp, L., 1952, "Steel Axes for Stone Age Australians," *Human Organization,* **2,** 17–22. Reprinted in Hammond 1975.

Sherzer, J., and R. Bauman, 1972, "Areal Studies and Culture History: Language As a Key to the Historial Study of Culture Contact," *Southwestern Journal of Anthropology,* **28,** 131–152.

Shivaraman, M., 1973, "Thanjavur: Rumblings of Class Struggle in Tamil Nadu," in K. Gough and H. Sharma (eds.), *Imperialism and Revolution in South Asia.* Monthly Review, New York, pp. 246–264.

Sieber, R., 1962, "The Arts and Their Changing Social Function," *Annals of the New York Academy of Sciences,* **96,** 653–658.

Silverberg, J. (ed.), 1968, *Social Mobility in the Caste System in India.* Mouton, The Hague.

Silverman, S., 1970, "'Exploitation' in Rural Central Italy: Structure and Ideology in Stratification Study," *Comparative Studies in Society and History,* **12,** 327–339.

Simpson, G. E., 1940, "The Vodun Service in Northern Haiti," *American Anthropologist,* **42,** 236–254.

———, 1945, "The Belief System of Haitian Vodun," *American Anthropologist,* **47,** 37–59.

———, 1965, *The Shango Cult in Trinidad.* Editorial Cultura, Mexico D.F., Mexico.

———, 1970, *Religious Cults of the Caribbean: Trinidad, Jamaica, and Haiti.* U. of Puerto Rico Press, Rio Piedras.

———, and P. B. HAMMOND, 1960, "'Discussion' of 'The African Heritage in the Carribean,'" in V. Rubin (ed.), *Caribbean Studies: A Symposium.* U. of Washington Press, Seattle, pp. 46–53.

———, and J. M. YINGER, 1972, *Racial and Cultural Minorities.* Harper, New York.

SINGER, A., 1973, "Marriage Payments and the Exchange of People," *Man,* **8,** 80–92.

SINGER, M., and B. S. Cohn (eds.), 1968, *Structure and Change in Indian Society.* Aldine, Chicago.

SINGER, S., E. J. HOLMYARD, and A. R. HALL (eds.), 1954, *From Early Times to the Fall of Empires.* Vol. 1 of *A History of Technology.* Oxford U.P., London.

SINGH, P., 1974, *Neolithic Cultures of Western Asia,* Seminar, New York.

SINHA, S., 1967, "Caste in India: Its Essential Pattern of Socio-cultural Integration," in A. de Reuk and J. Knight (eds.), *Caste and Race.* Little, Brown, Boston, pp. 92–105.

SKEAT, W. W., 1902, "The Wild Tribes of the Malaya Peninsula," *Journal of the Royal Anthropological Institute,* **32,** 124–141.

———, and C. O. BLAGDEN, 1906, *Pagan Races of the Malay Peninsula,* 2 vols. Macmillan, London.

SMITH, A. E., 1947, *Colonists in Bondage: White Servitude and Convict Labor in America, 1607–1776.* U. of North Carolina Press, Chapel Hill.

SMITH, R. J., 1975, *Ancestor Worship in Contemporary Japan.* Stanford U.P., Stanford.

SMITH, T. C., 1970, *The Agrarian Origins of Modern Japan.* Stanford U.P., Stanford.

SNOW, D., 1968, "Wabanaki 'Family Hunting Territories,'" *American Anthropologist,* **70,** 1143–1151.

SOEN, D., and P. DE COMARMOND, 1972, "Savings Associations Among the Bamilèkè: Tradition and Modern Cooperation in South West Cameroon," *American Anthropologist,* **75,** 1170–1179.

SOLHEIM, W., 1972, "An Earlier Agricultural Revolution," *Scientific American,* **226,** 34–41.

SPENCER, H., 1883, *Social Statics.* Appleton, New York. Original edition 1850.

SPENCER, J. E., 1966, *Shifting Cultivation in South East Asia.* U. of Calif. Press, Berkeley.

SPENCER, R. F., and others, 1965, *The Native Americans.* Harper, New York.

SPIER, R., 1973, *Material Culture and Technology.* Burgess, Minneapolis.

SPINDLER, G. (ed.), *Being an Anthropologist: Field Work in Eleven Cultures.* Holt, New York.

SPIRO, M., 1952, "Ghosts, Ifaluk, and Teleological Functionalism," *American Anthropologist,* **54,** 497–503.

———, 1967, *Burmese Supernaturalism: A Study in the Explanation and Reduction of Suffering.* Prentice-Hall, Englewood Cliffs, N.J.

SPOONER, B. (ed.), 1972, *Population Growth: Anthropological Implications.* M.I.T. Press, Cambridge, Mass.

SPRADLEY, J. P., and B. J. Mann, 1975, *The Cocktail Waitress: Woman's Work in a Man's World.* Wiley, New York.

SPUHLER, J. N. (ed.), 1965, *The Evolution of Man's Capacity for Culture,* Wayne State U.P., Detroit.

SRINIVAS, M. N., 1959, "The Dominant Caste in Rampura," *American Anthropologist,* **61,** 1–16.

STACK, C., 1970, "The Kindred of Viola Jackson: Residence and Family Organization of an Urban Black Family," in N. Whitten, Jr., and J. Szwed (eds.), *Afro-American Anthropology.* Free Press, New York, pp. 303–311. Reprinted in Hammond 1975.

STARR, C. G., 1973, *Early Man: Prehistory and the Civilizations of the Ancient Near East.* Oxford U.P., New York.

STAUDER, J., 1971, "The Domestic Group: Labour and Property," in his *The Majangir.* Cambridge U.P., New York, pp. 45–51. Reprinted in Hammond 1975.

———, 1972, "Anarchy and Ecology: Political Society Among the Majangir," *Southwestern Journal of Anthropology,* **28,** 153–168.

STENNING, D., 1957, "Transhumance, Migratory Drift, Migration; Patterns of Pastoral Fulani Nomadism," *Journal of the Royal Anthropological Institute,* **87,** 57–73.

STEWARD, J. H., 1938, *Basin Plateau Aboriginal Socio-Political Groups,* Bureau of American Ethnology, Bulletin 120, Smithsonian Institution, Washington, D.C.

——— (ed.), 1946/1950, *The Handbook of South American Indians,* 6 vols. Bureau of American Ethnology 143. Smithsonian Institution Press, Washington, D.C.

———, 1955a, *Theory of Culture Change: The Methodology of Multilinear Evolution.* U. of Illinois Press, Urbana.

———, 1955b, "Development of Complex Societies: Cultural Causality and Law: A Trial

Formulation of the Development of Early Civilizations," in J. H. Steward, *Theory of Culture Change.* U. of Illinois Press, Urbana, pp. 178–209.

———, 1955c, "The Patrilineal Band," in J. H. Steward, *Theory of Culture Change,* U. of Illinois Press, Urbana, pp. 122–242.

———, 1955d, "The Great Basin Shoshonean Indians: An Example of a Family Level of Sociocultural Integration," in J. H. Steward, *Theory of Culture Change.* U. of Illinois Press, Urbana, pp. 101–121.

———, 1970, "The Foundations of Basin-Plateau Shoshonean Society," in E. H. Swanson (ed.), *Languages and Cultures of Western Northern America.* Claxton, Caldwell, Idaho, pp. 113–115.

———, and L. Faron, 1959, *Native Peoples of South America.* McGraw-Hill, New York.

Story, R., 1958, *Some Plants Used by the Bushmen in Obtaining Food and Water.* Botanical Survey of South Africa Memoir 30, Johannesburg.

Strathern, A., 1970, "Male Initiation in New Guinea Highlands Societies," *Ethnology,* **9,** 373–379.

———, 1971, *The Rope of Moka: Big Men and Ceremonial Exchange in Mount Hagen, New Guinea.* Cambridge U.P., New York.

———, 1972, *One Father, One Blood: Descent and Group Structure Among the Melpa People.* Tavistock, London.

———, and M. Strathern, 1971, *Self-Decoration in Mt. Hagen.* Toronto U.P., Toronto.

Streuver, S. (ed.), 1971, *Prehistoric Agriculture.* Natural History Press, New York.

Strickon, A., and S. Greenfield (eds.), 1972, *Structure and Process in Latin American Patronage, Clientage, and Power Systems.* U. of New Mexico Press, Albuquerque.

Sturtevant, W. C., 1964, "Studies in Ethnoscience," in A. Romney and R. D'Andrade (eds.), *Transcultural Studies in Cognition.* American Anthropologist Special Publication 66, Part 2, No. 3, 99–131.

——— W., 1968, "Anthropology, History, and Ethnohistory," in J. Clifton (ed.), *Introduction to Cultural Anthropology.* Houghton Mifflin, Boston, pp. 450–475.

Suggs, R. C., 1960, *The Island Civilizations of Polynesia.* Mentor, New York.

Swadesh, M., 1971a, "Out of Animal Cries into Language," in his *The Origin and Diversification of Language.* Aldine, Chicago, pp. 157–181.

———, 1971b, *The Origin and Diversification of Language.* Edited by J. Sherzer. Aldine, Chicago.

Swanton, J. R., 1905, *Contribution to the Ethnography of the Haida.* American Museum of Natural History Memoir 8, New York.

Swartz, M., V. Turner, and A. Tuden 1966, (eds.), *Political Anthropology.* Aldine, Chicago.

T

Tabb, W. K., 1972, *The Political Economy of the Black Ghetto.* Norton, New York.

Tax, S. (ed.), 1975a, War: Its Causes and Correlates. Mouton, The Hague.

——— (ed.), 1975b, *Women Cross-Culturally.* Mouton, The Hague.

Tegnaeus, H., 1952, *Blood Brothers, an Ethno-sociological Study of the Institutions of Blood Brotherhood. With Special Reference to Africa.* Statens Ethnografiska Museum Publication 10, Stockholm.

Thomas, D., 1974, "An Archaeological Perspective on Shoshonean Bands," *American Anthropologist,* **76,** 11–23.

Thomas, E. M., 1959, *The Harmless People.* Knopf, New York.

Thomas, K., 1970, "The Relevance of Social Anthropology to the Historical Study of English Witchcraft," in M. Douglas (ed.), *Witchcraft Confessions and Accusations.* Tavistock, London, pp. 47–79.

Thompson, R. A., 1973, "A Theory of Instrumental and Social Networks," *Journal of Anthropological Research,* **29,** 244–265.

Thompson, R. F., 1969, "Àbátàn: A Master Potter of the Egbádo Yorùbá," in D. Biebuyck (ed.), *Tradition and Creativity in Tribal Art.* U. of Calif. Press, Berkeley, pp. 120–182.

———, 1974, *African Art in Motion.* U. of Calif. Press, Berkeley.

Tiffany, S., 1975, "Giving and Receiving: Participation in Chiefly Redistribution Activities in Samoa," *Ethnology,* **14,** 267–286.

Tippett, A. R., 1968, *Fijian Material Culture: A Study of Cultural Context, Function, and Change.* Bishop Museum Bulletin 232, Honolulu.

Tobias, P., 1956, "On the Survival of the Bushmen," *Africa,* **26,** 124–186.

Treistman, J., 1972, "Styles," in her *The Prehistory of China: An Archaeological Exploration.* Doubleday, New York, pp. 103–134. Reprinted as "The Beginning of Civilization in China" in Hammond 1976.

Tringham, R., 1971, *Hunters, Fishers and Farmers of Eastern Europe, 6000–3000* B.C., Hutchinson U. Library, London.

Tritton, A. S., 1954, *Islam, Beliefs and Practices.* Hutchinson U. Library, London.

Tuden, A., 1966a, "Ila Property Relations and Political Processes," in M. J. Swartz (ed.), *Local Level Politics.* Aldine, Chicago, pp. 95–105.

———, 1966b, "Leadership and the Decision Making Process Among the Ila and Swat Pathans," in M. J. Swartz, V. W. Turner, and A. Tuden (eds.), *Political Anthropology.* Aldine, Chicago, pp. 275–283.

Tumin, M., 1967, *Social Stratification: The Forms and Functions of Inequality.* Prentice-Hall, Englewood Cliffs, N.J.

——— (ed.), 1970, *Readings on Social Stratification.* Prentice-Hall, Englewood Cliffs, N.J.

Turnbull, C., 1965, *The Mbuti Pygmies: An Ethnographic Survey.* Anthropological Papers. American Museum of Natural History, New York.

———, 1968, "The Importance of Flux in Two Hunting Societies," in R. B. Lee and I. DeVore (eds.), *Man the Hunter.* Aldine, Chicago, pp. 132–137.

Turner, T., 1969, "Tchikrin: A Central Brazilian Tribe and Its Symbolic Language of Bodily Adornment," *Natural History,* **78,** 50–59, 70.

Turner, V., 1974, *Dramas, Fields, and Metaphors: Symbolic Action in Human Society.* Cornell U.P., Ithaca.

———, 1975, *Revelation and Divination in Ndembu Ritual.* Cornell U.P., Ithaca.

Tyler, S., 1969, *Cognitive Anthropology.* Holt, New York.

Tylor, E. B., 1865, *Researches into the Early History of Mankind and the Development of Civilization.* Murray, London.

———, 1889a, "On a Method of Investigating the Development of Institutions Applied to the Laws of Marriage and Descent," *Journal of the Royal Anthropological Institute,* **18,** 245–272.

———, 1889b, *Anthropology: An Introduction to the Study of Man and Civilization.* Appleton, New York.

U

Uberoi, J. B. S., 1971, *Politics of the Kula Ring.* Manchester U.P., Manchester.

Ucko, P., 1969, "Penis Sheaths: A Comparative Study," *Proceedings of the Royal Anthropological Institute for 1969,* 24–67.

———, and A. Rosenfeld, 1967, *Paleolithic Cave Art.* McGraw-Hill, New York.

———, R. Trimingham, and G. Dimbleby (eds.), 1972, *Man, Settlement and Urbanism.* Warner Modular Publications, Andover, Mass.

Udy, S., 1959, *Organization of Work.* Human Relations Area Files, New Haven.

Underhill, R., 1957, "Religion Among American Indians," *Annals of the American Academy of Political and Social Sciences,* **311,** 127–136.

V

Van Baal, J., 1971, *Symbols for Communication: An Introduction to the Anthropological Study of Religion.* Humanities, Atlantic Highlands, N.J.

Van Gennep, A., 1960, *The Rites of Passage.* U. of Chicago Press, Chicago. Original edition 1908.

Van Lawick-Goodall, J., 1972, *In the Shadow of Man.* Dell, New York.

Vansina, J., 1965, *Oral Tradition: A Study in Historical Methodology.* Aldine, Chicago.

———, 1971, "The Bushong Poison Ordeal," in M. Douglas and P. Kayberry (eds.), *Man in Africa.* Doubleday, Garden City, N.Y., pp. 245–261.

———, 1973, "Cultures Through Time," in R. Naroll and R. Cohen (eds.), *A Handbook of Method in Cultural Anthropology.* Natural History Press, New York, pp. 165–179. Reprinted in Hammond 1975.

Vayda, A., 1961, "A Re-examination of North West Coast Economic Systems," *Transactions of the New York Academy of Sciences,* **23,** 618–624.

Vaughn, J., Jr., 1970, "Caste Systems in the Western Sudan," in A. Tuden and L. Plotnicov (eds.), *Social Stratification in Africa.* Free Press, New York, pp. 59–92.

——— (ed.), 1970, *Environment and Cultural Behavior: Ecological Studies in Cultural Anthropology.* Natural History Press, New York.

———, 1971, "Phases of the Process of War and Peace Among the Marings of New Guinea," *Oceania,* **45,** 1–24. Reprinted in Hammond 1975.

———, 1976, *War in Ecological Perspective.* Plenum, New York.

———, and A. R. Rappaport, 1968, "Ecology: Cultural and Non-cultural," in J. A. Clifton (ed.), *Introduction to Cultural Anthropology.* Houghton Mifflin, Boston, pp. 476–497.

Veblen, T., 1953, *The Theory of the Leisure Class.* American Library, New York.

Vogel, E., 1971, *Japan's New Middle Class.* U. of Calif. Press, Berkeley.

Voget, F., 1975, *History of Ethnology.* Holt, New York.

Vogt, E., 1952, "Water Witching: An Interpretation of a Ritual Pattern in a Rural American Community." *Scientific Monthly,* **75,** 175–186.

———, 1960, "On the Concepts of Structure and Process in Cultural Anthropology," *American Anthropologist,* **62,** 18–33.

von Gruenebaum, G. E., 1961, *Medieval Islam.* U. of Chicago Press, Chicago.

W

Waddell, E., 1972, *The Mound Builders.* U. of Washington Press, Seattle.

Wagley, C., 1948, "Regionalism and Cultural Unity in Brazil," *Social Forces,* **36,** 457–464.

Wagner, N., and M. Haug, 1971, *Chicanos: Social and Psychological Perspectives.* Mosby, St. Louis.

Wagner, R., "Incest and Identity: A Critique and Theory on the Subject of Exogamy and Incest Prohibition," *Man,* **7,** 601–613.

Wallace, A. F. C., 1958, "The Dekaniwidah Myths Analyzed As the Record of a Revitalization Movement." *Ethnohistory,* **5,** 118–130.

——— 1961a, *Religious Revitalization: A Function of Religion in Human History.* Institute on Religion in an Age of Science, Boston.

———, 1961b, "Mental Illness, Biology, and Culture," in F. Hsu (ed.), *Psychological Anthropology: Approaches to Culture and Personality.* Dorsey, Homewood, Ill., pp. 255–294.

———, 1966, *Religion: An Anthropological View.* Random House, New York.

———, 1970a, *Culture and Personality.* Random House, New York.

———, 1970b, *The Death and Rebirth of the Seneca.* Knopf, New York.

———, and J. Atkins, 1960, "The Meaning of Kinship Terms," *American Anthropologist,* **62,** 58–80.

Wallenstein, I., 1974, "The Rise and Future Demise of the World Capitalist System: Concepts for Comparative Analysis," *Comparative Studies in Society and History,* **16,** 387–415.

———, 1975, *The Modern World System.* Academic, New York.

Warner, W. L., 1964, *A Black Civilization: A Study of an Australian Tribe.* Harper, New York. Original edition 1937.

Washburn, S., and J. Lancaster, 1971, "On Evolution and the Origin of Language," *Current Anthropology,* **12,** 384–386.

———, and R. Moore, 1973, *Ape into Man.* Little, Brown, Boston.

Wasserman, M., 1967, "White Power in the Black Belt," *New South,* **22,** 27–36.

Waterbolk, M., 1968, "Food Production in Prehistoric Europe," *Science,* **162,** 1093–1102. Reprinted in Hammond 1976.

Waterman, R. A., 1952, "African Influences on the Music of the Americas," in S. Tax (ed.), *Acculturation in the Americas: Proceedings of the 29th Congress of Americanists,* **2,** 207–218.

Watkins, M. H., 1943, "The West African 'Bush School,'" *American Journal of Sociology,* **48,** 666–674.

Watson, W., 1971, *Tribal Cohesion in a Money Economy.* Humanities, Atlantic Highlands, N.J.

Wax, M., and R. Wax, 1963, "The Notion of Magic," *Current Anthropology,* **4,** 495–518.

Wax, R., 1971, *Doing Field Work: Warnings and Advice.* U. of Chicago Press, Chicago.

Weaver, M. P., 1972, *The Aztecs, Maya, and Their Predecessors: Archaeology of Mesoamerica.* Seminar, London.

Weber, M., 1958, *The Religion of India: The Sociology of Hinduism and Buddhism.* Translated by

H. Gerth and D. Martindale. Free Press, New York.

WEIL, P., 1971, "The Masked Figure and Social Control: The Mandinka Case," *Africa,* **4,** 279–293.

WEIR, S., 1970, *Spinning and Weaving in Palestine.* Shenval, London.

WEISS, M., and A. MANN, 1975, *Human Biology and Behavior: An Anthropological Perspective.* Little, Brown, Boston.

WELMERS, W. E., 1949, "Secret Medicines, Magic and Rites of the Kpelle Tribe of Liberia," *Southwestern Journal of Anthropology,* **5,** 208–243.

WENZEL, M., 1972, *House Decoration in Nubia.* Toronto U.P., Toronto.

WERNER, A., 1914, "The Galla of East Africa Protectorate," *Journal of the Royal African Society,* **13,** 121–142, 262–287.

WERNER, O. 1973, "Structural Anthropology," in R. Naroll and F. Naroll (eds.), *Main Currents in Cultural Anthropology.* Prentice-Hall, Englewood Cliffs, N.J., pp. 281–307.

———, and J. FENTON, 1970, "Method and Theory in Ethnoscience or Ethnoepistemology," in N. Naroll and R. Cohen (eds.), *A Handbook of Method in Cultural Anthropology.* Natural History Press, New York, pp. 537–578.

WHARTON, C. (ed.), 1970, *Subsistence Agriculture and Economic Development.* Aldine, Chicago.

WHEELER, M., 1968, *The Indus Civilization.* Cambridge U.P., New York.

WHITE, L. A., 1948, "The Definition and Prohibition of Incest," *American Anthropologist,* **50,** 416–435.

———, 1949, *The Science of Culture.* Grove, New York.

———, 1959, *The Evolution of Culture.* McGraw-Hill, New York.

WHITING, J. W. M., 1961, "Effects of Climate on Certain Cultural Practices," in W. Goodenough (ed.), *Explorations in Cultural Anthropology.* McGraw-Hill, New York, pp. 511–544.

WHITING, J. W. H., and I. CHILD, 1953, *Child Training and Personality: A Cross Cultural Study.* Yale U.P., New Haven.

———, R. KLUCKHOHN, and A. ANTHONY, 1958, "The Functions of Male Initiation Ceremonies at Puberty," in E. Macoby, T. Newcomb, and E. Hartley (eds.), *Readings in Social Psychology.* Holt, New York, pp. 359–370.

WHITTEN, N., 1968, "Personal Networks and Musical Contexts in the Pacific Lowlands of Colombia and Ecuador," *Man,* **3,** 50–63. Reprinted in Hammond 1975.

———, 1974a, "The Ecology of Race Relations in Northwest Ecuador." In D. Heath (ed.), *Contemporary Cultures and Societies of Latin America* (2nd ed.). Random House, New York, pp. 327–340.

———, 1974b, "Blackness in Northern South America: Ethnic Dimensions," In his *Black Frontiersmen; A South American Case.* Halstead, New York, pp. 174–201.

WHORF, 1956, "A Linguistic Consideration of Thinking in Primitive Communities," in J. B. Carroll (ed.), *Language, Thought, and Reality: Selected Writings of Benjamin Lee Whorf.* Wiley, New York, pp. 65–86.

WIENS, H. J., 1951, "Geographical Limitations to Food Production in the Mongolian People's Republic," *Annals of the Association of American Geography,* **41,** 348–369.

WILLIAMS, B. J., 1968, "The Bihor of India and Some Comments on Band Organization," in R. B. Lee and S. DeVore (eds.), *Man the Hunter.* Aldine, Chicago, pp. 126–131.

WILMSEN, E., 1973, "Interaction, Spacing Behavior, and the Organization of Hunting Bands," *Journal of Anthropological Research,* **29,** 1–31.

WILSON, B. R., 1973, *Magic and Millenialism: A Sociological Study of Religious Movements of Protest Among Third World Peoples.* Harper, New York.

WILSON, F., 1972, *Migrant Labour in South Africa.* Spro-Cas, Johannesburg.

WILSON, M., 1951, *Good Company: A Study of Nyakyusa Age Villages.* Beacon, Boston.

———, 1971, *Religion and the Transformation of Society: A Study in Social Change in Africa.* Cambridge U.P., New York.

WINGERT, P., *Art of the South Pacific Islands.* Beechurst, New York.

WINKLER, E. Z., 1970, "Political Anthropology," in B. Siegel (ed.), *Biennial Review of Anthropology, 1969.* Stanford U.P., Stanford, pp. 301–386.

WITTFOGEL, K., 1964, *Oriental Despotism: A Comparative Study of Total Power.* Yale U.P., New Haven. Original edition 1957.

WOLF, A., 1970, "Childhood Association and Sexual Attraction: A Further Test of the Westermarck Hypothesis," *American Anthropologist,* **73,** 503–515.

WOLF, E. R., 1964, *Anthropology.* Prentice-Hall, Englewood Cliffs, N.J.

———, 1966, *Peasants,* Prentice-Hall, Englewood Cliffs, N.J.

———, 1969, *Peasant Wars of the Twentieth Century.* Harper, New York.

———, 1971, "Peasant Rebellion and Revolution," in M. Miller and R. Aya (eds.), *National Liberation Movements.* Free Press, New York, pp. 48–67.

WOLF, M., 1968, *The House of Lim: A Study of a Chinese Farm Family.* Appleton, New York.

WOLFE, A. W., 1969, "Social Structural Bases of Art," *Current Anthropology,* **10,** 3–44.

WOLFRAM, W., and N. CLARK, 1971, *Black-White Speech Relations.* Center for Applied Linguistics, Washington, D.C.

WOODBURN, J. C., 1968, "An Introduction to Hadza Ecology," in R. B. Lee and I. DeVore (eds.), *Man the Hunter.* Aldine, Chicago.

———, 1972, "The Future for Hunting and Gathering Peoples," in *!Kung.* Humanities, Atlantic Highlands, N.J., pp.1–3.

WOOFTER, T. J., JR., and others, 1936, *Landlord and Tenant on the Cotton Plantation.* U.S. Government Printing Office, Washington, D.C.

WORSLEY, P., 1957, *The Trumpet Shall Sound: A Study of Cargo Cults in Melanesia.* MacGibbon and Kee, London.

———, 1970, *The Third World.* Chicago U.P., Chicago.

WRIGHT, G. A., 1971, "Origins of Food Production in Southwestern Asia: A Survey of Ideas," *Current Anthropology,* **12,** 447–470.

WU, D. Y. H., 1974, "To Kill Three Birds With One Stone: The Rotating Credit Associations of the Papua New Guinea Chinese," *American Ethnologist,* **1,** 565–584.

Y

YALMAN, N., 1967, *Under the Bo Tree.* U. of Calif. Press, Berkeley.

YAMAMOTO, G., and T. ISHIDA (comps. and eds.), 1971, *Selected Readings on Modern Japanese Society.* McCutchan, Berkeley.

YETMAN, N. R., 1970, *Life Under the "Peculiar Institution": Selections from the Slave Narrative Collection.* Krieger, New York.

YOUNG, A., 1975, "Magic as a 'Quasi-Profession': The Organization of Magic and Magical Healing Among Amhara," *Ethnology,* **14,** 245–265.

YOUNG, F. W., 1962, "The Function of Male Initiation Ceremonies: A Cross-Cultural Test of an Alternative Hypothesis," *American Journal of Sociology,* **67,** 379–396.

———, 1965, *Initiation Ceremonies: A Cross Cultural Study of Status Dramatization.* Bobbs-Merrill, Indianapolis.

YOUNG, M. W., 1972, *Fighting with Food.* Cambridge U.P., New York.

YUSUF, A., 1975, "Capital Formation and Management Among The Muslim Hausa Traders of Kano," *Africa,* **45,** 167–182.

Z

ZARETSKY, I., and M. LEONE, 1975, *Religious Movements in Contemporary America.* Princeton U.P., Princeton.

Index

A

D

E

U

V

W

Y

BIBL. UNIV. LAUR. UNIV. LIB.
3 0007 00210856 0

DATE DUE
ÉCHÉANCE